Global Marketing

Foreign Entry, Local Marketing, and Global Management

Johny K. Johansson
Georgetown University

IRWIN

Chicago · Bogotá · Boston · Buenos Aires · Caracas
London · Madrid · Mexico City · Sydney · Toronto

© Richard D. Irwin, a Times Mirror Higher Education Group, Inc. company, 1997

Irwin Book Team

Publisher: *Rob Zwettler*
Sponsoring editor: *Nina McGuffin*
Senior developmental editor: *Nancy Barbour*
Marketing manager: *Colleen Suljic*
Project editor: *Beth Cigler*
Production supervisor: *Dina L. Genovese*
Interior designer: *Kay Fulton/Michael Warrell*
Cover designer: *Michael Warrell*
Cover photographer: *Mel Lindstrom*
Photo research coordinator: *Keri Johnson*
Prepress buyer: *Jon Christopher*
Compositor: *Carlisle Communications, Ltd.*
Typeface: *10/12 Janson Text*
Cartographer: *Maryland Cartographics*
Printer: *R. R. Donnelley & Sons Company*

▼▼ **Times Mirror**
◣◹ **Books**

Library of Congress Cataloging-in-Publication Data

Johansson, Johny K.
    Global marketing : foreign entry, local marketing, and global
management / Johny K. Johansson.
        p.   cm.
    Includes bibliographical references and index.
    ISBN 0–256–16051–1
    1. Export marketing.   2. Export marketing—Management.   I. Title.
HF 1416.J63   1997
    658.8'48—dc20   96–21836

Printed in the United States of America
1 2 3 4 5 6 7 8 9 0 DO 3 2 1 0 9 8 7 6

To my parents,
Ruth and Nils Johansson

THE IRWIN SERIES IN MARKETING

About the Author

···

*J*ohny K. Johansson was named the McCrane/Shaker Chairholder in International Business and Marketing at Georgetown University in 1989. An expert in the areas of international marketing strategy and consumer decision making, especially as applied to Japanese and European companies and markets, Johansson has published over 70 academic articles and chapters in books. He is the author (with Ikujiro Nonaka) of *Relentless: The Japanese Way of Marketing*, HarperBusiness, 1996. He has conducted numerous executive seminars in many countries, including Japan, West Germany, Sweden, Hong Kong, Thailand, and India. He has also been a consultant to companies in many countries, including Standard Oil of Indiana, General Electric and General Telephone and Electronics in the United States, Ford Werke AG in West Germany, and Mazda and Fuji Film in Japan.

Before joining Georgetown's faculty, Johansson held faculty positions at the University of Washington and the University of Illinois. He also has held many visiting appointments in several countries. He was the first Isetan Distinguished Visiting Professor at Keio Business School (Japan) and the first Ford Distinguished Visiting Professor at University of Cologne in West Germany. He also has been a visiting professor at New York University, Dalhousie University (Canada), Stockholm School of Economics, the Catholic University of Leuven (Belgium), the National Defense Academy (Japan), and the International University of Japan. In 1988 he was a Phelps scholar at the University of Michigan.

Johansson earned Ph.D. and M.B.A. degrees from the University of California, Berkeley, and his undergraduate degree (Civilekonom) from the Stockholm School of Economics. A Swedish citizen, he lives in Georgetown, Washington, D.C., with his wife Tamiko, and their two daughters, Anna, and Sonja.

Preface

Global marketing is one of the most exciting—but also one of the most challenging—fields of business today. It requires not only a good grasp of marketing principles and an understanding of the global environment, but also how the two interact, and how the environment impacts the applicability of the marketing principles.

The challenge when writing a text in global marketing is how to avoid being overwhelmed by all the curious and amazing differences in the marketing environments among foreign countries. So, the key approach of this text is to focus on the marketing decisions that have to be made, and then to deal with the environmental factors which directly impact those decisions. This text discusses the complexities of global marketing and clarifies the managerial roles involved without getting bogged down by the many environmental issues which are only marginally relevant.

Special Features

When compared to other texts in global marketing, the text has three main distinguishing features:

1. There are no designated chapters on the international environment of politics to discuss finance, legal, and economic regions. With the exception of culture, the book covers such variables on an as-needed basis in the various chapters.

2. As opposed to the view of the traditional "marketing manager," the typical global marketing manager's job consists of three separate tasks: foreign entry, local marketing, and global management. For each task the global marketer needs skills that the home market experience (or the standard marketing text) has rarely taught. This text's recognition of the three roles helps to dispel the notion that "there is no such thing as international or global marketing, only marketing."

3. The material is based on a theoretical foundation of the multinational firm. This is not for academic credit but rather because the theory helps the marketing manager to understand what drives the company expansion abroad, and it helps the manager understand how and when to adapt the various marketing functions involved.

Standard Material

This text also contains much of the standard research and teaching material that global marketers in business and academe have contributed over the years. This material is reflected not only in the chapter text, but also in the several cases that can be found at the end of each of the four parts. My intent has been to retain and update much of the teaching and instructional material that has made global marketing such a successful class in many business schools (and made for such an exciting managerial career) and to fit the material into a structure which reflects the current aspects of global marketing tasks.

To further illustrate the principles, the book incorporates cases at the end of each part. Many of these cases have been written by outstanding contributors to the field of global marketing, and I am very pleased to be able to introduce them here. Most of the cases are brief, as they are meant to serve as discussion material in class and not as a substitute for the longer Harvard-style cases which occupy entire sessions. In the teacher's manual I give suggestions for suitable longer cases for the various parts.

Target Audience

The text is aimed towards the executive, the M.B.A., or the senior undergraduate, none of whom is completely new to marketing or to the global environment. I have in mind a reader who is familiar with the basic marketing principles and who has had some exposure to the international environment and the thrust toward a global economy. I have avoided unnecessarily complicated jargon; the global marketing job is inherently complex, and any opportunity to "keep it simple" has been capitalized on.

Possible Courses

The three-way partition of the book makes it possible to construct several alternative course outlines from its content.

- A complete course on global marketing, possibly using additional Harvard-style cases, is the "full-course" treatment alternative.
- A shorter global marketing course, perhaps for executives, could go straight from the introductory first three chapters to the global management part starting with Chapter 11.
- An international marketing course could focus on the local marketing and the global management parts.
- An export marketing course could select the foreign entry chapters, and then do the local marketing chapter plus the pricing and distribution chapters in global management.
- At Georgetown I have used the text in a second-year M.B.A. class entitled "Foreign Market Development," for which I assign all of the

foreign entry and local marketing parts, but only the first two chapters of the global management part.

Supplements

Teaching a global marketing course requires more supplementary material than usual because of the amount of information about foreign countries which has to be provided. I am pleased to say that the editorial staff at Irwin has helped me put together what I think is a very strong resource package.

The supplements are especially designed by marketing professors to help teachers of this course be more effective. We have taken care to offer the best supplements we could make available.

Instructor's Manual: This manual is designed to assist instructors in meeting the varied curricular and pedagogical challenges inherent in teaching an International or Global Marketing course. The authors of this manual have been particularly sensitive to the needs of various kinds of global marketing classroom situations, concerning themselves with syllabus construction, pacing of topic coverage and other teaching suggestions, lecture outlines, discussion of end of chapter questions and supplemental readings based on the varying perspectives and needs of the instructor. Included in this supplement are discussions of the electronic transparencies, videos, and readings.

Test Bank: The Test Bank consists of more than 1,400 questions designed to thoroughly test the comprehension of basic terminology and concepts as well as the student's ability to apply those concepts. The material in each of the text's eighteen chapters is tested by a battery of sixty multiple-choice, ten short-answer and ten essay questions. The computerized version of the test bank, Computest 4, is available in DOS and Windows format.

Electronic Transparencies: A complete set of slides, including both in-text and out of text graphics, are presented on the PowerPoint software disk. Information about the slides is included in the Instructor's Manual.

Videos: The videos are comprised of numerous segments which highlight important aspects of global marketing. The videos are intended to provide unique footage of global marketing in action.

International Readings Booklet: This booklet, available in some packages, reprints current global business articles.

I have tried to make the text as enjoyable and interesting to read as possible. You will, of course, judge for yourself whether I have succeeded.

Acknowledgments

This textbook would not have been possible without the help and inspiration of many people. The environment at Georgetown's School of Business was ideal, with its emphasis on "international" as a school theme, the support of the Dean and the resources made available through the McCrane/Shaker chair, including a reduced teaching load and an outstanding secretary, Jennifer Barker. Then there were colleagues like Michael Czinkota and Ilkka Ronkainen, friends and competitors, and my other colleagues in marketing and international business, who all convinced me that a new text was needed, and who provided a stimulating environment for its completion. Andrea Alexander, May Guo, Niels Nielsen, and Kerri Olson were very able research assistants.

The content of the book owes much to colleagues at foreign academic institutions as well. First and foremost is Ikujiro Nonaka, professor at Hitotsubashi University in Tokyo, who has been a coauthor and friend over many years. Others in Japan include Tadao Kagono at Kobe University, Akihiro Okumura at Keio Business School, and Kiyonori Sakakibara, now at London Business School. I also learned from Masaaki Hirano at Waseda, Mitsuo Wada, when I was a visitor at Keio Business School, from my colleagues at IUJ in Urasa when I visited there, and from the many Japanese marketers I have met over the years through my academic friends.

In Europe, Professor Richard Koehler at Cologne University was very helpful as I learned more about the European integration effort. In Belgium, Piet Van den Abeele was a stimulating colleague. My Swedish colleagues— Gunnar Hedlund, Jan-Erik Vahlne, Lars-Gunnar Mattsson, Orjan Solvell in Stockholm, and Mats Forsgren and Jan Johansson at Uppsala—have been a source of inspiration over many years. Insead's Reinhard Angelmar and Jean-Claude Larreche have influenced my thinking about European companies more than they know. Tage Madsen at Odense is another colleague who has helped me understand what sets the Europeans apart.

Here in North America, I owe a lot to Alan Rugman at Toronto, who first introduced me to the new theory of the multinational, and whose writings I have used liberally. Susan Douglas was a great colleague during my two years at New York University. Tom Roehl, then at University of Washington now at University of Illinois, has been constantly provocative about the Japanese marketers. During my time at University of Washington, I also enjoyed Jerry Sullivan's different perspective on things Japanese, as well as Dick Moxon's and Fred Truitt's international business know-how. The work of Hans Thorelli at Indiana, Tamer Cavusgil at Michigan State, David Tse, now at City University of Hongkong, Philip Rosson at Dalhousie, Saeed Samiee and Tulso, Warren Keegan at Pace, and Masaaki Kotabe at Texas has had a strong impact on my thinking. When it comes to global strategy, I have been greatly influenced by George Yip at UCLA, a good friend and co-author, by Kamran Kastiani at IMD, and also by John Onto at the University of Melbourne and Nick Binedell at the University of Witwatersrand in Johannesburg.

Among marketing colleagues, I first want to thank Philip Kotler at Northwestern University and Jagdish Sheth, my former collegue at Illinois who is now at Emory University, both of whom have strongly influenced my thinking about the relationship between global and local marketing. I also want to single out Dominique Hanssens at UCLA, John Graham at Irvine, Arieh Goldman at Hebrew University in Jerusalem Dave Montgomery at Stanford, and Claes Fornell at Michigan, all five of whom have helped bridge the gap between international and noninternational marketing research. So has the strong group of researchers associated with Wharton, including Jerry Wind, John Farley, Bruce Kogut, George Day, and Erin Anderson. All have influenced what is in this text.

Some of the practitioners I have had the fortune to meet and learn from should also be thanked. Chong Lee at Lucky Goldstar Korea, Bruce Wolff at Marriott, Kevin Jones at McKinsey Japan, Ron Hosogi at Microsoft, Mitchell Reed of Grey Daiko, John Stabb at Microlog, and Chris Ericksen, then at GTE, stand out. So do Osamu Iida, Shumpei Hasegawa, Norimoto Otsuka, and Saburo Kobayashi at Honda, Chris Wada at Sony, Mitsuya Goto, then at Nissan, Karl Herman Gistren at Gadelius Japan, Ted Hirose of Shin-Nippon Wex in Nagoya, Hideo Shimoda of Jetro in Tokyo, Kiyofumi Matsumoto at Canon, Hiroe Suzuki at Dentsu, Hiroshi Ohnishi of Core Concept in Osaka, and Norio Nishi at the Commonwealth Bank of Canada in Tokyo. Hans Olov Olsson and Rune Lundberg at Volvo, Klaus Tarlatt at Ford AG in Cologne, and Jan Segerfeldt in Stockholm also have influenced my thinking.

Several of my present and former students provided valuable input of one kind or another. Eric Crabtree of CMT, Inc. in Moscow, Jim Hubbert, now at Disney Japan, Casey Shimamoto now at Daiwa Securities, Tsuyoshi Mano from Kyocera, Masumi Natsuzaka of Kao, Peter Munns at the International University of Japan, and Mitchell Murata at Georgetown have taught me much about global marketing.

Special thanks are due to the case writers who graciously allowed me to use their material in the book: Pamela Adams at SDA Bocconi, Tamer Cavusgil at Michigan State, Wolfgang Breuer and Richard Köhler at Cologne University, Tage Madsen at Odense University, Philip Rosson at Dalhousie, George Yip at UCLA, and Eddie Yu and Anthony Ko at City University of Hong Kong.

The editorial staff at Irwin deserves a great deal of credit. Rob Zwettler and Nina McGuffin are fun to work with, Nancy Barbour was a great slave-driver, and Beth Cigler knew where things were at. Harriet Stockanes in permissions and Michael Hruby behind the photos made me understand that there is more to a book than just the writing of it.

I also wish to express my appreciation to the following colleagues who reviewed this text and provided many helpful insights and suggestions:

Zafar U. Ahmed
Minot State University

David Andrus
Kansas State University

Jessica Bailey
The American University

Daniel Butler
Auburn University

Joan Buckley
University College Cork, Ireland

Tamer Cavusgil
Michigan State University

Paul Chao
University of Northern Iowa

Newell Chiesl
Indiana State University

Carol Felker Kaufman
Rutgers University

Josep Franch
ESADE, Spain

Pervez Ghauri
University of Limburg

Kate Gillespie
University of Texas

John Graham
University of California-Irvine

Bonnie S. Guy
Appalachian State University

John Hadjimarcou
University of Texas

David Jamison
University of Florida

Bail Janavaras
University of St Thomas-St. Paul

Joby John
Bentley College

William J. Kehoe
University of Virginia

Diana Lawson
University of Maine

Mike Mayo
Kent State University

Sam Okoroafo
University of Toledo

Stanley Paliwoda
University of Calgary

Daniel Rajaratnam
Baylor University

Catherine Rich-Duval
Merrimack College

Carlos Rodriques
Governors State University

Dennis Schorr
UCLA

Bernard Simonin
University of Washington

Nader Tavassoli
Massachusetts Institute of Technology

Tyzoon Tyebjee
Santa Clara University

Bronis Verhage
George State University

Cynthia K. Wagner
University of the Pacific

Jeryl Whitelock
University of Salford

Van R. Wood
Virginia Commonwealth University

My wife, Tamiko, and two children, Anna and Sonja, claimed to suffer greatly during the writing, but as far as I could see, their claims were exaggerated. Shattering a myth, my wife taught me that unlimited patience is no longer a Japanese virtue.

To all these people I say thank you. I hope the effort has not been in vain.

Contents in Brief

Contents

Part Two

Foreign Entry

Part Three

Local Marketing

Part Four
Global Management

18 The Future of Global Marketing 642

The complexity of operating in the global marketplace makes many demands on a marketer. Not only are there important decisions about which countries' markets and segments to participate in and what modes of entry to use, but a marketer must also help formulate the marketing strategies in these countries and coordinate their implementation. He or she must speak for the local markets at headquarters but also explain the need for global standardization to local representatives. It is a job in which proven marketing techniques and face-to-face contacts are invaluable and one that requires a thorough grasp of marketing fundamentals and use of global communications.

Part One of this book shows how the demands of these complex tasks force the marketing manager and his or her organization to reevaluate their marketing strategies. The primary issue for both the small firm marketing abroad for the first time and the large multinational corporation trying to implement a global campaign is the feasibility of their marketing plan. It means knowing not only what the company should do, but what it can do. This is never more relevant than in global marketing with its new and unfamiliar challenges, not the least of which is communicating well and doing business in a foreign culture.

The Global Marketing Job

"Brave new world"

After studying this chapter, you should understand the following global marketing issues:

1. The increase in international trade and investment, the emergence of free trade blocs, and the opening of previously closed economies have led to greater global market opportunities than ever, but also to the threat of increased competition at home.

2. In addition to seeking revenue and profit growth, the company entering a foreign market might do so to challenge a competitor, learn from lead customers, or simply diversify its demand base.

3. To compete effectively in the global marketplace requires skill building. The marketer needs to learn how to enter markets and how to manage the marketing effort in the local foreign market. To gain these skills, the global marketing manager needs to have hands-on marketing experience in one or more foreign countries.

4. The job (and career path) of the global marketing manager can be divided into three different tasks: foreign entry, local marketing, and global management.

CHAPTER 1 DESCRIBES the reality facing the marketing manager in today's global firm. As trade barriers are lowered, new growth opportunities in foreign markets open up, and new markets need to be entered. At the same time, foreign competitors enter local markets and previously unchallenged market positions need to be defended. The firm whose managers have a narrow view of its capabilities and its market will fall short. The purely domestic company often does not have enough managerial skill, imagination, and competence to respond to the opportunities or the threats of a global marketplace. Only by going abroad into competitive markets will a company stretch its resources and build the capability of its managers to a competitive level.

Chapter 1 illustrates how foreign markets and competitors have changed the face of marketing and how the global marketer must become more than a functional specialist. Today's marketers must develop skills that help to determine the overall strategic direction of the firm. This chapter shows how the complex new marketing can be subdivided into three main tasks—foreign entry, local marketing, and global management— each task an important component of the strategic capability of the manager and the firm.

Global Marketing Lays Foundation for Citicorp's Success

While stiff competition in the banking industry is swallowing up many banks, Citicorp maintains a competitive advantage by cultivating its global reach. The company boasts operations in over 90 countries, as well as a presence in developing countries with profitable specialties ranging from currency trading to credit cards. Citicorp's strategy for reinforcing its strengths is to skillfully manage its unparalleled international presence.

For chairman John S. Reed, the focus has been on global cooperation among employees. Instead of funding a separate development division, Citicorp expects its 15 operating divisions to share their innovations. Reed regularly brings together the Group of 15 (G-15 for short) or the executives who head the operating divisions.

Once a month, the G-15 meets to determine how the divisions can contribute to Citicorp's performance. At these meetings executives take turns describing the quality of their loan portfolios and the method of resolving any problems, as well as discussing methods for raising capital, cutting costs, and increasing revenue.

The G-15 executives have the authority to influence marketing decisions, but Citicorp's credit policy office carefully tracks the company's overall lending patterns. If the company invests too much of its assets in particular industries or regions, all divisions have to contribute to a solution.

This organizational culture compels the G-15 executives to balance their own wishes against Citicorp's overall needs. The company once had to choose between opening new facilities in Connecticut or Taipei, Taiwan. Since the Taiwanese branches were expected to become profitable more quickly than the Connecticut branches, Taiwan received the funding. Such decisions have helped Citicorp pull out of a slump. After building profits to record levels, the company was able to fund other projects, including the Connecticut branches.

To carry out its strategy, Citicorp needs managers who can contribute a global outlook, and this is a criterion met by each of the G-15 executives: Their offices are located in the United States, Europe, Asia, and Latin America, and eight of them were born outside the United States.

Globalization is one of the major forces changing marketing practices and Citicorp is one of countless organizations that need international expertise to fuel marketing success. Increasingly, organizations are turning to executives with the global experience and vision to lead them into the 21st century.

Sources: Saul Hansell, "Uniting the Feudal Lords at Citicorp," *New York Times*, January 16, 1994, sec. 3, pp. 1, 6; Martin Everett, "Soup to Oil? Hiring Marketers from Other Industries," *Across the Board*, July 1994, pp. 37–41; Thomas A. Stewart, "Welcome to the Revolution," *Fortune*, December 13, 1993, pp. 66–68.

GOING GLOBAL

A lot of businesses are going global today. Ten or 15 years ago global business was mainly in the hands of a select number of multinational giants. Small and medium-sized businesses concentrated on their home markets and perhaps one or two neighboring countries. Not so any longer. Even the smallest businesses have realized that they have something to market in far away countries, many of which have recently opened to foreign competition. Today, companies of all sizes in various industries from many countries are actively competing in the world's markets.

Behind the development toward a more global marketplace lies the revolution in global communications. Satellite television broadcasts have eliminated national borders in mass media. Fax machines and other advances in electronic telecommunications have made it possible to develop company information networks that rival government intelligence operations. Today it is possible for headquarters to participate directly in decision making in any subsidiary. Managers can direct operations any place on earth from airplanes and automobiles, even while they're on vacation.[1]

As long as world markets remain open, there is no stopping the spread of global competition. No markets are immune, as even government procurement business is opened to foreign suppliers. Deregulation and privatization confront sleepy public utilities with new and vigorous competitors, sometimes from countries in the same trading bloc.[2] Efficient foreign competitors from leading countries enter previously protected country markets and flush local companies out of comfortable market pockets. The lesson for all is that no market position is secure without attention to customer satisfaction and constant innovation.

Prominent movers in this raising of the competitive stakes have been Japanese, but companies in many other countries have risen to the challenge. European companies, aided by the European integration (EU), have consolidated and rationalized to protect themselves, and have in many cases become hunters on their own. Germany's BMW, Braun, and Beiersdorf; France's Thomson and Alcatel; Ciba-Geigy, Nestlé, and ABB in Switzerland; Italy's Benetton; and Sweden's Ericsson are some of the success stories. Others, like Volkswagen, General Motors, Electrolux, Fiat, Olivetti, Nixdorf, and Volvo, have had their ups and downs. Operating in the new global environment requires skills not easily mastered, especially when the traditional position was bolstered by trade barriers and government protection.[3]

North American companies have also taken up the challenge. Although many withered under the Japanese onslaught, others revived, stimulated by the new ideas learned and incorporating them into their own operations. Companies such as Xerox, General Electric, and Canada's Northern Telecom have successfully reengineered their operations and raised quality, and are coming through the difficult years stronger than ever. Companies with less-intense foreign competition, such as Hewlett-Packard, Microsoft, and Boeing, have kept their operations lean and their rates of innovation high, and have reinforced their global reach. Even U.S. automakers seem to be emerging from their long drought, although they have been helped considerably by the strong yen of the early 1990s. But as elsewhere, U.S. companies without international competitiveness—consumer electronics manufacturers, large steel producers, shoe makers—have had much more trouble defending their traditional market turf.

Even many Japanese companies have not fared well against international competition. Japanese markets were long protected by various tariff barriers, now removed, and also by nontariff barriers, some of which still remain. As standard economic theory suggests, such barriers often have the effect of supporting inefficient companies.[4] While Japanese automakers and electronics companies are generally very competitive worldwide, this is not the case in chemicals, pharmaceuticals, paper, medical machinery, and other industries. While rivalry among auto companies and among electronics companies is fierce, companies in less successful Japanese industries have been content with covert collusion not to compete.

The lesson is that intense competition at home and abroad forces a company to be internationally competitive. Today's global marketing manager must understand and learn from foreign competitors and from foreign customers.

A HISTORICAL PERSPECTIVE

The global perspective in marketing has become prominent in the last 5 or 10 years. It is useful to set this development in its historical perspective.

The Multinational Phase

In the two decades after World War II, American companies emerged as dominant multinationals. While the previously warring countries were preoccupied with rebuilding their nations, American **multinational companies (MNCs)** found great opportunities in Europe, Asia, and Latin America. Maintaining control over their manufacturing and technical know-how, and overcoming tariff barriers, through wholly owned subsidiaries, the American MNCs became suppliers to the world.

In those days marketing was technically much less advanced than it is today. Because of their obvious needs, foreign markets could be penetrated easily. Since production was often localized, products could be adapted to local markets. **Multinational marketing** meant marketing to different countries with local adaptation of products and promotions. At home in the States meanwhile, the growth ignited by the baby boom among other factors allowed companies to succeed with relative ease. Nevertheless, the size of the U.S. market, the relatively low U.S. tariff barriers, and competition between large firms stimulated development of more advanced marketing techniques.

Market segmentation, dividing a given market into more homogeneous subgroups, became a well-known conceptual tool toward the end of the 1950s, and the marketing mix with its 4Ps of marketing (product, price, promotion, and place) appeared in the early 1960s. Product positioning, the idea that a product or brand can be placed in a specific location in the consumer's perceptual map of a product category, became popular from the late 1960s onward. At the same time, marketing research techniques grew increasingly sophisticated with the impetus coming from academicians in business schools who were funded first by the Ford Foundation and later directly by companies. In the 1960s and into the 70s, the American marketers were, if not the best, at least the most technically proficient marketers in the world. Marketing textbooks from the U.S. established a leading global position, which they still seem to hold.

Gradually, as national markets grew and the American MNCs expanded production into new countries, these countries developed manufacturing and marketing capabilities of their own. While the American firms were still strong in new technology, they were no longer competitive in the manufacture of products embodying more standardized technology. Over time the United States became an importer of products it had originally invented, including textiles, electronics, and sports equipment. This process became known as the *international product cycle phenomenon* and retains a certain validity in today's globally integrated world.[5] It explains, for example, why a high-wage country such as Germany attempts to focus on high-technology industries. However, as increasing numbers of countries can handle high technology, companies in advanced countries may have to develop competitive advantages other than technology.

The Global Phase

The global phase, which involves much more standardization of products and integration of activities across countries than had been the case in the multinational phase, started during the 1970s, and was seen as early as 1968 in an article by Buzzell proclaiming the advantages of standardization.[6] The phase did not get commonly recognized, however, until 1983 when Ted Levitt at Harvard published an article arguing that world markets were growing more and more homogeneous.[7]

One of the major forces behind the emergence of the global perspective was the appearance of strong foreign competitors to U.S. firms in the United States. In particular, Japanese companies had entered the U.S. market with spectacular success in markets such as autos and consumer electronics, where American firms had long held dominant positions. From the mid-1970s on, foreign firms were no longer makers of the low-technology and low-priced entries, or luxury niche marketers as some Europeans had tended to be, but competed successfully in the core of the American marketplace.

Initially, the inroads by Japanese companies were explained as a consequence of tariff and nontariff barriers in their home markets that afforded them a ready supply of cash and preferential treatment as members of industrial groupings, allowing them to pursue low-price strategies overseas. The Japanese government also prioritized certain export industries, making low-interest loans and lenient tax treatment available. This line of explanation is still maintained today and underlies the push by other countries toward further opening of the Japanese markets.[8]

Gradually, however, the explanation for the success of the foreign entrants shifted more toward business-based factors. The availability of highly educated engineers, and skilled labor, and the companies' focus on manufacturing quality became a new line of explanation. The growth of suppliers in related industries and increasingly demanding customers served to explain an increasing rate of new product innovation. The existence of rival producers and intense competition helped enhance the firms' attention to customer satisfaction.[9]

By the end of the 1980s, Porter's work on the **competitive advantages of a nation** served to codify these factors.[10] No longer was Japan a special case; successful industries and companies in other countries shared similar characteristics. Companies with well-known global brand names such as Benetton in Italy, Swatch in Switzerland, Mercedes-Benz in Germany, and Sony and Toyota in Japan were shown to owe their success to favorable productive environments in their respective home countries.

While Porter's analysis is valid, it explains only part of the global performance of these companies. The main missing part is the marketing side. How can home country factors be important in foreign markets? Levitt in 1983 argued that markets around the world were becoming more similar because of technological advances in mass communications and the increase in international travel. People everywhere now are exposed to the same products and messages, and their preferences become more **homogeneous.** Accordingly, companies that offer standardized products with low prices and high quality win out over local competitors offering adapted products at higher prices. The large-scale advantages of **standardization** mean that the global company can be profitable while selling at a lower price, and the company can amortize investments in R&D and design over many markets. Global products, although not adapted to specific local preferences, can offer a superior quality-to-price ratio. This is why the Japanese succeeded against U.S. firms in the United States.

Although Levitt's argument was initially met by skepticism among marketing professionals, subsequent developments have tended to converge toward the global marketing view. Although local preferences have sometimes demanded product adaptation, there have been many surprising successes for standardized global products. Markets once thought to be very different across countries have been impacted by global brands. Consumer goods such as beer, food, and apparel, and services such as accountants, lawyers, and even retailers are some of the categories where global firms have been successful against locals in many countries. Add to this the typically global markets in many industrial products, high-tech products, and consumer durables such as cameras, watches, and VCRs, and in some ways the markets look more homogeneous today than even when Levitt was writing. Increasing similarity of preferences has led to the success of global products, which in turn has fostered further homogeneity of markets. Hamel and Prahalad, in a final twist, argue that in many cases new products lead and change preferences, so that the global firm should introduce many alternative new products, innovating and creating new market niches instead of trying to precisely target an existing segment.[11]

DRIVERS TOWARD GLOBALIZATION

Today, four classes of variables propel companies toward globalization: Market, competition, cost, and government variables are sometimes referred to as the four major **globalization drivers**.[12]

Market Drivers

Market factors are the strongest driver of global marketing. There are five major features of international markets that drive companies toward global marketing strategies. They are:

1. Common customer needs.
2. Global customers.

3. Global channels.
4. Transferable marketing.
5. Leading markets.

When customers in different countries have the same needs in a product or service category, **Common customer needs** become a compelling factor for companies. With technological progress and global communications, consumers in many countries are exposed to similar messages and products. For many industries, free trade and unrestricted travel have created homogeneous groups of customers around the globe. Preferences tend to become less localized or provincial and approach a *global* standard.[13] However, some markets—typically culture-bound products and services, such as foods, drinks, apparel, and entertainment—stubbornly resist the shift toward globalization and remain **multidomestic,** with different customer preferences and differentiated products across countries.[14]

Global customers are companies that have needs across several countries. As these customers go global, they want to do business with suppliers or vendors providing global service. This is why supplier firms in the automobile industry, such as German Bosch, Japanese Nippon Denso, and American Delco, have gone abroad. Global customers have spurred the development of global hotel chains, global ad agencies, and global communications. Hilton Hotels, McCann Erickson Worldwide, and Federal Express are prominent examples of

Companies serving multinational firms stress their global capability, as in this ad for DHL Worldwide Express.

Courtesy DHL Worldwide Express.

American companies following their customers abroad, in the process putting pressure on competing local services in various countries.

Global channels have had a similar positive effect on the emergence of global marketing strategies. Firms can in many cases expand internationally only if the requisite developments in the channel infrastructure keep pace. Thus, the multinational spread of large financial institutions, distributors of grain and other commodities, and even seemingly localized retailers such as supermarkets (Delhaize of Belgium, for example, is now present not only throughout Europe but also in the United States) and department stores (mainly by acquiring existing stores, but also opening new stores) makes it possible for marketers to sell their products through new integrated networks.

Transferable marketing is using the same marketing ideas in different countries. This can mean the same packaging, advertising, brand names, and other marketing mix elements. As campaign ideas in one country prove successful, the global company can use the same or a slightly adapted campaign in other markets as well. This is how good ideas get leveraged. For example, Nike's successful American ad campaign featuring basketball star Michael Jordan was used in many other countries as well. The multilanguage packaging of many consumer goods has made it possible to offer the same packages with the same colors and the same brand names in many countries.

Leading markets are markets where customers are particularly sophisticated and demanding.[15] The existence of such markets and the need for the firm to be in such markets push the firm toward global strategies in order to take full advantage of the benefits gained from leading markets. Although there is no need for the marketing strategy within a leading market to be identical to the strategy in other markets, there is good reason to share market research from leading markets with markets in other countries. Thus, the firm with the capability of implementing a global marketing strategy can draw on lessons from competitors and customers in leading markets to design the strategy. For example, while a semiconductor firm such as Texas Instruments has trouble making money in Japan, the lessons it learns in that difficult market help it to design entry strategies and service support elsewhere in the Asian region.

Competitive Drivers

The presence of foreign competitors in a firm's domestic market increases the need for the firm to venture abroad, if for no other reason than to counterattack in foreign markets. Benetton's success in the United States has led The Gap and The Limited, two U.S. competitors, to go abroad. The emergence of strong global competitors has served to develop the necessary facilities and infrastructure for domestic companies to go global. For example, global businesses tend not only to sell their products abroad, but also to transfer skills and technology across countries, making it easier for domestic companies to expand globally. The typical head of international operations at a novice entrant abroad has often been hired away from a more successful global company.

These kinds of competitive effects put pressure on companies to globalize their marketing activities. Even for the firm active in most foreign markets already, the competitive synergy achieved from synchronizing marketing across countries can be significant. Simultaneously introducing new models in several countries puts pressure on competitors, a strategy first used by Microsoft when introducing the new "Works" software. Monitoring competitive prices in several markets and coordinating price changes make it possible to match competitive prices in some markets and aggressively attack in others, as has been done by German automakers in the United States. Global coordination is also important when competitive signaling is to be interpreted. When Kodak was hesitant about sponsoring the 1984 summer Olympics in Los Angeles, the news was first relayed from the London office of Fuji film to American Fuji, which immediately offered to sponsor the games at the asking price. By the time Kodak had reconsidered, the competitive coup was already a fait accompli.[16]

Cost Drivers

In industries such as automobiles that require large-scale plants to be efficient, single markets are rarely sufficient to generate *scale economies*, and one plant needs to supply multiple markets. When a new plant is established, it is often designed to assemble one model only, shipping it to neighboring countries in order to gain such scale advantages. Toyota's new Kentucky plant, for example, produces the Camry model for the NAFTA market, and the new BMW plant in South Carolina will focus on the 325 model, supplying the North American market.

Even where there are no scale economies, *economies of scope* (gains from spreading activities across multiple product lines or businesses) can push businesses to globalize. Thus, in consumer packaged goods, where the dominant global firms have small plants in many countries, they gain scope economies by marketing a wide selection of products. Unilever, Colgate-Palmolive, and Procter and Gamble have mostly uniform product lines and brand names across the EU, but have manufacturing plants in all the major European countries.

Other cost drivers include global *sourcing advantages*, such as supplying from a low-wage country, improved logistics and distribution systems, which serve to make transportation cheaper, and the growth of inexpensive global telecommunications. Also, high product-development costs relative to the size of the national market and fast-developing technology serve to reinforce the need for global strategies to help recoup the investment.

These cost drivers generally induce companies to implement global strategies and some of these strategies further encourage globalized marketing. Thus, scope economies tend to favor globally uniform brand names and communications, and improved logistics and telecommunications make it possible to manage distribution of products and services centrally. Federal Express is now well known in many places across the globe, and its computerized

A few of Colgate-Palmolive's 493 new products introduced in 70 countries in 1994. Brand extensions, where a strong global brand is used to introduce new and related products, offer instant recognition and reduce promotional cost.

Courtesy of the Colgate-Palmolive Company.

tracking system makes it possible to monitor the progress of shipments 24 hours a day.

The most important cost savings from global marketing are usually the gains in avoiding *duplication* across countries. Designing different products for different markets, coming up with different promotional campaigns, creating localized slogans and brand names, and using different packaging in different markets are all signs of waste that can often be eliminated without a loss of goodwill. The original impetus toward global marketing is often management's desire to eliminate duplication and create better synergy across country markets.

Of course, there can also be a negative impact on global marketing from cost factors. For example, to capitalize on economies of scale in production several markets have to be supplied from a central location, creating a need for local warehousing facilities and local parts supplies. This investment may reduce some of the large-scale efficiencies. Furthermore, the large scale leads to inflexibility. For example, if a sudden change in demand creates a temporary market glut of one model and a shortage of another, a large specialized plant will be more costly to retool to satisfy the shifting demand.

Similarly, when product design is carried out in a leading market, local differences in preferences cannot always be taken into account. The same is true for prototypical advertising done in order to save money and for product-line pruning which eliminates local favorites too expensive to carry. Generally speaking, when marketing strategies are globalized to generate savings only, the local marketing effort suffers. Global marketing cannot be based on costs alone.

Government Drivers

The government globalization drivers include favorable trade policies, acceptance of foreign investment, compatible technical standards, and common marketing regulations. All of these factors have a direct and unequivocally positive effect on global marketing efforts. In the past, governmental barriers to foreign market entry kept local markets protected, and made global marketing an impossibility. Despite the continued progress toward open markets and free trade, it is important to keep in mind that such barriers can be raised again and that political complications can ruin the best-laid global marketing plans.

A good example of the effect of governments on globalization is the recent introduction of **ISO 9000**, the EU-wide new standard of quality certification (ISO stands for Industrial Standards of Operation). Faced with myriad conflicting regulations of products and services in the different member countries, the EU Brussels Commission decided to start with a clean slate and create a set of new standards to supersede existing national standards. Of course, each product or service category (telephones, consumer electronics, autos, pharmaceuticals, etc.) has its own category-specific standards. In addition, however, the Commission developed an umbrella code in ISO 9000 that serves as a guide for all companies wanting to do business in the EU. A Board of Examiners was created to certify companies under the code, which includes requirements on the safety of facilities, treatment of raw materials, quality inspection procedures, and even customer satisfaction measures. Although approval under the code is not a legal requirement as yet, many companies, European as well as non-European, have decided to expend resources to improve their operations and gain certification. This gives them a competitive edge over competitors not yet certified.[17]

ISO 9000 naturally encourages globalized marketing, since it is European-wide. Furthermore, the return on the investment in improved operations to gain certification is higher the more countries the company does business in. At the same time, the higher standards encourage uniformity of operations everywhere.

WHAT IS GLOBAL MARKETING?

Global marketing refers to marketing activities integrated across multiple country markets. The integration can take the form of standardized products, uniform packaging, identical brand names, synchronized product introductions, similar advertising messages, or coordinated sales campaigns across markets in several countries. Despite the term "global," it is not necessary that all or most of the countries of the world be included. Even regional marketing efforts, such as pan-European operations, can be viewed as an example of global marketing. The point is an integrated effort across several countries—and the principles are roughly similar whether one talks about 10 or 50 countries.

International marketing is an older term encompassing foreign trade analysis, environmental differences, and all marketing efforts in foreign countries, whether coordinated or not. There is also "foreign marketing," meaning merely marketing in some foreign country. As described earlier, in our historical perspective, "multinational marketing" meant marketing strategies that assumed all markets to be "multidomestic," or having strong local preferences, and is a predecessor term to *global marketing*, with its emphasis on standardization and integration.

In practice, these distinctions are not sharp, and the marketing activities they describe naturally progress from one to another. In order to perform the *global management* task successfully, the marketing manager needs to have some understanding of all the basics of international business and the characteristics of the market environments in foreign countries. The manager needs to have as keen a sense as possible of trade barriers, different market environments, and social and cultural biases—including of course his or her own. The successful global marketing manager gets intensely involved with these issues before attacking the global management job.

Marketing versus Manufacturing

To avoid confusion, it is important to emphasize the difference between global marketing and global manufacturing. *Global marketing* refers to marketing activities that are globally coordinated, often from a central headquarters location, involving a certain amount of uniformity, be it in products, prices, promotion, or distribution. Global marketing involves using the same marketing approach in many countries because the cost savings more than offset the disadvantages of a lack of local targeting.

Global manufacturing involves coordinating *manufacturing* activities across the globe. The term may imply the technology transfer that leads to some uniformity in manufacturing processes in different plants. More commonly, however, *global manufacturing* means specializing plants in different countries to play different roles in the global network. A common result of globally rationalized manufacturing production is that the company ends up shipping a large number of components and parts among its various plants. These intracompany shipments can reach large proportions. A common estimate is that in round figures about a third of external trade going to and from the United States is transfers between different units of the same company.

This book is about global marketing. Global marketing can occur without global manufacturing. Many of the Japanese companies have long practiced global marketing, but are newcomers to global manufacturing. Global manufacturing and global marketing executed together demand very complicated coordination. For example, in planning and executing a global advertising and promotional campaign for a standardized product line, a marketing manager is no longer affecting just one factory's production and shipment schedule, but a whole network of company plants in different countries.

Global marketing strategy will be dealt with in more detail below. Here it is sufficient to point out that in many cases it is easier to execute a global marketing campaign when the production side is not globalized. Because of this, non-American auto companies' foreign transplants almost always concentrate on specific models—Toyota Camrys in Kentucky, for example, and Volkswagen Golfs in Brazil—choosing models which sell well in different markets. Global marketing then involves selling these models in other parts of the world, shipping them from wherever the plant happens to be located.

Nonglobal Marketing

Many firms do a large international business without engaging in global marketing. For example, European companies like Germany's Siemens, France's Thomson, and Dutch Philips tend to treat their operations in different markets as independent profit centers. Their main markets are sufficiently different that there seems to be no immediate need for globalization. Their marketing can be characterized as more multinational or multidomestic than global. Other companies, such as many medium-sized exporters, tend to direct their overseas marketing efforts from home without an explicit aim to coordinate across countries. Their marketing effort abroad can be characterized as "international" rather than global.

However, the surge toward globalization in customer preferences, technology, and communications makes today's local markets candidates for global efforts tomorrow. One recurrent theme in global marketing is the degree to which previously domestic-only markets have become globalized as regulations and trade barriers are relaxed. It is difficult to argue that some markets will

The Rolm company in Austin, Texas, which develops and produces digital telephones for the American market, is owned by Siemens of Germany. The Rolm name is kept because it has credibility with existing customers and avoids demoralizing local employees.

Courtesy Siemens AG.

never be globalized, even though, as we will see later, there is often room in the market for local variants underneath the umbrella of global products and brands. The nonglobal firms need to make sure that they are not blindsided by the entry of strong global rivals.

A Managerial Approach

Taking a managerial approach, this book relates all important topics to the situation of the individual marketing decision maker in the firm or its subsidiary abroad. In this it differs slightly from other texts. Rather than treating the important environmental factors (political, economic, social, etc.) in separate chapters, we bring them into the decision-making setting explicitly, as additional problems or opportunities for the manager. As an example, a country's strict environmental code can be a constraint for some companies but serve to define a new market opportunity for others. Lack of commercial advertising opportunities in a country can force a company to turn to satellite TV and start developing global advertising copy.

We do not automatically assume the global company's home market is in the United States. The book covers companies headquartered in other countries and also takes a look at the United States as a foreign market. For many companies in other parts of the world, the United States is the main foreign market, and it should be of interest to Americans to recognize how they look from the outside. Incidentally, American managers who are disheartened by foreigners' in-depth knowledge of U.S. customers should keep in mind that because of the size of the United States, foreign managers tend to know more about the American market than about their other foreign countries' markets.

Terminology

Many global companies, as disparate as CNN and Honda, have banned use of the term "foreign" in their communications. They want to avoid the sense that some countries are separate and strange. The companies want their employees to view the world as an integrated entity and not favor the home country over others. While such avoidance is useful as a device to foster a global organizational culture, this book uses the word "foreign" freely. This is because "foreign" well describes the kind of situation global marketing managers often find themselves in. For managers of a company with established presence in the world's markets such as CNN or Honda, the various countries should be familiar enough to make use of the word unnecessary. For a textbook that teaches students how to get to that level of familiarity, however, "foreign" has just the right connotation of a slight (or severe) shock to the preestablished way of looking at the world (see box "Mercedes' Old-Fashioned Cars").

𝒢etting the Picture

Mercedes'
Old-Fashioned
Cars

ALTHOUGH MERCEDES-BENZ, the German carmaker, prides itself on the up-to-date technology it uses in its cars in the West, in other markets it is decidedly old-fashioned. Why? Because it has gone back to basics and become customer oriented.

In Saudi Arabia, auto engines are plagued by sand entering the cylinder blocks, gradually building up deposits until the engine cracks. But not Mercedes cars. Most new cars use light aluminum alloys in their engines because their hardness increases engine performance and is fuel efficient. By using older-style softer steel alloys, Mercedes cars lose the efficiency race, but keep running when the sand filters in. The hard silicon in the sand simply gets buried inside the softer metal of the cylinder heads.

In Poland, Mercedes' market share is on par with the Japanese cars' combined. Reason? The Poles are as rich as the oil sheiks? No. But for some models Mercedes has gone back to the old way of building cars from simple parts instead of using the integrated components and sub-assemblies that have served so effectively to increase Japanese manufacturing productivity. The problem with the modern techniques is that doing your own repairs is almost impossible, and repair costs rise since, when something breaks, whole assemblies are needed to replace a broken part. This matters less in Western countries where a big part of repair costs comes from the high cost of labor, and the new subassembly can be replaced quickly. But in Poland, labor is cheap. Mercedes sells well because spare parts are simple and inexpensive, and its cars can be fixed by the owner who can take his time to repair the car the do-it-yourself way or have a mechanic who is affordable fix it.

Moral: "Back-to-basics" marketing requires imagination and an understanding of usage situations.

Source: M. Wolongiewicz, student report, International University of Japan, June 1994.

GLOBAL MARKETING OBJECTIVES

The need to market overseas goes beyond pure marketing considerations. For example, presence in leading markets is necessary to keep track of new technological developments for tomorrow's products and services. Siemens, the German electronics giant, views its foreign market participation as one way to keep abreast of changes elsewhere and to maintain a global presence among present and prospective customers. Nissan's initial involvement in European auto markets—as well as its decision to drop the Datsun name and adopt the company name for its product line—was based partly on a desire to be better known among investors in the Eurobond market.

The main objectives the firm going abroad might pursue, often simultaneously, are as follows:

1. *Exploiting market potential and growth.* This is the typical marketing objective.

2. *Gaining scale and scope returns at home.* Longer production series and capital investment increase productivity.

3. *Learning from a leading market.* Many small market shareholders make no money in very competitive markets, but learn about new technology and about competition.

4. *Pressuring competitors.* Entering a market where a firm's main competitor has a stronghold might seem doomed to failure. But increasing the competitive pressure in the stronghold market might help divert the competitor's attention from other markets.

5. *Diversifying markets.* By adding new countries and markets to the company portfolio, the firm's dependence on any one market will be lessened. Although this is often a secondary objective, many companies attempt to maintain a balance between countries ("not more than 25 percent of revenues from any one foreign market") since currency fluctuations can affect revenues severely.

6. *Learning how to do business abroad.* This is mainly a spillover effect from marketing in a foreign country, but its value should not be ignored. For example, entering Poland may be a first step to entering Russia, in learning how to deal with former communist countries.

The potential diversity of objectives is one reason why marketing in the global company involves more than the traditional one product–market case typically treated in textbooks. But this does not mean that the local marketing efforts have to take a backseat to the global strategy. Satisfying the local customer is still the ultimate yardstick of performance in marketing. In a competitive market nothing less will do. Still, for the global marketer, the way to the goal involves more than finding out what the local customers want, designing the product or service, and then putting together a supportive marketing mix.

AN EXPANDED MARKETING REPERTOIRE

The new tasks of the global marketing manager are illustrated nicely by the experiences of P&G managers in Europe and Japan (see box "Procter and Gamble's Global Managers"). The experiences of P&G's Jager and his colleagues demonstrate the need for an international perspective in many marketing activities today. It is not only that many companies find their growth potential at home limited, and have to turn to markets abroad for new opportunities. It is also that even if a company decides to prioritize its home market first, foreign competitors are likely to enter, and the best defense is often an attack abroad. Motorola's semiconductor plant in Japan was established partly to keep the Japanese domestic companies busy at home, forcing them to pay less attention to the U.S. market.

Getting the Picture

Procter and Gamble's Global Managers

DURK JAGER is the president and COO at Procter and Gamble in Cincinnati, Ohio. A Dutchman by birth, Mr. Jager was educated in Europe and the United States, and worked initially for P&G in Germany. Having participated in several successful marketing introductions in Europe, in the early 1980s Mr. Jager was sent to Japan as P&G's effort there was faltering. After five long years, Mr. Jager managed to turn P&G in Japan around by breaking away from P&G's approach in Europe and elsewhere.

Mr. Jager is a very accomplished marketing manager in the global marketplace. He has been successful in Europe, in the U.S., and in Japan—but had to unlearn some lessons along the way. In Europe, P&G had been successful with a modified U.S. approach to product design and promotion. Japan was different. The company was forced to reconsider its marketing know-how, and to start looking at its products from the Japanese consumers' eyes.

As Mr. Richard Laube, advertising manager in Japan, states: "The striking thing is how simple the basics were. For example, we finally realized that disposable diapers should not be advertised as convenient if they could not be disposed of properly—as happened in Japan with its crowded conditions. We also realized the importance of carefully thinking through distribution. Again, it was extraordinarily simple questions which baffled us most. For example, we could not use in-store promotions for the Cheer brand of detergent simply because the stores were too small to stock enough product on the shelf."

The European experience did play a role in making management aware of potential pitfalls and the need to keep one's eyes open. Product design is one area where customer needs will blindside you if you are not careful. Ed Artzt, company president, and previously head of European operations, says: "We spent a lot of effort developing Vizir liquid detergent without remembering the fact that many German two-income households load their wash at night, but are not allowed to do the wash until the morning because of city noise regulations. The wash is ready to be started when people leave for work in the morning—by which time the liquid had drained through to the sink in the bottom of the washing machine."

The experience in Japan has been healthy for the company. Mr. Jager comments: "The Japanese companies are of course strong competitors. They do not hesitate to learn from their competitors—there is no 'not invented here' syndrome. P&G had to rethink its philosophy on this point, and we were successful in Japan only by incorporating competitive improvements on our products in our own new products. By the way, we are now selling our Japanese product versions in other countries as well. For example, our new Pampers diaper is the Japanese design. In fact, since we have a stronger global network than some of our Japanese competitors, we have been able to take their innovations global before they did. For example, the condensed detergents P&G now markets around the world are based on Kao's pathbreaking brands in Japan. That's what global competition is all about."

Sources: Yoshino, 1990; Natsuzaka, 1987; Artzt, 1988; and personal interview with Mr. Richard Laube, P&G Japan Advertising Manager, Osaka, June 3, 1991.

The global marketer draws on other markets and competitors for new products and services that go beyond the expressed desires of local customers. The global marketer has to learn to identify in what markets the state-of-the-art products are most likely to surface, what new competitors may blindside existing products, and which customers should be interviewed and observed closely for clues to new uses and benefits of existing products and for new product ideas. The global marketer has to identify to what extent competitive advantages in advertising and distribution are contingent on local marketing infrastructure and are thus not transferable. Hardhitting TV campaigns don't work well where markets need straightforward usage information (such as explanations of detergents for hard water in developing countries). They don't work well in countries where softsell is preferred because stores offer information (such as over-the-counter drugs in many European countries). Neither do they work well where TV advertising is banned—although new satellites have removed this "trade barrier" in some countries.

That is only the beginning of the list of additional considerations for the global marketer. There is simply a widely expanded marketing repertoire global marketers have to master. And as if this were not enough, the environments in which marketing decisions are made differ drastically between countries at different stages of economic development, markets at different stages of the product life cycle, with different competitors in the markets, and with consumers' cultural traditions and social norms widely divergent.

What these added complexities amount to is a reorientation of the marketing manager's perspective and an expansion of the skills necessary to be successful. Imaginative ideas about what can be done in a local market can come from any other market or any other competitor, as well as from the firm's own R&D. The global manager with a wider grasp of the possibilities stands a better chance of coming up with a winner. At the same time, the successful global marketer needs to be attentive to the local requirements, where traditionally he or she is thought to lack insights when compared to a local marketer. This is why local hires are so important, and why part of the new job of the global marketer is the acquisition of good talent (see box "Acquiring International Skills").

In the end, the globally savvy marketer's greatest advantage may lie in the ability to spot implicit assumptions in the traditional marketing know-how—and to go beyond them and think creatively. It is the purpose of this book to help develop such a sensitivity to the limits of traditional marketing know-how, and to show how global marketing can help the company not only to achieve profitability in a foreign country but also to expand the capabilities for success.[18]

LEARNING BY DOING

"Doing marketing" in a foreign environment helps develop what is sometimes called a **learning organization**. Learning organizations are organizations whose competitive advantage is not only lodged in existing assets and capabili-

*G*etting the
Picture

Acquiring
International
Skills

THE QUICKEST WAY for a company to beef up its global marketing capability is often to hire international specialists from outside. A case in point is Copley Pharmaceutical Company in Boston, a medium-sized (annual sales $50 million) drug maker 51 percent owned by Hoechst, the large German pharmaceutical concern. With Copley's development of promising new antihistamines and asthma drugs, Hoechst has set an aggressive goal for Copley's growth (sales of $1 billion within a few years), most to come from overseas sales.

Lacking international management skills, in May 1995 Copley appointed Gabriel R. Cipau, a Hungarian-born chemist and executive from Burroughs Wellcome of Britain, to be president

and chief executive. The new CEO most recently spent two years as president of Nippon Wellcome K. K in Japan. Copley also appointed its founder, Jane C. I. Hirsh, to a new position—president of international business interests. The previous president was let go.

Copley has joined forces with the Chia Tai Health Care Group of Hong Kong to form Chia Tai-Copley International Ltd., preparing for its China entry. Copley is also part of a joint venture in Russia, where its Mir Pharmaceutical unit is developing generic drugs. Cipau, the new chief executive, has set the growth strategy: Bring new products to new markets.

Source: Stewart, 1993; *New York Times,* May 16, 1995, p. D3.

ties, but in the ability of the organization to innovate, to create new products, to develop new markets, to adopt new distribution channels, to find new advertising media, and to discard outdated products and tired sales routines.[19] These companies do not exist only in high technology and high–value-added products—Microsoft, Hewlett-Packard, Mercedes, and Sony—but also in more mundane businesses such as consumer packaged goods. How does this learning work?

To illustrate how the learning happens, it will again be useful to relate the experiences of Procter and Gamble in Japan, and how that company had to change its ways of marketing.[20]

A well-known characteristic of the P&G marketing organization was long its reliance on the **brand management** concept it helped originate. Briefly, a brand manager's task is to support the brand in the marketplace through advertising and in-store promotions, and also to coordinate shipments to warehouses and stocking on store shelves. The job also involves helping to coordinate factory production schedules with special promotional drives, to do market research, and to suggest improvements to the developmental laboratories. For P&G the system also involved direct competition with other P&G brands in the same product categories. There was a conservative element built into the system in terms of managers' preoccupation with their existing brands.

New Products

As for new products, P&G evolved a system where any proposed introduction needed to be thoroughly tested in laboratory clinics, by home use, and through test marketing. The tests were to be summarized in one-page memos, ideally giving three strong reasons for the advocated action (the famous "keep it simple" memos). Only if definite preferences over existing product formulations were achieved in blind tests would the company give its go-ahead. In one case, involving Pringle's potato chips, the market tests lasted well over five years. The company wanted to ensure that the product represented a discernible improvement in quality and features over existing offerings.

This system works very well in mature and relatively slow-moving markets where the premium is on incremental improvements to maintain brand loyalty, tracking competitors and customers, and rapid reaction to competitive promotions. It works less well where the competitive edge goes to the firm with the newest product innovation and where customer preferences change fast. The latter are characteristics of the Japanese marketplace, where a premium is paid for speed and flexibility, with functional quality taken for granted. Thus, in Japan P&G found it could no longer rely on a great product well supported to be successful. It needed to be able to introduce new products more quickly.

The company tried to revamp its brand management system in Japan and placed brands under group management to avoid the individual responsibility that prohibited brand managers from taking risks. In order to speed up new-product introductions they also tried to limit "the Pringle syndrome," by making test evaluations quicker and less cumbersome. Because of the new management system, the company now is able to diffuse experiences from different countries throughout the organization faster than before. Reformulated products which succeed in one market are quickly introduced by managers elsewhere. The new compact detergents from P&G were developed in Japan and have now been introduced in most Western markets. The thinner diapers also emerged out of Japan. In both of these cases, P&G could move faster than its Japanese competitors because of its existing global network—but only after the "not invented here" syndrome typical of the narrowly focused brand management system had been eliminated.

Advertising

Long well-known for TV commercials depicting P&G products as problem-solvers for the harassed homemaker needing to impress her mother-in-law, the teenager looking for peer approval, or the young man who desperately needs a date, P&G went into Japan displaying Pampers diapers as a solution to a problem. Assuming that a wet baby posed a problem for the young mother, the company positioned Pampers as a new way of dealing with a hassle.

Realizing that grandmothers were important influences in Japan, the P&G commercials made sure the storyboard demonstrated approval from the

Labor of love. Pampers succeeded in Japan when P&G realized through market research that Japanese mothers did not think of their babies as an "inconvenience".

Caroline Parsons/Gamma-Liaison.

mother-in-law. Understanding that the homemaker who used the convenient paper diapers could be perceived as lazy, the commercials made sure that the baby's satisfaction showed, as the baby changed from crying to smiling. The commercials also adopted a big sister–little sister format, showing how the young Pampers-using mother followed in the footsteps of the already successful mothers.

Despite such seemingly excellent fundamentals, the advertising failed. The main reason was straightforward: The young Japanese mother simply did not view the baby as a "problem." Sure, there was wetness—but this only meant that diapers had to be changed. To leave the baby unchanged after an accident was unacceptable—regardless how "absorbent" the diaper was. Only by inventing a color-change wetness indicator could the paper diapers succeed, because then the mother could change the diapers right away after simply checking the color indicator. The indicator was convenient because it helped the mother take better care of the baby. And the idea of better care the Japanese mothers responded to, not to more convenience.

Needless to say, this benefit is contingent on the mother's not working outside of the home. But it can be transferred to Western markets, by focusing separately on segments of "mother at home" households.

Distribution

Upon entering Japan, P&G learned how strongly the implementation of large-scale in-store promotions depended on sufficient channel throughput. Several distribution layers in Japan are necessary because stores have very limited space, sometimes need replenishment daily, and have little capacity to handle a rush of buyers.

The solution to the distribution problem became the invention of new-product formulations and new packaging techniques. Thus, condensed detergents now allow limited store space to be more efficiently utilized. Similarly, thin diaper designs are preferable since they lead to smaller packages. Vacuum-packing techniques are used to compact the fluffy diapers, which then pop up when the smaller packages are opened. All these innovations, born in Japan, are now used by P&G in other country markets.

Skill Benefits

Over time, P&G's Japan operation has slowly turned profitable, as trial and error has been used to hone the marketing effort. For our purposes, it is important to recognize that these experiences have helped P&G improve marketing performance in other countries. The Japan episode has built global marketing capability further in an already successful company.

It should be said that the fact that the Japanese market is different does not cast doubt on the benefits of standardization. The experience in Japan would seem to suggest that the successful company there has to customize its marketing effort. Yet the P&G Japanese innovations have been successful elsewhere—and of course Japanese companies have succeeded overseas. What does this mean?

The explanation is that Japan functions in certain product categories as a *leading market*. This means that since customers in Japan are more demanding and thus more difficult to satisfy than elsewhere, if they are satisfied, the offering has a better chance in a follower country. This is not a new notion. It is popularly expressed as "If you can succeed here, you can succeed anywhere." Cosmetics and wine in France, autos in Germany, movies and computer software in the U.S., bacon in Denmark, and eelskin in Korea, for example, all fall in this category of products that must meet demanding standards in knowledgeable leading markets. Although adjustments to product features have to be made for local conditions (such as different voltages and regulations—a process we will call "localization"), by and large preferences in leading markets are ahead of those elsewhere, and thus predictive of the future.

To summarize at this point, major benefits from global marketing include:

1. *Capitalizing on the growth potential of the foreign market and neighboring countries.* This is the most obvious benefit for a marketer.

2. *Transferring competitive information and new products from those markets to other markets,* including the home market. Management shares information across countries, and the organization has "learned."

3. *Stretching and building up the firm's marketing capability,* not only in terms of implementation and execution, but also in terms of generating new ideas and concepts for strategic actions. Again, managers and the organization learn.

THREE HATS

To get a better grip on the complex job faced by the global marketing manager, it is useful to distinguish between three roles he or she may assume as a company goes global and becomes more extensively involved in international markets.

The Foreign Entry Role

First there is the **export manager** in charge of international sales. In many small and medium-sized companies—but also in some larger domestically oriented companies such as department stores and beer brewers—foreign sales account for perhaps less than 10 percent of the total turnover. As orders from abroad trickle in, someone takes charge of the international sales. As the business grows, this person gradually gains status in the organization, and the foreign business needs to be managed more systematically. The marketing activities initially involve learning about how to export and how to locate reliable middlemen overseas, often carried out with little or no attention to the larger picture. But as sales grow and the potential overseas is recognized by the company, more careful screening of markets overseas becomes desirable, and the possibility of establishing more permanent representation in key markets needs to be considered.

This is the **foreign entry** phase of the marketing manager's job. The manager has to learn the intricacies of doing business overseas, of finding the right middlemen, of quantitatively and qualitatively evaluating foreign markets, negotiating for joint marketing ventures, helping to set up a sales subsidiary, and learning to understand foreign customers' product and service requirements. Internally, he or she becomes the company leader in "internationalizing" the company. Externally, the manager becomes the company's spokesperson to the middlemen and customers in the markets entered.

These tasks verge close to a general management position, and the export manager in these companies has to shoulder more tasks than pure marketing. If the overseas entry involves manufacturing, marketing know-how is usually not crucial. But when the company enters a foreign country to gather access to markets, naturally marketers are needed. Nevertheless, many of the basic questions are organizational: setting up a logistics function and a network of middlemen, and developing reporting and control mechanisms back to headquarters. It's really basic marketing management—getting products to the customers, and getting paid for them.

The Local Marketing Role

But in many countries the company can't be satisfied using independent middlemen for the marketing effort. Especially in leading markets, the company needs to be closer to the ultimate consumer. Establishing a sales subsidiary and sending some expatriates to work there is common. In this way the company can ensure that the potential of the market is exploited, that the company capabilities are properly leveraged, that customer trends are monitored, and that moves by the competition are anticipated. In addition, the expatriate marketing manager has to direct the more tactical local marketing effort.

This **local marketing** role involves skills largely the same as those required in the domestic setting. This is the "marketing in Germany" or "marketing in China" hat. The basic marketing skills remain those of the typical textbooks, although the environment is of course different. This is the situation that tends to teach the manager a thing or two, not only about marketing skills but also about other cultures and behaviors, and, ultimately, about himself or herself.

Because of the different environment, the local marketing effort is usually carried out with the help of several natives. In some countries, the political, economic, social, or cultural environment differs so much that the expatriate becomes ineffective and a drag on the organization. Japan is notorious in this respect, and several foreign companies have decided to rely on Japanese employees altogether. This unfortunately removes many of the learning benefits that come from operating abroad. The typical approach today is to leave day-to-day management to natives, and let western managers play a more strategic role.

In many companies, the senior managers of foreign subsidiaries are expatriates. The joint ventures and strategic alliances common today feature expatriate managers in senior positions. They have to learn that, because of the different environment, some of their marketing skills may not be applicable in the local market. Market segmentation is difficult without reliable demographic and economic data. Domestic companies may be protected by tacit agreements between government and industry. In-store promotions run up against uncooperative retailers. The local marketing part of this book is intended to help the expatriate manager leverage marketing skills learned at home in this new environment.

The Global Management Role

The third hat of the global marketer, and often the next step on the career ladder, is the truly global part of the job. Using the learning and experience gained from foreign entry and local marketing, the marketer is now working on deriving global benefits from the firm's presence in various markets. The idea is to capture the scale advantages and other synergies to be created by more coordinated marketing.

Global management involves questions of standardization of products and services, uniform pricing around the globe, prototype advertising with a similar theme across countries, global brand names, and international logistics. The basic notion is to rationalize the global marketing operations in order to capture scale advantages and lower costs, and to coordinate the marketing campaigns across countries for maximum effect. This is easier said than done. The main body of this book develops the promises and the potential drawbacks of global marketing in much more detail.

A GUIDE TO THE CHAPTERS

As we have just seen, the three tasks the global marketing manager may face at different levels require various marketing skills and know-how. Matching the marketing skills required against the three tasks will help you to see how the various chapters of this book fit together. See Exhibit 1.1.

In Exhibit 1.1, the major marketing skills have been divided into three parts: market analysis, formulating strategy, and implementing and executing. **Market analysis** typically involves marketing research to find out about customers and competitors in various markets and to forecast sales and share figures. Research skills, analytical models, and statistical techniques are important factors in this stage. **Formulating strategy** in terms of segmentation, positioning, and the 4Ps flows naturally from the analytical stage. Strategy formulation requires imagination and intimate understanding of customers' situations and competitors' intentions and also the firm's own capability, in order to develop viable strategies. The **implementing and executing** phase deals with the development of systems and operating routines that get the strategy into the field and with the control of progress and performance in the specific market. Although it is sometimes useful to distinguish between implementation ("how to do it") and execution ("doing it"), for our overview the two can be treated together here.

EXHIBIT 1.1   Global Marketing *(Matching Skills and Tasks)*

Marketing Skills	Marketing Tasks		
	Foreign Entry (Part Two)	Local Marketing (Part Three)	Global Management (Part Four)
Market Analysis	Country potential; barriers to entry (Chs. 4,5)	Local buyer behavior, local marketing research (Chs. 7,8)	Globalization pros and cons; global customers and competitors (Ch. 11)
Formulating Strategy	Mode of entry; expansion paths (Chs. 5,6)	Localized marketing strategy (Chs. 9,10)	Formulating global marketing strategies (Chs. 12–16)
Implementing and Executing	Finding middlemen; negotiating with partners (Chs. 3,5,6)	Marketing in developed and developing countries (Chs. 9,10)	Implementing global strategies; motivating locals (Chs. 17,18)

In Exhibit 1.1 these three main marketing skills are matched against the three tasks facing the global marketer: foreign entry, local marketing, and global management. Where tasks match skills in the matrix, the main marketing problems have been identified. These are the main topics of the book's individual chapters. The book deals with foreign entry problems in Part Two, local marketing questions in Part Three, and global management issues in Part Four.

In **Part One** of the book, global marketing management skills and know-how fundamental to all global marketing tasks are introduced. Chapter 2 deals with the theoretical issues related to the question, "What business does a company have doing marketing in a foreign country?" Chapter 3 discusses the cultural fundamentals that tend to make marketing abroad a much more complicated affair than at home.

Foreign entry (Part Two). All marketers have to be able to do *market analysis*, undertaking research when necessary to understand customers and predict competitors. But the process differs considerably among the three tasks. In foreign entry the aim is usually to evaluate the market potential for a product or service in a foreign country about which relatively little may be known a priori. Such an analysis involves not only an assessment of market size and growth potential, what market segments exist and how to reach them, and strength of actual and potential competitors; the analysis also has to cover the height of various barriers to entry, including tariff and nontariff barriers, transportation costs, access to foreign middlemen, distribution availability, unfamiliar customs of doing business, and government regulations and policies favoring domestic producers. An otherwise very attractive market may be economically unreachable because of the height of the entry barriers. Chapters 4 and 5 will deal with these issues in more depth.

When it comes to *formulating strategy*, again the know-how required differs among the three tasks. In the foreign entry phase, the questions are usually not those of the typical marketing strategist (market segmentation and product positioning, for example) but rather questions of mode of entry. How should the foreign market be approached, via exporting or through a wholly owned subsidiary? Should a partner be licensed, or should we set up a joint venture? To what extent are the choices limited by regulation or government policies? Not only are many of these choices important for control over the marketing effort and product technology in the foreign country; the marketer also needs to understand how effective different relationships and linkages can be, and to what extent the firm can manage the relationships effectively. It is also important to recognize the implications of the chosen mode for learning about doing business abroad, and the role an entry plays in marketing to other neighboring countries. These issues are discussed in Chapters 5 and 6.

The *implementation and execution* phase is the most challenging one for many companies. Evaluating alternative countries for foreign entry and deciding upon the best mode of entry can be done with some certainty once data have been gathered. Setting the strategy in motion, however, involves a lot of travel to foreign countries, telephone and facsimile communications, often in a foreign language, locating and evaluating potential distributors, and personal negotiations with potential middlemen. The marketer executing an entry strategy needs to have a lot of energy, interpersonal skills, cultural sensitivity, and be able to sell himself and his company in a foreign country. It is not surprising to find that the difficulties of the task are such that a company often turns its back on foreign markets. While Chapter 3 covers the culturally related negotiation issues, Chapters 5 and 6 deal with the specific entry issues involved.

Local marketing (Part Three). The *market analysis* in the local marketing situation is quite similar to what is typically faced in the home market. Once inside a country, the marketer's aim is to generate information from market research on variables to be used for market segmentation, product positioning, and management of the marketing mix. There are complications—some marketing research techniques can't be used, for example, and consumer behavior can seem strange to an outsider—but the systematic application of fundamental marketing principles is still feasible. Chapter 7 discusses the ways in which assumptions about consumers and industrial buyers may have to be changed in foreign countries, while Chapter 8 deals with the marketing research complications.

In local marketing, the formulation and implementation of strategies become essentially a matter of adjusting to the foreign environment. The differences among countries' economic development, their cultural and social traditions, their regulatory environments, and other institutional factors combine to change the range of feasible strategies that can be considered. The local marketer, experienced in another country, may have to rethink a number of "tried-and-true" practices.

In terms of *strategy formulation*, the life cycle stage of the product in the new local market may be different. Segments identified in mature markets may not yet have crystallized in an emerging market. Positioning may have to change when the level of sophistication of the consumer makes certain attributes not salient. Differences in usage situations may make "obvious" benefits into negatives. Dominant competition may close out distribution alternatives favored at home. Sometimes the same distribution channels are not even available in the local market, and so on. The local marketer often has to be willing to take a fresh look, do some lateral thinking, "think outside the box"—in short, cast aside blinders—in order to succeed in a new local market.

The same problem afflicts *implementation and execution*. Point-of-purchase tactics that work in one country may be prohibited in another market. Package sizes may have to be reconfigured to fit store and consumer storage facilities. Credit extension for installment purchases may be unworkable because of banking regulations. Translating advertising copy may lead to unwanted word associations in another language, and so on. One of the frustrations of the local marketing manager is always the gap between what he knows is possible elsewhere, and what can be done in the local environment—and explaining that reality gap to impatient headquarters managers.

Chapters 9 and 10 offer more details on these problems, dealing with countries at different stages of economic development. Developed and developing countries present very different environments to the marketer, a difference to some degree captured by the traditional distinction between marketing in advanced, mature markets versus new, emerging markets. These chapters present a general approach to these disparate markets and offer in-depth discussion of the major markets in countries and regions of the globe.

It's important to emphasize that the adjustment to local conditions we mean when we discuss "local marketing" in Part Three is distinct from the common question of "standardization versus local adaptation." The adjustment in local marketing is best viewed as *localization* of the marketing effort, making it possible for the local marketer to be effective in the local context. However, *standardization* may be desirable from the headquarters' perspective now or later. It is precisely this shift in perspective that creates the headaches associated with global management efforts—and to understand the stress placed on local managers, the global marketer needs to put himself in their place. Part Three of the book does just that.

Global management (Part Four). From a local marketing perspective, globalization often seems suicidal. Instead of adapting to local customers' needs and preferences, global strategy means that products and services are uniform. Instead of recognizing important differences in cultural traditions and social mores, standardization gives everybody the same choices. Instead of using creative tactics to deal with the strengths and weakness of local competition, global strategies impose limits on local flexibility. In this sense, global marketing is fundamentally at odds with a market orientation.

In the *market analysis* stage, the global marketer basically attempts to identify the pros and cons of globalization and its accompanying standardization. The factors initially favoring globalization are likely to be found on the supply side rather than the demand side. Production economies of scale and scope, cost efficiencies as wasteful duplication across countries is avoided, and the possibility of investing more money in R&D are some of the factors. There are also competitive factors, as global competitors, reaping the benefits of these resource efficiencies, pose a threat to local companies.

But there are also market factors at work. Some customers, such as large multinational companies and even individuals who travel on business or vacation, need to be reached in many diverse places with a distinct and uniform sales message. Furthermore, because of the growth of global communications and technological diffusion, customer preferences in different parts of the world are converging toward a common standard in many product categories. The success of standardized products with global brand names in a wide variety of countries shows that adapting to existing local preferences is not always necessary or desirable. Strong global products can set new standards in local markets when they are marketed effectively.

These issues are dealt with in Chapter 11. This sets the stage for the global *strategy formulation* of the various elements of the marketing mix covered in Chapters 12 through 16. These chapters deal also with those *implementation and execution* problems unique to the various mix elements.

Questions associated with global products and services are discussed in Chapter 12. The centerpiece of any global marketing strategy is the question of how much adaptation to local preferences is necessary and it often leads to conflict between headquarters and the field. Chapter 13 discusses the issues involved in global pricing, where implementation and execution problems (including exchange rate shifts) often make a uniform global price unobtainable.

Global distribution (Chapter 14) is a topic that has increased in importance as trade barriers have fallen and global channels have opened up. Distribution has traditionally been considered a local marketing problem. A catchphrase has been "You have to distribute through local middlemen." However, the growth of global transportation, the emergence of global express mail, global credit cards, and global hotel reservations, and similar developments have made local sales possible without a local presence.

The most visible aspect of global marketing is perhaps the growth of global advertising and global promotions. Chapters 15 and 16 discuss the growth of global communications, including television networks and advertising agencies with global reach and customers linked via the "information superhighway." Chapter 16 also covers personal selling and direct marketing, an increasingly powerful global marketing avenue.

Chapter 17 deals with the organizational implications of global marketing. A major issue in implementing a global strategy is how to motivate the local subsidiaries and middlemen to support a global strategy that often constrains what they can do. Chapter 18 is the wrap-up chapter in which we look into future developments and evaluate whether the new communication possibilities, including the Internet, can help make the often-heard phrase "Global localization" become more than just a clever play on words.

SUMMARY

This chapter has emphasized the need for marketers to develop a global mindset. As markets grow more homogeneous across countries and global competitors win out locally, there is *no avoiding globalization*.

Firms pursue several objectives in their global expansion. Although sales and profitability are important, firms will go global in order to track, monitor, and challenge competitors, learn from lead customers and leading markets, and diversify away from reliance on a single market. Thus the marketing manager may find himself or herself in a foreign land, and the stint abroad will often seem unsettling, jarring the manager away from

preconceived notions and assumed know-how. In the process, the marketing manager will gain useful experience and learn new skills, which often can be put to good use at home and in other parts of the firm's global network.

The world of the global marketer is complicated, with not only new countries but also new tasks to deal with. It is useful to simplify the situation by separating the job into three parts: foreign entry, local marketing, and global management. The division is not always clearcut, and the roles of course overlap. But the tasks involved are quite different. Furthermore, the division mirrors the career path of many present and future global marketing managers: first, helping to evaluate and enter new foreign markets, then managing the marketing in one foreign country, and finally coordinating the global effort back at headquarters. These three hats of the global marketer help provide the structure for this book.

KEY TERMS

Brand management p. 21
Common customer needs p. 9
Competitive advantages of a nation p. 7
Export manager p. 25
Foreign entry p. 25
Formulating strategy p. 27
Global channels p. 10
Global customers p. 9

Globalization drivers p. 8
Global management p. 26
Global manufacturing p. 14
Global marketing p. 13
Homogeneous preferences p. 8
Implementing and executing p. 27
International marketing p. 14
ISO 9000 p. 13

Leading markets p. 10
Learning organization p. 21
Local marketing 26
Market analysis p. 27
Multidomestic markets p. 9
Multinational companies (MNCs) p. 6
Multinational marketing p. 6
Standardization p. 8
Transferable marketing p. 10

DISCUSSION QUESTIONS

1. What are the factors that seem to drive the globalization of the automobile industry? Why is the computer industry not spread more evenly around the globe?

2. Try to find some examples of a foreign competitor's gaining a large market share against domestic competitors. Then analyze whether the foreign firm was particularly good, the domestic firms were unskilled, or if good or bad luck played a role.

3. What would a marketing manager learn in the U.S. market that could be useful in Europe?

4. How would having served an internship in a Japanese company help you when you applied for a job at an American firm?

5. Why would "learning by doing" be particularly important when developing international marketing skills? In terms of marketing, would high-technology products require less or more direct experience with the local market than consumer packaged goods?

NOTES

1. Drucker, 1994, is as usual very perceptive in discussing how technology, information, and knowledge affect management.

2. Naisbitt, 1994, painstakingly documents the paradox of global economic integration coupled with political and ethnic fragmentation.

3. Lazer, 1993, spells out some of the implications of the new global order in more detail.

4. Nonaka, 1992, discusses how the creative inertia in some Japanese organizations has been overcome.

5. See Vernon, 1966. The international product cycle will be discussed in more detail in Chapter 2, which deals with foreign direct investment as a mode of entry.

6. See Buzzell, 1968.

7. See Levitt, 1983.

8. In his recent book, Chalmers Johnson reiterates this line of argument—see Johnson, 1995.

9. A prominent example of this second line of explanation is Womack et al., 1990.

10. See Porter, 1990.

11. See Hamel and Prahalad, 1991.

12. See Yip, 1992. This section draws directly on Yip's treatment of global strategy.

13. Levitt, 1983, was the first to recognize this trend.

14. Hout et al., 1982, first introduced the concept of "multidomestic" industries.

15. More on leading markets will be presented in Chapter 4 on country attractiveness. Leading markets are often attractive despite intense competition.

16. This incident is from Johansson and Segerfeldt, 1987.

17. ISO 9000 guidelines are available directly from the EU Commission in Brussels, and also from Department of Commerce offices. Consultants specializing in helping firms get ISO 9000 approval are also available in many countries. For an excellent overview of companies' response to ISO 9000 guidelines, see Prasad and Naidu, 1994.

18. The perspective on global marketing management adopted here is quite similar to what is advocated in the last chapter of Urban and Star, 1991.

19. The recent book by Barlett and Ghoshal, 1992, places strong emphasis on the importance of learning in global and "transnational" organizations.

20. The references used here include Yoshino, 1990, and Natsuzaka, 1987. In addition, this section is based on interviews with Mr. Richard Laube, Advertising Manager for P&G Japan in Osaka, and with Ms. Jennifer Sakaguchi of Grey-Daiko, an advertising agency in Tokyo. A final source is a student report, "Pampers in Japan," by Mike Ando, Yasu Mori, Kazal Roy, and Masa Tanaka, International University of Japan, June 1991.

SELECTED REFERENCES

Artzt, Ed. "The Vizir Development and Introduction." Presentation at the University of Washington's School of Business, March 17, 1988.

Bartlett, Christopher A., and Sumantra Ghoshal. *Transnational Management*. Burr Ridge, IL: Irwin, 1992.

Buzzell, Robert. "Can You Standardize Multinational Marketing?" *Harvard Business Review*, 46 (November–December 1968), pp. 98–104.

Drucker, Peter. *Post-Capitalist Society*. New York: Harper & Row, 1994.

Hamel, Gary, and C. K. Prahalad. "Corporate Imagination and Expeditionary Marketing," *Harvard Business Review*, July–August 1991, pp. 81–92.

Hout, Thomas, Michael E. Porter, and Eileen Rudden. "How Global Companies Win Out," *Harvard Business Review*, September–October 1982.

Johansson, Johny K., and Jan U. Segerfeldt. "Keeping in Touch: Information Gathering by Japanese and Swedish Subsidiaries in the U.S." Paper presented at the Academy of International Business Meeting in Chicago, October 1987.

Johnson, Chalmers. *Japan, Who Governs? The Rise of the Developmental State*. New York: Norton, 1995.

Lazer, William. "Changing Dimensions of International Marketing Management," *Journal of International Marketing* 1, no. 3, (1993), pp. 93–103.

Levitt, Ted. "The Globalization of Markets," *Harvard Business Review*, May–June 1983, pp. 92–102.

Naisbitt, John. *Global Paradox*. New York: Morrow, 1994.

Natsuzaka, Masumi. Class report, "Kao and Procter and Gamble in Japan," University of Washington School of Business, December 1987.

Nonaka, Ikujiro. "The Knowledge-Creating Company," *Harvard Business Review*, November–December 1992.

Porter, Michael E. *The Competitive Advantage of Nations*. New York: Free Press, 1990.

Prasad, V. Kanti, and G. M. Naidu "Perspectives and Preparedness Regarding ISO 9000 International Quality Standards," *Journal of International Marketing* 2, no. 2 (1994), pp. 81–98.

Stewart, Thomas A. "Welcome to the Revolution," *Fortune*, December 13, 1993, pp. 66–77.

Urban, Glen L., and Steven H. Star. *Advanced Marketing Strategy*. Englewood Cliffs, NJ: Prentice Hall, 1991.

Vernon, Raymond "International Investment and International Trade in the Product Cycle," *Quarterly Journal of Economics*, May 1966.

Womack, James P.; Daniel T. Jones, and Daniel Roos. *The Machine That Changed the World*. New York: Rawson Associates, 1990.

Yip, George. *Total Global Strategy*. Englewood Cliffs, NJ: Prentice Hall, 1992.

Yoshino, Michael. *Procter & Gamble Japan (A)(B)(C)*. Harvard Business School case nos. 9-391-003, 004, 005, 1990.

Theoretical Foundations

"What are we doing here?"

After studying this chapter, you should understand the following global marketing issues:

1. The firm contemplating global marketing needs to identify whether its firm-specific and country-specific advantages are sufficient to overcome the additional costs of doing business abroad.

2. Because marketing strategy attempts to leverage the firm's competitive advantages, the theory of the multinational firm is the natural starting point for business-level strategy formulation.

3. Internalization is the process by which the firm leverages its advantages on its own by exporting or investment, while externalization is the process by which the firm licenses its know-how to a foreign firm.

4. A market-oriented perspective needs to be combined with a resource-based perspective when the firm is contemplating global marketing.

THE AIM OF CHAPTER 2 is to introduce some of the fundamental building blocks of global market participation. The chapter first introduces the traditional economic theory of international trade and the theory of the multinational firm. The important concepts of *country-specific* and *firm-specific advantages* are introduced, and the role of marketing in leveraging these advantages is explained. The chapter applies and extends the economic principles to actual marketing examples, showing what the theories imply for global marketing strategy. The aim is to show how a few simple but powerful theoretical concepts can help guide the international marketer in the global marketplace.

In Chapter 2 we then define and explain the differences between a market-based and a resource-based strategy, and show how the two complement each other. The distinction between strategy implementation and execution is introduced and the importance of the "doing" part of international marketing is highlighted. The chapter ends by relating the market-based and resource-based strategies to the three functional tasks of the global marketer: foreign entry, local marketing, and global management.

"Made in Brazil" Becomes Badge of Pride

When it first started exporting products, the Brazilian subsidiary of Stanley Tools had to omit the "Made in Brazil" labels from at least half its products because customers had a negative impression of Brazilian quality. Five years later, only one Chilean customer wanted tools without the label.

Brazil has recently emerged as the nation with the third largest trade surplus. In other words, Brazil's exports exceed its imports to a degree unmatched by any other nation except Japan and Germany. And current available data on imports and exports do not actually show the full extent of Brazilian companies' foreign marketing because some organizations invest in foreign operations. For example, Tintas Renner S.A., Brazil's largest paint company, recently entered into joint ventures to establish paint factories in Argentina, Chile, Paraguay, and Uruguay. What happened to give Brazil this status in the world marketplace?

If "Made in Brazil" was once synonymous with shoddy work, that is no longer the case. Brazil far surpasses its Latin American neighbors in receiving certificates of quality from the International Organization of Standardization (known as ISO). Over 400 Brazilian companies have received ISO certification, which means that their products meet international standards of quality. By one forecast, 5,500 companies were expected to be certified by the end of 1997. An example of an ISO-certified company is Grupo Siemens, the Brazilian subsidiary of German-based Siemens AG. In a recent four-year period, exports from Grupo Siemens quadrupled, reaching an impressive $80 million.

Besides showing they can deliver world-class quality, Brazilian companies keep their prices competitive by improving productivity. At BASF da Amazonia S.A., productivity improvements saved the subsidiary of the German conglomerate from shutdown. The Brazilian factory now exports tapes to Europe, Latin America, and the United States. During the first half of the 1990s, Brazil's steel industry doubled its productivity to a level rivaling Japanese firms. During the same period, total manufacturing of Brazilian industry improved at the outstanding rate of 30 percent.

Brazilian companies are becoming a formidable presence in the world economy.

Sources: James Brooke, "A New Quality in Brazil's Exports," *New York Times*, October 21, 1994, pp. D1, D6; James Brooke, "Brazil Looks North from Trade Zone in Amazon," *New York Times*, August 9, 1995, p. D3; James Brooke, "More Open Latin Borders Mirror an Opening of Markets," *New York Times*, July 4, 1995, p. 47; Geri Smith, "Why Wait for NAFTA," *Business Week*, December 5, 1994, pp. 52–54.

INTRODUCTION

We have all come to take for granted a large number of imported products in our markets, and we tend to pity people who have no ready access to these products because of government restrictions or low incomes. Among such imports, we often associate certain products with certain countries, and may even prefer some products because of their country of origin. Examples include German cars and chemical products, Italian and French designs, Colombian coffee, Japanese VCRs, Swiss watches, computers and airplanes from the United States, and so on.

If we try to explain why these countries' products are preferred, it is easy to say, "These countries are best at it." Probing further, we say the reason for their superiority is "They have the right kinds of resources" or, "They've been doing it for a long time." When considering why these countries export their products to other countries in the first place, we find the same kind of commonsense answers: "The home market is too small for growth," or "They can make it cheaper than other countries," or "There is a great sales and profit potential in other countries."

If we ask why the product is sold by a particular company, a little more thinking is necessary. We might say, "This company is the best one at home, so it will be the logical one to export," or, "This company is not doing so well in its domestic market so it must export" (an equally plausible explanation). Similarly, if we inquire why this company is assembling its product in the market country while another is exporting directly from its home base, we might point to different tariffs and transportation costs, but, again, the answer is not always obvious.

In what follows, the theoretical foundations for these circumstances will be developed. The commonsense rationale behind a country's exports and imports will be examined. The theoretical justification for a country's exports is the well-known principle of **comparative advantage,** which refers to advantages in the resources available in a particular country. These can be termed *country-specific* advantages (CSAs). As to the question of which company will produce the product, it is possible to identify analogous *firm-specific* advantages (FSAs). And when it comes to how the foreign market will be supplied, we will see how barriers to trade (such as tariffs) may eliminate exporting as an option in favor of licensing know-how ("externalization") or investing in production abroad ("internalization").

This theory has relatively little marketing content per se, because the discussion centers on the justification of international operations of a business in general rather than the marketing function. Nevertheless, marketing issues are a necessary part of the package, and implications for marketing strategy and tactics can and will be derived.

Marketing has the task of demonstrating to customers that the net payoff from country-specific and firm-specific advantages (and disadvantages) is such that at the given price the company's product should be the preferred choice. So a clear understanding of exactly what the company's advantages are is a prerequisite for effective marketing strategy and tactics.

THE THEORY OF INTERNATIONAL PRODUCTION

Country-Specific Advantages (CSAs)

The principle of comparative or **country-specific advantage** provides the fundamental rationale for the existence of international trade. Free trade between two countries yields economic payoffs to the countries (in terms of higher welfare) provided the countries have different endowments of resources, that is, different advantages. It is not important if one country is better than another in producing all kinds of products. One country might have an *absolute* advantage (its resource inputs show higher productivity) for all the products involved and trade will still yield positive benefits to both countries. The requirement is rather that in one country the production of a product involves less of a sacrifice in the output of other products than it does in the other country, so that there is a *relative* advantage in production.

The original theory held that the country-specific resource endowments meant only natural resources and labor. Some countries have mineral resources, others have oil, others forests, and so on, and because of educational and social

*G*etting the
Picture

Which Country
Has What
Comparative
Advantage?

SINCE THE PRINCIPLE of comparative advantage applies at the country level, there have been several attempts at identifying exactly what the advantages are in different countries. A now classic example is Dunning's study in 1981, which arrived at the following conclusions:

Japan—Textiles, clothing, consumer electronics

United Kingdom—Food and tobacco products

Sweden—Mechanical and electrical engineering

United States—Transportation equipment

(West) Germany—Chemicals

It should be recognized that although some CSAs persist over time (such as those based on natural resources), there will be changes as new skills among labor are developed and technological innovations force new production processes to be employed and new raw materials to become scarce.

Source: Adapted from Dunning, 1981.

differences, the populations exhibit varying labor skills; all of these are factors that create differences in the countries' comparative advantages as well as the absolute advantages (see boxes). In extensions of the theory, other CSAs have been identified. They include proximity to the final markets (and the increased understanding of the demand structure that follows) and the ability to deal with a complex legal and commercial environment. Transportation costs, for example, are now often viewed as a country-specific disadvantage of foreign manufacturers.

For country-specific advantages to be decisive in international trade patterns they have to be actually fixed to a particular location. Over the years, the increased mobility of labor (the "importation" of south European workers to the northern European countries, the use of Indian laborers in the Saudi oil fields, and the "brain drain" from the U.K. to the U.S., for example) has made labor less of a country-specific factor. At the same time, the location of plants for textiles, electronic subassemblies, and sporting gear in Southeast Asia is obviously dictated partly by low labor costs. However, on the whole, the theory of comparative or country-specific advantage still explains many of the international trade patterns between countries, especially for raw materials, where location is indeed fixed.

For comparative advantages to be effective it is necessary that trade be free. In the absence of free trade, each country has to be more self-sufficient, and less specialization is possible. If the market is large, multinational firms may try to overcome trade barriers by investing in manufacturing within the country. Such import-substituting FDI by the multinational firm is a response to non-free

EVEN THOUGH one country has a comparative advantage in say, labor skills, it does not follow that its labor is the most skilled. The principle of comparative advantage means only that its labor skill when compared to its other productive inputs is higher than the corresponding ratio for other countries. It is often of interest, however, to identify what countries tend to have an *absolute* advantage in the sense that its resources show high productivity.

Productive Factor	*Country or Region*
Cheap labor	China, Philippines, Ghana, Indonesia, Brazil, India
Skilled labor	Japan, Taiwan, South Korea, North America, and Europe
Financial resources	United States, Japan
Natural resources	Russia, Middle East, China
Advanced technology	Japan, United States

Source: Adapted from Dunning, 1981.

trade, which is a second-best solution, since now production is not located according to the principle of comparative advantage. Because of the need for several productive inputs in any one manufacturing location, however, the MNC will also usually transfer resources to locations with different advantages. These **technology transfers** serve to give a dynamic character to CSAs. A country with low labor skills, for example, will gradually improve skill levels under such transfers.

The multinational firm also exploits both differences in tariff barriers between different countries as well as differences in tariff rates for parts and components, as opposed to fully assembled products. By investing in a country with cheap labor to make simpler parts and exporting to its assembly plant elsewhere, the multinational can draw upon country-specific advantages of different countries. For example, a Toshiba television set destined for the U.S. market may have a picture tube (the most critical component) from Japan with standard circuit boards and chassis added in its Malaysian plant and final assembly done in Canada, arriving in the United States with lower labor costs and lower tariffs than if it were imported from Japan directly.

The International Product Cycle

A strong position in a foreign country can be undermined quickly by a competitor who develops the product domestically, or by another importer whose product is manufactured in a low-cost country. What at one point were seemingly unassailable market positions in Western markets for autos, calculators, stereos, watches, steel, and so on, have been lost with sometimes amazing speed to new producers from lower-wage countries.

The working of the so-called **international product cycle** tends to make once economically justified production locations uncompetitive as new countries develop the requisite manufacturing technology and know-how. Country-specific advantages change over time.

The international product cycle (IPC) is different from the well-known product life cycle (PLC) long employed in marketing analysis. The PLC describes the various stages that a product's unit sales go through from time of introduction to maturity and decline in a given market. The IPC, by contrast, depicts the dynamics of international production, dealing with the gradual shift of production from the originating country to the low-cost mass producer in another country.

The IPC was initially proposed by Raymond Vernon in 1966, who used it to demonstrate how the manufacturing of new products in the United States shifted over time to new locations overseas and in the process affected trade patterns.[1] The process is depicted in Exhibit 2.1. In the initial stage, the innovator produces and markets the product at home to a growing home market. As production increases above the home market demands, the firm turns to exports and develops markets in other developed countries. Then, as these new markets grow and their domestic production of the product gets under way, trade shifts again to Third World markets. As the production know-how gets more widespread, however, these countries gradually develop their own manufacturing capability, helped by the processes and the technology by now standardized. As low-cost production in these Third World (or newly industrialized) countries gets under way, their imports give way to exports back to the original country's market. The cycle has come full circle, and the original inventor now imports the product.

As many countries other than the United States have become adept at inventing new products and processes, the international product cycle as originally developed has become outdated, and Vernon and others have amended it.[2] Today, for example, it is not uncommon to find that a country that started production of a certain innovative product continues as the foremost manufacturing site. The American supremacy in computer design is a good example. This process has been documented in detail by Porter.

Porter's National "Diamond"

In an important extension of the theory of comparative advantage, Porter has introduced what he calls the **diamond of national advantage**.[3] The diamond comprises four factors that make up the competitive advantage (or disadvantage) of a country:

1. *Factor conditions.* The nation's position in factors of production, such as skilled labor or infrastructure, necessary to compete in a given industry.

EXHIBIT 2.1   The International Product Cycle

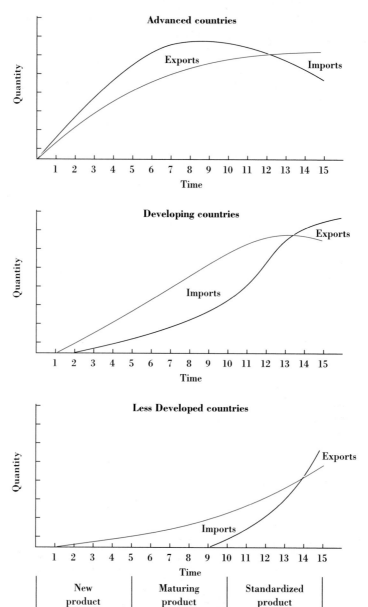

Source: Reprinted with the permission from the Journal of Marketing, ''A Product Life Cycle for International Trade.?'' by Louis T. Wells, July 1968, pp. 1–6. © 1968 by the American Marketing Association.

2. *Demand conditions.* The nature of the home demand for the industry's product or service.

3. *Related and supporting industries.* The presence or absence in the nation of supplier industries and related industries that are internationally competitive.

4. *Firm strategy, structure, and rivalry.* The conditions in the nation governing how companies are created, organized, and managed, and the nature of domestic rivalry.

Exhibit 2.2 shows how these factors interrelate. A nation's competitive advantage—and, consequently, the country-specific advantages for firms from that country—depends on the strength of each of these factors. Favorable factor conditions include the traditional endowment of natural resources that was the basis of the original theory of comparative advantage. Porter argues that, over time, vigorous competition in the industry will help develop stronger firms, and support growth and improvement among supplier firms. Furthermore, sophisticated and demanding customers at home help hone the competitive skills of the industry further.

Porter's is a dynamic theory, showing how over time a nation can build up and sustain its competitive advantage in an industry. While firms' relying on factor cost advantages (lower cost labor, for example) can provide the initial stimulus for economic growth, other countries will appear with even lower factor costs. In order to sustain growth, the nation's competitive advantage will

EXHIBIT 2.2   Porter's Determinants of National Advantage

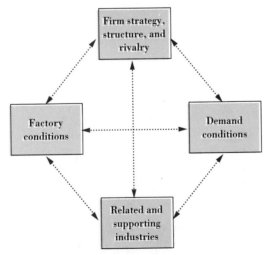

Source: Adapted and reprinted with the permission of the Free Press, a division of Simon & Schuster, from *The Competitive Advantage of Nations*, by Michael E. Porter. Copyright © 1990 by Michael E. Porter.

Getting the Picture

Porter's Related Industries

PORTER EXPLAINS how a globally competitive industry spawns the development of globally competitive firms in related industries in the listings below. As can be seen, many of the prominent industries in the world market have been built on more basic innovations in other industries.

Nation	Industry	Related Industry
Denmark	Dairy products, brewing	Industrial enzymes
Germany	Chemicals	Printing ink
Italy	Lighting	Furniture
Japan	Cameras	Copiers
Korea	VCRs	Videotape
Singapore	Port services	Ship repair
Sweden	Automobiles	Trucks
Switzerland	Pharmaceuticals	Flavorings
United Kingdom	Engines	Lubricants, antiknock preparations
United States	Electronic test and measuring equipment	Patient monitoring equipment

Source: Porter, 1990, p. 105.

have to be extended by capital investments in upgraded machinery and technological development in the industry. But for a nation to sustain its advantage it is also necessary that related and supporting industries follow by upgrading their facilities and expertise (see box "Porter's Related Industries") and that home market customers become more demanding, expecting the best.

It is important to recognize that Porter's diamond implies that a country can remain competitive in an industry even as its manufacturing costs rise. Thus, the diamond goes counter to Vernon's original IPC theory. While the IPC explains the "hollowing out" of a nation's industrial base, with manufacturing moving to low-wage countries, Porter's diamond suggests that competitive rivalry and capable business management can help nations develop new skills and renew their competitive advantages. While Vernon's IPC concludes that advanced nations will trade for standardized commodities and focus on innovation and new industries ("get out of televisions, and focus on computers"), Porter's diamond shows how the creation of favorable conditions can make a nation stay competitive in a given industry for a long time ("automobiles is what we do best"). Actually, in most economies of the world, both tendencies are at work simultaneously.

A 3M worker in Bangalore, India. A locational advantage in labor is not simply a matter of low wages. It can mean a well-educated workforce and a concentration of firms where workers can get valuable work experience.

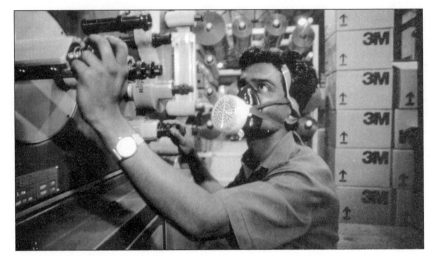

Dilip Mehta/ Contract.

The New Trade Theory

In a related development, it has been demonstrated that the trade patterns between countries depend on man-made, Porter-style, locational advantages.[4] For example, as advanced technology centers arise around strong research universities and innovative new firms, the local labor force develops skills unique to specific industries, and companies will find it increasingly attractive to locate in those areas. This **new trade theory** explains the development of high-technology areas such as "Silicon Valley" south of San Francisco, Bangalore in India, and the Stuttgart-Munich area in Germany. Similarly created CSAs include the skilled labor force in other industries, such as apparel in Italy, optical instruments in Japan, and chocolates in Belgium. These country-specific factors shift the comparative advantages away from what natural resources alone would suggest.

Of particular interest to marketers, Krugman and other "new trade" theorists point out that the products traded are generally differentiated and not homogeneous. Accordingly, international trade patterns will not necessarily follow the original theory's predictions. For example, there is a great amount of intraindustry trade between nations, with a country such as Germany both exporting and importing a large quantity of cars, for example. This still begs the question why Germany would not produce all its desired cars and then trade for other products. Krugman first demonstrated how the pure theory needs to be augmented to incorporate skills developed. *Differentiation leads to specialization and the creation of firm-specific advantages that come from learning by doing.* German automakers become good at certain types of cars, not others. From a marketing viewpoint this is hardly surprising, since these cars tend to be differentiated and to target alternative market segments.

·······························
EXHIBIT 2.3   Two Sets of Synonyms for FSAs and CSAs

Level	Synonyms
Country (CSAs)	Comparative advantages; location-specific advantages
Firm (FSAs)	Differential advantages; ownership-specific advantages

As a strategy, this process is variously known as organizational learning or knowledge creation.[5] It represents the process by which companies develop new resources. This learning of new skills is of course very much a theme of this text, since the global marketing manager's experiences with foreign countries serve to expand marketing know-how.

Importantly, Krugman's ideals, although perhaps self-evident to marketers, strike at the heart of the pro–free trade argument, since a country can become efficient in the production of goods in which it starts with little or no comparative advantage. This notion suggests a need for early industry protection and lies behind the discussion about more active industrial policy in many countries.

Firm-Specific Advantages (FSAs)

The fundamental premise of any enterprise is that it can transform valuable inputs into even more valuable outputs—this is the essence of "production" as opposed to "consumption." The rule for survival of a company is that it provide some desired benefit to the customer better than other enterprises provide. The company entering markets abroad must have some advantage which outweighs the increased costs of doing business in another country in competition with domestic firms. This advantage should not be available to competitors and is, therefore, to some degree monopolistic. It is called a **firm-specific advantage,** to emphasize that it is unique to a particular enterprise. (Since different writers and we too sometimes use different terms, Exhibit 2.3 gives some alternative synonyms, for FSAs and CSAs.)

Firm-specific inputs may be of several kinds. They could consist of a patent, trademark, or brand name or be the control of raw materials essential to the manufacturing of the product or simply control of distribution outlets. These advantages could also include process technology, managerial capacity, or marketing skills. They might well have their source in country-specific variables, but the essential point about them is that they can be used by the company alone. If mobile, they can be transferred to other locations by the company through exports or foreign direct investments.

These firm-specific factors are necessary but not sufficient to explain international expansion. Without them, there is no particular reason why the individual firm would contemplate going abroad. It has no competitive advantage to help it overcome the extra costs of going abroad. Assuming there is some firm-specific advantage, however, the question arises how the company will choose to exploit its advantage. Where it will produce is then a matter of the country-specific advantages of different countries.

The firm also needs to decide how it should enter the various country markets, and from what manufacturing plant the necessary supplies and final products should be procured. This component of the theory of international production is sometimes viewed as an explanation and justification for the emergence of multinational firms in itself and is denoted the theory of "internalization."

INTERNALIZATION THEORY

In the so-called **eclectic theory** of multinational production, FSAs will explain which companies will supply demand in a market and CSAs will determine from which countries this will be done.[6] The way in which the market will be supplied—the mode of entry—is determined by the companies' need to internalize their know-how.

Mode of Entry

There are a number of ways in which a company can enter a given country market. They will be discussed in detail in Chapters 5 and 6 on entry strategies. In principle, three different modes can be identified: straight exporting, licensing, and direct foreign investment (in production or selling capabilities). In *pure exporting* the product is simply exported to a distributor appointed in the market country; *licensing* "transfers" some ownership advantages via a contractual agreement to an enterprise in the market country; and *foreign direct investment (FDI)* means the company invests money in subsidiary operations in the country. As will be seen in Chapters 5 and 6, in practice there are many variations on these three types, but for theoretical purposes these distinctions are sufficient.

The question of choice of mode boils down to how the company with the owner-specific advantage can get a reasonable payoff or return on its know-how. Generally speaking, such a company could sell its superiority (be it in patents, brand names, or process technology) to a local buyer for use. This is the licensing or "externalization" option. If the market for such advantages were efficient, the price the firm could obtain would mirror directly the worth of the advantage in the final market. There are, in fact, a number of such contractual arrangements, some persisting over time (like Coca Cola's licensing of bottlers in different countries), others employed primarily in the initial stages of expansion owing to financial and other constraints (such as Mitsubishi's entry into the U.S. auto market using a tie-up with Chrysler Motor Corporation).

Delivering Coca Cola in Guangdong, China. Coca Cola's typical entry mode into foreign markets is to license independent bottlers in a franchising arrangement. But in some emerging countries Coca Cola invests directly in the bottling plants to control quality.

Ron McMillan/Gamma-Liaison.

One problem with the licensing option is that the foreign company will not have an opportunity to learn about the new market and to expand its skills repertoire. Furthermore, policing the licensee and overseeing the royalty payments (usually some percentage of sales) can be difficult. As the licensee develops the requisite skills of production and marketing, there is a risk that payments will not made, that the transferred know-how will be used for export production, so that over time the firm-specific advantage will be gradually eroded. This **dissipation** problem could be reflected in the prices of licenses, but with less than perfect foresight it would be difficult for the firm to assess the appropriate level of return. Generally, according to the theory, firms turn away from licensing because they can get higher returns on their FSAs by "internalizing" them.[7]

Where licensing is thus deemed to be too risky and learning is important, the company has a choice between exporting and FDI. Both avenues imply that the company has decided to retain control over its owner-specific advantages, either by producing at home (the export option) or investment to produce abroad (the FDI option). This is the meaning of **internalization.** In the exporting case, the firm-specific advantages are embodied in the product marketed abroad but may still need some protection against dissipation (see box). In the FDI case, the advantages are employed to generate returns in a subsidiary, and then the payoffs are repatriated by way of transfer prices or simply profit taken home. The usual definition of a multinational firm is one having a number of foreign production sites and thus a number of internal markets. The pure exporting firm is usually denoted an international company. From this perspective many of the European automobile companies are less multinational than international. For example, Mercedes and BMW build the vast majority of their cars in Germany, and the recent decision to establish assembly in the United States is a big step for both. Volvo, Renault, and Fiat have only limited manufacturing abroad, Volvo in Belgium, Fiat (previously) in Spain (Seat) and Russia. French Renault's investment in American Motors failed to resurrect the latter, and Renault is now back on home ground. Contrast this with Ford and General Motors, true multinationals that have built cars in Europe for a long time, and with Volkswagen and Honda, which have a number of plants outside their home countries.

Transaction Cost Theory

The emphasis on FSAs in the internalization theory can be given an equivalent theoretical interpretation in terms of Williamson's transaction costs.[8] Since this framework has proven useful in determining mode of foreign entry, the theory is of relevance to the global marketer.[9]

Generally speaking, **transactions costs** are costs incurred when completing a transaction between a buyer and a seller. Apart from obvious costs such as transportation charges, sales taxes, and brokerage fees, there are often other costs incurred as well. Examples include how to establish contact between buyer and seller, translations in order to communicate in different languages, the risk that the product might not follow agreed-upon specifications, misunderstandings in price negotiations, and so on. These obstacles create the costs incurred by the parties in the transaction, and unless sufficient gains from the exchange are obtained, the costs may prohibit trade.

The activities that are required to overcome these barriers can be termed "market-making" functions. Since specialization tends to reduce costs, a sufficient volume of transactions of a certain kind is likely to spawn different agents who specialize in these activities. The most direct examples of these kinds of institutions occur perhaps in financial markets, where banks and brokerage houses serve to link buyers and sellers across borders and rely on their global information network to spot trading opportunities in which they can fetch a profitable commission.

As an alternative to employing external agents or market-makers, a firm might assume such functions itself. The seller of a product might provide the credit, storage, or insurance necessary for the completion of the transaction, while the buyer might take the responsibility for the transportation, for example. These cases of (forward or backward) vertical integration represent examples of the principle of internalization. In the framework of transaction cost theory, internalization occurs when the most efficient (least-cost) means of effecting a transaction occurs within the firm itself.

A typical firm-specific advantage is a globally recognized brand name. From a transactions costs viewpoint, an established brand name serves to lower the cost of the exchange since the buyer can trust the quality of the product, and his "search" costs are reduced. If this trust is misplaced because company operations abroad are not properly controlled, transaction cost theory would predict that future purchases will not materialize. To ensure against such an event, the company will be likely to enforce rigorous quality control, possibly via FDI and 100 percent ownership. The transaction cost argument thus creates the same rationale for internalization as the FSAs do. In both cases, the aim is the protection of the benefits from the completed transaction, in one case by maintaining a sufficiently low transaction cost, in the other by protecting the FSA embodied in the brand name.

Exporting versus FDI

The choice between pure exporting and foreign direct investment (FDI) in manufacturing hinges on, among other things, the number and height of the obstacles to free trade. In the case of free trade (the situation usually associated with the original development of the theory of comparative advantage), there is no particular reason to engage in FDI just to service a market. Because of varying tariffs and nontariff barriers, however, the case for FDI is often quite strong. The investment in productive capacity induced by these types of barriers is often denoted "import-substituting" FDI, since such barriers tend to eliminate trade. For the marketer who likes to follow the trade conflict debates between various countries, it is good to remember that FDI often replaces exports and leads to a negative trade balance.

From a company viewpoint, however, there are usually additional factors that need to be considered in choosing between exports and FDI. Unless excess capacity is available in the home plant, the serving of other countries might well involve the establishment of additional manufacturing capability. When such a step is necessary, the country-specific advantages of producing in other countries need to be considered (better access to raw materials, cheaper labor, and lower transportation costs are factors that enter into this calculation). Furthermore, the

*G*etting the Picture

Country-Specific Advantages and FDI: Rossignol

FOREIGN DIRECT INVEST-MENT can be preferable to exporting even if the formal trade barriers are small. One reason is the country-specific advantage associated with manufacturing in the market country. The French ski manufacturer Rossignol's experience represents one of these cases.

As its share of the French market reached saturation, the management of Ski Rossignol realized that further growth was only possible through expanded international involvement. Initially the company sought to do that by exporting from France, establishing sales offices (commercial subsidiaries) in many of its target country markets, and improving its distributor network.

Because of problems with floating exchange rates and bad experiences with dock strikes and long transportation delays, the company decided to turn to FDI in manufacturing. It established plants in Switzerland, Italy, Canada, Spain, and the U.S. all within a span of about four years.

These sites, except Spain, were chosen because of their proximity to large ski markets (low labor costs influenced the Spain location). The company management stated: "Skiing trends change quickly, and with differences across countries. Furthermore, skiing conditions vary among countries and even (the case of Canada and the U.S.) between neighboring countries. With the rapid changes compounded by national and international differences, we needed to stay close to the large individual target markets in order that these trends be anticipated correctly."

The basic know-how of ski-making was not something Rossignol would lose control over by licensing. But in this case the choice of FDI was not undertaken because of trade barriers per se. The country-specific advantage of market proximity was the driving force.

Source: Thorelli and Becker, 1980, pp. 21–23.

case might arise where the firm-specific endowments are not strong enough to overcome the locational disadvantages of home production, but would be if the manufacturing were done in a third country closer to the market. With the emergence of trade regions, such patterns are common; for example, EU markets are often supplied from Ireland, and the American market from Mexico.

Thus, the firm will not in general choose between exporting and FDI as an either/or proposition, but rather make a decision on the basis that production abroad might well make profitable exports to other countries not served before. Where production will take place depends on CSAs coupled with the barriers-to-trade encountered from the countries where manufacturing occurs. "Pure" exporting from a home country is simply a special case in which CSAs at home and the firm-specific advantages are great enough to offset the locational disadvantages (including transportation costs and lack of market familiarity—see box "Country-Specific Advantages and FDI").

MARKETING IMPLICATIONS

From this discussion it should be clear which company will supply a market (it depends on its firm-specific advantages), from where it will do so (it depends on country-specific endowments); and how it will do it (it depends on the efficiency of contractual markets and the barriers-to-trade). Next, let's examine the marketing implications of the theoretical discussion.

Production-Based Advantages

The firm shifting from exporting to manufacturing in a country can both gain and lose some marketing advantages in the process. However, being closer to the customer is always a gain for a firm. For example, distributors can feel more secure about supplies, and customers can rely on after-sales service. The firm becomes more of an insider because it is able to hire a domestic workforce and create goodwill by being a good citizen. Company managers become more attuned to the way of doing business in the country and come to understand the market better.

But, there can be drawbacks. If the company is seen as an intruder, replacing a former domestic competitior, there may be more ill will than goodwill. Domestic competitors may mount a campaign against the newcomer, and since it is unlikely that all former employees can be hired, media can come to focus on the lot of some displaced workers. These are typical negatives for most countries, and the firm needs to conduct itself with care to minimize the potentially negative market reaction.

There is also a possiblity that a country-of-origin quality effect comes into play. As we have seen, the exported products embody the production know-how and skills, including the country-specific advantages, of the company at home. Some customers will question whether these can be transferred successfully to the plant in the new country. When Volkswagen started to build its Rabbit model in Pennsylvania in the 1970s, customers rushed to buy the last imports of the model from Germany. The typical strategy to overcome such consumer doubts has been to avoid emphasizing where the product was made. Of course, this approach forgoes the positive benefits of manufacturing within a country, and so a more constructive approach is to reexport the product back home. Honda, the Japanese car company, exports its Honda Accord coupe made in Marysville, Ohio, to Japan, thereby assuring the American consumers that the quality of the car is up to Japanese standards.

Marketing-Specific Advantages

Marketing decision making must also recognize that the source of the firm-specific advantage might lie in specific market know-how. For example, large consumer goods manufacturers (Nestlé, Unilever, Procter and Gamble) have

A company with vast global experience such as Unilever understands that marketing execution may differ across countries. Here is a promotional campaign for Vim, a new detergent bar, designed to complement traditional washing methods in India.

Peter Hince.

accumulated experience and skills in many foreign markets that give them an edge over competition. These skills include techniques for analyzing and segmenting markets, developing promotional programs and advertising campaigns, and administering massive introductory campaigns for new products. Similar skills in the marketing area might be said to lie behind some of Caterpillar's and IBM's successes in many markets (Caterpillar's policy that a serviceman can reach a site within 48 hours, for example) and also the close relationship with distributors nurtured by many companies in Japan.

A question that arises when marketing skills are important is the degree to which these skills can be transferred to other countries. Not all of them can be (see box, "Marketing FSAs").

Certain factors make the employment of marketing skills difficult in other countries. Where commercial TV is not available, it is difficult to leverage the skills developed in the area of TV advertising. Procter and Gamble's reluctance to enter the Scandinavian markets is one illustration of this, now partly alleviated as satellite TV and new channels open up the market to TV advertising. When the FSAs are in distribution channels (as in the Electrolux case—see box, "A Marketing Skill Transferred"), going abroad might involve having to create new channels in the local market. In some of these cases, production in the market country might make the local marketing effort easier.

Getting the Picture

Marketing FSAs

MOST COMPANIES have several marketing strengths, but are sometimes characterized by one or two major FSAs. Among global companies with strong marketing, the following FSAs stand out:

Strong brand names—Coca Cola, Sony, Mercedes.

Products with state-of-the-art technology—Microsoft, BMW, Canon.

Advertising leverage—Gillette, Unilever, Nissan.

Distribution strength—Kodak, Canada Dry, Panasonic.

Good value for the money—Ford, Ikea, Toyota.

Other companies have marketing FSAs not easily exploited overseas:

Budweiser's great brand name asset derives from an original Czech beer still brewed and sold, complicating sales in Europe. Also, its light taste relative to most countries' beers slows expansion.

German Henkel's (detergents) strong presence in the European market has been difficult to leverage elsewhere, as it depends on strong distribution and brand loyalty based on special washing traditions with respect to water hardness and temperatures used, less use of tumble dryers, and frequency of washing.

Kao's (detergents) and Shiseido's (cosmetics) strengths in distribution at home in Japan, where they have control at both wholesale and retail levels, cannot easily be duplicated elsewhere.

It could, for example, make it easier to recruit capable distributors and dealers, since host country production can be used to assure the channel members that supplies will be forthcoming.

A major difficulty in transferring marketing skills abroad is that these factors often represent intangibles, not skills "embodied" in the product itself (as technology typically is). The principal means of completing the transfer is by employing personnel transfers and education of local people.[10] Because of the new environment in which expatriates have to work, and the uncertain results of the educational effort, marketing skills will often not be transferable at a reasonable cost. Conversely, where marketing skills provide the basic firm-specific advantage, the incentive to go abroad is not as strong as where the advantage rests on factors that can be embodied in the product. An exception to this rule is the growth in franchised services, in which a specific mechanism is created to transfer marketing skills. Successful service companies such as McDonald's, Kentucky Fried Chicken, and Hilton Hotels have standardized their services and relied on training local franchisees in each specific detail of the day-to-day operations, to ensure uniform quality across countries. For manufacturing companies, such an investment in technology transfer is often not necessary, since the final product embodies the advantages already.

*G*etting the Picture

A Marketing Skill Transferred: Electrolux in Japan

THE SWEDISH MANUFAC-TURER of vacuum cleaners, Electrolux, has long sold its product through door-to-door salesmen demonstrating the virtues of the product in the home of a prospective customer. Over the years considerable refinement in the sales approach was developed and taught to new salesmen. The sales technique became one of the company's distinctive skills.

Entering Japan, Electrolux found initial reactions among the trade people toward this type of selling approach negative. It was said that the Japanese were not used to having unknown people enter their homes and would not allow the salesmen's entrance. Electrolux first decided to follow the standard Japanese approach of selling through department stores and specialty shops. For a period of several years the company attempted several variations on this approach, all with the same result: Sales were too small to cover costs, and the higher price of their product (be-cause of transportation costs, tariffs, and distributors' markups) was not considered sufficiently offset by better performance. Competitors among the domestic producers (Toshiba, Hitachi, and others) continued to dominate the market.

Believing that with a proper demonstration of performance the price differential could be justified, management of Electrolux decided against all odds to introduce their particular selling method in Japan. After extensive training of their Japanese salesmen, the door-to-door approach was introduced. The result: an immediate success. Electrolux became a market leader at the upper end of the market.

Electrolux's experience vindicates the idea that we should concentrate on doing what we do best. It also demonstrates the fact that in a new country one does not necessarily have to do things the way they have always been done, not even in a relatively isolated country like Japan.

Marketing Strategy

The understanding of "why we are here" in terms of firm-specific advantages is a key issue for the formulation of a marketing strategy in a country, especially for market segmentation and product positioning. The first point to note is that the firm-specific advantage might well vary across countries. In other words, the differential advantage that products enjoy over competition might be different for customers in different country markets. It becomes important to identify exactly what the advantages are for the particular country. Marketing research needs to be carried out in order that customer needs and competitive offerings be properly identified and matched against the firm's product. Such an analysis will yield guidelines for what features of the product need to be stressed in various countries, so as to place it in as advantageous a position vis-à-vis competitors' offerings as possible.

This logic underlies the many multinational firms' practice of providing different products from their complete line in different countries. In autos, few of the U.S. makes are sold abroad—they have a differential disadvantage. Many smaller European makes are not introduced in Japan where competition among small cars is intense. Black and white television sets are sold in the less-developed countries (LDCs).

Product positioning needs to be carried out with a clear understanding of what segments are to be targeted with a differential advantage. Because of weak infrastructure, in developing countries the needs of the customers are often quite different. For example, with voltage surges common, many home appliances need "shock fuses" to protect against breakdowns. A more rugged and basic version of a product might be designed in order to satisfy customer needs (the "small is beautiful" syndrome). But it's important to gauge the extent to which the FSAs can be kept when redesigning a product, since often if they are lost, the company enjoys no differential advantage and should probably not enter. The big American cars of the 1950s guzzled too much gas and were built too low to be useful on bad roads, so the American automakers exported from their European base rather than from the United States.

The character of firm-specific advantages sets limits on standardizing the marketing effort. Volvo, the Swedish car, is positioned as a luxury car in some overseas markets, but at home it is a practical and reliable transportation vehicle. Needless to say, the Swedish advertising is not particularly useful as a starting point for Volvo's marketing overseas. Although more will be said on this topic in a later chapter, it needs to be stressed here how the FSAs must be carefully analyzed so that the opportunities (and pitfalls) of a standardized program (with its associated lower costs and improved control possibilities) can be fully realized (or avoided).

RESOURCE-BASED VERSUS MARKET-BASED STRATEGY

As we have seen, when it goes abroad the firm usually can't be certain that the home advantages can be leveraged in foreign markets. Customers will not have the same preferences and competitors will be different. The transfer of advantages into foreign markets is fraught with dangers: Can service be kept at the desired level? To what extent is the marketing infrastructure different? Can the product perform as well in a new environment? When is high quality no longer high quality? These are uncertainties that challenge the marketing strategic plan.

Before the recognition of the learning effects of specialization discussed by Porter and Krugman, the economic theory of international trade and the theory of the multinational firm were basically static, "equilibrium theories" in economic jargon. As we have seen, the global perspective powerfully challenges a static mindset, and suggests that advantages are not a given and fixed fact. "Going global" stretches the firm's capabilities.

The dynamic benefits of foreign entry come from competing against new competitors and supplying new and demanding customers. This is what helps build new FSAs and sustain the competitive edge. Global markets are important not only for their market opportunities, but also for the opportunities they offer to expand the resources of the firm. It is in the constant re-creation of the company's assets and competencies that the dynamic benefits from global marketing come. The global marketer is always learning new concepts and techniques.

Always Market Oriented?

Most students and practitioners of marketing have learned about the advantages of a **market orientation.** "Don't think of the product sold, but the customer need fulfilled." "Deliver customer satisfaction, not just what you think is a quality product." "Your dealer is also your customer." "Understand the consumer better by listening to complaints." "Don't just read research reports but go meet your customers in the store."

For the marketing manager, it is natural to think about overseas opportunities in terms of customer needs and wants. It suggests that the main issue is whether there is a demand for the product. But this is only a start. More importantly, the manager has to identify what the firm has to offer abroad, and whether it can deliver on the promise.

The crucial factor for the firm is to understand the basis of its own success at home or elsewhere. The firm contemplating going abroad should identify its key strengths and whether its local success is just that, local. Only if there are good reasons to assume that some strengths are applicable in another country should it start examining markets abroad. It is possible to look at foreign entry in terms of learning and increasing competitiveness, but even then existing strengths and weaknesses have to be carefully assessed.

When countries are less developed as market economies, adopting a market orientation is often ineffective. The assumed infrastructure is weak or nonexistent, making "middlemen as customers" a moot idea. Customers with sophisticated needs are few and far between, making customer satisfaction a matter of providing the most basic products and services. Warranties and liberal return policies are difficult to administer and easy for customers to abuse. After-sales service can often not be offered without risky investments in new buildings and machines and additional training of dealer employees.

Knowledge-Based and Resource-Based Capability

Much has been written recently on the topic of the **knowledge-based organization.**[11] Market-based explanations for sustainable competitive advantages have given way to analysis of factors internal to the firm. If competitive advantages traditionally resided in a superior offering in the marketplace, recent rapid changes in products and services have suggested to analysts that competitive sustainability lies more in a company's speed and flexibility to change products and services.[12] These knowledge capabilities are not embedded in the products themselves—their features, quality, image—but involve know-how, skills, and experiences of the company and its employees. Such know-how can be difficult to articulate and teach, more art than science.

This ad for SAS, the Scandinavian Airlines System, emphasizes the airline's frequency of flights, in-flight comfort and service, as well as the firm-specific advantages and resources which define what SAS can offer the business traveler.

Courtesy Scandinavian Airlines System.

Knowledge is one of the resources of the firm. **Resource-based strategy** defines the firm not in terms of the products or services it markets, nor in terms of the needs it seeks to satisfy, but in terms of what it is capable of. From the resource-based perspective, the first question is what the firm *can* offer in terms of technology, know-how, products, and services. Only then may the issues of selecting markets and developing a competitive global strategy be successfuly tackled.

A good example of how a market orientation can be wedded to a resource-based approach is the strategy adopted by SAS under Jan Carlzon (see box, "SAS and Strategic Flexibility").

An internal focus on strengths and weaknesses seems to go counter to the marketing concept but, as the SAS example shows, in reality it complements it. Whereas a market orientation focuses on competitive advantages in the marketplace, the resources perspective fosters a view of the company as a leveraging force for its resources. It generates an appropriate mindset of "getting a return on the assets" philosophy, in which the key management question is how the resources should be deployed to generate the best return.

The Value Chain

For the global marketer, the change in perspective that comes with the resource-based view can be illustrated by the value chain concept. The **value chain** concept suggests that the firm's activities in transforming raw materials

Getting the Picture

SAS and Strategic Flexibility

WHEN SAS (Scandinavian Airlines System) needed a new CEO after a dismal year in the early 1980s, they turned to Jan Carlzon, the president of the Swedish domestic airliner Linjeflyg. Savvy industry observers expected Carlzon to pursue the same strategy at SAS as he had pursued successfully at Linjeflyg: cut-rate prices and targeting the tourist class. But Carlzon surprised them.

"The international market was not the same as the domestic," Carlzon explained in his 1987 book, *Moments of Truth*. "In the international marketplace, service was a neglected but important attribute, not price." After analyzing the available airline routes and the existing collection of airplanes, he decided on a contrary strategy. SAS defined itself as the businessman's airline, concentrated on business class excellence, and limited tourist class. This is market-based strategy.

Industry observers immediately questioned whether SAS could execute such a strategy, given the airline's existing capabilities. In fact, SAS went to considerable effort to improve its service delivery resources before promoting its service. The company sent employees to customer satisfaction seminars and training sessions, gave on-the-job training, and, perhaps most important, eliminated layers of supervisors, empowering front-line people to make decisions and take initiatives. SAS was profitable within one year, and was voted the world's best business airline a year later.

Alas, that was not the end. Other airlines copied the strategy, boosted their service capabilities, and soon Thai and Singapore airlines as well as British Airways and German Lufthansa could be seen advertising their preflight and in-flight service. With no airline having a distinct advantage in service anymore, competition shifted to routes and network connections, leading to a number of strategic alliances to develop global reach. SAS struck up an ill-fated deal with Continental Airlines for the U.S. market, an alliance that became a burden as Continental went into bankruptcy, and Carlzon lost his job.

Source: Carlzon, 1987; *New York Times*, April 5, 1994, p. D2.

and other inputs to final goods can be viewed as a collection of complementary and sequential tasks, each adding value to the product.[13] Some tasks are in operations (purchasing, design, manufacturing, and marketing), others are support activities (finance, personnel). The concept is an elaboration of the value-added notion in economic theory, which does not specify the activities inside the firm but simply views the firm as a transforming agent between inputs and outputs.

The value chain is the "internalized" sequence of operations undertaken by the firm. The vertically integrated firm has a long value chain, while a less integrated firm only focuses on some of the operations. "Deconstructing" the value chain is equivalent to externalization. The way McDonald's, the American fast-food restaurant chain, operates in different countries is instructive. In the United States the company has externalized major activities by hiring independent firms to supply the beef, potatoes, bread, and other ingredients, and by allowing independent entrepreneurs to open franchised outlets. However,

EXHIBIT 2.4 Value-Added Analysis for Consumer Electronic Products

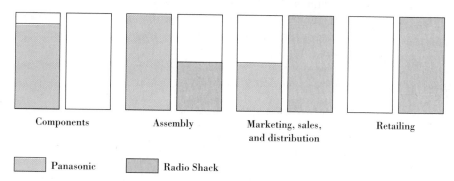

| Components | Assembly | Marketing, sales, and distribution | Retailing |

Panasonic   Radio Shack

McDonald's inspects operations and keeps tight quality controls on all phases of business. In Europe, suppliers are also independent local producers, but some key franchised locations, (including one on Paris' Champs Elysees) are owned by McDonald's itself, mainly for purposes of quality maintenance. In Moscow, McDonald's found it necessary to develop its own suppliers, since the local suppliers could not provide the necessary quality.

Exhibit 2.4 shows how two competing companies, Panasonic and Radio Shack, have configured their value chains in consumer electronics differently. While giant manufacturer Panasonic has no direct involvement at the retail level, Radio Shack, primarily a retailer, does no component manufacturing of its own. This shows how the firms' differing FSAs can be leveraged at different levels in the value chain for electronic consumer goods.

In global marketing, the stage of the value chain that can best be leveraged might not be the same as at home. For example, in markets in which the firm has limited experience or in which products are at a different stage in the life cycle, licensing a technology to a local manufacturer might be preferable to making and selling the product. Starting with a market perspective, by contrast, tends to lock management into a narrow focus on selling to foreign markets the same type of product sold at home.

This "externalization" of activities can be contrasted with the "internalization" principle discussed above that helps explain the emergence of the multinational corporation with wholly owned foreign subsidiaries. In Chapter 6, when entry modes are discussed, strategic alliances will be seen as one example of externalization.

The value chain can change over time, as new ways of combining activities appear and entrepreneurs grasp opportunities to simplify the entire flow, from raw materials to ultimate consumer (a process called industrial rationalization). For example, the Swedish furniture retailer Ikea developed a new formula for selling home furniture. Instead of showcasing finished furniture in downtown stores and later shipping merchandise to buyers' homes as traditional furniture retailers did, Ikea created a self-service store where purchasers could bring home their furniture the same day. Designing furniture in easily assembled pieces, and locating in suburban shopping malls where customers came by car, the company has been able to offer bookcases, tables, chairs, and even beds in easily transportable cardboard boxes. The assembled showroom furniture is clearly labeled with prices, stocking numbers, and units available, and the customer can walk around and make up a buying list without assistance. Having presented the list to the cashier, and made payment, while the order is relayed automatically to the stock room, the customer drives to the back door and picks up the packaged boxes. Ikea has in fact developed a new value chain, in which the customer does more work than before. In return, the prices are much lower. Ikea soon ventured abroad, and has become the first successful furniture retailer on a global scale.[14]

Internationalization

The resource-based perspective explains a commonly observed empirical regularity in foreign entry: Companies tend to expand first into countries close in terms of what may be thought of as "psychic" distance. Geographical proximity, cultural similarity, and economic development help make up a measure of psychic distances between countries, which helps describe the foreign expansion paths of firms quite well. The firms gradually enter ever more distant countries. This framework is often called the **internationalization** paradigm (not to be confused with "internalization"), showing how companies gradually expand overseas.[15]

The reason behind the pattern is mainly a desire to limit transaction costs. Going far away from home, in terms of geography, culture, or economic development, increases transfer costs for products and people and reduces the chances that the home market skills will be useful. However, as more countries are gradually entered in an expanding circle away from the home market, the company learns to do business globally, understands how to analyze foreign environments, and gains capability and a widened repertoire. In short, the firm develops new resources. Naturally, foreign market potential also matters—but in the beginning even a great potential in a psychically distant market may not be exploited because of the additional transaction costs. As experience is gained, the possibilities open up, and the firm goes global (Chapter 5 discusses the global expansion paths of companies in more depth).

Role of Technology

Because of increased spending on R&D and the successful appeal of so many recent innovations, many global markets are driven by technological developments. This is true not only for high-tech computers, telecommunications, and biotechnology, but for many ostensibly low-tech products such as diapers, detergents, cosmetics, drugs, and foods. New and modified products are often introduced not because customers ask for them but because of technological advances themselves.

In such a market, a focus on customers will not be sufficient to sustain loyalty and sales. The firm needs to develop technological capabilities to be able to compete by introducing new products. Although such competencies ultimately have to be matched against customer needs, there is often little in the way of consumer feedback or market research suggesting potential or latent needs with any degree of reliability. Only when the product emerges on the market do needs and wants crystallize. Examples of this phenomenon are too numerous to need mention.

To avoid spending resources on blind "trial and error" introductions of new products, companies often resort to close monitoring and quick imitation of new competitive offerings. As the speed of technological development has increased, intense competitive rivalries have led to a proliferation of new products in many markets, many of them "me-too" variants. This reinforces rivalry, making strategic execution factors, such as speed and flexibility, rather than uniqueness and differentiation, which place a premium on superior segmentation and positioning strategies, key for success. As managers often say, "If you execute well, when things don't turn out right you know it's the strategy that is faulty. If your execution is flawed, you don't know if the strategy is right or wrong."

Once again, the manager evaluates global marketing strategies with an eye to the firm's resources and true competencies as much as to potentialities in the foreign market.

STRATEGY IMPLEMENTATION AND EXECUTION

At this point it will be useful for us to distinguish between strategy implementation and execution. A "strategy" can be defined as a "unifying theme that gives coherence and direction to the various decisions" of the firm.[17] In global marketing, as we have seen, strategy formulation means specifying exactly how competitive advantages will be established: what customer segments to target, how to position products, and what internal resources to exploit to deliver them.

"Implementation" is how the strategy will be carried out. *Marketing implementation* involves choice of product features and price level to accomplish the desired positioning, selection of promotional vehicles and distribution channels to reach the target segment, and all the tactical decisions regarding the 4Ps of marketing.

If strategy formulation determines the "what to do" of strategy, and implementation the "how to do it," *execution* is the actual "doing it." For example, the strategy might call for entry into a foreign country with a product positioned at the low end of the market. Setting a low price for the foreign importer and launching an expensive introductory free sample campaign, the strategy is implemented through a month-long roll-out schedule in the new country. Execution is shipping the product to the importer on time, getting it through customs without delay, trucking it to dispersed distribution points, stocking warehouses and stores, developing the promotional material, monitoring the media vehicles announcing the introduction, and supervising the free sample offering. It is easy to see why execution is easily bungled in a new market, especially if intermediaries and specialists with local capabilities are not readily available.

Incrementalism

The difficulty of execution in foreign markets has led many companies to engage in **incremental strategies,** where entry is on a small scale initially, in order to build up experience in the new market. The Western entries into Eastern Europe and Russia illustrate this approach. Entering a small upscale niche ("beachhead") of the market, firms gradually establish their presence by learning to deal with former communist bureaucrats, finding joint venture partners that can be trusted, checking domestic products, updating and improving the distribution channels, and so on, before taking the next small step. It is a "two steps forward, one step back" kind of process.

A major weakness of an incremental strategy is that it takes longer to penetrate a market. This is particularly damaging when the product or service

A kiosk for Mars' Snickers and other candies in Moscow. Helping small Russian entrepreneurs to open such low-investment kiosks in larger cities, U.S.–based Mars gains entry into the emerging Russian market without great risk exposure.

Peter Blakely/Saba.

to be marketed is at a leading edge, as would be the case if a technologically new product was introduced in mature Western markets. Then a tentative entry would flag competitors who could quickly imitate the offering, introduce a "me-too" version, and capture the first-mover advantages of customer recognition and loyalty.

Western companies have traditionally relied on patent protection and access to unique resources to dominate certain market segments. By contrast, the Japanese solution has been to speed up the stepwise process considerably and continually improve their products. Competiton from the Japanese has made speed and flexibility of execution more important than otherwise and forced Western competitors to improve their execution capabilities. Part Four, "Global Management," discusses these issues in more depth.

Emergent Strategies

Because of the importance of execution ("Nothing happens until a sale is made"), some thinkers conceive of strategies as **emergent,** meaning they grow out of execution.[18] Reversing the logical sequence of formulation, implementation, and execution is useful in that it shows the importance of feedback from the marketplace. As the strategy in a foreign market is executed, the feedback from customers and middlemen will teach the marketing manager about the new marketplace. This learning experience is of real value to the manager and the firm, since it helps to build competence in the new setting. This is why it is so important that the manager entering a foreign market travel there to learn first-hand what the situation is. As new understanding is gained, erroneous assumptions can be replaced, mistakes rectified, and misguided strategies redirected.

STRATEGY AND THE THREE HATS

As a firm begins to market globally, and the marketing manager wears first the hat of foreign entry, as an export manager, then of local marketing, perhaps as an expatriate, and finally the hat of stratigic global management, first a resource-based analysis of the firm's assets and capabilities is most relevant, then a market analysis of customers and competitors.

In the *foreign entry* phase, after the market potential has been initially researched, the resources perspective will dominate. The firm must decide what it has to offer, what it can do well, and how it should enter abroad. Foreign entry is frequently initiated by an order from a foreign country for a company's product. Especially in the early stages of global expansion, the assessment of the market, customer segments, and competitive offerings is often done through informal methods and by independent middlemen. The most pressing question is whether middlemen are reliable.

The *local marketing* phase requires analysis of customers and competitors, the typical market-based approach. The managerial headaches come, as usual for the marketing manager, from unforeseen shifts in customer preferences, potential channel conflict, uncertainty about advertising effectiveness, and competitors' price cuts. The company's resources obviously make a difference for what kind of market strategy can be contemplated and whether an expensive competitive battle can be sustained, but the overriding concern in local marketing is in-depth analysis of customer needs and wants, evaluation of actual and potential competitors' strengths and weaknesses, tactical decisions across the life cycle stages of the product, and issues of quality and customer satisfaction.

With *global management*, the focus shifts back to headquarters and the resource perspective. The task for the global marketing manager is now to synchronize strategic moves in various countries across the globe, standardizing products and services, coordinating activities, and timing new product entries, all in hope of synergistic efficiency. Will savings from standardization more than offset potential loss of revenues in some countries? How can subsidiary managers be soothed when a new product is rolled out in another country first? How can we get our agent in country X to report quickly any moves by competitor Y? Which are the leading markets for our product? For these kinds of questions, the firm needs to understand its strengths and weaknesses well. Part Four of the book will show how the marketing manager can mold and stretch company resources into a globally effective marketing machine, using global strategies to find the optimal trade-off between local suitability and scale economies.

SUMMARY

In this chapter the economic theories underlying the global marketing effort were reviewed. The "eclectic" extension of traditional trade theory of a nation's comparative advantage was first discussed. Country-specific advantages (CSAs) determine in which nation production takes place. Firm-specific advantages (FSAs) determine which firm will most likely succeed in a given market. The entry mode depends on the transaction costs and the risks of not internalizing the use of the firm's know-how.

The discussion also highlighted Vernon's international product cycle (IPC), Porter's "diamond of national advantage," and Krugman's new trade theory. Although fundamentally the theories are about countries and industries, and not about companies, they help the manager understand the global economic forces making for dynamic shifts in competitiveness between countries and regions. These are the "megatrends," and the global marketer will have a greater chance of success going in their direction.

Chapter 2 then explored specific marketing implications of the theories, and showed how CSAs and FSAs can be translated into strategic advantages for the firm. These advantages are crucial to help overcome the natural disadvantage of being a foreign marketer abroad. Contrasting a market or customer orientation, the resource-based perspective on strategy shows how the foreign marketer will often have to build up new skills to serve a given market and identify the internal knowledge the company has that will give it an edge. We made the distinction between implementation and execution of strategy, emphasizing how marketing activities that seem simple at home are often difficult to execute in the global marketplace. Chapter 2 ended with a look at how resource- versus market-based strategy impacts the three global marketing tasks—the "three hats." The resource-based perspective ("Can we do it?") is very important in foreign entry and then again later in global management, while the local marketing phase is dominated by market-based considerations ("What do customers want?").

KEY TERMS

Comparative advantage   p. 37
Country-specific advantage   p. 37
Diamond of national advantage   p. 40
Dissipation   p. 47
Eclectic theory   p. 46
Emergent strategies   p. 63

Firm-specific advantage   p. 45
Incremental strategies   p. 62
Internalization   p. 47
Internationalization   p. 60
International product cycle   p. 40
Knowledge-based organization   p. 56

Market orientation   p. 56
New trade theory   p. 44
Resource-based strategy   p. 57
Technology transfer   p. 39
Transactions costs   p. 47
The value chain   p. 57

DISCUSSION QUESTIONS

1. How does internalization theory explain the use of wholly owned subsidiaries as opposed to licensing?

2. What might be the marketing advantages of establishing a manufacturing subsidiary in a country, as compared to simple exporting? Any potential marketing disadvantages?

3. How does a market orientation explain entry into the Japan market? A resource-based view? Why are both perspectives useful?

4. When would a market-based strategy suggest withdrawal from a foreign market, while a resource-based view suggest the opposite? Under what conditions would the converse be true?

5. What is the difference between implementation and execution in foreign market entry?

NOTES

1. See Vernon, 1966.
2. See Vernon, 1979, in particular. The later extensions involved introducing dynamic competitive conditions and firm-level rise and decline explicitly. The multinational in the early stage is an innovation-based oligopoly, turning into a mature oligopoly, and then a senescent (aging) oligopoly.
3. See Porter, 1990.
4. See Krugman, 1988.
5. See, for example, Grant, 1991, pp. 204–9.

6. See Dunning, 1988.

7. The dissipation problem and the issue of getting a reasonable return on the firm's assets are headaches for managers, since licensing is a very convenient option not requiring much in terms of resources. See Rugman, 1979.

8. See Williamson, 1975.

9. See, for example, Anderson and Gatignon, 1986.

10. Kogut and Zander, 1993, report on these practices.

11. See, for example, Nelson and Winter, 1982; Grant, 1991, ch. 9; and Kogut and Zander, 1993.

12. See Itami and Roehl, 1987.

13. See Porter, 1985.

14. This extension of the value chain is from Norman and Ramirez, 1993.

15. See Johanson and Vahlne, 1990, for an up-to-date discussion of their internationalization paradigm.

16. Much of the following material is from Kotler et al., 1985.

17. From Grant, 1991, p. 1.

18. See, for example, Quinn, 1980, who discusses both incremental strategies and the way strategic patterns emerge from the small, incremental steps firms take.

SELECTED REFERENCES

Anderson, Erin and Hubert Gatignon. "Modes of Foreign Entry: A Transaction Cost Analysis and Propositions," *Journal of International Business Studies*, no.3 (1986).

Carlzon, Jan. *Moments of Truth*. Cambridge, MA: Ballinger, 1987.

Dunning, John H. *International Production and the Multinational Enterprise*. London: Allen-Unwin, 1981.

_____. "The Eclectic Paradigm of International Production," *Journal of International Business Studies*, Spring 1988, pp. 1–31.

Grant, Robert M. *Contemporary Strategy Analysis*. Oxford: Blackwell, 1991.

Itami, H., with T. W. Roehl. *Mobilizing Invisible Assets*. Cambridge, MA: Harvard University Press, 1987.

Johanson, Jan and Jan-Erik Vahlne. "The Mechanism of Internationalization," *International Marketing Review* 7, no. 4 (1990), pp. 1–24.

Kogut, Bruce. "Designing Global Strategies: Comparative and Competitive Value Chains," *Sloan Management Review*, Summer 1985, pp. 27–38.

_____, and Udo Zander. "Knowledge of the Firm and the Evolutionary Theory of the Multinational Corporation," *Journal of International Business Studies* 24, no. 4 (1993) pp. 625–46.

Kotler, Philip, Liam Fahey, and S. Jatusripitak. *The New Competition*. Englewood Cliffs, NJ: Prentice Hall, 1985.

Krugman, Paul R. *Geography and Trade*. Cambridge, MA: MIT Press, 1988.

Nelson, Richard R., and Sidney G. Winter. *An Evolutionary Theory of Economic Change*. Cambridge, MA: Belknap, 1982.

Normann, Richard, and Rafael Ramirez. "From Value Chain to Value Constellation: Designing Interactive Strategy," *Harvard Business Review*, July–August 1993 pp. 65–77.

Porter, Michael E. *Competitive Advantage*. New York: Free Press, 1985.

_____. *The Competitive Advantage of Nations*. New York: Free Press, 1990.

Quinn, James Brian. *Strategies for Change—Logical Incrementalism*. Burr Ridge, IL: Irwin, 1980.

Rugman, Alan M. *International Diversification and the Multinational Enterprise*. Lexington, MA: D. C. Heath, 1979.

Thorelli, Hans B., and Helmut Becker, eds. *International Marketing Strategy*, revised ed. New York: Pergamon, 1980.

_____, and S. Tamer Cavusgil, eds. *International Marketing Strategy*, 3d. ed. New York: Pergamon, 1990.

Vernon, Raymond. "International Investment and International Trade in the Product Cycle," *Quarterly Journal of Economics* 80 (May 1966).

_____. "The Product Cycle in a New International Environment," *Oxford Bulletin of Economics and Statistics* 41 (November 1979).

Wells, Louis T. "A Product Life Cycle for International Trade?" *Journal of Marketing*, July 1968, pp. 1–6.

Williamson, O. *Markets and Hierarchies: Analysis and Antitrust Implications*. New York: Free Press, 1975.

Chapter 3

Cultural Foundations

"Different strokes for different folks"

After studying this chapter, you should understand the following global marketing issues:

1. Culture is not only a fundamental dimension of any society but a very visible force affecting managerial behavior.

2. Culture tends to affect strategy implementation and execution, "how" things are done, more than strategy formulation.

3. Our own culture has given us certain useful behavioral skills. In new situations, those skills may be useless and even counterproductive.

4. Complete adaptation to a new culture may not be productive, since such behavior is unexpected and might erode trust.

5. Cultural differences are examples of market entry barriers, and can be overcome with sensitivity, hard work, and a superior product or service.

A GLOBAL MARKETER can't avoid the obvious truth that people in Hong Kong, Oslo, or Johannesburg are different, despite the growth of global travel services, global media networks, global hotel chains, and global product offerings. Since marketing is a people-oriented function, this affects the global marketer powerfully.

Culture has two main effects on the global marketer. First is the effect on demand. Differences in culture make it difficult to predict customer reactions and understand consumer behavior. Customers around the world have varying needs, face disparate economic constraints, use contrasting choice criteria, and are influenced by different social norms. Although much of our general discussion about cultures in Chapter 3 will be useful for customer analysis, the demand issues will be dealt with in more detail in Part Three, "Local Marketing," starting with Chapter 7 on buyer behavior.

The second effect of culture is on the "soft" skills of management. National culture affects organizational culture, how managers deal with subordinates and other employees, how they negotiate contracts, how they control the independent middlemen needed to enter a foreign market, how they establish trust with joint venture partners, and how they manage distribution channels. Simply stated, culture has a direct effect on what people-skills the global marketer needs in the foreign environment. This is the main topic of Chapter 3.

Euro Disney Tries to Rekindle Marketing Magic

Just a year and a half after opening its gates, the Euro Disney theme park situated outside Paris was teetering on the brink of bankruptcy. The company reported disappointing revenues and an unexpected $900 million loss for its first full year of operation. Unless it could negotiate financial help from its creditor banks and parent Walt Disney Company, Euro Disney would have to shut down. What went wrong?

At one point, Euro Disney seemed to be a promising concept: Based on Disney's success in Japan and North America, the company's theme park concept seemed to have worldwide appeal. However, park attendance at Euro Disney was less than expected, and the visitors who came did not spend much money. Perhaps most devastating to Euro Disney's bottom line was that the resort had constructed too many hotel rooms. Tourists did not book rooms for visits to the park as expected.

Disney responded by modifying its marketing approach, renegotiating the financial package, and changing the way it treated its employees. The familiar "Disney culture" was relaxed to fit the local culture and the expectations of the European managers and workers. A number of the French employees did not take lightly to the idea of being lectured about personal grooming, what makeup to use, and what clothes to wear, even coming and going to work, as they felt such demands were tantamount to invasion of privacy. And European middle managers cared more about prestige and status than the democratic ideals of American management. For these reasons, Disney eased up on its strict behavioral code.

Other changes involved adaptation of the "product." For instance, the French—over one-third of Euro Disney's visitors—expect wine with their lunch, so the park has loosened Disney's no-alcohol policy. And, contrary to the eating habits of snacking Americans, the French visitors expected their lunch promptly at 1 P.M., causing long lines and some frustration. So, the park opened additional restaurants to accommodate local tastes and habits. In addition, Euro Disney invested in a spectacular new ride, the Space Mountain roller coaster, reportedly the fastest Disney attraction in the world, to generate excitement and lure new visitors. Euro Disney also set more affordable prices—up to 20 percent less for tickets, food, and hotel rooms.

The initial results of Disney's new approach were somewhat encouraging. The theme park finally has begun to generate a profit. However, observers are cautious about forecasting long-term success. To hold down costs, Euro Disney has had to postpone building a version of a Disney-MGM studio attraction, which had been expected to draw many visitors. Euro Disney's expenses will also rise in 1997, when it begins paying interest on its renegotiated loans. Thus, only time will tell whether the "Disney magic" has finally caught Europe in its spell.

Sources: Roger Cohen, "When You Wish upon a Deficit," *New York Times*, July 18, 1993, sec. 2, pp. 1, 18–19; Roger Cohen, "Euro Disney '93: $90 Million Loss," *New York Times*, November 11, 1993, p. D4; Roger Cohen, "Euro Disney in Danger of Shutdown," *New York Times*, December 23, 1993, p. D3; "Euro Disney Rescue Approved," *Japan Times* May 21, 1994, p. 6; Nathaniel C. Nash, "Euro Disney Reports Its First Profits," *New York Times*, July 26, 1995, p. D3.

INTRODUCTION

Although the aim of business may be the same everywhere, the way to do business varies considerably across countries. The advent of global markets and global firms has to some extent reduced the disparities among countries, but it has also meant that the successful executive travels to more and more countries. Whereas in some firms a stint in the London or Paris or New York or Tokyo office serves as a step on the career ladder, in others the career stopovers are likely to include Kuala Lumpur, Mexico City, and Kiev. "Culture shock" is a potent threat to the high-flying international marketer—and his or her family.

Cultural differences affect the applicability of the experienced marketer's professional skills directly. In the new setting a great marketer is no longer necessarily a great marketer, perhaps not even a good one. The experienced marketer will often have a frustrating time getting back to the basic fundamentals of the marketing effort. When Pepsi Cola entered Japan many years ago, they selected a young executive who had been very successful in the U.S. marketplace. His age and impetuous nature, key ingredients in his American success, set back Pepsi's introduction severely. While Coca Cola gained market leadership with the help of Japanese leaders, Pepsi still has to recover from the initial mistake.[1]

Situations can differ so drastically that experience is a misleading guide. Nestlé sold its infant formula in Africa, where it was mixed with unclean water and heavily diluted, causing tragedy. Products that seem to fill needs instead create more problems.[2] Or, the experienced marketer, who has learned the importance of tracking sales, may be misled in a foreign culture, resulting in disaster for the marketing effort. Reliance on store sales data might be dangerous in cultures where habitual manipulation of records has been fostered by inequitable tax regulations.

It's "back to basics" time. Some Japanese companies have a policy of sending new and untutored marketing representatives abroad, even when seasoned managers with experience of the particular country are available. The assumption is that the neophytes will perceive customers without preconceptions, and be able to come up with fresh ideas. While this is an extreme approach, the point is the same: When there are great cultural differences between countries, the marketing manager often has to start from scratch again.

Chapter 3 begins by discussing the meaning of culture and how cultures differ across nations. It then explains the process by which culture affects managerial skills and negotiation strategies. It cautions against overadaptation, and concludes with culture's impact on the managerial tasks of foreign entry, local marketing, and global management. (The many cultural effects on demand—needs, wants, tastes, and choices—will be discussed in Part Three, "Local Marketing," starting with Chapter 7.

At the outset it is useful to look at some examples of what culture involves (see box, "Cultural Idiosyncrasies"). As the illustrations in the box suggest, there are hundreds of potential cultural clashes every day in various parts of the world. Some of them are recognized, others are not. Every manager's behavior conveys intended or unintended meanings to his or her counterpart. **Body language,** the often unintended signals that a person projects through dress, body position, hand and eye movements, fidgeting, and so on, may provoke all sorts of culturally slanted interpretations. In countries with a homogeneous population, such as Italy, a gesture is often sufficient for information to be shared. A "Hai" in Japanese usually means "I see" rather than the more definite "Yes" which is its literal translation. A "Hai" accompanied by a slight bow is a stronger statement (unless, of course, the response is to a speaker of higher status, in which case again it simply means "I see"). And so on and so forth.

The global manager needs to learn to be a good observer of individual behavior, to become sensitized to the potential manifestations of cultural

*G*etting the Picture

Cultural Idiosyncracies

AS MORE and more of a global marketplace emerges, managers' dress and appearance may seem to be growing increasingly similar across countries. In terms of what kind of behavior is considered acceptable, however, wide differences persist. As a rule, it is not necessary to behave as Romans do when one is in Rome—unless one is Roman. Nevertheless, a few items are sufficient to indicate what kind of misunderstandings may occur.

When an Indian shakes his head, it does not mean "no" as in the West, but "Yes, I understand." When a Scandinavian speaks slowly, he is serious and sure, not uncertain and deviant, as might be the case elsewhere. When an American speaks, he or she wants to make eye contact, while a listener from Japan wants to give room and avoid a direct glance.

Continental Europeans often have supper around 10 PM. A relatively formal dinner party might not be over until 3 or 4 AM. To leave at midnight, which is late by U.S. standards, requires a solid excuse and needs to be announced before the start of proceedings. Drinking water only is pretty much an insult to others at the party, not deeming them worthy of serious companionship.

In Japan, and other countries as well, being drunk is by and large an excuse for insolent behavior. In the United States, drunkenness is not forgiven, regardless of the situation. While Japanese consider inebriation to bring out the true person, U.S. managers insist on self-control at all times. "Don't trust a man who doesn't drink" may have been coined by W. C. Fields, but it does not represent corporate America as much as some other countries.

Stylish dress sits badly in conservative American corporations, where Brooks Brothers attire is appreciated. In the U.S., managers dress for other managers, while elsewhere, the aim is often for the opposite sex and "bella figura," even among top managers. The stated objective among Americans is that dress should not be the focus. The result, however, tends to be that appearance matters more than elsewhere, since deviations stand out. Of course, the Japanese blue or grey suit easily wins first prize in the race to be unnoticeable, but actually serves to proclaim its wearers members of the same caste, a subconscious but prized benefit in all matters Japanese.

Sex is, of course, a tricky subject in any business circle, especially in Muslim countries, but also among Americans with their puritan roots. In European countries the topic is usually closer to the surface but needs to be approached with flair ("Everyone to his taste" as Prince Orlofsky puts it in the Fledermaus operetta). Similarly, religion is usually a no-win topic of conversation. One reason the American insistence on human rights has encountered resistance in a country such as China is that it reflects a missionary zeal to convert others—Buddhism offers more of a "live and let live" ideology.

Sources: Durlabhji and Marks, 1993; Hall, 1976; Hall and Hall, 1990.

idioms. At the same time, the manager will begin to understand his or her own cultural heritage and biases. Just as foreign travel teaches you about a foreign country, it also teaches you about yourself. This is why the immersion in at least one foreign culture gives the manager a wider repertoire of skills and greater sensitivity to alternative behaviors. Great global marketers don't need to start from scratch all the time, but they need to be flexible and always ready to question their own past experiences.

THE MEANING OF CULTURE

Culture is the underlying framework that guides an individual's perceptions of observed events and personal interactions, and the selection of appropriate responses in social situations. The framework consists of *objective* reality as manifested in societal institutions and *subjective* reality as socialized predispositions and beliefs.

Culture is manifested in **learned behavior.** What is called "culture" is not an abstraction but physical reality. The functions of a society—the "what a society does"—are not very different across countries. Everybody has to get food, lodging, a job, money, clothes, a significant other, success, career, status, social recognition, pride, comfort, peace of mind, a center for his or her existence, power, some influence over others, and all the other things! These are the objectives of people's behavior all over the world. The relative amount of time and resources allocated to these activities may vary, but the tasks remain. The question is *how* these tasks are accomplished and this varies a great deal across cultures.

The modern conception of culture focuses directly on observable behavior. It suggests that culture not only predisposes the individual toward certain behavior but eliminates other behavior. Consequently, culture creates a repertoire of behavioral skills.[3] Culture directly influences what people will do and what people can do. This narrowly focused interpretation of culture is very useful for global marketing managers. It suggests that culture is more important for *how* managers should decide, less to *what* the decision should be. *Culture affects implementation and execution of strategies more than their formulation.*

CULTURES ACROSS COUNTRIES

What kinds of cultures are there in the world? There are several useful ways of classifying cultures across countries. First, however, one needs to recognize that cultures and countries do not necessarily go together. Countries with large populations such as India, China, Russia, and the United States are really **multicultural,** meaning that they contain a wide variety of cultures within their borders. The same goes for some smaller nations, such as former Yugoslavia, Belgium, Canada, and South Africa. In other cases, several countries can be seen as one cultural grouping. Examples include the Scandinavian countries (Denmark, Norway, Sweden) and Latin American countries (Venezuela, Colombia, Ecuador, but not necessarily Brazil).

High Versus Low Context Cultures

An important distinction between cultures suggested by Hall is that between **high and low context** cultures.[4]

In high context cultures the meaning of individual behavior and speech changes depending on the situation. Nonverbal messages are full of important—and intended—meanings. Even if no words are spoken, individuals communicate. And when words are spoken, "reading between the lines" is important. High context cultures require a similarity of backgrounds, a commonness of purpose, and a homogeneity in society. These result from careful enculturation and socialization starting at an early age in the family. The process continues naturally in homogeneous countries, with one religion, one language, centralized broadcast media, coordinated educational system, and so on.

In "low context" cultures, by contrast, intentions are expressed verbally. Propositions have to be justified and opinions defended openly. In low context cultures the situation is not allowed to change the meaning of words and behavior—the context conveys little or no information. This is quite useful and effective in a country that is multicultural and where people's value systems and attitudes can be very different.

High context cultures can be found in a variety of countries, including most of the European countries, some of the Latin American (Chile, Mexico, perhaps Venezuela and Argentina), and many of the newly industrializing Asian countries (but not China or India). In countries with high context cultures—such as

East meets West in Dubai. High- or low-context culture is not a matter of modern buildings or a comfortable outdoor setting but of individual values, social norms, and subjective perceptions.

Derek Berwin/The Image Bank.

Saudi Arabia and Japan—a written contract is not always enforceable if the situation changes or if new people move into executive positions.

Americans, because of their **diversity,** have a low context culture. Low context cultures can also be found in ethnically diverse countries such as India, China, Russia, and in countries such as Australia and New Zealand with large immigrant populations that have nevertheless blended.

"Silent Languages"

In a famous article, Hall also pointed out the important role of "silent languages" of international business.[5] He identified the use of five different silent languages: space, material possessions, friendship patterns, agreements across cultures, and time. All of the factors have some meaning in interpersonal communication, but are not necessarily spoken of. For example, one's conception of *space* relates to matters such as the distance between two people conversing. In the Middle East men will maintain an intimate distance, often too close for comfort for Western people. *Material possessions* of course always speak volumes about one's station in life, particularly where social hierarchies are well developed so that people learn what to look for. The emphasis on well-known brands in Asian markets, for example, reflects a need to clearly identify one's position with signals other people understand.

Friendship patterns, that is, whom you treat as a friend, are not only reflective of your own cultural upbringing but also involve questions of trust and responsibility. In a business deal, it would not be strange for an American to assure a prospective partner that a third person "will agree because he is my friend." By contrast, in a country like Japan, the person might well say, "I cannot speak for him because he is my friend." *Agreements across cultures* are also interpreted differently. While Western business people rely on explicit contracts, and keep the letter of the law, Eastern cultures rely more on general agreement and the basic intent of the partners.

Perceptions of *time* vary considerably between even relatively close cultures, and studies have documented the varieties of problems connected with different time perceptions.[6] Latin Americans' perception of their being "on time" even when 30 minutes late for an appointment is counterbalanced by East Asians who think it safest to show up 30 minutes early, just to be on time. While northern people might not like to "waste" time on "small talk" in a business meeting, Latins tend to spend more time on nonbusiness conversation. Differing perceptions of time and its use are responsible for many problems in business negotiations, a topic to be discussed later.

It is important also to recognize that time has an additional dimension. Whether one's cultural background says so or not, in global competition "time is money," so *time* has a strong economic component. For example, the famous JIT or "just-in-time" inventory system of Toyota, the automaker, is really a "much-before-time" system, with supplier trucks waiting outside the plants in the early morning hours. When German supermarkets close at 6 PM, the clerks' understanding, codified in their labor agreement, is that no checkouts be done after that time (whereas in most other countries doors close at 6 PM, but customers already in the store are checked out). Needless to say, in Germany store customers line up by 5:45 PM, but in the end half-filled shopping carts are often left in the aisles or at the register. One would perhaps have expected that with increased competition through the EU integration, customer service would improve, but the outcome is still unclear.

When interpreting various cultural manifestations in different countries, the marketer needs to remember that self-referencing can be misleading. *Self-referencing* is a process by which we form judgments about others. It involves judging others' behavior against our own past experiences and our own conception of self.[7] Other information is often used when judging people—the particular setting, the other people involved, verbalized motivations, and so on. But such information, even when available, is often difficult for us to interpret when we face people from a foreign culture. Therefore, self-referencing is common when judging people from abroad—we see others through ourselves.

This can lead to misperceptions. When people dress casually while you are in a dark suit, when they avoid eye contact while you look steadily at them, when they speak slowly and you speak purposefully, when they smile while you are earnest, information comes to you, but it does not necessarily mean what you think it means. Before reaching any hasty conclusions, you must check with people familiar with the culture, and perhaps bring a knowledgeable companion to any meeting. The bottom line is, learn about the culture, don't trust first impressions—and play down self-referencing in favor of more objective information. **Cultural adaptation** as a skill to be honed must be high on the manager's list of priorities, but as with all valuable acquisitions it can't be had on the cheap.

Hofstede's Cultural Dimensions

The high versus low context distinction and "silent languages" provide useful concepts by which to think about various cultures. Hofstede's questionnaire study of IBM's employees around the globe in 1980 is a much more systematic assessment of cultures across countries.[8] Although the world has changed considerably since the study was done, cultures have changed less—and judging from recent events in Eastern Europe and Russia, ethnicity and cultural roots are stronger than ever.

According to Hofstede's survey findings, countries can be classified along four basic **cultural dimensions.** The first cultural dimension is **individualism versus collectivism.** In a collective society, the identity and worth of the individual is rooted in the social system, less in individual achievement. A second dimension is high versus low **power distance.** High power distance societies tend to be less egalitarian, while democratic countries exhibit low power distance (see Exhibit 3.1).

....
EXHIBIT 3.1 The Position of the 40 Countries on the Power Distance and Individualism Scales

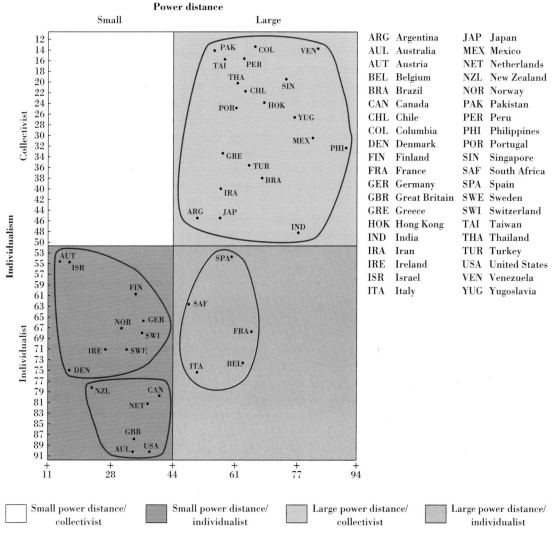

Power distance

Small   Large

ARG	Argentina	JAP	Japan
AUL	Australia	MEX	Mexico
AUT	Austria	NET	Netherlands
BEL	Belgium	NZL	New Zealand
BRA	Brazil	NOR	Norway
CAN	Canada	PAK	Pakistan
CHL	Chile	PER	Peru
COL	Columbia	PHI	Philippines
DEN	Denmark	POR	Portugal
FIN	Finland	SIN	Singapore
FRA	France	SAF	South Africa
GER	Germany	SPA	Spain
GBR	Great Britain	SWE	Sweden
GRE	Greece	SWI	Switzerland
HOK	Hong Kong	TAI	Taiwan
IND	India	THA	Thailand
IRA	Iran	TUR	Turkey
IRE	Ireland	USA	United States
ISR	Israel	VEN	Venezuela
ITA	Italy	YUG	Yugoslavia

☐ Small power distance/ collectivist   ▨ Small power distance/ individualist   ☐ Large power distance/ collectivist   ▨ Large power distance/ individualist

Source: Reprinted by permission of the author from *Culture's Consequences*, published by Sage Publications, © 1990 by Geert Hofstede.

As can be seen from the "map" in the Exhibit, Australians and Venezuelans tend to be diametrically opposite each other on these two measures. While Australians are individualistic and democratic, Venezuelans are much more collectivist and believers in formal authority. It is important to recognize that the distances between countries on the map are proportional to the degree to which they differ culturally.

Exhibit 3.2 The Position of the 40 Countries on the Uncertainty Avoidance and Masculinity Scales

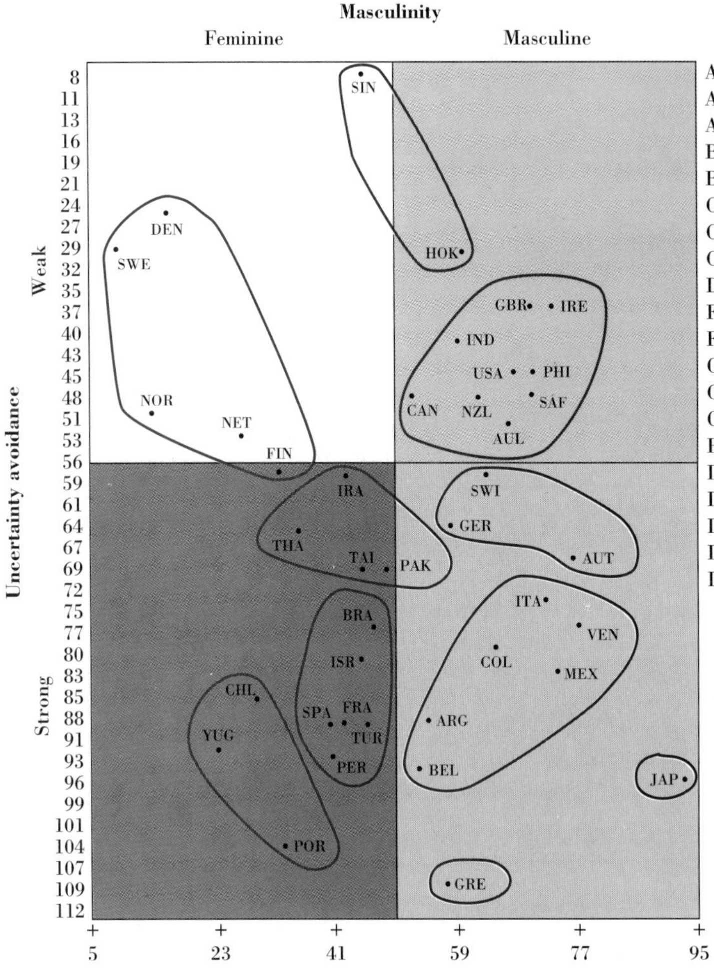

ARG	Argentina	JAP	Japan
AUL	Australia	MEX	Mexico
AUT	Austria	NET	Netherlands
BEL	Belgium	NZL	New Zealand
BRA	Brazil	NOR	Norway
CAN	Canada	PAK	Pakistan
CHL	Chile	PER	Peru
COL	Columbia	PHI	Philippines
DEN	Denmark	POR	Portugal
FIN	Finland	SIN	Singapore
FRA	France	SAF	South Africa
GER	Germany	SPA	Spain
GBR	Great Britain	SWE	Sweden
GRE	Greece	SWI	Switzerland
HOK	Hong Kong	TAI	Taiwan
IND	India	THA	Thailand
IRA	Iran	TUR	Turkey
IRE	Ireland	USA	United States
ISR	Israel	VEN	Venezuela
ITA	Italy	YUG	Yugoslavia

Weak uncertainty avoidance/feminine
Strong uncertainty avoidance/feminine
Weak uncertainty avoidance/masculine
Strong uncertainty avoidance/masculine

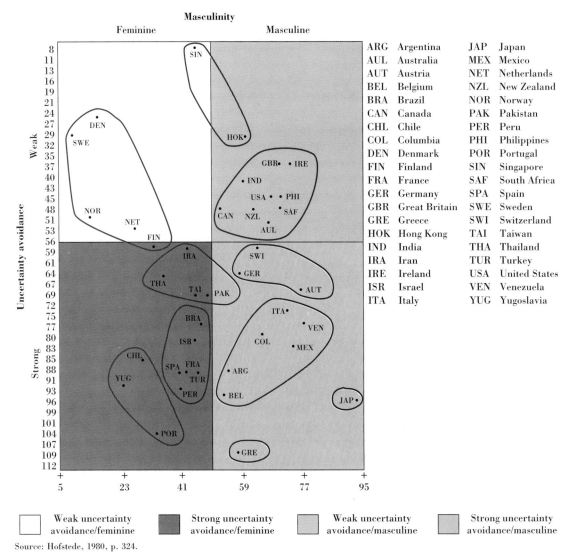

Source: Hofstede, 1980, p. 324.

Hofstede's third dimension, **masculine versus feminine,** captures the degree to which a culture is dominated by assertive males rather than nurturing females. Finally, **weak versus strong uncertainty avoidance** rates nations according to the level of risk tolerance or risk aversion among the people (see Exhibit 3.2).

As can be seen from the map in Exhibit 3.2, Australia and Venezuela are not as far away from each other this time. Both cultures tend to be dominated more by males than females, and although Venezuelans are more eager to avoid risks, the distance—and thus cultural difference—is not that great. The difficulties managers from the two countries might face in dealing with each other would likely revolve around individualism and differences in the use of power. While an Australian would act alone and treat others as equals, the Venezuelan might feel better seeking support among peers and then imposing decisions on subordinates.

In some later applications Hofstede has added a fifth dimension, **Confucianist dynamics,** to distinguish the long-term orientation among Asian people, influenced by Confucius, the Chinese philosopher, from the more short-term outlook of Western people.[9]

The Hofstede mapping of countries is useful in that it offers a snapshot of the cultural distances between countries. Marketers can anticipate the degree to which marketing programs, especially communications and services, might need to be adapted to a new culture. Also, for the multinational company with different product lines in different countries, a choice can be made about which line should be introduced in a new market. For example, when Kentucky Fried Chicken expanded into Korea and Taiwan, they started with the menus already developed for Japan rather than the American selections.

Managers can also evaluate how difficult it may be to do business in a country culturally distant from their own and how much of a cultural shock they and their families are likely to get when moving to the country. As Exhibits 3.1 and 3.2 suggest, the typical American manager might find it very difficult to run a subsidiary in a country whose culture was much more oriented toward less individualism, more power distance and authority, and more avoiding uncertainties (see box, "Business Here Is Business There").

The cultural distances measured by Hofstede underlie the gradual pattern of global expansion suggested by the so-called "internationalization" process discussed briefly in Chapter 2. We will get back to it in Chapter 5 dealing with export expansion.

Gannon's Metaphors

In a recent book, Gannon proposed a novel way of looking at cultures.[10] He suggested the use of descriptive metaphors for different cultures, characterizing cultures in such a way as to anticipate what people's reactions might be in different situations. The **metaphors** offer a mental anchor for the manager who has to deal with a new culture and cannot foresee all contingencies.

In practice, it is impossible for the global marketer to learn about all cultures. According to Gannon, learning a smattering of individual "don'ts" ("don't prop your feet on the table, don't blow your nose, don't compliment anybody's wife, don't cross your legs, don't touch your host's son's head," and

Getting the Picture

Business Here Is Business There—With a Twist

CULTURAL DIFFERENCES can be managerial headaches.

Raytheon, the U.S. chemical firm, hired Italian-Americans to manage operations in Sicily but found that this strategy did not produce the desired results. The problem related to the origins of the managers. They were from Northern Italy, and not very much liked or trusted among the Sicilians with their closely knit family ties.

In another case, a firm introduced a technical product into a market relatively free of competition. Anticipating few problems with the entry, the firm did not pay sufficient attention to the person chosen as its European sales manager located on the Continent. As it happened, the man chosen disliked the French, and made no effort either to learn their language or culture. His treatment of the French sales force reflected this attitude, lowering morale and performance. A competing firm entering later was able to attract much of the original company's sales force and go on to become the market leader.

The standard advice in negotiations and selling is to get any agreement in writing. This advice is not so well taken in many cultures where the business decision is made at one level with a word and a handshake, and the actual closing with order specification, cost figures, and final signing taken care of later. Lack of understanding and finesse on this score lost the contract for one Western firm in Japan. Selling kitchen equipment for restaurants, the firm's sales manager pressed the president of the purchasing company for his signature on a written contract just after an oral agreement had been reached. Making two mistakes in one move, showing distrust of the oral agreement and asking for a signature at the wrong time, the manager failed to close the deal.

Sources: Hall and Hall, 1990; Salacuse, 1991.

so on) from the typical "how to" books is likely to create confusion when more than one culture is covered. Gannon argues that it is more effective to develop a holistic sense of a culture by creating an image (a metaphor) representing how the people think and behave. By planting the image in the back of one's mind, Gannon suggests, one can more comfortably interpret what someone in that culture is trying to say or do. If the metaphor is correct and fairly deeply understood, one's own reactions and responses can become more genuine and instinctive.

Some of Gannon's proposed metaphors are given in Exhibit 3.3. As can be seen, Gannon suggests that the metaphor of American football captures many of the features of American culture, with its emphasis on competition, specialization of individual functions, strong leaders calling the plays, and the desire for individual recognition. By contrast, Italians can be described in operatic terms, where speeches are like tenor and soprano arias, the "bella figura" of Italian dress is represented by the costumes and stage setting, and the major players are all given time to shine in the spotlight.

EXHIBIT 3.3   Gannon's Metaphors

1. *American football*: Individualism and competitive specialization; huddling; ceremonial celebration of perfection.
2. *The British house*: Laying the foundations; building the brick house; living in the brick house.
3. *The German symphony*: Orchestra; conductors; performance; society, education, and politics
4. *The French wine*: Purity; classification; composition; compatibility; maturation.
5. *The Italian family opera*: Pageantry and spectacle; voice expression; chorus and soloists.
6. *The Swedish summer home*: Love of nature; individualism through self-development; equality.
7. *The Japanese garden*: Wa and shikata, harmony and form; seishin, spirit of self-discipline; combining droplets.
8. *The Chinese family altar*: Confucianism and Taoism; roundness, harmony, and fluidity.
9. *India: cyclical Hindu philosophy*: The cycle of life; the family cycle; the social cycle; the work cycle.

Source: Martin Gannon, "Cultural Metaphors," *Understanding Global Cultures*, pp. v–vii. ©1994 by Martin Gannon. Reprinted by permission of Sage Publication.

The German culture can be characterized by the classical symphony, with its strict discipline under a leader, and skilled individuals performing together, like a well-oiled machine. And so on. However simplified such metaphors are, Gannon argues, they give the manager the right mindset with which to approach bureaucrats, distribution middlemen, potential partners, and customers in the foreign culture.

CULTURE AND MANAGERIAL SKILLS

Culture influences how management skills—the way managers plan, decide, act, and control—can be applied. Not only are there obvious implications for the way managers treat subordinates and other people, there are also definite cultural biases influencing the effectiveness of subsidiary management and the capability of marketing implementation.[11] These things will be pursued further below in the context of salesmanship and negotiations. First, it is useful to outline briefly how culture leads to skills.

The Skill Development Process

The linkage that connects national culture to managerial skills can be described as a sequence of steps.

1. Culture defines a set of acceptable behaviors and a set of unacceptable behaviors. "Don't prop your feet up on the table," and "You must wear a suit and tie" are typical examples. These form social norms for behavior. In business they form the "way of doing business."

2. Individuals learn to perform to these behavioral norms. Managers learn how to do business. These are the processes of enculturation and socialization. They determine how individuals will behave as consumers in the marketplace, how demanding they are, how they voice complaints, and so forth.

3. Over time, individuals become skilled at acceptable behaviors—and less skilled at unacceptable behaviors. They will simply not be able to engage in "learning by doing" certain behaviors. Complaining to someone making noise during a Beethoven recital is difficult for many people, since they will then be too upset to enjoy the performance anyway—a "lose-lose" situation. The savvy concertgoer will have no such qualms, because he or she has done it many times. The American marketer will be good at succinctly present his or her point of view—while the Japanese counterpart will be good at listening.

4. Acceptable behavior in the business firm is usually a reflection of acceptable behavior in society, especially if the company is large. In large companies employees cannot know each other personally and thus have to rely on more arm's-length relationships based on the general culture. Smaller companies can be less orthodox, with an organizational culture that is unique and unrelated to the larger society.

5. Successful managers tend to be good at acceptable behaviors—and at avoiding unacceptable behaviors. A particular organizational culture is created. Sometimes, of course, this can be dysfunctional, as when change is forced on the organization. Thus, "organizational rebels" or "change agents" often play important roles in rejuvenating companies.

6. Successes and failures in the past generate managerial "experience"—and successful behavior will be repeated elsewhere. This is because of the positive reinforcement received when behaving in a culturally acceptable way.

Managerial Styles

Because of this skill development process, culture tends to generate different **managerial styles** in different countries.[12] This can be illustrated with a comparison between companies from the so-called "Triad," Japan, North America, and Europe. First, we need to analyze the cultures of these three regions.

As we saw in Exhibits 3.1 and 3.2, Hofstede's research produced the rough classification for the countries in the Triad seen in Exhibit 3.4.

EXHIBIT 3.4   Hofstede's Classification of Triad Countries

	Japan	North America (Canada, United States, Great Britain)	W. Europe Northern	Continent
Individualism	low	high	high	high
Power distance	high	low	low	high
Masculinity	high	high	low	high
Risk tolerance	low	high	high	low
Context	high	low	high	low

Note: "Context" added.

Source: Adapted from Hofstede, 1980.

Great Britain is included among the North American countries in Exhibit 3.4, while Mexico is excluded, based on their respective scores in Exhibits 3.1 and 3.2. Also, because of their great differences from one another on the Hofstede maps, the European countries were divided into Northern Europe (Scandinavia, Finland, and The Netherlands) and Continental Europe (the rest, except Great Britain). "Context" has been added as a fifth dimension to account for differences between high and low context cultures.

According to Exhibit 3.4, the Western regions are high on individualism, as one might expect, but differ on the other three dimensions. Power distance is low in democratic North America and Northern Europe, less so in continental Europe. The only region low on masculinity is Northern Europe, where gender equality is more of an established fact. The tolerance for risk is higher in North America and Northern Europe, while Japan and continental Europe tend to avoid uncertainty. Japan's group orientation and hierarchical society are reflected in their low score on individualism and high power distance. Japan and Northern Europe are high context societies, while North America and Continental Europe are less so, needing more clarification and verbalization.

How do these national cultures affect managers who are sent abroad? Some of the well-known stereotypes of various country managers can easily be derived from these dimensions.[13] One understands why Japanese travel in groups, and insist on careful preparation of meeting protocols, why they listen well and slow down their decision making. Western managers can be expected to take responsibility on their own, being individually more confident and trusting their ability to problem solve and improvise. At the same time, Continental Europeans tend to want clear agendas and organization of meetings, and are more likely to insist on a clear structure of agreements and solutions. The high context cultures of Japan and Northern Europe make it less important to justify everything verbally and explicitly, since most managers will be able to "fill in the missing pieces" on their own. In those countries, less is more, when it comes to talking.

Managing Subordinates

These cultural differences suggest that different types of leadership skills will be needed in managing marketing overseas.

Going to a high context culture from another such culture will in general be easier than going to a high from a low context culture. Managers from a high context culture will have sensitivities to nonverbal cues that go unnoticed or are ignored by low context cultures. The person from a low context culture is easily seen as a "bull in a china shop" in a high context culture. The American managers are brought up to tolerate and respect others' convictions, but are, because of their low context culture, not sensitive to nuances and not used to placing themselves in somebody else's position.

It is not surprising if people from high context cultures feel uncomfortable when managers from low context cultures arrive to run a subsidiary. People from high context cultures tend to be fine-tuned—they pay attention to nuances, and omissions; they indulge the speaker and fill in the unspoken meaning on their own. In the United States, being drunk is no excuse for badmouthing one's boss to his face—while in a country such as Japan, that is the managers' unspoken but understood purpose of after-business drinking. The typical manager from a low context culture has no ability or will to indulge subordinates to that extent: "If words are spoken, they are meant. There is no excuse."

To help managers to cope with—or, even better, avoid—such cultural clashes, most companies offer new expatriate managers (and their families)

A graduating multinational class of new employees at Andersen, the global accounting and consulting company. Following the cybernetic law of requisite variety, Andersen tries to match its global and culturally varied client base with an equally multicultural workforce.

© John Abbott.

predeparture workshops and briefings about the new culture they are to encounter. As important, most companies make sure that their professional development programs are open to a multinational group of employees. In this way the managers will naturally get "cultural sensitivity training" as a side benefit from internal executive courses.

CULTURE AND NEGOTIATIONS

So far the discussion has dealt mainly with how to deal with people inside the organization. But cultural effects on management extend also to outside activities. They affect the way the manager can and should deal with customers and with suppliers, with middlemen and potential alliance partners. Culture affects negotiations, and it is hardly possible to overstress the need for **cultural sensitivity.**

Since culture affects the people-skills of the manager, it is not surprising to find that most writings on business negotiations across countries stress the cultural problems involved. Even though such face-to-face negotiations usually involve more than just marketing issues, they are important in all three phases of global marketing management. Foreign entry via licensing or a joint venture necessarily involves finding contract partners. Local marketing puts the marketer in direct contact with channel members who need to be convinced to carry the product. Global management involves trade-offs between local subsidiaries' autonomy and headquarters' need for standardization. Cross-cultural negotiations are a fact of life for the global marketer.

There are several good books on cross-cultural negotiations, and these are recommended for the prospective negotiator.[14] In general, each different culture will require its own particular approach. The Hall, Hofstede, and Gannon frameworks discussed above offer some preliminary insights, but in actual negotiations more detailed advice is necessary. Following are a few basic cultural generalities.

Know Whom You Are Dealing With

In most negotiations, knowing something about the cultural background of the opposite partner is considered a must. It is important to know not only the nationalities involved, but also the particular ethnic background. This holds not only for today's obvious cases in Yugoslavia, Russia, and Belgium (Flemish versus Valloons), but also more subtle differences between ethnic backgrounds in the United States, Nigeria (Ibos versus Hausas), and Singapore. It is important not to treat these different subcultures as parts of the larger homogeneous unit, since differences, especially in nonverbal behavior, can be striking (see box, "Different Strokes").

But it is important never to forget that beyond cultural differences, personality can dominate cultural stereotypes. Thus, there are soft-spoken

THE CONDUCT at the negotiating tables varies a great deal across cultures. Where Americans want a prompt answer, Scandinavians can take their time. By contrast, Latin Americans are likely to interrupt when they understand where a speaker is going and are prone to argue a point. Japanese often close their eyes—some even actually do sleep. Arabs may leave the table because of a telephone call, and simply return later. Mexicans are notorious for arriving late. Italians pay much attention to looks and how an impressive statement can be made. The French often speak among themselves when another speaker is talking. The Germans insist on starting with background information before getting to the point. Chinese are very argumentative among themselves.

These crude generalizations do not always hold up, of course, but it is useful for the negotiator to understand that what seems to be strange behavior is not necessarily so. Leaving the table may seem insulting to some, but is perfectly natural to others. They may not even give it a second thought, since in their own culture it is the way things are done. And in that culture it fills a useful function. Coming late does not mean laziness or carelessness and is usually not even intentional. But in a society where clocks are rare, a 10 o'clock meeting means "sometime in the morning." When the costs of tardiness increase, people will come on time. This is why now in Mexico City, business meetings are much more in sync with the Western world.

However, it is important that the negotiator recognize when cultural oddities are merely guises for delaying tactics and, in fact, represent snubs. The reason is not only the personal affront but also the question of respect for the other side. In many instances there is a subtle power gambit being played, where the foreign negotiator is being tested. By indicating that one recognizes what game is being played, and threatening to pull out, the negotiations can often be put back on track.

Sources: Graham, 1983; Hall and Hall, 1990; Salacuse, 1991.

Americans, emotional Japanese, calm Brazilians, and informal Germans. But such persons may also have decided to accommodate a partner's different style, as when a Russian tries to be easygoing in a negotiation with a Brazilian. The experienced negotiator can usually diagnose the case in which the deviant behavior is genuine. And remember, without genuine behavior, **trust** is difficult to establish.

Know What You Are Saying

The second caution from experts is the possibility of discrepancies between what the manager thinks he or she is communicating and what is actually received by the other party.[15] Direct and straightforward speech still leaves many things unsaid—and "plain speaking" is in many cultures a typical way to hide something (one might do well recalling Othello's "honest Iago"). If something needs to be hidden, one ploy is to stress other points strongly, deflecting attention in the same way that most magicians do their tricks. This works against the typically open and direct American negotiators who may not have anything to hide—but who are nonetheless suspect because of the haste and eagerness with which they push negotiations along.

Managers need to remember that what they may think is a harmless and friendly question may not be so elsewhere. Chatting during a coffee break, and asking, "Do you have children?" can in the United States sometimes lead to a protracted explanation of a person's legal divorce and custody proceedings, whereas in a country such as Saudi Arabia it is akin to an intrusion on privacy.

All these issues teach you as much or more about your own culture's special characteristics as they do about foreign cultures.

Nonverbal communication is always a mysterious ingredient in negotiations. Research on negotiations has consistently found the other party's attractiveness to be a strong contributor to positive negotiation outcomes.[16] Although in some cases the causal direction seems to be the reverse—we like the person we have just concluded an agreement with—for the most part the effect goes the other way. If we like the appearance of someone, we are more likely to conclude an agreement. Although analysis of proposals and well-timed strategic concessions are the basic components of any successful business negotiation, most managers agree that appreciation of intangibles such as dress, looks, and nonverbal behavior can make for a much more satisfying negotiation experience and may count for more than we think. All the more so in the context of intercultural negotiations.

Know When to Say What

The typical approach by American negotiators is to take a problem-solving view of negotiations, in which the parties are oriented toward information exchange. They try to convey their own preferences and identify those of the other party by focusing on facts, asking questions, probing, and looking for specific data. Members of other cultures are more likely to assume a broader perspective and take a longer-term view of the negotiations, attempting to assess the potential of a general relationship beyond the specific contract agreement. To Americans, this is likely to be viewed as wasting time and avoiding critical issues. The difference is particularly important—American negotiators should take note of this—in foreign entry, at which time initial importing agreements may be too quickly struck and later turn out to be constraints on further penetration. Although it is difficult and time-consuming to fully evaluate the long-term consequences of a tie-up, it is important that the early negotiators not ignore the potential (or lack of it) for future and more broadly based collaboration, that is to say, spend some time and effort relationship-building if necessary.

Graham has analyzed negotiations in many cultures and identified four sequential stages that characterize information exchange in most business negotiations:[17]

....
EXHIBIT 3.5   Four Stages of Business Negotiations

Stage	Japanese	Americans
1. Nontask sounding	Considerable time and expense devoted to such efforts is the practice in Japan.	Relatively shorter periods are typical.
2. Task-related exchange of information	This is the most important step— high first offers with long explanations and in-depth clarifications.	Information is given briefly and directly. "Fair" first offers are more typical.
3. Persuasion	Persuasion is accomplished primarily behind the scenes. Vertical status relations dictate bargaining outcomes.	The most important step: Minds are changed at the negotiation table and aggressive persuasive tactics are used.
4. Concessions and agreement	Concessions are made only toward the end of negotiations—a holistic approach to decision making. Progress is difficult to measure for Americans.	Concessions and commitments are made throughout—a sequential approach to decision making.

Source: Adapted from John L. Graham, "A Hidden Cause of America's Trade Deficit with Japan," *Columbia Journal of World Business*, Fall 1981, p. 14.

1. *Nontask sounding.* This is an initial period when the conversation consists mainly of small talk, designed to get the partners to know each other better.

2. *Task-related exchange of information.* An extended period when the main issues are brought out, facts are presented, and positions clarified.

3. *Persuasion.* This is the stage when the parties attempt to make each other see the issues their way, when there is further explanation and elaboration of positions, and questioning of the other side's evidence.

4. *Concessions and agreements.* Toward the end of most negotiations is a period when mutual concessions might be made, when there is some yielding of fixed positions in order to reach an agreement.

Applying the framework to negotiations between Japanese and Americans, Graham and Sano found the significant cultural differences outlined in Exhibit 3.5.[18] As can be seen, the length and the importance of the stages differ between the two countries. The Americans use less time for nontask soundings than the Japanese, and they are brief with explanations, while the Japanese are more thorough. The Japanese are likely to wait with concessions until the very end, while the Americans move toward an agreement by gradually yielding ground. Against this background it is hardly surprising if trade negotiators from Japan and the United States sometimes seem to be in disagreement about how negotiations are progressing.

EXHIBIT 3.6   Type A and Type B Negotiators

Trait	Type A Negotiator	Type B Negotiator
Goal	Contract	Relationship
Attitudes	Win/lose	Win/win
Personal styles	Informal	Formal
Communications	Direct	Indirect
Time sensitivity	High	Low
Emotionalism	High	Low
Agreement form	Specific	General
Agreement building	Bottom-up	Top-down
Team organization	One leader	Consensus
Risk taking	High	Low

Source: Chart from *Making Global Deals*. Copyright 1991 by Jeswald W. Salacuse. Reprinted by permission of Houghton Mifflin Company. All rights reserved.

Negotiators from different cultures may be classified as proactive "A" types or reactive "B" types. Exhibit 3.6 identifies the major traits of the two types of negotiators. The type A negotiator starts with the easily agreed-upon smaller details and works up, while the type B negotiator first wants to agree on the overall framework of the agreement. Most of the traits in the list are self-explanatory. The "agreement building" trait refers to the process through which the agreement is formulated. As the list suggests, the type A negotiator is a more dynamic, energetic, and risk-taking entrepreneur while the B type is a slow, seasoned, mature individual who avoids risk. The A type is closer to the American managers in Exhibit 3.5, the B type closer to the Japanese managers. As Salacuse stresses, both approaches can work—which one is best depends on the cultures involved.[19] It's when they clash that there may be trouble.

THE LIMITS TO CULTURAL SENSITIVITY

Although the advantages of understanding and adapting to a foreign culture are evident, there can sometimes be "too much of a good thing." There are limits to which the marketing manager should go to try to accommodate the foreign culture if he or she wants to be effective sometimes depending on the situations.

Nonadaptation

There is a case to be made for **nonadaptation.** First, it is important to recognize that when a country is ready for change, a different culture can be attractive. This is easiest to see in the formerly communist nations. Russians want genuine Americans, not adapted versions. They can do the adaptation on

An unusual nego-tiation between one Japanese and two Americans. It is still uncommon to see a single Japanese negotia-tor, and for him to be flanked by two Americans suggests a lot of pressure. Not a good recipe for a favorable deal.

Richard Laird/FPG.

their own and expect the "real thing." The politically mandated changes in these countries have eroded the old norms and paved the way for new approaches. Here, attempting to adapt would be a mistake, since the locals want to learn from a successful foreign culture. It is important for the marketing manager to understand the historical and human context in which the firm's business dealings are taking place.

A second, more obvious caveat should be stated. There are limits to the effectiveness of cultural sensitivity as an accommodation strategy. Most trans-actions between buyers and sellers are based on the intrinsic costs and benefits to the parties, more than on the perceived appropriateness of the partners' dress and behavior. Once the particular needs and constraints of the prospective customer have been recognized and taken into account, even less-than-sensitive behavior can be overcome. Put simply, all behavioral refinements to the contrary, if the offering does not meet the needs of the buyer there is no transaction.

There are two other reasons why attempts at adaptation to another culture can be counterproductive. First, they may be only superficial, and thus lack any deeper meaning or conviction. While they are likely to engender the same kind of sympathy as flattery does, they are also clearly prone to misinterpretation, and may even create distrust.[20] The businessperson who wants to establish trust needs to present himself or herself sincerely and unequivocally. Hearing Japanese businessmen speak in straightforward and easygoing English and their American counterparts displaying Japanese-style sensitivity suggests Johnson's famous comment about the dog walking on two hind legs: "It is not done well, but one marvels at the fact that it is done at all." Such behavior can appear suspiciously similar to a smokescreen.

Keeping One's Center

A final reason why cultural adaptation can be counterproductive is that the manager runs the risk of losing his or her bearings. Management skills, as well as marketing skills, are learned through experience and reading. These skills are usually internalized and have become second-nature to be called on at a moment's notice to evaluate a situation. When the manager is busy paying attention to his or her behavior in an unfamiliar setting, however, it is very difficult to be intuitive. It is, in fact, difficult to think. What come to mind in such situations are often only random bits and pieces of know-how, and with bad luck, the manager can come out worse in the process. It takes preparation and a certain nerve to do what one does best. To illustrate, it is useful to think of the new cultural encounter as a performance. As performing artists know well, in the actual performance the individual's skills are rarely 100 percent. Rather, by practicing and preparing, the artist can make sure of success even at an 80 percent performance level. In the unfamiliar global setting, even 80 percent is a lot. As the performing artist knows, it is important not to get overly concerned with audience reaction or one loses one's center. Adaptation to the customer's culture, while a nice gesture, should not be allowed to interfere with the intrinsic merits of the proposal.

One should always try to understand one's customer or partner. But it is one thing to understand why and how the other side does things, and quite another to try to do things like that oneself. This view, finally—respect the other person's space and assume that he or she will respect yours—is the best approach. The transaction has to be based on intrinsic business merits, not on personal likes and dislikes. The notion that one should let personal likes and dislikes influence a business relationship, so popular in the early discussions of European, Japanese, and even American business, has been torpedoed as too expensive in the open competition in global markets.[21] Even in Japan, loyalties to suppliers and distributors who are not competitive have vanished into thin air as the market has opened up.[22]

A Global Low Context Culture?

Will there be—or is there already—a **global culture?** People in Europe and elsewhere ask why it is that the American culture seems to be dominating other cultures in the world's marketplace. Although it is important not to confuse popular culture with culture that guides managerial behavior, it is clear that the English language and the American business schools often determine the framework. One explanation lies in the international transferability of American culture.

The American culture travels light. Low context cultures are not as tied to the particular country of origin. A high context culture depends on common background and implicit understandings—it enables fine-tuning, but also limits the repertoire. A manager from a high context culture will need time to build up business in a new country. The American businessman can move much more rapidly since the focus is on the intrinsic merits of the transaction only—good products and services, customers who need them—and less on adapting to the particular cultural environment in the new country.

In today's world markets, high context cultures are high cost, both in terms of entry barriers and managerial inefficiency. They cherish the notion that every country is unique and no outsider can understand "us." This is possibly correct, and holding onto tradition is perhaps a desirable feature in itself. But it is counterproductive in the global economy, since it limits the inflow of new ideas into a company's managerial ranks, it reduces the pool of suppliers considered, and it keeps superior foreign goods out of markets. Globalization means that people in every country will have to decide the degree to which their own unique ways of doing business are worth preserving. These are difficult decisions. But in the global economy and the global firm, old ways don't promise success.

CULTURE'S IMPACT ON THE THREE GLOBAL MARKETING TASKS

Culture impacts the three roles of the global marketing manager in different ways. Generally speaking, when foreign entry is contemplated, the skills will involve correct interpretation of some cultural signals and a fair knowledge of local middlemen in the particular country. In the local marketing phase, the specific culture needs to be understood at a much deeper level since customer requirements and consumer preferences have to be deciphered. When it comes to global management, the cultural issues revolve broadly around the question of the extent to which adaptation in the marketplace is always necessary, or whether cultural norms can be challenged.

Foreign Entry

Culture is intimately tied to the "way of doing business" in a country. Whether signed contracts are necessary or a simple handshake is sufficient is largely a matter of custom, or business culture. When evaluating potential importers and distributors, not only their financial standing but also their social standing often matters. Establishing trust without personal friendship is impossible in some cultures—but "friendship" may be counterproductive. There are numerous incidents of principals feeling betrayed by their friendly local middlemen in a foreign market.

It is important to bear in mind that culture influences the "how" of business, but not necessarily the "what" of business. The functions of middlemen remain the same everywhere. The product shipped has to be guided through customs at the border; it has to be inspected, stored, and delivered to the appropriate outlets. Installation and after-sale service have to be completed where required, payments have to be made and remitted, and so on. What does differ between cultures is the way these functions are carried out, by whom, how fast, at what price, and so on.

For the marketer planning an entry into a foreign market, therefore, the analysis of its culture should center on what signs indicate a trustworthy and effective middleman or licensee, what are danger signals, and what behaviors suggest strengths and weaknesses. In this analysis there is little use for one's home culture, unless the countries are fairly similar. It is the lack of familiarity with foreign cultures that has made the "psychic" distance between countries a prime determinant of patterns of early expansion abroad. Europeans trade among themselves, Americans go to Canada, and the Japanese focus on Asia. Managers feel more comfortable with people similar to themselves, and have more confidence in their evaluation of potential partners. As more experience accumulates, the managers learn to accept and assess very different cultures.

When investment in foreign manufacturing is contemplated, the risk exposure generally increases, and there is a greater need for more expert input. External legal advisers, political risk analysts, and financial intermediaries might all be needed. In addition, it becomes important to predict how cultural factors will affect the management and efficient operation of the plant. This requires specialist advice in local labor relations and a keen appreciation of how culture affects the workers in the country. The expatriate manager needs to have spent some time in the country, to have at least moderate language capability, and be willing to adapt to some of the local customs. One reason foreign direct investment is sometimes foregone in favor of granting a license to a local manufacturer is the cultural complications arising in managing a foreign labor force.

Local Marketing

When we come to local marketing, cultural factors relate directly to the marketplace. Rather than simply being a matter of managerial behavior, culture is a strong determinant of consumer demand. For the marketer it is no longer sufficient to develop cultural sensitivity and to learn to accept individuals who act in strange ways. Now culture is involved in understanding and predicting buyer behavior (the topic of Chapter 7).

For the manager, there is now no escaping the need for first-hand personal experience of the people in the local market. Although market research reports can suggest the needs, wants and desires of potential and actual customers, it is always necessary to interpret survey findings and related statistics in the context of the actual buying situation. Experience in the domestic setting where the context is familiar and therefore not so salient blinds one to this fact. In a foreign market, where the type of outlets, retail assortments, infrastructure, and other contextual factors are different, demand analysis needs to account for underlying cultural drivers and other basic forces.

A few examples will illustrate these points. The first automatic laundromats introduced by Americans in Germany after World War II failed because

German housewives, although eager to clean the family clothes, were not about to show their dirty linen in public. Despite a strong demand for Western ice cream, ice cream parlors did not take off in Tokyo until intensive promotion and advertising made it "hip" for young people to stand on the street and eat their ice cream (high rent for space prohibited seating in the parlors). Wearing Western brand name clothes in the former communist countries was an act of protest and daring as much as a statement of taste and preference.

Western markets tend to be analyzed in terms of individual consumer behavior, treating social and cultural factors as subservient to internal psychological mechanisms for product and brand choice. Although these issues will be covered in more detail later, it should be noted here that this represents a significant bias to be recognized when marketing locally in foreign countries. Of course, in all markets the actors are individuals. But the notion that social and cultural factors in some way are subordinated to the cognitive and affective processes that the individual goes through is sometimes misleading when predicting choices and buying decisions of consumers in foreign cultures. The decisive factors can often be the social and cultural norms.

Examples abound, and not only from group-oriented societies. The desire to belong to a certain social class makes people buy a Mercedes although they would perhaps rather have a BMW. The force of popular pressure makes people order coffee when they want tea. In Germany, and in many other places, the need not to be too different leads consumers to forgo innovative new products in favor of the tried-and-true. More on these factors will be presented in Chapter 7 on local buyer behavior.

While such behavior is usually interpreted by Western observers as a simple trade-off between individual preferences and social norms, the process at work is often subtler. The products are not bought to satisfy individuals, but to satisfy others, such as peers and relatives. Of course, one can always argue that "really" the person is satisfying his or her individual desires, but the fundamental lesson is that to predict choices and buying decisions, individual preferences are not so important.

A somewhat extreme example can be used to drive home this point. While in the West most people would marry because they find their partner attractive, in a society where marriages are arranged, as is often the case in India and Japan, the idea that your wife should be attractive is not so important. An attractive partner may attract unwanted attention and even interfere with your life and work—something not completely unknown in the West! When agreeing to an arranged marriage—or buying a car, a house, a suit, a television set—the individual's particular likes or dislikes thus may be much less important to the decision maker than the desire to keep all involved parties at ease. In poorer countries, the focus on the individual can be even more misleading. After all, if you are the decision maker in a large family, your own tastes perhaps should be the last to be satisfied.

Trying to convince a buyer to use disposable, nonrecyclable packaging does not accomplish much when social worth is measured by the sacrifice involved in recycling. In local marketing, it is absolutely necessary to understand the local culture, the moral norms, the social forces which impinge on the individual. Unless this is done, the decision maker cannot interpret market research correctly, since responses and words can mean so many different things in different contexts. Here the manager needs to know when he or she *doesn't* understand—the first step to "enlightenment."

Global Management

When the task is global integration of the marketing effort across various countries, understanding cultural forces means something quite different again. *Here the marketer needs to understand the extent to which cultural forces are malleable and perhaps already changing.* The task involves less of any particular knowledge about the content of various cultures, and more an astute judgment of what the dynamics are and in which direction a country might be heading. Globalization, and any accompanying standardization, often involves going against cultural traditions.

An example will illustrate some of the issues involved. There is less reason to engage in an in-depth assessment of cultural norms in Russia today. The political and economic changes sweeping over the country suggest that a new order is slowly emerging, and the lawlessness and lack of direction reported in the news media are an expression of a culture where traditional guideposts lack legitimacy and credibility. Russia's mandate is for change—and the promise of American culture and capitalism has opened the door for entrepreneurs who would not have been listened to before. To try to "adapt" to Russia's norms today would be counterproductive and even impossible, since those norms are not yet worked out.

For global management, the issue of standardization of products, services, promotions, communication systems, and control procedures is paramount. To coordinate activities in multiple countries, comparability is necessary, and thus standardization becomes critical. By its very nature, standardization will cut across cultural lines. What the manager has to do is evaluate which lines can (and which cannot) be crossed with impunity, and which particular country's standards should be chosen as the general guide. An assessment of the degree of flux in a country needs to be carried out, and a seasoned judgment about the real and imagined obstacles to standardization has to be made. This is transnational management at its most fundamental level, and much more will be said on this topic later.

··

SUMMARY

This chapter has introduced the central role of culture in global marketing management. Culture should be interpreted broadly, in- cluding not only behavioral patterns inculcated by parents and peers, but practices embodied in religious institutions, ancient traditions, education, and the political process. Change in culture is slow even when people want to change because institutions aim to preserve the status quo and so cultural differences are here to stay. In organizations, the corresponding attitude is "We don't do things that way around here."

Chapter 3 discussed the frameworks for cultural analysis developed by Hall, Hofstede, and Gannon, identifying some major cultures around the world. We showed how culture helps develop certain managerial skills—and downplays others—which explains why managers from different nations tend to behave differently even though what they want to achieve is the same. This is why culture tends to affect implementation and execution more than strategy formulation, and why a degree of cultural adaptation is so urgent.

The effects of culture on negotiation skills were explained and illustrated with specific examples. It is important to recognize how one's own words and behavior will be perceived by the potential partner. While some adaption to the behavioral norms of a host country is necessary, too easy attempts at complete familiarity may backfire by eroding trust. Indeed, the potential mistrust generated by someone's consummate ease in a foreign culture may trigger the intuition that the fully adaptive individual's integrity is questionable, merely achieved to gain advantage. As always a high degree of judgment and sensitivity in these matters is crucial.

The confrontation with a foreign culture is useful because it teaches managers about their own cultural biases. This self-awareness is likely to be disconcerting at first, since it challenges the manager's sense of identity. But if faced in a constructive spirit, it helps the individual manager to grow and to understand other people's motivations better. It teaches managers how to empathize with others and place themselves in the other's situation. This is particularly important when managing marketing in countries with high context cultures where the meaning of words depends on the situation. One needs to know why and how one's foreign counterpart does what she or he does.

Culture plays a different role in each of the three marketing tasks. In foreign entry, culture has a direct impact on negotiations with potential middlemen and alliance partners. In local marketing, the question is how to treat local employees and, in particular, how consumer demand is affected. In global management, it's often "forget the cultural differences" time, and then cultural analysis is useful for assessing the amount of potential damage that can be absorbed in a strategy of standardization.

KEY TERMS

DISCUSSION QUESTIONS

1. An American manager can often be heard to start out saying, "Well, the way I see it . . ." while a Norwegian as often will start with, "Well, as we all know . . ." What cultural explanation can you find for this?

2. Discuss the advantages and the drawbacks for a manager's career in a company when she or he is posted abroad. Remember to consider the external labor market in addition to the internal career path in the company.

3. Find three examples of high context cultures and three examples of low context cultures. Justify your selections.

4. Why is it that Americans are considered bad listeners while the Japanese are considered very good listeners?

5. In negotiations it is often said that "silence is golden." Give an example of what this might mean. Can you find an example where the rule does not hold?

NOTES

1. Coca Cola's success in Japan is discussed in more detail by Huddleston, 1990, pp. 177–8.

2. See "Nestle Alimentana S.A.—Infant Formula," Harvard Business School case no. 9-580-118.

3. From Bellah et al., 1989. The view of culture as a determinant of behavioral skills is quite recent, complementing the more standard definition of culture as simply an underlying predisposition to behave in a certain way. The new emphasis on *skill* suggests that some people are not able to do what culture demands, even though they know what is asked. It is not easy for the new overseas manager, who is asked to eat ceremonial foods, to speak slowly, smile, and be patient, while not even understanding the language.

4. See Hall, 1976.

5. See Hall, 1960.

6. See, for example, Anderson and Venkatesan, 1994, and Levine and Wolf, 1985.

7. See Sujan, et al., 1993.

8. See Hofstede, 1980.

9. See Hofstede, 1988.

10. Gannon, 1994.

11. Good examples of these cultural effects can be found in Harris and Moran, 1987, and Barsoux and Lawrence, 1991.

12. See, for example, Barsoux and Lawrence, 1991.

13. These characterizations draw on Durlabhji and Marks, 1993; Hall, 1976; and Harris and Moran, 1987.

14. See, for example, Hall and Hall, 1990; Graham and Sano, 1984; March 1990.

15. See Tung, 1988, for example.

16. See, for example, Tung, 1988, and Graham et al., 1994.

17. See Graham, 1983; Graham and Sano, 1984; and Graham et al., 1994.

18. See Graham and Sano, 1984.

19. See Salacuse, 1991.

20. See Francis, 1991.

21. See, for example, D'Aveni, 1994.

22. See, for example, Blustein, 1995.

SELECTED REFERENCES

Anderson, Beverlee B., and M. Venkatesan. "Temporal Dimensions of Consuming Behavior across Cultures." Ch. 9 in Hassan, Salah S., and Roger D. Blackwell, eds., *Global Marketing: Perspectives and Cases.* Fort Worth, TX: Dryden, 1994.

Barsoux, Jean-Louis, and Peter Lawrence. "The Making of a French Manager," *Harvard Business Review,* July–August, 1991, pp. 58–67.

Bellah, Robert et al. *Habits of the Mind.* Berkeley: University of California Press, 1989.

Benedict, Ruth. *The Chrysanthemum and the Sword.* Tokyo: Charles E. Tuttle, 1954.

Blustein, Paul. "Giant Trading Companies Battle to Preserve Japan Inc.'s Edge," *Washington Post*, April 12, 1995, pp. A18, A19.

D'Aveni, Richard. *Hypercompetition.* New York: Free Press, 1994.

Durlabhji, Subhash, and Norton E. Marks, eds. *Japanese Business: Cultural Perspectives.* Albany, NY: SUNY Press, 1993.

Francis, June N. P. "When in Rome? The Effects of Cultural Adaptation on Intercultural Business Negotiations," *Journal of International Business Studies*, Third Quarter, 1991, pp. 403–28.

Gannon, Martin and Associates. *Understanding Global Cultures: Metaphorical Journeys through 17 Countries.* Thousand Oaks, CA: Sage, 1994.

Graham, John L. "Business Negotiations in Japan, Brazil, and the United States," *Journal of International Business Studies* 14 (Spring–Summer 1983), pp. 47–62.

———, and Yoshihiro Sano. *Smart Bargaining with the Japanese.* New York: Ballinger, 1984.

———, Alma T. Mintu, and Waymond Rodgers. "Explorations of Negotiations Behaviors in Ten Foreign Cultures Using a Model Developed in the United States," *Management Science* 40, no. 1 (January 1994), pp. 72–95.

Hall, Edward T. *Beyond Culture.* Garden City, NY: Anchor, 1976.

———. "The Silent Language in Overseas Business," *Harvard Business Review*, May–June 1960, pp. 87–96.

———, and Mildred Reed Hall. *Understanding Cultural Differences.* Yarmouth, ME: Intercultural Press, 1990. A comprehensive statement summarizing some very influential cultural notions relevant to managers.

Harris, Philip R., and Robert T. Moran. *Managing Cultural Differences.* Houston, TX: Gulf, 1987.

Hofstede, Geert. *Culture's Consequences.* Beverly Hills, CA: Sage, 1980.

———. "The Confucius Connection: From Cultural Roots to Economic Growth," *Organizational Dynamics* 16, no. 4 (Spring 1988), pp. 5–21.

Huddleston, Jackson N., Jr. *Gaijin Kaisha: Running a Foreign Business in Japan.* Tokyo: Charles Tuttle, 1990.

Levine, R., and E. Wolff. "Social Time: The Heartbeat of Culture," *Psychology Today*, March 1985, p. 35.

March, Robert M. *The Japanese Negotiator.* Tokyo: Kodansha, 1990.

Salacuse, Jeswald W. *Making Global Deals.* Boston: Houghton Mifflin, 1991.

Sujan, Mita; James R. Bettman; and Hans Baumgartner. "Influencing Consumer Judgments Using Autobiographical Memories: A Self-Referencing Perspective," *Journal of Marketing Research* XXX (November 1993), pp. 422–36.

Tung, Rosalie. "Toward a Concept of International Business Negotiations," in *Advances in International Comparative Management*, Richard Farmer, ed. Greenwich, CT: JAI Press, 1988, pp. 203–19.

CASES

Case 1

CANADA'S THRIVING EXPORTERS

Canada is a country with 31 million inhabitants dispersed in a vast country occupying the northern half of North America. Most of its population lives within a few miles of the United States border to the south, but the country has vast agricultural land, forests, and minerals. Two successful export ventures, the Versatile Farm Equipment Company and TannerEye Ltd., show how entrepreneurial flair can take advantage of (or succeed in spite of) country-specific advantages and disadvantages.

Versatile Farm Equipment Company

"Product differentiation is the key to our success. If we had a conventional product—no matter how good—we would not be here today," says Paul M. Soubry, president of Versatile Farm Equipment Company in Winnipeg, Manitoba.

In reviewing the depressed state of the world farm equipment industry, Paul Soubry emphasizes the vital importance to his company of their "nichemanship" approach in building an international reputation through the production and sale of four-wheel-drive (4WD) agricultural tractors.

Founded in 1947 by two Toronto entrepreneur-inventors, Versatile Farm Equipment Company became in 1966 the first company in the world to commercialize an integral 4WD agricultural tractor. Demand in western Canada for these powerful but simply-designed units proved strong, and with duty-free entry to and from the United States, sales to large-scale farms in the Dakotas and Montana soon followed. Australian farmers also found that the Versatile tractor suited their requirements and traveled to Winnipeg to purchase a number for use at home. International sales were further boosted when the Canadian International Development Agency funded the purchase of 300 of the tractors for use in Algeria. Thus overseas sales quickly became an important source of income for this small but growing Canadian-owned company.

In 1977, the company was acquired by Cornat Industries Ltd. of Vancouver (later renamed Versatile Corporation), and a new

Source: Case compiled from Phillip Rosson, Mary Brooks, Shyam Kamath and Donald Patton, "Excellence in Exporting: Advice and Comments from Canada Export Award Winners," Centre for International Business Studies, Dalhousie University, 1985.

management team headed by Paul Soubry, obtained support from the board of directors for a growth strategy based on aggressively seeking international sales. An early step in implementing this strategy was to tighten control of marketing in Australia by buying out its distributor and establishing its own operations. In 1980, Versatile entered into a marketing arrangement with Fiat Trattori in which Fiat agreed to purchase 4WD tractors from Versatile for international distribution in specified markets. The tractors sold under this arrangement were marked "Manufactured in Canada by Versatile." In the United States, the company's marketing efforts were continued through their two U.S. offices and extensive distribution network. Other international sales were handled directly from Winnipeg.

The following year, the demand for agricultural equipment began a precipitous decline, with the total number of 4WD tractors sold worldwide falling from a peak of 16,000 in 1977 to 5,700 in 1984, and with sales of only 4,000 projected in 1985. Lying behind this gloomy trend were such factors as increased protectionism in agriculture, slower rates of economic growth, excessive international indebtedness by Third World countries, currency fluctuations, and high interest rates in major markets.

Surviving in a shrinking market has required the use of bold strategies to cut costs and increase product differentiation. Accordingly, overheads have been reduced, and new numerically controlled production equipment as well as CAD/CAM processes have further contributed to cost-effective production. In 1983, the decision was made to reach a broader market by investing over $26 million in plant expansion and in the design, production, and marketing of a scaled-down, lower priced 4WD—the Series 200. At the same time, Versatile has carried out a major R&D blitz (yielding as many as 76 new patents), successfully redesigned its biggest units, licensed company technology, know-how and brand name to overseas manufacturers, and has entered into joint venture arrangements.

According to Paul Soubry, Versatile's relatively small size (approximately 2,500 employees worldwide) has advantages in these turbulent times, as does his firm's lean management structure and quick decision making. With 65 percent of sales coming from exports, Versatile's five-year strategic-planning process pays careful attention to future trends in farm incomes, expected government policies at the national and international levels, as well as the anticipated actions of competitors. With its strategic overview, capable management, and skilled work force, Versatile's carefully chosen market niche may well prove a fully defensible and profitable base for long-term survival and growth.

As a seasoned executive in the farm implements industry, Paul Soubry holds no illusions about the future. "I think it's going to be very challenging for the next three or four years. But those who survive—and we intend to be one of them—will emerge leaner and more cost efficient, ready to progress when the market improves."

TannerEye Ltd.

"We went into business against unbeatable odds—and survived," says vice president and marketing director, Michael Jardine, as he looks back over seven years of steady growth in his company's operations. What's more, he says, "our first sale was an export sale—we established in business to export."

From an initial investment of only $7,500, TannerEye Ltd. has grown so that today it employs well over 100 people at its plant in Charlottetown, Prince Edward Island. President G. Peter Leunes and his partners have succeeded in carving out a profitable niche for the company in a most unusual product and service area—covering high quality eyeglass frames, mostly manufactured by others, with a thin layer of decorative leather facing. TannerEye also produces complete sets of eyeglass frames from blocks of special plastics imported from Europe and the United States for the customer's brand label.

Small company size is no disadvantage in the modern eyewear industry, which increasingly requires flexibility to respond to rapid change in market requirements. More and more wholesalers and manufacturers in the United States, Europe, Japan, and elsewhere are looking to companies like TannerEye to come up with the 50 or so new frame styles, designs, and color changes demanded each year. Attractive designs, recognized craftsmanship, unique skills, reliable delivery, and a strong customer orientation give TannerEye an edge over the hundreds of Italian, French, German, Japanese, and other competitors in this truly international industry.

The company's Prince Edward Island location may seem remote or inconceivable to some, but the island location has advantages, not the least of which is a lifestyle that is attractive to many in the design field. Also, Prince Edward Island is sufficiently beautiful so that many overseas customers find reasons to justify a visit to the company's production facilities, especially in summer. Increased use of electronic data transmission, especially the telecopier, is reducing the distance between TannerEye and its customers, and airfreight services have proved satisfactory for bringing in needed raw materials and shipping out finished eyewear.

However, the road to success has not been smooth. At the outset TannerEye found that one or two large customers took almost all of the company's production—a promising beginning. But things soon turned sour when customer bankruptcies left large accounts unpaid and TannerEye in crisis. Fortunately, TannerEye had export development corporation coverage and was eventually reimbursed for these bad debts. On the basis of this experience, Mike Jardine advises others who are starting out to be wary of overdependence on large customers and to pay strict attention to the terms of the sale and financing methods used in export sales. TannerEye now uses a range of export financing tools for its overseas markets.

Mike Jardine characterizes the spirit of this enthusiastic and capable young company when he says, "We're survivors. We have good instincts and operate well under pressure." TannerEye is rightly proud of its seven-year history. Not content to rest on its laurels, the company has ambitious plans for the future.

DISCUSSION QUESTIONS

1. What are the country-specific advantages behind Versatile's success? Any disadvantages? Are there location-specific factors which are not country-specific?

2. What are the country-specific advantages behind TannerEye's success? Are there any location specific factors which are not country specific?

3. Do you think "Made in Canada" is a positive factor in Versatile's success? In TannerEye's?

4. What firm-specific factors play a role in Versatile's success? In TannerEye's?

Case 2

IKEA'S UNLIKELY EXPANSION (A)

*I*kea, the Swedish furniture store chain virtually unknown outside of Scandinavia 25 years ago, has drawn large opening crowds to its stores as it has pushed into Europe, North America, and Asia. Along the way it has built something of a cult following, especially among young and price-conscious consumers. But in contemplating its United States entry, the company managers realized that they faced their biggest challenge so far.

Company Background

Ikea was founded in 1943 by Ingvar Kamprad to serve price-conscious neighbors in the province of Smaland in southern Sweden. Early on, the young entrepreneur hit upon a winning formula, contracting with independent furniture makers and suppliers to design furniture which could be sold as a kit and assembled in the home of the consumer. In return for favorable and guaranteed orders from Ikea, the suppliers were prohibited to sell to other stores. Developing innovative modular designs whose components could be mass produced and venturing early into Eastern Europe to build a dedicated supplier network, Ikea could offer quality furniture in modern Scandinavian designs at very low prices. By investing profits in new stores, the company expanded throughout Scandinavia in the 1950s.

Throughout the following years, the Ikea store design and layout remained the same; Ikea was basically a warehouse store. Because the ready-to-assemble "knockdown" kits could be stacked conveniently on racks, inventory was always large, and instead of waiting for the store to deliver the furniture, Ikea's customers could pick it up themselves. Stores were therefore located outside of the big cities, with ample parking space for automobiles. Inside, an assembled version of the furniture was displayed in settings along with other Ikea furniture. The purchaser could decide on what to buy, obtain the inventory tag number, and then either find the kit on the rack, or, in the case of larger pieces, have the kit delivered through the back door to the waiting car.

This simple formula meant that there were relatively few sales clerks on the floor. The sales job consisted mainly of making sure that the assembled pieces were attractively displayed, that clear instructions were given as to where the kits could be found, and making sure that customers did not have to wait too long at the checkout lines. Ikea's was a classic "cash-and-carry" approach, except that credit cards were accepted.

European Expansion

In the 1960s and 70s, as modern Scandinavian design became increasingly popular, expansion into Europe became a logical next step. The

Source: Case compiled from Rita Martenson "Innovations in International Retailing," University of Gothenburg, Sweden: Liber, 1981. Richard W. Stevenson, "Ikea's New Realities: Recession and Aging Consumers," *New York Times*, April 25, 1993, p. F4.

company first entered the German-speaking regions of Switzerland, thereby testing itself in a small region similar to Scandinavia. Yet expansion so far away from Sweden made it necessary to develop new suppliers, which meant that Kamprad traveled extensively, visiting potential suppliers and convincing them to become exclusive Ikea suppliers. Once the supply chain was established, the formula of consumer-assembled furniture could be used. After some resistance from independent furniture retailers who claimed that the furniture was not really "Swedish" since much of it came from other countries, Ikea's quality/price advantage proved irresistible even to fastidious Swiss consumers.

The next logical target was Germany, much bigger than Switzerland, but also culturally close to Ikea's roots. In Germany, well established and large furniture chains were formidable foes opposed to the competitive entry and there were several regulatory obstacles. The opening birthday celebration of the first store in 1974 outside Cologne was criticized because in German culture birthdays should only be celebrated every 25 years. The use of the Swedish flag and the blue-yellow colors was challenged because the Ikea subsidiary was an incorporated German company (Ikea GmbH). The celebratory breakfast was mistitled because no eggs were served. Despite these rearguard actions from the established German retailers, Ikea GmbH became very successful, and was thus accepted, being voted German marketer of the year in 1979. The acceptance of Ikea's way of doing business was helped by the fact that Ikea had enlarged the entire market by its low prices, and some of the established retailers adopted the same formula in their own operations.

To get the stores abroad started, Kamprad usually sent a team of three or four managers who could speak the local language and had experience in an existing Ikea store. This team hired and trained the sales employees, organized the store layout, and established the sales and ordering routines. Although the tasks were relatively simple and straightforward, Ikea's lean organizational strategies meant that individual employees were assigned greater responsibilities and more freedom than usual in more traditional retail stores. Although this was not a problem in Europe, it seemed to pose one in North America.

North American Entry

To prepare for eventual entry into the United States, Ikea first expanded into Canada. The Canadian market was close to the U.S. market, and creating the supply network for Canada would lay the foundation for what was needed for the much larger U.S. market. Drawing upon a successful advertising campaign and positive word-of-mouth, and by combining newly recruited local suppliers with imports from existing European suppliers, the Canadian entry was soon a success. The advertising campaign was centered around the slogan, "Ikea: The impossible furniture store from Sweden," which was supported by a cartoon drawing of a moose's head, complete with antlers. The moose symbol had played very well in Germany, creating natural associations "with the north," and also creating an image of fun and games which played well in the younger segments the company targeted. The Canadians responded equally well to the slogan and the moose, as well as to Ikea's humorous cartoon-like ads poking fun at its Swedish heritage ("How many Swedes does it take to screw in a lightbulb? Two—one to screw in the lightbulb, and one to park the Volvo"), which became often-heard jokes.

The United States presented a much different challenge, as it offered a much larger market with its population dispersed, great cultural diversity, and strong domestic competition. The initial problems centered around which part of the United States to attack first. While the East Coast seemed more natural, with its closer ties to Europe, the California market on the West Coast was demographically more attractive. But trafficking supplies to California would be a headache, and competition seemed stronger there, with the presence of established retailers of Scandinavian designs.

Then, there was the issue of managing the stores. In Canada, the European management style had been severely tested. The unusually great independence and authority of each individual employee in the Ikea system had been welcomed, but the individuals often asked for more direction and specific guidance. For example, the Swedish start-up team would say to an employee, "You are in charge of the layout of the office furniture section of the store," and consider this a perfectly actionable and complete job description. This seemed to go against the training and predisposition of some employees, who came back with questions such as, "How should this piece of furniture be dis-

played?" Ikea's expansion team suspected that the situation would be possibly even more difficult in the United States. The team also wondered if the same slogan and the moose symbol would be as effective in the United States as it had been in Germany and Canada.

DISCUSSION QUESTIONS

1. What is Ikea selling?

2. What are Ikea's firm-specific advantages? Country-specific advantages?

3. Why is expansion abroad in retailing difficult? What has made it possible in Ikea's case?

4. What could be the cultural reasons for Ikea's problems with store managers and employees in North America?

5. In terms of demand potential, the United States would seem to have good potential for Ikea. Can the U.S. entry make good use of its unique skills and resources?

Case 3

THE ELUSIVE MARKET POTENTIAL OF EASTERN EUROPE

*M*r. Jim Fisher, a senior executive of a Western pharmaceutical company, reflected on his last several days in Budapest as he sipped his drink at the Hilton Hotel terrace overlooking the beautiful Duna River. People sitting at other tables were busy discussing the importance of the historic day, as on that day, 19 June 1991, the last Soviet soldier was scheduled to leave Hungary. It wasn't difficult to read the excitement and enthusiasm in the faces and expressions of especially the local people.

This was Fisher's third visit to Budapest over the past year. During the same period, he had also visited Prague, Bratislava, Warsaw, and Moscow. His assignment had been to evaluate the business opportunities in pharmaceuticals in Eastern Europe for his company. By June 1991, he had spent more than two months traveling through the region and concentrated much of his attention on investigating potential export and investment prospects for his company. Enjoying the beautiful view of Duna River that afternoon, he felt a sense of frustration. Despite all the time and effort he put into this task over the past year, no tangible opportunity was yet apparent. He felt quite uncomfortable not being able to provide his company with the blueprints of a potentially fruitful deal.

Market Opening

What prompted Fisher's company to assign him the task of exploring business opportunities in Eastern Europe and the Soviet Union was, of course, the dramatic opening of these markets to the west, which began largely in 1989. The desire by the former Soviet Bloc countries to move toward a free market system and to privatize their enterprises was quite strong.

The early reports that came out of the region pointed toward a tremendous business opportunity in pharmaceuticals and medical products. Recalling his discussions a year ago with John Rosthorn of ICI Pharmaceuticals, Fisher felt confident that the opportunities were outstanding. Rosthorn had commented that the drug industry had a strong opportunity because of poor longevities in the large and aging populations, a reasonable health care infrastructure, harsh social and environmental conditions, and growing health care awareness and European affinities. The former Soviet Union is thought to be the fourth largest drug market in the world. Although spending for drugs per capita is low, the growth potential is high. Rosthorn thought that more than one strategy would be needed

Source: Case written by S. Tamer Cavusgil, Director, International Business Development Center, and professor of marketing and international business at Michigan State University.

to approach East European markets because of heterogeneous populations and political instability. Rosthorn estimated that it would cost under 10 percent of net sales to sell into East European markets, even with poor communications systems and the lack of well-trained sales personnel or adverse reaction reporting.

Reports coming out of the former Soviet Union indicated that plants to formulate insulin, antibiotics, vitamins, and a variety of other drugs are desperately needed. Soyuzvneshstroimport, the Russian minister for the medical industry, has been seeking bids on such projects and has noted that the money for these projects would be made available despite general budget constraints.

In the eastern states of Germany, a barrage of Western products has been available since the two Germanys' currencies were united in July 1990. Companies based in western states are now supplying some 75 percent of the food and consumer items sold in eastern stores. But products of eastern German marketers who often lack marketing knowledge and sometimes have either no image or negative images, are at a disadvantage to these incoming Western products. Generally, thousands of little firms—once part of government-owned conglomerates—are having a tough time marketing their goods to Soviets and other Eastern Bloc markets.

Privatization

Throughout the East Bloc, many state-owned businesses are to be sold to investors as the communist way of life fades into the past. The process started with the sale of reasonably well functioning firms in order to lure investors and set a precedent for further privatization of not-so-successful firms. The firms that might be sold initially in Hungary, for example, include a travel agency and numerous pharmaceutical companies. In Poland, a chocolate company and an organization that preserves historic buildings may be sold. In Czechoslovakia, a shoe company may be offered.

Each country is developing a timetable for the sale of government firms. Hungary wants to sell 100–150 firms in the next 20 months, and Poland wants to sell 100 firms in one year, while Czechoslovakia and eastern German states are moving more slowly to sell off enterprises. Perhaps 90 percent of industry in East Europe is government owned, and assets totaling $100 billion could be sold to investors. The sales will not only bring in hard currency and improve management and efficiency, but will also transform society, producing entrepreneurs and a middle class.

By 2000, perhaps 50 percent of industry in East Europe will be privatized, but the other 50 percent may be too inefficient to ever be privatized. Yet some critics are now attacking capitalism as not much better than socialism, recognizing drawbacks such as longer work days, layoffs, the development of social classes, and so on. And some deals privatizing companies have been criticized as giving away state property for ridiculously low prices. Privatization also faces the problem that many citizens don't have enough money to buy food and clothing, so there certainly isn't any money for buying stock in a company. As a result, some governments are considering ways to make it possible for workers to buy stock cheaply. Another problem is a fear of foreign domination as Western companies move in.

Market Potential

Mr. Fisher's travels through Eastern Europe and the former Soviet Union as well as his conversations with more than three dozen business executives and government representatives have nonetheless confirmed the extraordinary nature of market potential in the region. The region, with its 430 million inhabitants, accounts for about 17 percent of the world GNP. Three leading countries in the region, Hungary, Czechoslovakia, and Poland, have a combined GNP greater than the Peoples' Republic of China. And wage rates are still low in the region—below those of Spain, Portugal, and Greece.

Within the region, there is considerable diversity. Countries differ radically in terms of market size, cultural traditions, quality of infrastructure, pace of economic reform, and political stability. Indeed, ethnic diversity, which had been suppressed by 45 years of communist regime, is now surfacing strongly in Yugoslavia, the former Soviet Union, Czechoslovakia, and to some extent in Romania.

Local Work Force

Fisher's own observations led him to believe that Central Europe, including Hungary, Czechoslovakia, and Poland, still represents a prime region for new business ventures. There appears to be a tremendous amount of production capacity available in many industries. Western companies can enter Central Europe and negotiate arrangements that will allow them to use this vast capacity with very low costs. For example, General Electric's recent joint venture with Tungsram of Hungary (together with acquisition of Thorne, Ltd., of the United Kingdom has made the company the worldwide leader in lighting.

In addition to production capacity, Central Europe has an abundance of well-educated manpower. People appear to aspire for western life styles and seem ready to work hard in order to improve their standards of living.

On the negative side, Fisher has recognized several deficiencies of available manpower. First, knowledge of modern business practices is very limited: basic accounting and finance concepts and instruments are not well known; and management education is only now making an entry into the curriculum. Second, industry sector knowledge is also limited; for example, knowledge of banking, transportation, and communications practices is also inadequate. Third, sales and marketing mentality is not widely shared.

How to Do Business

Leaving these thoughts temporarily, Fisher's eyes searched for a waiter who could replenish his drink. Just then, he saw Mr. Brad Simpson enter the terrace with another man. Fisher asked them to join him for a drink. He had met Brad Simpson a few days earlier at an informal gathering of foreign business executives in Budapest and was impressed with his insights on Central Europe. Simpson introduced Fisher to Mr. Gyorgy Balogh, who was accompanying him. Balogh, as it turned out, was an executive in the Budapest office of an international management consulting firm.

After ordering some drinks and preliminary discussion, Fisher decided to bounce off his frustrations on the two men, who seemed to have a much more thorough understanding of the business climate in Hungary and elsewhere in Central Europe. As the most senior executive in Hungary of a large British telecommunications company, Simpson had a decade of experience in the region. As a management consultant, Balogh worked with a large number of western companies seeking joint ventures and acquisition opportunities in Hungary.

Simpson commented that the lack of sales and marketing capabilities was largely the result of past upbringing and values. Since all marketing was performed by state trading organizations, manufacturing companies did not concern themselves with marketing.

There were also some cultural idiosyncrasies, Balogh added. First, "making a sales call" is foreign to people in Central Europe. In the state enterprises, the markets were fixed by the top authorities; the managers just had to worry about producing. Second, "calling high" is a difficulty. People entering sales positions are reluctant to call on people who might be at higher social hierarchies. Therefore, salespeople may be comfortable calling on data processing managers but not the real decision makers at higher levels of the organization.

Third, new salespeople are afraid to make calls because of not knowing "what to say." Some are petrified about the sales encounter. Fourth, the concept of account management is completely new to the people. Fifth, proper follow-through is missing. Once an order is placed, considerable follow-through is needed to ensure that the customer gets the product on time, and that they are installed and working properly. The follow-through mentality and sense of urgency are not yet widely established. Finally, competition is a new phenomenon. Since manufacturing companies are generally given a production quota and simply asked to deliver it, managers have a difficult time of adjusting to competition, especially by western firms.

Simpson wondered about how to encourage individual initiative. If people could be motivated by a mix of monetary and other incentives, businesses could expect greater productivity. Unfortunately, however, the incentive pay system is not at all well established. There are also serious impediments to setting up differential pay scales based on qualifications and effort.

Decision-Making Process

The discussion soon centered on what both Simpson and Balogh considered the key deficiency: the decision-making processes of client companies. Both men observed that there is no predictable pattern to decision-making processes of Hungarian executives, and that the process seems to be endless and follows no logical progression. The shift from the centrally planned system to a free market system requires decisions at the enterprise level, but managers do not seem to embrace this responsibility with open arms. In the previous regime individuals were not allowed to or asked to make decisions. Thus by not making decisions, the possibility of being wrong was eliminated. Further, decisions were arrived at collectively, so no one individual was put in the position of making a mistake.

Simpson mentioned that his company now actually assists prospective clients develop a procedure for arriving at decisions. This is certainly a new twist—a supplier teaching its customers how to make decisions!

There was consensus that a massive training effort is needed to instill modern business mentality and practices. Several western-style business educational institutions are now in place, such as the International Management Center in Budapest and the International Business School in Moscow. Established institutions such as the Budapest University of Economic Sciences (formerly the Karl Marx University) are also stepping up management education programs. Finally, many short-term management training programs are being offered under the auspices of western European and U.S. governments (yet not always with a relevant and applied curriculum). Nevertheless, much more has to be done to make a real impact on the thousands of managers needed to guide the transition economy.

As he thanked his guests and headed for his hotel room, Fisher felt good about the new insights he gained about the economic and social climate in Hungary and elsewhere in Central Europe. At the same time, he couldn't help wondering about a potential action agenda he might present to his management upon returning to his office.

DISCUSSION QUESTIONS

1. Should his company continue to pursue a potential venture in Eastern Europe, or should they abandon the project for a while?

2. Where in Eastern Europe should the company concentrate its efforts?

3. Should the company be on the lookout to acquire an existing business? Should they seek a local partner?

4. Should the company consider local production? Should the priority be on catering to the local market or on entering export markets?

5. What type of a time horizon is appropriate for a profitable operation in middle Europe?

6. What other advantages could be gained in the long term from the company's involvement in Eastern Europe?

Case 4

TOYS R US JAPAN (A)

Company Background

Toys R Us, Inc. is a children's specialty retailer concentrating on toys and children's clothing headquartered in Paramus, New Jersey.

Toys R Us is, by all accounts, the largest toy retailer in the world, with about 20–25 percent of the U.S. market, and 2 percent of total international sales. It was founded in the late 1940s by the current chairman, Charles Lazarus, as the first "toy supermarket," and was acquired by department store chain operator Interstate Inc., in 1966. Interstate went bankrupt in 1974 after becoming overextended through buying a number of discount chains, but it continued to build more Toys R Us stores through a court-ordered reorganization. After this was finished in 1977, Interstate divested all its other assets and became Toys R Us, Inc.; Lazarus became chairman and CEO. Toys R Us grew fast through the late 1970s and 1980s by an aggressive expansion campaign which undercut existing retailers. The first Kids R Us stores were opened in 1982; and the first international stores were opened in 1984. Since going public in 1978, sales have risen every year, although earnings showed only nominal gains between 1989 and 1991.

The company currently operates 1,032 stores, with 581 Toys R Us stores and 217 Kids R Us stores in the United States, and with 234 Toys R Us stores operated through international subsidiaries in 18 countries. Sales in

1993 were $7.9 billion, making Toys R Us the 50th largest retailer in the world and the 22nd largest in the United States. By comparison, Japan's largest retailer, Daiei, had about $14 billion annually in sales. After-tax profits of $483 million were realized in 1993, and 18 percent of total sales and 14 percent of profits were from the international operations.

Company Strategy

Toys R Us has succeeded by using a "category killer" strategy, which combines strong advertising to promote name recognition and discounts on the most popular items (loss leaders such as diapers) to create a perception that everything is discounted, with large stores offering a wide selection of brand name merchandise. Such stores are the progenitors of the low-cost, low-service, warehouse-style discount store concept that is currently taking a large share of the U.S. market. In the United States, a computerized inventory system is used to track demand on a regional and store-by-store basis to maintain low standing inventories and capitalize quickly on trends. This system is being upgraded with even better communications technology and improved regional warehouse facilities. Toys R Us also owns and operates its own fleet of trucks, to save on shipping. Industry power from the high market share is occasionally wielded by

Source: Case compiled from report developed by Michael Chadwick and Jeong-Soe Won, Waseda–Georgetown Graduate Business Program, Tokyo, 1994.

Toys R Us to keep its producers in line. Prices on most goods are competitive with other retailers, but in general they are not deeply discounted. Over the past year, Toys R Us has used coupon promotions aggressively in the period before Christmas to increase market share over their major sales period.

Toys R Us International

The long-term strategy for Toys R Us is to expand primarily in international markets. Toys R Us International operations follow the home country strategy, but as competition from other large-volume discount-type stores is less in most of the international markets, prices are correspondingly higher. Inventory is chosen with more than half from the Toys R Us U.S. inventory, and the rest is chosen to reflect local tastes. As of 1993, Toys R Us has started making franchising deals to enter foreign markets with local partners; deals to enter six such markets have been made, primarily in oil-rich developing countries in the Middle East. Of the 115 stores Toys R Us plans to open over this year, 70 will be in other countries.

The Japanese Toy Market

As in many product categories, the toy retail market in Japan is dominated by small specialty stores and general retailers. Of the 29,413 stores which had toy sales as a significant percentage of overall sales in 1991, 11,628 were toy and hobby specialty retailers (including computer game shops), and 12,582 were small general retail shops; an additional 2,772 were convenience stores, and 1,227 were large toy specialty retailers; less than 500 larger general retailers made a significant portion of their income from toy sales. By comparison, in 1987 the United States had only 9,629 stores which fell into the specialty retailer category, and a significant percentage of total sales were made by large general retail chains such as Kmart, Sears, and Wal-Mart.

Japanese statistical reporting does not separate toys from other leisure goods, but statistics indicate that yearly sales for toys, sporting goods, and musical instruments were approximately ¥3.3 trillion ($25 billion at 1991 exchange rate of ¥130/$1) in 1991. The largest exclusive toy retailer in Japan, Kiddyland, had 1992 per store sales of ¥230 million ($1.8 million) from 52 stores for a total of ¥11.96 billion ($92 million), as compared to Toys R Us' $7.9 billion from 1,032 stores ($7.6 million per store). All in all, there are 21 toy/hobby store chains (defined as having more than one store) in Japan, with the largest, Pelican, having 71 stores.

The 29,000 toy and sporting goods retailers are serviced by a network of 5,692 wholesalers and deal almost exclusively in Japan-made products. There are upwards of 15,000 toy manufacturers in Japan, but only six of all of these (including game giants Nintendo and Koei) employ more than 50 people; the vast majority are one or two person operations. The most popular products are computer games and dolls or toys with linkages to animated television characters.

The average Japanese household spent ¥83,724/year in 1992 ($650) on health and leisure products (again, the two are not differentiated in statistical analyses). There are approximately 39 million households in Japan, which ranks Japan with the United States and Europe as one of the three largest and wealthiest markets in the world for leisure products. In general, they are motivated as much by quality as by price, and show a preference for established brand-name merchandise over lesser known goods.

Barriers to Entry

Before Toys R Us entered the Japanese market, a number of issues were pointed to and voices were raised to suggest that Japan was not ready for the retailing revolution Toys R Us represented. The issues took a number of forms: suggestions that Toys R Us would not be able to get the necessary permissions and empty space it needed to open huge stores; statements that major Japanese manufacturers would not be willing to enter into direct deals with Toys R Us, instead preferring to work through middle wholesalers and preserve their traditional trade links; analyses that claimed that Toys R Us, like many other multinationals, would find that the tools which worked so well in the rest of the world would come up short when confronted with the sensitive Japanese consumer; and contentions that discount retailing was antithetical to the Japanese psyche, which linked quality with price, and so Toys R Us, by competing on price, would class themselves out of the market.

DISCUSSION QUESTIONS

1. What is the basis for Toys R Us success in the United States?

2. What are the problems in transferring Toys R Us firm-specific advantages to a foreign market?

3. Why should Toys R Us internalize the firm-specific advantages rather than licensing another retailer abroad?

4. Does Japan look like a good market opportunity for Toys R Us?

5. What are the entry barriers into Japan? Any culturally based barriers, in terms of how to do business? Do you think there are any cultural obstacles to product acceptance?

Global marketing can be implemented only after the firm has entered foreign markets. In Part Two, we turn to the process of market entry and global expansion. Although conceptually there are many similarities between a national roll-out of a new product and international expansion to new countries, going across borders poses new difficulties.

When a business enters a foreign country, exposure to political risks needs to be managed. When products have to be shipped across borders and into another country's distribution channels, foreign middlemen have to be identified and put under contract. When transactions are across borders, exchange rate fluctuations and customs duties affect revenues. When sales have to be promoted overseas, advertising agencies with a local presence must be used. These are only some of the complications of choosing which country to enter, what mode of entry to use, and what global expansion path to follow.

Although much of the material in Part Two deals with the novice exporter, large multinationals that operate in many markets must follow the same principles. Exporting mechanics and customs barriers directly affect where a multinational will locate new facilities. An MNC will often have to change the chosen entry mode when its strategic objectives change. If political or economic conditions in a country change, an MNC will sometimes exit and then reenter as conditions improve. And for even the largest multinationals, there are usually still markets left to conquer.

Chapter 4

Country Attractiveness

"But this is not Kansas!"

After studying this chapter, you should understand the following global marketing issues:

1. Assessing a country's attractiveness for entry involves not only issues of market potential and growth, but also considerations of trading bloc membership, competitive intensity, and entry barriers.

2. A systematic quantitative screening of candidate countries should always be undertaken when comparable data are available.

3. Attractiveness factors need to be weighed against each other systematically, and the sensitivity of the final choice to possible shifts in objectives should be considered.

4. To forecast sales for a country the manager will often have to combine subjective estimates with whatever objective data are available.

5. There are many independent research agencies that provide up-to-date economic and political data on countries and regions and that will provide customized analysis on specific products and markets.

In theory there are several reasons for the firm to enter a foreign market. From a pure marketing perspective, it is most natural to view expansion abroad in terms of entering new countries because of their market potential. But as we saw in Chapter 1, the firm may also enter in order to get access to a larger regional trade bloc, to learn from customers and competitors in a leading market, or to attack a competitor's major market. A country can look attractive not only because the firm can sell a lot of products but also because the firm can derive other benefits from a presence there.

Chapter 4 will outline the principles and techniques involved in systematically evaluating a foreign market before entry. Early entry considerations are usually broad economic, social, and political indicators, a matter of making sure that the "basic fundamentals" are in place. More in-depth analysis is then used to forecast sales and choose among the most promising countries or regions. Chapter 4 describes various data sources, but also emphasizes the importance of first-hand experience before making a final choice.

Can KFC Be Politically Correct in India?

Was it the MSG? That's what officials of Bangalore, India, said. The city government shut down India's first Kentucky Fried Chicken (KFC) restaurant, claiming that tests on chicken samples showed dangerously high levels of monosodium glutamate. Disputing the report, the Pepsico subsidiary that operates KFC in India obtained a court order to keep the restaurant open.

The problem, company managers maintain, is not the restaurant's quality. In fact, Sandeep Kohli, managing director of Pepsico Restaurants International, says, "Ours is the cleanest restaurant in the whole of India." Rather, the local government was responding to political pressure from anti-Western forces. The closing of the KFC restaurant followed weeks of protests by a local group of farmers which is associated with a broader campaign to curb foreign investments.

Ever since 17th-century British colonial forces acquired dominance of the country's economy, many Indians have been ambivalent about—and even hostile toward—attempts by Westerners to invest in their country. In particular, left-wing and nationalist groups have called for strict limits on foreign investment. These groups accept high-tech investments but want to exclude foreigners from operations they believe India has the capability to handle (for example, food processing, agriculture, and the production of consumer goods). Besides KFC, protesters have targeted the Coca-Cola Company, the Kellogg Company, McDonald's, and Pepsico's Pizza Hut and Frito-Lay units.

Similarly, political pressure became a great burden for the Enron Development Corporation, and its $2.8 billion power plant to be built in the Indian state of Maharashtra. After five months of work and $300 million invested into building the plant, which would have been India's largest power plant, the state government backed out of the contract. The cancellation of the project caused many American and other foreign investors to reevaluate the prospects of the Indian marketplace.

In spite of any political downside, India's economic and demographic characteristics nonetheless present enormous potential. Impressed by statistics of a population of 900 million, with 200 million in the middle class, many companies remain committed to marketing in India. Hyundai Motor Company, for instance, is moving ahead with plans for a joint venture.

With up to 1,500 customers a day in its first months, KFC plans to stay in Bangalore. Comments managing director Kohli, "At the end of the day, in India as elsewhere, it is the customers who will decide."

Sources: John F. Burns, "India Effort vs. Foreign Business Upsets American Chain," *New York Times*, September 14, 1995, p. D6; John F. Burns, "India Project in the Balance," *New York Times*, September 6, 1995, pp. D1, D3; John F. Burns, "India Now Winning U.S. Investment," *New York Times*, February 6, 1995, pp. D1, D3; "Hyundai Plans Joint Auto Factory in India," *New York Times*, November 24, 1995, p. D12; Juman Dubey, "Kellogg's Invites India's Middle Class to Breakfast of Ready-to-Eat Cereal," *The Wall Street Journal*, August 29, 1994, p. 83B.

....

INTRODUCTION

From one angle, choosing the country or countries to enter is very similar to selecting *target segments*. The candidate segments are screened using broadly based criteria such as size, growth rate, basic fit between customer preferences and the existing product line, and competitive rivalry. Next, more detailed data on ease of entry, synergy with existing know-how, and long-term prospects are used to narrow down the choice set. The final targeting is done by matching resources against obstacles to forecast likely sales over the planning horizon.

This idealized picture is, of course, not always a true representation of how target segments get chosen in practice. The data on segment size and growth rate might well be reliable, but good data on preferences and on competitive rivalry are not always available in foreign countries and are often out of date. As to the possible entry barriers and synergy with existing know-how, subjective assessments from experienced managers are often the only source of information. Judging the future potential of the segment involves forecasting competitive actions and customer reactions, always an uncertain task. The final choice of targets involves a good deal of subjective judgment by managers.

It is hardly surprising to note that choosing countries to enter in a systematic way is fraught with problems. Even though vast improvements have come with the emergence of global databases, international on-line data services, and global research agencies, market-level data quality is still usually uneven and comparable data across countries are often nonexistent. Lack of familiarity with conditions abroad means that predictions of customer preferences and long-term prospects are even more hazardous. The notion of matching the company know-how against foreign opportunities might be good in principle, but in reality it is very hard to do.

So what is a rigorous and systematic approach to country selection that is realistic? The answer comes in two parts. First, the initial screening should be based on a well-articulated vision of why the company wants to go abroad and what kinds of resources it can marshall. The nonsales objectives the company might entertain and any limiting constraints should be clarified and be used to screen countries out of contention as early as possible. Second, when more than one country remains in the choice set, the final choice should be made only after in-country visits have confirmed hunches about entry barriers, the available published data on market size, growth, and the competition's market shares, and primary data on preferences and competitive strengths have been collected. By narrowing choices sufficiently, such personal visits will be feasible. The iron rule is never to commit resources without first-hand information.

Chapter 4 delineates this process in more detail. It shows how to do attractiveness screening in terms of *market potential* and *resource demands* of different countries. We present systematic screening procedures based on available data and discuss how to handle various obstacles and special factors complicating the systematic process. We then present different approaches to forecasting sales in a foreign country.

It should be emphasized at the outset that in Chapter 4 "entering a market" means simply to make the firm's existing products or services available in a foreign country. There might be some localization requirements that force the firm to modify the offering, but basically the products or services are known. This is the typical situation a company is faced with in screening countries. The important question of global standardization versus adaptation is not an issue until the company has global presence, and will be dealt with later in Part Four.

BASIC EVALUATION PROCEDURE

The process of evaluating candidates for foreign market entry can be divided into four stages: *country identification; preliminary screening; in-depth screening; and final selection.*[1] The discussion of each stage will be illustrated by an actual application at a company called Microlog. See box, "Microlog Goes to Europe (A)."

Stage 1—Country Identification

In the **country identification** stage, the candidate countries are identified and listed. In principle the company can start with most of the world's more than 200 countries, but most often the list includes a more limited set of alternatives. Typically the company decides to enter a particular trade area. For example,

*G*etting the
Picture

Microlog Goes
to Europe (A)

MICROLOG INC. is a small ($12 million annual turnover in 1993) company located in Germantown, Maryland, just outside the Washington, D.C. beltway. Its business is in telecommunications. The company markets and services voice processing systems, that is, computerized electronic telephone systems that help direct incoming calls, record messages, and generally serve as an on-line mail and audio information service. Such integrated hardware-software systems saw tremendous growth in the United States in the early 1990s. Microlog is one of the many small companies that helped develop the systems.

Its domestic market includes local businesses, as well as the United States government.

The company wants to expand overseas. Domestic markets are growing, but competition is intense. Microlog management has decided that the best strategy is to capture first-mover advantages in new and growing foreign markets such as the EU. Once a system is installed, a company will not change vendor, and the servicing brings in business. Furthermore, word-of-mouth from successful entry travels fast to geographically close companies.

Source: Adams et al., 1993. Used with permission from Microlog Corporation.

companies opt to focus on Europe or Latin America or East Asia, and then do a more in-depth analysis within each of the regions to identify where to place their sales headquarters, and which countries to enter first.

The choices in this first stage are broadly based on easily available statistics on population, GNP, growth rates, and media reports on political and economic developments. It is useful for the manager to have a sense of the economic size of the countries. Japan is often claimed to be a "small" country by the Japanese themselves. The truth is that with its 125 million people and high GNP it is a giant.

Just population size itself is sometimes useful for comparisons. Everybody knows about China's more than a billion and India's 800 million people, making them the biggest countries on the earth, and potentially very attractive once markets are opened up (see box, "All or Nothing at All?").

Population comparisons are crucial for the global marketer to get an initial grasp of a country's potential. Indonesia has 178 million people, while Malaysia has 17 million, a big difference. The unified Germany has about 80 million people, biggest in Europe (not counting Russia), much bigger than another country with German culture, Austria, at 8 million. France and the U.K. have about 55 million each, while Sweden has 8 and Denmark 5 million people, much smaller markets. Hungary at 11 million is small compared to Poland's 40 million, and in Latin America, Chile at 13 million is small compared to Brazil at 150 million. Japan is 2.5 times as large as South Korea's 44 million, while another "tiger," Hong Kong, has a limited home market of 5 million people.

Such figures should always be in the back of the global marketer's mind. The scale of the task, the resources needed, and the market potential make it a different ball game to enter Germany's huge market versus entering Switzerland with its 5 million citizens. Firms enter markets such as Hong Kong and Hungary and Denmark looking beyond the small countries' national borders to the neighboring countries.

*G*etting the Picture

All or Nothing at All?

WITH ALL the newly emerging markets, many countries that previously seemed of low potential and of no interest to marketers have suddenly opened up. There is opportunity in Russia, in China, in Brazil, in South Africa. Leading statesmen from various countries travel the globe selling their countries to multinational investors in the hope of getting their economies on to the fast growth track. Trading blocs help boost trade between countries, and international investments are facilitated. Free trade and special economic zones help open up previously closed economies, allowing these countries to generate hard currency by reexporting assembled products, and as a result become more attractive to foreign marketers.

How do companies choose among these riches? For some it seems easy.

"Just take it all," as Jack Welch, the CEO of General Electric, wants to to do. "We are in most of the world's markets, and doing well in the leading ones. But look at the markets of the future. Where are they, and what is our presence? It's India. GE pulled out when ownership restrictions on the FDI were imposed in the 1960s. We have to get back. It's China. We have to be there now that it is opening up. And then Latin America. Sure, we have lost money there as has almost everybody else. But Latin America is coming back, and we better get back in full-scale."

The huge and growing markets of the emerging economies look very attractive when economic and political fundamentals are in place.

Sources: Dubey, 1993; Smart et al., 1993.

Bicycle riders in Shanghai. As economic growth continues at a blazing speed, Chinese are demanding more consumer goods.

Greg Girard/Contact.

Getting the Picture

Microlog Goes to Europe (B)

TO SCREEN candidate countries, the marketing director and his assistant first decided among three regions: Southeast Asia, Latin America, and Europe. All three regions showed promise, with increasing penetration of telephones and promising economic prospects. Southeast Asia showed the fastest growth, while Latin America was bound to get a boost from the NAFTA accord. Europe was very attractive because of the 1992 homogenization of regulations. Given their limited resources, the two managers decided to first focus on Europe, partly because of their own ease and comfort there (the manager had extensive experience in Europe, and the assistant was British). They also sensed that Europeans might be more culturally prepared for a computerized response to a telephone call than the other regions (although partially correct, later acceptance in the Southeast Asian countries proved to be even quicker).

Source: Adams et al., 1993.

The firm's objective at this stage is often to gain presence in one or more of the emerging trade regions of the world. With the growth of international coverage in major newspapers and broadcast media, and the increase in on-line international news services, these broad strategic choices are often made early in the selection process by top management.

The country identification process at Microlog is described in the Microlog (B) box.

Stage 2—Preliminary Screening

After the candidate countries have been identified, the **preliminary screening** stage begins. This involves rating the identified countries on macrolevel indicators such as political stability, geographic distance, and economic development. The idea is to weed out countries from consideration. For example, if profit repatriation or currency convertibility is questionable, the country may be eliminated. Also countries with signs of political instability may be ruled out at this stage. Generally, exchange rate volatility is an important indication of underlying economic or political problems.

At this stage, the anticipated costs of entering a market should be broadly assessed, to match financial and other resource constraints. In addition to data on transportation costs and customs duty which are comparatively easy to assemble, costs involve storage and warehousing, distribution in the country, and supporting the product in the market. These usually have to be rough estimates, drawing on industry experts and personal experience in the country.

Japan often gets crossed off the list at this stage because the costs of entry and operations tend to be prohibitively high. While the Japanese might complain that Western companies do not adopt the necessary long-term perspective when evaluating Japan, the economic facts are that Western companies have trouble making ends meet in Japan, and that other markets often offer better prospects.

Preliminary screening by Microlog is described in the Microlog (C) box.

<table>
<tr>
<td>

*G*etting the
Picture

Microlog Goes
to Europe (C)

</td>
<td>

TO COLLECT preliminary screen-
ing data on the European countries, the
marketing manager asked for help from
a team of MBA students at a nearby uni-
versity. The five-member team collected
U. N. data on the size and growth of the
GNP, population size, infrastructure,
and level of industrial activity from the
university library. Visits to the World
Bank yielded information on political
risk factors, ethnic diversity, and po-
tential language and cultural problems.

</td>
<td>

Informal interviews with fellow
European MBA students and faculty
members with European experience
were used to verify information and
check indicated ratings.

The preliminary screening led to a se-
lection of 11 countries for in-depth eval-
uation. The set of countries included
Belgium, Denmark, France, Germany,
The Netherlands, Ireland, Italy, Norway,
Spain, Sweden, and Switzerland.
Source: Adams et al., 1993.

</td>
</tr>
</table>

Stage 3—In-Depth Screening

The point of preliminary screening is to make it possible to limit the more
expensive and time-consuming in-depth screening to countries which show
obvious promise and are in the feasible set. The **in-depth screening** stage is
the core of the attractiveness evaluation. Data here are specific to the industry
and product markets, if possible even down to specific market segments. This
stage involves assessing market potential and actual market size, market growth
rate, strengths and weaknesses of existing and potential competition, and height
of entry barriers, including tariffs and quotas. Where possible, in-country
segmentation should also be explored, with an eye to capturing more precise
target segment forecasts. Furthermore, at this stage the company resource
constraints—money, managers, supply capacity and so on—should be revisited
to make sure that contemplated entries are feasible.

Several screening criteria for the in-depth stage can be useful to the prospective entrant. Generally, studies have shown that almost all entrants use information
relating to *market size and growth rate, level of competition, and trade barriers.*[2]

Market size: A direct measure of market size can be computed from local
production, minus exports, plus imports. An indirect measure can be derived
from the widely available GNP measure, population size, growth in GNP, and
imports of relevant goods.

Market growth: Growth estimates can be obtained by getting the market
size measures for different years and computing the growth rates. When
deriving the growth rate in this manner, it is important that cyclical changes in
the economy are accounted for. When the business cycles turn up, even
slow-growing mature markets will show strong growth.

Competitive intensity: Level of competition can be measured by the number
of competitors in the market, and the relative size distribution of market shares.
The U.S. Department of Commerce tracks such shares for many industries in
different countries in its *Market Shares Report.*[3] Competition is generally
toughest where a few large domestic companies dominate the market. When

*G*etting the Picture

Microlog Goes to Europe (D)

AFTER THE CHOICE of the 11 countries had been accepted by Microlog's manager, the team and the manager discussed the selection of in-depth screening criteria. The selected criteria are shown in Exhibit 4.1.

As can be seen, the criteria involved market size, growth potential, a "loose brick" factor indicating ease of entry, competitive factors, distribution possibilities, cultural distance to the U.S., technological development, likely receptivity to voice processing, and importance of the market in the EU.

Once the criteria were agreed upon, the team set about collecting data, scor-ing each of the 11 countries on the selected criteria. This entailed some hard legwork. For example, regulatory data of the telecommunications industry were collected from the countries' consulates in D.C., a laborious job divided up among the team members. Competitive data came from Microlog's management, trade association figures, Department of Commerce publications, and computer searches across various publications. In the end, many of the ratings came from the team's (and the manager's) subjective judgments.

Source: Adams et al., 1993.

existing companies all have small shares, or when foreign companies have already made successful entry, the competitors will generally be less concerned about a new entrant.

Trade barriers: Tariffs, taxes, duties, and transportation costs can be ascertained from official government publications. One problem in analyzing such data is that the level of the barriers depends on the exact specification of the goods entered. The company can often decide to do some assembly in the foreign country to avoid high tariffs on finished products, for example, or it can decide to purchase a component from a local manufacturer in another country to get a better rate because of increased local content. Accordingly, the country rating on tariff bar-riers can only be assessed accurately after preliminary decisions have been made as to whether a final or some intermediate product will be shipped to that country.

Depending on the particular industry, other criteria are useful. In telecom-munications, for example, an important aspect is the degree and kind of government regulation. A potentially large market such as Germany suffers from a centralized and bureaucratic regulatory structure that has been an obstacle to pan-European standards. In food products, most countries feature some protection of their local agricultural industry which may affect the realizable potential for a foreign entrant. In professional services (lawyers, doctors, accountants, engineers), certification requirements in many countries make it necessary to work with local partners.

The in-depth screening stage at Microlog is described in Microlog box (D).

Stage 4—Final Selection

In the **final selection** stage, company objectives are brought to bear for a match, and forecasted revenues and costs are compared to find the country market which best leverages the resources available. Typically, countries similar

EXHIBIT 4.1 Microlog Country Criteria and Stores

Criteria	Factor Weight	Belgium R	Belgium A	Denmark R	Denmark A	Germany R	Germany A	France R	France A	Ireland R	Ireland A	Italy R	Italy A	Netherlands R	Netherlands A	Norway R	Norway A	Spain R	Spain A	Sweden R	Sweden A	Switzerland R	Switzerland A
Growth potential (10 = high growth potential)	20.00%	8.00	1.60	7.00	1.40	9.00	1.80	6.00	1.20	7.00	1.40	10.00	2.00	8.00	1.60	6.00	1.20	10.00	2.00	8.00	1.60	8.00	1.60
The "loose brick" factor (10 = the loose brick)	20.00%	10.00	2.00	7.00	1.40	4.00	0.80	1.00	0.20	7.00	1.40	9.00	1.80	10.00	2.00	3.00	0.60	9.00	1.80	5.00	1.00	9.00	1.80
Competition (1 = strong)	13.00%	7.00	0.91	4.00	0.52	6.00	0.78	1.00	0.13	8.00	1.04	6.00	0.78	7.00	0.91	6.00	0.78	8.00	1.04	2.00	0.26	6.00	0.78
Distributors	12.00%	7.00	0.84	8.00	0.96	7.00	0.84	8.00	0.96	9.00	1.08	5.00	0.60	7.00	0.84	7.00	0.84	5.00	0.60	4.00	0.48	6.00	0.72
Technological development stage—telecommunications (10 = United States)	7.00%	8.00	0.56	9.00	0.63	9.00	0.63	10.00	0.70	8.00	0.56	5.00	0.35	8.00	0.56	8.00	0.56	4.00	0.28	8.00	0.56	9.00	0.63
Hofstede's culture score	7.00%	1.00	0.07	8.42	0.59	4.71	0.33	1.31	0.09	7.04	0.49	3.14	0.22	5.28	0.37	5.91	0.41	2.01	0.14	7.23	0.51	5.21	0.36
Technological development stage—computer (10 = United States)	6.00%	7.00	0.42	9.00	0.54	10.00	0.60	9.00	0.54	8.00	0.48	7.00	0.42	7.00	0.42	10.00	0.60	5.00	0.30	10.00	0.60	9.00	0.54
Receptivity	6.00%	6.00	0.36	8.00	0.48	7.00	0.42	7.00	0.42	10.00	0.60	6.00	0.36	10.00	0.60	7.00	0.42	6.00	0.36	10.00	0.60	5.50	0.33
Size of market-GDP (ranked with 1 as smallest)	5.00%	0.96	0.05	0.65	0.03	10.00	0.50	7.23	0.36	0.21	0.01	6.67	0.33	1.38	0.07	0.65	0.03	2.33	0.12	1.38	0.07	1.40	0.07
Importance of market vis-à-vis the rest of Europe /EEC (10 = influential)	4.00%	5.00	0.20	5.00	0.20	9.00	0.36	10.00	0.40	4.00	0.16	5.00	0.20	5.00	0.20	1.00	0.04	3.00	0.12	5.00	0.20	4.00	0.16
Total	100.00%		7.01		6.75		7.06		5.00		7.22		7.06		7.57		5.49		6.76		5.00		6.99

Source: Adams et al., 1993. Used with permission from Microlog Corporation.

to those the company has already entered show lower entry costs, less risk, and quicker returns on the investments required to build up the market franchise. With a longer time horizon, less risk-averse management, and lower target rates of return, the firm can select countries that show greater long-term prospects and that promise to expand the firm's capabilities.

The firm's objectives in contemplating foreign entry can be used to assign importance weights to the various criteria, such as costs, to get a weighted sum across the criteria. There are several ways to assign scale numbers to the ratings and the importance weights. The process leads to a ranking of the countries from highest to lowest attractiveness for the firm.

Where the objective is to find the country with the highest sales and market share prospects in the relatively short term, the importance weights will be high for those criteria relating directly to the market acceptance of the product and the competitive intensity in the market. Accordingly, market size and growth potential will be weighed against competitive rivalry. Where profitability is the objective, the costs of trade barriers and resource costs will also be rated important. The attractiveness rating then will be quite similar to a preliminary cost-benefit analysis.

Other considerations also affect the weights. If the company has limited resources, for example, the trade barriers and the cost ratings can be used to screen out promising but too costly entries. As another example, being the first entrant sometimes offers extra benefits in terms of better access to middlemen and easier creation of customer loyalty. If such first-mover advantages are great, the absence of global competitors will be important, and the competitive situation in general will be given extra weight. Where the aim is to simply test the waters and learn more about doing marketing abroad before venturing to other countries, a geographically close country with low cultural barriers can be chosen in order to minimize exposure if things turn bad.

The final selection stage of the team's assessments in the Microlog case is described in Microlog box (E).

Direct Experience

The final selection of the country to enter cannot and should not be made until personal visits have been made to the country and **direct experience** acquired by the managers. There is no substitute for on-the-spot information and the hands-on feeling of a new market. There are lessons to be learned from the flexibility with which the hotel staff responds to unusual requests, the language capabilities of the average person in the street, the courtesy, or lack of it, in stores, the degree to which a doctor responds to a client's questions, the ease with which a telephone connection home can be made, and the speed with which currencies may be exchanged.

There is the general sense of the country once the relative comfort of the intercontinental hotel has been abandoned in favor of some local culture. While visiting a potential partner, it is useful to observe the spirit of the company

Getting the Picture

Microlog Goes to Europe (E)

BEFORE CALCULATING the attractiveness scores for the various countries, the team met with the manager and his assistant in order to come up with weights reflecting the importance of the various criteria for the voice processing system's market success. The cultural and linguistic similarity with the United States and the compatibility of the phone system and its regulation were judged to be particularly important. The manager had visited Europe and decided that even though the voice recordings on the system would have to be in the native tongue, for Microlog to transact business in any other language than English would be difficult. At the same time, size of the market was seen as unimportant or even slightly negative, since it was deemed that entry into a smaller market to start with might be a more manageable task for the firm. Also, in one of these meetings the ease of expansion from the entry base into other countries emerged as an important criterion.

The final report contained the weights and attractiveness scores given in Exhibit 4.1. As can be seen, the countries rated highest were the Netherlands and Ireland. In both cases the telecommunications market was well developed, the industry regulations were not as severe as elsewhere, and the countries seemed to be natural entry gates for the Northern European market. The Scandinavian countries, although attractive in many ways, were not sufficiently close to continental Europe to be good gateways. In addition, Sweden's Ericsson was a feared potential competitor. Germany was ruled out mainly because of its byzantine regulatory system that raised barriers and made entry costly. France's regulations were also a barrier, which was raised further by the dominance of Alcatel, the French telecommunications giant and a potential competitor. Because the team considered the Netherlands' location more favorable than Ireland's, it recommended the Netherlands for initial entry. As a second alternative for an entry into Southern Europe, the team recommended Italy.

Source: Adams et al., 1993.

Western contractor and Kuwaiti government official chat with construction workers in Kuwait. To understand local customs and markets nothing beats hands-on research and personal visits.

Jane Lewis/Tony Stone Images.

THE FINAL CHOICE? The Netherlands. A first trip to the European CeBIT fair in Hanover yielded several contacts, including a couple of leads to distributors in The Netherlands. Rerouting his return trip through Hilversum, the manager met with executives at Philips, the big electronics manufacturer. Philips was interesting not simply as a prospective customer, but as a partner in the European market. With the kind of strong European connection provided by Philips, Microlog would be able to quickly establish credibility, and create a base for future European expansion. As the manager put it: "We wanted Philips to be the long pole in our European tent." For its part, Philips'

management recognized the potential value of Microlog's voice processing system, and was interested in having Microlog provide an OEM system to be marketed under the Philips name in their telecommunications division. Signing a nonexclusive "best efforts" contract with Philips enabled Microlog to gain immediate credibility in Europe, and gain a strong base for further expansion via independent value-added resellers (VAR). In this way, Microlog could gain entry into several European markets by piggybacking on Philips' sales force and also selling via the VARs under its own brand name.

Source: Adams et al., 1993.

employees. In stores, the degree to which customers examine products and talk to store clerks and the speed with which they make choices suggest whether store employees need special incentives, information, and training. The supermarket shelves show to what extent competitive products compete in-store as well as between stores; the crowds in buses or subways and the vehicles in the parking lots suggest what kinds of transportation is used to get to the stores; and so on. Countless such observations may be made on the local scene. And the visits will often have serendipitous effects, creating marketing opportunities not recognized before, as happens to Microlog in box (F).

SPECIAL CRITERIA

A few special factors create obstacles, complicate matters, and can change the country attractiveness ratings dramatically. Some relate to country or company characteristics, others to entry objectives.

Political Risk

For many firms the standard first question asked about a country concerns **political risks.** There are many ways of analyzing the risk and of assessing the level of exposure, and the sources of information vary from very detailed statistical reports on the history of the country's political development to impressionistic tales by recent visitors to the country.[4] The factors that need to

EXHIBIT 4.2   **Political Risk Factors**

Factors	Examples
Level 1 : *General Instability*	Revolution, External aggression
Level 2 : *Expropriation*	Nationalization, Contract revocation
Level 3: *Operations*	Import restrictions, Local content rules, Taxes, Export requirements
Level 4: *Finance*	Repatriation restrictions, Exchange rates

Source: Steven J. Kobrin, "Political Risk: A Review and Reconsideration," *Journal of International Business Studies* 10, no.1 (1979), p. 67–80. Reprinted by permission.

be considered can be arranged in a descending order of importance for the investor, as in Exhibit 4.2.[5]

Political risk analysis proceeds from the first to the fourth level in the table. The data used will usually come from any one of the several firms offering political risk analysis.[6] If at any of the levels the risk is deemed unacceptable, the investment project receives a "No-Go" stamp and is discontinued in favor of FDI elsewhere or simply export or licensing negotiations. Even though in several cases the economics of an FDI project are quite acceptable—in the sense that projected discounted returns well pass the hurdle ROI rate—the political risks have been great enough to stop the project. This is more likely to happen when the investment is aimed at the acquisition of raw material or low wage costs than when the penetration of markets is at stake. But Coca-Cola's early experience in India shows that even in the latter case political risks matter (see box, "The Real Thing").

The rise of international terrorism activities is a new type of political risk. The Iran uprising, politically motivated murders in South America, and the crime wave in newly capitalist Russia have made multinational companies and their expatriate managers very uneasy and eager to purchase insurance. Although terrorism's international reach can make almost any country unsafe, as the bomb explosion at the World Trade Center in New York showed, terrorism and escalating crime have put an especially dark shadow on certain countries' and regions' attractiveness. For example, in a December 1993 Gallup survey of British executives' evaluation of political risk in various countries, Russia was rated as "difficult" by 57 percent followed by Africa (47 percent), and South America (46 percent).[7] High-risk countries included Angola, South Africa, Zaire, Colombia, Haiti, Papua New Guinea, Turkey, and Israel's West Bank and Gaza Strip.

As governments change and new regimes come to power, political risk can be temporary, but it is important that the company makes sure to follow risk indicators closely and keep them updated.

COCA-COLA had been marketing in India for may years when in 1977 the Indian government decreed that the secret formula for the cola and 60 percent of the equity of its Indian subsidiary must be transferred to local nationals. The equity transfer was accepted by Coca-Cola, but the company refused to divulge the formula and also insisted that it must supervise the quality control of the manufacturing process. The Indian government, set on local control, argued that this would still make the Indian company only a reseller of the American company's know-how and product. The government wanted to exercise local control over manufacturing and also stop the outflow of foreign exchange. In the end, Coca-Cola decided to withdraw from India (a small market for them in the global picture) rather than jeopardize their firm-specific advantages, leaving the market to domestic imitators.

But things change. Under the liberalization in the early 1990s following Mr. Rao's election as Prime Minister, foreign direct investment in India is picking up. Less-restrictive investment and repatriation conditions and a booming home market have made India attractive again. In 1993 Coca-Cola decided to return, and consumers in India are now able to taste "The Real Thing" again, and not just imitations.

Source: Dubey, 1993; *New York Times*, September 22, 1993, p. D4.

Multiproduct Firms

Many firms, large and small, offer multiple product lines, and thus entry into a country involves deciding which of the products and country segments should be evaluated. For example, a computer software firm might sell off-the-shelf application software to architects and apparel designers with localized after-sales support, and also market customized software for newspaper editing and layout design. These products and market segments may show various market potentials within a given country, so the method of attractiveness screening needs to accommodate various combinations of products and segments. For example, if the company can limit its foreign entry to off-the-shelf software and train the local distributor to do the after-sales service, this can be one option considered. This is the standard arrangement for American software houses abroad. Alternatively, it might be feasible to enter the country by creating a new overseas organization, which could handle a larger product line.

Once such alternative value chain choices about products and segments have been mapped out, the multiproduct company needs to collect data for the various combinations of products and segments. In this case a country may be represented more than once, with alternative mixes of products and segments. Consistent and comparable data at the segment level can be difficult to find and collect, and the company often must rely a great deal on experts and subjective assessments by experienced "country hands."[8] To improve the accuracy of the ratings, the companies try to get data from a number of sources and weigh them together.

Competitive Entry

When the aim of the foreign entry is competitive, the evaluation process is naturally quite different from the one presented above. The aim can be to attack a competitor's cash-generating home market or another market where a competitor is dominant. In other cases, the aim is to preempt or disrupt a competitor's entry into a new market by entering first or increasing the firm's marketing support. In either case, the choice of country is often a given. However, the firm must recognize the resource implications of fighting these kinds of battles. They may not generate much revenue and could be costly. The firm has to carefully evaluate whether the gains in other countries over time will justify these excursions. Procter and Gamble lost money for more than 10 years on its Japanese operations but was willing to do so partly to provide a competitive check on Kao, its Japanese rival.

Choosing Leading Markets

The choice of country is made differently yet again in the cases in which a company goes abroad to learn from customers and competitors in leading market countries. Then the company aim is primarily to gain further strengths and expand capability, and tapping market growth is only a secondary goal, at least in the short run.

Leading markets (or lead markets) tend to be large, strong at the high-end of the product line, free from government regulation and protective measures, with strong competitors and demanding customers.[9]

Leading markets are generally found in different countries for different products. Strong domestic competitors emerge because of a country's location-specific advantages, such as natural resource endowments, technological know-how, and labor skills. Over time, these advantages enable domestic firms to accumulate experience. The customers of these firms are sophisticated and demanding, making these markets bellwethers for follower markets. The United States PC market, the Japanese camera market, and the German automobile market are examples of such leading markets.

The actual location of a leading market in an industry may also change over time. This is partly a result of the workings of the international product cycle discussed in Chapter 2. As follower markets mature and customers become more sophisticated, and as domestic producers develop new competitive skills, the follower markets may become the new leading markets. A good example is Japan in consumer electronics. Conversely, leading markets may lose their status. For as Japan rose, the United States lost its lead in consumer electronics.

An industry can have several leading markets, for different segments of the total market, as in the automobile industry. In automobiles, apart from Germany, also Japan, Italy, and perhaps even the United States can lay claims to preeminence. However, different leading markets involve some market segmentation and product differentiation. German buyers place a premium on advanced auto technology, which is why other automakers have located engineering centers there. Italy has a well-developed luxury sports car market, and even German firms such as Porsche hire Italian designers. The Japanese provide mass manufacturing state-of-the-art knowledge, and their domestic customers get perhaps the best value for the money. The United States still provides a sophisticated market for large luxury cars, even if the domestic producers have not performed particularly well.

COUNTRY DATA SOURCES

Despite the important role of personal visits to the top candidate countries, most of the data used in the screening of countries come from secondary not primary sources. Since the assessment usually has to be done in the home office, the manager needs to rely mainly on published data available at home. Of course, it would be ideal to have in-depth data on customer preferences and buying behavior in each country, but such data can rarely be made available at reasonable cost before entry (although market research agencies are certainly able to provide survey studies).

A large number of organizations—consulates, commerce departments, newspaper and magazine affiliates, information agencies, and ordinary market research firms—can be helpful in providing data for the global firm. Some of the more prominent organizations are listed in Exhibit 4.3.

Generally speaking, data on economic and political indicators are not so difficult to obtain, although not always up-to-date. The more difficult task is usually to get data specific to an industry.

The Data-Gathering Steps

The steps in putting together the data usually go along the following lines. Start with the United Nations publications, followed by Department of Commerce and other government offices, and then, if possible, international organizations such as the EU Commission, World Bank, and the International Monetary Fund (IMF). Then start researching the computerized data banks, CD-ROM or on-line news services, to get the most recent data and developments. The rise of Internet, on-line services, and computerized data banks such as Lexis-Nexis, have transformed the data-gathering tasks in the last few years. Magazines and newspapers can be screened in this phase, using keyword searches to find recent articles.

So far, the effort can usually be handled by newly hired employees or by college students, as in the Microlog case. But now the search should be turned over to professional data-gathering organizations. Business International, Dun & Bradstreet, and The Conference Board are some possibilities. By now the data will cost money, but usually syndication keeps report costs down to reasonable levels for most firms (under $1,000). The advantage tends to be the recency of the figures—these organizations have to provide the most recent data available.

EXHIBIT 4.3   Country Data Sources

United Nations

Conference of Trade And
Development
Palais Des Nations
1211 Geneva 10
Switzerland

Publications
Room 1194
1 United Nations Plaza
New York, NY 10017

Statistical Yearbook
1 United Nations Plaza
New York, NY 10017

International Business Organizations

A. C. Nielsen Co.
150 N. Martingale Road
Schaumburg, IL 60173

American Marketing Association
250 S. Wacker Drive, Suite 200
Chicago, IL 60606

Dun & Bradstreet
World Financial Center
Building A, 31st Floor
New York, NY 10281

American Demographics, Inc.
108 N. Cayuga Street
Ithaca, NY 14851

Burke Marketing Research
2621 Victory Parkway
Cincinnati, OH 45206

European Community
Information Service
200 Rue de la Loi
1049 Brussels, Belgium and
2100 M Street, NW, 7th Floor
Washington, DC 20037

American Management Association
440 First Street, NW
Washington, DC 20001

Conference Board
845 Third Avenue
New York, NY 10022

Frost and Sullivan
106 Fulton Street
New York, NY 10038

Computer On-Line Services

America On-Line
8619 Westwood Center Drive
Vienna, VA 22182

Lexis/Nexis
Reed-Elsevier Inc.
P.O. Box 933
Dayton, OH 45401

Prodigy Services Co.
445 Hamilton Avenue
White Plains, NY 10601

Miscellaneous

Economist Intelligence Unit
111 West 57th Street
New York, NY 10019

Europa Year Book
Europa Publications Ltd.
18 Bedford Square
London WC1 3JN England

Media Guide International
Business/Professional Publications
Directories International, Inc.
150 Fifth Avenue, Suite 610
New York, NY 10011

Business Week
McGraw-Hill Publications Co.
1221 Avenue of the Americas
New York, NY 10020

International Financial Statistics
International Monetary Fund
Publications Unit
700 19th Street, NW
Washington, DC 20431

Yearbook of International Trade
Statistics
United Nations
United Nations Publishing Division
1 United Nations Plaza
Room DC2–0853
New York, NY 10017

Doing Business in. . . . Series
Price Waterhouse
1251 Avenue of the Americas
New York, NY 10020

Market Share Reports
U.S. Government Printing Office
Superintendent of Documents
Washington, DC 20402

Frost & Sullivan Inc.
90 West Street, Suite 1301
New York, NY 10006

Finally, specific market research reports might be needed. Here the choice is between general agencies such as Nielsen's and Burke's or more specialized organizations. The latter can be accounting firms—Andersen Consulting, for example, does a fair amount of international market research in services—or legal professionals, or industry-specific research firms (wood products, automobiles, airlines, and computer software, for example). The reason specialization occurs is simply that the research firms have to invest a great deal of time to be sufficiently well informed about the global situation for an industry, and the payoff comes when more than one client can be served on the basis of the same material. This does not mean that the firms send the same customized report to all clients—rather that the customization is done on top of a common data set for the industry.

In what follows, data gathering in the various stages of the attractiveness analysis will be discussed.

Country Identification

In the country identification stage, the analysis usually has to make do with general information. A good place to start is with the United Nations annual compilation of world economic and social data, which will give a broad picture of the various countries. These data will help to narrow down the set of countries to consider further.

A common approach used with these kinds of data is to use the computer to **cluster countries** into groups with similar economic and social conditions and therefore similar demand. **Clustering maps** show a picture of which countries are similar and which are far apart (recall Hofstede's similar approach to culture discussed in Chapter 3). To incorporate more than two criteria at a time, it is common to do an initial factor analysis before clustering the countries. The factor analysis helps combine all the criteria into a manageable few dimensions, although at the price of making interpretation of the dimensions less clear. The interested reader is referred to the many available statistical texts.[10]

An example of a country clustering map is provided in Exhibit 4.4. As can be seen, at this level the groupings usually turn out to be similar to the East-West and North-South categories typically employed in U.N. policy analyses. Although such groupings should not be mistaken for market segments, these very broad indicators serve to indicate strength of markets and socioeconomic distance to the home market.

In one application, Cavusgil used six variables (population growth, median age, number of children per household, infant mortality, life expectancy, and GNP per capita, all available in published U.N. data) to come up with market-based clusters of countries.[11] He then proceeded to name the clusters, and to describe their distinguishing features. Finally, he outlined the marketing implications. The results are presented in Exhibit 4.5. As can be seen, even these relatively crude measures are useful to judge country attractiveness, uncover market opportunities, and suggest interesting marketing implications.

EXHIBIT 4.4   A Two-Dimensional Country Clustering Map

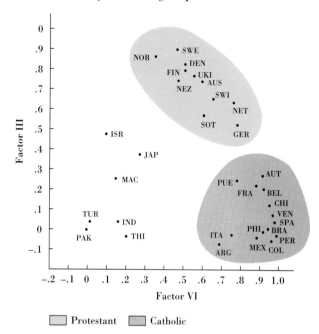

Protestant   Catholic

Factor number	Name and number of descriptors	Selected descriptors
I.	Aggregate economic, of level of development (47)	Gross national product, radios in use, passenger kilometers flown
II.	Population size (31)	Total midyear population
III.	Personal economic, or standard of living (32)	Income per capita, newsprint consumption per capita, birth rate (negatively related)
IV.	Canada—conditions on which Canada ranks highest (12)	Newsprint production, visitor arrivals in the U.S., geographic area
V.	Linguistic affinity (10)	Adults who read English or speak it
VI.	YC—Code for private descriptors (11)	Brand and industry sales of a consumer product, number of Roman Catholics
VII.	International participation (22)	Membership in international organizations, foreign tourist arrivals, airfare to Tokyo
VIII.	Trade capacity (12)	Exports, number of Protestants
IX.	Climate or price stability (10)	Sunny days per year, temperature of key city, price index (negative)
X.	Mortality (5)	Infant death rate, number of Moslems

....

EXHIBIT 4.5   A Market-Oriented Clustering of World Markets

Cluster	Demographic make-up	Marketing implications
Dependent societies		
Most countries in Africa, Asia, and a few in South America	Population growth: 3% Median age: 16 Children: 5 + Infant mortality: 100 per 1,000 births Life expectancy: 40 years GNP per capita: less than $300	Demand goods and services related to food, clothing, housing, education, and medical care. Investments related to extractive activities (agriculture and mining) are undertaken. Government/state economic enterprises are the major buying groups. Poor infrastructure and access to rural markets are major impediments.
Seekers		
Most Latin America; some in Asia, (Indonesia, Thailand, Philippines), and some in Africa, (Morocco, Tunisia, Egypt)	Population growth: 1.5 to 2.5% Median age: 20 Children: 4 + Infant mortality: 50 to 100 per 1,000 births Life expectancy: 60 years GNP per capita: less than $900	Infrastructure-related projects are high priority (construction equipment, machinery, chemicals, etc.) Good opportunities for technology sales and turnkey projects. Independent trading groups and a few large holding companies have much influence. Increased urbanization but a "mass market" does not yet exist.
Climbers		
Brazil, Venezuela, Portugal, Mexico, Taiwan, Malaysia, Turkey, South Korea	Population growth: under 1.5% Median age: slightly higher than 20 Children: 2 to 3 GNP per capita: Less than $2,000	Industrialization and service sector expenditures assume greater importance. Private enterprises have become more dominant than the state agencies. Good opportunities for joint ventures and technology agreements. Growing mass market.
Luxury and leisure societies		
United States, Canada, Japan, United Kingdom, Australia	Zero or very little population growth Median age: 30 + Children: 2 Reaching maximum longevity GOP per capita: greater than $8,000	Substantial discretionary income and availability of credit. Restructuring of economy. Maturing markets. Intense competition. Relocation away from large population centers.
The rocking chairs		
West Germany, Switzerland, Luxembourg, The Netherlands	Fertility rates below replacement level Median age: 37 Children: less than 2 Peak life expectancy GNP per capita: greater than $10,000	Dominance of service economy and high-technology sectors. Highly segmented markets. Ideal distribution and communications channels.

Source: Cavusgil, 1990, pp. 206–7. Reprinted by permission of Butterworth-Heinemann, Ltd., and the author.

Preliminary Screening

One data source for the preliminary screening phase is the *Business International Market Report*, published annually for the last thirty years. The report gives weighted indicators of market size, growth, and market intensity for the world's markets. The *market size* data are based on a combination of measures including population size, urban percentage, private consumption expenditures (disposable GNP minus private savings), ownership figures for telephones, cars, and televisions, and electricity production. The *market growth* indicator is basically the average shift in market size over five years. The *market intensity* measure is intended to capture the dynamics of the marketplace by double-weighting the private consumption expenditures, the car ownership figures, and the proportion of urban population.

The BI indices, now published by the Economist Intelligence Unit, are particularly useful for identifying promising growth countries and thus suggest newly emerging markets where a global marketer may want to have a presence. The indices need to be buttressed by political risk indicators and some data on the degree to which the market is open and free of government interference. Such data can be obtained from the *Political Risk Yearbook*, published annually by Political Risk Services in Syracuse, New York. These data provide expert assessments of political instability in a country, including the chances of a violent change in government and the degree of social unrest. They also contain summaries of restrictions on business, such as limitations on foreign ownership and constraints on the repatriation of funds. Countries that score high on political instability and restrictions on business can usually be eliminated from consideration early.

For the most up-to-date information on the political risk situation in a country, the semi-annual credit ratings published by *Institional Investor*, a financial markets periodical, can be very useful. Published in the March and September issues, the tabulations give a quick overview of recent volatility, useful in the preliminary phase. Exhibit 4.6 shows selected volatility ratings for 1995.

In-Depth Screening

In the in-depth screening stage, when data on specific markets are needed, the data availability varies by industry. Trade associations are usually the place to start, followed by government agencies. The U.S. Department of Commerce, and its counterparts in other countries publish some data at the industry level, even some market share data for various countries and products. Where trade conflicts have occurred, more data tend to be available. In highly visible industries such as automobiles, computers, and consumer electronics, reasonably good data are usually available from the trade press. There are also syndicated data. Frost and Sullivan in New York, for example, provide worldwide studies of market growth and potential for specific industries. The problem in the in-depth screening stage is the lack of comparability between

....

EXHIBIT 4.6   Changes in Institutional Investor Credit Rating for
Selected Countries

Country	Six-month change in credit rating*	One-year change in credit rating**
Brazil	3.1	4.6
Canada	−1.1	−1.7
Czech Republic	3.0	6.1
Iran	−1.2	−2.3
Iraq	−0.7	0.7
Israel	1.4	4.5
Lebanon	1.7	5.1
Oman	−0.8	−0.5
Peru	2.7	6.2
Philippines	2.5	4.9
Poland	2.6	5.2
Qatar	−0.3	−0.8
Saudi Arabia	−1.6	−2.8
Slovenia	0.1	6.1
Sri Lanka	2.0	4.7
Sweden	−0.6	−0.1
Turkey	−1.2	−4.9
United States	−0.4	0.7
Venezuela	−2.9	−4.5
Vietnam	2.6	5.7

*   The six-month change covers the period of September 1994–March 1995.
** The one-year change covers the period of March 1994–March 1995.
Source: *Institutional Investor*, March 1995, Vol. 29, 3, pp. 124-25. This copyrighted material is reprinted with permission from *The Journal of Portfolio Management*, a publication of Institutional Investor, Inc., 488 Madison Avenue, NY, NY 10022.

countries and the incompleteness of some countries' data. The dynamic potential of a country such as Italy, for example, with its large underground economy, is difficult to capture in published statistics. The lack of information serves, in fact, as a barrier to entry.

Clustering using detailed data on product-specific criteria can be useful as well for the in-depth screening. In the Microlog case the team clustered the countries on two criteria at a time. Exhibit 4.7 shows the resulting clusters for the mapping of "Competition" against "Growth Potential." In the upper northwest corner is a cluster of countries with high growth potential and relatively weak competitive intensity, obviously presenting more opportunity than France, with so-so growth and a high degree of competition (1=strong competition). This graph alone quickly suggests why France may be a bad choice for Microlog's entry into the EU.

EXHIBIT 4.7 EXHIBIT 4.7   Microlog's Country Clusters

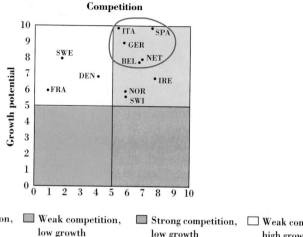

Source: Adams et al., 1993. Used with permission from the Microlog Corporation.

Final Selection

The final selection stage requires no new secondary information in principle, but it is here that the subjective judgments and experiences during the visits to the prospective country play a bigger role. Now managers can substitute subjective "guesstimates" for missing data and correct other data which seem out of line. Although this may introduce bias into the final assessment, it is at least clear where it comes from. Thus, it is possible to do a sensitivity analysis and evaluate the extent to which the overall ratings vary for potential biases in either direction.

FORECASTING COUNTRY SALES

The first part of the country attractiveness analysis dealt with the market **potential** in a foreign country. The potential identifies what could be achieved under "ideal" conditions, while a **forecast** assesses what is likely to be obtained given the likely situation and contemplated strategies. Here the focus is on the derivation of sales forecasts at two levels: market (or industry) and company.

The forecasting of market sales and market share involves quite technical skills, many of which are valid in any market. But there are additional factors that need to be considered in foreign markets. Economic and demographic data might not be available or not be comparable because of different classifications.

Getting the Picture

Mazda's Shorthand Forecast

EVEN BEFORE 1981, when their agreement to voluntarily restrict exports to the U.S. took effect, the Japanese auto companies had an easy time forecasting their American sales (after 1981 the Japanese simply divided up their market share among themselves). Mazda, for example, was able to employ a "shorthand" type of quick forecasting method. First, projected industry sales, in units, were polled from various sources, including economists in Washington D.C. Second, the market share going to imports as a class was identified, also provided by these same sources. Next, the Japanese share among these imports was estimated on the evidence of past performance and projected competitive developments worldwide—the Japanese Automobile Manufacturers' Association (JAMA) was instrumental here. Finally, the share falling to Mazda from the Japanese piece of the pie was estimated on the basis of in-house data and probable developments in styles and specifications, and against previous performances abroad. Computing the forecasted sales then was simple. They equalled Industry sales × Import share × Share for the Japanese × Share for Mazda among the Japanese. Time and cost to develop the forecast? Negligible. Accuracy? Almost perfect.

Source: Personal interview with company spokesmen, Mazda North America, July 23, 1984.

The marketer often has to leverage past data from other markets, including the home market, into a kind of "bootstrap" forecast of what is likely to happen in a new market. Forecasting sales in a foreign market is a matter of combining technical skills and country knowledge imaginatively.

A Basic Equation

Few companies are as fortunate as Mazda when it comes to forecasting sales in foreign markets (see box, "Mazda's Shorthand Forecast"). The Mazda approach provides the basic components that companies have to estimate in order to generate a forecast:

$$\text{Sales} = \text{Industry Sales} \times \text{Market Share}$$

The division between industry sales and market share serves to isolate what factors need to be considered. To develop an estimate of *industry sales*, the well-known determinants such as economic growth, disposable incomes, social and political developments, as well as dynamics of the product life cycle need to be incorporated. The *market share* prediction, on the other hand, relates directly to factors such as competitive situation and marketing effort. The basic idea tends to be that what affects the market size is one thing, what affects the share we get in the market is another. Although in international marketing this represents an oversimplification because of various trade obstacles (tariff and nontariff barriers), such factors can be incorporated and accounted for as we will show.

Stage of the Life Cycle

An important aspect of the international forecasting problem is the stage of the life cycle (PLC). These stages vary by country, even for a given product. In the early stages, relatively little data are usually available for statistically based forecasting, and more inventive methods have to be relied on. In later stages, more sophisticated methods can be employed.

THE EARLY STAGE OF THE PLC

In the early stage of the product life cycle, market share is usually less important—what matters is the size and growth rate of the total market. Three types of forecasting techniques can be used. One is the evaluation via a "build-up" method from industry experts and distribution channel units; another is forecasting by analogy, doing a comparison with a lead country. When all else fails, judgmental methods have to be used.

The Build-Up Method

For the early stages of introduction the best estimates of future sales usually come from industry experts and knowledgeable channel members. If the company can contact some of these individuals—travel is usually necessary—an estimate of the market size can be based on their information. The **build-up** connotation comes from the fact that the market sales are estimated on the basis of separate estimates from individuals knowledgeable about certain segments of the market. These single estimates of various parts of the market are aggregated ("built up") into an evaluation of total market size.

For example, when one company attempted to forecast sales in Europe of a new consumer audio product, it divided each country market into three segments each served by different channels. The teenage segment purchased mostly through convenience outlets. The high-performance segment purchased through specialty stores. The family user purchased through general merchandise and department stores. The company then collected estimates from each of these channels in the main European countries to build up a forecast.

Given that these estimates are subjective, it is important that the marketer gather additional information from whatever other sources are available so as to develop a sense of the reliability of the subjective estimates.

The information from the build-up method should always be compared to managerial experiences of the product in other countries—provided of course there are other countries further along the product life cycle process. In these cases forecasting by analogy has become quite popular.

Forecasting by Analogy

The basic premise underlying forecasts by **analogy** is that the sales in one "lagging" country will show similarities to sales in another "leading" country where the product is already marketed. Since the 1960s, when the theme of global interdependence and convergence first emerged strongly, such similarities have been used to forecast a similar rate of acceptance of a new product in many different countries, especially those belonging to a common regional grouping. A standard example was television, its introduction in the United States had been shown to exhibit a growth curve replicated with minor modifications in a number of other countries (the so-called "demonstration effect"). Most examples fall within the durable category of products, where market penetration in terms of first-purchase rates is used as a standard indication of stage of market development.

According to this technique a reasonably quick and cheap way of assessing the sales potential at a given point (and for the future) in a country where a product introduction is contemplated would be to ascertain at what stage of the growth curve (the product life cycle) the product will be when entering the new market. If the product is new, the assumption is made that the growth curve will have approximately the same slope as in a "lead" country where the product is already introduced. Empirical analyses have demonstrated that the speed of adoption tends to be quite similar in new countries—but also that (because of differences in economic rates of growth), the saturation level will be lower (or higher). These differences are usually adjusted for judgmentally when the final forecast is developed.

An Illustration: TV Penetration

An example of the possible use of forecasting by analogy is provided by the introduction and market penetration of TV sets in various countries at different points in time.[12] Exhibit 4.8 shows the percent of ownership and annual increases in sales for three countries.

According to the exhibit, the penetration rate was slightly faster in the United States compared to Germany and the U.K., and large annual increases occurred correspondingly earlier in the life cycle. Other countries showed different patterns. Sweden, for example, exhibited a penetration rate steeper than that of the United States, often ascribed to the "demonstration effect" of the United States and other countries in which TV stations came on the air earlier.

Exhibit 4.8 illustrates the opportunities and problems in forecasting by analogy. Yes, the patterns are the same, generally speaking. But the timing of the takeoff and rapid growth stages are different, and the lags involved are not identical. By introducing variables to explain the variations in the penetration curves it is possible to adjust the forecast by analogy to more properly reflect the likely time path.

EXHIBIT 4.8 Yearly Increase in Household Ownership of TV Sets, 1946–70

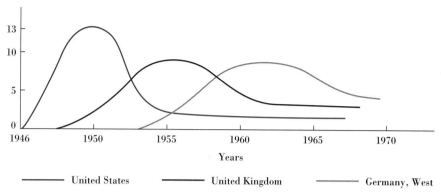

Years

——— United States ——— United Kingdom ——— Germany, West

Source: Lindberg, 1982. Adapted with permission. © 1982 by the American Marketing Association.

To account for the difference in size between countries, the sales figures are usually weighted by a measure such as GNP or population size. For example, forecasted sales might be computed from an expression such as the following:

$$S_b(1995) = [S_a(1991)/GNP_a(1991)] \times GNP_b(1995),$$

where S stands for unit sales, the subscript "a" stands for the leading country, "b" for the lagging country, and there is a lag of four years (1995–1991). In words, the ratio of sales to GNP in the lead country in 1991 gives the unit sales per dollar GNP. By multiplying this factor into the lagging country's GNP in 1995, a sales forecast is arrived at.

It goes without saying that such a simple formula requires a careful assessment of the comparability between the two countries. What is relevant is whether there is any reason to expect the ratio between sales and GNP to differ between countries. The United States and Canada are two quite different countries in some respects—but there might be little reason to expect these differences to be very important once the discrepancy in the size of population has been taken into account. On the other hand, comparing Japan and West Germany, countries with quite comparable economic output records, might be more difficult: The TV might play a very different role in the Japanese household with the absent husband working until 11 P.M. as compared to the German household in which the larger homes and less time on the job allow the family to spend more time together. These differences might induce the suspicion that GNP will not account for differences in sales (as it turns out the penetration ratio is higher for Japan where color TV has become more of a status symbol than in Germany).

Judgmental Forecasts

If the product has no history in any comparable country (as might be the case when entering the former communist countries), analogies can be misleading. Furthermore, channel members may know too little for a build-up method to have any validity or reliability. Purely judgmental methods may have to be used.

Judgmental forecasting techniques generally attempt to introduce a certain amount of rigor and reliability in otherwise quite arbitrary guesses.[13]

THE JURY TECHNIQUE   The use of executive judgment based on first-hand experience and observation in estimating foreign sales is indispensable. The **jury technique** is basically a structuring of the standard executive committee meetings, in which the members are asked to submit their separate forecasts, either before or after intensive discussion. The individual forecasts are then pooled and the results again evaluated before a final figure or range is arrived at. The concept is that a group of experienced executives would have more insights when combined than any single one. When coupled with the Delphi method (see below), the method gains additional power.

It is important that whatever data exist are made available to the jury and also that staff members from overseas are included in the process. It should be emphasized that this type of managerial judgment becomes especially important in decisions involving major commitments and high risk, since then the consensus arrived at by the jury automatically assigns responsibility to the whole group, not a single individual manager. In this respect, foreign entry is more naturally the domain of several executives rather than a small number or one person with good knowledge of operations in one country but not in others.

EXPERT POOLING   There is no doubt that consultation with experts (**expert pooling**) on the country contemplated will always be a cornerstone in sales forecasting where new entry is concerned. Without a firm's having previous experience in a new country's markets, the reliance on independent experts (academicians, consulting firms, or host country nationals) is almost unavoidable. Judging from the literature on export initiation it is precisely this type of information source about market potential that best serves the process of exploring entry into a new country.

The **panel consensus,** much like the jury of executive opinion, tries to pool the available information from more than one source. The Microlog team used this type of pooling to arrive at country ratings on the selected criteria, essentially taking averages across each team member's subjective rating. The Delphi method is a more systematic approach.

The **Delphi method** consists of a series of "rounds" of numerical forecasts from a preselected number of experts. These experts may or may not know the identity of the other members of the panel. They are asked to provide individual estimates, independently of their colleagues. The estimates are tallied, the average forecast is computed, and summary statistics (but not individual estimates) are returned to the experts. Another round of estimates is collected, tallied up, and the summary is again distributed. As these rounds continue, the feedback provided will tend to bring the estimates into line. The expert whose initial estimate is far off the average forecast will tend to converge towards the mean—unless, of course, he has strong prior beliefs that his estimate is more correct. In either case, the process gradually converges, as those with weaker opinions yield to those with strong opinions under the influence of the pressure to adjust toward the average forecast received.

The Delphi method has been discussed widely, and has come in for its share of criticism. The basic problem is that "bad estimates might drive out good estimates" when the panel members show unequal degrees of stubbornness. In general, however, the type of pooling of various opinions offered by this technique has been its greatest advantage. When judgmental analysis is carried out by using several individuals with some experience or direct knowledge of a country's market, it serves to prohibit one particularly strong personality (a headquarters executive, for example, or the general manager of a subsidiary) from dominating the proceedings. The anonymity provided serves to ensure that everybody "has a voice."

THE LATER STAGES OF THE PLC

When the product in the market country has reached a more mature stage in the product life cycle, forecasting using past data becomes possible. There are essentially two approaches available for carrying out these forecasts. One is based on historical data of industry sales alone, simply extrapolating past trends into the future. The second allows for more in-depth analysis, incorporating the variables that underlie sales developments in the country. This method is based on regression analysis.

Time Series Extrapolation

Time series data represent a form of "history in numbers." In other words, statistics are based on past performance, behavior, and developments, and the statistical analysis of the data generated by these histories will simply ferret out what happened in a more comprehensive and objective manner than subjective evaluations. Thus, the primary requirements for statistical forecasting of foreign sales are (l) that data are available, (2) that past events are relevant for the future, and (3) that statistics will be a better judge of what happened than more informal or anecdotal accounts. Although in domestic forecasting the reliance on statistical analysis often seems great (because the requisite data *are* indeed available), in international marketing all three requirements typically pose problems. For example, recent dramatic political and economic changes in

Asia, Eastern Europe, and Latin America suggest that historical time series may be a poor guide for the future.

Extrapolation refers to the method by which a time series of (sales) data observed over some periods in the past is extended into the future. It represents, in a sense, the purest form of forecasting, in that the concern is entirely with the future: The current level of sales provides but one data point among many. At the same time it represents a very naive form of forecasting in that the only information employed is the numbers of the sales series in past periods. The focus of the forecaster's job is on detecting patterns in these numbers to be projected into the future. There are many excellent texts on this topic, and since the international context adds little to these treatments, they will not be covered here.[14]

Regression-Based Forecasts

The first considerations in developing a **regression forecast** involve the use of some prior knowledge to develop a forecasting equation. First, the relevant dependent variable of interest needs to be determined. Is it a matter of annual industry sales, in units (the most common choice)? In dollars? The growth rate of sales per annum? The import sales alone?

Second, the forecaster must try to identify what factors will affect the dependent variable selected. For most country analyses, GNP and population figures become relevant since they tend to measure the "size" of the market. But more specific measures are often needed. How many people or firms could one consider to be potential customers, or, stated differently, what is the "in-the-market" proportion? If a country has a large population but few single-person households, the market for labor-saving prepared foods might be correspondingly smaller. Where a large number of small manufacturers exist, but only few large-scale corporations, the market for mainframe computers and associated software might be minimal, despite a high GNP per capita.

Getting the Picture

Armstrong's Regression Model

ARMSTRONG FORECASTED camera sales in a given country in three steps. First, a *regression* was specified to predict camera sales per potential buyer:

$$R = f(E,P,B,T,W,C,G)$$

with E = Beckerman's standard of living index

P = Price of camera goods

B = Buying units index (households per adult)

T = Temperature

W = Rainfall

C = Proportion of children in the population

G = Growth of per capita income per year.

This regression equation combines the *willingness* and *ability* to buy into a forecast of *average of sales per potential buyer (R)*. It was estimated using data on camera sales for existing country markets.

The second step specified the size of the potential market using a *multiplicative chain:*

$$M = (T) \times (L) \times (A) \times (N),$$

with M = Number of potential buyers

T = Total population

L = Literacy rate (proportion)

A = Proportion of population aged 15–64

N = Proportion of nonagricultural employment.

This equation was not estimated since the variables were straight proportions. These are *segmentation* variables, eliminating people outside Kodak's target segments. For example, Kodak's experience showed that most sales occurred outside the nonagricultural segment.

The third step combined *sales per potential buyer* and the *size of the market* to derive the forecasted sales:

$$S = (R) \times (M)$$

where S = forecasted camera sales in units per year for the given country.

Source: Armstrong, 1970.

THE SIZE COMPONENT It is useful at this stage to break up the independent variables into different categories. One set deals with "size": how many firms, or people, are potential customers, for example. A useful approach is sometimes to *segment* the total number into homogeneous subsets: how many heavy industry firms, how many in services, or, for consumer goods, how many households with children, how many with incomes over a certain level, how many in the big cities versus the rural areas, and so on depending upon the product. This type of evaluation can usually be done using the "chain ratio rule," in which the initial figure of size is broken down by the percentages falling into the separate segments: For example, the size M of one segment may be calculated as

M = Number of households × Proportion with children × Proportion with incomes over $10,000 a year

WILLINGNESS TO BUY   A second group of independent variables influences the willingness to buy the product. In consumer goods, need for the product among types of consumers, existing attitudes toward foreign products, and fit between product use and buyer life-styles are all important considerations. In industrial markets, sophistication of the process technology employed in manufacturing, attitude towards foreign products, special features the product offers, and other similar considerations are relevant here. Needless to say, this portion of the analysis must be based on intimate knowledge of the country's people, be it through formal market research or personal experience.

ABILITY TO BUY   The last category relates to consumers' ability to pay for the product. Variables here are income, per capita expenditures on related products, profit performance of company customers, and other similar economic factors. It's important to identify trends in these figures so that precautions can be taken and future opportunities are not missed.

SALES PER CUSTOMER   Customers' willingness and ability to buy are combined into a total sales estimate. Using the market size multiplied by the average sales per customer, a simple version of the model is:

$$S = M \times s$$

where s is the average sales per customer (in units or money).

FORECASTING MARKET SHARE

After forecasting industry sales it becomes necessary to predict what portion of total industry sales the particular company can obtain. This entails a forecast of market share.

Predicting Competition

Market share forecasts involve prediction of competitive moves. This requires not only knowing who actual and potential competitors might be in a given country but assessing competitors' strengths and weaknesses. Hard enough when it comes to understanding what is currently going on, when attention is directed toward the future, the forecasting problem becomes very thorny. Small wonder that subjective managerial judgment plays a relatively great role.

Market share forecasts are usually done best by breaking up the problem into its separate components. First, the *likely competitors need to be identified,* including domestic firms and multinational companies operating in the country. Second, *country-specific advantages of the domestic companies* over foreign competition should be well understood. Third, the *company's strengths against the other firms* have to be objectively assessed, particularly against other foreign firms operating in the country.

IDENTIFYING COMPETITORS   Drawing on informal in-house knowledge and on selected contacts in the market country, a list of competitors is compiled. One difficulty is identifying what future entries may be made—here also less formal research methods will be reliable indicators. It is important that *potential* entrants be included, particularly when the product in the new country is at an early stage in the life cycle while in other countries its development has progressed further. When a competitor is already well established in other markets, entry into a new market can be undertaken quite quickly. A good example is the burgeoning auto market in Saudi Arabia that was rapidly covered by major automakers from Europe and Japan once the oil revenues had radically increased the spending power of the population.

DOMESTIC COMPETITION   The fact that tariff and nontariff barriers make entry difficult by raising foreign firms' prices and giving advantages to domestic producers needs to be considered very carefully. Not-so-prohibitive existing barriers could be changed all too quickly after an entry has been successfully made, and the possibility of direct foreign investment needs to be considered at this stage. For forecasting purposes, the critical figure is the proportion of the market available to nondomestic countries ("country share"). In most countries there are (possibly unstated) limits on market capture that the entering firms

U.S. lawmakers use sledgehammers to smash a Toshiba radio after the Japanese company sold submarine technology to the USSR. This 1987 incident ignited a political furor as Americans were already concerned about Japanese incursions into American markets, but consumers continued to buy Toshiba television sets and laptop computers.

Bettmann.

can reach without inducing protectionist measures. Managerial judgment and informal inquiries might disclose what those limits are. The forecasted share might well need be to constrained a priori using this information, with the understanding that the company will have an upper limit on the share it can obtain in the market.

Apart from such political considerations, the forecaster needs to evaluate the strength of a possible "pro-domestic" attitude on the part of buyers. There is sometimes covert or overt pressure on buyers to stay loyal to their domestic companies, the "Buy American" movement being one example. In addition, there are attitude differences toward products from different countries, as well as formal requests to companies that entry into certain other countries be restricted (at the time of this writing, certain Arab states demanding that suppliers not do business with Israel, for example).

In addition to these extra-economic considerations, the forecaster needs to be aware that many domestic producers provide a product or service that is particularly well suited to the special needs and wants of the country, even though it might make little headway in the international marketplace. America's big cars, the dark beer of England, "small-is-beautiful" farm equipment in India may be hard to compete with in local markets. In these cases the evaluation of the competitive strengths of the domestic producers needs to be adjusted beyond a straightforward application of strengths and weaknesses of products. Needless to say, such adjustments become subjective and judgmental.

In the end, the forecaster should be able to come up with a reasonable estimate of the market share "available" to imports (import share versus domestic share). This step serves well in accounting for factors affecting market performance that are not encountered in the home market.

COMPETITION AMONG IMPORTS   How well will the company fare against other *foreign* competitors in the local market? Here more objective data are sometimes available, since these firms might have been encountered in other world markets. Motorola can assess fairly directly how well its products may perform relative to Siemens, L. M. Ericsson, or Hitachi using its experience with these companies in other parts of the globe. Market share estimates can't be assumed equal to those in other markets, but a fair evaluation can be made.

If appropriate, this last step can be broken down into evaluating foreign competitors first and then firms from the company's home country. Westinghouse might first assess a probable U.S. share, and then go on to comparing itself to General Electric. We saw Mazda's approach, first identifying the probable Japanese share and then comparing its strength against Japanese competitors. This breakdown becomes particularly necessary when the tariff, quotas, and other nontariff barriers (including country-of-origin stereotyping and attitudes) differ for different home countries. A typical example would be automobiles in the EU. Semi-official quotas help Italian and French authorities keep domestic auto firms' market shares up to protect employment. Once the "desired" domestic share has been ascertained from industry experts, the foreign automakers can focus on the remaining available market share.

SUMMARY

Chapter 4 examined how companies evaluate countries' attractiveness for foreign market entry. The evaluation proceeds in stages, with an initial identification of a set of countries based on the company's strategic intentions, such as a desired presence in a particular free trade region or cluster of similar countries. A preliminary screening using broad socioeconomic indicators reduces the set, after which an in-depth screening of the most promising candidates reduces it further. The in-depth screening focuses on the market and market segments targeted for entry, and attempts to assess the degree to which competitive advantages can be leveraged and objectives met. A variety of data sources exist for these assessments. Clustering techniques "map" countries' differences and similarities. The screening requires trips to the top candidate countries to get a direct feel for the market and marketing infrastructure. Such "hands-on" contact by managers with the new market should never be missed.

Sales forecasting techniques applicable in domestic markets need to be modified for foreign markets because of data differences and differences in product life cycle stages, among many other factors. The standard breakdown of the forecasting problem into industry sales and market share forecasts as separate issues can be elaborated by introducing "import share" to deal with tariff and nontariff barriers and "country share" to deal with country-of-origin attitudes.

It's important that several independent forecasts be carried out, if feasible, and the results "pooled" to arrive at the best forecast possible. This pooling effort draws on many individual judgments, based on managers' valuable direct personal experience with the country in question. The unlikelihood of intimate knowledge of every country on the list makes group consensus forecasts generally superior to an individual's projections.

KEY TERMS

Build-up method p. 139
Clustering countries p. 132
Clustering maps p. 132
Country identification p. 117
Delphi method p. 142
Direct experience p. 124
Expert pooling p. 142
Extrapolation p. 144
Final selection p. 122
Forecasting by analogy p. 140
In-depth screening p. 121
Jury technique p. 142
Leading markets p. 129
Market share forecasts p. 146
Panel consensus p. 142
Political risks p. 126
Potential versus forecast p. 137
Preliminary screening p. 120
Regression forecasts p. 144

DISCUSSION QUESTIONS

1. Company spokespeople are often heard to say, "We have to be in that market." What is a likely explanation for this statement if the market is (a) China; (b) Germany; (c) Brazil; (d) Japan; (e) the United States? Give examples of products or services.

2. What factors would you consider when help-ing an already global manufacturer of house-hold vacuum cleaners choose between Mexico, India, and China as the next country to enter?

3. Try to trace and analyze the emergence of Japan as a leading country in automobiles. Consider France in wines, the United States in computers, and similar *traditional* leaders. What do their differences with Japan tell you about the leading markets of the future?

4. In what kinds of product categories would you expect *industry forecasts* could be gener-ated from extrapolation of historical data? *Market share* forecasts?

5. New hi-tech products—such as the Sony Walkman was—are often said to generate their own demand. What does this imply about the possibility of forecasting sales when such a product is first introduced? How could one forecast sales for it when later entering a market such as Russia?

NOTES

1. This section draws on Douglas and Craig, 1983, and Kumar et al., 1994.

2. See, for example, Wood and Goolsby, 1987.

3. See Exhibit 4.3 for how to get these reports.

4. See De la Torre and Neckar, 1990.

5. Adapted from Kobrin, 1979.

6. These firms include, for example, Business Inter-national and Frost & Sullivan—see the discussion on country data sources, and Exhibit 4.3.

7. See "War Cited as Top Risk to Business," *Chicago Tribune*, January 17, 1994, p. 1.

8. Kumar et al., 1994.

9. This section draws on Johansson and Roehl, 1994.

10. A compact and accessible treatment of both factor and cluster analysis can be found in Churchill, 1994.

11. See Cavusgil, 1990.

12. This example is adapted from Lindberg, 1982.

13. This section draws on Armstrong, 1985, and Makridakis, 1990.

14. Armstrong, 1985, is useful and relatively accessible for the nontechnical reader. Lindberg, 1982, and Makridakis, 1990, offer interesting applications.

SELECTED REFERENCES

Adams, Jonathan, Shubber Ali, Leila Byczkowski, Kath-ryn Cancro, and Susan Nolen. "Microlog Corporation: European Market Evaluation." Class project School of Business, Georgetown University, May 12, 1993.

Armstrong, J. Scott. "An Application of Econometric Models to International Marketing." *Journal of Marketing Research* VII (May 1970), pp. 190-8.

———. *Long-Range Forecasting*, 2d ed. New York: Wiley, 1985.

Cavusgil, S. Tamer. "A Market-Oriented Clustering of Countries." In Thorelli, Hans B. and S. Tamer Cavusgil, eds. *International Marketing Strategy*, 3d ed. New York: Pergamon, 1990.

Churchill, Gilbert A., Jr. *Marketing Research: Methodologi-cal Foundations*, 6th ed. Dryden, 1994.

De la Torre, Jose, and David H. Neckar. "Forecasting Political Risks for International Operations." In Vernon-Wortzel, H., and L. Wortzel, eds. *Global Strategic Man-agement*, 2d ed. New York: Wiley, 1990.

Douglas, Susan, and Samuel C. Craig. *International Mar-keting Research*. Englewood Cliffs, NJ: Prentice Hall, 1983.

Dubey, Suman. "After 16 Years Away, Coca-Cola to Re-turn 'The Real Thing' to India." *The Wall Street Journal*, October 22, 1993, sec. A, p. 9E.

Johansson, Johny K., and Thomas W. Roehl. "How Companies Develop Assets and Capabilities: Japan as a Leading Market." In Beechler, Schon, and Allan Bird, eds. *Emerging Trends in Japanese Management*, vol. 6 of *Research in International Business and International Rela-*

tions, ed. Manuel G. Serapio, Jr. Greenwich, CT: JAI Press, 1994, pp. 139–60.

Kobrin, Stephen J. "Political Risk: A Review and Reconsideration." *Journal of International Business Studies* 10, no.1 (1979), pp. 67–80.

Kumar, V., Antonie Stam, and Erich A. Joachimsthaler. "An Interactive Multicriteria Approach to Identifying Potential Foreign Markets." *Journal of International Marketing* 2, no. 1 (1994), pp. 29–52.

Lindberg, Bertil. "International Comparison of Growth in Demand for a New Durable Consumer Product." *Journal of Marketing Research*, August 1982, pp. 364–71.

Makridakis, Spyros G. *Forecasting, Planning and Strategy for the 21st Century*. New York: Free Press, 1990.

Naisbitt, John. *Global Paradox*. New York: Harper & Row, 1994.

Porter, Michael E. *Competitive Strategy*. New York: Free Press, 1980.

Smart, Tim, Pete Engardio, and Geri Smith. "GE's Brave New World." *Business Week*, November 8, 1993, pp. 64–70.

Thorelli, Hans B., and S. Tamer Cavusgil, eds. *International Marketing Strategy*, 3d. ed. New York: Pergamon, 1990.

Wood, R. Van, and Jerry R. Goolsby. "Foreign Market Information Preferences of Established U.S. Exporters." *International Marketing Review*, Winter 1987, pp. 43–52.

Export Expansion

"Over the river and into the trees"

After studying this chapter, you should understand the following global marketing issues:

1. Barriers to entry include not only tariffs, quotas, and elaborate customs procedures, but also restrictive government regulations, limited access to distribution channels, and pro-domestic consumer biases.

2. Barriers to entry sometimes will sometimes force the firm to unbundle its value chain and identify intermediate products, or components of the final product, to export.

3. The firm can let its agent and distributor handle the local marketing or it can control marketing by establishing a foreign sales subsidiary.

4. Export expansion into several countries involves strategic questions about whether to focus on a few culturally similar countries to leverage existing know-how, or to diversify more widely to gain risk protection and increased learning.

5. The marketing mix alternative is extension versus localization, depending on demand conditions in the foreign market.

AFTER IDENTIFYING various opportunities in a foreign country or countries, the question becomes how the chosen country or countries should be entered and what strategy the global expansion should follow.

For marketing, it helps to distinguish between modes of entry that *sell the product* to the selected market and those that *transfer know-how* to the host country. *Licensing, franchising, strategic alliances, and investment in manufacturing* are entry modes that share technology and know-how with host country partners and local employees, while *exporting* is the standard exchange of product for money. Exporting is more straightforward, since it is expansion into new markets with an existing product line, while transfer of know-how involves trade in markets for intermediate goods. Selling Coke is different from selling the formula. This is why many firms expanding abroad start with exporting.

Chapter 5 will concentrate on the export mode of entry and expansion. Exporting is the international equivalent of trade across geographical regions, often the preferred mode when trade barriers (including tariffs and transportation costs) are low. The local marketing effort can be directed through independent middlemen, but it is usually preferable to establish a foreign sales subsidiary.

Cartoons Capture Kids' Hearts from Guadalajara to Guangdong

Betty Cohen, president of the Cartoon Network and TNT International, has a friend who grew up in Mexico, and like many children, she enjoyed watching cartoons. When Cohen's Mexican friend moved to the United States, she was astonished to discover that Fred Flintstone could speak English as well as Spanish.

People around the world have sought out popular entertainment born in the United States for years. Although the United States has lost its dominance in marketing the "hardware" of entertainment—televisions, VCRs, CD players, and so on—consumers are still eager to snap up the "software," from audio recordings to movies.

Marketers are therefore crafting strategies to expose U.S. popular entertainment and culture to new audiences, and they target children's programming as a market ripe for global expansion. Fox and Nickelodeon are creating new shows with partners abroad, while other companies are tailoring existing products to foreign markets. Fred Flintstone and his animated colleagues of Hanna Barbera are owned by the Cartoon Network, which has teamed up with Ted Turner's TNT cable network as Cartoon-TNT to provide global television programming. Cartoon-TNT has 28 million subscribers in Europe, 2 million in Asia, and 4.5 million in Latin America. The Cartoon Network offers up its huge cartoon library as a global product, adapting cartoons by dubbing them in several foreign languages. It also uses ratings data to select offerings for particular regions.

Hollywood also has been targeting its movies to eager audiences in developing countries. Movie studios have been experiencing flat profits domestically but have enjoyed rapid growth in Latin America and Southeast Asia, and China's huge population offers tantalizing opportunities for expansion. When Walt Disney Company originally released *The Lion King* there, it expected to gross $3 million. The movie surpassed all expectations, grossing that much in just 10 days, and subsequently the company doubled its forecast.

Unfortunately for U.S. popular entertainment and culture marketers, consumer demand is only one facet of the global marketing environment. Selling popular entertainment and culture in developing nations also poses some challenges. China, for example, heavily taxed the revenues generated by *The Lion King*, cutting deeply into the movie's profits. In addition, studios must contend with a slow-moving government bureaucracy wary of exposing the country to foreign entertainment. Further, piracy is rampant in many countries, including China and Thailand. Consumers there can buy unauthorized videos, CDs, and other products without generating any royalties for the artists or studios. The Motion Picture Association of America has pegged losses to piracy of movies alone at well over a billion dollars annually.

Still, enormous potential remains. Already, MTV has become the world's top brand of music videos, CNN is number one in television news, and ESPN sports has become a global leader. Perhaps it's just a matter of time before Fred Flintstone is speaking Chinese.

Sources: Lawrie Mifflin, "Can the Flintstones Fly in Fiji?" *New York Times*, November 27, 1995, pp. D1, D4; Seth Faison, "A Chinese Wall Shows Cracks," *New York Times*, November 21, 1995, pp. D1, D4; John Huey, "America's Hottest Export: Pop Culture," *Fortune*, December 31, 1990, pp. 50-53ff.

INTRODUCTION

Several strategic questions arise about how to enter foreign markets and conduct an orderly global expansion. What should the mode of entry be? How fast should new country markets and new products be added to existing ones? What is the best expansion path, considering the learning and experience already accumulated? Will similar countries be preferable or should one strike out into new ground completely? What added advantages would a product and country diversification strategy entail? How should new entries be chosen so as to maximize total benefits?

Immediate global expansion into all markets is usually not feasible. Financial, managerial, and other resource constraints often dictate a more sequential approach. Even if the company is resource-rich, prudence suggests the company take a more deliberate approach. The company needs to establish defensible market positions in each country before moving on to other countries. Foreign direct investment might be avoided at the early stages because of the risk exposure. The learning associated with exporting and doing business abroad needs to be assimilated and diffused to benefit company managers.

Chapter 5 first introduces the major modes of entry and discusses each briefly, then turns to the impact of entry barriers on mode choice, followed by the main exporting tasks involved in entering a single country. The functions independent middlemen and the key issue of control over the local marketing effort are dicussed. The effect of "cultural distance" on the internationalization path of firms' expansion (already discussed in Chapter 2) and the important concept of learning how to do business abroad are taken up again. The benefits and costs of export diversification versus a focused global expansion strategy are discussed and the main product and promotion alternatives are reviewed.

Modes of entry that transfer know-how are discussed in more depth in Chapter 6.

FOUR MODES OF ENTRY

It is useful to distinguish between four **modes of entry** into a foreign market: exporting, licensing, strategic alliance, and wholly owned manufacturing subsidiary. These four modes break down into several different activities. A typical breakdown is given in Exhibit 5.1.[1] These alternatives will be discussed in detail in this and the next chapter. At the outset, we take a quick look at the options available.

EXPORTING   **Indirect exporting** refers to the use of home country agencies (trading companies, export management firms) to get the product to the foreign market. "Piggybacking" is the use of already exported products' transportation and distribution facilities. Consortia are used by some smaller exporters banding together to sell related or unrelated products abroad. **Direct exporting** by contrast, means the firm itself contacts the buyers abroad, be they independent agents and distributors or the firm's own subsidiaries. There is also *direct marketing*, including mail order and telemarketing, a new but rapidly expanding mode of foreign entry particularly useful for small businesses and for initial entry. Since direct marketing is an outgrowth of direct mail promotion, it is discussed in Chapter 16 on global promotion.

LICENSING   **Licensing** involves offering a foreign company the rights to use the firm's proprietary technology and other know-how, usually in return for a fee plus a royalty on revenues. Among licensing modes, **franchising** has become a

....

EXHIBIT 5.1   Entry Modes for Foreign Markets

Exporting	*Strategic alliance*
Indirect exporting via piggybacking, consortia, export management companies, trading companies	Distribution alliance
	Manufacturing alliance
	R&D alliance
Direct exporting, using market country agent or distributor	Joint venture
Direct exporting, using own sales subsidiary	*Wholly owned manufacturing subsidiary*
	Assembly
Direct marketing, including mail order and telemarketing	Full-fledged manufacturing
Licensing	Research and development
Technical licensing	Acquisition
Contract manufacture	
Original equipment manufacturing (OEM)	
Management contracts	
Turnkey contracts	
Franchising	

Source: Adapted with permission from Root, *Entry Strategies for International Markets, Revised and Expanded.* The New Lexington Press, Simon & Schuster International Business and Professional Group, p. 16.

well-known alternative with the expansion of global hotel and fast-food chains. In franchising, the firm provides technological expertise to the reseller abroad and also helps with the management of the franchise and often with the capital investment that is needed for start-up. The other licensing options are all similar, differing mainly in the type of know-how transmitted. *Turnkey* contracts provide for the construction of whole plants and often the training of personnel capable of running the operations; *contract manufacture* is hiring a firm to produce a prespecified product (jeans produced by Filipino and Chinese textile mills for overseas manufacturers).

STRATEGIC ALLIANCES (SAs)   **Strategic alliances** are collaborations between companies, sometimes competitors, to exchange or share some value activities. Examples include joint R&D, shared manufacturing, and distribution alliances. Strategic alliances in the form of **joint ventures** also involve capital investments and the creation of a new corporate unit jointly with a foreign partner. Such joint ventures have long been common especially in countries such as India where government mandates participation by locals and in countries such as Japan where market access is difficult for outsiders.

Joint ventures are a type of strategic alliance in which partners create an equity-based new unit. In recent years, non–equity-based strategic alliances have become very common. An international strategic alliance is typically a *cooperative collaboration* between companies, even between potential competitors, across borders. The alliance could encompass any part of the value chain—

although the focus is often limited to manufacturing, R&D, or distribution. In distribution alliances, the partners agree contractually to use an existing distribution network jointly. A typical example is the linkup between Lufthansa and United Airlines to pool route information and passengers.

WHOLLY OWNED MANUFACTURING SUBSIDIARY   When production takes place in the host country through a wholly owned manufacturing subsidiary, the company commits investment capital in plant and machinery that will be at risk in the country. This is traditional **foreign direct investment (FDI).** A wholly owned subsidiary in manufacturing can involve investment in a new manufacturing or assembly plant (such as Sony's TV plant in San Diego), or the acquisition of an existing plant (such as Matsushita's purchase of Motorola's TV plant outside Chicago). The presence of actual manufacturing operations helps support marketing activities. For example, a local plant is more likely to provide a stable flow of products, and it will be easier to adapt the products to the preferences of local customers than with a plant located outside the country's borders.

It is important to recognize that FDI usually leads to exporting. As manufacturing is established abroad through direct investment, parts and components are often shipped (exported) from the home country. About a third of U.S. international trade involves such shipments between units of the same company.[2] Although such intraorganizational transfers are quite different from market exchanges, more and more companies set transfer prices at market levels and allow subsidiaries to buy from local suppliers if quality and price are more favorable. This means the supplier plant has to engage in "internal" marketing, satisfying internal customers in the subsidiaries abroad.

A **sales subsidiary** is fundamentally different from a wholly owned *manufacturing* subsidiary. A sales subsidiary manages distribution and marketing of the product in the local market. Usually the product is exported from the home country or from another foreign plant. Volvo North America, located in Northbrook, Illinois, imports and distributes Volvos shipped from Europe.

Establishing a sales subsidiary requires relatively low levels of capital investment. Although operating costs for even a small sales office can be high in a country like Japan, with major expenditures for "general administrative and sales," the investment exposed to risk is often low. At the same time, establishing a sales subsidiary involves taking control of the marketing in the country and is thus strategically important. For marketing effectiveness, the control of the sales effort should generally be in the hands of the company itself.

THE IMPACT OF ENTRY BARRIERS

Before examining exporting and the other entry options in more detail, we look at the barriers that always exist to entering a foreign market. *The height and nature of the market entry barriers directly influence the entry mode chosen by a company.* Entry barriers increase the cost of entry and constrain the options available, and where they are high, the company might have only one choice of entry mode or else have to stay out.

Entry Barriers Defined

The concept of **entry barriers** comes from the economics of industrial organization. It generally connotes any obstacle making it more difficult for a firm to enter a product market. Thus, entry barriers exist at home, as when limited shelf space prohibits a company from acquiring sufficient retail coverage to enter a market. Overseas it can mean that customs procedures are so lengthy that they prohibit an importer's fresh produce from getting to the stores before spoiling.

In global marketing it is convenient to classify the entry barriers according to their origin. Although gradually less important because of dramatic improvements in technology, *transportation costs* sometimes force new investment in manufacturing to be close to the market. Proximity of supplies and service still matters when transportation costs are high. **Tariff barriers** are obvious obstacles to entry into the country. Less visible **nontariff barriers**, for example, slow customs procedures, special product tests for imports, and bureaucratic inertia in processing import licenses, can also make entry difficult. **Government regulations** of business, domestic as well as foreign, constitute another set of market barriers, sometimes creating local monopolies. A special subset of these barriers are regulations directly intended to protect domestic business against foreign competitors.

One of Europe's traffic bottlenecks, the border crossing between France and Spain. As the EU integration continues and the customs checkpoints are eliminated, market entry barriers have quite literally been dismantled.

Raphael Galliarde/Gamma-Liaison.

Other barriers are more subtle. *Access* to manufacturing technology and processes, component suppliers, and distribution channels can be restricted by regulation, territorial restrictions, competitive collusion, or close ties between transacting partners. These barriers constitute artificial value chain imperfections and become important for the marketer to consider when deciding the configuration of the overseas operation. There are also "natural" entry barriers that arise because of competitive actions. Many of the typical marketing efforts—creation of brand loyalty, differentiation between products, high levels of promotional spending—are factors that, when successful, lead to barriers or defenses against competitive attack.

The Cost of Barriers

The economic costs of entry barriers are well known. The inefficiency created by barriers translates into higher prices for consumers. What this means to the marketer is that the barriers create additional costs for the foreign entrant.[3]

Regardless of the source of the barriers, their existence means that some firm or individual (**gatekeeper**) will have a chance to profit ("capture rent" in economists' terminology). For example, where tariff barriers exist, the payment goes to the foreign government (unless, of course, corrupt bureaucrats pocket the money). Where a domestic company has built a viable defense for its products with a strong brand image, it can collect "rent" by charging premium prices. Where close ties in distribution channels are necessary, natives with good contacts garner considerable fees by simply arranging a meeting between two prospective partners. The cost of doing business is very high in some countries because of such barriers.

Although there may be no major cost differences between these barriers, they are very different in their effect on the foreign entrant and what can be done about them.

Tariff and Nontariff Barriers

The firm on its own or through its trade association or local chamber of commerce can attempt to lobby its own or the host government for a reduction in tariffs and nontariff barriers. Examples abound. American companies demand that the U.S. trade representative pressure Japan to open its markets. The European companies appeal to the GATT/WTO to help reduce tariffs on steel from the EU into the United States. The automobile quotas on foreign cars in Italy are under pressure from the EU Commission. These negotiations are sometimes emotional and clouded by national pride and are always difficult.

The firm should analyze the tariff base carefully to identify how the tariff rate is calculated.[4] Most often the tariffs are higher for a complete assembly, lower for parts and components. In the early 1980s when the United States raised the tariff rate for imported trucks to 25 percent, Nissan shipped every truck in two parts, the body and the flatbed, which could be assembled in a one-step operation. In this way the trucks entered as unfinished goods, with a lower tariff rate of 2.5 percent. Such "screwdriver assembly plants" exist in various parts of the world precisely as a way of avoiding high tariffs, but governments are also learning to write more stringent classification codes for the imported parts to capture more of the rent or profit generated.

It is common to lower or even waive a tariff when the imported product or component has a certain level of "local content" or when imports involve production for reexport. The foreign entrant has an incentive, therefore, to add parts and labor from the foreign market. When such parts are not available, it is not uncommon for the entrant to help establish a supplier of the parts in the country so as to obtain the lower tariff rate. This is an example of how tariff barriers can lead to foreign investment in plants.

In general, trade barriers will lead the foreign entrant to reexamine the firm's existing integration of activities in its value chain, from supplies to final sale. It becomes important to identify if some activities in the chain need to be broken out and to internalize only those activities that cannot be done better elsewhere. For example, when Volkswagen entered Japan, the difficulty and expense of establishing its own dealer network made the company decide to contract with a competitor, Nissan, to distribute Volkswagens in Japan. Thus, even though the barriers represent imperfections in the market, skillful management can help reduce the negative economic effects from these imperfections. As economists have shown, where trade is prohibited by tariffs, multinational production is often an efficient response, with gains for the firm and the country as well.[5]

A final tactic, increasingly employed as regional trade agreements proliferate, is to establish manufacturing in a member country in the regional trade group. Then the firm can export to the market country in the region at lower tariff rates from the transplant operation inside the region.

Government Regulations

When it comes to government regulations of business—involving questions ranging from "Who can start a business?" to "Can free product samples be sent in the mail?"—the foreign firm can do little but to adapt to them. Some assistance from the home government might be available. The U.S. government's negotiation in the late 1980s of the so-called "Structural Impediments Initiative" (in which Japan was asked to change things like its retail store regulations) is an interesting example of intrusion into a country's domestic policies by a foreign nation.[6] The EU homogenization of a myriad of regulations is another example of how government rules are changing in the globalizing economy.

The foreign entrant will need to study in detail the specific regulations affecting its industry and the sales of its products and services. In this process the foreign services of government offices (including the consulate abroad) and the local chambers of commerce can be of help. In other instances, the company needs to hire professional specialists who can decipher the foreign regulations. International law firms are often a good place to start.

Government regulations may be so severe and limiting that the company can do little without a native partner. As a member of a joint venture or some other collaborative alliance, the native partner can be assigned the task of carrying out negotiations with government authorities and local regulators. When Toys R Us established its operations in Japan, it selected Mr. Den Fujita, the general manager of McDonald's Japan, as its representative. The most pressing problem, getting building codes and retail regulations changed, required a strong local presence. Once in, the firm became an insider with claims on the same local protection as domestic firms.[7]

Distribution Access

In many countries it is very difficult to get members of the distribution channels to carry the firm's product. Retailers have no shelf space, they carry competing brands, and they don't trust that the new brand will sell. Wholesalers can't depend on supplies from overseas, they are not familiar with the distributor, and they need extra rebates if they are to take a new brand on. Again, tracking the new brand requires that price and packaging information be entered into the computer so the scanners will work, and so on. In many countries, including the United States, new brands need to pay a "slotting" fee—a "tip" or bribe—to get the trade interested. The difficulty of getting **access to distribution channels** means that the firm, even after successful entry, might compete with a handicap. As seen in Chapter 2, this is not an unusual situation in foreign markets (since such network ties lower transaction costs and are thus economically justified).

There is a downside to close distribution or supply ties. When the channel members or suppliers are not efficient, the ties may be more a burden than a benefit. Thus, some smaller parts manufacturers in Japan who are suppliers for Nissan, say, lack scale economies and may not be as efficient as suppliers in South Korea, Taiwan, or even Europe and the United States, especially when the yen is very strong. In a similar vein, the vertical integration by Mercedes through its purchase of the electronic component business of AEG, one of its German suppliers, might not be very profitable if AEG quality is weak.[8] Where free market supplies are available, free competition typically ensures competitive prices and consequently lower costs.

Lack of access to distribution channels usually means that the firm has to consider a strategic alliance or even sell the product unbranded in an OEM (original equipment manufacturing) arrangement with a firm already established. Volkswagen distributes Toyota trucks in the EU countries. Mitsubishi cars are sold in the United States through Chrysler dealers. Ricoh copiers have been marketed under the Savin brand name in the West for many years. There is also the (usually expensive) alternative of establishing a new channel. When Honda motorcycles entered the United States, the company saw fit to help train and finance new dealerships across the country.

Another access barrier is the possibility that the firm cannot hire capable local talent. Where people find working for a domestic firm preferable, either because of pay or some status-related reason, the firm may have trouble entering the market alone. This is especially striking when the market is very new to the firm, so that access to local workers is important. On the other hand, in some countries, especially developing countries, working for a foreign firm may be seen as desirable, and to that extent foreign entry is facilitated.

Natural Barriers

Competition among several differentiated brands tends to create so-called **natural barriers,** allowing strong brand names to charge a premium price over more generic or no-name competitors. This is the case in "pure domestic" markets, in which all companies compete on an equal footing (hence "natural").

Market success and customer allegiance are the factors behind natural barriers. When customer satisfaction and brand loyalty are high, or country-of-origin biases favor a domestic brand, it may be difficult to break in. Further, if advertising expenditures are large and price promotion common—typical of North American markets—the prospective entrant has to offer something special and match promotional spending. This is where firm-specific advantages are important. Natural barriers depend as much on subjective consumer perceptions as on real differences between products. Thus, it may not be sufficient to have a "superior product" in terms of objective tests. The marketing effort in the new country has to convey the superiority effectively.

Advanced versus Developing Nations

In developing countries, the important barriers are usually tariffs and other government interventions into the free market system. If the firm is able to invest in product assembly in order to get under the tariff barrier, the markets are generally less competitive and a strong position can often be gained at relatively low cost. Pepsi gained entrance to the Soviet Union with the help of President Nixon, and dominated the Russian market for colas until the fall of the Berlin Wall.

By contrast, in advanced countries it is usually natural barriers that are high. Here entry may be easier, but it is difficult to establish a strong and defensible position. This is important to remember when evaluating the firm's strategy for learning and gaining expertise in global markets. Advanced countries with open markets are a learning ground for marketing strategy and tactics. Developing countries with their tariff and nontariff barriers and myriad government regulations produce subsidiary managers with savvy about negotiations with foreign governments.

When gains have been easy because the company was one of the first foreign entrants and local protection was forthcoming, the firm may have learned less and developed less capability for more open markets. To achieve success in fiercely competitive open markets, firms have to acquire marketing skills and flexibility. In highly protected markets what matters most is skill in negotiating with government officials and powerful bureaucrats. Despite Pepsi's marketing skill elsewhere, Pepsi management in Russia seems to have been taken by surprise by Coca Cola's entry after the Berlin Wall fell.[9]

Exit Barriers

The firm usually faces **exit barriers** after entry—nonrecoverable investments have been made, people hired, contracts signed—and if there is likelihood of a forced exit, a firm will be reluctant to commit. Another consideration for the marketer is the potential loss of goodwill accompanying withdrawal from an important and visible market. The French automaker Peugeot probably lost a a great deal of brand equity (and money) in the U.S. market before finally exiting in 1992.

When future exit is a distinct possibility because of uncertainties, an otherwise attractive foreign market can be entered by choosing a less visible and less committed mode of entry, such as OEM manufacturing or licensing. If a global brand name might be hurt by withdrawal, the company could conceivably market the product under another name. With the advent of global markets, however, companies are less willing to forgo the advantages of leveraging a global brand name. In the era of global marketing, the company needs sufficient resources and capability to nurture and sustain its products and brands, thus surmounting exit carriers by never having to face them.

Effect on Entry Mode

In sum, barriers to entering a foreign market make entry mode decisions more complex than just the arithmetic of a simple geographical expansion.

The company can expand into some markets only by *unbundling* its know-how. That is, even though the company may want to be a player in final product markets everywhere, in country markets where government regulations or the company's lack of market knowledge would force the use of joint ventures, the company might opt only to *sell components*, so as not to give up crucial know-how. An obvious instance is China's insistence that foreign auto manufacturers entering the Chinese market team up with a Chinese joint venture partner. "Unbundling" is one of the possible outcomes of negotiations by potential foreign entrants into China's auto industry.

Where local-content requirements are high, the company may contract with a local producer to contract manufacture simpler versions of the products. Toshiba television sets are assembled in the Czech republic in a plant built by Toshiba but operated by local Czechs, with Toshiba's reward being a royalty on the sales.

In other markets where distribution is complex or customer requirements idiosyncratic, the company might opt to engage in a *distribution alliance with a competitor*. In order to gain quick market penetration, Japan's Ricoh produced

Ford cars in a Tokyo showroom. Ford's alliance with Japanese automaker Mazda has helped propel Ford cars into becoming best sellers in Japan.

Caroline Parsons/ Gamma-Liaison.

OEM (original equipment manufacturing) and let the Savin company sell their first copiers in the United States. The global expansion path is often more complex than simply a question of where the firm's final products will be sold.

Many companies develop managerial expertise with a particular mode of entry, and this entry mode becomes the preferred mode of expansion. Some Western multinationals have long preferred wholly owned subsidiaries, run by an American expatriate. This mode has been sustained even when the cost of financial exposure and the growth of local management expertise weakened the rationale for them. Companies such as Union Carbide, IBM, Honeywell, Philips, and the American auto companies fall into this category. Other companies, such as small technology-based entrepreneurs, will often expand through licensing or joint ventures. The reason for one sustained company policy or another is usually that management feels more comfortable with it having developed skills dealing with that form of overseas involvement.

Each mode of foreign entry involves quite different managerial skills. Overseeing a number of licensees in various countries is one thing, running a network of wholly owned subsidiaries quite another. Direct exporting involves learning about overseas transportation, international trade credit, tariff barriers, and so on, quite an investment for the beginner. The growth of various forms of cross-border strategic alliances in the recent past has been accompanied by the emergence of a cadre of international contract lawyers and managers skilled in international negotiations. The start-up costs of learning to manage any one of these modes of entry are considerable, and it is not surprising that companies tend to leverage their particular skills by staying with the same approach.

Consequently, even though the firm's value chain may be broken up to get under a certain country's barriers or in accordance with government regulations, its expansion path will be likely to follow the same mode of entry everywhere. Xerox and 3M are good at running international joint ventures; IBM and Ford like wholly owned subsidiaries; and Benetton and McDonald's prefer franchising. Staying with the "tried-and-true" leverages the company's expertise properly, minimizes the obstacles to entering, and maximizes the chances of success. When these companies have used another mode of entry, chances are they were forced to do so by government regulation or some other market access barrier.

THE EXPORTING OPTION

For the newcomer to the international scene, the exporting option is often the most attractive mode of foreign entry. Then, sometimes it is just through the experience of exporting that the idea of a full-fledged market entry is developed. At any rate, when unsolicited orders have started flowing in from abroad, the firm begins to pay more attention to the potential in foreign markets, and exporting becomes the natural first step.

Indirect Exporting

The simplest way to manage the firm's export business is to employ outside specialists. The firm may hire a **trading company,** which becomes the "export department" for the producer (see box, "Japan's Giant Traders"). In the United States the arrangement whereby an **export management company (EMC)** performs all the transactions relating to foreign trade for the firm has a similar character. EMCs are independent agents working for the firm in overseas markets, going to fairs, contacting distributors, organizing service, and so on. They serve basically as an external "export department" for the firm, an example of value chain deconstruction. This type of "indirect" exporting has its great advantage in the fact that the firm avoids the overhead costs and administrative burden involved in managing their own export affairs. On the other hand, there is the disadvantage that the skills and know-how developed through experiences abroad are accumulated outside the firm, not in it.

In most cases, the domestic firm wants to make only a limited commitment to its facilitating agencies, keeping open the option of taking full responsibility for its exporting at a later date. This is one reason why EMCs lead rather precarious lives. If they are too successful, the producer may decide to break the contract and internalize the exporting function.

Direct Exporting

Direct exporting has the advantage over indirect exporting in the control of operations it affords the producer. Going through an intermediary trading company, the firm may not even know in which country the product is sold.

*G*etting the Picture

Japan's Giant Traders

ALTHOUGH TOYOTA may employ more people, the biggest companies in Japan in terms of total turnover are the giant trading companies. The big traders do business in all kinds of products all over the world. They finance salmon fishing in Alaska and sell the fish in Hong Kong; they ship iron ore from Australia to Japan and steel from Korea to Indonesia; they ship cars to Europe and bring beer back to Japan. They are active in oil exploration, build paper mills in Peru and chemical plants in China, and organize international consortia for the exploration of minerals in New Guinea. Their take is usually a small commission or fee on the transactions created, but they also speculate in the spot market for various commodities, sometimes winning, and sometimes losing. Their global information network is the envy of any spy ring, and they announced the Iranian revolution before the CIA learned about it.

The largest trading companies and their sales in 1990 are shown in the table below.

Each of these traders belongs to "keiretsu" groupings in Japan, which bring together a number of companies in different industries. Thus, Mitsubishi Corporation is part of the Mitsubishi group, which also includes Mitsubishi cars, Mitsubishi Bank, Mitsubishi Electric, and about 50 other companies.

These traders are able to help many companies enter foreign markets. Thus, Marubeni was active in assisting Nissan in its initial stage in the United States, and in Algeria, Toyota trucks are still sold by a trading company. Non-Japanese can also employ these traders, provided they are not competitors of keiretsu members. It is important to keep in mind, however, that these companies are always on the lookout for new deals and will sometimes develop a competing business. For example, the Swedish Nobel company, maker of dynamite, found that its trading partner in Japan had initiated domestic production in direct competition with Swedish imports.

Name	Sales (billion yen)	Employees
Itohchu	14,762	7447
Mitsui Bussan	14,179	8882
Marubeni	13,246	7418
Sumitomo Trading	13,077	6366
Mitsubishi Corp.	12,660	8552

Sources: Eli, 1991. Emmott, 1992.

With direct exporting the firm is able to more directly influence the marketing effort in the foreign market. The firm also learns how to operate abroad. Without involvement in the day-to-day operations of overseas affairs, the firm will not generate much in-house knowledge. It is not until the firm decides to hire its own staff that a more strategic involvement in foreign markets becomes feasible.

....

EXHIBIT 5.2   Direct Exporting Functions

Product shipment	*Legal issues*
1. Transportation to the border	1. Export license
2. Clearing through customs	2. Hiring an agent
Local distribution	3. Transfer of title/ownership
1. Finding a distributor	4. Insurance
2. Screening distributors	*After-sales support*
3. Personal visit	1. Service
4. Negotiating a contract	2. Parts and supplies
Getting paid	3. Training of locals
1. Checking creditworthiness	4. Creating a sales subsidiary
2. Getting paid in local currency	
3. Hedging against currency losses	
4. Converting funds to home currency	
5. Repatriating the funds	

Source: Adapted from Root, 1987, p. 6.

For the direct exporter, the principal choice is between establishing a sales subsidiary or employing independent middlemen. The latter option means an *agent* to manage sales and administration paid through fees and commissions and a *local distributor* who supplies the product to the trade and adds a markup to the cost. The choice between a sales subsidiary and independent middlemen depends on the degree to which control of the marketing effort in the country is desired and the resources the firm can muster. To strike the optimal balance, the volume of operations (current and anticipated), the firm's willingness to take risks, and the availability of suitable local distributors are critical determinants. Investing in a wholly owned sales subsidiary is a bigger commitment and requires more resources than the use of independent people. But where the market is potentially large, the firm would generally be better off with more central control of operations and, in particular, the marketing effort.

The Exporting Job

There are many separate functions to be taken care of in direct exporting. The major tasks are listed in Exhibit 5.2.

The exhibit and the discussion to follow cover only the major tasks. Some of them, such as those relating to legal issues, are only marginally related to marketing, while others, such as after-sales support, directly relate to customer acceptance. Many of the functions can be handled by independent specialists who can be found through Department of Commerce contacts, at industry fairs and conventions, through the local telephone directories or by contacting the

Consulate. Associated with these tasks are numbers of different documents needed for exporting. Exhibit 5.3 gives a list of the principal documents. They will also be discussed below.

Product Shipment

TRANSPORTATION   The shipment of the product to the border of the country is usually handled by an independent freight forwarder in combination with a shipping agency. In the typical case, freight forwarders who might specialize in certain types of products or countries pick up the product at the factory, transport it to the embarkation point, and load it onto the transnational carrier. Federal Express and DHL serve as freight forwarders in the case of express mail, and they usually own their own transportation fleets (although some shipments, such as air transport to Africa, might go by a regular airline).

CLEARING THROUGH CUSTOMS   Unloaded at the national border, the product will go from the ship or airline to a customs-free depot before being processed through customs. This depot can be a large free-trade zone, such as the one outside of Canton in China or in Gibraltar at the bottom of the European continent. From this free-trade area the product can be shipped to another country, never having crossed the border. In the typical case, the free-trade

EXHIBIT 5.3   Principal Documents Used in Exporting

Required by . . .	
Foreign customer	*U.S. Government*
1. Pro forma invoice	1. Export declaration
2. Acceptance of purchase order	2. Export license (strategic goods and shipments to designated unfriendly nations)
3. Ocean (airway) bill of lading	
4. Certificate (or policy) of insurance	*Foreign governments*
5. Packing list	1. Certificate of origin
Exporting manufacturer	2. Customs invoice
1. Purchase order	3. Consular invoice
2. Letter of credit or draft (trade) acceptance	*Exporter's bank*
Freight forwarder	1. Exporter's draft
1. Shipper's letter of instructions	2. Commercial invoice
2. Domestic (inland) bill of lading	3. Consular invoice
3. Packing list	4. Insurance certificate
4. Commercial invoice	5. Ocean (airway) bill of lading
5. Letter of credit (original copy)	

zones allow workers to further add value to the product. For example, along the Mexican border with United States, the so-called maquiladors are small factories located in the free-trade zones, and Mexican workers can be used to work on the products with no cross-border shipment of products. Thus, they can be shipped anywhere in the United States after the Mexican labor value added, without having to cross custom lines.

The customs officials will process the goods for entry once a claimant appears. This is usually the buyer, but can also be an independent importer or customs facilitator who specializes in getting the customs procedures done quickly. By presenting shipping documents—the **bill of lading**—the buyer or his agent can get access to the goods after paying the assessed duty. The tariff rate is decided on by the local customs official on the spot. In some countries, this is where there is often a temptation for bribes, the buyer "inducing" the customs official to assign a lower tariff classification.

After entering the country, the goods will often require storage, and there are usually facilities in the destination port to be rented. The price is often quite high—as is the daily storage rental for goods waiting to be processed in the free trade zone. Companies try to save money by getting the goods through customs quickly and warehoused at a less expensive location.

Local Distribution

FINDING A DISTRIBUTOR   The next step is to get the product into the distribution channels. The most common approach is not to try to create new channels, but to use existing ones. Although there are some instances where the creation of new channels has been instrumental in a company's success (the Italian apparel maker Benetton's franchised stores in the United States, for example, and the U.S. cosmetics firm Avon's door-to-door system in Asia), in most cases existing channels will have to do. This means identifying one or more independent **distributors** who can take on distribution to wholesalers and retailers. These distributors usually take ownership of the goods, paying the producing firm, and often will handle the importing and customs process, in addition to storage and distribution in the country. Generally, the firm appoints one distributor for the whole country, with an exclusive territory. However, in large nations such as the United States overseas-based companies often have two or three distributors in various parts of the country (East Coast, Midwest, and West Coast, for example).

It is crucially important for the firm to find the best distributor available. According to one report, exporters find that the range of distributor performance can vary from zero to 200 percent of what is expected.[10] There are only a few excellent distributors in any one country, and the best ones are often not interested in taking on another supplier unless offered a well-known global brand.

Identifying potential distributors can be done with the assistance of governmental agencies. Many countries maintain trade facilitation agencies to assist in the search for local distributors. The U.S. Department of Commerce,

A Benetton store in Warsaw. Benetton's thoroughly tested system for management training helps the global expansion of the company, especially into emerging markets where local entrepreneurs with good experience are hard to find.

© Ed Kashi.

for example, will assist in identifying the names and addresses of many potential distributors in various countries and industries. But more commonly, potential distributors will be found at product **fairs** and international conventions. At these fairs, held in places such as Frankfurt, Cologne, Hong Kong, and Las Vegas, distributors will come to spot new products that might have a market in their country and try to establish a relationship with a vendor. The export manager participating in a fair should try to identify beforehand potential distributors who might come to the fair and arrange meetings ahead of time, but this is of course not always possible.

SCREENING DISTRIBUTORS   Once a few select candidates have been identified, they need to be screened on key performance criteria. In many cases a late entrant to the country market might have trouble finding a good distributor, making it particularly important that the screening process does not miss some key characteristic. The criteria include the ones given in Exhibit 5.4.

Which of these criteria are judged important and which not depends on the situation and the significance the company attaches to the criteria. For example, consumer nondurables typically require little after-sales service. The financial strength of the distributor is less important if the firm can support the company in the start-up period. Distributor strength can even be a drawback when the initial arrangements are seen as temporary, to be superseded by a more permanent, FDI position if the market is as large as expected.

....
EXHIBIT 5.4   Criteria for Choosing Distributors

> Previous experience (products handled, area covered, size)
>
> Services offered (inventory, repairs, after-sales service)
>
> Marketing support (advertising and promotional support)
>
> Financial strength
>
> Relations with government
>
> Cooperativeness
>
> Whether or not handling competing products

Source: Adapted from Root, 1987, pp. 63–65.

PERSONAL VISIT   Once some promising leads have been developed, a personal visit to the country is necessary. On the trip managers should do three things:

- Talk to the ultimate users of the equipment to find out from which distributors they prefer to buy and why. Two or three names will be likely to keep popping up.
- Visit these two or three distributors and see which ones you would be able to sign up.
- Before making the final choice, look for the distributor who has the key person for your line. This is a person who is willing to become the champion for the new product line. Experience has shown that the successful distributor is the one who has one person in the organization willing to take the new line to heart and treat it as his or her own baby.[11]

NEGOTIATING A CONTRACT   The contract has to be very specific as regards the rights and obligations of the manufacturer and the distributor, the length of the contract, and conditions for its renegotiation. A checklist is given in Exhibit 5.5. The conditions under which competitive product lines might be added and the degree of exclusivity that the distributor is granted figure prominently among the rights and obligations. Although local regulations and the letter of the law naturally must be followed, the usual situation is one in which the actual formulation of these contracts hinges directly on the size and strength of the two parties.

As we saw in Chapter 3, in Western countries these negotiations tend to be rather open and confrontational so that all key points get hammered out fast while in Eastern and other nations negotiations can be protracted, indirect, and often quite trying on Westerners' patience. Regardless, the spirit of the contract should be reflected in the subsequent actions of both the manufacturer and the distributor. Where it is not, neither of the parties will be happy. The relationship between the two should not be a zero-sum game, but a win-win proposition. (See the discussion of negotiations in Chapter 3.)

....

EXHIBIT 5.5   Master Foreign Distributorship Agreement Checklist

Appointment	*Confidental information*
Appointment	Sales literature
Acceptance	Advertising literature
Territory-Products	Quantities
Sales activities	Mailing lists
Advertising (optional)	*Trademarks and copyrights*
Initial purchases (optional)	*Subdistributors*
Minimum purchases (optional)	*No warranty against infringement*
Sales increases (optional)	*No consequential damages-indemnity*
Orders	*Product warranty*
Distributor resale prices	*Relationship between parties*
Direct shipment to customers	*Effective date and duration*
Product specialists (optional)	Effective date and term
Installation and service	Early termination
Distributor facilities (optional)	Breach
Visits to distributor premises	Insolvency
Reports	Prospective breach
Financial condition	Change in ownership or management
Business structure	Foreign protective act
Competing products	*Rights and obligations upon termination*
List prices	No liability for principal
Prices	Return of promotional materials
Taxes	Repurchase of stock
Acceptance of orders and shipment	Accrued rights and obligations
Acceptance	*Noncompetition*
Inconsistent terms in distributor's order	*No assignment*
Shipments	*Government regulation*
No violation of U.S. laws	Foreign law
Passage of title	U.S. law
Defects, claims	Foreign Corrupt Practices Act
Returns	*Force majeure*
Payments	*Separability*
Terms	*Waiver*
Letter of credit	*Notices*
Deposits	Written notice
Payments in dollars	Oral notice
No deduction by distributor	*Arbitration*
Set-off by principal	ICC rules
Security interest	Jurisdiction
	Article titles
	Entire agreement and modifications
	Entire agreement
	Modifications

Source: Adapted from Hall, 1983, pp. 65–66. Courtesy of Unz & Co.

Getting Paid

Getting paid can be a headache, especially if the country imposes convertibility restrictions. Today in China, India, Russia, Mexico and other countries, it is very difficult to get access to hard currencies like dollars, yen, or D-marks. The local currency is either very weak (Mexico) or not easily convertible (China, India). And despite heroic efforts to participate in global capital markets, many former communist countries (Russia, Bulgaria) still have trouble paying for their imports in hard currency.

In most countries, checking on the creditworthiness of the buyer can usually be done through banking connections. Regardless, many exporters avoid relying on credit, not shipping goods until an intermediate bank, preferably in the seller's country, guarantees payment. This is traditionally done via some form of **letter-of-credit.** This is arranged for by the buyer. Exhibit 5.6 shows the linkages involved. As can be seen, once the buyer approaches the local bank, opening a credit line, this bank will contact its corresponding bank in the selling firm's country. This latter bank will inform the seller that a letter of credit has been issued, assuring the seller that payment will be made. Once the seller ships

....
EXHIBIT 5.6   Letter of Credit Model

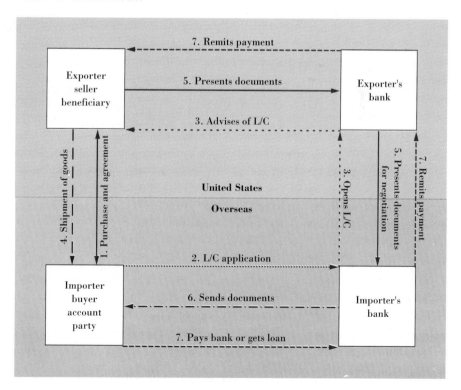

the goods, the bill of lading can be presented to the bank, which will contact the overseas bank in the buyer's country, and will pay the seller. This transaction usually takes place before the goods have reached the buyer's country. Once they arrive, the buyer can claim the goods at customs against the bill of lading sent by the bank.

Because letters of credit involve several intermediaries and a fair amount of administrative work, the fees tend to be high. Importing companies try to reduce costs by negotiating standing letters of credit, amounting to an international credit line. In other cases, the buyer will try to induce the seller to simply accept payment within 30 or 90 days of delivery, similar to typical domestic arrangements. As international financial markets and banking institutions become further integrated, payment is likely to become less of a problem. For example, the problem of repatriating funds from a weak currency country has made financial intermediaries develop so-called "swaps," through which the funds will be exchanged (at a discount) against funds elsewhere. There are also, of course, various ways of hedging against shifts in exchange rates, and many importing firms use futures options to purchase funds in a currency they know will have to be used in the future.

For the marketer, it becomes important to stay close to the financial managers in the company and make sure they are consulted before an order from a new country is accepted. Standard sales techniques, such as offering delayed payments, installment pay schedules, or no-money-down credit sales might have to be forgone in favor of more prudent pricing schemes.

Legal Issues

Many products require an **export license**—usually issued by the Department of Commerce—to be shipped out of a country. In the Cold War era, many computers and other electronics products could not be exported from the United States—exporters could not get an export license. The issue of national security concerns was used to block many exports on the grounds that the Soviets might get hold of technology with military value. Even today, when many license requirements have been voided or are approved liberally, there is often a need to get a pro forma license. In the importing country, especially where currency restrictions are in place, import licenses are needed for many foreign products. The local Department of Commerce office will offer help on the license matter.

The **title** or ownership to the exported goods generally follows the bill of lading. Whoever holds the bill of lading has access to the goods. The business risk—and thus exposure to normal loss, such as lack of sales in the marketplace—shifts with the title. The local distributor who borrows money to pay for the goods will be exposed to risk at the point when the bill of lading is accepted by the seller's bank—or, sometimes, as the seller's bank delivers the bill of lading to the buyer's bank.

If damage to the goods occurs during transit, **insurance** questions arise. The common procedure is for the seller to quote a price **c.i.f.** (cost, insurance, freight), in which case the seller will arrange for insurance and shipment to the border. This simplifies the whole exporting process but also makes the seller responsible for following up with insurance claims. Alternatively, the seller can quote **f.o.b.** (free on board), in which case the buyer is straddled with the need to arrange for shipment and insurance. Good marketing thinking suggests that the company should quote its prices at the higher c.i.f. rate, and not bother the buyer with extra work.

The seller needs to pay attention to legal matters in the market country. Product liability and warranty issues can become a problem, after-sales service responsibility questions may come up, conflicts with distributors about contracted quotas and sales efforts may arise, and so on. Since most countries do not allow foreigners to work on legal questions, a company representative, an **agent,** is needed.

The agent will be the legal representative of the firm (the principal) in the local market, usually working for a retainer fee and a contract that provides hourly compensation on special cases. Exhibit 5.7 offers a checklist of things to consider when hiring an agent. Where their responsibilities involve some sales activities—such as, for example, visiting distribution outlets to monitor in-store support—agents can also be remunerated via a commission percentage of revenues. Many agents work for more than one principal, but not for competing firms. Agents can be found through the same sources as distributors.

After-Sales Support

In order to support the local marketing effort, the firm needs to establish after-sales service, stock spare parts and supplies, and train local staff. These tasks are often managed by the distributor, aided by the agent. The contract specifying the responsibilities of the distributor (see Exhibit 5.5) should make clear what marketing role he should play, and the agent is expected to enforce the contract.

As the firm's sales in a country grow larger, control of the local marketing effort becomes a very important issue. Not only does after-sales support need to be monitored more closely, but the whole marketing program (pricing, product line offered, promotion, and channel management) might need more effective management. A single agent and one or two independent distributors can't usually be counted on for that kind of marketing support.

This is when the company often decides to establish a sales subsidiary, staffed with locals and a few top managers from headquarters.

Such a sales subsidiary will run the local marketing effort, conducting market research, dealing with local advertising agencies, monitoring distributors' performance, providing information on competitors, on market demand, and on growth, and generally managing the local marketing mix—sometimes going against top management's recommendations and shared wisdom. More on this will be discussed in Part Three "Local Marketing."

·····················

EXHIBIT 5.7   Master Foreign Agency Appointment Checklist

Appointment	*Product Warranty*
Territory-Products	*Effective Date and Duration*
Sales Activities	Effective Date and Term
Promotional Efforts	Breach
Introductions (optional)	Insolvency
Prices	Prospective Breach
Acceptance	Change in Ownership or Management
Agent Representations	Foreign Protective Act
Minimum Orders (optional)	*Rights and Obligations upon Termination*
Increase in Orders (optional)	No Liability of Principal
Agent Facilities	Return of Promotional Materials
Competitive Products	Re-Purchase of Stock
Confidential Information	Accrued Rights and Obligations
Reports	*Indemnity*
Operations Report	*No Assignment*
Credit Information	*Government Regulation*
Visits to Agent Premises by Representatives of Principal	Foreign Law
	U.S. Law
Sales Literature	Foreign Corrupt Practices Act
Trademarks and Copyright	*Force Majeure*
Acceptances of Orders and Shipments	*Separability*
Acceptance	*Waiver*
No Violation of U.S. Laws	*Notices*
Commissions	Written Notice
Commission Percentage	Oral Notices
Accrual	*Governing Law*
Refund	*Arbitration*
Discontinuation of Products	*Article Titles*
Repair and Rework	*Entire Agreement and Modifications*
Relationship Between Parties	Entire Agreement
Sub-Agent	Modifications
No Warranty Against Infringement	

Source: Adapted from Hall, 1983, pp. 67–68. Courtesy of Unz & Co.

CULTURAL DISTANCE AND LEARNING

The many new tasks and foreign ways of doing business facing the beginning exporter are daunting. Understanding what has to be done is one thing—being able to execute is another. Not surprisingly, many companies begin exporting tentatively, try to learn "on the job," and commit resources only gradually. Research has shown that "going global" for many companies simply means expanding into a few culturally similar countries. Although from a pure marketing viewpoint such a myopic focus seems counterproductive—first-mover advantages are potentially lost, for example—when the analysis is

An advertisement for CP Rail System (Canadian-Pacific Railroad) targeting U.S. customers. For many American and Canadian firms, the first export business is across the border to the next-door neighbor. It helps build skills in doing business abroad.

Courtesy of the CP Rail System.

broadened to include managerial learning and organizational capabilities, the incrementalism seems more justified. Companies often can't market what they *should* market, but only what they *can* market.

The "Cultural Distance" Effect

There is a basic rule of thumb for firms when they first expand abroad. Companies find it natural to look for countries abroad where their experiences in the home market would be most useful, where the intercultural synergy would be maximized. This "reasoning by analogy" leads to selecting countries with conditions similar to the home market's. Most of the **export expansion paths** followed by firms begin in countries "psychologically" or "culturally" similar to their own or to countries they already export to.[12] Geographical proximity plays a role but is only one part of the broader notion of "cultural distance" at the heart of expansion-by-gradually-internationalizing. (See the Hofstede graphs in Chapter 3.)

The **cultural distance** effect works so as to create very natural "biases," which are not necessarily counterproductive, since they are often supported by the success of the actual entry. Factors that make for cultural proximity also make previous experience relevant, and if the company is successful in one country, it might profit nicely from doing the same thing in another similar country. In general, however, the blind acceptance of the easy cultural distance path leads to a superficial analysis of possibly very real differences among the

AN INTERESTING example of the principle of "cultural distance" is the relationship between old colonial powers and their dominions. One would have expected that because of the historical events preceding independence many colonized countries would spurn companies from the colonial powers. In many cases, however, this has not happened. British companies are still very active in India, Australia, and countries in Southeast Asia, and French firms do a lot of the international business of their old colonies in West Africa. The reasons are basically to be found in the cultural ties and traditions established during colonial rule. The foreign language used for business, the educational system of the country, the financial connections with the outside world, the newspapers read, and expatriates staying in the country after independence are all factors that contribute to a paradoxical degree of dependence on the previous colonizers on the part of many newly independent countries.

countries and also to a predictability of company action that can be a disadvantage from a competitive standpoint.

There are numerous examples of the cultural distance effect at work. The United States and Canada are each other's most important trading partners, and many small businesses in Wisconsin, for example, trade more with Canadian businesses than they trade with California or the East Coast. Japan's exporting companies generally started trade with the Southeast Asian countries before moving on to Latin America and Australia. Most European companies export first to their immediate neighbors, an old habit much encouraged by the establishment of EU ties.

The International Learning Curve

The cultural distance path can be justified not only on the basis that it seems to achieve a maximal capitalization on previous experience. It also allows the gradual accumulation of learning how to do business abroad. At least in the initial stages of expansion, this learning effect is a common rationale for choosing countries to enter.

The same **learning curve** is at work when the experienced international marketer eyes new and important country markets, such as the American market. For most European and other firms, entry into the U.S. market represents the capstone of success. Traditionally, the U.S. market for many products has been the biggest, most competitive, and most difficult to penetrate. Consequently, much preparation generally goes into entry into it and much care is exercised in developing the appropriate strategy and tactics. As part of the preparation, companies attempt to develop skills and savoir faire by entering markets with characteristics similar to the U.S. market's. European firms enter the U.S. market via Canada, allowing time to elapse before crossing the border. The Swedish furniture retailer Ikea entered the European markets,

TOYOTA, the Japanese automaker, exported overseas first to its Southeast Asian neighbors, then to Australia. As a former export manager remembers: "The Asian markets we were familiar with, and the expansion was natural. Australia we didn't know very well, but it was sort of a rehearsal for entering the United States. We had decided that Toyota needed to be in the U.S. because of its market potential and for the status it carried here at home. Europe? Well, that's different." He smiles sheepishly.

"This Danish businessman came to Tokyo in 1958, I think, and wanted to be our representative in Denmark. We didn't know what to do, but he simply ordered a few cars from us, prepaid, and we had to ship them. That's how Europe got started. No systematic planning—but the Danish businessman made good, and Denmark is still one of our strongest European markets."

Source: Personal interview, Toyota sales headquarters, Tokyo, June 1982.

established a strong market position there, and waited until its Canadian operations were fully mature before entering the United States. The size and competitiveness of the U.S. market make it the "Mount Everest" of consumer markets, according to Ikea representatives.[13]

Learning periods are routinely incorporated into the expansion paths of Japanese firms, which tend to enter Southeast Asian markets along the cultural distance path first and then, looking for diversification, enter Latin American markets (focusing on the Japanese expatriate markets). As skills and confidence grow, the companies eye the U.S. market with its great potential. Before entering it (or the European market), however, many Japanese companies will enter the Australian market to make sure they will be able to sustain penetration in a country with similar characteristics. Only with sufficient success and learning in the Australian market will they attempt to enter the U.S. market.[14]

The Internationalization Sequence

The cultural distance effect generates the typical *internationalization* sequence of multinationals. Initially, countries that are similar are entered, especially ones geographically close. Thus the early markets for German autos included France, Benelux (Belgium, the Netherlands, and Luxembourg), and the Scandinavian countries. As more know-how and skill in international affairs are accumulated—the learning curve phenomenon—management becomes less culturally "biased" and more "off-beat" markets are explored. At this stage there might not be any systematic analysis across the globe but impromptu analysis of those countries from which the firm receives unsolicited orders, countries someone discovers through personal contacts or visits, or countries a manager simply takes a personal interest in. Thus at some stage an excursion into a country far away culturally takes place, often by chance (see box, "Seizing the Moment").

From Germany an early 20th century wave of emigration shifting from North to South America, laid the groundwork for the entry of German businesses years later. The cultural distance from Germany to Latin America was initially very great, greater than that to North America, but as German settlers in Latin America provided information, an incipient market, and general know-how, the German multinational companies both before and after World War II showed a greater interest there (in particular in Argentina, Brazil, and Chile) than they would have on the basis of cultural distance alone. That is, German personal contacts lessened the distance and stimulated the early exploration of these markets.

EXPORT EXPANSION STRATEGY

After building up experience and confidence, internationalizing companies start considering a more orderly and strategic export expansion. When companies find that over 10 percent of their revenues comes from overseas markets, management starts paying more attention to overseas potential.[15] Then an export expansion strategy seems needed to manage the increasing dependence on overseas markets.

Macrosegmentation

With more than 200 independent country markets to consider, many exporters find it difficult to develop a comprehensive global attack. Therefore companies tend to break down the field into regional groupings such as the EU, NAFTA, or ASEAN or simply geographical regions, Southeast Asia, Oceania, the Middle East, Western Europe, and treat these markets as relatively autonomous organizational units. Alternatively, the country clustering maps discussed in Chapter 4 are revisited to discern possible synergies and untapped opportunities. The typical question is which countries seem to go together from a market opportunity standpoint. This is a form of macrosegmentation.[16]

Macrosegmentation consists of grouping countries on the basis of common characteristics deemed to be important for marketing purposes. These variables typically include sociodemographic data on population size and character, disposable income levels, educational background, and primary language(s), as well as indicators of level of development, infrastructure, rate of growth in GNP, and political affiliation. The choice of variables must take into account the possible lack of data comparability across many countries and will generally vary across products (for industrial products, a manufacturing intensity index is often used as an indicator of general level of economic activity, for example).

To identify regional groupings (macrosegments) of countries, it is possible to use computerized techniques such as cluster analysis. Alternatively, the experienced manager will often be able to spot groupings by simply looking for "profiles" formed by the scores of the countries on the relevant variables.

Automobiles provide an illustration. The initial grouping into macrosegments identifies regions on the basis of general factors thought to affect purchases of autos directly or indirectly. These indicators will probably include income levels, average household size, and state of the roads (infrastructure) in the country. One region will then comprise countries with similar figures on GNP/capita, household size, and infrastructure. In this way most Western European countries plus North America, Australia, New Zealand, and Japan might be considered one "region." Countries with reasonably high income levels but poor infrastructure—say the Middle East countries, Northern Africa, some South American countries (Argentina, Venezuela, and Brazil, say), and a few East Asian nations (perhaps Singapore and Hong Kong)—would be a second region. Other countries, all relatively poor, might form a "Third World" region.

With the proper selection of discriminating indicators, the company contemplating auto sales in these three regions could infer that the type of auto, its promotion, distribution, price, and service (i.e., its marketing mix) should look very different across the three macrosegments.

As for the first "region," those countries will generally be more demanding in styling, luxury, options, and comfort. If the macrosegmentation analysis has been handled correctly, these preferences can be further analyzed and evaluated independently of the countries of regions number two and three. Again, some producers might well decide to target the specific segment region two, avoiding the intense competition between automakers in region one. This has been done by Russian automakers whose cars are not competitive in region one and by truck manufacturers whose special "tough terrain" four-wheel-drive cars are especially suitable for rough roads.

The second macrosegment might show more potential but because of the poor infrastructure, the cars demanded need stiffer handling characteristics and shock absorbers, will need to ride higher, and will need to feature a simplified engine and transmission package. The company needs to decide if targeting this group of countries is worth the extra costs of adapting to these needs.

The last region might show too small a potential to be worth entering. Even though the cars desired by countries in the Third World don't differ very much from cars targeted for the second segment, the buying power of the population might be too low for entry. It is, of course, important to take into account the possibility of future growth and the potential from supporting an already emerging economy.

The homogeneity of the countries in each cluster suggests that a standardized product can be successful in any of the regions. A standardized product for the first cluster can be successful in another cluster of countries, although it will need different positioning. A product targeted at the core markets of countries in cluster one could be marketed in cluster-two countries as an upscale luxury item. For example, the Canon AE-1 automatic camera was positioned as a "convenient" single lens reflex (SLR) product in Japan but as a technological marvel in Europe. Part Four of the book will deal with the standardization question.[17]

Diversification Benefits

In developing an export expansion strategy, some companies make an effort to balance market countries so that the international "portfolio" of countries provides **diversification** protection against the risk of large losses. Exporting itself can provide initial diversification.

How does such a protection work? The basic concept is simple. If, say, a company is entirely dependent on one company in the home country for all its sales (e.g., as a domestic supplier to a large company such as Boeing), any factor that affects the customer adversely will have serious repercussions for the supplier firm as well. A good example is a lack of airline orders for Boeing due to recessional factors, followed by fewer purchases by Boeing of aircraft parts and supplies. The solution for the small (or large) supplier lies in the diversification of its customer base to other firms, perhaps international customers in the same industry (e.g., getting an Airbus contract from France). Most companies that sell abroad show a more stable pattern of sales and earnings than firms concentrating on one or two markets at home.[18] Strong sales in a large market at home might not be so easily defended by the company with extensive commitments abroad, but neither will sales be affected so dramatically when the bottom falls out of one key market.

To implement the concept, the manager needs to have an idea of the degree to which countries tend to move together, meaning the degree to which sales fluctuations in one country will be mirrored in another. If two countries belong to the same economic union (as, for example, France and Italy do), global economic and political developments are likely to affect both countries similarly. Accordingly, the two countries do not combine well in terms of diversification benefits.

By contrast, where the countries involved are France on the one hand, say, and Saudi Arabia on the other hand, a very different picture emerges. Not only are the two countries very different, it might even be that the very factor that makes demand among the Saudis great (say, an increase in oil prices) also makes for a weakening franc and lower demand in Paris. By establishing a distribution base for the product in Saudi Arabia, rather than trying to penetrate Italy as a simple extension of the Paris operations, the firm has become diversified and has a much better protection. This *negative* interdependence between market countries is useful when developing a well-balanced country portfolio from a risk perspective.

Examples of diversification strategies are common. Volvo, the Swedish car maker, limited its U.S. market involvement to 25 percent of total output for many years. In personal interviews with top management, Toyota executives reported feeling uneasy when their exports take more than 50 percent of their home market demand. The recent tendency is for Japanese exporters to limit their unit shares going to the U.S. market, not only in autos but in electronics. The fear of too great a reliance on the U.S. market is palpable, especially at a time when the United States seems to be vacillating in its adherence to free trade.

Diversification versus Focus Strategy

Even though there may be strong diversification benefits from entering several markets or regions, a case can be made for **focusing** on a few select markets. These markets can be given more attention and market positions fortified. If the countries are relatively similar, spillover effects can be shared more easily. Product lines can be the same. Good advertising copy is more likely to play well in a similar country. How should a company strike a balance between overextending itself and being too dependent on a few single markets? Exhibit 5.8 shows some of the market factors that need to be considered.

As can be seen in the exhibit, high-growth markets require more marketing support for a brand, and a focused strategy tends to be desirable. On the other hand, instability and competitive rivalry in the market increase the benefits of diversification. When decisions have to be custom-tailored to the local market, there is greater need for focus. The "marginal sales" condition refers to the shape of the sales response curve to increased marketing expenditures. If the market responds strongly to an increase in expenditures (the sales response curve shows a region of increasing returns), it will pay to focus and spend more, since every dollar spent brings in increasingly more sales.

Empirical research has shown that generally diversified strategies tend to lead to greater export sales, while concentrated or focused strategies tend to result in somewhat higher profitability.[19] One prime determinant of exporting success is that expansion follows a coherent and clear strategy, something which is easier in focused strategies.[20] In firms whose objectives and intentions are clearly articulated, export expansion proved more successful than in companies with more diffuse objectives. Even though export expansion paths may seem random at times, the firm that develops a more structured approach, be it concentrated or diversified, seems to do better.

EXHIBIT 5.8   Market Factors Affecting Choice of Expansion Path

Factors	Diversify if:	Focus if:
Growth rate	Low	High
Demand stability	Low	High
Competitive lag	Short	Long
Spillover	High	Low
Need to adapt product	Low	High
Need to adapt promo	Low	High
Marginal sales	Diminishing	Increasing
Need for control	Low	High
Entry barriers	Low	High

Source: Adapted with permission from Ayal and Zif, 1979, p. 88. © 1979 by the American Marketing Association.

A Comparison of Two Industries

The point of the factors in Exhibit 5.8 is that even though diversification may seem desirable from a portfolio and risk point of view, market factors may dictate a need to focus on only a few country markets. A comparison between a mature industry such as cameras and a new industry such as personal computers will help to illustrate the trade-offs involved.

Single-lens reflex cameras constitute a product category characterized by global marketing and slow growth. A new product such as Minolta's Maxxumm needs to be introduced in most major countries almost simultaneously. Competitive lead time is short, there are considerable spillover effects across countries, and little need for adaptation. The major strategic task is to capture first-mover advantages in the global marketplace. A rapid diversification roll-out to the various countries is clearly called for.

By contrast, the fast-growing PC hardware market is a more difficult case. Localization of supporting software packages is time-consuming, demand fluctuates wildly in response to economic shifts, and it is important to capture increasing return by establishing local monopolies with the help of installations and service support. The global market, not surprisingly considering these conditions, has remained fragmented, with different companies concentrating on defending their local markets. As growth slows down and markets become more stable, one would expect a shakeout and a trend toward globalized markets with major players dominant. The recent successes of American PC makers in Japan and Europe signal that this development is under way.[21]

Marketing Strategy

The questions of entry mode and expansion strategy can be viewed as questions of distribution—one part of the marketing mix. Some basic decisions about the product, price, and promotional package also need to be made.

As Keegan has suggested, there are typically four marketing alternatives to be considered when export expansion is contemplated.[22] The most common is **product-communications extension**, simply extending the existing product line, pricing policies, advertising appeals, and promotional themes to the new countries entered. This approach naturally costs less and is convenient but does not always work. It seems to fit a company such as Coca-Cola, since consumer preferences and competitive conditions for colas tend to be similar across countries. On the whole though, it works best where cultural distances are small and is a natural for a company adopting a focus strategy to expansion.

A second marketing alternative is **product extension–communications adaptation.** When use conditions are the same or similar as those in the domestic market but the need to be fulfilled is different, the product line can be extended but the communications must adapt. This involves repositioning a standardized product. The Minolta Maxxumm is a good example. The product is basically standardized but the positioning varies across countries. In Japan and Europe it is a camera for serious amateurs, young adults who are interested in the technology. In the United States, on the other hand, the camera's appeal is to a broader group of people, including families and older adults.

A third strategy, **product localization–communications extension,** can work well when use conditions change, but positioning is the same. The well-known Exxon slogan, "Put a Tiger in Your Tank," has worked well across the globe for many years. The gasoline itself, however, has been adapted by the use of additives to account for differences in climate, season, and performance requirements in various countries.[23]

The fourth strategy alternative is **dual adaptation,** involving both product localization and communications adaptation. This case is most likely to be necessary when a diversification strategy is attempted, entering countries where use conditions and positioning requirements differ. This alternative involves higher costs and often more uncertainty as well, since cultural distance is likely to be larger and market know-how less. Benetton, the Italian apparel maker, has faced this problem in Southeast Asian markets. Because Asians tend to have shorter arms and legs relative to body length than Westerners, the designs have to be altered. Also, attempts to extend Benetton's politically charged European advertising has met with resistance from local retailers whose customers are willing to buy the Italian design image but not the societal concern.

Keegan suggests a fifth strategy alternative, **product invention,** which he recommends for global strategies. It involves developing entirely new products for the market abroad, less common as an entry strategy since it presupposes thorough knowledge of market conditions. Global companies with presence in many countries do this often. The Nissan Primera was developed for the European market, the Volkswagen Rabbit was developed for the American market (on the European Golf platform), and Procter and Gamble's Vizir detergent was developed for Europe. More will be said about this in Part Four, the "Global Management" part of the book.

SUMMARY

In this chapter the discussion has centered on the exporting mode of entering foreign markets and the ways companies tend to expand their global market reach. Four major entry modes were identified: exporting, licensing, strategic alliances, and wholly owned subsidiary in manufacturing. The impact of entry barriers on the choice of an entry mode was discussed. Barriers restrict the company's choices. We discussed the exporting option in some detail, showing the various functional tasks, many of them new to the typical marketing manager, which will have to be carried out if export expansion is embarked on.

Typical patterns followed by exporters into foreign markets reflect the cultural distance effect and the internationalization process. As the company gradually develops confidence in its ability to market abroad, expansion into new countries takes on a more orderly and structured character. The firm has to decide whether it should follow a diversification strategy, with its risk-reducing benefits, or a focus strategy, selecting only those countries where potential revenues are highest. Research findings have shown that

the main point is to develop a clear and coherent strategy for expansion, whether a diversification or a focus strategy.

KEY TERMS

Agent p. 175
Bill of lading p. 169
c.i.f. p. 174
Cultural distance p. 177
Direct and indirect exporting p. 155
Distribution access p. 161
Distributors p. 169
Diversification p. 182
Dual adaptation   p. 185
Entry barriers p. 158
Exit barriers p. 163
Export expansion path p. 177
Export license p. 174
Export management company (EMC) p. 165
f.o.b. p. 175

Fairs p. 170
Foreign direct investment (FDI) p. 157
Focus strategy p. 183
Franchising p. 155
Gatekeeper p. 159
Government regulations p. 158
Insurance p. 174
Joint ventures p. 156
Learning curve p. 178
Letter-of-credit p. 173
Licensing p. 155
Macrosegmentation p. 180
Modes of entry p. 155
Natural barriers p. 162

Nontariff barriers p. 158
Product-communications extension p. 184
Product extension–communications adaptation p. 184
Product localization–communications extension p. 185
Product invention p. 185
Sales subsidiary p. 157
Strategic alliances (SAs) p. 156
Tariff barriers p. 158
Title p. 174
Trading companies p. 165

DISCUSSION QUESTIONS

1. How can control over local marketing be managed in exporting? In licensing?

2. What might be the *natural* entry barriers against foreign cars, if any, in the United States? Against foreign foods? Any differences across the country?

3. For an industry or product of your choice, use library sources, Department of Commerce publications, and trade publications to find out when and where the major international fairs and conventions are held, and estimate how much participation would cost for

a company (registration fees, booth charges, travel, food and lodging, preparation of pamphlets, etc.).

4. How does the learning involved in internationalization add a dynamic aspect to the expansion path that exploits a firm's existing FSAs?

5. In what way do the new regional trade groupings offer diversification benefits? To what extent do they reduce diversification benefits?

NOTES

1. Adapted from Root, 1989.

2. From U.S. Department of Commerce statistics.

3. The costs of entry barriers are not an issue of free versus managed trade. All agree that barriers cost money and that consumers have to pay more for products and services. The policy difference is rather in terms of whether the added costs are worth it for the nation, since barriers protect firms and jobs, however inefficient, at least in the short run. In the longer run, the added economic benefits from lower barriers are supposed to result in new investment and new job opportunities in competitive industries. At least that is the theory. Since the foreign marketer will be confronted with sometimes hostile reactions from workers who have lost their jobs because of trade (as now happens in Eastern Europe), this theory should be kept in mind. It provides some defense.

4. The Department of Commerce will have the tariff schedules for many countries and be able to give advice on how to analyze them. Also, some direct experience is, as always, useful. Watching a customs official decipher the schedules to assign the correct tariff instills some sense of humility and respect for government officials.

5. Recognizing FDI and the multinational firm as an efficient response to barriers is one of the core propositions of the modern theory of the multinational—see Buckley, 1987.

6. See Czinkota and Kotabe, 1993.

7. Personal interview with Mr. Isoda of Daiwa Securities, June 5, 1993.

8. Although the close company groupings in Japan called "keiretsus" have been acclaimed as a source of their overseas success and a barrier to foreign entry, they are now also a burden as the high yen means that inefficient partners can no longer be supported by other members—see Emmott, 1992.

9. See Elliott, 1995.

10. See Beeth, 1990.

11. Ibid. offers a brief but enlightening discussion of what makes for a great distributor.

12. The cultural distance and internationalization effects were first brought out by researchers at Uppsala in Sweden—see Johanson and Vahlne, 1977, 1992.

13. See "Ingvar Kamprad and IKEA," Harvard Business School case no. 390-132.

14. As their annual reports show, these are the typical steps taken by Japanese firms in autos, electronics, and heavy equipment.

15. The figure of 10 percent keeps coming up in many informal conversations with executives. It is of course not a hard and fast figure—overseas potential should always be considered—but it seems that at about 10 percent of revenues, overseas markets develop enough "critical mass" to demand more attention. The actual figures for most multinationals lie closer to 50 percent even though American MNCs tend to be somewhat lower because of the large home market.

16. This term was first proposed by Wind and Douglas, 1972.

17. This example is from Takeuchi and Porter, 1986.

18. See Johansson, 1982.

19. See Piercy, 1982.

20. See Piercy, 1982, and Lee, 1987.

21. See Hall, 1983.

22. This section draws on Keegan, 1969.

23. In Keegan's original formulation, the third strategy alternative involved product "adaptation" rather than product "localization" as used here. When adaptation is to actual *use* conditions, as is the case here, the term "localization" is preferable. "Adaptation" can then be reserved for the case of adapting to different customer *preferences*, a more complex question. "Localized" products can still be standardized, as most cars are, while adapted products are not standardized. This issue will be dealt with in more detail in Part Four, "Global Management."

SELECTED REFERENCES

"A Success Story for U.S. PC Firms," *Asahi Evening News*, July 6, 1994, p. 7.

Ayal, I., and J. Zif. "Market Expansion Strategies in Multinational Marketing," *Journal of Marketing* 43, (Spring 1979) pp. 84–94.

Beeth, Gunnar. "Distributors—Finding and Keeping the Good Ones." In Thorelli and Cavusgil, 1990, pp.487–94.

Buckley, Peter J. *The Theory of the Multinational Enterprise*. Studia Oeconomiae Negotiorum 26. Uppsala, Sweden: Acta Universitatis Upsaliensis, 1987.

Contractor, Farouk, and Peter Lorange, eds. *Cooperative Strategies in International Business*. Lexington, MA: Lexington Books, 1988.

Czinkota, Michael R. and Jon Woronoff. *Unlocking Japan's Markets*. Chicago: Probus, 1991.

Czinkota, Michael R., and Masaaki Kotabe. *The Japanese Distribution System*, Chicago: Probus, 1993.

Eli, Max. *Japan, Inc: Global Strategies of Japanese Trading Corporations*. Chicago: Probus, 1991.

Elliott, Stuart. "At Coke, a Shift to Many Voices." *New York Times*, January 20, 1995, pp. D1, D6.

Emmott, Bill. *Japan's Global Reach*. London: Century, 1992.

Hall, R. Duane. *International Trade Operations*. Jersey City: Unz and Co., 1983.

Hanssens, D. M., and J. K. Johansson. "Synergy or Rivalry? The Japanese Automobile Companies' Export Expansion." *Journal of International Business Studies*, Spring 1990, pp. 34–45.

Johanson, J., and J. E. Vahlne. "The Internationalization Process of the Firm—A Model of Knowledge Development and Increasing Foreign Market Commitments." *Journal of International Business Studies*, Spring–Summer 1977, pp. 23–32.

_____, and _____. "The Internationalization Paradigm: A Review and Assessment." *International Marketing Review*, 1992.

Johansson, J. K. "A Note on the Managerial Relevance of Interdependence." *Journal of International Business Studies*, Winter 1982, pp. 143–45.

Keegan, Warren J. "Multinational Product Planning: Strategic Alternatives." *Journal of Marketing*, January 1969, pp. 58–62.

Lee, Chong Suk. *Export Market Expansion Strategies and Export Performance: A Study of High Technology Manufacturing Firms*. Doctoral dissertation, University of Washington, 1987.

Piercy, Nigel. "Export Strategy: Concentration on Key Markets vs. Market Spreading." *Journal of International Marketing* 1, no.1 (1982) pp. 56–67.

Porter, Michael. *The Competitive Advantage of Nations*. New York: Free Press, 1990.

Root, Franklin R. *Entry Strategies for International Markets*. Rev.ed. New York: D. C. Heath, 1987.

Takeuchi, Hirotaka, and Michael E. Porter. "Three Roles of International Marketing in Global Strategy." In Porter, Michael E., ed. *Competition in Global Industries*. Cambridge, MA: Harvard Business School Press, 1986.

Thorelli, H. B. and S. Tamer Cavusgil, eds. *International Marketing Strategy*, 3d ed. New York: Pergamon, 1990.

Vernon, Raymond. "International Investment and International Trade in the Product Cycle." *Quarterly Journal of Economics*, May 1966.

Wind, Jerry, and Susan Douglas. "International Market Segmentation." *European Journal of Marketing* 6, no.1 (1972).

Licensing, Strategic Alliances, FDI

"Can't we be friends?"

After studying this chapter, you should understand the following global marketing issues:

1. The marketer plays fundamentally different roles when nonexporting modes of entry are used.

2. Since licensing and strategic alliances involve transfer of know-how, the marketer needs good interpersonal skills to deal effectively with partners in foreign countries (who may be competitors in some product markets).

3. Regardless of the product mode of entry, the firm can exercise control of the marketing effort via a wholly owned sales subsidiary.

4. The optimal mode of entry is to first find a way over entry barriers and then make trade-offs between strategic posture and the product/market situation.

EXPORTING might be the mode of entry into foreign markets that most closely resembles market expansion at home. But it is only one mode of entry, and because of transportation costs, tariffs, and other entry barriers, companies find it necessary to contemplate using other modes of entry involving *technology transfer and know-how sharing*, in which the FSAs are sold unbundled, not simply embodied in the final product. These modes are licensing, strategic alliances, and FDI (foreign direct investment) in wholly owned manufacturing subsidiaries. The global marketer needs to understand how these modes operate and how the deconstruction of the value chain affects the marketing effort. In licensing and strategic alliances there may be no need—or no role—for local presence of marketers from the company, as the partner becomes responsible for the local effort. By contrast, FDI in a manufacturing plant might lead to a marketing effort not only in the country itself but throughout a whole trade region.

Firms Partner Up to Crack Telecommunications Market

Once upon a time, "telecommunications" meant local and long-distance phone service provided by monopolies. Today, not only are there many more ways to communicate electronically, but telephone systems are opening up to competition. Old and new firms are partnering to gain a share of foreign markets.

Despite the recent problems with the peso, an important battleground is Mexico, where existing service is notoriously bad and the long-distance market is valued at $4 billion. Mexico's telephone monopoly, Teléfonos de Mexico, is scheduled to end on January 1, 1997, and the Mexican government is granting licenses to organizations that want to compete for a share of the market. To receive a license, an organization must prepare five-year plans for investment, marketing, and finance.

The first company to receive a license was a joint venture between MCI Communications (a U.S. company) and Grupo Financiero Banamex-Accival (Mexico's biggest financial group), and this venture is the first in line to negotiate with Teléfonos de Mexico and to start constructing a national network. With the effort expected to cost $600 million over three years, the involvement of a financial services partner in the venture makes business sense, while MCI will contribute its technical and marketing expertise. MCI's chairman, Bert C. Roberts, Jr., is undaunted by the current difficulties plaguing the Mexican economy. He observes that organizations and individuals try to cut their expenses during a recession and that MCI's marketing strategy is generally to "[capitalize] on a situation like this."

As shown with the MCI-Banamex deal, joint ventures are the norm for entering the high-stakes telecommunications marketplace. Other joint ventures seeking to operate in Mexico include one between GTE and Grupo Financiero Bancomer (Mexico's second-largest financial group), and another between AT&T and the Mexican Grupo Alfa conglomerate.

And, even bigger expansion plans are possible. Of the four largest telecommunications markets, only two are still monopolies: France and Germany. The U.S. government has been applying pressure on these governments to open up their telecommunications markets.

In the meantime, U.S. firms are not remaining idle; they are already building partnerships. France Télécom and Deutsche Telekom have invested in U.S.–based Sprint to create a new venture, which is subject to government approval. AT&T has joined alliances with other European carriers and is also considering offering service directly to French and German customers by purchasing capacity on the lines owned by their national utilities.

Sources: Anthony DePalma, "MCI Wins Mexican Long-Distance License," *New York Times*, September 7, 1995, p. D5; Anthony DePalma, "Telmex Gains in Attempt to Buy Cable-System Stake," *New York Times*, June 22, 1995, p. D6; "Dutch-Swiss Team Wins Czech Phone Bid," *New York Times*, June 29, 1995, p. D7; Mark Landler, "Can U.S. Companies Even Get a Bonjour?" *New York Times*, October 21, 1995, pp. D1, D7; Elizabeth Malkin, "Mexico: He Just Might Lock You in Until You Do a Deal," February 26, 1996, p. 54.

INTRODUCTION

Exporting no doubt introduced a new set of activities for the beginning global marketer. But complicated as exporting is to manage in a practical sense because of the number of tasks and the various middlemen involved, conceptually it is a natural extension of traditional market expansion. This is not the case for the alternative modes of entry. Licensing, alliances, and FDI all involve management skills and concepts different from the standard marketing repertoire. This chapter will cover the basic new points.

Licensing used to have a bad name as an entry mode. As we saw in Chapter 2, licensing runs the risk of *dissipation*, that is, a firm's know-how will easily leak to its competitors. The oft-told stories about American companies like RCA, Honeywell, and GE selling technology licenses cheap to the Japanese after World War Two only to witness the later incursions of Japanese companies into Western markets have helped put licensing in a bad light. In recent years, however, as technology sharing between competitors has become commonplace, licensing is no longer the black sheep. Also, as more countries accept the new World Trade Organization (WTO) intellectual property regime, enforcing patent protection is becoming easier. Technological leaks can be prevented more effectively now that international law is enforceable—and anyway technological change is often so fast that licenses lose their value before the clones and copies appear.

Still, many firms prefer to invest in wholly owned manufacturing subsidiaries abroad rather than run the risk of dissipating their firm-specific advantages and not getting sufficient upfront compensation for the use of their patented know-how. In fact, the standard definition of a *multinational* corporation is not simply a company that sells its products in many markets but one that also has several manufacturing and assembly plants operating abroad.

The chapter starts with a brief history of the growth of multinationals from various countries. An understanding of the larger global forces helps explain how technology transfer and trade in know-how, rather than products, arise in emerging and protected economies. We discuss the three nonexporting modes of entry: licensing (including franchising), strategic alliances, and manufacturing subsidiaries. The chapter ends with a sketch of the optimal entry mode under different assumptions of company strategic objectives and market maturity.

HISTORICAL BACKGROUND

Multinational companies are so commonplace it is sometimes difficult to remember they were not always so omnipresent. The historical background behind the emergence of these companies with their presence in many if not most of the major countries in the world is interesting for the light it throws on the current trend toward global strategies.[1]

Even before World War II, Western companies had established a presence in many foreign countries. Singer, the American sewing machine company, built one of the most prominent buildings in prewar Leningrad as its Russian headquarters. Philips, the Dutch electronics company, was strong in Southeast Asia, part of which was known as the Dutch East Indies. Bayersdorf, the German maker of the global skin cream Nivea, had established many country subsidiaries, which became independent companies after the German capitulation. Multinational business is not only a post–World War II phenomenon, but was common much earlier.

After the end of World War II, companies in the victorious countries were intent on restoring prewar operations abroad. But compared to the Americans, the Europeans were weak—the war had been largely fought on their territory. Thus after the war, European companies were content mainly to leave their far-flung operations to fend for themselves. By contrast, the Americans insisted much more on strong central control—something made much more feasible by advances in communication technology and management techniques honed by the war effort. Thus after World War II, the American multinational companies (MNCs) became a dominant force in the global markets. Their style was based on wholly owned subsidiaries run by expatriates from the United States, with products adapted and manufactured for local markets, but with strong financial control from headquarters.

The Europeans necessarily took a different route. Foreign subsidiaries were given wide latitude in decision making and product selection and were used mainly to market products in their immediate market area. Control and coordination mechanisms from headquarters were weak, and subsidiaries often acted as independent companies. While the Americans insisted on multinational consistency in some key areas such as brand names, use of technology, and resource allocation criteria, European MNCs ran their subsidiaries more loosely, and their home country operations centered on the European markets. As a consequence, even today there are many brand names well-known in Europe but without global reach—while many of the best-known brand names in the world are American.

In the mid-1960s, Japanese exporters started appearing in Western markets, and a new era had begun. While initially their attacks on American and European markets were easily countered by the domestic firms, the persistence and continual adaptation by the Japanese companies gradually began taking effect. The market penetration efforts were orchestrated out of Japan, with high productivity, high quality, and strong service making it possible to offer good products at low prices. In contrast to the Europeans and the Americans, the Japanese effort capitalized on advances in transportation and telecommunications to serve the global markets via exports only. Coupled with open markets in the West, this meant that there was limited need to invest in production overseas. The Japanese could establish global brand names, standardize products of high quality, and provide effective after-sales service with only sales subsidiaries in the market countries. This kind of export-led global expansion is today followed by companies from other emerging countries in Asia and elsewhere.

Today, the Japanese may be able to operate with this model no longer. Protectionist sentiment, trade barriers, and a high yen are forcing them to invest in production overseas. But the Japanese are still intent on maintaining the fundamentals that made them such a strong force in the first place, and indications are so far that they are succeeding—at least in making foreign workers perform to exacting Japanese standards.

Today, when the potential lies in global operations, the Europeans find themselves straddled with headstrong local managers in semi-independent subsidiaries. The Americans are trying to rein in their local subsidiaries in order to capture global synergies in marketing and production without sacrificing motivation. The Japanese are carefully investing in new production locations, trying to maintain their worker base at home but still avoid trade barriers. All these companies are aware of the need to "globalize" their strategies—but the idea of the best way to do this differs drastically among them. Their historical expansion paths have set the parameters for their globalization efforts, the limits as well as the possibilities. We will come back to this issue repeatedly in Part Four, "Global Management."

LICENSING

Licensing refers to the offering of a firm's know-how or other intangible asset to a foreign company for a fee, royalty, and/or other type of payment. Its advantage over exporting is its avoidance of tariffs and other levies that might be assessed against an imported product. For the new exporter, it also has the advantages that the need for market research and knowledge is reduced and that, as opposed to the use of a distributor, it is often possible to induce the licensee to support the product strongly in the market. This is because from licensing, the firm in the host country gets specific know-how from the licensing firm and thus is able to develop some skills on its own; it does not just resell the product as the distributor does. Licensing is therefore a form of *technology transfer*—but this is also its greatest weakness for the licensor. Because the licensee gets access to certain firm-specific knowledge, it will share in the competitive advantage of the licensor—and can then potentially use this knowledge in further applications other than the ones specifically stated in the licensing contract.

To avoid this *dissipation* of firm-specific advantages, the licensing firm needs to handle contract negotiations with considerable skill. Exhibit 6.1 shows some of the elements of the typical licensing contract. It is important, for example, to limit the geographical area within which the licensee might sell the product so as not to engender competition with the firm's own sales in other countries (see box, "How Not to Do It"). It is also important to make sure what the conditions for terminating the contract are, what the time limit is, and how the specific know-how is to be used. Contracts identify the level and kind of marketing support the licensee is supposed to generate and the appropriate steps to be taken should this support not be forthcoming. The licensor, for his part, pledges his supply of the requisite transfer of knowledge, including managerial and technical support, patents with or without trademark, or brand name transfer.

The royalty level and payment structure vary with different forms of licensing. **Straight licensing** of a certain technology in processing, for example, tends to bring **royalties** of 5 percent of gross revenues, sometimes more (the Disney World Corporation receives 7 percent from its Japanese licensee), sometimes less. Occasionally there are also payments in the form of technical assistance *fees* and the possibility of *lump-sum royalties*, paid out only intermittently. Another attractive alternative is to negotiate for an equity option in the licensee's firm, that can be exercised when further in-depth penetration into the country market is desirable.

Franchising

Special interest has arisen in recent years in two types of licensing modes. One is franchising, the other is turnkey projects. They both offer certain advantages and disadvantages over straight licensing. *Franchising* has become particularly popular because it allows a much greater degree of control over the marketing efforts in the foreign country.

....

EXHIBIT 6.1   Elements of a Licensing Contract

Technology package	*Compensation*
Definition/description of the licensed industrial property (patents, trademarks, know-how)	Currency of payment
	Responsibilities for payment of local taxes
	Disclosure fee
Know-how to be supplied and its method of transfer	Running royalties
	Minimum royalties
Supply of raw materials, equipment, and intermediate goods	Lump-sum royalties
	Technical assistance fees
Use conditions	Sales to and/or purchases from licensee
Field of use of licensed technology	Fees for additional new products
Territorial rights for manufacture and sale	Grantback of product improvements by licensee
Sublicensing rights	Other compensation
Safeguarding trade secrets	*Other provisions*
Responsibility for defense/infringement action on patents and trademarks	Contract law to be followed
Exclusion of competitive products	Duration and renewal of contract
Exclusion of competitive technology	Cancellation/termination provisions
Maintenance of product standards	Procedures for the settlement of disputes
Performance requirements	Responsibility for government approval of the license agreement
Rights of licensee to new products and technology	
Reporting requirements	
Auditing/inspection rights of licensor	
Reporting requirements of licensee	

Source: Adapted from Hall, 1983, pp. 67–68.

The basic "product" sold by the franchisor is a well-recognized brand name, nurtured carefully through global advertising and promotion, including sponsorship of various events. The franchisor also provides a wide range of market support services to the franchisee, in particular local advertising to sustain the brand name, of which the franchisee usually will pay a portion. Training manuals for employees, help with product lines and production scheduling, accounting manuals, and occasional assistance with financing are some of the services provided to the franchisee. In return, the local franchisee raises the necessary capital and manages the franchise, paying an initial fee and a royalty percentage on total sales to the franchisor.

In franchising, product lines and customer service are standardized, two important features from a marketing perspective. Although cultural differences might require adaptation—in Europe, McDonald's serves beer, and in Asia, rice is added to the menu—the franchising concept works precisely because of standardization of product and service. Products should be predictably the same ("too good" can be as dangerous as "too bad" since customers rely on "what to

Getting the Picture

How Not to Do It

A NEOPHYTE American firm decided to avoid managerial and research expense to explore foreign markets and to simply license the manufacturing and sales of their product to a U.K. firm. The English firm was granted the right to sublicense the process know-how to other parts of the world. After a few years the foreign markets for the company's product increased greatly in potential, but the U.S. company gained only a small share of the increase revenues. It had already "sold" those markets to the English company and could only watch as that company's sales took off.

Adapted from M. L. Mace, "The President and International Operations", *Harvard Business Review*, November–December 1966, p.76.

expect"). The same for service—"personal service" in franchising should perhaps be called "impersonal service," since even the smiles are obligatory.

One drawback of franchising is the need for careful and continuous quality control. If the franchisor does not perform, the company might have to terminate the contract. When the McDonald's restaurant on Champs Elysées in Paris gave mediocre service in unclean premises, the McDonald's corporation stepped in and took over. Such close supervision of the various aspects of far-flung operations requires well-developed global management systems and labor-intensive monitoring. Because of the managerial skills required, international franchising has become successful largely among those businesses having long experience with franchising at home before venturing globally. Examples include the successful American fast-food purveyors, McDonald's and Kentucky Fried Chicken, the British-based Body Shop, and Italy's Benetton. Because franchising is a common mode of global expansion in services, it will be discussed in more detail in Chapter 12, "Global Products and Services."

Turnkey Projects

A **turnkey** project is the production of a complete manufacturing plant, possibly including the actual operation of the plant. It often involves many different subcontractors in addition to the main contractor for the project and the host government often signs as one of the parties on the buying side. As such, it suffers from the risk of political instability and change of regime. For the smaller or newer company, it is usually a project too big and risky to undertake. There are, on the other hand, many firms for which the first venture abroad takes the form of subcontracting participation in this type of project. More will be said about turnkey projects in Chapter 13, "Global Pricing."

Original Equipment Manufacturing (OEM)

In terms of the theory of the multinational, **OEM** usually falls in the "exporting" subcategory, involving shipments of components from home to overseas. From a marketing viewpoint, however, it fits better with licensing and strategic alliances since the company brand name is suppressed, usually not the case in exporting. OEM is like selling a generic brand.

In OEM, a company enters a foreign market by selling its unbranded product or component to another company in the market country. This company then markets the final product under its own brand name. For the supplier firm, there is little or no expense in marketing its product overseas, and the buyer gets a product ready to use and to market. The supplier has to give up its own effort to market the product overseas, but often tries to change its strategy later if the overseas market for its product is strong.

Some examples will illustrate the principles. Canon provides the cartridges for Hewlett-Packard's very successful laser printers and also for Kodak's copiers, both OEM arrangements. After several years of successful market development, Canon now also markets its own copiers with success. Esco, an Oregon-based heavy machinery firm, supplies parts OEM to Mitsubishi Heavy Industries, to be distributed under Mitsubishi's name as spare parts in Komatsu and Caterpillar earth-movers.

The large Korean consumer goods manufacturers such as Samsung and Lucky-Goldstar have opted for the OEM entry mode in the U.S. market. By selling unbranded color television sets, microwaves, and VCRs to resellers such as Sears, Amana, and Emerson, they have avoided the need to spend money on establishing a brand image in the market. At the same time, however, they have given up the chance to establish their own recognizable identity in the way the Japanese have done. Opting for a Canon-like approach, the Korean automaker Hyundai decided to establish its own dealer and service network in the States. The pros and cons of the two approaches are still hotly debated among observers, but so far the Hyundai investment has been successful.

STRATEGIC ALLIANCES

An international *strategic alliance* (SA) is typically a collaborative arrangement between firms, sometimes competitors, across borders. The joint venture is today often viewed as an equity-based SA, while new forms of alliances involve nonequity-based collaboration (partnerships, agreements to share, contractual participation in projects).[2]

SAs are a new type of entry mode increasingly prevalent in the last decade. Because they often represent collaboration between potential competitors, one effect has been to weaken the tie between ownership advantages and company control. Strategic alliances are based on the sharing of vital information, assets, and technology between the partners, even though they might in the process lose their proprietary know-how. Thus, alliances tend to be akin to licensing agreements, with the exception that the royalty and fee payments to one partner are replaced by active participation in the alliance by both partners.

The Rationale for Nonequity SAs

Since nonequity strategic alliances, especially between competitors, are a relatively new form of entry mode, we explain why they have emerged now.

The economic gains from strategic alliances are usually quite tangible. A company accesses technology it otherwise would not get. Markets are reached without a long buildup of relationships in channels. Efficient manufacturing is made possible without investment in a new plant, and so on.

However, given the risks of losing control of the firm's know-how, one wonders why alternative organizational forms—joint ventures, wholly owned subsidiaries, licensing, or mergers, for example—have proven insufficient. The reasons quoted by companies include the sheer size of the financial investments required, the speed with which market presence can be established in SAs, and the lessened risk exposure.[3]

Two other factors play a role as well. One is the crumbling of the value of control itself. As we saw above, leading know-how is being diffused faster than ever, products and manufacturing processes embodying new technology are now readily copied through widespread reverse engineering and competitive benchmarking. Companies that have presence in most leading markets will have quick access to most new technologies. Even though patents can be policed across borders, the speed with which technology ages makes leakage less of a problem.[4]

A second factor is the new urgency about competing in several country markets at once. Having a presence in leading markets is often necessary to observe customers, monitor competitors, and to disturb competitors' sources of cash. Alliances allow firms to expand the use of existing managerial resources.[5]

Hence, nonequity SAs represent more of an expansion of a company's repertoire than the replacement of existing forms of business venture. The company can now do things it could not do before. SAs allow two companies to undertake missions impossible for the individual firm to undertake. Strategic alliances constitute an efficient economic response to changed conditions.

Distribution Alliances

Since their marketing implications differ considerably, we will distinguish between three types of nonequity alliances: distribution, manufacturing, and research and development (R&D).

An early and still common form of SA is the shared distribution network. The tie-up between Chrysler and Mitsubishi Motors to distribute cars in the United States is one example. So are Nissan's agreement to sell Volkswagens in Japan, the licensing of Molson's of Canada to brew and sell Kirin beer in North America, and the tie-up between SAS, KLM, Austrian Air, and Swiss Air to share routes in European air corridors.

These types of arrangements are not new. In the traditional textbooks they fall under "piggybacking," "consortium marketing," and licensing. Their strategic rationale usually lies in improved capacity load and wider product line for one partner and in inexpensive and quick access to a market for the other. Assets are complementary, and the partners can focus on what they do best.

One drawback of these SAs is that over time the arrangement can limit growth for the partners. The partner with the established distribution network

Deutsche BA is an example of one of the many alliances in the airline industry. In 1992 British Airways increased its presence in the German market by buying 49% of a local airline, renaming it Deutsche British Airways.

Raphael Gaillarde/Gamma-Liaison.

may want to expand its product line, competing with the other partner's products. It may want to expand into other markets, shift resources from the existing markets, and thus give less support to distribution than the other partner would find acceptable. Growth will be constrained.

As for the other partner, the arrangement hinders its learning more about the market and how to market the product in the foreign country and thus creates an obstacle for further inroads. If this partner decides to develop greater penetration in the market, adding products to the line and increasing marketing support, it might be competing with the first partner's products, and also tax the capacity limitations of the existing channel network. Mitsubishi's lackluster performance in the U.S. auto market is partly due to the difficulty of working through Chrysler's dealer network and the late creation of an independent dealer network. Its growth has been stymied.

Because of such limits to growth, this type of SA does not last long when market expansion is an important goal of a partner.[6] The association can be convenient and economical, however, and when there is less pressure to grow, the alliance is justified.

Manufacturing Alliances

Another early form of strategic alliance is shared manufacturing. In Japan, Matsushita has agreed to manufacture IBM PCs, using up excess capacity. Volvo and Renault are sharing certain body parts and components, even though their full-fledged merger was scrapped. Saab engines are now made by GM Europe in its Opel factories (an alliance emerging from GM's purchase of 50 percent of Saab stock).

It is not always easy to distinguish these arrangements from OEM and similar agreements. The difference is that OEM arrangements are simple contracts for selling unbranded components to another manufacturer. Potentially they sell the components to many customers. By contrast, the SAs illustrated here involve the brands of both manufacturers with existing capabilities in the manufacturing of the parts; the subcontracting is a special arrangement for both partners.

These alliances are complementary more in economics than in technology. The arrangement is convenient, saves money, and is similar to a distribution agreement. The partners fill unused capacity and save money and time by not having to invest in new plant and equipment. From a marketing viewpoint, the alliance is sometimes a drawback since the sales organization has to deal with two principals in charge of production. It is harder to get the alliance to listen to customer feedback.

As in the case of distribution tie-ups, these SAs are likely to put a constraint on further growth. Limits to further expansion come from limited capacity, less learning from the partner, and difficulty in changing the product mix for further expansion. A change in growth objectives may spell the end of the arrangement.

R&D Alliances

SAs in R&D are different from those in distribution and manufacturing. In addition to providing favorable economics, speed of access, and managerial resources, R&D alliances are intended to solve critical survival questions for the firm.[7] R&D tie-ups with competitors are a means of keeping pace while making sure that competitors work toward the same technological standards. In essence, the amount of funding involved in R&D leads the company to hedge its bets and try to make sure the direction of research is the same throughout the industry. The firms have confidence in their own implementation of the new technological ideas, and marketing can be the competitive edge when technology can no longer be.

This is a striking departure from past practices, at least in the West. The R&D labs of the major companies provided the basis for their competitive edge, with supersecret research patented and policed for infringements and with full-fledged new discoveries emerging unannounced. Today, the companies are eager to announce the start of their research rather than its completion; they want competitors and customers to know what they are working on; and they listen attentively for news from competing firms. When differences in standards threaten to emerge, the firms gather eagerly under the auspices of the industry association to iron out differences. As one company introduces a new product based on a new technology, customers know that competitors will announce similar products within a few months. If a competitor misses a beat, it can spell disaster.[8]

Microsoft, the PC software giant, has always made a special effort to protect the integrity of its unique software. However, recently it has decided to share some technological developments with actual and potential competitors

The assembly line at the Suzuki-Maruti joint venture plant in India. The joint venture demanded by the Indian government was a necessary price for entry, but has now placed Suzuki in a favorable position as India is opening up.

Robert Nickelsberg/Gamma-Liaison.

in order to induce other software writers to use the Microsoft standard. Furthermore, it is now under pressure from several industry SAs, including one (Taligent) between Apple, IBM and Hewlett-Packard, and Microsoft has also found it necessary to license the new Java network software from Sun Microsystems.

Increasing R&D activity has been accompanied by a proliferation of new products in the markets, which in turn has increased competitive rivalry. To compete effectively companies have been forced to increase and speed up their R&D efforts even more or risk losing their technological competencies. Strategic alliances provide one way of doing this and alleviating the accompanying financial strain on the organizations.

In many markets the products have to embody the new technology even to be considered by buyers. While once a Saab car could tout the special advantages of an aerodynamic shape and front-wheel drive, now even anti-lock brakes, air bags, and 16-valve turbo engines are standard. It is this relentless emphasis on the most recent technology in new products that has raised the ante of global participation in so many industries and has led to the need for SAs in R&D. As we will see in Part Four, "Global Management," technology has changed the nature of marketing in many global markets.

Joint Ventures

Even though *joint ventures* (JVs) have undeniable strengths from a marketing viewpoint, many corporations have been reluctant to enter into JV agreements unless forced to by government regulations or pressure. The JV involves the transfer of capital, manpower, and usually some technology from the foreign

$\mathcal{G}$etting the
Picture

A Happy
Marriage

SOME "MARRIAGES" are happy. One managing director of a JV between a Swedish company and a firm in another industrialized country says: "We in the local firm wanted to enter this new product line and saw that the Swedish subsidiary was not doing so well in our country . . . . We offered the Swedes a ready and functioning sales organization and, in addition, a manufacturing unit that could produce the product about 30 percent cheaper . . . This is a happy marriage. We need each other equally."

Source: L. Otterbeck, "The Management of Joint Ventures," in Otterbeck, 1981, p. 283.

partner to an existing local firm, whose main contribution tends to be expertise and understanding of the local market.[9]

The transfer of technology is the main problem. Since the JV implies that equity is shared among the partners, there is a decided risk that the know-how (and thus the firm's specific advantage) will become diluted by the necessary sharing of information. The point is well illustrated by the protracted negotiations that preceded the GM-Toyota JV agreement in 1982 to produce a small car for the U.S. market. The U.S. Justice Department was reluctant to approve the agreement between two of the world's largest automakers on antitrust grounds. From Toyota's perspective there was little about car manufacturing or marketing to be gained from the venture, as compared to GM's potential gains and the company was reluctant to share its manufacturing know-how with a competitor. However, Toyota saw the agreement as defusing the concern about Japanese imports that threatened (and still does) to force U.S. lawmakers into a protectionist stand. Consequently, Toyota could be indifferent to the delays caused by the U.S. government. At least for some time, the political risks could be "managed" by Toyota in this manner.[10]

The key decision in JVs is the selection of a partner. Very few hard and fast rules apply here, apart from the obvious one of picking a partner who is willing and able to share company resources and skills and whose skills complement those of the partner. In general, the venture is best off when contract negotiations identify exactly what the mutual expectations are and where the limits on the responsibilities should be drawn. It is also common to specify procedures to be followed for a dissolution of the partnership. The contract guiding the formation of a JV has often been likened to a marriage contract and for good reason. (see box, "A Happy Marriage").

MANUFACTURING SUBSIDIARIES

Foreign direct investment **(FDI) in wholly owned manufacturing** subsidiaries is undertaken by the international firm for several reasons. The aims could be to acquire raw materials, to operate at lower manufacturing costs, to avoid tariff barriers and satisfy local content requirements, and/or to penetrate local markets.[11] The last rationale is of prime interest in the marketing context.

Manufacturing FDI has several advantages in market penetration. First, local production means price escalation caused by transport costs, customs duties fees, local turnover taxes, and so on can be nullified or drastically reduced. Availability of goods can usually be guaranteed to resellers, minimizing potential channel conflicts over allocation decisions and eliminating delays for ultimate buyers. Location of production in the market country may lead to more uniform quality, although in some cases the basis of initial reluctance to go to manufacturing abroad may well have been the risk of lowered quality.

The most striking marketing advantage of local production is usually the projection of an ability and willingness of the company to adapt products and services to the local customer requirements. Examples include U.S. automakers' production of cars for European markets and French ski manufacturer Rossignol's location of plants in the United States and Canada. In both cases there was a desire to be closer to major markets and to be able to anticipate and quickly adapt to major changes.

There are certain distinct disadvantages to FDI in manufacturing. The major one is the risk exposure that comes with a resource commitment on the scale usually required. Even joint ventures are not free from this commitment and risk since most agreements stipulate heavy costs for one partner's withdrawal. Also, since FDI generally means the company becomes a more or less full-fledged member of the local economic and social scene, the predecision information gathering and research evaluation process is heavy. Much of this research centers on assessing the "investment climate" in the foreign country, especially the political risk (see the "political risk" section of Chapter 4).

There is a potential problem in overseas manufacturing when country-of-origin effects are strong, that is, for products whose quality consumers tend to judge by the "made-in" label. In such cases, as the Toyota example shows, going abroad is not usually the preferred option (see box, "Taking the Plunge"). Research shows there can be a significant effect on product and brand evaluation from a shift in manufacturing location.[12] This can work to the disadvantage of the firm establishing production in a low-wage country where workers have lower skills. In some cases, as customers realize that what they intended to buy is actually manufactured in a developing country, they reject the product.[13]

The solution adopted by companies is to shift lower-skill operations overseas, keeping more advanced operations at home. Although companies are criticized for this strategy, it is often justified not only because it protects product quality and established brand equity, but also because it is a natural step in the gradual upgrading of labor skills in the low-wage countries. Finally, companies with global brands strive very hard to ensure that quality standards are met, and research suggests that a strong brand image can override any negative country-of-origin effects.[14]

Getting the Picture

Taking the Plunge

"WITH OUR FLEET of specially built ships we would rather build the cars here in Japan and export them to the U.S. and Europe. There is no economic reason for us to invest in an assembly plant in those countries. Now, of course, with the European trade barriers and the U.S. protectionist voices becoming louder, we may have to make some local investment and meet the local content requirements. But how will our customers react if we cannot maintain our quality level? So, we decided to start with the joint venture with GM in Fremont to see whether we could manage the work force in the U.S. and satisfy our quality conscious customers. Finally, I think we have succeeded."

Source: Toyota spokesman in 1986 before Toyota started assembly plants in Derbyshire, England, and in Kentucky.

Financial Analysis

The economic analysis of the investment project usually takes the form of a discounted cash flow analysis. There is no need to go into depth here concerning this application of a well-known method. The standard approach of projecting streams of costs and revenues over the planning horizon (usually the payback period or the lifespan of the commitment) is directly applicable, and despite the complications involved in forecasting these series in a foreign country, the principles stay the same. The forecasting techniques discussed in Chapter 4 are directly relevant here.

On the revenue side, the possibility of using the proposed manufacturing location for exports to third (and, of course, home) countries needs to be considered. In many cases the investment calculation is complicated because the host country market is only one potential area where sales might go. Also, the forecasting of cost streams should take into account the possibility of importing subassemblies from other plant locations rather than manufacturing all components from scratch. The in-depth analysis of all these factors is beyond the scope of a marketing text.

Where political risk is low enough for the FDI project to get off the ground, it is still customary to incorporate a risk premium into the hurdle rate. Since the political risk tends to vary with regime shifts, new elections, and so forth, the risk premium needs to be adjusted over time and as new capital infusions are considered. In the discounted cash flow computations, adjustments of the discount figure should be made, generally raising the figure for each successive year.

Acquisitions

Rather than establish the wholly owned subsidiary from scratch (a **greenfield** investment), the multinational company can consider the **acquisition** of an existing company. The advantage lies in the speed of penetration: An existing company will already have a product line to be exploited, the distribution network and dealers need not be developed from scratch, and the company can simply get on with marketing its new product(s) in conjunction with the existing line. German Siemen's purchase of compatriot Nixdorf to improve penetration in the European minicomputer market is a case in point. Another example is the purchase of American Borden by Swiss Nestlé in order to expand in the U.S. dairy food market.

The disadvantages of acquisition are many, however. In a narrow sense, the existing product line and the new products to be introduced might not be compatible, and prunings and adjustments that have to be made require reeducating the sales force and distribution channels. In general, it is not so easy to find a company to acquire that fits the purposes of entry very well. In many countries the acquisition of a domestic company by a foreign firm is not looked upon favorably by the government, employees, and other groups. From a marketing viewpoint the particular advantage of acquisition lies in the market acceptance of the company's products, gaining sales as a spillover from goodwill toward the acquired company's lines. But this benefit can be gained from a joint venture, and many of the political drawbacks of acquisitions are eliminated with a joint venture.

ENTRY MODES AND MARKETING CONTROL

The effect of entry mode on the degree to which the firm can exercise control over its local marketing effort is not simple and direct. It is important to distinguish between the question of where and by whom the product or service is produced (which is the main concern of the preceding discussion on mode of entry) and the way the marketing is managed.

It is useful to separate three alternative ways of organizing the local marketing effort. They are, in increasing order of control: (1) independent agents and distributors; (2) alliance with a local marketing partner; and (3) a wholly owned sales subsidiary.

There is a rough correspondence between the modes of entry and the means of organizing the marketing. As we saw in Chapter 5, exporting typically involves independent agents and distributors. As we saw in the preceding discussion, the local partner in a strategic alliance is often also in charge of local marketing. FDI in manufacturing often means the creation of a wholly owned subsidiary that may also handle the local marketing.

But in practice, the picture is not so simple. For example, exporting is often undertaken from a home country plant to a wholly owned sales subsidiary abroad. This is a common organization when the local market is large and the company has had some success in the market, as in the automobile industry. European and Japanese cars are generally shipped to the U.S. sales subsidiary of the automaker. When FDI in assembly and manufacturing is undertaken, such as Nissan in Tennessee, the companies create a freestanding manufacturing subsidiary, which sells and ships its cars to the sales subsidiary.

In the case of sales subsidiaries handling the marketing, the logistics and the distribution may still be handled by independent carriers and distributors.

The sales subsidiary is in charge of promotion, including advertising, pricing, market research, and the management of the channels of distribution.

It is actually quite common to find real-world cases in which the preferred marketing control mode is different from the product entry mode. Exhibit 6.2 shows some of these cases.

The example of Absolut Vodka (from Sweden) sold in the United States represents an instance of pure exporting, with Seagrams functioning as the independent agent with territorial marketing control in the United States. A Toshiba-EMI joint venture in Japan markets EMI's music recordings in Japan, many localized by translations of covers into the Japanese language. Volvo cars exported to the United States are marketed by the company's U.S. subsidiary located outside of Chicago.

Licensing usually means less control over the marketing effort, as in the case of Disneyland in Chiba outside Tokyo. The Japanese marketing effort is controlled by the independent Japanese licensee. In the case of EuroDisney, in which Disney took a joint venture stake in the operation, the marketing effort is basically under the control of the local European partners. Microsoft's early entry into Japan was via ASCII, an independent licensee (although disagreements over the local marketing strategy later forced Microsoft to establish its own Japanese subsidiary which markets the software in Japan). And Nike, the athletic shoe-maker, has licensed manufacturing in Asia, but controls the marketing.

To enter via a strategic alliance and then allow the marketing to be done independently is unusual, since the partner is a natural marketing agent. However, some new joint ventures in China seem to be planned according to this model. For example, in autos the marketing may have to be controlled by the Chinese government. On the other hand, for other products, with Western

....

EXHIBIT 6.2   Product Entry and Marketing Control Can Be Different

| | Marketing control | | |
Mode of entry	Independent agent	Joint with alliance partner	Own sales subsidiary
Exporting	Absolut vodka in the U.S.	Toshiba EMI in Japan	Volvo in the U.S.
Licensing	Disney in Japan	Microsoft in Japan (initially)	Nike in Asia
Strategic alliance	Autos in China	Eurodisney	Black and Decker in China
FDI	Goldstar in the U.S.	Mitsubishi Motors in the U.S.	P&G in the E.U.

manufacturers establishing plants in joint ventures with Chinese government affiliated manufacturers, the marketing is managed separately by Western sales subsidiaries. An example is American Black & Decker, maker of power tools, which has its own marketing subsidiary in China.

Entering via FDI in manufacturing and then allowing independent agents to do the marketing can be illustrated through an OEM agreement. Lucky-Goldstar, a Korean company, has invested in a television plant in Arkansas, which builds television sets for the Sears private label. The lack of control over marketing is a drawback, and in the long run most companies would like to take over the marketing and establish their own brand name as Goldstar is now doing.

Mitsubishi Motors now manufactures cars in Illinois that are marketed through its joint venture with Chrysler (although the arrangement is being gradually phased out as Mitsubishi establishes a parallel dealer network to gain more control over the marketing). The combination of wholly owned manufacturing plants and sales subsidiaries is common. Procter & Gamble operates several plants in Europe, with products marketed through its European sales subsidiaries, of which the German is the largest.

Two major lessons from these various cases should be emphasized.

1. Local marketing control often can be effectively exercised via a sales subsidiary, regardless of the entry mode of the product.

2. Even with a sales subsidiary, however, product entry mode is not irrelevant. For example, reliable and timely supplies to the local market cannot be ensured through exporting when protectionist pressures mount or when transportation is long and hazardous. Licensees may not perform as agreed, and partners in alliances may or may not prove to be good partners when conditions change.

In the end, choosing the best entry mode depends not only on marketing factors, but also on the business strategy as a whole, including the strategic objectives of the involvement in the foreign market. The last section will deal with this issue directly.

OPTIMAL ENTRY STRATEGY

Which mode of entry into the foreign market should be chosen? Can an optimal entry strategy be found?

With all the factors internal and external to the firm to be taken into account, it's impossible to give a single answer to this question. A mode that offers protection from political risk (such as licensing) may offer little help with control of product quality. A mode that maximizes control over company-specific advantages (such as FDI in manufacturing) involves the maximum political risk, and so on.

One approach is to use the mode of entry which minimizes **transaction costs.** As we saw in Chapter 2, the costs involved in entering a foreign market can be viewed as "market-making" investments. Minimizing such costs means choosing a mode of entry which leverages a firm's FSAs abroad at least cost. If the firm needs to invest in after-sales service abroad in order to generate sales (as is the case with autos, for example), the best mode might require investment in a subsidiary. This means transaction costs will be high, and the firm needs to be sure that the market potential is great. To lower costs and risk exposure, but also weaken the market presence, the company may enter through an alliance with an existing dealer network, as Volkswagen did with Nissan in Japan.[15]

Practical Considerations

It is clear from the transaction cost approach that different conditions require different entry modes. These conditions are constraints and objectives of the firm and the conditions in the market country, in particular the barriers to entry. Entry barriers will be dealt with in more detail below. Some practical considerations need to be discussed first.

For the resource-poor firm, FDI is usually out of the question. The financial requirements can't be met. This leaves exports, licensing, and alliances, all three of which require some start-up work. The small firm with a patentable or else protectable firm-specific advantage might well go into licensing. The advantage is the relatively low involvement necessary once the licensing contract has been negotiated. The biggest headache tends to be the identification of good licensees abroad and the skill and manpower required to guide the negotiations to a successful contract resolution, one that does not preclude future changes in levels of involvement. The licensing option has the distinct advantage over exports in that there is little political risk—future changes in the country's trade policies, for example, can largely be ignored.

For the company that wants to enter incrementally and keep future options open, the exporting mode is preferable at the entry stage. The contracts signed with distributors can usually be made less restrictive in regard to the future than licensing agreements. As experience with the market accumulates, sales branches are established and control is gradually assumed over the marketing effort. The OEM path should be followed with caution since then it is difficult to build up expertise, and the partner may be a direct competitor.

When the market abroad needs to be penetrated quickly, either because competitive entry is imminent and/or because technological change is very rapid, a distribution or manufacturing alliance, such as a joint venture, is often the best mode of entry. Licensing is a weak solution, in that it does not ensure control over the local marketing effort, and so it is likely to be preferred only when the company can't identify a strong alliance partner. Exporting and the establishment of a wholly owned subsidiary both have the disadvantage that it takes time to develop the presence in the market and the channels of distribution necessary for strong and quick penetration.

Acquisition and joint venture have the advantage in common with licensing that an existing network can be used. Because the commitment is so great, however, it becomes very important to determine if quick penetration means

WHEN KIKKOMAN, the top Japanese soy sauce producer, decided to enter the U.S. market, no one in the company was prepared for the size of advertising expenditures required for penetration. Entering cautiously, the nationwide roll-out from the beachhead in San Francisco gradually pushed through the United States during a 13-year period. But the necessary education of new customers entailed TV advertising, making the entry expensive. Headquarters in Japan had to support their subsidiary's advertising budget for 20 years, until sales in the United States were finally great enough to generate sufficient advertising dollars. The dollar advertising budget is small relative to U.S. standards for packaged goods—about 9 percent of sales. But compared to Japan, where sales of $350 million are generated by a $5 million budget, the advertising/sales ratio is stunningly high for the home country executives.

Source: Thorelli & Cavusgil, 1990.

the presence in the foreign market will be short run. When quick penetration is necessary and the market might be short run (as for fads), the preferred mode of entry tends to be indirect export via established facilitators such as trading companies or export management companies.

Another practical consideration is the degree to which a *massive marketing* approach is needed. In markets such as North America it is usually quite difficult to enter without considerable resources available for the marketing effort. Most foreign companies enter some smaller geographical segment of the United States (such as the East Coast approach favored by the Europeans), but even with such a limited focus, the intensity of competition demands marketing support as the Kikkoman example shows (see box).

Strong competition favors FDI or an alliance with a strong partner, such as the Toys R Us tie-up with McDonald's in the Japanese market. The marketing effort needs to be large enough to get across a threshold level before any expenditures will be effective—advertising messages otherwise will be drowned out by competing advertising (diminishing returns set in only after large amounts are expended).

A similar kind of concentrated or focus strategy is sometimes warranted when market *growth rate* is very high. In fast-growing markets it becomes important to give the product sufficient support to make sure that the market share is not eroded by furiously charging newcomers. The firm must maintain control over the marketing effort—something requiring at a minimum the establishment of a wholly owned sales subsidiary, often also FDI in assembly and production. In the cases where product localization becomes absolutely necessary (such as for electrical appliances in many countries), such FDI is even more likely to be required.

When the "product" offered for sale is actually a service (legal, accounting, hotels, consulting), the franchising mode often offers the best way to maintain the quality of the service and to transfer the requisite know-how. Since a service usually embodies people-skills, franchising provides an opportunity for developing skilled personnel away from the home country while still maintaining quality control. It

EXHIBIT 6.3   An Optimal Entry Mode Matrix

Company strategic posture	Product/Market situation			
	Emerging	**High-growth**	**Mature**	**Services**
Incremental	Indirect exports	Indirect exports	Direct exports	Licensing/Alliance
Protected	Joint venture	Indirect exports	Alliance/Licensing	Licensing
Control	Wholly owned subsidiary	Acquisition/ Alliance	Wholly owned subsidiary	Franchising/Alliance/ Exporting

is the strictly standardized service component of the fast-food industry that is the basis of success for its franchising operations. In services, alliances can also be useful in order to make it possible to adapt to the local culture more easily.

An Optimal Entry Mode Matrix

Pulling together these practical considerations, we can distinguish several strategic situations and the preferred mode of entry in each. The entry strategy is affected both by company factors (firm-specific advantages) and by market factors (opportunities and threats).

The company factors can be grouped into three strategic postures. The market factors are different in advanced and emerging economies and in high-growth and mature markets. Services need to be treated separately. (See Exhibit 6.3.)

STRATEGIC POSTURE   One company posture is when few resources can be dedicated to entry, the usual case when entry is the first step in the internationalization process. The major characteristic of the entry strategy then tends to be its tentativeness and the desire to keep future options open. This strategic posture will be called "incremental".

A second strategic posture is when the firm possesses a well-protected trade secret or patentable know-how whose potential abroad is clear, but needs to learn about the market and develop more local familiarity. This situation will be denoted "protected." Typical examples would include the Coca-Cola formula, the computer-on-a-chip, and electronic banking technology. In such cases there are usually real or self-imposed limits to the resources (manpower, operating capital) allocated to the entry.

In a third strategic situation the company has well-established firm-specific advantages, is large enough to encounter relatively few resource obstacles to expansion, and offers a product with definite potential abroad. This is the typical "global" situation, with the company committed to expanding abroad without jeopardizing any of its firm-specific advantages. This will be called the "control" posture.

PRODUCT/MARKET SITUATION   The various product/market conditions that might prevail in the market country can be grouped into four different categories. A first distinction is between products and services. The characteristics of service markets are different from those of markets for physical products when it comes to entry mode considerations. Whereas the product embodies many of the firm-specific advantages in its physical attributes and can thus be viewed separately from the actual transaction through which ownership is exchanged, the quality and benefits of services reside in the transaction itself. This is why export of services often takes the form of people's travel (professionals in various fields, doctors, engineers, consultants, and so on) to perform the service.

Among product markets it is useful to distinguish between three situations. Emerging markets are those recently opened up because of political changes, and which show generally weak infrastructure, difficulty in accomplishing market-based exchanges, lack of distribution alternatives, and risk of default on payments. Some less-developed countries also fall into the emerging category.

A second situation is high-growth markets, such as some high-technology markets in advanced economies and markets in many fast-growing countries, including the newly industrialized countries. The main marketing issues tend to be to quickly establish presence in the country and to support the product sufficiently in the marketplace so as not to lose out against competitors. The sales growth will go to the entrant who quickly establishes leadership and captures first-mover advantages in the high-growth market.

A third situation is the market in the mature stage, when the name of the marketing game is market share, including dominance in at least a niche in a well-differentiated marketplace. Many markets in advanced economies are mature. The emphasis in entry in mature markets is not so much on speed of penetration as on the total amount of marketing expenditure needed to establish presence and maintain loyalty.

Entry Barriers

Since entry barriers may limit the available choices of entry modes, it is useful to first evaluate what they are. They are likely to differ considerably among the four product/market situations.

Emerging markets are the most straightforward. In many of these markets, the government is actively controlling which new companies can enter and by what mode. China, for example, does not allow wholly owned subsidiaries, but insists on joint ventures with the Chinese partner (often a government-owned factory) holding a controlling interest. Finding qualified distributors and agents can be a headache in emerging economies, thus ruling out direct exporting. Indirect exporting through trading houses specializing in the country's trade is often feasible, and entry into Eastern Europe and Russia, China, and many less-developed countries often involves using intermediaries with special connections.

In these markets tariff barriers tend to be high for certain products deemed to be unnecessary luxury imports, which can include "necessities" such as cars, bicycles, televisions, and refrigerators. The problem of getting hard currency to pay for the imports makes even indirect exporting questionable. In many cases, the only entry mode available may be a joint venture with a government-affiliated factory to which the entrant offers know-how and modern machinery in return for a share of the profits and, it is hoped, a foot in the door for future expansion.

The high-growth markets tend to offer a fuller range of entry mode options. There could be some attempt by governments to protect a fledgling "infant" industry, as when the semiconductor industries in Japan and Europe tried to fend off the Americans. This protection usually involves nontariff barriers, including requirements for testing, changing standards, and customs inspection. In general, it is difficult to create effective barriers to entry in high-growth markets since entrepreneurial spirits on both sides of the border conceive of new ways of circumventing them. When quotas on semiconductor sales from Japan into the United States were established in the mid-1980s, Americans would drive into Canada to receive chips sent from Hong Kong and simply transport them across to the United States in their briefcases. This is not one of the modes of entry considered here, however.

In more advanced economies, the barriers to entry tend to be "natural." The mature markets are often difficult to break into because of the strength of well-established competitors who dominate distribution and can count on customer loyalty. In today's free-trade world, tariff barriers in mature economies are usually relatively low, but nontariff barriers and government regulations could exist. Quota or tariff protection of certain industries is common, forcing the entrant to establish at least assembly inside the borders. Examples include the protection of food products in Europe, autos in the United States, and rice in Japan. In general, where there is protectionist sentiment among politicians, a company might have to avoid entry or make an equity-based entry and sell products with at least some local content.

Service markets face their own special entry barriers. Services are often subject to strict government and local regulations. Opening hours for retail stores and banks, what financial services can be offered, whether restaurants can serve alcohol, even what hotels can charge per room are some of the standard regulations. Often government has a monopoly—on airwaves, telecommunications, airline routes—and in many cases the services can be offered only by natives, as in legal services, medicine, and accounting. It is rare that services can be performed without a local partner, and alliances and joint ventures become a necessity.

Optimal Modes

Given that the feasible choices of entry mode are constrained by entry barriers, the next step is to find out what the best choices may be. For preferred choices among the alternative modes see again Exhibit 6.3.

INCREMENTAL The resource-poor entrant that wants to stay flexible for the future will most likely be best off with exporting. For emerging markets, indirect exporting may be the only feasible option. If the market in the country is growing quickly, indirect exporting might be preferable since the start-up costs are lower and market presence can be established more rapidly. In services, the actual start-up usually requires people to be sent abroad (a form of "direct exports") but also requires some continued presence from local people, making licensing the preferred option.

PROTECTED   The firm with strong and protected know-how but without very keen interest or skills in foreign markets might also be best off with indirect exporting in high-growth markets (if speed is of the essence). An alliance with a local competitor with distribution capability might be a viable alternative. Where slower penetration is acceptable, the alliance alternative should be expanded to include the possibility of a joint venture or possibly licensing, should a suitable partner be found. In an emerging market, against its better judgment as it were, the firm may have to accept a joint venture, keeping its partner in check to the extent possible. If the offering is a service, licensing should be the first alternative. It would run relatively low risks of dissipation because of patents or other protection and would allow the proper adaptation to local market conditions.

CONTROL   The larger firm interested in global expansion and control over production and marketing in various countries would usually do best with some type of FDI in manufacturing and local sales subsidiaries. In emerging markets, a wholly owned subsidiary may be the only viable option. If the market is growing rapidly, acquisition of (or an alliance with) a local firm may be the most advantageous alternative. Where the market is large, establishing a manufacturing subsidiary with 100 percent ownership is more easily justified. However, if there are large economies of scale in manufacturing (the case in autos, but not in electronics, for example), the company would do better focusing all manufacturing in one or two plants and sourcing worldwide from there through exporting. Tariff barriers against imports might preclude such an option, of course. If the company's business is in services, the use of franchising is probably the best bet. It offers good control possibilities coupled with local adaptation (of great importance in most services) and also allows local capital to be used, an advantage from a political risk point of view.

Real World Cases

The suggested entry modes can be illustrated with reference to some real-world examples (see Exhibit 6.4).

INCREMENTAL STRATEGY   Supervalu, a wholesaler of food products from Washington state, has entered the Russian food market on a small scale. An intermediary trading company located in Boston specializing in Russian trade approached the wholesaler about exporting packaged food products to Russia. The products were to be sold in a Moscow supermarket the intermediary had established. Reluctant at first, Supervalu finally agreed when the financial risk

EXHIBIT 6.4   Entries under Different Conditions

Company strategic posture	Product/Market Situation			
	Emerging	**High-growth**	**Mature**	**Services**
Incremental	Supervalu to Russia	North American fish to Japan	Rossignol skis to U.S.	Dialogue to Europe
Protected	Pharmaceuticals in China	Sun Energy technology to Europe	Coca-Cola bottling; Toyota-GM tie-up	Disneyland in Japan
Control	New FDI in India	Matsushita in U.S. TV market	IBM Worldwide; autos into U.S.	Hilton, Sheraton; McDonald's

was assumed by the trading company and its Russian partner. The wholesaler is now attempting to increase its presence in the Russian market, with or without the help of the intermediary.[16]

The U.S. fishing industry, characterized by numerous small establishments, has found a large and rapidly growing market in Japan, whose supplies from northern waters have been effectively cut off by Russian ships. But, by necessity, sales to Japan are characterized by *indirect exports* via the large Japanese trading companies. Despite some attempts by the Americans to join together and establish some profitable processing followed by direct exports, the market knowledge and financial power of the trading companies has made the fishing industry on the American West Coast simply raw materials suppliers to Japanese processors.

A more positive experience of an incremental exporter maintaining flexibility is the case of Rossignol, the French ski maker mentioned in Chapter 2. The initial entry into the North American market was via *direct exports* to American distributors. This choice was predicated on the lack of financial clout and market knowledge possessed by the company. As its experience and success in the European (primarily French) market grew, so did the recognition that the U.S. and Canadian markets were not only important but also quite different from the European in terms of skiing conditions, customer preferences, and so on. The decision was then made to establish wholly owned manufacturing in both countries to enable the company to adapt its products and stay in close touch with market developments. The initial choice of direct exports allowed the company the requisite time for learning and for accumulating resources before a more committed move was undertaken.

A small consulting firm in the computer software business, Dialogue, Inc., operates out of New York City. The demand for its services abroad is growing rapidly, and the company has had problems identifying the right mode for serving this market. The strategy the company has evolved consists of *service and distribution alliance* tie-ups with different consulting firms in various European countries, sharing the software know-how with them through seminars and training sessions both in Europe and in New York and then using the company's established sales force and local market presence to help sell the software with the requisite quality control and backup services.

PROTECTED KNOW-HOW   Western pharmaceutical companies eyeing the vast Chinese market see tremendous opportunity. There is little need for the companies to worry about leakage of formulas, since China has a very different tradition in medicine, and there are few pharmacologists educated in the West. But the unfamiliar market, the need to establish good relationships with government agencies, and, not least, the Chinese government's rules mean that joint ventures are the only entry mode for Schering-Plough, Merck, Pfizer, and the rest.[17]

The Atlas International Company of Seattle, Washington, is an export management company (EMC) specializing in sales of U.S.-developed sun energy technology. The innovating companies are too small and too unskilled at marketing abroad to be able to take advantage of the opportunities that present themselves and have turned to *indirect exporting* using Atlas. Many of the rapid growth markets are a consequence of government resource allocations to the sun energy field, and Atlas provides a service by keeping abreast of the rapidly developing opportunities in different countries. Nevertheless, Atlas recognizes that if for any one company's exports start taking a large share of total sales, that firm will look for ways of managing "its" part of the business.

Coca-Cola's *licensing* of local bottlers is its standard approach in overseas markets, sometimes aided by a *joint-venture* ownership structure. The protection of the formula is the keystone of this policy—the bottlers are given a concentrate and instructions for adding carbonated water to produce the drink but do not get access to the formula itself. Another case of a joint venture in a mature market is Toyota's tie-up with General Motors in Fremont, California, where small cars under the Chevrolet Nova name are marketed. To questions about the possible dissipation of Toyota's firm-specific know-how, the company has said little, but observers tend to agree that the effects are small. Not much of the actual know-how has been transferred, since many of the assembly tasks have been adapted for American workers. In addition, by now the technology from Japan represents quite standard process knowledge, available to most if not all carmakers in one form or other already. The basic strength of the agreement seems to be that GM gets Toyota's people to implement the new procedures and assembly technology.

In a reverse situation, Disney World agreed to *license* its name for use at the new entertainment park in Chiba outside Tokyo. Satisfied with a substantial 10 percent of gross sales in royalties and the provision that quality controls would be stringent, the Disney company apparently judged its expertise in the Japanese market insufficient for a wholly owned subsidiary operation. At the same time, the agreement will tend to limit the accumulation of experience

Pepsi-Cola's licensed bottlers target the same consumers in Moscow as else-where. The Pepsi entry into Russia was helped by then U.S. president Nixon, and Pepsi came to dominate the market.

Sarah Leen/Matrix.

abroad and thus limit the possibility of going into other Asian markets. (The company was a bit more secure in its knowledge of the European market and opted for an equity investment in a joint venture with French partners, but as we saw in the opening vignette of Chapter 3, it is encountering a fair number of problems.) Whether or not Disney World will enter any other Asian countries may be a question not only of what its top management is thinking but of what the Japanese licensee has in mind.

CONTROL POSTURE Now that India has relented on its ban on foreign ownership, many companies are coming back. Whether through greenfield investments, acquisitions, or reacquisitions of abandoned facilities, companies are establishing wholly owned subsidiaries in which they can control operations and use of their know-how. These companies include American and Japanese car companies, Korean conglomerates, and European electronics manufacturers, eager to cash in on the future growth of the Indian market.

When the American color TV market took off toward the end of the 60s, the Japanese electronics giant Matsushita (brand name Panasonic) faced the choice of establishing production in the United States or being left behind. Trade barriers were high and Sony was already present at its San Diego plant. By *acquiring* the troubled Motorola TV plant outside Chicago, Matsushita at great cost managed to kill two birds with one stone. One, it acquired the desired manufacturing base in the market and could enter quickly (especially since they kept the Motorola brand name Quasar), and two, political pressures were assuaged, especially since the plant was scheduled to close. The cost was the problem inherited at the plant of low productivity and fragmented labor-management relations. After considerable effort (including the introduction of some of the vaunted Japanese management techniques such as quality control circles), productivity was again on the rise within a spectacularly short period of time (less than one year).

The control strategy of IBM in the mature markets of Europe and Asia has been based specifically on 100 percent ownership of sales and manufacturing subsidiaries for its mainframe computers. The objectives of protecting its hard-won technical know-how and maintaining its corporate philosophy of providing outstanding service to back up its products were factors in determining the FDI strategy. In personal computers, by contrast, the company has been more willing to engage in alliances, including joint ventures. IBM's know-how in the PC field is much less on the cutting edge than in mainframes.

Scale returns in manufacturing have made automakers in Europe and Japan hesitant about setting up plants abroad. Although transportation costs to the large North American market are relatively high, all the Japanese and European automakers have followed basically the same path of *direct exports* marketed through wholly owned *sales subsidiaries*. Establishing a dedicated distribution network, an expensive and resource-consuming undertaking, the marketing effort can be controlled without investing in manufacturing or assembly. In 1976, Volkswagen established production in Harrisburg, Pennsylvania, in order to be closer to its main overseas market, but quality problems forced the company to close the plant after five years. It was not until the voluntary quotas with Japan were enacted in 1981 that Japanese automakers started manufacturing in the United States. In 1994, both Mercedes and BMW announced plans to start manufacturing in the United States, reducing transportation costs of sports models specially designed for the North American market. When economies of scale in manufacturing are great, exporting worldwide from one or two plants is preferable, unless entry barriers to major markets are high.

The *franchising* of fast-food companies such as McDonald's is well known in many parts of the world. The main ingredient in this successful global expansion is the emphasis on (control of) standardized service more than the product itself (the food). This is generally true also in the companies' domestic market. The hotel chains that have sprung up in many metropolitan centers of the world, the Hiltons and the Sheratons well known to many travelers, are not wholly owned subsidiaries as one might have thought but franchise operations typically capitalized by local interests and supported by world-wide promotion and advertising.

These services aim less at a local market and more toward a global market of international business people and tourists. The standardization of the service has a distinct "consumer confidence" or "trust" aspect to it—the customer using these services avoids taking chances with unknown offerings. This is why franchising, with its greater possibilities of controlling quality, is preferable to alliances or simple licensing of a trademark or brand name.

SUMMARY

This chapter described the three nonexporting modes of entry: licensing, strategic alliances, and FDI in wholly owned manufacturing subsidiaries. The marketer's role differs in these entry modes from that of simple exporter, since the company is marketing its FSAs directly rather than embodied in the final product. Against a historical background the characteristics of the modes were shown to depend on various trade barriers and the modes shown to provide various opportunities for the global marketer. Each mode has advantages and disadvantages for the entrant from a marketing perspective, and examples were used to demonstrate that a wholly owned sales subsidiary can be used successfully with any mode of entry.

The vexing question of what the optimal mode of entry should be was then discussed. The theoretical answer is to choose the mode that maximizes the discounted net cash flow. The practical answer depends on a number of strategic and situational considerations that favor one mode over another. These practical considerations were summarized in a matrix of strategic market and resource situations facing the entrant into a country. Matching typical company postures (incrumental, protected, or control) and typical market situations (emerging, high-growth, mature, service), the marketing manager gets a feel for which mode may be preferable as a first choice. Several real-world examples were used to demonstrate the application of the choice-of-mode matrix and to show how companies have actually attempted to make entry decisions recently that are good for today and also leave room for future change and growth.

KEY TERMS

acquisition p. 205
FDI in wholly owned
manufacturing p. 203
Greenfield investment p. 205

Original equipment
manufacturing (OEM) p. 197
Royalties p. 195

Straight licensing p. 195
Transaction costs p. 209
Turnkey p. 197

DISCUSSION QUESTIONS

1. While Disney World entered the Japanese market by licensing a Japanese company Euro-Disney outside Paris is established as a joint venture with European backing but with Disney holding majority control. To what would you attribute the difference in entry mode? Given the lack of success so far in Europe, do you think another entry mode would have been better? Why or why not?

2. Because it is located in the southern hemisphere, Chile's strong fruit-growing industry has the advantage in many northern markets of counterseasonal harvesting. What entry mode would be most suitable for these markets? What trade barriers would Chilean fruit-growers face with this entry mode?

3. What are the pros and cons of a strategic alliance versus a joint venture with the same

partner in a high-tech industry (a) to enter a mature market? and, (b) to enter a high-growth market?

4. Why has franchising become the most common mode of entry for multinational hoteliers?

5. What are the pros and cons of indirect exporting for a small maker of ceramic art works? For a small company producing PC software? What alternative modes of entry would you suggest?

NOTES

1. This section draws on Otterbeck, 1981, and Hamel and Prahalad, 1988.

2. The terminology varies between writers. Some keep joint ventures separate from strategic alliances, arguing that the latter do not involve equity investments but are simple collaborations. From a marketing perspective, however, joint ventures and strategic alliances pose similar problems. See Contractor and Lorange, 1988, and Varadarajan and Cunningham, 1995.

3. See, for instance, Hamel, Doz, and Prahalad, 1989, and Bleeke and Ernst, 1991.

4. See Johansson, 1995.

5. See Terpstra and Simonin, 1993.

6. Bleeke and Ernst, 1991, and Parkhe, 1991, show the lack of durability of many strategic alliances.

7. Bleeke and Ernst, 1991.

8. Hamel et al. 1989, give an upbeat view of competitive collaborations.

9. See Contractor and Lorange, 1988, and Geringer and Hebert, 1991. There are many other forms of international ventures which are quite different organizationally—for example, the American Beth-lehem Steel and Swedish Granges JV for the mining of iron ore in Liberia—but such alliances are of less interest here.

10. See Hamel, 1991.

11. This discussion of FDI in overseas manufacturing is necessarily brief. A lot has been written on the topic, and the interested reader can find a good comprehensive statement of the modern FDI theory in most multinational texts, including Rutenberg, 1982.

12. See Johansson and Nebenzahl, 1986.

13. See, for example, the reaction of Chrysler buyers to learning that the cars were built in Mexico (Nag, 1984).

14. See Tse and Gorn, 1993.

15. Anderson and Gatignon (1986) develop the application of transaction cost theory to entry mode in depth.

16. This example is from "Food Distribution in Russia: The Harris Group and the LUX Store," Harvard Business School case no. 9-594-059.

17. See Beamish, 1993.

SELECTED REFERENCES

Anderson, Erin, and Hubert Gatignon. "Modes of Foreign Entry: A Transaction Cost Analysis and Propositions." *Journal of International Business Studies*, no. 3 (1986), pp. 1–26.

Beamish, Paul W. "The Characteristics of Joint Ventures in the People's Republic of China." *Journal of International Marketing* 1 no. 2, (1993), pp. 29-48.

Bleeke, J., and David Ernst. "The Way to Win in Cross-border Alliances." *Harvard Business Review* 69, no. 6 (November–December 1991), pp. 127–35.

Contractor, Farouk, and Peter Lorange, eds. *Cooperative Strategies in International Business*. Lexington, MA: Lexington Books, 1988.

Geringer, J. Michael, and L. Hebert. "Measuring Performance of International Joint Ventures." *Journal of International Business Studies* 22, no. 2, (1991), pp. 249–63.

Hamel, Gary. "Competition for Competence and Inter-Partner Learning within International Strategic Alliances." *Strategic Management Journal* 12 (Summer 1991), pp. 83-103.

Hamel, Gary, and C. K. Prahalad. "Creating Global Strategic Capability." In Hood, Neil, and Jan-Erik Vahlne, eds. *Strategies in Global Competition*. London: Croom Helm, 1988.

Hamel, Gary; Yves Doz; and C. K. Prahalad. "Collaborate with Your Competitors—and Win." *Harvard Business Review*, January–February 1989, pp. 133–39.

Johansson, Johny K. "International Alliances: Why Now?" *Journal of the Academy of Marketing Science*, Fall 1995.

Johansson, Johny K., and Izrael D. Nebenzahl. "Multinational Expansion: Effect on Brand Evaluations." *Journal of International Business Studies* 17, no. 3, (Fall 1986), pp. 101–26.

Nag, Amal. "Chrysler Tests Consumer Reaction to Mexican-Made Cars Sold in the U.S." *The Wall Street Journal*, July 23, 1984 Sec. 2.

Otterbeck, L., ed. *The Management of Headquarters-Subsidiary Relationships in Multinational Corporations*. Aldershot, U.K.: Gower, 1981.

Parkhe, Arvind. "Interfirm Diversity, Organizational Learning, and Longevity in Strategic Alliances." *Journal of International Business Studies* 22, no.4 (1991), pp. 579–601.

Pucik, Vladimir. "Strategic Alliances, Organizational Learning, and Competitive Advantage—The HRM Agenda." *Human Resource Management* 27, no.1 (Spring 1988), pp. 77–83.

Root, F. R. *Foreign Market Entry Strategies*, 2d ed. New York: Amacom, 1989.

Rutenberg, David P. *Multinational Management*. Boston: Little, Brown, 1982.

Terpstra, Vern, and Bernard L. Simonin. "Strategic Alliances in the Triad: An Exploratory Study." *Journal of International Marketing*, 1, no.1 (1993), pp. 4–25.

Thorelli, Hans B., and S. Tamer Cavusgil, eds. *International Marketing Strategy*, 3d ed. New York: Pergamon, 1990.

Tse, David K., and Gerald J. Gorn. "An Experiment on the Salience of Country-of-Origin in the Era of Global Brands." *Journal of International Marketing* 1, no.1 (1993), pp. 57–76.

Varadarajan, P. Rajan, and Margaret H. Cunningham. "Strategic Alliances: A Synthesis of Conceptual Foundations." *Journal of the Academy of Marketing Science*, Fall 1995.

CASES

Case 1

HONDA GOES TO BRAZIL

I am going to speak to you about Honda's approach to opening new markets. To help you better understand how Honda actually works to open a new market, I would like to start from my own experience.

When I joined the company over a quarter of a century ago, Honda was primarily a motorcycle manufacturer, having begun automobile production just three years earlier. At this time, I was engaged in developing overseas markets for motorcycles and I spent most of my time in Latin America. Although this was an area plagued by political instability, which remains to this day in many parts of the region, Honda believed that there was great potential to develop motorcycle markets there. No matter where people live, they have a need to move from one place to another, and Honda believed that because it provides an affordable and convenient means of transportation, the motorcycle would surely have a role in Latin America.

Now, let me ask you a question. Suppose there was a country that had a population of 130 million, which is a huge market, but a per capita income of less than $700 per year. In this country, motorcycle sales for the past three years were no more than several thousand units per year while the auto industry produced nearly 1 million units annually. In this country, the import duty for motorcycles was 105 percent, the industrial product tax was 24 percent, and the merchandise circulation tax was 17 percent, making the landed cost of imported goods three times as high as the FOB price. In addition, business practices dictated that payment terms were draft 180 days and the financial situation was always tight. Borrowers were charged 50 percent per annum, including inflationary compensation. What would you do to penetrate that market?

There are only 4 possible answers to this question.

1. Give up.
2. Wait for better conditions.
3. Get in anyway but minimize your risk.
4. Make a big investment to create a market and develop your products at the same time.

I consulted with the local people, with people in Japan, and others. Their recommendations were of two types. Some recommended that under these conditions it was impossible to access the market. Others advised that to realize the potential of this market, one must make a large investment and dive right in.

Source: Speech by Osamu Iida, Executive Vice President, Honda North America, March 28, 1996.

The answer that my colleagues and I chose was number 3. Our proposal to Honda management was to establish our own subsidiary.

As you may have realized, the country I have been speaking of is Brazil. We decided to establish Honda's own, 100 percent subsidiary in Sao Paulo in the fall of 1971. It was the ninth subsidiary that Honda had established overseas by then. Our business plan was very modest. The projected break-even point was sales of only 150 motorcycles per month. I and two other colleagues were dispatched from Japan, and we started business in Brazil by renting a warehouse in the backyard of an old sheet metal shop.

In the beginning, our strategy was to build up a firm and solid foundation for future business while learning every aspect of things Brazilian. For that purpose, we had to do things that were quite contrary to prevailing business practices at the time. For example, we sold to dealers on a strict cash basis. We also required dealers to stock a minimum of spare parts while we were developing a spare parts supply system.

You can hardly imagine how painstaking it was to establish our parts business. We had to obtain import licenses and every part required a Portuguese name. We were forced to invent names for some parts. Obtaining customs clearance for every single part was a bureaucratic nightmare. And everything had to be done by hand without the help of computers.

While the population of Brazil was 120 million at this time, it was widely known that only about 30 million of the people were economically active. Our own research done by Honda without the help of any outside consultants told us that an effective demand for the product we were offering would only be possible with 1 million people. Just counting on that 1 million people, we estimated that the market could be developed into 100,000 units per year over a 5 to 10 year period.

Just to give you an idea of the price for the small 50cc motorcycles we were selling, they had a price tag of around $1,100. The Volkswagen Beetle, which was produced at a huge VW plant in Brazil, cost $3,600. Who would buy a small motorcycle that cost nearly one-third the price of a car? We believed that unless we could establish a new image or concept around motorcycles in Brazil, we would never succeed. We sent the message that the motorcycle was a new product for a new age by showing sound usage by sound people. To spread the new image of the motorcycle, we focused on various grassroots activities instead of a huge, budgeted advertising campaign that we could not afford. Our grassroots activities included participating in local auto shows with elaborate displays, establishing circuit riding safety schools in small towns that provided motorcycle riding safety training while also serving as promotional events, and advertising in upscale magazines. Featuring our 50cc model, these ads presented motorcycles as "lithe machines for the accomplished" to foster a mature yet innovative image for Honda motorcycles.

We were very encouraged by the growing demand for our motorcycles. In 1973, for example, Honda imported more than 10,000 units. But the oil shock of 1973 and an increase in the import duty from 105 percent to 205 percent in 1974 made the price of motorcycles inaccessible to almost everyone. Then, in 1975, the Brazilian government prohibited imports of almost everything. So, the question was what should we do now?

Even while we were carrying out our initial market research before establishing Brazilian Honda, we recognized that the market would not be fully developed unless we successfully established manufacturing operations there. Because our 50cc motorcycles cost one-third as much as a car in Brazil, it was imperative that we do everything possible to lower the price. One way to achieve this was to establish manufacturing operations in Brazil. Toward the middle of 1974, our manufacturing plan was ready for governmental approval. This also required a lot of work and after it was approved, we set out to construct our factory, which we completed with unimaginable speed. Our first motorcycle came off the line in Brazil in 1975, one year after construction of the plant began.

The factory was located in Manaus, a city located about 1,000 miles up the Amazon River from its mouth. You may ask why we located our factory in Manaus in the heart of the Amazon jungle where there was little or no infrastructure in place and a huge distance from our markets in the southern part of the country. The Amazon region had been a free market region since 1968, as part of the Brazilian government's regional development plan to bring investment to the area. To ensure that our factory was able to produce products at least equal in quality to imports from Japan, it was necessary that we equip it with the most suitable machines and guarantee an uninterrupted supply of critical parts to be imported. The lack of import restrictions allowed us to import the most modern equipment for our plant, and the location provided us with an abundant, unskilled but trainable work force. These advantages outweighed the disadvantages and allowed us to get the same level of quality and cost equal to that which we enjoyed before the oil shock and the increase in the import duty.

After that, business went successfully as we planned. And today in Manaus, we have a modern, full-fledged motorcycle factory amid the tropical jungle, with an annual capacity of 120,000 motorcycles. Our operations at this facility include engine manufacturing, complete with aluminum die casting, computer controlled machining, plastic injection, stamping, welding, plating, painting, and final assembly.

Our market for Honda motorcycles in Brazil soon reached 100,000 units per year, which proved that our initial research was not far off the mark. During the 1980s business did not always go smoothly. There was a huge credit crisis in Latin America that was particularly severe in Brazil. And in a reaction to the country's democratization effort, a serious political crisis occurred in Brazil. Despite all this, Brazilian Honda has remained an ongoing, dynamic business, riding over such waves like an expert surfer. Today, Brazilian Honda exports motorcycles to many of its Latin American neighbors, as well as to Europe and Asia.

Honda's experience in Brazil illustrates the two key components of its strategy for opening new markets. First, Honda showed that to be successful, a company must make a clear and firm commitment to the new market it wants to develop. Despite the various obstacles that the company will encounter—cultural differences, different business practices, various regulatory obstacles which some people may consider trade barriers—these should not be overestimated. While tough to overcome, these obstacles must not prevent the company from successfully entering the market. Second, the company must consistently ensure high levels of customer satisfaction, always striving to exceed their expectations. In all of Honda's activities, from new product development to after-sales service, we always put the customer first. Even as far back as 1956, Honda recognized this and made it a basic company principle.

DISCUSSION QUESTIONS

1. Why did Honda decide to invest in a manufacturing plant in Manaus, Brazil? What alternatives did the company have?

2. What risk factors led many other companies to avoid investing in Brazil?

3. What were the causes for the market success of the company's motorcycles?

Case 2

BARRETT FARM FOODS: FROM AUSTRALIA TO EUROPE

*I*n late spring, 1994, Philip Austin, general manager of Barrett Farm Foods, was joyous, having just returned from the food industry fair in Cologne—world's largest food and beverage fair. He was so enthusiastic about the prospects of exporting Barrett's products to the European Community that he immediately called for a meeting of his senior managers.

Barrett Farm Foods, based in Victoria, is Australia's sixth-largest food company. It distributes both bulk agricultural commodities and processed food products. Among others, it sells macadamia nuts, cereal bars, garlic, ginger, dried fruits, and honey all over Australia. The company has had a healthy rate of growth over the past decade, and its sales reached $158 million last year. Barrett is committed to serving the domestic market; it also intends to expand its canned foods business substantially over the next two years.

What prompted Mr. Austin to attend the Cologne fair was a recent report from the Australian government trade commission (Austrade) which highlighted the tremendous potential of Australian exports of foodstuffs. For example, Australian food exports to Europe exceeded $4 billion last year. Austrade believes that highly processed foodstuffs are the coming thing and plans to boost the export of them to about $6 billion this year.

Austrade notes that Australia's raw agricultural commodities export amounts to $80 billion annually. This figure illustrates the dilemma. If just 10 percent of that value-adding were done here, Australia's balance of trade problems would disappear. Austrade believes that meat, cereal, sugar, dairy commodities, and marine products have the most potential for food processing.

While Barrett Farm Foods has had little experience with export customers, it has always received unsolicited inquires from foreign distributors and agents. No one in the organization was able to follow up on these prospects. Yet Mr. Austin is aware that other Australian food processors are doing a steady level of export business. His impressions from the Cologne fair confirm a significant potential. Those who stopped by the company stand at the fair and sampled its products, such as the nut and honey-based cereal bar and vegemite-like spread, had some very kind words to say.

In particular, Mr. Austin was encouraged by his encounters at the fair. Mr. Luigi Cairati, a senior executive with the Italian supermarket chain Standa, was keen on doing business with Barrett Foods. He pointed out that, over the past decade, there has been a explosion in the interest among European supermarkets and food stores for exotic food and vegetables, with each group competing to display produce from

Source: Case written by Professor S. Tamer Cavusgil, Michigan State University.

all around the world. Standa is interested in searching for new products from other countries and also in meeting off-season demand for fruit and vegetables.

Mr. Jean-Marc Donce, purchasing manager for the French food group Fauchon, confirmed their interest in showcasing exotic and high-quality food in their stores. He added that Australia is a very fashionable country in Europe. It is seen as exotic and pollution-free and in general producing a quality product. It also appears that the market for canned fruit is opening up as the fruit crop from trees in Europe diminishes.

Mr. Austin also met Mr. Peter Telford, a UK agent who showed great interest in representing Barrett Farm Foods in the European Community. Mr. Telford talked about his knowledge of the market, extensive contacts, and prior business experience. He also noted that other Australian firms, such as Goodman Fielder Wattie, Burns Philip, Adelaide Steamship, and Southern Farmers, are already doing business in the region. He pointed to several success stories, including Sydney-based pastry manufacturer, C & M Antoniou. C & M Antoniou has now established a small plant in Britain as a way of avoiding the considerable wall of duties surrounding the EC market. The company is now supplying several of the country's major supermarket chains, including Marks and Spencer, Tessos, and Safeways. Another Australian group, Buderim Ginger, has recently expanded its operations from Britain into Europe by opening an office in Germany.

Philip Austin immediately created a three-person task force among his senior managers and charged them with the task of implementing an export drive. He felt that an export volume of $20 million for the first year was reasonable. For products to be exported to Europe, the company would examine its cur-

rent product offerings. It would appoint Mr. Peter Telford, or another suitable agent, to facilitate sales to European customers. Philip Austin had returned from Cologne with dozens of business cards, so there were numerous potential customers who could be contacted for immediate sales. Given the considerable distance to Europe, Austin thought that an additional 30 percent markup was appropriate for export customers. The company could also forward some product and company literature used in Australia to its export customers in case they wished to use this material for local promotion.

DISCUSSION QUESTIONS

1. What problems do you see in Mr. Austin's plans for European expansion? What are critical deficiencies in his marketing plan? In particular, comment on the following components of the marketing plan and offer your recommendations for enhancing Barrett Food's prospects in Europe.

2. What factors will determine Barrett's product potential in Europe? What role will product packaging and country-specific standards play? What other issues need to be resolved in determining customer acceptance?

3. How should Barrett Foods be represented in Europe? What types of channels need to be tapped? How will they access them? What difficulties do you anticipate? What are the ideal characteristics of their prospective distributor(s)?

4. Is the simple "cost-plus" approach suggested by Mr. Austin realistic? What cost factors should be taken into consideration? What procedure should the company follow in setting prices for export customers? What choices do they need to make with respect to positioning?

Case 3

TOYS R US JAPAN (B)

Toys R Us first made public its plans to enter the Japanese market in 1989, signing a high-profile deal with McDonald's Japan under which a new subsidiary, Toys R Us Japan, was established with Toys R Us owning 80 percent and McDonald's Japan holding the remaining 20 percent. The long-time president of McDonald's Japan, T. Fujita, came on board as vice chairman of the new joint venture, and almost the entire staff was locally hired. There are no foreign permanent employees at Toys R Us Japan's headquarters in Kawasaki City, 20 minutes outside central Tokyo. The two companies presented a formidable team to local competitors; Toys R Us, with its commanding share of the U.S. market and excellent marketing strategy, had the industry power and experience in cracking foreign markets, while McDonald's, so firmly established in Japan that it is almost considered a Japanese company by many, had the depth of market knowledge and research skills, as well as the communications lines to the target groups of children and young families. As part of the deal, McDonald's has the right to establish a restaurant in any location Toys R Us picks for a store.

The first store was opened in Ibaraki Prefecture in December 1991, and since that time, Toys R Us has opened 15 more stores, with more expected before the end of the year. Toys R Us has relied on McDonald's market research to target suburban areas with young families as a primary growth base. City stores have so far been limited to Osaka and Nagasaki, but most stores are near enough to major cities that they can be reached within a one-hour drive. Despite the high cost of land, the stores are provided with ample parking. They are still lagging a bit behind the ambitious plan announced in 1991 to have 31 stores open by the end of the year, but are on target for 100 by the year 2000, if their luck and the lack of any serious competition holds out.

Their primary advertising media strategy is the use of colorful inserts in newspapers, rather than television or radio, which are far more expensive and scattershot, not necessarily reaching the targeted audience. Newspaper inserts for home deliveries ensure that advertising reaches the home, where mothers and children, the primary targets, are more likely to see them. It is also possible in this way to localize advertising to areas near stores; there are as yet too few stores in operation to make television a valuable alternative.

Land and Approval

The timing of the Toys R Us market entry was fortunate. In 1989, the bubble economy was in full swing, but by December 1991, when the first store opened in Ibaraki, the economy had lapsed into recession. The slogan "Everyday Low Prices" was therefore appealing to many who were looking for value as well as quality, and the minimal level of service (no gift-wrapping) was more acceptable as fewer gifts were being given.

Source: Case developed by Michael Chadwick and Jeong-Soe Won, edited by J.K. Johansson, (Georgetown University).

The entry was also well timed in coinciding with an antistructural impediments initiative by the Bush administration. The Japanese government, looking for positive PR, pushed the Ibaraki regional government to waive the "Big Store" laws under which existing retailers can veto the entry of a large retailer into the area. The first store, at 3000 square meters and offering 18,000 items in inventory, was the perfect example of what has come to be called in America a "category killer": By creating an overwhelming advantage, it is intended to stop competitors from opening opposing stores before they start.

Direct Deals with Manufacturers

As Toys R Us Japan imports more than half of its supply from the U.S., this was not the pressing issue it was first painted to be. Only one major Japanese manufacturer has signed on to ship directly to Toys R Us stores, but that one is Nintendo, which extended its American direct-shipping agreement to cover Japan as well in June 1991, before the first store in Japan was opened. On the other hand, neither is it true that, with this deal, "the Japanese toy distribution system, hit by a wave of internationalization, has taken a first step toward significant reform," as no other manufacturers have made a similar deal, and no other toy retailer has been able to crack the distribution network and deal direct. Toys R Us has adopted a flexible strategy in approaching the distribution issue, working through existing channels in Japan where necessary, but utilizing the central Kobe warehouse as a waystation so they can control their in-store inventory more precisely.

U.S. Methods in the Japanese Market

Before entering the Japanese market, Toys R Us had operations in eight other countries. It drew on these experiences, especially those of its successful stores in two other Asian cultures, Hong Kong and Singapore. There was thus a willingness to be open in methods and changes; for example, although corporate policy dictates that no store should be less than 3,000 square meters, the Japan group decided that the new store in Himeji, Hyogo Prefecture, could be viable at 2,800 square meters, and succeeding stores were sometimes even smaller than that.

Just as importantly, Toys R Us was able to draw on the successful experience of McDonald's, another American firm which was able to adjust to Japanese rules while still maintaining its innovative nature (as the first Western-style fast food chain) to become a market leader. When McDonald's came to Japan, it faced and beat the same issues of establishing distribution and supply channels, and its experience was valuable for Toys R Us to draw on.

Large-Scale, Discount Retail in a Small Store Market

Toys R Us also copied McDonald's in another important respect: it viewed its fundamental system as a positive innovation that provided value to Japanese consumers, and marketed it as such. Toys R Us marketing, rather than focusing on "Everyday Low Prices," promised unparalleled inventory, essentially guaranteeing that even the most popular items would be in stock at all times, which small local retailers were unable to do. Rather than being forced to get up at 4 AM and get in line to get the new Mortal Combat 4 the day it came out, all a consumer had to do was come to Toys R Us any time to be sure they could get the game.

The relative lack of service, while offputting to some Japanese consumers, is not unique to Toys R Us. At the same time, other discount stores such as Topos have made inroads, offering a wide selection, low prices, and economy packaging. Only Toys R Us, however, has combined the by now accepted discount store with the specialty retail niche; but given its success, it would seem likely that Home Depot, CompUSA, and other large-scale niche retailers are following the progress of Toys R Us very carefully.

Competition

Interestingly, in Japan it has been two footwear dealers that have taken the lead in opening shops modeled on Toys R Us. Chiyoda's "Harrowmark" chain and Marutomi's "BanBan" are both expanding nationwide, offering low prices in line with Toys R Us, but unable to finance the same stores or inventories. The price wars that have been spawned may well cut into Toys R Us Japan's bottom line for some time. Other stores have adopted nonprice techniques to compete, such as "do-it-yourself" toy days, where children are helped to build models or stitch together dolls, or the hiring of "toy consultants" to get into kids' heads and guess the next big hit so stores can stock up.

Just as threatening is a move by smaller retailers to unite in opposition to Toys R Us. The ostensible goals of the 600 company–member Toy Shop Specialist Council (Gangu Senmontei Kai) are to research new management techniques, examine the possibility of making direct deals with producers, and cooperate to establish a new joint distribution system, all laudable goals. However, they have also taken less benign steps, approaching distributors and asking that they boycott Toys R Us for its policy of dealing direct. While they have had some successes, few distributors want to cut off hope of dealing with the toy giant, and so are taking a wait and see approach. "Distribution retribution" has not yet come to hurt Toys R Us.

Cost

Toys R Us Japan, while unwilling to release operating results, has indicated that it is willing to carry a lot more debt than is the low-leverage parent firm, in line with the practices of Japanese competitors. They also lease their land on short-term leases, a concession made as part of the price of goodwill, but not a serious drawback in the current depressed land market. Despite the low rents and interest rates, in general, operating costs are three times as high as in the U.S. They also import a lot of goods, and are now profiting from the cheap dollar. However, this triple positive of cheap land, cheap money, and cheap imports will have to end sooner or later, and sharp swings upward in any or all of them will certainly have a negative effect on the bottom line.

Positioning

While value is important to the Japanese consumer, quality has traditionally been more of a watchword than price. Given two equivalent products, the consumer will choose the cheaper one; differentiate them and quality will win over price in most product areas in Japan. It is important for Toys R Us to steer clear of the part of the low-price zone where it veers into being equivalent to low quality. To that end, their policy of only carrying established brand name items is good, as is the marketing emphasis on inventory rather than price, but in the future, as price competitors arise, it will be important for Toys R Us to walk a fine line between becoming too expensive for the young target market it aims for and so cheap that consumers decided the store has nothing else going for it.

The Future of Toys R Us Japan—Less Rosy Than the Present?

Discussions with Toys R Us Japan executives indicate that they feel that Japan is an almost untapped market, easily capable of supporting five times as many stores as are now in operation. At the same time, they discount the idea of competition rising to fill that niche before Toys R Us can preempt it. However, examples of other American companies that took a lead in market share, then became sanguine and saw that lead slip away, are legion. While Toys R Us to date has shown no tendency to give in to wishful thinking, it is still necessary to look at the challenges to be faced in the future. These include not only increasing competition, but also increasing costs, possible positioning problems, and the danger of a consumer and supplier backlash if the U.S.–Japan trade situation continues to deteriorate.

DISCUSSION QUESTIONS

1. Is Japan an attractive market for Toys R Us? What are the pros and cons of its entry?

2. How did Toys R Us manage to cross the entry barriers into Japan? What alternative modes of entry could have been tried?

3. How did the domestic competition react?

4. Does the Japan entry of Toys R Us seem a success? What are the long-term prospects?

Case 4

DALOON A/S (A): THE INTERNATIONALIZATION PROCESS

At the end of 1990 the newly appointed managing director Hemming Van was taking stock of how far his company, Daloon A/S, had come since his father started the business in 1960. After years of hard work, the small Danish-based start-up was now a leading producer of frozen snack products, and Europe's largest producer of spring rolls. Daloon was living up to its Chinese name: "The Great Dragon."

The Company

Daloon differed from most firms in the food industry in that the company's business concept was not based on the processing of specific raw materials, but was based on a product concept, Chinese pancake rolls. Hemming Van's father, Sai-Chiu Van, came to Denmark from China as a very young man in 1935. Starting his own business at the beginning of 1960, in basement premises, he made 240 rolls

Source: Daloon A/S parts (A) and (B) were prepared in 1993 by Professor Tage Koed Madsen, Department of Marketing, Odense University, as a basis for discussion rather than to illustrate either effective or ineffective management. The case is based on information made available by Daloon A/S. The case is not to be used or reproduced without prior permission.

for a stall in Tivoli Gardens in Copenhagen. That year Sai-Chiu Van sold about 50,000 rolls to various small restaurants and wine bars, and the foundation was prepared for the firm now employing almost 300 persons, producing almost 150 million rolls, and selling a total of about 300 million DKK in 25 countries.

Internationalization

Daloon's internationalization process began in 1970, at a time when the individual markets only to a much smaller extent than now were characterized by international competition and cooperation across national borders. Up through the 1970s Daloon did not have the required capital resources to head directly for the consumer market. That was the major reason why the catering market was always the first target at the entry of a new national market. The retail market was considered too unstable, unreliable, and expensive to enter. An exception, however, was made in Switzerland, where Migros became a partner as early as the beginning of 1974. Today in 1988 Daloon had more substantial capital resources and much better development resources internally. This meant that the firm was now better capable of entering the retail market directly. (This was first done in Spain in 1990 when Daloon concluded a private label agreement with one of the most important retail chains.)

It was characteristic of Daloon that a brand name strategy as well as a private label strategy was pursued. Fundamentally, it was the opinion of the Daloon management that the earning opportunities were just as good as a specialized private label supplier as they were as a brand name supplier. This went for the consumer market as well as the catering market. Frequently, life was easier in the catering market as most catering wholesalers were not very particular about the product's carrying producer names or the name of the individual wholesaler. Brand identification was not the decisive factor

in obtaining customer loyalty; many other qualities in the wholesaler's market were more decisive and the brand name was therefore not a dominating competitive parameter for them.

Products

The basis for practically all activity at Daloon was the fundamental product concept that comprises many different aspects of "rolls." It was a standardized product in the sense that the outside of all rolls was made of the same sort of pancake. There was, however, some variation to the effect that some rolls were to be prepared in a deep-fat frier (declining sales), whereas others could be prepared on a frying pan or in the oven. At present, efforts were being made to develop a roll that was microwavable. The problem related to microwaving was that the rolls do not get crisp when microwaved. The development so far indicated that the rise in the number of microwave ovens did not represent a threat to Daloon's sales of the existing products.

The filling of the individual types of rolls varies (savory rolls, China rolls, pizza rolls, gourmet rolls, etc.). In some cases the filling contains different meat products whereas other rolls contain only vegetable filling. Low-calorie rolls were marketed under the name of Daloon-Light. The continued product development at Daloon had the effect that the rolls were today considered wholesome fast food providing the consumer with great flexibility when preparing the food. Rice, salad, vegetables, and so on could be chosen by the individual consumer to go with the rolls.

Daloon put great emphasis on supplying a wholesome and uniform high-quality product. This meant that Daloon was very meticulous in the selection of proper raw materials and took great care that they could be seen as well as tested in the finished product. Furthermore, efforts were made to use as few additives as possible (colorings, flavorings, preservatives).

It was considered an advantage that the firm had no ties to raw material producers as the composition of the raw materials in the filling could be changed without any problems. This resulted in great flexibility and negotiation strength vis-à-vis the raw material suppliers. The raw materials cost about 20 percent of the amount (excluding VAT) the customer paid for a Daloon product.

The production machinery was tuned in such a way as to achieve the optimum balance between advantages of scale and product change flexibility. In practice, this meant that the individual process lines were arranged so that the outside (the pancake) of the rolls was practically the same for all rolls whereas the filling could be changed very quickly. In that way it was possible to produce small series of specialized rolls without losing the low-cost advantages of large-scale operations. Daloon had developed a substantial part of its machinery—and had taken out the corresponding patents.

At Daloon the product development department had recently merged with the quality control department as it was frequently hard to distinguish between fundamental product development and minor adaptations (belonging to quality control). In the day-to-day activities it was considered much more appropriate to deal with such questions generally. This meant that all product-related decisions were dealt with by Daloon's product development group consisting of the R&D manager, the technical manager, the sales manager, the financial manager, and the managing director. The group convened regularly. The individual salespeople had direct access to the members of the group. This had the effect that feedback from the market could be incorporated very quickly in the internal product development and product adaptation work.

Competition

It was difficult to define Daloon's market because the rolls and also the other Daloon products were considered highly varied substitutes by the consumers, on the consumer market as well as the catering market. In principle, all fast-food products competed with Daloon's products. This applied of course to other rolls and soufflés, but also sausages, pizzas, breaded fish, and all possible ready-made dishes or dishes that were easily and quickly prepared and that could be bought in flexible portions. This market situation offered advantages and disadvantages. The advantage was that the sales opportunities were practically unlimited for a company the size of Daloon. The disadvantage was that it was often difficult to point out direct causes of declining sales in the market. This meant that no special importance was attached to the traditional analyses of market shares, consumer familiarity with Daloon's products and repurchase percentages. Instead they rely much more on personal contact with the actors in the market when Daloon assesses its position in the market.

In the European market only four producers supplied rolls that were directly comparable with Daloon's rolls. The firms in question were four Dutch companies that individually were smaller than Daloon, but combined were bigger. Compared with them Daloon had a production technical lead and was capable of producing at lower costs. In addition Daloon had established much stronger sales organizations in Scandinavia, Britain, and Germany than these competitors. The Dutch companies were started in the same way as Daloon, namely by a person immigrating from the Far East and starting production of rolls. The Dutch firms, however, had their roots in Indonesia where the rolls were somewhat drier than in China. The Dutch firms had stuck to this tradition. Also, their fillings contained more chicken and more bean sprouts as these raw materials were relatively low-priced in the Netherlands.

A line could be drawn from Paris over southern Germany marking the north-south border in Europe as to the perception of what a roll was or should be. France, for instance, was characterized by the Vietnamese cuisine with its tradition for rolls with much thinner pancakes and a minced meat filling including prawns and crabs. Such rolls were not part of the Daloon program at present, but Daloon was now in the process of developing this type of roll. The French agent had for several years urged Daloon to produce such rolls. At Daloon they had, however, been occupied developing products on the basis of the requests made by their own salespeople. This was one of the reasons why Daloon had been reluctant to start development activities aimed especially at the French market.

DISCUSSION QUESTIONS

1. What are the firm-specific advantages of Daloon over its competitors? The country-specific advantages? Any disadvantages?

2. To what extent does the international expansion by Daloon demonstrate the "cultural distance" effect at work?

3. What alternative modes of foreign entry might Daloon consider for further expansion?

Case 5

DALOON A/S (B): ENTERING THE GERMAN MARKET

At the beginning of 1992 managing director Hemming Van was able to look at a year that had brought new and great challenges to Daloon A/S.[1] After a couple of years with large expansions and rapid growth he was proud to ascertain that Daloon had finally broken into the retail and catering markets in Germany.

The German Entry

The German market had seen a virtual explosion in sales in recent years. Sales had almost quintupled since 1988. Now the German mar-

ket was as important to Daloon as the Danish and British markets, each representing about 30 percent of Daloon's total sales.

It had been very difficult for Daloon to make sales and marketing work on the German market through the 1970s and 80s. As a matter of fact the retail market was about to drop out in early 1989 and the catering market was stagnating. An important reason for the imminent collapse of the retail market was that the oven rolls introduced were of low quality. The finished ready-made roll had neither a structure nor a presentation that came up to consumers' expectations. This was due to the

[1]For source and company background, please see Case 4, "Daloon A/S (A)."

fact that rolls were not adequately pretreated by Daloon. The consequences were failing sales and delisting by the chains.

The Retail Market

Following intensive product development activities, in 1989 Daloon could offer the retail market new and improved rolls that were prefried by Daloon in Nyborg, Denmark, and that could easily be prepared in an oven. The new assortment was introduced to Aldi, a leading supermarket chain, and Aldi took the products as a mixture of brand name and private label; the package was specially developed for Aldi, but carried Daloon's name and logo. From the outset the products sold well in Aldi stores and this meant that other chains were included among the customers (with genuine private labels). Aldi's great success had the effect that the consumer market now suddenly accounted for the majority of Daloon's sales in Germany, which is still the case. In Nyborg the consequences were very tangible as the German progress was the major motive behind the decision to invest 80 million DKK in new manufacturing equipment which was ready for production at the end of 1991.

The Catering Market

In the German catering market Daloon pursued a brand name strategy as well as a private label strategy, dependent on the requests of the individual customer and the opportunities available. Most important, however, was the brand name strategy. Daloon had been active in this market since 1970 and sales had developed quietly and steadily over the years, and by a giant leap in recent years. Even before the German reunion Daloon had extended its activities to include former East Germany by the employment of a junior salesman. The German catering market was more accessible to Daloon than the Danish market in that Germans traditionally had a hot meal at noon.

Daloon's target groups were as follows:

- Industrial and staff canteens (i.e., within industry, insurance, banking, etc.).
- University canteens, etc.
- Institutional canteens (hospitals, nursing homes, etc.).
- Military canteens.

This segmentation of the market was the result of various circumstances. The fundamental target group were industrial and staff canteens (cafeterias) representing the most important market potential. Very often the canteen customers work hard physically and this is reflected in the choice of the canteen. University canteens were special in that the customers were almost exclusively young people who often had attitudes and eating habits different from the average German. Within institutional canteens the food was prepared in a centrally located kitchen and then delivered to the different wards of the institution. The composition of the menu must reflect the special demands made by such wards. Military canteens were a relatively new target group. The reason for this was that the former practice of letting the soldiers be in charge of the preliminary preparation of the food had been abandoned. Now the kitchen staff had suddenly to be paid and this resulted in demands for more pretreated products in these canteens. A corresponding development had been ascertained by Daloon in other target groups where reductions had taken place in the kitchen staff. In that way time had been on Daloon's side; this also went for the more general acceptance of convenience food.

Distribution Channels

These target groups were served by a total of about 300 catering wholesalers of whom about half carried Daloon's products. As Daloon products were carried by the major wholesalers, this corresponded to somewhat more than half the sales in this part of the German catering market. An ever increasing concentration was taking place among wholesalers. During the latest 10 years the number of independent wholesalers had been halved and Daloon expected a corresponding reduction within the next 10 years. Part of the concentration had been caused by mergers, part by some wholesalers growing big enough to oust others that simply had to close down. City Grossmarkt was an example of a wholesale firm that had grown rapidly in recent years. Furthermore, more and more wholesalers are entering into some sort of purchase cooperation.

Generally, the wholesaler was in charge of the entire distribution of Daloon's products just as invoicing had always been effected via the wholesaler. In a few cases where quantities were extraordinarily large, Daloon delivered directly to a canteen. Daloon had its own warehouse in Paderborn. From this warehouse deliveries were made twice a week to wholesale warehouses all over Germany. These warehouses carried stocks and delivered to the individual canteens. The wholesalers had their own agents influencing the individual canteens. Depending on sales, each wholesaler had between 1 and 80 salespeople in the field. The small and medium-sized wholesalers were regional whereas the major ones were national, covering the entire German market. The trend was that more and more were becoming national as the small wholesalers were the ones ousted. The small canteens were increasingly being served by "cash & carry" stores like Metro.

Daloon was only a small unit in the assortments of the wholesalers. A large wholesaler might carry 5 or 6 Daloon articles out of a total number of 4,000 articles in the wholesaler catalog. This meant that Daloon could not expect the individual wholesaler to make a special effort for Daloon's products. Daloon had to work in the field on its own and influence the decision makers of the individual

canteens. Traditionally, Daloon had done so by participating in the great gastronomy fairs in Germany as well as in the so-called Hausmessen (house fairs), held locally by the wholesalers for chefs and the like. Annually, Daloon participated in about 50 so-called house fairs. The chefs had once placed orders during these house fairs, but this was not done very much any more. All this made it necessary for Daloon to get into closer contact with the canteens in other ways.

Industry Trends

Simultaneously, competition had grown keener within convenience products, categories. The four Dutch competitors were strong in the Ruhr district where eating habits better matched the Indonesian rolls. The Dutch firms of course tried to oust Daloon in other parts of Germany. Simultaneously, recent years had seen a number of new launchings. National German producers like Pfanni, Packfisch, and Hanna had launched potato dough with filling, puff paste with meat and vegetable filling, cordon bleu with chicken, etc. Danish Prime was active with meat balls, lasagna, etc. The Unilever firm VandenBerg had developed a fish roll with vegetable filling. These were all examples of products competing more or less directly with Daloon's rolls. The large actors in the market like VandenBerg, Iglo, and Oetkers were furthermore independent of wholesalers as they distributed directly to medium-sized and large canteens.

In addition to the ordinary catering wholesalers Daloon cooperated with more specialized actors in the catering market. A substantial customer was ARA, which was a system gastronomic firm. Daloon's brand name products were included in the ARA menu sold by ARA's sales organization especially to small canteens and the like. A minor customer was Luckart, specializing in vegetable products. Daloon's vegetable products (rolls and soufflés) were included in Luckart's assortment as private labels. For Daloon this represented new opportunities in the consumer market as the firm was free to exploit the product concepts developed for Luckart over the years.

....

DISCUSSION QUESTIONS

1. Why was the German market so difficult for Daloon to enter? What was required to make entry successful?

2. How did the distribution differ between the retail and the catering markets in Germany?

3. What did Daloon do to counter the lack of attention given to its product line by the German distributors? What else could it have done?

*I*n Part Two, *Foreign Entry*, we focused on how the firm establishes its presence in foreign countries. Part Three now looks at the local marketing activities in the new countries.

The marketer is no longer at headquarters but located abroad. This shift has several important consequences. First, the marketer must analyze and segment markets, manage distribution channels, introduce products and services, develop effective promotions, capture market share, and increase sales. Even though the main strategic objective of the firm's presence in the country might be to check competition, monitor leading customers, or cross-subsidize a business elsewhere, the marketing job is still to be as successful as possible within the global corporate constraints.

Second, the marketer must learn more about the environmental factors, as the political, financial, and legal restrictions on business can create unforeseen headaches. Also, the social and cultural networks among customers and competitors work in new and mysterious ways. The marketing infrastructure has developed under different conditions, so that the functions performed by wholesalers, retailers, advertising agencies, and other middlemen may deviate from expectations.

Co-workers speak a different language, pledge allegiance to their own nation, believe in a different religion, and behave in unfamiliar ways toward each other.

Third, the focus is no longer on national boundaries. The local marketer is now concerned with the *market*—and the market may or may not be the same as the nation. The market could be larger, a free trade area or geographically close countries, or it could be smaller, ethnic or urban subgroups within a country.

In our discussion of marketing in Part Three, the manager will be seen as a marketer who is working within the special constraints created by a new and unfamiliar environment, with an arm's-length relationship to the home office. Chapter 7 presents the conceptual models underlying the marketer's understanding of customers and describes how the firm's treatment of its customers must be adapted to different cultures. Chapter 8 discusses the marketing research necessary to analyze and understand local markets. Chapters 9 and 10 show how the different market environments in maturing and emerging economies affect the local marketing effort. These chapters deal with strategy formulation, implementation, and execution under quite different conditions.

Local Buyer Behavior

"Buyers everywhere are the same—only different"

After studying this chapter, you should understand the following global marketing issues:

1. Despite cultural differences, customers all over the world are "rational" in the sense that they do what they do for a reason.

2. Because of widely differing circumstances surrounding product purchase and use, the core benefit of a product or service can vary considerably across countries.

3. Understanding customers involves conceptual skills and imaginative rethinking more than new analytical marketing skills.

4. Existing concepts and models of consumer behavior and industrial purchasing behavior are useful tools when examining buyers in local markets, but underlying assumptions need to be reconsidered.

5. Regardless of the specific local motivations behind buyer behavior, customer satisfaction remains the goal of the marketing effort.

CUSTOMERS FUNDAMENTALLY may want and demand the same things, but their specific product and service needs and preferences vary considerably between markets. The underlying reason is differences between cultures and environments, that is, the conditions under which products and services are used and consumed. These affect buyer behavior directly and influence how local marketing is performed indirectly. A good deal of the local marketer's work consists in adjusting her or his understanding of how and why customers and competitors behave as they do in local conditions.

This adjustment is not a matter of advanced marketing skills but of basic conceptual skills. To the extent they are relevant and applicable, most of the *technical* marketing skills required in a local market are very similar to those at home. This chapter will not deal extensively with those. On the other hand, there are sophisticated *conceptual* skills needed, especially when the local market is a leading market. To understand customers and competitors, the local marketing manager needs to develop a ''theory'' of what motivates the people. As a start, it is useful to get back to relatively simple models of buyer behavior—concepts such as the stages of consumer decision making, how information is processed by consumers, what external influences play a role in buying decisions, and how the individual buyer handles risk-taking—and reevaluate the assumptions underlying these models. Such conceptual rethinking requires a stretch of the imagination and constitutes part of the learning that goes into marketing abroad. The local marketer will develop conceptual skills, fresh ways of thinking about marketing, which can in the future be usefully applied in other parts of the world. And the significant features of the buyer behavior in the home market will be understood more clearly when contrasted against buyer behavior in other countries.

Customers Keep South African Brewery on Its Toes

Keeping customers' goodwill and (business) can be tricky, and it is especially so for countries experiencing social turmoil. National Sorghum Breweries is a South African company that markets sorghum beer, a thick, pinkish brew with a very short shelf life. Sorghum beer has deep roots in the African culture; it is traditionally the first drink served at an African wedding or funeral. Early in this century, however, the South African government took control of brewing and sales of the traditional beer and essentially made other alcoholic beverages unavailable to black

South Africans. Not surprisingly, ambivalence and even some hostility grew toward the product that was no longer controlled by the black majority.

During the changes that transformed the country in the 1990s, the South African government decided to return the industry to black ownership. Given its history, marketing sorghum beer might have seemed daunting. Nevertheless, Mohale Mahanyele, who led the investor group that bought what was to become National Sorghum, saw advantages. Sorghum beer had sprung from the African culture, and National Sorghum had an exclusive license to brew it. Plus, Mahanyele had fought apartheid peacefully through a group that demanded return of industries to the people, so consumer attitudes could perhaps be changed.

Although Mahanyele had to contend with massive turnover (most of the white employees quit rather than work for a black manager), National Sorghum's operating profit doubled in two years. But then came some crippling problems. The company purchased Jabula Foods, provider of packaged meals to the prison system and mining companies. When the acquisition became public, Afrikaner officials canceled the prison contract, costing Jabula more than half its income. Also, social upheaval in 1994 affected sales and distribution of the sorghum beer. Rioters burned some beer halls, and drivers were afraid to make deliveries. Sales suffered.

Consumer perceptions of the product had other effects. Black South Africans tended to view sorghum as a drink for poor people. When possible, they drank other beers. To expand its market, National Sorghum developed its own lager beer. However, it went head to head with South African Breweries, the country's largest brewer. SAB is better positioned to court retailers with special deals and freebies. The beer in a pub's refrigerator is therefore likely to be SAB's.

Despite these problems, National Sorghum has built its annual sales to $160 million, and in mid-1995, it sold 30 percent of the company to an Indian firm for about $1 a share—almost four times what its investors originally paid. Building the company's competitiveness and consumer loyalty should be easier with this additional backing.

In sharp contrast to the challenges National Sorghum faces are surprises in buyer behavior experienced by marketers elsewhere. For example, consumer goods marketers in China have been delighted to discover that Chinese consumers spend more freely than their official incomes would indicate. Apparently, they have more resources than the government realizes. And in Japan, many marketers are pleased to see consumers emphasize value, forcing the traditional, high-priced retailers to permit the opening of new channels. Apparently, where consumers are concerned, it's not safe to assume anything.

Sources: Donald G. McNeil, Jr., "Not Thriving in Its Homeland," *New York Times*, October 3, 1995, pp. D1, D4; Brian Bremner, " 'Made in America' Isn't the Kiss of Death Anymore," *Business Week*, November 13, 1995; James Sterngold, "The Awakening Chinese Consumer," *New York Times*, October 11, 1992, pp. D1, D4.

INTRODUCTION

Good marketing basics are good marketing basics everywhere. Understand buyer behavior, and treat the customer right. Offer products and services appropriate to the local usage conditions, have some competitive advantage, and offer quality that justifies consumer loyalty. Forget the kind of "pride in the product" that translates to "Since it's good enough at home, it's good enough here." Empathize with the customer's situation, don't fight it. Fight the headquarters instinct that says, "What we do is what they get."

It is not always true that one has to adapt to local cultural norms, do it exactly the way the locals want it, or forget about one's own heritage or pride in what one's company produces. There are times when breaking rules is good. Foreign companies successful even in idiosyncratic markets warn against overplaying the "cultural sensitivity" theme. Offering superior value to customers is as good a recipe for success in Asian, Latin American, and European markets as in the United States. *It is just that what constitutes "value" differs depending on actual usage conditions, what functions are really needed, and culturally contingent expectations about performance.*

The major factors that influence buyer behavior in a local market are summarized in Exhibit 7.1. As the diagram shows, *cultural* factors are a major influence on buyer behavior and are a source of wide variations in buyer behavior across countries. The various cultural forces discussed in Chapter 3 need to be assessed when predicting buyer behavior in local markets. Other external factors are important as well, including economics, technology, and

Exhibit 7.1   Diagram of Major Factors Influencing Local Buyer Behavior

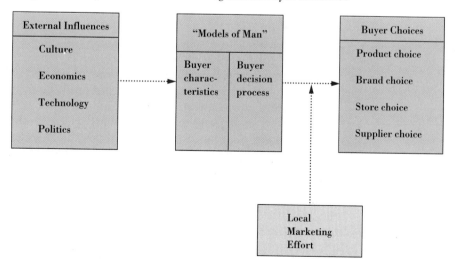

politics. These and related external influences determine the overall context in which the local buyer makes purchasing decisions.

The buyer box in Exhibit 7.1 involves the psychological and sociological models of man, which underlie how the marketer thinks customers should be approached. Buyer characteristics, such as personality, age, marital status, and life cycle stage are internal determinants of behavior and will be useful when segmenting the local market. In industrial purchasing, this box also includes the characteristics of the buyer's organization. The buyer decision process relates to the way the buyer processes information and makes purchasing decisions, which is a major issue for the local marketer since processes vary across markets and cultures. Finally, as the purchasing decision is made, the firms's controllable marketing factors (including product design, price, promotion, and distribution) become important influences on the choices made.

This chapter focuses on the "models of man" that underlie local marketing decision making in consumer and industrial goods. The aim is to explain what to look for in buyer behavior in the widely different cultures the local marketer might encounter. The chapter starts by discussing sociological and psychological factors important for understanding local customers. Next it covers decision making by consumers and how they go through the various steps in the buying process. The last section deals with buyers in business-to-business markets, emphasizing sensitivity to organizational culture and the pursuit of relationship marketing.

UNDERSTANDING BUYERS

Understanding people in foreign countries is often a baffling business. We see that they are born, experience childhood and adolescence, have common human needs, grow up, fall in love, and establish families, work hard, grow old. Everybody has a life. But what kind of life, and what do people choose to make of it, and why?

Of course, many groups of people are not in the position of being able to choose. A great number of people in the world live under such poor economic conditions that showing them vast choices of brands, products, or lifestyles would be pointless. They are stuck and just as likely to resent the inaccessible materialism they see advertised on the global communication highway.

But even among very poor people there are those who can and do, within limits, choose. The choices made will often astound an outsider. In a mud hut in Central Africa, where clean water is scarce, one will find a Sony TV set. In India, a paradigm of a developing country, a poor farmer is happy to show off his new Philishave electric razor. In the reopened China provinces, one can see Nissans and Toyotas navigating roads intended for oxcarts and pedicabs. And when the consumers in recently opened Eastern Europe go shopping, the result can be surprising for other reasons (see box, "Shopping but Not Choosing").

*G*etting the
Picture

Shopping but
Not Choosing

IN 1989 the East Berliners were first allowed free access to West Berlin's stores. Their surprise at the variety of products was palpable. In one case a couple with two carts strolled through the aisles of a supermarket, loading up on products at every step. Queried why they bought so many units of each selection, they responded: "How can we be sure these brands will be available when we come next time?" Another couple in a shoe store was surprised to find out that sales clerks were helpful in surveying the selections, locating the right sizes, and suggesting alternatives. "The way we see it back home," they explained, "clerks are there to guard the merchandise."

Sources: *The Wall Street Journal,* February 11, 1990; "A New Brand of Warfare," *Business Central Europe,* April 1994.

Consumption patterns are unpredictable without a feel for local culture. In affluent America, people in expensive Boss suits are happy with junk food but insist on the latest PC upgrade. In Germany, the food seems less important than unsurpassable beds, while in neighboring France, not to mention Belgium, food is a passion. The Japanese, those sticklers for quality details, seem oblivious to leaking roofs patched with plywood and corrugated sheets of plastic.

A Universal Trait in Local Form

The good news is that there is at least one simple truth about buyer behavior in all markets. *It is that most people are doing what they do for a reason.* Consumers perceive a link between behavior and desired results. Buyers do not choose products or services for no reason, even in the most fatalistic of cultures. Buyers are **goal oriented.**[1]

Thus, if one can find out what people in a local market are trying to achieve, one can start to understand their behavior. The local marketer should start by attempting to find out what *motivates* buyers by asking them what and why they buy, or by observing them buying certain products or choosing certain brands. (see box "Finding the Hidden Motivators"). Marketing research on motivation is not easily done, even in the United States, with the most straightforward customers. First, as psychoanalysis tells us, behavior has **hidden motivators.** They are not only willfully suppressed or denied by the buyer—choosing the rich dessert to finish the meal "just this one time." Motivators may be unconscious—choosing colors "I like" that have been suggested by fashion.[2] The result is that direct questions often fail to uncover the true reasons behind behavior, since the buyer does not necessarily perceive these drivers consciously. He or she may very well give very "sure" and "true" answers to direct questions; a fair amount of marketing research is based on the simple notion that people are willing and able to tell the truth. But psychoanalysis tells us this model can be misleading in any market.

---

*G*etting the Picture

Finding the Hidden Motivators

W H E N Marriott opened up a new luxury hotel in Jeddah, Saudi Arabia, it became an instant attraction for local luminaries and international travelers. The grandly decorated lobby with its large windows and magnificent entrance drew not only travelers and hotel guests but also local visitors. The large number of people crowded in the lobby delayed check-in and check-out operations, and long lines formed in front of the service counter. Managers of the Marriott headquarters in the United States soon determined that it was necessary to install the quick check-out system already in place in many of its hotels worldwide, which would allow the guests to leave quickly-without waiting in line.

But when the system was proposed to local management, objections were immediately raised. The managers explained that the customers of the new Marriott wanted to spend time in the lobby, to see and be seen, and to enjoy the status it conveyed; the long lines supplied a simple but legitimate reason for doing this. It was decided that a more rapid check-out process would be a negative benefit and the proposal was scuttled.

Source: Bruce Wolff, Vice President of Distribution Sales, Marriott Hotels.

A second consideration is that the **sociocultural** context within which the buyer acts not only influences behavior but also the perception of its motivators. In the West it is common to attribute choices to individual decision making. This goes well with individualism and the idea of "taking responsibility for one's own actions." In Eastern cultures it is less common to view the purchase as simply an outcome of individual deliberation. Responsibility is diffused among members of the extended family, relatives, and peers, and the decision is often justified at the group level. Individually motivated behavior is frowned on, even though it is common enough! Still, one does not want to talk openly about it or by seeming too ego-centered to open oneself to criticism. A similar reluctance to seem "materialistic" is of course detectable in Western countries.

A third complication is that the "means-end" relationship in buying can be more subtle than simply functional. One no longer chooses products or brands because they offer certain functions—the "demanding" customer takes those for granted. Instead the gratification is **emotional**—one likes the "look" of the new television set, the "feel" of the new car, and does not even know or understand many of the specific features. This has led marketers to say that consumers "buy the sizzle, not the steak." Thus, in some mature markets brand image and status are often assumed to be all-important. But this can be a misleading guide for a new local marketer who has to remember that quality and functionality are indeed taken for granted.[3] A global brand might be desired by local customers—but the product has to perform under local conditions, which the marketer must understand.

African villagers watching a soccer game on television. Their gathering in front of a single television set is not necessarily a sign of poverty but of a desire for a shared experience.

John Chiasson/Gamma-Liaison.

Perceived Risk

Most buyers make decisions under pressure. Tension comes not just from the trade-off between different features in different brands and the question of whether some extra option is worth the extra cost but from the buyer's aspirations and expectations and the expectations of relatives, peer groups, and colleagues. To an outsider, these pressures are often invisible.

The term **perceived risk** was coined by Raymond Bauer in the early 1960s to describe this tension in choosing.[4] Leon Festinger and his students at Stanford developed a related insight in their concept of **cognitive dissonance** to describe the emotional letdown of failing or thinking one had failed to make the right choice.[5]

These early developments in thinking about consumers occurred in sociology. Bauer and Festinger both emphasized peer group support in the way individuals handled risk. Generally speaking, sociology is the study of the impact of social forces on individuals and how individual behavior is molded by society. As the United States developed into a premier consumer market and the individualistic tendencies of the self-centered consumer society surfaced in the 1960s, the major aim of the economic system became the gratification of the individual consumer. The preface to the 1978 edition of a prominent American consumer behavior text illustrates this:

One of the most remarkable developments in the last two decades is the dynamic emphasis on the consumer as the focal point of the economic system . . . In part the awakened interest in the consumer is the result of a dramatic shift in demand-supply relationships, a change that has, in effect, placed the consumer in the fortunate position of being free to choose from many options. Thus business firms are now compelled to design and sell products that conform to the consumer's desires. "Consumer orientation" by the business firm, in turn, requires a solid basis of fact. It is not surprising, then, that analysis of the consumer has assumed a new importance.[6]

After the 1960s, the new models of the consumer in the United States emphasized psychology and treated societal forces as constraints on the individual that could be freely adhered to or transgressed. Increasing affluence led consumers to greater economic freedom, and, not surprisingly, to less reliance on family, group, or societal norms. Individuals were expected to decide what they wanted to be, and then make themselves into that person. The standard American marketing textbook followed suit, with environmental forces on the consumer occupying a minor role compared to individually based perceptions, cognitions, attitudes, affect, intention, and action.[7]

But this is misleading elsewhere in the world. Not many countries have gone through such a transformation yet. Economic affluence is still far away. Furthermore, in more socially homogeneous countries, even affluence is unlikely to engender the same tendencies towards individualism. The cultures of countries such as France, Saudi Arabia, and Japan are all based on a conception of a unique national tradition and show few signs of weakening social control even as the inhabitants grow increasingly well off. The reason is that social forces are not only negatives. They enable people to live in safety, protect individuals in need, help one get a job, alleviate the need to always justify one's actions, improve communication, generate a spirit of solidarity, and facilitate teamwork.

When a society is internally strong and orderly, social and other environmental influences on purchases are necessarily stronger. The weak social structure of the United States creates a bias in American marketing toward individual choice. Individuals are the focus, and even children are treated as decision makers. In other societies, the individual is less important. The typical man or woman dresses as he or she does because someone or something has suggested it. To understand these consumers, the local marketer has to pay attention to the sociologically important environmental influences.

Marketing and Materialism

Marketing actions are basically undertaken in the belief that more and better goods will bring an increase in consumers' standards of living, an increase in their satisfaction, and perhaps even more happiness. This assumption is often justified, but in emerging markets where capitalist dogma remains suspect, and in markets where religious and other cultural factors combine to denigrate materialism, marketers have to tread softly. For example, advertising "puffery," the use of innocuous exaggeration, may have to be avoided. What seems to be innocent play on words ("best in the West") in one context may not be seen as

Getting the Picture

Useful Economic Theories

EVEN THOUGH ECONO-MISTS have been ignored by most consumer behavior analysts in recent years, traditionally, understanding consumers was the job of economists. Some of the old economic theories are useful in countries where the marketer does not have immediate access to market research data on customer attitudes and motivations.

James Duesenberry's *relative income hypothesis* states that consumers' well-being is a function of how much income they have relative to their peer groups—absolute income levels matter less. Another economist, Milton Friedman, has proposed that what determines an individual's consumption is his **permanent income**, defined as the regularly expected income, without "transitory" factors that lead to a temporary increase or decrease in take-home pay.

These behavioral effects are useful to keep in mind when analyzing local consumers as well as local employees. Although from a psychological perspective they are superficial, not spelling out the exact mental processes involved, they offer useful insights when more in-depth psychological data are missing. A similar case can be made for the **conspicuous consumption** concept developed by Thorstein Veblen, an economist active around the turn of the century. Conspicuous consumption refers purcha produc ity to sumer behavior thinking goes further and deals with the underlying psychological processes, but the basic concept is still valid in many cultures.

Sources: Brooks, 1981; Veblen, 1899.

such in another cultural context. And many high-minded guardians of national culture will be offended by extravagant claims, regardless of merit.

When anticipating customers' reactions to new products and increased product choices, it is important to consider the very real limitations to which material affluence can generate happiness; Consumers have more products and enjoy more of the material—and also spiritual and cultural—things marketers bring. They lead "richer" lives. But richer is relative. Richer than what? As James Duesenberry, the Harvard economist, hypothesized several decades ago, the psychologically effective impact of rising incomes is that of the **relative income** not the absolute income level (see box, "Useful Economic Theories").

World Cup players from Europe making less than $250,000 a year are pitied in the media. In the United States, a cornerback in pro football making only $600,000 is cause for newspaper comparisons with more appreciated players.[8] Cornerbacks are by no means the highest paid players on a pro football team, and what matters is relative riches.

The fruits of progress are never distributed equally among a people, nor among nations. Even as one consumer gains, another gains more, and the first has lost, relatively speaking. This is why most of the emerging-world's consumers feel under so much tension. The past had a certain order and predictability that made them feel good, and they might long for or still depend on that security, while at the same time, from the media, store windows, and their peers they know the many things available in the marketplace—things the developed world enjoys. How can they be happy without them?[9]

The bottom line is that the new foreign entrant in a local market should recognize that the entry is not necessarily welcome universally. Of course, some emblematic arrivals are celebrated, such as McDonald's, Coca-Cola, and Marriott. But for many potential customers, not to mention competitors, new entrants create a lot of pressure. Over time, the spread of affluence may be viewed as good, but in the short run, the potential for a backlash always should be recognized by the marketer. And it is always important that the marketer ensure that the product and service offered can solve problems as promised.

CONSUMER DECISION MAKING

An adapted version of the flowchart model of individual consumer decision making first introduced by Engel, Kollat, and Blackwell helps in the analysis of how local consumers make decisions.[10] The authors distinguish between five hierarchical stages of a consumer decision process (see Exhibit 7.2).

This flowchart can be useful to understand consumers anywhere. Buyers uncover needs or problems, look for alternative ways of satisfying their needs (where alternatives are available), evaluate the alternatives against each other, make a choice, and get satisfied or not. But local market environments differ, affecting both how these steps are taken and what starts and ends the process. The flowchart can't be applied the same way everywhere. Understanding the American consumer of detergents does not mean understanding the German consumer of detergents. To paraphrase the well-known Rumanian playwright Ionesco, consumers are not consumers—in fact, detergent is not detergent.

The Meaning of a Product

A necessary preliminary step in analyzing local consumers is to question what the product or service "means" to them. What does the product or service do for the buyer? How does it fit into the consumption and use pattern of the buyer? What are the core benefits?

This is not a question of lifestyle or preferences of the consumer but rather a question of what the product represents generically, what the **core benefit** is. And the core benefit often differs between local markets.

EXHIBIT 7.2   **Consumer Decision Process**

Source: Engel et al. 1978, p. xi. Reproduced with permission of the publisher.

Some examples will clarify this. While the core benefit of an automobile may be transportation in some countries, especially large ones with a well-developed road network such as the United States, the auto is often a status symbol in less-developed countries. While disposable diapers may be bought for convenience in some countries, they are used for health reasons elsewhere. A credit card may offer more security and convenience than cash in some countries, while in others it offers a chance for parents to indulge their teenage offspring.

While these benefits are intermingled in most markets, and some segments of a local market will emphasize some over the others, the identification of a different core benefit is a necessary first step in analyzing local customers. Misunderstanding what the core benefits of a product are in a local market is sometimes a fatal mistake.

Because the product or service has already been marketed at home and perhaps elsewhere, most local marketers—and their headquarters counterparts—assume the core benefits of their offerings are well-known. But core benefits are not independent of the local environment. In fact, the core benefits of a product are a direct function of the environment. *The generic function of a product depends more on the local environment than on innate individual preferences.*

The core benefit of a car in the middle of Tokyo, for example, is hardly a matter of transportation. Still many families do own one to safeguard their social standing and boost their self-perceptions. Ice cream is bought for its healthy milk in India. Coca-Cola is recommended instead of local water in many countries. Disposable bottles are *not* convenient when space is limited and garbage is difficult to dispose of. Credit cards are convenient only when they are generally accepted and safe only when the charges from a stolen card can be stopped easily. Membership in a low-price club works only when bulk storage at home is possible. Even a simple product such as apples is not the same everywhere (see box, "Fresh Fruit in Japan").

So, the product often takes on a different meaning—or no meaning at all—in a local market. This means that certain products have no market—yet—in some countries. In others their core benefits have to be reformulated. In fact, the product or service itself may have to be reformulated or "localized." And, to repeat, this reformulation *is not adaptation to consumer preferences but to the local conditions of use.* The core benefits differ not because people are different but because the local infrastructure differs.

Problem Recognition

Problem recognition is what happens when an individual perceives a difference between an ideal and an actual state of affairs. The tension generates a motive for the individual to start the buying decision process in order to satisfy the need. New products often lead to tension and a recognized "problem," the way underarm deodorants suggest that "humans smell."

$\mathcal{G}$etting the Picture

Fresh Fruit in Japan

ONE OF THE LONG-ENDURING trade conflicts between Japan and other countries has been in the fresh fruit industry. Oranges from California, apples from Washington State, grapes from Chile, and bananas from the Philippines are only a few of the cases where entry has been denied at the border. Japan's domestic fruit industry is small but strong politically. Gradually, however, the foreign producers have been granted entry and are doing quite well.

The typical justification for keeping products off the Japanese markets is that they do not meet the standards expected by Japanese customers. Although this tends to hide the more important reason of wanting to protect the domestic industry, for fresh fruits there is a grain of truth in this argument. This is not because Japanese consumers want quality per se—it has to do with the core benefit of fruit in Japan. Until recently, fresh fruit in Japan was viewed as a specialty, even luxury product, usually bought during the gift-giving season. It had no particular role to play as a daily food supplement, in salads, for snacks, and so on. Thus, in the beginning, the imported fresh fruit was judged according to standards for apples at $5 apiece, cantaloupe at $40 a melon, and boxed grapes for $70, all turned out in beautifully wrapped gift sets. Not only did the customs officials deem the imported fruit below par, the consumer could not accept it. It was not until fresh fruit took on the new core benefit of a daily food supplement that the imported fruit was accepted. The industry acceptance was helped by the fact that creating a new core benefit amounted to enlarging the generic market for fresh fruit, also benefiting the domestic growers.

It should come as no surprise to the reader that the education of the Japanese consumer as to the new core benefit involved quite an effort in media advertising, in-store and magazine information about diets, and the promotion of fruit in American-produced TV programs broadcast in Japan. What is also interesting is that many of the foreign producers adopted advice by the Japanese officials about packaging, storing and handling the fruit, as well as adhering to demands about pesticide treatments. The imported apples offered for sale in Japan today are not only less expensive than the domestic varieties, but are literally the cream of the crop from the foreign producers. And, in a final twist of what global markets mean, the fresh fruit offered for sale in Western supermarkets today is more healthy, packaged better, and more carefully handled than before as a consequence.

Sources: Clifford, 1993; "300 Growers Protest U.S. Apple Imports," *Mainichi Daily News*, July 8, 1994, p. 5.

Because the core benefits may differ between local markets, the ability of a product or service to create a problem and satisfy the ensuing need will differ as well. The buyer may not perceive the offering as relevant or suitable, and the product will not be considered—the brand will not be included in the "evoked set." Large, Western-style furniture, for example, is simply not considered in some Asian markets—it is more or less useless for the Asian consumers' needs in their smaller homes.

In other cases, the introduction of a new foreign product or service leads to an increased awareness of new possibilities. The "ideal state" is changed; the consumer is made aware of the deficiencies of what was available before; the buyer's aspiration level is raised; and the offering "educates" the consumer. The new entry has "created a need," although one can argue that at some deeper level there was a latent need for this offering.

For the local marketer it is important to recognize that education about the core benefits might be necessary in order to create a demand for the product. But such promotion must first ensure that the core benefits are deliverable in the local market. To advertise "smooth ride" in a country with no paved roads will backfire.

This type of consumer education is not only about raising functional performance standards with new products or services. It is also about teaching the consumer to make finer distinctions between alternatives. These issues become important not only in the "evaluation of alternatives" stage of the decision process but also serve to create the stimulus for problem recognition. Increased awareness of what a product or service can deliver—a new shampoo with rinse and conditioning in one, for example—will create new criteria for choice. When entering a local market, such "firm-specific advantages" may have to be taught before the consumers recognize that they have a "problem" with their less-advanced existing products. This "need-stimulating" aspect of opened-up trade is one reason why foreign products are sometimes viewed by public policymakers as problem creators rather than problem solvers.

Search

The next step in the process, a consumer's **search** for alternative ways to solve the problem, is closely related to his or her level of involvement with the product category. For products with which involvement is high—because of a large money outlay, interesting products, or high perceived risk—search tends to be more comprehensive and time consuming, although previous experience and brand loyalty can reduce the effort. For convenience and habit purchases, the decision process is shorter, with little need for extended searches or alternative evaluations.

However, the search intensity is also dependent on the perceived availability of alternatives. In markets which have been closed to trade, consumers have had less exposure to alternatives, and then searching for alternative choices has not been worthwhile. The motivation to search is low, and the consumers' incentive to make an effort needs to be stimulated by the new entrant. There is often an aversion to innovations in such markets, the old product having a monopolistic advantage the consumer initially assumes is based on true superiority. No one really wants to find out that the tea they like so much is really not as good as the new varieties on the market, or that the old beloved manual SLR camera is inferior to a new automatic. The introduction of these new versions often needs to be done with a fair amount of persuasion by a credible spokesperson.

One advantage for products with high global brand awareness is that this initial distrust is easier to overcome. In many emerging markets the consumers have long waited for the arrival of these brands. There is a pent-up demand that the newly arrived global marketer can capitalize on. It is important to realize, however, that such a release will not automatically translate into future success. Once the mystique of a long-desired goal is dissolved, the consumer is likely to engage in more sober evaluation of the product's benefits.

Search and Innovations

The new local marketer should recognize that in many cases the new product represents an innovation to the consumer, and the level of search activity is influenced by the individual's psychological acceptance of new things. There are three useful categories for classifying such innovations: consumption substitution innovations, new want-creating innovations, and income-adding innovations.[11]

Consumption substitution innovations do not involve much new learning by the consumer. Already well acquainted with the product category, the consumer might turn to a new offering because of some new feature, or for the sake of variety, or because of brand image. Standard marketing know-how for mature markets—segmentation and positioning—are applicable here.

New want-creating innovations are the ones likely to create "problems" for the individual by raising levels of aspiration. Here the marketing problem is similar to a truly new product problem, with the same difficulties in educating the consumer about benefits, convincingly demonstrating how the new product satisfies the awakened wants, and then making it easily available at an acceptable price. As has been emphasized above, even if the product has been introduced elsewhere first, the local marketer can't assume that the core benefits are the same in this new market.

Income-adding innovations are the new products and services that promise to reduce the costs of solving the consumer's problem. This is not only a matter of offering lower prices, but of transmitting the core benefits at a lower total cost for the consumer in terms of time and money. Automated services often fall into this category. Buying an airline ticket over the phone using a credit card is generally less expensive in the total picture than for the customer to visit the travel agent personally. These kinds of innovations might have trouble being accepted in many countries not so much because the consumers "like" to talk to the agent but because the consumer can't trust the completion of the transaction, not understanding "how the system works." In addition, without proper protection from credit regulations, the credit purchase may be associated with high risk.

Thus, with new products—the typical situation for new local marketers—one can't expect that the new offering will necessarily be welcomed with open arms. For the consumer to start reconsidering loyal choices, he or she has to be given special reasons to consider a new product. This leads to the next stage of the decision process.

Young Japanese enjoying a novel kind of breakfast: cold cereal with milk and fruit. Many commonplace products taken for granted in certain countries in fact represent innovations in new markets.

Kellogg's® and Kellogg's® Almond Flakes are trademarks of Kellogg Company. Used with permission.

Evaluation of Alternatives

Once the new product or service is in the consumer's evoked set of alternatives, the highly involved individual will process the available information, matching the pros and cons of the alternatives against preferences.

There are several ways that consumers deal with these kinds of **multi-attributed evaluations.** Consumers can, for example, use gradually less-important features to successively screen out alternatives (a "hierarchical" decision rule) or consider all features simultaneously (a "compensatory" rule). The choices depend on factors such as involvement, product experience, and time pressure. Where customers are sophisticated, as in leading markets, compensatory evaluations are likely. Japanese buyers of cameras often spend a lot of time in stores comparing and assessing features. By contrast, in follower markets, especially in the early stages of the product life cycle, consumer evaluations tend to be more hierarchical. A desirable country of origin or the cachet of a Levi's or Nike, can be sufficient for purchase (see box, "One People, One Mind).

Even when more attributes are evaluated, which features are important can vary considerably between markets. Part of the reason is that the core benefits can vary. While a Mercedes may be bought for its luxury status in the United States, a used Mercedes may be bought for its dependability in Eastern Europe. While Levi's are practical and functional in the United States, they may convey status in Germany.

In markets such as the North American, where many similar products vie for attention, simple functional superiority is not easy to gain or sustain. At this point, the consumer is likely to focus on less-tangible benefits, such as brand image, up-to-date features, and aesthetics. The success of the Jeep in Australia

*G*etting the
Picture

One People,
One Mind

LEVI'S JEANS seem to be in demand in every corner of the world. American tourists abroad sell their pairs to local citizens at inflated prices, and foreign tourists flock to American shopping malls to buy jeans. As trade barriers and distribution inefficiencies in different local markets disappear, the global market opens up and pricing becomes more uniform. But differences in competitive intensity and exchange rates mean that wide price differences persist, and Levi's continue to be status products in most markets except at home in the United States.

The newest development is a demand for used Levi's from the vintage years of the 1950s and 60s, when James Dean, Johnny Cash, and Jack Kerouac first established jeans as the protest wear of rebels. Roaming through flea markets around the United States, bargain hunters from Europe, Asia, and elsewhere pay cash for used jeans, repair them as needed, and resell them at home and elsewhere. A true vintage pair can fetch as much as $3,000, and many sell for as much as $100. The markets span the globe, from Finland and Poland to Australia, Japan, and Thailand.

Sources: Janofsky, 1994; Quintanilla, 1995.

and Japan is not based on the functional aspects that dominate in the United States but on its status. The local marketer should not forget the functional aspects, however, since quality performance is a necessary condition for purchase. Inferior performance on essential features will not go unpunished.

For low involvement purchases, it is well known from market research that the time and effort required for a thorough evaluation of the available information are often too demanding on the average consumer,[12] who resorts to simplified rules of thumb, such as "choose the brand with the second-lowest price." Such rules are difficult to discern without keen observation on the part of the marketer and an understanding of the foreign culture (as well as his or her own culture).

Choice

The final choice of which alternative to select or try is influenced by social norms and by situational factors, including in-store promotions.

SOCIAL NORMS   Where group pressures to comply are strong, as in many non-Western cultures, one can expect influence of **social norms** to override any multiattributed evaluation. The social norms can be usefully analyzed by the so-called extended Fishbein model.[13] A flow diagram of the Fishbein model, as simplified and adapted to marketing, is given in Exhibit 7.3. Fishbein hypothesizes that a person's behavioral intention derives from the multiattributed evaluation of the alternatives but is modified by the social norms (Fishbein originally used the term behavioral norms) affecting the choice. The multiattribute evaluation results in an overall ranking of the alternatives in order of

EXHIBIT 7.3   The Extended Fishbein Model

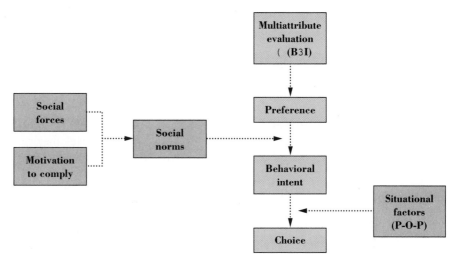

B = beliefs about product attributes; I = importance of the beliefs, P-O-P = point of purchase.
Source: Adapted from M. Fishbein and I. Azjen, *Belief, Attitude, Intention, and Behavior*, p. 334. © 1975
Addison-Wesley Publishing Company, Inc. Reprinted by permission of Addison-Wesley Publishing Company,
Inc.

preference. As Exhibit 7.3 shows, the social norms involve two aspects: the social forces themselves and the individual's motivation to comply.

Social forces represent the pressures and normative suggestions that come from an individual's family, peer groups, social class, and other external forces. For example, an autoworker in Germany will face some pressure to buy a German car, regardless of individual preference. A successful pension fund manager in the City of London is more likely to wear an expensive analog Rolex rather than a cheap digital watch however versatile and reliable.

Motivation to comply relates to the willingness of the individual to listen to what others say and think. This is very much a matter of culture. In high context and homogeneous cultures where norms are both enforceable and enforced, the motivation to comply will usually be great. Most people will know what products, features, brands, and stores are "acceptable," and adhering to the norm will have tangible benefits. Buying the right brand brings memberships, invitations, and opportunity. You "belong." Individualism, on the other hand, which represents low motivation to comply with others' demands, will be costly, since sanctions can be enforced. You are an "outsider," not unattractive in low context cultures where sanctions can't be effectively imposed. James Dean, the quintessential American outsider, is used by Levi's to advertise its jeans in Japan. Paradoxically, but not surprisingly, for the "young rebels" in Japan, wearing Levi's means that they "belong."

The high value placed by Confucian cultures on the importance of social norms suggests that, in general, Eastern cultures show much more of an impact from social norms than do Western cultures. This was borne out in one study of athletic shoes comparing behavioral intentions of Koreans and Americans. As hypothesized, Koreans showed a significantly greater willingness to consider peer group influence than did Americans.[14]

SITUATIONAL FACTORS Exhibit 7.3 also shows how the **situational factors** impact behavioral intentions. Situational factors vary from lack of shelf space and inability to get the product stocked by stores, to problems in controlling the prices faced by the ultimate buyer, to prohibitions against in-store promotions to help induce trial. There is no excuse for the local marketer not to get a firsthand look and feel for what the obstacles may be at this level of the decision process. This is where "the rubber meets the road" and there are numerous situational factors that could ruin the best-laid plans.

One issue needing attention is who the buyer is. Is the decision maker the father, the mother, or the children—or someone else—in the family? Who executes the decision in the store? To what extent is the choice made before the store is entered, and, accordingly, who needs to be targeted via media advertising messages?

As before, knowledge from home markets or elsewhere may be misleading. Many European husbands buy the groceries in supermarkets as wives with higher incomes stay at work. Teenage children are prime deciders of automobile choice in Japanese families. Choices of schooling and careers for children are made by many American fathers; these are a matter of the children's preferences in European countries; in Japan it's a mother's issue of getting her children into the best school. Who makes decisions about what food to eat, what clothes to wear, and whether to take a vacation varies widely across cultures, and the local marketer can't make assumptions. Find out!

Outcomes

The degree to which consumers achieve satisfaction with their purchases also varies across cultures, as recent satisfaction surveys amply demonstrate.[15] This is not surprising, considering what factors make for high satisfaction.

The most obvious determinant of satisfaction is the actual performance of the product or service when used or consumed. But basic functionality does not necessarily mean that satisfaction is high. As we saw in the evaluation section, where product and service quality are high, basic performance is not necessarily a big factor in consumer evaluations. That the car starts in the morning is usually no cause for rejoicing—unless, of course, one's expectations are very low, as must have been the case with buyers of the notorious Trabant in former East Germany. Satisfaction is very much influenced by the expectations of the buyer.

Customer satisfaction tends to be high when expectations are exceeded and the consumer is pleasantly surprised. It is important to recognize that the competition existing in the local market already has generally set the requirements for the new arrival's acceptance. The new entrant has to offer something new or special. This is why entries from a leading market have a better chance of success than others.

Another determinant of satisfaction is previous experience—or lack of it—with the product category. To some extent, this experience helps form the expectations about acceptable performance. In markets where products have only recently become available, expectations are based on reputation, not previous experience. This, however, does not mean that expectations are low. Unverified stories and word-of-mouth information in emerging markets have made many consumers hold unrealistic expectations about the general happiness they will experience when markets are flooded with products. Any one product's performance can generate dissatisfaction when expectations are unrealistically high.

The lack of supporting infrastructure can also be a problem in emerging and developing markets. The promise of a new shampoo might only be realized where showers are available and the water is clean. Expecting personal computers to significantly raise white-collar productivity might be unrealistic in societies where computer literacy in the educational system is low and company managers lack skills.

In the end, the consumer is back to the core benefits and the degree to which the use and consumption experience manage to validate those essential benefits, and possibly satisfy other, more esoteric desires. Consumer well-being is the aim of all marketing, and it is important that the new local marketer realize the challenge that the local consumer is confronted with. In many cases the need is not yet recognized by the prospective buyer, in others the new product may not be able to deliver because of lack of infrastructure support, and in yet others the new product may be out of reach of the customer's budget. New products and brands do not only bring improvement and a better quality of life. They create problems that need to be solved and wants that need to be satisfied. The local marketer must make sure the firm's offering can solve the problems and satisfy the needs.

LOCAL INDUSTRIAL BUYERS

Marketing to local industrial buyers is different from marketing to local consumers. Because buyers are also people, psychology comes into play to some extent, but the organizational context makes for a different decision process.[16]

The Local Business Marketing Task

At the outset it is useful to define the local business marketer's task more precisely. Five types of business-to-business buying situations can be distinguished:

1. Buying raw materials and industrial supplies on the open market.
2. Procuring parts and components for further processing.

3. Buying finished products from an original equipment manufacturer (OEM) for resale.

4. Buying products as a distributor.

5. Buying a complete system or "turnkey" operation.

Situation 1 is important in international business but does not require much in terms of understanding buyer behavior. A typical case would be a trading company buying oil on the spot market in Rotterdam. These kinds of markets tend to involve simple exchanges, often computerized, and with the buyer and sellers not in face-to-face contact.

Buying situations 2, 3, and 4 involve more in-depth contacts between buyers and sellers, and marketing becomes correspondingly more important. All three usually involve the creation of long-lasting relationships. In situation 2 the local marketer's role is as a supplier to the buying firm, and issues of quality control and punctual delivery become important. Situation 3 is similar, but here the local marketer needs also to evaluate the performance of the buyer as a marketer of the company's finished product and assess whether the OEM strategy is preferable to establishing its own brand. When selling to a distributor (situation 4), the local marketer needs to consider what assistance should be offered to market the product further down the distribution chain.

The purchase of a turnkey operation (situation 5) involves much wider considerations, since here the marketer usually works in tandem with other vendors. This type of situation will be dealt with further in Chapter 13, Global Pricing, since the decisions involve negotiations about contracts and costs.

Concentrating here on situations 2, 3, and 4, since they involve similar activities, the job of the local business-to-business marketer can be more clearly defined. He or she needs to establish the foreign firm as a dependable supplier to an independent business organization operating in the local market, where the buyer in the local organization is usually a native of the country. The local business uses the product for further processing or resale, in the OEM case under its own brand name. The competition consists of other suppliers, both domestic and foreign, who can also provide the parts and components, the OEM product, or the branded product to be distributed.

In this situation, a local marketer with the appropriate customer orientation has to understand the local buyer's position in the organization, the other people and factors in the organization which influence the buying decision, and the role the product (and the marketer) play in making the buyer successful in his or her organizational role. In short, the local marketer should help the buying organization succeed—and make the buyer look good. A challenging task, especially in a foreign country.

Individual Buyer Factors

Several personal factors influence how well the buyer performs the job. Typical variables to assess include age, income, and education relative to others in the organization, professional identification, personality, and, especially important

A Colgate sales rep makes a call on a store owner in Mexico City. In this kind of open-air market it is important for the salesperson to offer merchandising display tips, explain special promotions and rebates, help unload slow-moving inventory, and also to understand who really makes the decisions, the owner or his wife.

Courtesy of the Colgate-Palmolive Company.

in foreign markets, attitudes toward risk. In many countries, it is also important to assess the buyer's family background, and his or her past and likely future career path in the organization.

Depending on personality and underlying cultural conditioning, buyers tend to develop styles of dealing with vendors. A basic consideration is how the buyer treats the seller—as an equal, or less than an equal. American marketers steeped in a democratic tradition find it hard to accept the inequality and subservience in more hierarchical societies no matter where it's exhibited, but especially when it affects them, as sellers. But it is important to recognize that despite a more advanced product or service offering, the seller is in a sense there to serve, and what is important is to serve the needs of the prospective customer. It is only when competing suppliers are nonexistent that the seller becomes the equal of the buyer. Western companies have long prided themselves on technological uniqueness, but as global competition intensifies, even aristocrats have to adopt a "customer first" attitude.

Attitude toward risk is intimately tied to an individual's willingness to change. Changing from an existing domestic supplier to a foreign supplier is usually a very risky decision. First, it is not easy to evaluate the new supplier, especially when many of the engineers and managers are foreign. Second, the reliability of supplies is questionable, since many suppliers give priority to buyers in their own country or with whom they have done business for many years. Third, although it is natural to start out with a small order, this is also a means by which the patience and commitment of the foreign firm are tested further. Fourth, terminating an existing domestic supplier sometimes carries with it political negatives (unemployment, plant closings), which make it more than a simple cancelling of a business transaction.

Thus, to believe that the local marketer's job is just to present a better problem solution is naive. More has to be done. To signal a strong level of commitment to the new market, the CEO or another top executive might have to visit the prospective customer. Quality questions have to be answered promptly, local language product information has to be offered, and any questions about potential delivery delays due to time differences, geographical distance, or transportation problems have to be dealt with effectively. As further elaborated below, the risks involved in a buyer's adopting a foreign supplier lead to high up-front costs and require a long-term, relationship-building approach to the transaction.

Buying Process

Just as in consumer markets, the business buying process can be depicted as a sequence of steps. The flowchart in Exhibit 7.4 delineates these steps.[17]

Problem recognition can occur when quality inspections are done, when a breakdown occurs, or, in routine purchasing, when inventory controls show that supplies are low. In nonroutine cases, there follows a *need specification* phase, which determines the functions that a purchased product or service must perform. It is in this phase that reengineering often gets started. Reengineering involves questioning why the functions are necessary and whether a whole new approach might not be better. For example, rather than replace a broken water pump, why not shift to aircooling? Rather than install faster paper copiers, one company shifted the policy on internal memos to "e-mail only."

Next follows the *product specification* phase when the desired features of the product or service are specified. In this important phase existing suppliers often have an inside track, since they can ask for their particular attributes to be specified. This is a typical entry barrier, with new foreign entrants excluded because of what might seem nonessential requirements. For example, American office equipment firms selling to U.S. government offices lobby for "Buy American" rules in their business so as not to lose the government as a customer to a foreign supplier.

The next two phases are a *search for suppliers* and *proposal solicitation*. They can involve active search or passive announcements of a proposal opportunity. A major task of the local marketer is to make sure that local opportunities are effectively covered and leads followed up. Many foreign subsidiaries have local staff members in sales whose task it is to scan newspaper announcements for proposal solicitations and to maintain contact, perhaps daily, with larger accounts and prospects. Since one of the drawbacks of the foreign company is the fact that it is rarely an insider getting called on by the customer, the salesmen have to be very active and often initiate contact.

Industrial Buying Process

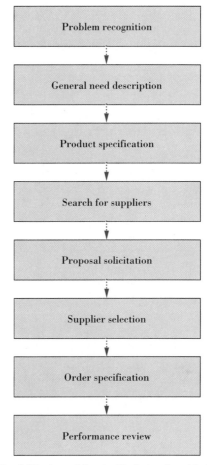

Source: Robinson, et al., *Industrial Buying and Creative Marketing*. Copyright © 1967. All rights reserved. Adapted by permission of Allyn & Bacon.

The final stages involve *supplier selection, order specification,* and *performance review.* By this time the main preselling task has usually been completed, and the attention shifts to closing and contracts, a domain in which the marketer often needs legal help. The performance review needs to be anticipated and designed by the time of order specification, and it is the marketer's role to see to it that after-sales service is strong enough to render a favorable review. Word-of-mouth spreads easily among companies in the same industry and in smaller countries, and the local marketer needs to realize that the early sales will become barometers of competitive advantage or disadvantage.

Not all the stages are passed through in each case. For example, companies often attempt to routinize many purchases after a supplier has proven its worth. So, the new local marketer's sales representative often must call on a prospective buyer even though no proposal has been solicited. The fortunate marketer is present at the beginning of the stage when the product specifications are set down, and can then perhaps become the sole qualifying supplier. More commonly, however, the newly arrived local marketer has to try to wrestle an account, away from a favored domestic supplier.

Organizational Influences

The buyer in an organization is usually only one of the actual decision makers. Buyers are persons with formal authority for selecting the supplier and arranging the terms of purchase. The users of the product or service—engineers, designers, manufacturing managers—often have more influence on the decision of which supplier to choose. Then there are upper-level executives who have to sign off on a purchase decision. In the organizational linkages between these groups there are various "gatekeepers" and influencers who can wield unseen authority.

These individuals have different impact at different levels of the buying process. Users are typically more influential in the early part of the process, up through product specification. The senior executives may have real influence early when resources have to be allocated, but the signing off on the selected supplier may be more of a pro forma step, especially in decentralized and bottom-up organizations.

Although ideally a local marketer may wish to establish a strong and trusting relationship with all these parties, such a perfect world rarely exists even at home, but especially not in a foreign setting. For example, in many Asian organizations formal position descriptions tend to be vague or misleading, making it very difficult to identify key people. But it is important anywhere to try to identify the degree to which the buying decision is based on group consensus or whether there is one influential decision maker, which is quite common among Asian companies, even in Japan. In many old-style and hierarchical European companies it is common for a buyer to affect independence and entrepreneurial initiative, while in fact the decision is made by a group of senior executives. The local marketer needs to remember that it can be slightly embarrassing for a buyer to admit that others in the organization make the decision. Or, as usual, buyers may use others' alleged need for consultation as an avoidance tactic or to postpone a decision.

The group decision making involved in many industrial purchases means that cultural influences will be strong, both from the organizational culture and the culture at large. As we saw in Chapter 3, most organizations reflect the culture of the country or region where they are located, although there are instances of geocentric organizations which try to remove ethnocentric cultrues from the organization (IBM, Philips, and Sony are some examples). In most instances, the local marketer, when approaching the customer, will have to be guided by both local cultural norms and the specific organizational culture involved.

Because of the complexity or unfamiliarity of organizational influences, it is not easy for the local marketer to define exactly what is needed by the buyer. Matters such as cost, quality, and dependability are usually as necessary abroad as at home, but may not be sufficient to make a sale in many organizational settings. Personal rapport with a senior executive may be more useful than a demonstration of technical superiority to an impressed engineer. There are countless stories of high-tech suppliers venturing abroad only to find their welcome less than enthusiastic despite their product's obvious advantages. The stated reason is often that a foreign supplier cannot be relied on, a sort of "company security" argument. More likely, the supplier is not able to satisfy the varying needs among the several people involved in the purchase. Shifting to a new supplier, for example, often involves a loss of face for some existing procurer in the organization who has demonstrated the strength of the previous supplier (see box, "Japan's Keiretsus").

Relationship Marketing

For the local marketer contemplating the business-to-business marketing task, it is helpful to anticipate establishing a long-term relationship with the buyer and the buying organization. **Relationship marketing** is the term applied to a marketing effort involving various personalized services, creation of new and additional services, and customizing a company's offering to the needs of a special buyer. Although the idea of relationship marketing is adaptable to consumer markets, it is obviously more applicable in business-to-business marketing. The Japanese vertical keiretsus provide good examples of what relationship marketing is about. As another example, Citibank has tried to attract and build strong relationships with wealthy customers in many countries by offering extended banking hours, a separate lobby with attractive decor, comfortable seating, and sometimes free drinks.

Relationship marketing takes a long-term view since without it the effort required to build a relationship is hardly worth it. The up-front costs of developing the mutual trust and confidence of a relationship are greater than the revenues from a single sale. A dependable relationship is beneficial to both parties in the long run. The buyer does not have to go through the buying process every time a purchase is required. The seller overcomes the barriers created against competitive entry, thus justifying the investment in learning about the organizational culture, the particular people involved, the product and service requirements, and the local culture. The relationship must create a win-win situation.

This is easier said than done, even between companies in the same country. On the seller's part there is a definite need for the people-skills discussed in

'I'd better write it down.' A representative of Thermofrost, an American company specializing in cooler equipment, explains the maintenance of a newly installed freezer display to a store manager in Britain. Getting customers off to the right start is important in relationship marketing.

Courtesy of the Parker Hannifin Corporation.

Chapter 3, "Cultural Foundations." There are several key things that the marketer can do to create a workable relationship.

Adopt the buyer's viewpoint. The aim of the local marketer is to be useful to the local buying organization. As always, this means that the product or service must fill the required specifications and after-sales support must be forthcoming. Perhaps even more so than at home, the supplier must pay attention to all the influential people in the organization, not only the buyer. In some foreign countries, gift-giving and so forth may come uncomfortably close to paying bribes and other unethical behavior. There is a fine line to walk as the local marketer gets acculturated. The guideline here should be the supplying firm's ethical standards and above all the individual's own standards of conduct. A good rule to adopt is whether one would do the same thing at home, considering all the possible ramifications.

Accept and demand transparency. Not based on a legally binding contract, the relationship has to be based on mutual trust, something achievable only with openness—especially across cultures. The buyer has to learn enough about the supplier and its operations to be able to gauge the credibility of the promises made. By the same token, the buyer needs to allow some insights into its operations and its personnel, so that communication concerning product and service modifications can flow easily. Local middlemen that can be trusted by both sides play a role here. The need for trust also excludes the use of "bribes" to middlemen, apart from the legal and ethical considerations involved in payoffs. A simply market-based relationship or arm's-length relationship is but a marriage of convenience. It does not generate customer satisfaction, provides no barrier to competitive entry, and will not help the foreign firm recoup investment made in the foreign entry.

Grow with the relationship. The long-term view implies that unavoidable changes due to unforeseen circumstances (common enough in global marketing) must be acceptable to both parties. The relationship should be established on the basis that both parties will grow together, a dynamic relationship providing satisfaction of current needs and potential for stretch into new areas and challenges. This is what foreign entry and marketing abroad are all about to begin with. The rewards of versatility were the rationale for the global effort. Thus, a static view is incompatible with today's global competition.

Be proactive. Make your company useful and irreplaceable to the buyer. Suggest novel solutions, point out potential problems. Stay close to the knitting. All these familiar exhortations are generalities which have to be invested with real meaning by the local marketer and the sales representatives, given the unique local environment and the buyer's organizational culture.

It is useful to distinguish between standardized off-the-shelf products and customized offerings. In the former case, the seller's task is usually to provide a steady supply to middlemen, offer a reliable product, and provide after-sale service, as necessary. "Proactive" here simply involves helping the customer get maximum benefit from the purchase and ensuring continued support given local needs and conditions. Examples include trucks, machine tools, and industrial supplies.

Being proactive takes on a larger role when products sold involve customization. In many situations industrial products are bought as "problem solutions" in the buyer's factory or office. Slow handling of customer orders, delays in warehouse shipments, and increased customer complaints are typical of some of these problems needing solutions. In such "reengineering," the buyer is likely to need more initial help in developing a solution. Buying some PCs off-the-shelf, adding a truck to the fleet, or adding a telephone operator might be just stopgap solutions. In these "consultative" selling situations, the proactive marketer needs to have more expertise, invest more time studying the client's business, and provide a "system solution" (see box, "Boeing's Sales Pitch"). Needless to say, such proactive relationship building requires a very strong global sales operation.[18]

It is important to keep a close watch on the costs incurred in servicing the customer. In some cases the buying firm has "turned the tables" and exploited the services of the supplier without counterbalancing through increased revenues. The Japanese subcontractors are sometimes exploited like this by their large customers, being forced to cut a greater percentage of costs than the buyer. Procter and Gamble's efforts at giving its large Wal-Mart account special attention soured when Wal-Mart unloaded costly inventory functions on P&G. When the supplier and the customer come from different cultures, such potential hazards are even more potentially dangerous.

As in all relationships, power becomes an issue. Bosch, the German supplier of auto components and parts to many European auto companies, strives to maintain a good relationship with its customers. But after the firm opened a modern plant in Japan for the production of ABS braking systems, customers demanded that their new ABS systems should come from the superior Japan plant. Wanting to preserve good relations, Bosch had no choice but to consent, even though it meant curtailing production at its German plant.

Networks

In industrial markets the creation of relationships between buyers and sellers has over time led to the formation of networks of independent companies. One well-known version of such a network is the so-called **keiretsu** of Japan, with a large number of firms collaborating. There are *horizontal keiretsus*, usually led by a large bank, with noncompeting firms in different industrial sectors combining to support each other, and *vertical keiretsus*, in which a lead manufacturing company links a large number of suppliers of components and parts and distributors for its products. An example of a horizontal keiretsu is the large Mitsubishi group; Toyota represents perhaps the best-known vertical keiretsu (see box, "Japan's Keiretsus" on p. 263).

Because of the access to other members in a network, becoming a member yields additional advantages over and above those of the single relationship. On the other hand, to become a member of a network is often difficult, since it involves acceptance by several seemingly unrelated companies. Thus keiretsus are often accused of keeping foreign suppliers out of the Japanese market.

Getting the Picture

Boeing's Sales Pitch

THE BOEING COMPANY, located in Seattle, Washington, is year in and year out the United States' largest exporter. The company's planes can be found in the fleets of most airlines around the world. What kind of sales pitch sells these planes against the competition of European Airbus and some smaller competitors?

As most newspaper reports suggest, pricing (that is, financing) is perhaps the most potent marketing weapon. The Export-Import Bank of the U.S. is an important ally of the Boeing company, helping to offer favorable financing terms. The product is perhaps second in importance, involving attributes such as safety record, advanced technology, fuel efficiency, and customer comfort. And the planes, although they seem to be "off-the-shelf" with standardized designations, same engines, and a few optional "body stretches," actually are somewhat customized in terms of seat sizes, color schemes, and cabin configurations.

In terms of service the company offers training programs for pilots and mechanics, and maintains a regular office with local staff in the cities of major customers (in London for British Airways, in Frankfurt for Lufthansa, in Tokyo for JAL and ANA, and so on).

The company also helps customers in business matters only vaguely related to airplanes, such as helping sons and daughters of high officials find appropriate schooling in foreign countries.

While some, if not all, of these efforts can be duplicated quite easily by accomplished competitors, Boeing relies on a trump card which in some cases is hard to match. The company gives the prospective buyer a complete system evaluation of the customer's existing fleet and route structure. Over the years, the Boeing aerospace engineers have developed very sophisticated computer software for forecasting air traffic demand, evaluations of various route structures, and the identification of optimal fleet configurations. In their sales presentations, the Boeing engineers will use the software to analyze the customer's need for new aircraft, given the existing fleet and its age, and suggest additions. As a hypothetical example, if the customer intends to buy two new A320 Airbuses, Boeing might be able to show how a combination of a 747 and two 737s will be more cost effective. The problem solution offered is validated by Boeing's years of experience and high-tech wizardry. This is proactive, relationship-building marketing.

In a long series of studies, Swedish researchers have expanded the notion of networks into the international arena. Analyzing large Swedish exporters of primarily industrial products (such as Ericsson in telecommunications, Asea in power generation, Volvo and Scania in trucks, and SKF in ball bearings), the researchers have identified the critical role of **network building** in the international operations of these firms.[19]

These networks of linkages between independent firms in different countries are a source of competitive advantage in local markets. Creating a strong relationship with a foreign buyer takes on a greater strategic role than a narrow focus on the particular transaction would suggest. Over time, the seller gains further understanding of the new market, expansion into related products, and access to other potential customers. Viewing the relationship as a long-term commitment that can grow and change, the Swedish companies attempt to overcome their natural weakness of a limited home market.

In the last few years, as the increased European integration and the growth of the regional trade blocs (NAFTA, ASEAN) have encouraged consolidation of such networks, the Swedish companies have been very active in forming strategic alliances and in mergers and acquisitions. The ties between the units in the networks have become closer, and competition in the markets is often between the networks rather than individual companies. What is important to point out here is that the local marketer, when establishing a supply relationship with a local buyer, may be planting a seed for a mutually beneficial long-term relationship to help ensure survival in the new globalized economy.

....

SUMMARY

As a new local marketer, one's assumptions about reasonable buyer behavior have to be put on hold. It is important to "zero-base" one's mind to the extent possible, and approach buyers with an open mind. It helps to remember that most people make purchase decisions for a reason, however vague or hidden. But it is necessary to keep in mind that the core benefits of the products or services in a foreign country might be very different from what they are at home. Understanding new customers abroad involves getting to know cultural strangers.

Once the core function of the product or service has been identified, it is useful for the marketer to look at how the consumer goes through the usual steps of decision making, from problem recognition to search and evaluation to final choice and outcome. At each stage of this decision process the cultural differences between different local markets will affect how the consumer acts and what happens next. Understanding the consumer abroad involves not only relearning the role the products play in a different context but also how local peer groups and other social influences affect the consumer's decision making.

At the business-to-business level, buyers are constrained by the people and other factors in their company, making organizational culture an important influence on buyer decision making. Since national culture is one important source, but not the only one, of organizational culture, the job of the local marketer is often to separate what he or she knows about the culture at large and what happens in the individual firm. The ultimate aim is to learn as much as possible about the main users, senior executives, and other influential people in the company, and then to use this knowledge to structure an offering that will help the buyer succeed too in a win-win relationship. Selling to industrial buyers involves creating a long-term, mutually beneficial relationship that is potentially the start of a global network.

KEY TERMS

Attitude toward risk p. 259
Cognitive dissonance p. 245
Conspicuous consumption
  p. 247
Core benefits p. 249
Customer satisfaction p. 256
Emotional gratification p. 244
Goal orientation p. 243
Hidden motivators p. 243
Keiretsus p. 266

Motivation to comply p. 255
Multiattributed evaluations
  p. 253
Network building p. 267
Organizational influences
  p. 262
Perceived risk p. 245
Permanent income hypothesis
  p. 247
Problem recognition p. 249

Relationship marketing
  p. 264
Relative income hypothesis
  p. 247
Search p. 251
Situational factors p. 256
Social norms p. 254
Social forces p. 255
Sociocultural context p. 244

DISCUSSION QUESTIONS

1. "Consumers everywhere are the same. Look at the way they adopt all the American products. I am sure that if the governments would only open up the markets, all consumers would in the end become just like us." Comment on this statement.

2. Give an example of how an individual purchase decision can be complicated by cultural forces. Give an example of cultural forces facilitating a consumer choice. Can you find a product or service for which in one country cultural forces complicate the choice, while in another country for the same product choice is made easier?

3. What would you see as the pros and cons of relationship marketing for a Western supplier to gain access to a Japanese overseas plant? For a small computer software American firm to gain access to a large European company?

4. What differences would you expect to find between the organizational culture in a large German multinational and that in an American MNC in the same industry? What factors might make the cultures very similar?

5. Identify a product with different core benefits for different local markets abroad? Motivate and explain your choice.

NOTES

1. The idea of goal-oriented consumer behavior is by no means new—see Solomon, 1994. But it is important to keep in mind, since some non-Western religions have a fatalistic bent, which tends to make human action pointless. Consumer behavior is not pointless.

2. Dichter, 1964, is the father of this line of reasoning.

3. See Solomon, 1994, p. 425.

4. The different sources of perceived risk are discussed further by Solomon, 1994, p. 228.

5. The original source is Festinger, Leon, *A Theory of Cognitive Dissonance* (Stanford, CA: Stanford University Press, 1957).

6. See Engel et al., 1978, p. xi.

7. This is still the typical approach—see, for example, Solomon, 1994, and the 8th edition of Engel et al., 1995.

8. From *The New York Times*, August 23, 1994.

9. There have been numerous features in daily newspapers about the plight of consumers in Russia and Eastern Europe. See, for example, *The New York Times*, August 21 and October 7, 1994, and March 10, 1995.

10. See Engel, et al., 1978.

11. See Sheth and Sethi, 1973.

12. There are many studies of "information overload," including Jacoby et al., 1974, and Keller and Staelin, 1987.

13. See Fishbein and Ajzen, 1975. An early application in marketing is presented in Ryan and Bonfield, 1975.

14. See Lee and Green, 1991.

15. Comparable satisfaction scores for various products on the market are now compiled annually for several countries, including the U.S., Japan, Germany, and Sweden (see, for example, Fornell, 1992).

16. This section draws on Robinson et al., 1967, and Rangan et al., 1995.

17. Updated from Robinson et al., 1967.

18. A detailed analysis of this so-called "interaction approach" to industrial marketing can be found in Hakanson, 1989.

19. See, for example, Hakanson, 1989; Forsgren and Johanson, 1992.

SELECTED REFERENCES

Brooks, John. *Showing Off in America.* Boston: Little, Brown, 1981.

Clifford, Bill. "Yes, Those U.S. Apple Growers Protest No Access." *The Nikkei Weekly,* April 19, 1993, p. 4.

Dichter, Ernest. *Handbook of Consumer Motivations.* New York: McGraw Hill, 1964.

Engel, James F., David Kollat, and Roger D. Blackwell. *Consumer Behavior,* 3d ed. Chicago, IL: Dryden, 1978.

Engel, James F., Roger D. Blackwell, and Paul W. Miniard. *Consumer Behavior,* 8th ed. Chicago, IL: Dryden, 1995.

Fishbein, Martin, and Icek Ajzen. *Belief, Attitude, Intention, and Behavior.* Reading, MA: Addison-Wesley, 1975.

Fornell, Claes. "A National Customer Satisfaction Barometer: The Swedish Experience." *Journal of Marketing* 56, no. 1 (January 1992), pp. 6–21.

Forsgren, Mats, and Jan Johanson, eds. *Managing Networks in International Business.* Philadelphia: Gordon and Breach, 1992.

Hakanson, H. *Corporate Technological Behavior: Cooperation and Networks.* London: Routledge, 1989.

Hochschild, Arlie Russell. *The Managed Heart: Commercialization of Human Feeling.* Berkeley, CA: University of California Press, 1983.

Hofmeister, Sallie. "Used American Jeans Power a Thriving Industry Abroad." *New York Times,* August 22, 1994, pp. A1.

Jacoby, J.; D. E. Speller; and C. Kohn. "Brand Choice Behavior as a Function of Information Load." *Journal of Marketing Research* 11 (1974) pp. 63–69.

Janofsky, Michael. "Levi Strauss: American Symbol with a Cause." *New York Times,* January 3, 1994, sec. C, part 1, p. 4.

Keller, K. L., and R. Staelin. "Effects of Quality and Quantity of Information on Decision Effectiveness." *Journal of Consumer Research* 14 (1987) pp. 200–213.

Lee, Chol, and Robert T. Green. "Cross-Cultural Examination of the Fishbein Behavioral Intentions Model." *Journal of International Business Studies* 22, no.2, (1991) pp. 289–305.

Quintanilla, Carl. "Not Your Ordinary Blue Jeans: Antique Levi's May Fetch $75,000." *Denver Post,* September 7, 1995, p. C-01.

Rangan, V. Kasturi; Benson P. Shapiro; and Rowland T. Moriarty. *Business Marketing Strategy: Concepts and Applications.* Chicago: Irwin, 1995.

Robinson, Patrick J.; Charles W. Faris; & Jerry Wind. *Industrial Buying and Creative Marketing.* Boston: Allyn & Bacon, 1967.

Ryan, Michael J., and E. H. Bonfield. "The Fishbein Extended Model and Consumer Behavior." *Journal of Consumer Research* 2, no. 2, (1975), pp. 118–36.

Sheth, Jagdish N., and S. Prakash Sethi. "A Theory of Cross-Cultural Buyer Behavior." Working paper, Department of Business Administration, College of Commerce, University of Illinois, Urbana, IL, 1973.

Solomon, Michael R. *Consumer Behavior.* 2d ed. Needham Heights, MA: Allyn & Bacon, 1994.

Veblen, Thorstein. *The Theory of the Leisure Class.* New York: New American Library, 1899.

Womack, James P.; Daniel T. Jones; & Daniel Roos. *The Machine That Changed the World.* New York: Rawson Associates, 1990.

Chapter 8

Local Marketing Research

"What is going on here?"

After studying this chapter, you should understand the following global marketing issues:

1. Although wide differences between countries exist, the globalization of markets has meant that there is a constant increase in data availability and research possibilities inside foreign markets.

2. There are numerous sources of errors in cross-cultural research, including mistranslated questionnaires, strong demand effects, and poor control over the administration of surveys.

3. With sensitivity and skill, marketing research techniques, including focus groups and questionnaire-based surveys, can be adapted and used in foreign cultures.

4. As with forecasting, the best approach is to always attempt to get more than one study or data source to support an important decision.

VARIOUS DATA GATHERING and research tasks were discussed in Chapter 4, "Country Attractiveness." The "unit of analysis" was the country or the larger trade region. In other words, the data all referred to country characteristics, that is, were aggregates of country data. In this chapter we get inside the country and focus on *local market* research, the typical application of traditional marketing research.

Finding out about customers and competitors in a local market is, in principle, not different between countries. The aim is to understand what motivates and satisfies customers, their needs, wants, preferences, and dislikes, and to understand competitors, analyze their behavior, and predict competitive intentions and reactions. Good marketing research involves a research design based on sound methodology, sampling that yields representative data for the target segments, questionnaires and other measuring instruments that generate accurate and unbiased responses, and data analysis that produces valid and reliable results. Good marketing research is good marketing research anywhere.

The problem is the *local environment*—or, perhaps more accurately, the problem is the marketer's foreignness. The differences from home in social and economic institutions, the educational level, the cultural and religious traditions, and other underlying factors affect directly the degree to which formal market research is possible and useful at all and what needs to be done to adapt it appropriately to local conditions.

The aim of the research is not so much to be scientifically correct as to be pragmatically correct in the often "rough-and-ready" local conditions. It is more important to ask the right questions than to ask the questions right, since asking the right questions in a foreign culture is an art in itself. Since the aim is to understand the customer and predict the competitor, research that gets the correct answer most efficiently is the best regardless of the elegance of the method. In this respect, the formal methods employed in traditional market research are sometimes not only inapplicable, but inappropriate, under foreign local circumstances.

Getting to Know the European Consumer

Despite all the talk about an integrated European Union, the European consumers are hardly homogeneous. According to Tom Broeders, an independent marketing consultant in Belgium, "Europe is a collection of different cultures related to language and habits." Often, differences in consumer behavior follow ancient boundaries. Thus, in Belgium, the people of the northern region of Flanders use margarine; those of the southern region of Wallonia use butter. Even as the West European countries lower economic and political barriers among themselves and pan-European products such as Procter and Gamble's Vizir detergent, Heineken's Buckler non-alcoholic beer, and Nissan's Micra are introduced, cultural and demographic differences persist and make systematic market research essential—but complicated.

Marketing research in Europe must blend flexibility, intuition, and knowledge of what information resources exist in each country. The researcher's first lesson is that multiple sources are usually necessary. For demographic data about European consumers, researchers must rely mainly on national and regional government agencies, such as each country's national statistical institute. However, privacy concerns in some countries limit data availability. In Germany, for example, the notion of a census was rejected for many years—Germans feared government interference in their private lives.

Each country also has its own way of organizing data collection, and countries often do not use the same breakdowns of simple classifications, such as income categories, occupations, and business size. European marketing research firms often segment consumers in a variety of ways, making cross-national comparisons difficult. The researcher must also be prepared to overcome obstacles ranging from intense concern about privacy to market researchers' limited access to computer systems.

Language differences make the creation of pan-European survey questionnaires difficult and expensive. These problems will diminish as the European nations begin providing more data for cross-national comparison and market researchers test pan-European strategies. One example is the joint European development of a standardized questionnaire that is administered annually and collects comparable data on a number of sociodemographic, political, and economic indicators. Called the Eurobarometer, it was originally written in French and English, translated by native speakers into 12 other languages, then back-translated into French and English to check for subtle variations in meaning.

Also on the positive side, studies comparing media use and buying behavior have designs similar to those conducted in the United States. People meters, scanners, and consumer panels are common tools in Germany, France, the United Kingdom, Italy, and The Netherlands. And with the increase in the number of market research firms with networks covering several countries, there are practical ways to overcome the hurdles that arise in international marketing research, including the not-so-trivial problem of coordinating data gathering and analysis across countries.

As always, researchers and other marketers should visit each country they want to serve. Looking around with the help of a good interpreter can enable them to develop their own insights about why potential customers would want to buy their product. Firsthand information about the local market still remains essential.

Sources: Blayne Cutler, "Reaching the Real Europe," *American Demographics*, October 1990, pp. 38–43; Thomas T. Semon, "Red Tape Is Chief Problem in Multinational Research," *Marketing News*, February 14, 1994, p. 7.

INTRODUCTION

Marketing research forms the basis for informed marketing decision making everywhere. Marketing research techniques are generally not culture-specific nor bound by markets or countries. Nevertheless, the applicability of various research tools can vary considerably between markets in different countries, because of institutional, cultural, social, and other environmental differences. Thus, even though marketing research is necessary, the local effort might be decidedly different from the typical textbook case.

This chapter will discuss research on the environment, then deal with the gathering of customer data. This is followed by research on competition. The final section will deal with research directed toward the various marketing decision areas. The chapter will start by briefly considering why research is valuable to the marketing decision maker.

THE VALUE OF INFORMATION

It is useful to understand the principles of when market information is valuable to a local marketer. There are four of them—and a fifth applicable just to foreign local marketing.

PRIOR KNOWLEDGE   One obvious reason marketing research is particularly important abroad is that the decision maker's knowledge of the marketing environment, of the customers and competitors, is often so weak. What motivates buyers, who the competitors are, and what channel members respond to are basic marketing questions about which understanding may be limited. Ignorance raises the value of information.

DECISION IMPACT   But ignorance alone is not a good reason for doing research. If it were, most entries would never be undertaken, since there are always things left to know. The important point is for the decision maker to identify what kind of information, and how much of it, will impact a decision. In other words, the question is what kind of research will make for a different decision about marketing strategy in the local market. For example, when companies enter the EU market, they often do it on the basis that "they have to have a presence there." For new information to change this conviction, it has to be very dramatic.

The local marketer's research is limited to the specific marketing actions that can be considered. Thus, to uncover that the local currency is volatile might make little difference. To learn that politics in the country is corrupt might similarly be interesting but won't affect marketing decisions. But some seemingly irrelevant environmental event might have strong impact. Privatization of the airwaves, for example, might lead to greatly enlarged possibilities for advertising. Downsizing a drug testing bureaucracy might make it more difficult to introduce new products quickly because test approvals could be delayed. This information would be good to have.

VARIABILITY   When customers can be expected to differ widely in their preferences, desired product attributes, and usage habits, the value of good market information increases. If on the other hand, education is standardized, populations are ethnically homogeneous, and religious and cultural traditions are strong, people are often quite similar in attitudes and behavior. If, at the same time, the news media tend to follow the same line, there is often a striking unanimity in people's understanding of themselves and the outside world. And when there is less variability, research can quickly generate a sense of the marketplace, and the value of more large-scale research is diminished.

This is often quoted as one reason why marketing research for segmentation purposes is so important in the United States—the diversity among people is greater than in many other countries. By contrast, research in more homogeneous countries such as Norway, Korea, and France can make do with smaller samples and less advanced data analysis.

LEVEL OF COMMITMENT   When the stakes are high, information becomes more crucial. The deliberations and data gathering before a new model is introduced or a new campaign theme is approved tend to be protracted. When the decision is irreversible, such as that of a major new product launch, firms collect a lot of information. In the case of Vizir, the pan-European liquid detergent from Procter and Gamble, the product was researched and tested for four years before the "go" decision was made.

If confidence in one's understanding of the market is low, the firm may opt for an incremental "go-slow" approach to a local market, releasing the product gradually with a slow roll-out through the market and distribution channels, moving into new areas only as sales rise and more is learned about the market. Alternatively, the company can do full-fledged test marketing, as was done for Vizir. Test marketing is usually a very expensive but sure way of getting data on product acceptance. The disadvantage of test marketing is also clear: It gives the local competitors plenty of warning and time to direct a counterattack, sometimes by introducing a "me too" version. At the same time as Vizir entered the European markets, Henkel, the German competitor of P&G, introduced a similar product.

These four factors are the principal determinants of the value of information in standard marketing research.[1] In foreign markets there is a fifth principle—the need to reconsider what to focus research on in local conditions.

FOCUS   The usual research project in home markets revolves around customer reactions to various contemplated marketing activities. In survey research, for example, primary data might be collected from consumers or business customers to assess buyer evaluative criteria, attitudes, and buying intentions. Testing advertising may involve exposing some consumers to a contemplated campaign theme and comparing their responses to those of a matched unexposed sample. These "fine-tuning" studies are rarely cost-effective in new foreign markets. What matters here is a better understanding of much more fundamental determinants of buyer behavior, to get deeper into the broad underlying environmental determinants of demand.

ENVIRONMENTAL DATA

Because foreign markets present new and different marketing environments, the most valuable marketing research for the local manager is often that which deals with very simple and basic—but easily overlooked—factors.

Back to Basics

First of all, remember that usage situations vary and they affect customer choices directly. It is not a matter of attitudes and preferences, but simply "reality." Home furniture does not sell well where homes are small. Electric toothbrushes are less than useful when electricity is expensive. Small cars and thin-soled shoes make big people uncomfortable with good reason. Placing a PC on the desk of an executive in many countries insults a status hard won. And so on.

It is not useful to research customer evaluation of a product if its basic functionality is not understood. One study tried to identify the demand for and desired course content of an international executive program by asking managers in Asia, Europe, and North America for rankings of various topics. The study sponsor did not realize that for many managers one major motivation to participate lay simply in the status it conferred upon the manager, independent of the content of the course, something uncovered when telephone callbacks were made.

Similarly, individual attitudes may be irrelevant when the buying determinants work at group level. In high context cultures, clothes and other personal items carry significant image connotations. Finding out through research that people are buying certain brand names because they "like the style and the quality" hides the real reason: strong social pressure. To make matters worse, this sort of cultural reason is often hidden and unconscious to the buyer and the harder for research to uncover, precisely because it's so fundamental.

Thus, in new local markets, the most valuable market research centers on very basic environmental determinants of consumption and buying behaviors. The local marketing campaign that goes wrong abroad often does so because of unexpected differences in environmental factors (different from the home market) that are missed or ignored. Especially in the early stage of local market penetration the unfamiliar environment mandates reassessment of what the firm's key success factors are. As the experience of the U.S. Department of Commerce in Thailand shows, research methods can be quite unconventional (see box "Market Potential in Rural Thailand").

Environmental Dimensions

For research purposes it is common to distinguish four **environmental dimensions:** (1) physical; (2) sociocultural; (3) economic; and (4) regulatory.[2]

PHYSICAL   The most obvious environmental factor affecting people's behavior is the *climate*. The humidity and heat of the Eastern Seaboard of the United States in the summer (and of many other countries as well) dooms polyester

---

$\mathcal{G}$etting the
Picture

Market
Potential in
Rural Thailand

MARKET RESEARCH in some countries requires novel and imaginative methods. When the U.S. Department of Commerce wanted to evaluate the market potential for various American manufacturers in Thailand, they were faced with a dearth of data on the Thai market. "Bootstrapping" the knowledge and experience of their embassy people in Bangkok, they developed an ingenious indirect method. They linked the potential of a trade area to the presence of various social and economic institutions and created a five-level grading scale of the potential in various areas. Trade area potential was ranked according to the presence or absence of buildings—town hall, temples, train station, and schools—easily ascertained through photographs or personal visits. The more buildings, the higher the potential.

Sources: Amine & Cavusgil, 1986; U.S. Department of Commerce.

---

fabrics, encourages air conditioning installations, and raises property values for summer houses in cooler places like Vermont or Maine. The heat and humidity should raise air conditioning sales also in Southeast Asia, but the soft housing construction, necessary because of the region's propensity for natural disasters, prohibits effective insulation. The cold of Russia has made furs a particularly common Russian export product, although the lack of adaptation to Western styles and to countries with less chill thus needing lighter furs has prevented further penetration of the best markets.

Researching the physical environment involves examining the geography of the country, studying the climate charts, and, especially, personal visits. Naturally enough, the impact of the physical environment on behavior is largely imperceptible and "hidden" to the people living in a country, so the best information comes from the newcomer's own observation. Here the lack of prior exposure to the country is a benefit. The Japanese are fond of sending very fresh people to the United States, because they are able to observe American behavior without prejudice. They are also more imaginative. As the well-known one-liner about Japanese marketing acumen goes: "People here go barefoot—what a great potential for shoes!"

Several levels are involved in tracing the marketing effects from the physical environment. Apart from its direct effect on clothing, fabrics, housing construction, and food and drink, the harshness, for example, of a physical environment has countless historical secondary effects. People in cold climates need more food, more sugar and fats, are bigger, use stronger designs, are harder on equipment, and demand individual space. Products need to be strong, reliable, and functional, since breakdowns can be punished by the harsh conditions. In softer climates products can be less reliable, people interact more easily, and there is less emphasis on individual self-sufficiency. Relationships between people are nursed, and products need to be acceptable and approved by one's social peers. The physical environment is responsible for a number of traits associated with national cultures that affect consumer "problems" and desire for products to solve them.

A Kodak bill-board at a bus stop in China. Transit advertising tends to be strong in densely populated areas, since many people use mass transportation. It is especially useful for brand awareness and the introduction of new features and products.

Reprinted courtesy Eastman Kodak Company.

SOCIOCULTURAL   Social and cultural influences are usually less obvious than physical factors, and the researcher needs to both observe and talk to people to collect the data. It is usually not sufficient to observe social gatherings, talk to experts and interpreters, or read treatises on the behaviors of the people in the local market. The marketer needs to develop a "feel" for these factors by immersing himself or herself in direct contact with the locals. This is not easy without language competency and is one of the major and very good reasons why there is such stress on learning a foreign language in "how to do business in . . . " literature.

Some of the important sociocultural aspects to look for are the following:

1. *To what extent is social interaction viewed as a way to pass on information versus simply building relationships?* Conversations in the United States, for example, can take on the character of question-and-answer interviews. In other cultures, the aim is to make the other person feel good, a sort of "making love" with words. Needless to say, things like word-of-mouth advertising take on a different role in such cultures.

2. *To what extent are interactions hierarchical versus horizontal?* In democratic countries, assumed equality tends to make people speak the same regardless of position. An observer can't judge who is the president

ALTHOUGH PAMPERS, the
Procter and Gamble diaper brand, had
well-documented problems in its early
years in Japan, the cause was not for lack
of market research. But the research that
was done during the introductory and
subsequent periods did not probe deeply
enough into the usage and functions of
disposable diapers in Japan. For example,
although research showed that the
mothers liked the product itself, it did
not tell P&G that they did not like the
way their babies looked in the diapers.
The bulky stuffing made little difference
to American mothers who were thinking
of function and convenience—so the
Japanese mothers were not even queried
on that point. Furthermore, since research
showed that the ease of changing
diapers was an important benefit, the advertising
featured fathers ably taking
care of the baby, a mistake. The research
did not catch the fact that although men
might influence purchases, traditional
Japanese fathers are usually proudly inept
in handling their offspring.

Sources: Yoshino, 1990; Richard Laube,
advertising manager, P&G Japan.

among a group of five. By contrast, in less democratic contexts, it is
clear who is speaking to whom and with what weight. Opinion
leadership, assumed to rest with one's peers in the democratic West,
takes on a different meaning when the opinion leader is one's superior.

3. *Do people take responsibility for one another, or do they treat each person as an
   independent risktaker?* Recommending a doctor or a vacation destination or
   a brand to one's friend is easy in the United States, since one is not
   responsible for the outcome. In other cultures it is necessary to make sure
   that the outcome will be a success—which also means that
   recommendations are offered less readily.

These are the kind of subtle sociocultural differences market research has to
uncover since they directly affect how customers make decisions about new
products and services. There are other, more obvious sociocultural factors that
can be accessed readily by the local marketer through *secondary data* analysis. The
role of women in the work force, the spending power of young teenagers, and
the influence of groups versus individual desire on purchasing decisions are
factors directly affecting marketing programs that can readily be discerned
through secondary sources. The local marketer needs all the information he or
she can get. In many countries, urban sprawl and efficient mass transportation
have made transit points major marketplaces. Transit advertising can be very
effective in such environments, especially among groups that can't be reached by
other promotions. White-collar workers in Southeast Asia who stay at work late
are more easily reached by transit and newspaper advertising than by TV advertising,
for example. Such relevant social phenomena are uncovered through
both means—studying secondary sources and making hands-on, personal visits.

The P&G Pampers story in Japan shows the impact of subtle sociocultural
factors on local marketing (see box, "P&G Pampers in Japan"). Doing the
proper market research as it is defined in one's home country does not ensure
that the right answers will come forth.

*G*etting the Picture

The Eastern European Customer

WHEN THE EASTERN EUROPEAN countries opened up after the fall of the Berlin Wall, most Western manufacturers assumed that the customers would be eager to buy their products. In many cases they were disappointed by customers who seemed reluctant to switch to the new and better brands. Price and purchasing power were a problem, but interviews with shoppers who stayed with their old brands showed that many of them had enough money to buy the new products. According to the interviews, the problem was that the consumers could not choose between the new variants on the market, since they simply did not have enough understanding of the different features. The Western brands in shampoos, for example, offered "conditioning" and "rinse" and other features such as "two-in-one" and "hair repair," confusing attributes which the Eastern European customers could not translate into benefits. The solution was to change the advertising copy and to offer in-store descriptions on the shelves.

Source: M. Wolongiewicz, student report, International University of Japan, June 1994.

ECONOMIC The level of economic development is naturally a major determinant of local buyer behavior. Disposable income data are easily available from secondary sources and are, by and large, reliable. But without more information on the income distribution and the social impact of economic well-being, income-per-household data can be interpreted incorrectly. For example, in some countries there can be a dramatic difference in spending power between the rich few and the many poor. In others, there can be a seemingly strange allocation of spending among the poor away from necessities and toward relative luxury goods. One can see many television antennas among the corrugated metal and plastic sheet shacks in the barrio encircling Mexico City, for example. What research needs to uncover is the effect of income on the buyer decision-making process.

The logical evaluation of a purchase in terms of quality and price is perhaps a realistic model for analyzing Western middle-class buyers but often too rational to capture the essence of buyer decision making elsewhere. Emotion, social status, processing deficiencies, and sheer lack of experience often lead to "suboptimal" choices by individuals in the poorer strata of society, even from the individual's own viewpoint.

Questionnaires need to be administered in person because of low literacy levels, and questions can rarely be structured as rigorously as is standard in the West. Open-ended questions designed to elicit verbal responses and probing to generate reflective comments are common methods for exploring how purchasing decisions are made. The aim is mainly to gain information about obstacles to product purchase and effective product use, and the research is explorative (see box "The Eastern European Customer").

REGULATORY The institutional framework within which markets function is designed to enable or prohibit certain business practices, in short, to regulate the markets. It is of course very important that on-the-spot research uncovers

---

*G*etting the Picture

Ikea in Germany

IKEA, THE SWEDISH furniture retailer, was able to break into Switzerland quite easily from a base in Zurich in the German language part of the country. Preliminary research—and the short cultural distance—suggested that Germany, the big neighbor to the north, would be a natural next target. But the story in Germany was decidedly different. German retailers organized a strong counterattack, with lawsuits and concerted efforts to cut off supplies. Even though the Ikea entry finally succeeded, it took the company much longer than expected after the Swiss entry. The German store regulations, although similar to the Swiss regulations, were enforced more effectively, something the research had failed to uncover. The German furniture retailers combined forces and challenged Ikea in the courts, while the fragmented Swiss retailers had acted reluctantly and independently. More research might have helped.

Sources: Martenson, 1981; Bartlett and Nanda, 1990.

exactly what is and is not possible under local laws and ordinances. In-store promotions, for example, are usually subject to various limitations the new local marketer needs to identify. Such research is best done through a research assistant who can contact government agencies, trade associations, and various libraries. Research also should be used to uncover the extent to which trade associations and similar networks of actual and potential competitors are present. This research usually involves the local marketer directly. For example, researching distribution in a local market is best done through lots of personal visits, face-to-face interviews, and talking to academic experts. It is important to find out who the movers and shakers are and how their network operates. Ikea's experience in Germany is instructive (see box, "Ikea in Germany").

While practices at home may or may not be similar to those in the new market, there are always nuances which can make or break an entry campaign. The local manager needs to learn as early as possible the main features of the regulatory environment and the paths through which the entry can best proceed.

CUSTOMER DATA

The most basic function of marketing research is to understand the customer. Thus most market research texts deal a great deal with techniques for collecting and analyzing data directly from consumers and industrial buyers. But for the global local marketer, in many local markets abroad, getting valuable information from the consumers directly is not so easy, and other sources have to be used.

Apart from the customers themselves, in foreign markets two important avenues through which to understand the customers are talking to the middlemen and observing the products on the market. Traditional market research emphasizes talking to the consumers, but in many foreign markets, even mature ones, these other avenues are equally useful and often less expensive.

The Stages of Consumer Research

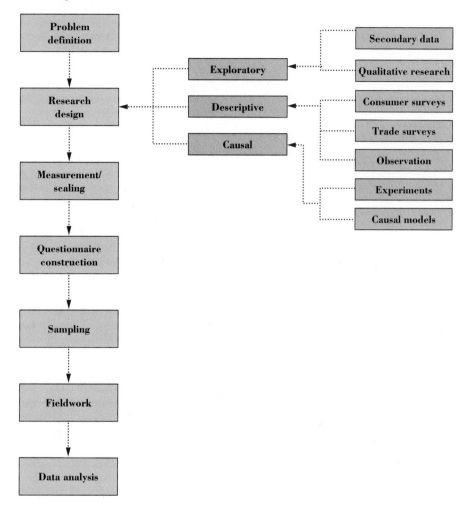

Research Stages

There are several stages involved in the typical consumer research project. They are given in Exhibit 8.1. Apart from the last stage, data analysis, all the stages of the research process can be affected by a foreign environment. They will be discussed in order.

PROBLEM DEFINITION   It is common to distinguish between the marketing decision problem and the marketing research problem. The decision problem in a market might revolve around the question of what to do about declining sales, and the research problem might be to assess customer attitudes and satisfaction levels. The same research might not be applicable in another market, even though the decision problem is the same.

For example, over several years the California Almond Growers Exchange was unable to penetrate the Japanese market even though there were no real trade barriers and domestic competition was weak or nonexistent. Planning to do a study of consumer attitudes toward almond nuts, the association first decided to do a marketing audit, tracing the sales through the distribution channels. The real cause of low sales was found to be the lack of distribution coverage. A deal was struck with Coca-Cola Japan, which had in place 15,000 salespeople and over 1 million sales locations throughout Japan. The association has now captured over 70 percent of a growing market.[3]

SECONDARY DATA   With the globalization of markets, the availability of **secondary data** (data already collected and available) on markets in different countries has grown exponentially. Various independent firms, from advertising agencies, to international research firms, to electronic news media, have emerged to gather and sell information on markets in different countries. Although such information is often most useful for the broader country screening process (see Chapter 4), there is an increasing amount of data available on buyer behavior in the different markets. Furthermore, leading firms are increasingly building representation and capability to do market surveys in different countries, including the emerging economies.

A useful start when doing research is always to look at the easily available *secondary data sources*, such as the U.N. publications, the OECD and GATT/ WTO reports, and the Department of Commerce reports in the United States. After that, the search should get more focused on in-market data such as consumption patterns and spending for various product categories. If available, syndicated data on consumer buying intentions and attitudes should be consulted before the usually expensive primary data collection starts. Some of the sources are listed in Exhibit 8.2.

....
EXHIBIT 8.2   Selected International Data Sources

The Economist Intelligence Unit (EIU): Marketing in Europe (product markets in Europe— food, clothing, furniture, household goods, appliances). EIU now also owns BI (see below).

Business International: BI data base (consumption patterns in different countries).

Frost & Sullivan: Syndicated market research for various industries in different countries.

Euromonitor: European marketing data and statistics (population, standard of living index, consumption).

Bates Worldwide: Global scan (spending patterns, media habits, and attitudes in different countries).

U.S. Department of Commerce: Global market surveys (research on targeted industries); country market surveys (more detailed reports on promising countries for exports); overseas marketing report (market profiles for all countries except the United States).

QUALITATIVE RESEARCH   Although there are many forms of qualitative research, the well-known **focus groups** have become standard for initial exploratory research in many markets.[4] Recruiting carefully screened users and potential buyers of a product, research companies gather 8 to 10 individuals around a table to share opinions about a product or service. Guided by a moderator's questions, the participants are encouraged to voice any misgivings about a design or dislikes about a color pattern, to point to ambiguities in translated advertising copy, and so on. The responses are taped, usually on video, and the sponsoring marketer can observe the proceedings from behind a one-way mirror.

In foreign markets focus groups have the advantage of being relatively inexpensive, can be completed quickly, and can reach local pockets of the total market. Unfortunately, they can also be **unrepresentative** because typical screening criteria are incorrect in the new environment or are not implemented correctly. For example, when the Italian maker of Campari, the aperitif, asked for a series of focus groups of "buyers" in the United States, the local research firm could not find any buyers to recruit. Agreeing to lower the screen to "users," the Campari maker was dismayed to find that the users recruited knew too little about the beverage to give any useful information. The Italian company refused to pay for the research.

In general, the small nonrandom sample sizes of focus groups make assumptions about representativeness tenuous at best. It is also important to remember that respondents get paid, and even if it is usually a small amount (typically $25 in the United States, about the same in Europe—the amount varies by city and by respondents' occupation, more than by country), this will tend to inhibit the expression of negative feelings. Another problem is that the moderators—and the research firms—are usually specialized in certain products and customers, and may be less than ideal for other consumer groups. A German company sent the videotapes of five focus groups to a Japanese client, who was surprised to observe the dominating attitude of the moderator toward his respondents. The moderator, not without pride, explained to the perplexed sponsor that he usually dealt with corporate customers for industrial products, not teenagers discussing audio tape design.

These and related problems can be overcome with careful planning of the focus groups. Representativeness in terms of geographical areas is usually dealt with by selecting certain cities that are leading markets for the products. In the United States, New York and Los Angeles are often viewed as trendsetters—in Germany, it is Berlin and Munich. Few U.K. studies can avoid London, and the same is true for studies in France (Paris), Italy (Milano), Spain (Madrid), and Scandinavia (Stockholm).[5] The moderators chosen should be professionals who can identify in some way with the subjects and make them feel at ease. The amount paid should be sufficient to make a difference and thus be an **incentive,** but not so large as to invite praise. The screening criteria should be related to the level of market sophistication. To get consumers in emerging markets to help adapt the product is often pointless, since they usually have little experience and no confidence in their own judgment. By contrast, local users in leading markets are often ideal key informers for the adaptation of a global product.

Consumer intercept survey for Colgate Plax at a hypermarket in Paris. As consumers globally face more choices, the importance of research increases. The "shopping mall intercept" method for selecting respondents has thus become increasingly common.

Courtesy Colgate-Palmolive Company.

CONSUMER SURVEYS   **Surveys** of relatively large (n=500 and above) random samples drawn from a sampling frame of representative product users constitute the "meat and potatoes" of traditional market research. Whether administered by mail, phone, or in person, such surveys are used for a variety of marketing purposes, including segmentation and positioning, concept testing, and customer satisfaction and competitive product evaluation. But the problems with survey research methods in certain markets have been well documented.[6]

There are many cultural aspects affecting the application of the kind of direct questioning involved in the typical consumer survey. In high context cultures the idea that one can understand consumers from their responses to a formal survey is naive. Open-ended questions are often left blank by respondents in hierarchical cultures who are not used to explaining their reasoning or are afraid of being too transparent. Answering truthfully to a stranger is not necessarily proper in some nations, especially those in which an authoritarian regime has made people wary of questions. Americans have no hesitation about fabricating an opinion on the spur of the moment—Europeans will leave questions unanswered "since they have no direct experience using that product." Asked for their "perceptions" of the gas mileage of a certain car model, Japanese respondents may ask for time to check automobile specifications in a car magazine.

Face-to-face interviews are prone to bias because of **demand characteristics,** that is, trying to answer in a way that satisfies the interviewer or the respondent's own ego. Such demand pressure is handled differently in different

*G*etting the
Picture

Telling It like
It Is

THE RESEARCHER followed the family on the weekly Saturday shopping trip to the local open-air market. The goal was to document spending patterns for various household products by urban families in a large Mediterranean country. Walking by the various stalls offering all kinds of produce, clothing, and electronic products, the observer dutifully recorded the family's bargaining for a better deal and the actual prices paid. Returning home, he discussed the trip with the husband, and double-checked the figures. The husband corrected him, doubling the price for the shirt bought, and lowering the price for the red wine. "But I saw how much you paid," protested the researcher. "You don't understand," responded the husband. "I can't wear such a cheap shirt, and I can't spend that much on wine."

Survey responses sometimes do not match reality.

Source: Doctoral researcher in anthropology at the University of California at Berkeley, at a Q&A session, June 1990.

cultures. Western people are known to either try to please ("yea-sayers") or go against ("nay-sayers") according to their attitude toward the assumed sponsor. Respondents everywhere may try to answer more or less conscientiously, often opting for the least inconvenient multiple-choice alternative. Or they may lie. For example, respondents may be eager to show off a socially desirable image (see box, "Telling It like It Is").

One drawback of surveys can be the attitude of the respondents toward the study itself. In Western as well as Eastern societies, there will be prospective respondents who refuse to divulge any opinions simply because they "do not want to be taken advantage of," distrusting the function of market research. In more insidious cases people will consent to participate only to fake their responses so as to distort findings. To handle these problems of respondent noncooperation, the firm does well to interview the research firm carefully so as to thoroughly understand the general sentiment in the local market vis-à-vis formal questionnaires. It is also a good idea to monitor the process by observing some pilot interviews if at all possible.

Even if surveys are afflicted by a number of problems and potential distortions in many foreign markets, they can be very useful. Many examples exist of primary market research using consumers that has been successful across cultures (see box, "Axia Strikes Out").

TRADE SURVEYS   The quickest, least expensive, and most commonly used method for learning about customers in a market is to survey the "trade," mainly people in the distribution channel and trade associations. These people can often explain the basic segments in the market, who the buyers are, the type of buying processes used, and the sources of buyer information. They can answer the who, when, what, and how-much questions but will usually not be able to more than speculate about the why. These people provide a good starting point for further data gathering and analysis.

Getting the Picture

Axia Strikes Out

IN 1988 when Fuji film, the successful Japanese company, attempted to diversify into blank audiotape and videotape, it faced a stiff challenge. It is a very competitive global market with strong Japanese competitors such as Maxell, TDK, and Sony, plus American 3M and Kodak, and German BASF. Based on the success of its newly introduced Axia brand name in Japan, however, Fuji decided to go global.

The company intended to use the Axia brand name in the global marketplace, but decided that it needed to test it against its own Fuji name. The Fuji name had been easily beaten by Axia in Japanese tests—Fuji was seen as "boring"—but the company suspected that other countries' consumers would feel differently about the Japanese association. Developing new global design prototypes, the company undertook painstaking and expensive survey research and focus groups with consumers in the United States (New York and Los Angeles) and in Europe (London, Paris, and Duesseldorf).

The result? Axia bombed—while the Fuji name was very attractive. In addition, the company was able to identify differences in design requirements. For example, while the Japanese consumers associate the color black with high quality, American and European consumers tend to favor silver and gold in high-quality images. Accordingly, the "global" tapes introduced under the Fuji name are similar between the United States and Europe—but in Japan the name and the look are different.

Source: Interview with an executive of the marketing research agency hired by Fuji, November 23, 1989.

In the United States, the use of **middlemen** for information about consumers is usually limited to the sales and scanner records of retailers and wholesalers. More attention is usually given to middlemen in the business-to-business sectors, if only because there are a limited number of ways to use formal research methods on business customers. In many other countries the middlemen are a much more important—and perhaps the only—source of information.

In countries with less social mobility and less diversity than the United States—and that includes a majority of the world's nations—key informants in the trade are good sources of information about buyers. Cultural homogeneity makes it possible to get a sense of people through a few personal interviews, since the informants usually can speak for a large share of the population. Furthermore, social stability means that many middlemen have been in the same position for many years, and they can speak from experience. In the United States, by contrast, people are diverse and no one person can speak for the many subcultures. And people are likely to change jobs frequently, not building up much experience in the trade.

Interviewing middlemen is, it should be remembered, only one aspect of getting data on the trade. Store visits to observe customers and talk to them directly, inspecting store layouts and atmospheres, and collecting sales and turnover data are other activities that yield market information.[7]

OBSERVATION   Research involving direct observation of customers buying and using existing products can be very beneficial. Existing products give important clues to customer preferences, especially in mature markets. In markets where access is free and the customers have well-developed preferences, the sales records of the various products constitute, in fact, a shortcut to understanding customer preferences. The products "reveal" consumer preferences.[8]

By analyzing best-selling products—and those that don't do so well—the local marketer can start to identify which features of a product are valued by the market and which are not. Although these points are in a sense obvious, Western marketers have been slow in exploiting this potential. The Japanese have been much faster. The Japanese successes in Western markets have not been based on thorough market research in the traditional sense.[9] Instead, they have learned about customers by analyzing the products that are successful in Western markets.

For example, the way drivers enter their cars has a direct bearing on design. The Japanese small cars were built originally for men, who can easily put one leg in and then sit down in the driver's seat pulling the other leg after. But in the West, the small Japanese cars became popular with women, whose skirts prohibited such an entry. Thus, the Japanese had to make the door larger, to allow the woman driver to first sit down, and then pull both legs in. This redesign came about when Toyota engineers traveled to Los Angeles and watched people get in and out of their cars. Similar research lies behind the lowered threshold of the trunk (to make it easier to slide baggage in and out), the coffee cup holders in cars, and the height of the fastback door.

This approach has been very successful—as a leading American businessman once said, "The Japanese have gotten the American consumers' number." But for the practice to work well in general, it is necessary to assume that current products reflect customer preferences. This assumption is likely to hold only in mature markets with no entry barriers. Where customers have been deprived of products because of trade barriers, consumer preferences might well display a yearning for something different. The same holds where economic development is too low for some products to be affordable. Such latent preferences can't be uncovered through observation. A better way would be informal interviews with experts in the trade.

CAUSAL RESEARCH   **Causal** marketing research involves more scientific methods of research design and data analysis. The aim is to establish the link between a decision variable such as price or advertising and a result measure such as brand preference or purchase. Typical research designs involve experimental methods and the estimation of links in causal models. The problems attacked tend to be the fine-tuning of price levels, testing of alternative advertising copy and visuals, and the connection between after-sales service and customer satisfaction. The basic notion underlying the research is that the local marketer needs to understand exactly what impact the contemplated marketing activities will have on the results.

In new foreign markets this kind of research is rarely worth the costs. The decisions to be made are much too basic to need that much fine-tuning, and the action alternatives facing the local marketer are often rather crude. The exception is advertising if there is good reason to try out some alternatives because the local consumers might not be receptive to the kind of advertising coming from headquarters. *Storyboard tests* with alternative copy, for example, are not expensive and can be done quite quickly.

For the firm with long-established presence in the country, on the other hand, the fine-tuning involved in causal research can very much be worthwhile. Then the standard marketing research approaches can be applicable. The use of scanner data and associated buyer panels, through which household spending patterns and demographic profile can be matched against sales promotion activities in stores, is becoming possible in most mature economies. The emergence of global markets has in this respect been accompanied by a globalization of market tracking measures, and the local marketer will do well to check out the available services in the new market.

MEASUREMENT AND SCALING   Measurement errors are likely to occur in any research, and the problems are magnified when dealing with a foreign culture. Here we can only suggest the flavor of the problems involved—expert publications in international marketing research should be consulted for further reading.[10]

In **attitude scaling,** the way of measuring an individual's intensity of feeling vis-à-vis some product or company, very basic factors can create headaches. Using numbers for scale points raises questions of cultural significance of different numbers (the number "4" carries negative connotations for some Chinese, for example, as "13" does for Western people). It also raises questions about the validity of numbers as indicators of emotions or value ("he's a 10" may be easy to grasp for Westerners used to quantification, confusing to others). There is always the question about how many scale points should be used. Since scaling numbers are designed to reflect underlying emotions, one would like to have an approximate verbal equivalent of any number (or—complicating matters much further—does the culture have "emotions without words"?). There is also the problem of equal-appearing intervals. Even in Western applications, it is not always clear that the difference between a "1" and "2" is equal to that between a "6" and a "7."

These are only a few of the problems associated with one technical question about scaling. On a more basic level, the cognitive and emotional concepts measured—such as *attitudes and preferences*—might not be equivalent across cultures. In some cases the corresponding mental state does not exist. For example, "assertive" is a notorious English language concept for which there are few counterparts in any language. In other cases, the same word has a different meaning—"love" has a much stronger sense of "obligation" in Asia than in the self-centered West. In yet other instances the foreign language has a much more nuanced set of emotions—the word "disagree," which is commonly used in attitude scales, can be expressed in at least five different ways in Japanese.

QUESTIONNAIRE CONSTRUCTION   The **questionnaire** employed in the typical consumer survey needs to be carefully pretested, especially if it is simply a translation from a standardized version in another country. Translated questions are often very prone to misunderstandings, even when literally correct, because of differences in context.

The local market researcher should first translate the original questionnaire into the foreign language and then have someone else **back translate** the questionnaire into the original language. Differences will appear, and they have to be resolved through discussions, pretests with target respondents, and repeated back translations. It is common for this process to yield a questionnaire of different length than the original, since different languages require different levels of polite indirectness.

Typical screening questions such as "Do you do most of the shopping in this household?" can be ambiguous because the meanings of the words "most," "shopping," and "household" depend on cultural norms and the family's economic situation. These difficulties can be overcome by careful design of the questionnaire and painstaking pretesting.

SAMPLING   The lack of comprehensive and reliable **sampling frames** from which to sample respondents has long been holding back market research in many countries. Telephone directories are not very useful when few households have telephones. Postal addresses won't work well when people are mobile, when one address covers many individuals in extended families, and when postal service is unreliable.

However, the problems involved in getting acceptable sampling frames are being gradually solved with the emergence of service firms that specialize in developing lists for direct marketing and survey research purposes. The increasing importance of global direct marketing (discussed in Chapter 16) has encouraged American research firms to invest in the development of lists in many foreign countries, using alliances and joint ventures with local entrepreneurs. The researcher who pays for the use of such lists can ask that customized lists be developed, using standard target segmentation criteria about geographic location, income, family size, and so on. Although an emerging country such as China might still be relatively uncharted, consumers in many other countries in Asia and Latin America are becoming accessible to local market researchers.

FIELDWORK   The fieldwork will typically be handled by a subcontracting market research firm, sometimes a full-service advertising agency. Here the choice is usually between a branch of a multinational firm, and an independent local firm. The multinational firm has the advantage when cross-national comparability is desired. Nevertheless, the local firm will often be more cost-efficient and will sometimes have better knowledge of local situations (even if, in general, the multinational firm will be able to attract very good local talent because they can offer career opportunities abroad). Independent local firms will in many cases be part of a wider international network of local research firms, and working with local firms in many different countries can still provide cross-country comparability without too severe coordination problems.

As always, it is important that the administration of the survey be carefully monitored, since it is tempting for interviewers to cheat by returning bogus questionnaires, especially when they get paid by the number of completed interviews. But in many countries it is difficult to completely control the process. In the United States, for example, it is not always legal for a representative of the sponsor to listen in on a phone interview, or even tape it, without the respondent's explicit permission. Callbacks making sure that a respondent was interviewed can be made, provided the respondent agrees.

Finally, it is important to emphasize that as economic growth occurs, mature markets with differentiated demand requiring formal and scientific market research applications will emerge in many countries. As consumers grow more sophisticated, so necessarily must the techniques used to track their preferences.

COMPETITOR DATA

In most markets the local marketer is faced with competition from both domestic and other foreign competitors, and research is important to identify who they are, what their strengths and weaknesses are, and how they are likely to react to the new entry.

The secondary data used to evaluate the attractiveness of the country (Chapter 4) will already have given the marketer a sense of who the competition is. In addition, analyzing the products on the market will naturally generate information about competition. There are more things to be done, however.

Strengths and Weaknesses

From company annual reports, if available, 10K or corresponding stock exchange filings, and similar sources, it is possible to get a sense of the financial capability of the competition. Recognize, however, that a company with a large consolidated financial base is not necessarily active in any one country market. It's important to judge the *strategic importance* of the market for the competition, and the strategic intent of the competitors operating there.

The overall importance of the market for the competitors is usually higher for domestic companies than for foreign entrants. However, FDI in manufacturing tends to make a foreign company an "insider" in the country and thus likely to behave similarly to a domestic company. IBM Japan is in many respects a truly Japanese company, with only a handful of Western employees, and not at the top level. Understanding the organizational structure of the competitors helps gauge their local strengths. A multinational such as Philips, the Dutch electronics company, with strongly independent country operations, is not likely to engage in massive support for a particular country's operations. By contrast, a company with a globally integrated strategy such as Caterpillar will be able to take a loss in one market and make it up elsewhere. Its country operations can draw on the global resources to a greater extent than can the Philips subsidiary.[11]

As for the local marketing efforts of competitors, research will identify whether strategies involve low prices rather than unique differentiation, will reveal the strengths and weaknesses of their distribution and after-sales service systems, and so on. This type of information is usually available from middlemen, trade magazines, and even newspaper articles. More often it's easier to "scoop out" the strengths and weaknesses of competitors than to get a handle on what motivates customers.

Competitive Signaling

The local marketer must read competitive signals to judge what competitors' future actions may be. In most markets, not only emerging ones, deregulation and the privatization of industry have led to chaotic conditions, and forecasting competitive behavior is not easy. This is especially true in high-technology areas such as telecommunications and computers where premature announcements are sometimes used to mislead competitors or foil a takeover bid.

Competitive posturing can be difficult to interpret for a new local marketer, and it may be necessary to hire experienced local talent precisely to deal with relationships with competitors, as well as with the public and with the authorities. In most countries the type of "hands-off" bureaucratic stance assumed in the United States is unusual, and it becomes important for the new manager to develop a network of contacts so that communication in the trade can be facilitated. Although from one angle such networks may be seen as collusive and anticompetitive, from another viewpoint they simply represent the way business is done in the foreign industry. With the advent of strategic alliances and related cooperative alignments between companies and competitors, the local marketer needs to study and learn how the network can be used to the firm's benefit.

RESEARCH FOR DECISION MAKING

Having done research on the environmental factors affecting customers and competitors, the marketer needs to research segmentation and positioning opportunities, as well as the probable market response to the various marketing mix elements.

Segmentation Research

The kind of large-scale market segmentation studies common in the United States, Japan, and Western Europe are relatively rare in other places around the globe. This is not only because they are expensive and require advanced analytical techniques. They also suffer from the problems of collecting data from individual respondents already discussed. And in many markets they are not necessary.

Differing segments exist, of course, in all markets. People's life styles, usage levels, demographics, and attitudes vary among any population. But to be useful for marketing purposes, segments have to possess the following characteristics. They have to be:

1. Identifiable (What distinguishes them?)
2. Measurable (How many?)
3. Reachable (How to distribute to, communicate to?)
4. Able to buy (Can they afford it?)
5. Willing to buy (Do they want it?)

It goes without saying that each of these requirements, except possibly the first one, can be difficult to satisfy in emerging and less-developed markets. If, in addition, the potential customers in these markets have only weakly developed preferences—because of a lack of exposure to products and services—research to identify market segments will be akin to searching for Atlantis, the mythical sunken city.

But in mature markets in developed countries there is always a payoff to *researching market segments.* And such research does not always have to be so large-scale or expensive. With the advent of global markets and global communications, there are sources for secondary data that can serve as very reasonable indicators of potential segments (see Exhibit 8–2). Bates Worldwide, for example, the global ad agency headquartered in New York, publishes its "Global Scan" database every other year. The database covers 20 countries and offers demographics and socioeconomic data for subgroups of the population of the various countries. The Euromonitor is another source that offers data on attitudes and opinions in addition to socioeconomic data on the European countries. The so-called VALS (Values and Lifestyles) program initiated by Stanford Research Institute has been expanded internationally, identifying lifestyle segments of many developed markets.[12]

Although such data will necessarily be only a crude start, they can give the marketer a good sense of the market segments, especially when compared to the market at home. Since in many cases the introduction of a new global product will create its own segment, there is perhaps less need for in-depth segment research than is common in the United States. But in most developed markets, many of the large research firms have branches that can carry out local research as advanced as that at home. The largest firms are given in Exhibit 8.3.

....
EXHIBIT 8.3   International Market Researchers (1992)

	Non-U.S. revenue (million US$)
A. C. Nielsen	$790
IMS International	391
Research International	122.6
MRB Group	64.7
Milward Brown	45.5
Information Resources	34.8
Louis Harris and Associates	14.4
McCollum/Spielman Worldwide	10.6
Gallup Organization	8.5
National Research Group	2.9

Source: Reprinted with permission from *Advertising Age*, January 1, 1994. Copyright 1994 Crain Communications, Inc. All rights reserved.

Positioning Research

The research that goes into product positioning strategy suffers less from the weaknesses of segmentation studies abroad. Good primary data are expensive to collect, but the number of respondents for positioning purposes can be more limited. Getting individuals to reliably and validly rate competing products on various features is not so difficult, even though pretesting is necessary to make sure that the salient attributes and evoked stimuli include the relevant items.

That consumers from different countries have different **perceptions** of a given brand or product is hardly surprising, since this can be true also of the market at home. A product's or brand's country of origin can bias perceptions.[13] Attributes defining the product may differ from those at home. The marketer needs to make sure that the offering is acceptable on aspects that might have been unimportant in the home market.

For many Western marketers, it will be tempting to rely on the image of the brand name as a major positioning tool. The local marketer should take a "reality check" of the company's perceptions against those of the local market. It is common to hear a newly arrived marketer proclaim that everybody knows and admires the company brands. Such "facts" need to be corroborated by research in the local market, among middlemen as well as among ultimate consumers. For example, while the Olivetti slimline design of word processors makes for an elegant and sophisticated Continental image, American customers found the image to be "fragile" and "effeminate."[14] Though Swedish products are considered functional and well made by big Swedes, they can seem stodgy and clumsy to smaller Asians.

Only research can uncover such potential positioning problems. Such research does not have to be very elaborate and expensive, but it should be an image survey done with the usual care. The respondents have to be representative, and the sponsor should not be identified.

Product Research

Product research in a local market usually involves usage analysis to see whether *localization* is necessary, and preference identification to assess the profitability of adaptation.

Product **localization research** requirements consist of finding out what factors affect the usability of a product. The size of parking spaces, the narrowness of streets, and the gasoline prices affect what size car is acceptable. Voltage levels, fire regulations, and circuit overloads affect what changes may be necessary in electrical products. Language, operating systems, and functions used affect what PC software applications may or may not be acceptable. When it comes to localization of a product (that is, removing obstacles to its convenient and proper local use), the research is not about user preferences but about usage constraints.

Observation is a particularly powerful method for uncovering localization requirements in an existing product. But it is important to recognize that the observer has to pay attention not only to unusual things, such as driving a car barefoot, but also to unremarkable manners, such as how much elbow room the

Campbell's product research lab in Hong Kong. The Asian palate is very different from the Western and so Campbell's, trying to leverage its brand name and experience in soups, is developing new products targeting the Asian market—and will perhaps bring the successful recipes back to Western markets.

Greg Girard/Contact.

driver uses. The hollowing out of doors in cars today came about not only because safety can still be ensured with stronger materials but because observation showed that with automatic transmissions, men drive with wide swings of the elbows.

In product **adaptation research,** the focus is on the adaptations that may give the product an advantage in the local customer's eyes. Such research is much more akin to product research at home. The techniques involve focus groups, concept testing with selected users, and test marketing.[15] These activities tend to be important in any developed market. One question often is, however, whether the uncovered preferences for an adapted product will be adhered to by headquarters (the issue of *adaptation versus standardization* will be discussed in more depth in Part Four, "Global Management").

When doing product research abroad, many companies find it useful to simply observe customers using the product. If the product is new on the market, recruited subjects can be given the chance to try the product in their home for a period of time and then report their experiences. This was done by Procter and Gamble when they introduced Pampers in European and Asian markets. It is done routinely by consumer goods companies going into emerging and developing markets, since it allows localization requirements to be uncovered. For example, when German electric irons were first introduced in Asia, their cords were too short. In Europe there are usually several electric outlets in the wall, while in Asia at that time electric outlets connected to the one bulb in the ceiling.

Traditional product research is based on the assumption that the individual consumer has well-developed preferences, that these can be identified and measured, and that then the design of a new product can target an unfulfilled need or provide a new benefit. When successfully accomplished, the results of the process can be impressive.[16] But in many new markets the assumption of well-developed preferences is unfounded. In new markets preferences may be embryonic or nonexistent. In many foreign markets the solicitation of preferences is flawed, as was seen above. Competitive reaction or preemptive introductions may make the process too slow as well.[17]

An alternative, Japanese-style approach short-circuits the process and speeds it up. By analyzing the leading brands and their attributes, they are able to understand what appeals to their customers. Targeting one of the brands, that brand's customers can be questioned directly for possible improvements. Reverse-engineering the brand, and producing a new version incorporating the existing leader's strengths minus the weaknesses—a so-called "me too plus" product—the Japanese have been able to capture large market shares abroad. Examples include the Toyota Lexus, Camry, and Corona, the Canon Sureshot, and the VHS development by Matsushita.[18]

In developed countries with mature markets, the target product approach has the drawback that the possibility of a striking innovation that completely changes market preferences will be missed. Targeting some leading brand and offering minor improvements is generally not enough to establish a sustainable advantage. The leading brand is likely to respond, and a cycle of actions and reactions will push prices down. This is a typical result of a Japanese entry in many markets. For the local marketer, it is important to recognize that establishing customer loyalty is as important in the foreign market as at home. The aim should not be the quick kill but the sustained satisfaction of the customer.

Although the standardization of products will be covered in Part Four, it is interesting to point out here that because of the globalization of markets, the ergonomics of products (the interplay between man and machine) have become an important part of design. Since the same basic product design ("platform") may be used in several countries by people of different culture, physical size, and gender, design has to be more carefully thought through. The result has been, as many observers have sentimentally remarked, a lessening of the variety in the marketplace and a proliferation of similar variants. Aesthetics and sentimentality aside, in terms of functionality the benefit is that the designers all use state-of-the-art techniques. Globalization has meant high quality at popular prices, but also a lot of similar designs.

Pricing Research

Pricing research asks two different kinds of management questions. One question refers to the *elasticity of demand* to price changes, a fine-tuning of what prices to charge. At home, these kinds of studies may involve in-store experiments or the analysis of historical time series data of prices and sales volume. The in-store data gathering often involves some kind of temporary promotional offering, to identify the extent to which deal-prone customers will react.

These studies are usually difficult to carry out in new local markets. Historical sales data are not available and access to stores and promotional tracking are often limited. The new entrant may have to check competitive prices to identify realistic price levels and then attempt the fine-tuning only after some data, perhaps from a test market, are in hand. Of course, in the case of a well-established multinational in a developed and mature market, the pricing research can easily be carried out in the more advanced typical way.

The second function of pricing research is to identify a *price level* congruent with the intended product position. This is usually a more important aspect of pricing research for the foreign local marketer. This type of research involves less formal methods than price sensitivity studies. In the typical market the research involves finding out about competition's price points and the proper alignment of the firm's own prices given the competitive strengths and weaknesses of its brand. Advanced methods such as trade-off and conjoint analysis can be useful for these purposes, since the basic task of comparing products and brands is real enough for customers to give reliable and valid answers.[19]

In emerging and developing markets where competition has been hampered by trade barriers, pricing has to take into account the effect of price on image. Generally, these markets will be more receptive to a higher price because the quality of their past products was low. This is seen today in Eastern Europe, where Western entrants tend to be the high-priced alternatives. But it is important for the firm to monitor competitive quality improvements and customer reactions to these, since an unwarranted price premium is a recipe for failure. Consumers' confidence in their own product evaluations, regardless of brand image, will generally increase as markets mature, and prices might have to be adjusted downward from a high initial base. Even though Unilever introduced their superior Timotei shampoo at a premium price in Eastern Europe, they had to revise prices downward within six months as local competitors came back with improved products.[20]

Another kind of pricing research involves monitoring "parallel" imports, unauthorized middlemen importing the identical products and brands from countries whose prices are lower because of exchange rates. Regardless of the price policy used, fluctuations in exchange rates tend to produce temporary misalignment in prices between countries. Entrepreneurial spirits in a country can exploit such arbitrage opportunities by purchasing the product abroad, shipping it to the market, and selling it at a discount. For example, it is estimated that as many as 20 percent of the Mercedes Benz cars sold in Japan in 1992 were sold as parallel imports from Europe and the United States[21] Since these entrepreneurs are usually protected under antimonopoly laws, the firms can do little directly to stop them. Instead, they tend to monitor the levels, do research on customer sensitivity to the price differentials, and, as necessary, adjust their prices downward. The firms also attempt to block the parallel imports by more or less subtle tricks such as refusing to honor warranties, delaying repair work, and so on.[22] More will be said about these issues in Chapter 13, "Global Pricing."

Distribution Research

When arriving in the local market, the marketing manager will naturally need to visit stores and dealers—**hands-on research**—to learn firsthand what the current state of the market is. Inspecting store shelves, observing customers in the stores, talking to dealers and to customers will be natural ways of conducting informal market research.

What products are on the shelves will give the marketer a quick feel for the competitive situation. It is easy to learn which are the leading brands and what the retail prices are. Middlemen can help explain the standard margins in the trade and what functions are performed by the various players. Coupled with sales data for competing brands and products, such information is a natural beginning to understanding the distribution system.

The hands-on activities employed by the Japanese have been described by Johansson and Nonaka (see box, "The Japanese 'Hands-On' Approach").

Getting the Picture

The Japanese "Hands-On" Approach

WHEN AMERICAN SALES of Minoltas overtook Canon sales in the early 1970s, Canon sent a three-man team over to the States. Their job was to suggest an alternative distribution strategy from the one originally employed. The original American distributor had been less than interested in pushing Canons in new camera stores and had been content with a few accounts where its own business in film cameras was strong. In contrast, Minolta's aggressive entry through discount store chains had been very successful.

The three-man team trekked across the U.S., visiting camera stores, talking to distributors, and posing as customers in many places. After two months, the new strategy crystallized. Detecting a strong ethnic prejudice on the part of the distributor against the new camera dealers, mainly European Jews, and little or no support in established specialty stores, Canon created a wholly owned subsidiary to import and distribute the cameras. Hiring and training a sales and service force of Americans, the company mounted a counterattack through the specialty camera shops. Crisscrossing the country to offer the dealers incentives and gathering customer information, Canon was back on top in sales with a premium product in less than one year.

Source: Johansson and Nonaka, 1986.

Distribution research also involves interviews with other key informants and experts on the local distribution system. It is very important to keep an open ear and mind to unaccustomed practices, such as rebates, return privileges, and payment practices. Simple matters can be uncovered and dealt with quickly. For example, a Japanese automobile executive found that out of 10 problems at a dealership level, a personal visit could resolve an average of 7 on the spot. One American hotel chain used to pay travel agents for their services by check, not realizing that cashing a foreign currency check in some countries can be very expensive. Participating in a travel convention in the Far East, the international sales manager learned the facts and was able to devise a new payment method of consolidating fees before sending a check.

Business books and trade magazines can be very helpful identifying which peculiar factors affect local distribution acceptance of the product and inducements it is necessary to offer. As Chapter 5 showed, much distribution research needs to be done before the entry mode is chosen.

Promotional Research

The role of advertising in the acceptance of a product or brand and the effectiveness of various sales promotion techniques are important factors to ascertain in local markets. Neither is easy without primary research, but a crude measure may be gotten by examining the advertising-to-sales ratios of major competitors and the level of in-store promotional activity. Reliable media data are often difficult to get and the spending levels can't be easily assessed with certainty, but rough guesstimates of the magnitudes can usually be derived from

A Unilever brand manager test marketing a new tea flavor in India gets consumer feedback. Introducing this new product involves the same considerations as in many other mature markets in the West and East. The success of the new brand Taaza came after research showed its significant preference advantage among consumers.

© Peter Hince.

middlemen and trade experts. It is important to develop a sense of the amount of spending needed to break into the market successfully so that the appropriate funds can be requested from headquarters.

Since market communications play an important role in any local marketing effort, the manager needs to thoroughly investigate the options available. Even in emerging and developing markets, TV and magazine advertising can be very influential in shaping customer evaluations. Research on copy and visuals is crucial in making sure to avoid the many pitfalls associated with foreign languages and cultures and especially translations from home country materials.

Major faux pas can usually be avoided by having local staff in the subsidiary and in the local agency review any proposed communication, but more careful testing of campaigns is always warranted. Focus groups with potential customers, pretesting of alternative storyboards, and follow-up with recall scores and attitude surveys are all useful tools regardless of level of market development. Remember that people in poor countries are also looking for emotional satisfaction, and image-related factors such as choice of spokesperson and background music can have a powerful differential impact that needs to be tested out.

Test Marketing

In emerging and developing local markets it is difficult to generate data prior to entry. As was seen above, there are quite formidable barriers to effective primary data collection, and secondary data are of uncertain consistency and may be lacking altogether. It is of course difficult to develop a marketing plan and proceed with a well-coordinated introduction in such markets. Accordingly, companies tend to approach these markets with care and use the initial entry points as **test markets** to learn more about the customers and competitors and to adapt the marketing program as sales results flow in.

The fact is that market response to new products is hard to predict anywhere.[23] Whether the markets are emerging, developing, or developed, the new local marketer faces uncertainties which are difficult to erase simply by doing more research. The customers can't give reliable and valid responses without direct experience with—or at least exposure to—the new product.

Similarly, emerging and developing markets are likely to exhibit the typical product life cycle characteristics of an introductory period followed by a growth period. In these cases, market research prior to test marketing is best focused on leading users and markets in other countries and on leading brands and products. As discussed in Chapter 4, leading markets may be used to develop a forecast by analogy, which then can help set expectations and targets for test marketing.

SUMMARY

Because of differences in country environments, the typical marketing research approach often has to be modified considerably when going into foreign local markets. In fact, an important part of marketing research involves the assessment of these environmental differences and how they influence customers and competitors. Such research uses more informal methods than typical consumer research and requires firsthand personal observation in the local marketplace.

Even though understanding customers is often the most important research target in local markets (as it is at home), the direct assessment of customer preferences in foreign markets often is less useful than interviews with middlemen and analysis of leading products on the market. The researcher has to support direct questions to customers with validations from experienced middlemen and revealed attribute preferences from observation of the products of local market-share leaders.

Chapter 8 concluded with examples of more specific research, including hands-on research, directed toward the various decision areas in marketing. The researcher has to be imaginative in adapting existing techniques to local conditions. While one may question the need to adapt products to all local preferences, there is no backing away from the need to adapt research methods. The aim of marketing research may be the same in all local markets—but the way to get meaningful results differs.

KEY TERMS

Adaptation research p. 297
Attitude scaling p. 290
Back translation p. 291

Causal research p. 289
Demand characteristics p. 286
Focus groups p. 285

Hands-on marketing research p. 299
Incentives p. 285

DISCUSSION QUESTIONS

1. List the various sources that could help you find out how the availability of credit cards has affected consumer spending in a country of your choice.

2. Discuss the pros and cons of the following methods for finding out what the local effect of outdoor advertising at a World Cup soccer game would be:
   a. Focus groups on brand image.
   b. Survey of brand attitude.
   c. Telephone survey of brand recall.
   d. Store sales data for the brand.

3. Analyze your own shopping behavior for various products from the beginning notion of need to the completed purchase. Where do environmental factors influence the process?

4. Locate secondary data sources in your library that give you an up-to-date profile of consumer spending for a product category of your own choice in the European Union (EU).

5. As a new local marketing manager in a country of your choice, describe how you would go about locating sources to help you find out about the competitive situation in the local market?

NOTES

1. See, for example, Churchill, 1994, ch. 3.
2. See Jeannet, 1981.
3. See Alden, 1987.
4. Malhotra, 1993, ch. 6, offers a thorough discussion of qualitative research with an international flavor.
5. The actual cities chosen depend of course on the type of product involved, where the target segment is located, and what the available resources are. In general, however, foreign entrants tend to have a predilection for choosing the capital or big cities, because that is where media headquarters and opinion leaders are located.
6. See Douglas and Craig, 1982. This book and the one by Churchill, 1994, are drawn on for much of the material in this chapter.
7. Johansson and Nonaka, 1986, give examples of how the Japanese companies do this.
8. The "revealed preference" theory in microeconomics is based on the same notion.
9. The examples of the Japanese approach to marketing research here and in several other places in this chapter are mainly drawn from an unpublished internal report compiled by the Chrysler Corporation in 1988–89 studying research methods at Toyota and Honda.
10. See, for example, Douglas and Craig, 1982.
11. See Hamel and Prahalad, 1989.
12. See Mitchell, 1983, ch. 10.
13. See Johansson and Thorelli, 1985.
14. See Dichter, 1964.
15. See Thomas, 1993, chs. 8 and 10.
16. See, for example, Urban and Hauser, 1980.
17. See the Buick Reatta case in Urban and Star, 1991. Several months of sophisticated product positioning research was undone because the Mazda Miata, a small sports car, was introduced just before the launch of Reatta, a Buick sports car.

18. See Cooper, 1994, and Hanssens and Johansson, 1991.
19. See Urban and Hauser, 1980.
20. From "A New Brand of Warfare," *Business Central Europe*, April 1994.
21. Personal interview in Tokyo with Hans Olov Olsson on July 12, 1994. Mr. Olsson is president of Volvo Japan.
22. The parallel trade into Japan is increasing dramatically as the yen rises in value but rigid distribution channels maintain domestic profits.
23. See Thomas, 1993, ch. 3.

SELECTED REFERENCES

Alden, Vernon R. "Who Says You Can't Crack the Japanese Market?" *Harvard Business Review*, January–February 1987, pp. 52–56.

Amine, Lyn S., and S. Tamer Cavusgil. "Demand Estimation in a Developing Country Environment: Difficulties, Techniques, and Examples." *Journal of the Market Research Society* 28, no. 1 (1986) pp. 43–65.

Bartlett, Christopher A., and Ashish Nanda. "Ingvar Kamprad and IKEA." Harvard Business School case no. 9-390-132, 1990.

Churchill, Gilbert A., Jr. *Marketing Research: Methodological Foundations*, 6th ed. Chicago, IL: Dryden, 1994.

Cooper, Robin. *Cost Management in a Confrontation Strategy: Lessons from Japan.* Cambridge, MA: Harvard Business School Press, 1994.

Dichter, Ernest. *Handbook of Consumer Motivations.* New York: McGraw Hill, 1964.

Douglas, Susan, and Samuel R. Craig. *International Marketing Research.* Englewood Cliffs, NJ: Prentice Hall, 1982.

Hamel, Gary, and C. K. Prahalad. "Strategic Intent." *Harvard Business Review*, May–June 1989, pp. 63–76.

Hanssens, D. M., and J. K. Johansson. "Rivalry as Synergy? The Japanese Automobile Companies' Export Expansion." *Journal of International Business Studies*, Third Quarter 1991, pp. 503–26.

Jeannet, Jean-Pierre. "International Marketing Analysis: A Comparative-Analytic Approach." Working paper, 1981.

Johansson, Johny K., and Ikujiro Nonaka. "Marketing Research: The Japanese Way." *Harvard Business Review*, March–April 1986.

Johansson, J. K., and H. B. Thorelli. "International Product Positioning." *Journal of International Business Studies*, Fall 1985, pp. 57–75.

Malhotra, Naresh K. *Marketing Research: An Applied Orientation.* Englewood Cliffs, N.J.: Prentice Hall, 1993.

Martenson, Rita. *Innovations in International Retailing.* University of Gothenburg, Sweden: Liber, 1981.

Mitchell, Arnold. *The Nine American Lifestyles.* New York: Macmillan, 1983.

Thomas, Robert J. *New Product Development.* New York: Wiley, 1993.

Urban, Glen L., and John R. Hauser. *Design and Marketing of New Products.* Englewood Cliffs, NJ: Prentice Hall, 1980.

Urban, Glen L., and Steven H. Star. *Advanced Marketing Strategy.* Englewood Cliffs, NJ: Prentice Hall, 1991.

Yoshino, Michael. *Procter & Gamble Japan* (A)(B)(C). Harvard Business School case nos. 9-391-003, 004, 005, 1990.

Local Marketing in Mature and New Growth Markets

"The customer as King"

After studying this chapter, you should understand the following global marketing issues:

1. A new marketing environment usually requires some rethinking of how to apply basic principles of good marketing. The principles might be applicable, but effective execution requires adjustments.

2. Not all mature markets are the same from a marketing perspective, regardless of how similar they seem on the surface.

3. Marketing in a high growth market in a newly industrialized economy is not the same as marketing in a high growth market in a mature economy. There is less stress on technology and product innovation and more on generic market development for existing products.

4. The reader should get a better understanding of—and a more forgiving attitude toward—local marketers who claim that "our market is not the same" when *global* strategies are imposed.

A S   W E   H A V E   S E E N in the previous two chapters, good marketing at home or in one country is not necessarily good marketing everywhere. Since each country has its own special character, the local marketing job is never exactly the same anywhere. But in countries in some broad categories, the job is in fact more approximately the same.

For local marketing purposes it is useful to divide countries into three categories: advanced economies with basically *mature markets*; newly industrialized economies (NIEs) with strong *growth markets*; and developing economies with gradually *emerging markets*. Mature markets include the so-called triad countries in Western Europe, North America, and Japan, Australia, New Zealand. The NIE growth markets comprise the "four Asian tigers" (Hong Kong, Korea, Singapore, and Taiwan, the original newly industrialized countries), and also other fast-growing markets such as Chile and other Latin American countries, several ASEAN countries, some Middle Eastern countries, Israel, and South Africa. Growth markets also include poorer Western European countries such as Greece and Portugal for which the EU membership has been very beneficial. Emerging markets include the newly democratized post-Communist nations, including China (still communist but with a more open economy) and other developing countries, including India. Many emerging markets have a history of central control that still colors their approach to free markets.

This classification is not necessarily the one used by public agencies or global companies. For example, "emerging" sometimes refers to all markets outside the triad, and an emerging country such as China also shows high growth in some product markets. Furthermore, there are product markets with high growth in mature economies, especially in high-technology industries. Nevertheless, the split serves to highlight the main distinctions with marketing relevance. The correspondence to the product life cycle is useful for marketing purposes, since the marketing problems encountered reflect the PLC stage the markets are in.

Warming Up U.S. Consumers to Unchilled Milk

A mericans may think they're the world's high-tech consumers, but they've been slow to try at least one new product: ultra-heat-treated milk requiring no refrigeration. U.S. consumers generally think of milk as most nutritious and appetizing when it is cold and fresh from the dairy.

Such ingrained attitudes are a major hurdle for Parmalat S.p.A., Italy's top milk producer, in the United States. Parmalat offers shelf-stable milk in U.S. supermarkets, but consumers are suspicious. Typically, they assume technologically sophisticated foods must be artificial. Many are afraid to drink Parmalat milk on the grounds that, to last six months without refrigeration, it must have been irradiated or laced with preservatives. (Both assumptions are false; the milk is treated only with very high heat.)

To convince consumers that its milk is safe and healthful, Parmalat relies on marketing communications. The company spends millions on television and print advertisements describing the product's convenience and health benefits. Leaflets in stores inform consumers that Parmalat preserves its milk only with heat, that little of the milk's nutrient value is lost in the process, and that modern processing techniques result in little change in taste. The milk cartons echo the message: "Not Irradiated" and "No Preservatives." These efforts set Parmalat apart from U.S. dairies, which view milk as a commodity and do not advertise it.

Appealing to U.S. consumers also required Parmalat to take a fresh look at its package sizes. Whereas European consumers, with little room in their refrigerators and pantries, prefer small cartons, Americans are used to buying milk by the gallon or half-gallon. Parmalat first offered only eight-ounce and one-quart packs, but has since added two-quart cartons.

Willingness to adapt and educate has helped Parmalat make inroads in the United States. Its sales rose 25 percent in a recent one-year period. It still has less than 1 percent of the American milk market, but Parmalat hopes to build its share to 10 percent—no small feat, since Americans are the world's top milk consumers.

One motive for Parmalat's expansion overseas is that sales have been stagnant in Italy—a problem that has inspired other Italian companies to try for a seat at the American table. Luigi Lavazza, Italy's largest coffee company, uses reliable follow-up service to snare American buyers for its espresso machines. Barilla S.p.A., Italy's biggest producer of pasta, and its smaller Italian competitors have enjoyed rising sales in the United States. Eager Americans are already indulging their appetites for pasta, exotic coffee, and other gourmet foods. Unlike Parmalat, these companies do not need to convince U.S. consumers to try something new—milk on a shelf does not exactly have the glamour of steaming espresso.

Sources: John Tagliabue, "Unchilled Milk: Not Cool Yet," *New York Times*, June 10, 1995, pp. 33–34; John Tagliabue, "Lavazza Takes a Ride on America's Coffee Bubble," *New York Times*, July 25, 1995, p. D8; John Tagliabue, "Imported Pasta's Rising U.S. Sales Draw Complaints," *New York Times*, September 5, 1995, p. D4; John Tagliabue, "Pasta Makers of the World, Unite," *New York Times*, October 28, 1995, pp. 33–34; "Canada Drops Curbs on Pasta from Italy," *Journal of Commerce*, June 1, 1995, p. 3A.

INTRODUCTION

In this first of two chapters that deal with local marketing in differing environments, the focus will be on *mature* and *new growth* markets. Since many of the standard marketing techniques are applicable in these markets, the emphasis will be on the adaptation of this know-how to local conditions and the differences between various types of markets. *Emerging* markets, especially newly democratized countries, are quite different, and Chapter 10 is devoted to them.

This chapter starts with a comparison of marketing in the three different environments. It then turns to a discussion of local marketing in mature markets, followed by the special case of Japan. Then marketing in the new growth markets of the NIEs is discussed, followed by the special case of marketing in Latin America.

THREE LOCAL MARKET ENVIRONMENTS

Marketing Environment

To get a grip on the local marketing environment, it is useful for the local marketer to compare three market situations (see Exhibit 9.1). As can be seen from the exhibit, the **emerging markets** are characterized by low levels of product penetration, weakly established marketing infrastructure (especially in terms of advertising media and distribution outlets), relatively unsophisticated consumers with weak purchasing power, and weak domestic competitors. Even with high tariffs, foreign products are potentially making inroads.

New growth markets in NIEs, by contrast, show greater purchasing power and more demanding customers. Consumers can buy more than just basic products, and brand names are important. Because of a high growth rate, there are some strong domestic companies, and foreign competitors face entry barriers. These markets possess a rapidly developing marketing infrastructure.

EXHIBIT 9.1   **Three Marketing Environments**

Feature	Product/Market Situation		
	Emerging	New growth	Mature
Life cycle stage	Intro	Growth	Mature
Tariff barriers	High	Medium	Low
Nontariff barriers	High	High	Medium
Domestic competition	Weak	Getting stronger	Strong
Foreign competitors	Weak	Strong	Strong
Financial institutions	Weak	Strong	Strong
Consumer markets	Embryonic	Strong	Saturated
Industrial markets	Getting stronger	Strong	Strong
Political risk	High	Medium	Low
Distribution	Weak	Getting stronger	Strong
Media advertising	Weak	Strong	In-store promotion

Most **mature markets** show slow growth apart from some high-technology markets. The customers in these mature markets are pampered by strong domestic and global companies who compete intensely for customer satisfaction. Although some of these markets are still protected by trade barriers, customers are able to choose from among the best products in the world and tend to be confident about their ability to make informed purchase decisions, such as, for example, separating high value from high price.

Even though there are many similarities, new growth markets in the NIE countries differ from the typical growth markets in mature economies. The latter are usually driven by product innovation and high technology, while NIE growth markets result from a general economic expansion and require much less product innovation.

Marketing Tasks

Execution of the key tasks for the various marketing functions differs in these three environments. Exhibit 9.2 shows some of the main dimensions. The marketing effort by the local marketer in emerging markets tends to focus on the development of a **marketing infrastructure,** enlarging market reach through improved logistics and establishing functioning distribution points.

EXHIBIT 9.2   **Dominant Marketing Dimensions**

Task	Product/Market Situation		
	Emerging	**New growth**	**Mature**
Marketing analysis:			
Research focus	Feasibility	Economics	Segmentation
Primary data sources	Visits	Middlemen	Respondents
Customer analysis	Needs	Aspirations	Satisfaction
Segmentation base	Income	Demographics	Life style
Marketing strategy:			
Strategic focus	Market development	Participation in growth	Compete for share
Competitive focus	Lead/follow	Domestic/foreign	Strengths/weaknesses
Product line	Low end	Limited	Wide
Product design	Basic	Advanced	Adapted
New product intro	Rare	Selective	Fast
Pricing	Affordable	Status	Value
Advertising	Awareness	Image	Value-added
Distribution	Build-up	Penetrate	Convenience
Promotion	Awareness	Trial	Value
Service	Extra	Desired	Required

Analyzing customer needs involves primarily on-location visits to assess feasibility of entry, and a major question is whether the company should be the first to enter or whether it would be better to wait and let others go ahead building up the infrastructure. A question mark is the degree to which disposable per capita incomes are sufficient for the market to take off, and the product offered is often a simplified and less-expensive version. Often the primary aim is to make the product available in selected locations, typically urban, and then build up from there by creating awareness and positive word-of-mouth.

In new growth markets, the typical strategic aim of the local marketer is generic **market development** to get more customers into the market and generate economies of scale for an existing product line. The aim of market research is to identify the dominant design requirements of demographic subgroups, and the local visits are meant to gain distribution in the leading channels. The product line now includes the top of the line, even though entirely new products are not yet common. Image, high price, and special service are all aspects that can be used to distinguish the offering at the high end, while the lower-end products tend to be less attractive because of the competition from domestic or other foreign brands.

In mature markets, the strategic focus for the local marketer is typically on gaining market share. This is when fine-tuning of the marketing effort is necessary, and sophisticated market research, new product introductions to develop new niches, and value-based pricing are used to appeal to a fickle and difficult-to-satisfy customer.

LOCAL MARKETING IN MATURE MARKETS

We focus first on the main issues that make a difference in the implementation and execution of traditional marketing know-how in foreign mature markets.

Market Analysis

An important feature in mature markets is the need for *market segmentation*. In mature markets customers are increasingly particular, with well-developed preferences; they are eager to satisfy varied and idiosyncratic tastes. Small differences in products and services make a big difference to the customer. The ability of firms to target increasingly narrow niches of the market increases accordingly. New media, such as cable TV and the Internet, as well as direct marketing techniques, such as telephone shopping and catalog sales, help manufacturers target narrow consumer segments.

The fragmentation of mature markets presents an opportunity but also a headache for the foreign entrant. The opportunity lies in the fact that there will often be a part of the market that has yet to find the kind of product desired. With the large populations of Europe, North America, and Japan, even small such niches may represent a large enough market. The problem is that the

*G*etting the
Picture

Citibank Goes
to Germany

THE BANKS OF GERMANY are among the strongest in the world. The largest, Deutsche Bank, has local branch offices covering every part of the country (and has now expanded into former East Germany). But as commonly happens in large banks, a focus on the biggest and best customers has made it neglect some smaller retail customers. For an individual, opening a checking account at Deutsche Bank can turn into a time-consuming and slightly intimidating experience.

In the early 1980s, Citibank, based in New York, saw an opportunity to draw on its retail banking software systems developed for the home market and expand into other countries. Creating supportive in-branch atmospheres with tellers and officers trained to deal with individual customers and using quick state-of-the-art technology for creditworthiness checks, the bank succeeded in drawing customers away from the German banks. It was especially successful in attracting customers from the "more common people," including the many Turkish "guestworkers" who had often felt neglected in German banks. Since much of the earnings of such guestworkers is saved and then transferred back to the home country, these customers make for a very good banking business. Citibank was able to create a very profitable operation in Germany with this and other niches.

Sources: Professor Ingo Walter, presentation at University of Southern California, Los Angeles, April 8, 1987; Various newspaper reports.

foreign entrant has to spot these niches. The stereotypical descriptions of the consumers in these markets will be misleading, and conventional wisdom has to be shunned.

There are many examples of this. Baskin-Robbins has done very well in Japan, even though "Japanese do not eat ice cream standing up." Now teenagers do, even if other people don't. Armani, the Italian designer, has been very successful in the United States, even though "American men don't want to look too stylish." Businessmen wear Armani suits after hours, if not on the job. Japanese autos are a big threat in Europe, despite the notion that "Europeans drive their cars too hard for the light Japanese autos." Not all Europeans drive like Arnold Schwarzenegger. And even in a staid and mature industry such as banking, segmentation can succeed (see box, "Citibank Goes to Germany").

Product positioning, the creation of a particular place in the prospect's mind for the product or service, goes hand in glove with market segmentation. In mature markets, successful products have to provide "something special."

For many foreign entrants from Third World countries, it is tempting to enter mature markets with low-end and inexpensive products. This may be unavoidable for them, but over the longer run such a strategy tends to be untenable. As industrial development progresses across the globe, other countries develop the requisite know-how and labor skill to become the new low-wage producer. In apparel, Hong Kong first gave way to the Philippines and now China has taken over. The solution is to upgrade, positioning the products at a higher end in the marketplace. Hong Kong is now a quality manufacturer of apparel.[1]

AT&T telecommunications equipment is delivered to a distributor in Saudi Arabia. The prominence of AT&T in a leading mature market such as the United States creates brand equity and facilitates entry into other countries.

© John Madere.

Since product positioning is a matter of customers' perceptions, this is where image, brand name, and country of origin enter the consumers' mental picture.

A strong *brand image* not only carries the benefit of status and recognition for the customer. The well-known brand name certifies that the product will function well—otherwise the image would have lost its luster. The global brand names that have emerged over the years represent considerable assets, or "brand equity."

The "made in" labels of foreign-made products can in the same way generate a **country-of-origin effect.** A country well known for high-quality manufacturing, such as Germany, offers an advantage to firms with products made in Germany, a country-specific advantage (CSA) in fact. When Volkswagen started the production of the Rabbit model in the United States in the late 1970s, some American customers rushed to buy the last German-made ones (for good reason, as it turned out, as the Pennsylvania plant had quality problems from the start). French fragrance products are rated highly, so in the early 1980s Shiseido, the Japanese cosmetics firm, hired Serge Lutens in Paris to do its new line of fragrances. Swatch, the very successful Swiss watchmaker, hired Italian designers for its initial line, knowing that "Swiss design" was not particularly good for styling. Companies recognize that country-of-origin effects can be useful marketing tools.[2]

As more countries develop the skills and know-how to produce quality products, one can expect such country-of-origin effects to change. The process is a matter of market success. For example, as Honda, the Japanese carmaker, successfully marketed its Ohio-assembled Accords back in Japan, the company made sure the news media knew about it. This had two results. One, it assured the American buyers that the Hondas built in Ohio were every bit as good as those built in Japan. Second, it made consumers reevaluate their perception of the ability of Americans to build reliable cars.[3]

Marketing Decision Making

PRODUCT Many Third World countries tend toward selling a low-cost **"me too" product** in a mature market. A "me too" product is basically a copy of another product, often with simpler features and at a lower price. The key to success of a "me too" is the price sensitivity of the marketplace. A tractor from the former Soviet Union, such as the Belarus, can be sold at a discount—the main uncertainty is the necessary amount of the discount. This can usually be researched. By contrast, a completely new product offers a more high-margin opportunity, but also poses a greater challenge.

The local marketer introducing a *new* kind of product to the market has the advantage of little or no competition. Being the first into a previously untapped segment generates what is called a **first-mover advantage.** Brand name recognition is often greater for the first entry. Customer loyalty and distribution networks are easier to develop. (Distribution accessibility tends to be more limited for latecomers.) Necessary product modifications can be spotted faster. Reputation as an innovator and pioneer can be capitalized on in advertising. These are firm-specific advantages (FSAs) that translate into a strong market position.[4]

Real world examples are plentiful. The Walkman has become synonymous with Sony all over the globe, despite determined copying of the designs by other Japanese electronics firms. Swatch is still the leader in fashion watches despite attempts by Seiko, Timex, and lesser competitors to challenge Swatch's leadership. Schick is still the leader in razor blades in Japan, where they entered before the world leader Gillette.

These advantages to the first mover are, of course, not automatic. It takes diligent management, staying close to the customers, supporting with strong market communications programs, and being willing to quickly modify the products as new technology develops. These things can be done by the local marketer, but only if the commitment to the foreign market is firm. If the support of top management at headquarters wavers, strong market positions can soon be eroded.

PRICING In mature markets it is common to think of pricing in terms of selecting a target position—high end or low end, depending on the positioning desired—and then using temporary deals and offers to attract customers—and to fight competitors—in the short term. By making the price cuts temporary, the brand can be maintained at the higher position, while still competing with

<table>
<tr><td>

*G*etting the
Picture

Why Americans
are Price
Sensitive

</td><td>

WHEN JOHN KENNETH GALBRAITH published *The Affluent Society* in the 1960s, his assertion was that prices do not matter much in a society where people are affluent. This led many foreign observers to assume that in America, the land of milk and honey, prices do not matter. Many of them were surprised to find that, in fact, the United States may have the world's most price-conscious consumers. The Japanese, for example, have long been wondering why Americans are so focused on price.

The explanation is simple. It has to do with something called intrabrand competition. Intrabrand competition means competition between two offerings of the same brand.

In most countries of the world, the manufacturer can usually control retail prices for his or her brand. Even where outright control over prices is prohibited, within limits, suggested retail prices are adhered to. In Europe, Japan, and other places, the price for, say, a Braun coffeemaker is largely the same in the different stores that carry it. This is not true in the United States—and is becoming less true in other countries as well as the trade is being deregulated.

In the U.S. marketplace, suggested retail prices can usually not be enforced. Attempting to not ship to stores that undercut suggested prices is illegal—and this is enforced through the legal system with its many lawyers. The

</td><td>

principle is that any store legitimately selling coffeemakers should be able to feature Braun models. The price they charge is theirs to decide, not Braun's. Neither can Braun charge the store a higher price than it charges other similar stores—again, a law that is actively enforced. When a big cost-cutting retailer begins to offer Braun's products, the company can try to avoid shipping, claiming lack of supplies or some other problem, but such defenses have been challenged successfully in courts and do not usually hold up.

The result is that a Braun automatic coffeemaker that in a department store retails for say, $95 can be had at a cost-cutting suburban warehouse for $49.95. A Ralph Lauren eyeglasses frame at $250 in the city can be had for $129 across a state line. London Fog coats are sold at a 40% discount in off-price outlets. And these are not copies, but the real thing (although knockoffs are also a big market). When the price competition hits intrabrand competition, no buyer is immune. Most individuals will feel ripped off when they find out that they could have bought the same $450 Olympus camera for $250 through a catalog house, and vow never to be caught again. American consumers are price sensitive for good reason, and American stores have also wised up, many promising to pay the difference if the customer can find the same product at a lower price elsewhere.

</td></tr>
</table>

lower-priced entries. Low-priced entries from the Third World countries can expect such competitive defenses from established brands.

One might think that in mature markets price would not be an important factor for consumers. However, competition in mature markets is often so fierce that pricing and discounts become very important competitive tools (see box, "Why Americans Are Price Sensitive").

As a counterpoint, it is important to remember that positioning also plays an important role in emerging markets. Contrary to popular belief, high prices may not be such an impediment to market success in these countries as one would expect. By focusing their spending on a few items, even poor consumers are able to spend for luxuries. In such instances, a low price can be a drawback, since a luxury image is automatically associated with a high price. Chapter 10 deals with this question directly.

PROMOTION   In many mature markets where market share is the criterion of success, sales promotions such as free samples, coupons, and point-of-purchase displays are used to break the habitual choice of the loyal customer. The supporting marketing communication attempts to increase the saliency of features on which the brand is superior to competitors offering unique selling propositions. This leads to the kind of hard-hitting ad campaigns so often derided by foreign visitors to the United States. Because of the immense media clutter in the United States, and the proliferation of product variety, marketing communications need to have an impact during the short interval the customer is exposed.

Advertising also helps add value to the brand by creating a positive image, high recognition, strong status appeal, and so on. Advertising intended for this purpose uses more of a soft-sell; such market communications tend to be favored in Europe and, perhaps especially, in Japan. When members of the distribution channels are able to furnish necessary product information (as in traditional European stores) or the consumers have time to examine products in the store (as in Japan), such softer advertising is often more effective.[5] But even in Europe the more specific and concrete benefits-oriented American style may work (see box, "American Advertising Comes to The Netherlands").

DISTRIBUTION   In mature markets the distribution system is usually well developed, and there are few or none of the infrastructure problems so common in emerging countries. But there is another problem—getting into the appropriate channel is often very expensive and sometimes impossible.

For example, to get a supermarket chain in a mature market to add a new foreign product on the shelf takes not only hefty dealer margins, promise of secure and timely delivery, and extensive promotional support but there are direct payments to be made—"slotting fees"—and a very short probation period. If the brand proves itself—a matter of quick turnover—the future might be bright. But a small mistake in execution—a slipped delivery date, a faulty package, inappropriate promotional language—can easily waylay the best promise.

Entry through department stores is hardly easier. Kao, the Japanese company, spent several unsuccessful years attempting to get its cosmetics line on the floor of the large German stores. And the perfumeries that offered an alternative distribution channel proved equally resistant. In autos, where the necessity of dealer service and trained repairmen make entry very expensive, many companies spend years developing a network. BMW, the German carmaker, found it necessary to create its own subsidiary in Japan to help

Getting the Picture

American Advertising Comes to The Netherlands

THE OPENING OF DUTCH broadcasting to commercial TV has made competition in previously staid industries more intense. An example is the insurance industry. The Dutch insurance company OHRA had developed innovative services for their clients, including direct payment to pharmacies, extended evening hours, and travel assistance abroad. The company wanted to advertise these new benefits, which were offered at a 15% discount under competitors' prices. Problem was, the soft-sell image-building advertising traditionally done in The Netherlands did not lend itself very well to explaining the new benefits.

The solution was to hire an American agency, Direct Resources Inc. out of New York. Its president, Mr. Cohen, had impressed the Dutch representatives during a direct marketing conference in Europe. A campaign of detailed, informative commercials was developed, although there were some setbacks at first. The first idea was to illustrate the theme "stay ahead of the pack" by using a duck followed by ducklings—only to find that "stupid duck" was a common Dutch expression. When Mr. Cohen wanted to shoot the commercials with rich people to emphasize the targeting of upper-to-middle incomes, the Dutch toned the effort down to less conspicuously wealthy Dutch households. When Mr. Cohen shot the commercials in New York with Dutch expatriates, the company rejected the audio portion as "obviously not real 'r's' by Dutch people."

Despite these missteps, the fundamental purpose was achieved. The Dutch company found itself with a more specific and concrete commercial that not only said that OHRA was a wonderful company but also detailed why. The commercial explained how the competitors had copied OHRA's innovations but had yet to offer the 15% discount that OHRA offered. The company was able to put across its innovative image together with specific benefits—by marrying Dutch restraint to American brashness.

Sources: TeleVeronique and TV 10, 1989; *New York Times*, August 22, 1994, p. D7.

support the independent dealers that dared stock its cars. Before that, a typical dealer showroom in central Tokyo might feature one car in a small one-room window. As the Japanese began to shop for cars outside the inner city, new dealers with larger showrooms on the outskirts of Tokyo could be established.

One distribution strategy is "piggybacking." In piggybacking an existing network controlled by another company, often a potential competitor, is used to distribute the product through contracting with the competitor to move products on a fee or commission basis. Toyota trucks are sold through Volkswagen dealers in Germany. Nissan sells some Volkswagen cars in Japan. The now common international alliances between airlines often involve the sharing of reservation systems for complementary routing. The large-scale dealers selling a large number of competing auto makes, the multiple-brand electronics stores, the personal computer stores, and other similar retail innovations initiated in the United States are spreading to other mature markets. As this transformation unfolds, one can expect better market access for foreign marketers in most of the mature markets.

Microsoft Works as advertised in Mexico. Developed by the Leo Burnett agency's local office in Mexico City, it reassures the buyer about local support services: "Me, Afraid? With Microsoft you will never be alone."

Courtesy Microsoft.

CUSTOMER SATISFACTION   In many mature markets intense competition has produced a management focus on **customer satisfaction** (CS), a need to make sure that existing customers will stay loyal.

Typically, two things make for a satisfied customer in these markets. First there is product *quality*, in a broad sense, including, functional performance factors (reliability, flexibility, and so on). Second are emotional factors, a matter of pleasing the customer. Here personal attention and after-sales service factors (delivery, warranty, and so on) become important. The idea of customer satisfaction also includes what is usually called "the surprise quotient," the degree to which the company can offer an unexpected technical feature or personal service.

Effective customer satisfaction strategy requires some rethinking on the part of the company, an effort to see things from the customer's perspective. Sony's approach to the Walkman design illustrates this idea (see box, "Sony's CS Rethinking").

While a lack of functional quality is certain to negatively affect satisfaction, managers can't assume that perfect functioning alone will produce any customer euphoria—in mature markets it may simply be taken for granted. The real satisfaction—which creates repeat business, customer loyalty, and positive word-of-mouth—comes from emotional factors, which are seen to yield "extra" or value-added quality. These relationships are depicted in Exhibit 9.3.

<table>
<tr><td>

*G*etting the
Picture

Sony's CS
Rethinking:
The Walkman
Case

</td><td>

ORIGINALLY about two-thirds of the Walkman repairs were caused by customers' accidentally dropping the units. This information was initially seen by Sony as a service problem, with standard questions about whether warranties should be extended in such cases and so on. Later, the information was fed back to the product design team, who tried to improve the design so the

</td><td>

Walkman would less likely be dropped. In the current stage, however, the design team has adopted the philosophy that the Walkman units must be designed sturdily enough to withstand an accidental drop. If customers use the product in active situations, they must be provided with products that do not restrict their activity.
Source: Johansson and Nonaka, 1993.

</td></tr>
</table>

A customer's typical experience with an automobile can be used to illustrate the way quality affects satisfaction in Exhibit 9.3. When the car does not start in the morning, or when the steering wheel rattles, functional quality is low. This kind of trouble leads to dissatisfaction (lower left-hand corner of the graph). Even a kind repair man will have trouble raising satisfaction levels. On the other hand, the fact that the car starts and the wheel does not rattle, does not generally lead to satisfaction—it is taken for granted.

In order to produce high levels of satisfaction, the customer needs to be given something not so obviously expected—something for which the "surprise" quotient is high. This can involve simple things such as a pickup when service is due, or a cleaned-out ash tray after service is done. It can also involve semi-functional things such as more elbow room for the driver, clear instrument

EXHIBIT 9.3   CS and Two Kinds of Quality

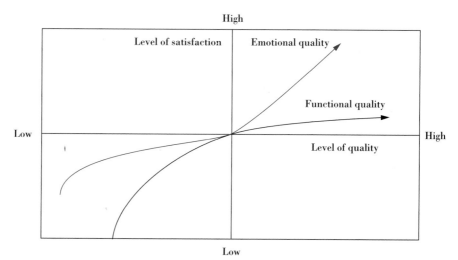

panels, and an easy-to-program radio. Although not necessary in a functional sense, these things often make the driver happier—they raise the emotional quality and therefore satisfaction (upper right-hand corner of the graph).[6]

In mature countries with mature markets and intense global competition, customers' expectations continue to rise, and they demand ever higher quality products and improved service—at competitive prices. This is a stiff management challenge, which must be successfully met for the local marketer to be successful in today's mature markets.

SPECIAL CASE: MARKETING IN JAPAN[7]

So far we have dealt with the basic strategies for mature local markets. The local marketer has, of course, to add specifics pertinent to his or her market's special environment. Japan's situation is sufficiently unusual that it deserves more treatment. European marketing today is best treated under global strategies, because of the EU integration, and we will do that in Part Four of the book. The North American market is not covered specifically, since many marketing texts more or less explicitly deal with that environment.

The key differences in Japan for a marketer involve the complex distribution system and a difficult-to-please customer. Before discussing those two issues, we assess the market potential of Japan.

Market Potential

Japan is a country the size of California with 120 million people concentrated in small pockets of inhabitable land. Its economic performance in the last 40 years has been phenomenal, per capita incomes growing from poverty level to the highest in the world. The Japan market has an enormous potential for foreign firms in a wide variety of products and services.

Japanese markets have not yet been penetrated very much by foreign firms. One reason is the country's relative isolation, geographically and culturally. Except for Australia and New Zealand, Japan is very far away from other developed countries. Its language and customs are different from other countries and difficult to learn or understand, even for other Asian people. And the country has a long history of deliberate isolation from the rest of the world.

Despite these obstacles, many Western firms have recognized the potential of the growing Japanese economy and its large population. But adapting products and services to the Japanese customers' requirements has been, and continues to be, a problem. As the Japanese economy took off after the Korean war, the customers in Japan were the beneficiaries of intense competition among Japanese domestic suppliers in many product categories. Even though the industrial policies developed by Japan's Ministry of International Trade and Industry (MITI) involved tariff protection from foreign competitors, domestic firms kept their rivalry going. Since foreign suppliers started with the handicap of not understanding how to do business in Japan very well, most customers in Japan, both industrial and ultimate consumers, preferred to deal with domestic suppliers who could be pitted against each other.

Today much of the tariff and other trade protection is dismantled; Japan has eased control over foreign capital investments; and consumers are more than willing to purchase foreign products. The combination of high incomes, high productivity workers, state-of-the-art technology, and success in exporting, has diminished the need for protection. Pressure from American and European trading partners and the threat of protectionist countermeasures have made the Japanese eager to attract foreign products to Japan. But marketing in Japan is not all that easy. The distribution system is complex and costly and the consumer is very demanding.

Distribution

FRAGMENTATION   The fragmented nature of the Japanese distribution system has frequently been noted by foreign companies. Western wholesale and retail middlemen are rationalized into large-scale units performing integrated functions; the Japanese system features several layers of small, specialized units, each handling small quantities of products. For each sale at the retail level, the product in Japan will go through many more hands, each siphoning off their fees and commissions. In 1988 the typical wholesale-to-retail ratio was 4:1 in Japan, while in the United States the corresponding figure was 2:1.[8]

The reason for the difference lies partly in the lack of the warehousing and storage space that makes large-scale distribution possible. There is a need to offer smaller packages, fewer units, and faster restocking of supplies. When Procter and Gamble introduced its Cheer detergent brand into Japan using point-of-purchase promotions and dealer rebates, the consumers often found the stores sold out; there was simply not enough shelf space available in the stores to do the necessary stocking up. Although the Japanese consumers are now able to shoulder some of the storage functions as their cars, houses, and refrigerators become larger, there is still a premium price paid for space. In addition, the distribution system serves to employ a large number of people, often elderly, in mom and pop–type outlets. While change is under way toward larger scale in distribution, Japan still lags behind many Western countries.

CLOSE TO CUSTOMERS   For the local marketer in Japan, the cost of the system is only part of the problem, however. The need for frequent and close contacts between middlemen creates a preference for dealing with the same people and an aversion to change. Each middleman is treated as a customer. For a newcomer to break into an established relationship is not easy—especially if the product or service offered competes with a domestic alternative. There are still cases in Japan where a retailer is threatened with a cutoff of supplies from a domestic manufacturer or wholesaler if a competing product is added to the shelf. Although illegal and thus kept as "an understanding," the pressure can be

*G*etting the Picture

Illegal Barriers—
Or Relationship
Marketing?

ACCORDING TO THE Eastman Kodak Company, makers of world-leading Kodak films, its Japanese competitor Fuji film has illegally blocked access to distribution in Japan. In a complaint lodged with the U.S. Trade Representative, Kodak charges Fuji with illegal rebates and strong-arm tactics to control the four largest film wholesalers in Japan and keep Kodak out of retail stores. Only about 15% of Japan's film retailers stock Kodak film, and Kodak has only 10% of the market to Fuji's 70%.

Fuji's view is, not surprisingly, different. It claims its rebates are legal and amount to cooperative sharing of channel members' promotional budgets. As for distribution access, Fuji film is sold everywhere, but so is Kodak film in the United States. The little green boxes are seen by Japanese everywhere from an early age. Schools receive complimentary supplies of the little green boxes for class photos, and high-school students on class trips carry Fuji disposable cameras. Past tariff protection is gone, and Japanese tariffs are at zero, while American duty on imported film is at 3.7%. And while Fuji has 70% of the market in Japan, it proves nothing: Kodak has nearly 70% of the market in the United States.

Moral: Relationship marketing creates natural barriers.

Sources: *Washington Post*, June 26, 1995, p. A12; *New York Times*, July 5, 1995, p. D4.

very real. These pressures are now relenting, but they kept American cigarettes, European beer, and Western PCs off the retail shelves for a long time. The Kodak example is illuminating (see box, "Illegal Barriers").

Creating a new distribution channel is possible, but very expensive. Not only is it difficult to entice existing middlemen to give up their existing business, the new people that may be attracted are often not the best. Add the cost of training and stocking and the cost of space and display locations, and the investment can be very large. It has been done successfully, as in the Toys-R-Us case but one can understand why many Western firms find it too expensive a proposition.

Customer Analysis

DEMANDING CONSUMERS   The demanding Japanese customer is another hard nut to crack for the newly arrived local marketer. Japanese customers are, in some ways, the most demanding buyers in the world.[9]

Japanese customers have long been accustomed to thinking that the only reason an imported product should be bought is that it provides something special. Western luxury brands and special cultural items with strong country-of-origin affiliation—such as Italian designs, French specialty foods, and American sports apparel—have been staple items in Japanese consumption. Of course, if Japanese producers were able to produce as good—and sometimes better—products by taking apart the foreign product (reverse-engineering) and making a similar version, Japanese consumers would often opt for the Japanese version.

However, the recession in the early 1990s seems to have made for a change in the consumer mindset that is likely to be favorable for the foreign marketer. Some of the major shifts in this mindset should be recognized.

CHANGING CONSUMERS   The SII (Structural Impediments Initiative) and related efforts by Western powers to pry open the Japanese distribution system have won some victories, including the easing of the limiting large-store law, putting pressure on entrenched domestic marketers.[10]

As the distribution system opens up, imports made cheaper by the rising yen pose a strong competitive threat to domestic companies in Japan. Not surprisingly, price sensitivity on the part of the Japanese consumer has increased considerably in the last few years. Lower-priced imports are now more generally available in the new distribution channels, and they have put price pressure on domestic retail prices. Some of these imports are private label brands of retailers. Accordingly, the consumer is faced with lower-priced alternatives not only in new discount outlets but also in established retail stores. The Japanese consumer today benefits from strong interbrand price competition and has learned from exposure to overseas markets and prices that lower prices do not always mean lower quality.

Furthermore, while traditional retail outlets try to sustain premium brand prices, discount outlets have begun to sell brand name products at reduced prices, and a good deal of the brand name products are direct imports from overseas. Accordingly, while uniform prices made comparison shopping useless in the past, because of parallel imports there is now price competition within brands. Even not-so-poor consumers get price sensitive when there are large savings to be gained.

SUBURBAN SHOPPING   The Japanese are finally finding it worthwhile to get into the family car, drive to the large supermarket or out to the suburbs, and do their shopping once a week. Improved storage conditions in the home, with efficient refrigerators and freezers, make it possible to buy in larger quantities. Packaging innovations, such as condensed detergents and vacuum packs, alleviate the still severe space problems. As Jeeps and four-wheel-drive off-the-road vehicles become ever more popular, the family today has a car that can carry the purchases comfortably. The Japanese are becoming more similar to Westerners in their leisure and shopping behavior, if not in their work habits.

LESS BRAND CONSCIOUS   When the Japanese consumers' disposable incomes were growing, there was a considerable amount of status-oriented consumption. Well-known global brand names fetched high price premiums, especially in the luxury product categories.

Although there are still signs of this behavior, things have now changed. Less secure financially, consumers take time to evaluate products and compare prices. They have become what one informant calls "value-conscious," and don't necessarily demand the very latest (although for some product categories and for some consumers this is of course not uniformly true). Rather than focusing on brand and all the latest features, many consumers are learning to make trade-offs between what they really need to have and what the price is.

QUALITY   This does not mean lesser quality is accepted. Quality does not reside in the features of a product. For the Japanese it is not an attribute defining the product. Quality for the Japanese simply means that the product performs the promised function without fault. The many new features desired before the present slowdown were all to come with zero-defect quality—which they largely did, thanks to the vaunted Japanese manufacturing skills. When the Japanese consumer trades off features and prices today, there is no compromise with quality.

Consumers can still demand quality because the Japanese companies have read the trend toward more value and are producing high-quality simpler versions of their upscale products. These simpler versions keep only the main features of the higher-end products and are sold at lower prices. They are still as reliable as the typical products associated with Japanese companies and carry their brand names. Panasonic video-camcorders now come with a minimum of features (no stereo audio and no manual zoom, for example) and simplified operations—and a price reduction of up to 35 percent. Toyota has introduced a small four-wheel-drive pickup with only one engine size, manual transmission, and bare-bones interior, including an AM-only radio. It sells briskly at a price level about 25 percent below Toyota's own comparable models, although the economic turnaround in the economy is making consumers gradually demand more features.

The insistence on quality extends to the increasingly popular imports, many of which are not of Japanese quality (see box, "The Japanese Take to Mail Order Buying").

DIFFERENTIATED SEGMENTS   With the new emphasis on price and value, the Japanese market has become more differentiated than previously. For each product category, there are (1) upscale segments, (2) middle of the roaders who buy the tried and true, and (3) those buying on price, looking for cheaper imports and private labels. In this way the Japanese market has become more similar to the American.

In sum, while Japanese customers were always demanding in terms of quality, service, and up-to-date technology and design, they are now also open to discounted prices. "Bargain" is no longer a dirty word.

LOCAL MARKETING IN NEW GROWTH MARKETS

The local marketer in a **newly industrialized economy (NIE)** with fast economic growth faces a situation not unlike that of early marketers in mature markets. Although some of the markets are small in terms of population—

Getting the Picture

The Japanese Take to Mail Order Buying

DESPITE CLAIMS that Japan's lack of Western imports is a consequence of Japanese consumers' reluctance to accept Western products, there are some recent successes to the contrary. Japanese have taken to ordering foreign products from mail order catalog houses.

From its headquarters in Freeport, Maine, L. L. Bean sends thousands of catalogs to consumers throughout Japan, now Bean's largest foreign market. Sales in 1994 reached $100 million, up 66% from a year earlier. Clothing and camping equipment, fishing tackle and hiking boots are sold in record numbers by companies such as Lands' End, REI, and Eddie Bauer.

Mail order packages bypass the notorious Japanese distribution system, tariffs are low (averaging 2.5%), and the yen is high, all factors behind the growth. In addition, the companies have issued Japanese language order forms and text, and have established warehouses in Japan to store the more popular items. Delivery from the U.S. generally takes 5–10 days, faster after the Tokyo International Post Office hired new employees and cleared a new floor to handle the giant mail sacks.

Still, consumer habits die hard. Japanese are afraid that sizes may be too large and hesitate when they cannot touch or feel the fabric. To overcome this resistance, L. L. Bean, Eddie Bauer, and other companies have opened complementary store outlets in Tokyo, even though this means that customers try on the clothes and run home to order by catalog at lower prices. And quality is still a problem. "With products imported from America, sometimes the buttonholes are not sewn very well so they come apart," says Kaori Morozumi, a 33-year-old jewelry designer who spends up to $1,000 on mail orders several times a year. "These are deficiencies that Japanese products just wouldn't have."

Sources: Updike and Kuntz, 1995; WuDunn, 1995.

Hong Kong and Israel at about 5 million, Singapore at a almost 3 million—others are in the range of the European mix of populations—or between Chile's 14 million and Korea's 44 million.

Market Analysis

Markets in NIEs tend to be in the growth phase of the product life cycle, which makes them attractive for entry. Certain markets might seem mature—food, basic household products, apparel—but there is generally potential for new variants and more international offerings. Other markets might be embryonic and in the introductory stage, including leisure products and services, Western furniture, and frozen food. But as incomes are rising, people in these countries are demanding the variety and experiences offered by the markets in more mature economies.

In NIE markets it is easy to observe the attention given to well-known brand names. Many people from these countries are aware of foreign products, either through travel or through the global communication network. Global brands carry a cachet, and companies capitalize on this by high-profile

Outdoor advertising for foreign brands in South Africa. While global brands often have an initial advantage over domestic brands in new growth markets, some native brands gradually regain competitiveness.

Pascal Maitre/Matrix.

promotions, including very visible outdoor and transit advertising. However, this does not mean that these customers are necessarily gullible; rather they are open to indulging themselves occasionally. For more basic and essential products and services—foods, household appliances, autos—the demand for quality and performance can be as high as in an advanced market.

These countries often use foreign technology and capital to fuel their growth, which tends to create a certain advantage for foreign entrants, since they represent the "real thing." Unlike more mature markets, domestic products tend to be seen as less desirable, even though their functional performance may be superior. This "neocolonial" attitude on the part of the customers does not mean that one particular foreign country is necessarily favored, although one is struck by the apparent preference for Japanese products in Korea and British products in Hong Kong and Singapore. Any country-of-origin effect generally reflects how the economic development of these countries has depended on these supplier countries to a great extent, and, consequently, the products on the market tend to come from these countries.[11]

Market segmentation in these countries differs from that in the developing countries primarily in the degree to which a core middle class is developed. The emergence of such a core group of consumers with some spending power in the NIEs means that segmentation techniques are directly applicable. In some cases, the requisite basic information—demographics, incomes, location—is unreliable because of large but hidden extended families . . . a desire to avoid taxes, and increased mobility of the populace. But as economic growth continues, consumer segments can be defined based on spending according to preferences rather than necessity. It becomes important to recognize this and augment the official data available with primary data collection and personal observation and interviews.

Marketing Decision Making

PRODUCT　There is no need to consider product or service adaptation in NIE markets in any way different from advanced markets'. Localization is a must, and customers are as demanding as elsewhere. Since there is some cachet to being "foreign" for certain segments and occasions, the "no adaptation" option should be given serious consideration. It is important that the brand name be strongly supported—generic products in these markets rarely stand a chance against the domestic variants.

PRICING　Pricing is important but can largely reflect the same considerations as in the advanced markets—demand, costs, competitive conditions. If the unique selling proposition involves status positioning, a high price is warranted. These markets are growing, and people are ready to spend money. At the same time, it is important that price not be too limiting—building a brand franchise with a large and loyal following is very much the name of the game.

PROMOTION　Products and services should be supported for the future potential benefits they offer. Creating a strong image for a brand is important. Sharing information and building trust among customers for industrial products is similarly important. The sales personnel need to be careful not to divulge trade secrets that can be used by domestic producers against the innovating firm. The NIEs have often shown themselves impervious to international copyright laws and patent enforcement. Microsoft, the large U.S. software producer for personal computers, has long had a policy of avoiding entry into Korea, Hong Kong, or Singapore because of these countries' copyright infringement practices (pirated Microsoft software still finds its way into these markets).

Nevertheless, with free trade issues still politically salient in attractive markets such as the United States and Canada, the NIEs will find it necessary to curb such activities in order to be part of the global trade system. Thus, promotional support, tie-ins with local representatives, and an open mind in regard to sharing with and trusting locals will be more justified in the future than in the past (see box, "Marketing in Korea").

DISTRIBUTION AND SERVICE　Distribution and service activities should also be viewed for the potential long-range benefits. Distribution is very important—and warrants larger margins and more support services than elsewhere. Participating in a growth market usually involves spending money to increase the number of outlets, the coverage of segments, and responding to competitive threats. These markets are not cash cows yet—except for the upper niche—but they will be later.

Getting the Picture

Marketing in Korea[12]

NOT ALL OF THE NIE'S are the same when it comes to marketing. While a country such as Taiwan has high trade tariffs and little regulation of how to do business, South Korea has lower tariffs, but when it comes to marketing regulations, it is considered by some observers to be one of the most restrictive countries in Asia. For example, most aspects of promotion are heavily regulated: how, what, when, where. Price cuts should not exceed 60 days per year, any one individual period being limited to 15 days for a manufacturer, 7 days for a retailer. Any one business can have only four promotions per year. The price cuts have to be related to the product value according to a complicated formula. Commercial TV is available, but until 1995 the advertising industry was strictly local. Liberalization of TV time buying and the advent of cable and satellite TV promise to increase competition for local agencies, which lag their foreign counterparts.

Distribution, a key element of the marketing mix since promotional tools are limited, has its own share of regulations. For example, store limits have been at 300 square feet for foreigners, roughly the size of an average 7-Eleven store. A liberalization package, passed on July 1, 1993 as a first step in a campaign to gain GATT/WTO membership for Korea, has led to increased store construction in the big cities by Korean entrepreneurs eager to position themselves ahead of an expected foreign influx. Most foreign firms enter via joint ventures, needing a local partner to handle the regulatory obstacles if not the business itself. Price Club/Cosco, the American warehouse retailer, established links with Shinsegae, and its low prices are revolutionizing the market, with prices 30% below Korean competitors.

With liberalization, the Korean market is very attractive. The 44 million people claim an annual income approaching $10,000 per capita. The Korean won is tied to the dollar, minimizing exchange rate problems for Western companies. Because past restrictions have favored producers and kept consumer choices down, there is a pent-up demand for foreign products, but retail and personal service are not at very high levels. Although older consumers are ambivalent about buying foreign products, which they are told is unpatriotic, younger consumers are more interested in the status and high quality of global brands. With liberalization and deregulation, one can expect the Korean consumer to follow the Japanese example, just as its manufacturers have.

Sources: Boddy, 1994; Taylor, 1994.

SPECIAL CASE: MARKETING IN LATIN AMERICA[13]

These general considerations provide a starting point for the local marketer in an NIE. But more details on local conditions are needed to formulate, implement, and execute strategy. Not all countries can be covered here; since Latin America is coming back as one of the growth markets of the world (see box, "Latin American Surge"), it will be useful to examine the Latin American countries further.

Getting the Picture

Latin American Surge

LATIN AMERICA'S drive toward free trade is surging. In customs lanes at the international airports of Rio de Janeiro and Sao Paulo, the police simply wave through thousands of passport bearers from Argentina, Paraguay, and Uruguay, Brazil's common market partners in Mercosur. Jets that shuttle hourly between Sao Paulo and Buenos Aires carried 1.3 million passengers in 1994, twice as many as four years earlier. Four times as many business executives from Mercosur countries visited Brazil as did executives from the United States.

Further north, the United States, Canada, and Mexico have agreed with Chile to start negotiating that country's entrance into an expanded NAFTA. In a mid-1995 meeting of 33 trade ministers from the Americas in Denver, the delegates agreed to start working on the creation, by 2005, of a hemispherewide customs union, the Free Trade Area of the Americas.

Since free trade talks are expected to take years, a complementary building block that crosses trade barriers more easily is taking shape—Latin-American multinational corporations. Telecomunicaciones de Chile has invested in telephone companies in Argentina, Colombia, Peru, and Venezuela. Tintas Renner S.A., Brazil's largest paint company, has joint venture partners in Argentina, Chile, Paraguay, and Uruguay. In recent financial ventures an Ecuadorean bank bought a Colombian bank, a Colombian bank bought a Venezuelan bank, and a Chilean bank bought a Bolivian bank. In 1995 there were 300 Brazilian and 170 Chilean companies operating in Argentina.

Sources: Brooke, 1995; Smith, 1994.

The economic growth in the Latin American markets is fueled by regional trading blocs, a political shift toward increased democracy, and a gradual emergence from a large debt burden in several of the countries. For the local marketer, of special importance is the culture (religious and ethnic heritage), which affects communication strategy in particular, an uneven income distribution, which affects segmentation strongly, and a drive toward pan-regional marketing. More on this below—first some background information.

Market Environment

Latin America is a geographical area that stretches from Mexico down through Central and South America to Cape Horn. It is tied together by a common cultural heritage of native Indians, colonial dominance by Spain and Portugal, and the Roman Catholic church. The language is Spanish except in the largest country, Brazil, whose 160 million inhabitants speak Portuguese. The total population is 460 million, of which Mexico accounts for 86 million.

Latin America exhibits a varied ethnic mix of descendants of the ancient, highly developed civilizations of Incas/Aztecs and the conquering Europeans—largely Spanish and Portuguese, but also German, Italian, and British. There are also African, Asian, and Polynesian influences and a significant Japanese presence in Peru and Brazil. These varied influences combine uneasily, with ethnic heritage strongly linked to social class. There is great disparity between the political, social, economic elite and the often illiterate, poor peasants of Indian heritage. Society is stratified with two classes (very rich and very poor). This has given rise to political/military instability, a history of revolutions and coups, and terrorism as a means of changing the status quo. Economic progress should serve to lower this propensity for violence, and there is some indication of a growing middle class.

The Roman Catholic tradition is still the most important religious influence; it has been shifting from its traditional role of supporting the oligarchy to supporting movements for social justice. There has been some growth in Protestantism and an evangelical movement (principally Pentecostal), heavily influenced by TV evangelism from the United States. The shift toward Protestantism goes hand in hand with the industrialization and urbanization of Latin America and the cultural shift toward democratization and self-reform.

Overall the region is poor, with at least 50 percent of wealth controlled by 20 percent of the people in almost all the countries in Latin America. Affluent consumers with buying power equivalent to that in developed countries are only about 10 to 20 percent of the population in most countries. Broadly speaking, these are countries in the process of moving from agricultural to industrial society.

One grievous problem in several Latin American countries has been a large external debt. Argentina, Brazil, Venezuela, and Mexico are countries still feeling the pain of the large debt burden incurred in the 1970s. Recent write-offs by private banks and support from the World Bank and the IMF have helped ease the burden considerably. Nevertheless, foreign exchange controls and hyperinflation constitute recurring business risks in Latin America. For example, 1993 inflation in Brazil reached 2,492 percent, forcing corporate planning cycles to be reduced sometimes to as little as one month. However, average inflation in large countries in Latin America (with the exception of Brazil) was actually down to 16 percent in 1993 versus 1,200 percent in 1990.

Other risks stem from political instability and difficulty implementing institutional reforms, particularly in Mexico, Brazil, and Venezuela. Slow or disappointing progress in democratic reforms and endemic corruption could cause a populist revolt against free market economies. The 1995 devaluation of the Mexican peso and the continuing high-level political corruption have threatened the stability of the entire region. While Mexico's exports are booming because of the weak peso, the expected market growth in the country has not occurred, and exporters to Mexico and foreign investors there still suffer. Gradually the economic situation is improving, and if the political situation improves as well, the NAFTA agreement can be extended further into Latin America as planned.

Regional Trade Agreements

Several regional trade agreements affect marketing in Latin America directly by enhancing the opportunities for regionwide marketing strategies. The agreements are as follows:

LAIA—Latin American Integration Association. This agreement between all South American countries and Mexico expands a previous free trade agreement (LAFTA) into a customs union with free flow of goods and a common tariff rate toward nonmembers.

ANCOM—Andean Common Market. In February 1993, Bolivia, Colombia, Ecuador, and Venezuela began operating a common market. ANCOM means reduced tariffs, increased intraregional trade, free factor mobility, and a political climate more favorable to foreigners.

MERCOSUR—Southern Cone Common Market. A common market consisting of Argentina, Brazil, Paraguay and Uruguay.

NAFTA—North American Free Trade Area. The 1994 ratification of NAFTA has meant that Mexico has moved closer to its northern neighbors. But rather than seeing this as a step away from the Latin American region, from a marketing viewpoint Mexico has become a natural entry gate to the larger Latin American market for North American businesses.

Market Segmentation

Market segmentation in Latin America is often based on the simple distinctions between urban and rural population, combined with age and income level. A typical rule of thumb says that 80 percent of the purchasing power is in urban areas, 20 percent in rural areas. Companies targeting affluent urban buyers can generally apply the same ideas and techniques as in the developed world. The urban segment is a status-conscious and aspiring market with working- and middle-class households sacrificing a large portion of their income to purchase the comforts and status symbols of the industrialized world, appliances, TVs, VCRs, and so forth.

Urban Latin America has a young, style-conscious segment. Approximately 56 percent of Latin America's population is under the age of 24. Many young adults live with their parents and spend disposable income on luxury and semiluxury items. The youth market can have a large influence on the buying patterns of their parents and other consumer groups. Cable TV is not yet available in most of Latin America. However, trying to capture the future potential of this market, MTV (Music TV) Latino is targeting the still small but rapidly growing Latin American pay-TV market (about 7 to 10 percent of Latin American households subscribe to cable TV).[14]

Companies have to rethink their strategies for reaching outlying markets/rural populations in Latin America. Face-to-face interviewing and observation are generally necessary to gauge reaction to promotions and products. It is very important to be sensitive to religions, political, ethnic, and cultural issues of all kinds. Cultural idiosyncracies, such as symbolism of certain colors, flowers, animals, and so on, have to be reckoned with in advertising and promotions. Many consumers have not had extensive contact with the developed world.

The cultural heritage of poverty and sometimes fatalistic religion creates a large tradition-bound core customer segment in rural Latin American markets. These are family-oriented segments, with authority centered in the father in a culture of "machismo" and the strong male figure. There is a willingness to leave things to destiny and chance, to view the future as inevitable, and to put off till the well-known "mañana" anything that can wait and will take care of itself anyway. Making promises of delivery, whether or not you expect to fulfill an order, is often the order of the day.

Marketers targeting the huge pool of low-income consumers have a tough challenge. Successful mass marketing can be achieved through creative packaging (small volume, low-price units), taking new product roll-outs one step at a time, establishing one product firmly before launching another, and spending heavily on advertising.

Marketing Communications

Marketing communications in Latin America are dominated by the need to overcome illiteracy. High illiteracy rates mean that there is a need for product identification through nonverbal/pictorial means. The accompanying music becomes very important—Brazilian commercials typically rely heavily on the popular dance music of the region. Package shape and design become very important. Repetition of identical posters and reinforcing the product and its name are useful, accompanied by easily memorized music. Sponsoring popular daytime soap operas on television allows the advertiser to reach a huge audience of women of all ages. Radio advertising can be very effective with semiliterate audiences. Because cents-off coupons can't be handled by retailers, inducing new product trial is a challenge. Companies have used inventive promotional tools such as vans and sound trucks stationed at markets to play music and offer free samples to passersby. Sponsorship of movies or sporting events is fruitful. Endorsements by well-known entertainers or athletes can be powerful. Cafe Pele, named after the soccer star, has been very successful for Brazilian coffee maker Cacique de Alimentos. When Gatorade featured soccer star Pele in a TV commercial in which he was seen drinking Gatorade after a game, no words were necessary. Sales took off and success was ensured throughout the region.

Ads aimed at Latin audiences can succeed by portraying the family, as households often have three generations under one roof. Women respond well to commercials that convey a sense of pleasing the family through traditional roles of caring for the home and making meals. The Hispanic culture is upbeat and happy, and Hispanics react most favorably to ads which portray them as colorful and lively.

Research has paradoxically also shown that adult urban Latin Americans want detailed product information in advertising and tend to reject image-oriented ads. They want to understand immediately what the commercial is for and what it claims to deliver. Product demonstrations and testimonials are effective.[15]

In general, Latin America, especially in the rural markets, is in its infancy in terms of knowledge and awareness of world-class brands and products. This means that even established brands will need to invest considerably in raising brand awareness and creating a market presence, and smaller brands have a unique opportunity to gain a foothold.

Distribution

Distribution in Latin America is moving toward the larger integrated units and the chain concept common in Western markets. For example, large supermarkets with expanded assortments of leisure products and home appliances—so-called hypermarkets—are growing in importance. Carrefour, the French chain of hypermarkets, has a large presence in Latin America.

The Dutch company SHV Holdings invested $60 million in the wholesale distribution sector in Venezuela, despite political and economic instability in the country. In 1993, the company expected to open three "Makro" megastores in Venezuela with another two under construction. The company already had 23 stores in Brazil and 4 in Argentina. Makro uses bulk purchasing, low operational costs, and elimination of transportation expenses to keep prices extremely low. One of SHV's basic strategies is to work with local partners to take advantage of their local capital, experience in distribution, and knowledge of local markets.

A joint expansion agreement between Wal-Mart and Cifra, Mexico's largest retailer, has led to the creation of a prototype store called Aurrera. This new store is a modern store with carefully planned layout, designed to improve traffic circulation by redesigning the entrance and pedestrian walkways and using large focal points to identify main departments.

Cifra's success in Mexico has been the result of a saturation approach targeting different income groups. Using access to Wal-Mart's financial resources, technology, and marketing expertise, Cifra plans to continue to expand rapidly, targeting the expected demographic boom in Mexico. Despite the peso problems, Wal-Mart is also opening its own stores in Mexico and is moving into Argentina with its own stores as well.

In terms of establishing distribution at entry, barriers exist. Some find a weak infrastructure creates problems (see box, "Getting Started in Mexico").

Foreign companies have found that it is a mistake to rely on selling products through large and established Latin American distributors, who may only take on products that are easy to sell and who do not have a commitment to specializing in their products. For Northern firms, joint ventures with strong local partners are advisable at entry to help open up the doors to Latin

*G*etting the
Picture

Getting Started
in Mexico:
Amway Finds
Localization
Leads to
Rapid Growth

WHEN ENTERING Mexico, Amway, the American direct home sales company, had to modify its system to conform to local laws and adjust for the lack of service infrastructure.

First was a change in the organizational system to avoid responsibility for social security payments and income tax withholdings for its individual distributors. Each Amway distributor must therefore register as an individual business so that there is absolutely no labor connection with the company.

Instead of the home delivery from a central warehouse used in the U.S. and Europe, the lack of adequate service by shippers in Mexico forced Amway to use eight distribution centers in six cities. It also works with a Mexican express delivery company for service to areas not covered by its own depots.

One challenge was the inadequate telecommunications system. The Mexican telephone company's (Telmex) rapidly expanding toll-free 800 service couldn't keep up with Amway's needs for quick order taking from its distributors. Service is still relatively inefficient and expensive. Also, Amway has had trouble securing a dedicated line for computer communication between HQ in Monterrey and outlying distribution centers.

Trademark registration and health authorization processes for imported products cause significant delays—average wait is up to three months versus one month in Europe.

Sources: Dreifus, 1992; American Chamber of Commerce in Mexico, 1992.

America's clubby business world. Some companies, such as the Philadelphia hospital company AMSCO, avoid allowing middlemen to define their markets and concentrate on learning the market and getting to know the end customers firsthand.[16]

Tropicana Dole Beverages International entered the South American market by launching its Pure Premium Orange and Grapefruit juices and Pure Tropics line of fruit juice blends in Argentina. Tropicana, in partnership with its sister company, Seagram de Argentina (both affiliates of Seagram), is currently in a joint venture with La Serenisima, Argentina's largest dairy, and is a partner with similar high quality products and brand loyal customers. The company chose entry into Argentina because of its strong economy, concentration of affluent consumers, and its lack of premium chilled juice competitors. Argentina is to be used as a springboard for entry into other key Latin American markets.[17]

Major Country Markets

Latin America has four major markets. Argentina, Brazil, and Mexico have large populations—Chile has the highest per capita GDP. Some marketing highlights:

In Argentina, where inflation has been reined in and the economy improved, significantly increased purchasing power has contributed to record sales in the soft drink market (seventh in the world in per capita consumption, with consumption growing at 8 percent per year for past 10 years). Fierce competi-

An Argentine advertisement for Tropicana orange juice, emphasizing its purity. The Spanish language ad is a logical pan-regional advertisement as Tropicana expands from its Argentine entry point to the rest of Latin America.

Courtesy Tropicana.

tion exists between Pepsi and Coke for brand penetration and customer loyalty. Both companies are targeting young consumers and installing large numbers of vending machines as well as sponsoring rock concerts and special promotions. After nearly reaching bankruptcy during the years of hyperinflation and price controls, Pepsi has recently been relaunched in Argentina, achieving a 39 percent market share. Coke has responded by restructuring its distribution channels to work more closely with supermarket chains, bars, restaurants, and other retailers.

In Brazil, the national passion for soccer translates into huge investments in marketing. The Brazilian national team's qualification for the World Cup finals meant an estimated $1 billion in marketing. If Brazil had not qualified, only approximately one-third this amount would have been spent. Advertising agencies in Brazil estimate that about $500 million was spent on media and promotions in the preliminary qualifying rounds, but the amount multiplied as the Brazilian team advanced to the final victory.

In Chile, the most vigorous example of recent Latin American growth, consumer markets are booming. Over $200 million was invested in new shopping malls in 1994. One-fifth of the Chilean population currently frequents shopping malls (versus three-fifths in the United States). The new shopping malls run from a $59 million luxury mall to Chile's very first outlet mall, where one-third of the new stores will be foreign chains.[18]

As in Argentina, credit card issuers are helping to fuel growth in spending by lowering the minimum household income required to obtain a card (for instance, Banco Santander requires only $500 to 600 monthly income, versus $1,000 previously).

In Mexico, direct mail is being used extensively for the first time because the postal service is now more reliable. The relative newness of direct mail is an advantage—Latin Americans receive little junk mail, and many tend to read every letter. Response rates for inquiries of 5 to 10 percent are common (versus 1 to 2 percent in the United States). However, the use of direct mail is affected by a shortage of reliable mailing lists. A 24-hour home shopping network was also introduced in Mexico in 1993.

Some marketers are trying integrated marketing approaches to reach consumers in Mexico. For example, the Kellogg's cereal company sponsored a conference on nutrition and fiber that generated a large amount of publicity. This was followed by an equally successful introduction of recipes and nutrition messages on cereal boxes.

Pan-Regional Marketing

Some observers argue that the Latin American market is **pan-regional** and that a marketing strategy aimed at the Latin American region overall will be effective.[19]

Advertising agencies such as McCann-Erickson and DDB Needham believe that there is a strong trend toward increased regionalization and integration in Latin America.[20] They anticipate that this will lead to more pan-regional advertising and media buying. However, cross-border advertising is currently hampered by the media infrastructure, which is still very localized and not very extensive in some countries.

Two American companies' Latin American strategies can be used to demonstrate how global marketers are approaching the region.

Burger King in Latin America: Burger King, the fast-food restaurant chain, plans an aggressive expansion into Mexico, Brazil, Chile, Peru, Argentina, Colombia, and Puerto Rico over the next five years. This expansion will take the form of joint ventures, franchise agreements, and alliances with U.S. consumer products companies such as Coca-Cola. Burger King will spend about $5 million in advertising annually to introduce its name into the region.

Burger King expects to have 600 restaurants in Latin America and the Caribbean by 1996. In 1991 there were no Burger Kings in Brazil, but the company's goal is to have 250 by the end of 1996. Similarly, in Mexico BK hopes to have 117 restaurants, versus only 3 in 1991. BK currently has 29 franchise groups in Latin America, and plans new franchise agreements in Argentina and Chile.

The company's objective in expanding in Latin America is to "think globally and act locally." The company has established headquarters for the Latin American division in Miami but is also establishing corporate offices in the local markets including Rio de Janeiro, Mexico City, and Sao Paolo.[21]

IBM in Latin America: IBM's long-term strategy for Latin America includes spending millions of dollars to bring computer technology to local schools in 11 countries. In five years, IBM has provided 800,000 children with access to computers and has trained more than 10,000 teachers. This program is intended to enhance the company's image and also create a market with loyal future customers for its products and services.

The computers are purchased by institutions and private firms and donated to the schools. IBM contributes in the form of teacher training and technical support and has invested millions of dollars in its Latin American Research Center, which advises countries on designing and implementing educational programs.

In Venezuela, IBM and Procter and Gamble have designed a donation scheme called Future Mission, where students, parents, and teachers collect proof of purchase seals from P&G products and redeem them for computer equipment for their schools. An extensive advertising campaign including press, radio, direct mail, TV, and in-store computer demonstrations has publicized the program.

In the end, however, it is misleading to believe that Latin America is a single, borderless market like what the European Union aspires to be. Manuel Mencia of the Beacon Council, a Florida economic development group, says that non–Latin Americans tend to ignore that "what divides Latin Americans is much more important than what binds them."[22] Marketers may do better understanding one country's culture at a time and, for the time being at least, emphasizing localization.

SUMMARY

In the mature markets of the advanced countries local marketing should become "just marketing." It can—but with a twist. Even among the triad nations of Western Europe, North America, Japan, Australia, and New Zealand, there are plenty of differences the marketer must take into account. This chapter has spelled out some of the more obvious differences, at least in respect to Japan, but has still really only scratched the surface. The local marketer has to develop a more in-depth sense of the local marketing scene in order to be effective.

Market segmentation is usually a "must" in mature markets, and new entrants will often have to enter with niche strategies, positioning their products not in the core of the market but in a specialty niche. Even when the entrant is a strong core brand in a leading market, the differences between mature markets can be great enough that the niche approach is preferable. On the other hand, when the product is new, as usual a new entrant has a chance to develop a new market and gain favorable first-mover advantages, something which takes resources, focus, and continuous monitoring of penetration.

New growth markets in the NIE countries differ from the typical growth markets in mature economies. What is important is further market development, helping to increase the total market size. The local marketer should work to improve the infrastructure to make products and services available to a larger number of potential customers, develop a communication strategy that is sensitive to local culture, language, and religion, and adapt packaging and pricing to accommodate smaller budgets. To take advantage of opportunities in the new growth markets of the NIEs, the local marketer needs to pursue a localization strategy and will benefit by working closely with local partners.

KEY TERMS

"Me too" products p. 314
Country-of-origin effects p. 313
Customer satisfaction p. 318
Emerging markets p. 309

First-mover advantage p. 314
Market development p. 311
Marketing infrastructure p. 310
Mature markets p. 310

New growth markets p. 309
Newly industrialized economies (NIEs) p. 324
Pan-regional Latin American marketing p. 336

DISCUSSION QUESTIONS

1. From library research, identify how a product and brand of your choice is advertised differently—or similarly—in a European country and North America. Are the differences (similarities) related to differences (similarities) in positioning?

2. Discuss the major factors that affect market acceptance of a consumer product such as a watch in a Latin American country. How would you as a local marketer help develop the market?

3. Other than offering low prices, what can a Third World country do to get its products accepted by consumers in a mature economy? Can you find an example of a successful entry from such a country?

4. What are the reasons why entry into the Japanese market is so expensive?

5. Why might a successful North American marketer not be the best one to head the company's marketing effort in Latin America? What kind of person is needed, and how would he or she be trained?

NOTES

1. The diffusion of manufacturing technology that drives this development exemplifies the Vernon international product cycle.

2. Country-of-origin effects have been the focus for a number of research studies for three decades or so. The sustained findings are that made-in labels matter for customers' quality perceptions. While consumers often protest that where a product is from does not matter, they still use country of origin as a clue to quality. It is less common, apparently, that consumers buy things because of some patriotic feeling. See Papadopoulos and Heslop, 1993.

3. As the multinational companies expand their manufacturing operations across the globe, the same process can be expected to make customers reevaluate their stereotypes of the countries. So, Indonesian-made calculators won't raise any eye-

brows. What seems to be happening, according to research by David Tse and others at the University of British Columbia, is that a strong brand name serves to reassure the buyer. A Hewlett-Packard printer made in Malaysia is still an H-P product. A Sony TV made in San Diego is still a Sony—and to many consumers, its positioning is still that of a "Japanese product." See Tse and Lee, 1989.

4. See Kerin et al., 1992.

5. See Johansson, 1994.

6. See Albrecht, 1992, and Fornell, 1992, for a fuller presentation of what customer satisfaction involves in different markets.

7. Thanks are due to Kennedy Gitchel for reviewing and updating the material in this section.

8. See Czinkota and Woronoff, 1991, p. 91.

9. Fields, 1989, paints a vivid picture of Japanese consumers.

10. This section draws on Johansson and Hirano, 1995. The structural impediments initiative (SII) was an agreement in the early 1990s between the United States and Japan to dismantle distribution and other barriers that prohibited entry into each other's markets.

11. Papadopoulos and Heslop, 1993, discuss many of these remnants of the past in chapter 2 of their book.

12. Thanks are due to Chong Lee and Stephen Gaull from whose research this section is drawn.

13. Thanks are due to Kerri Olson for drafting this section and to Ernesto Priego for reviewing and updating it.

14. These data come from the *Crossborder Monitor*, February 16, 1994.

15. See Sanchez, 1992.

16. From Barks, 1994.

17. From "Tropicana Enters South American Juice Market," PR Newswire (PRN) on ProQuest Business Dataline, February 21, 1994.

18. From *Crossborder Monitor*, November 24, 1993, p. 2.

19. See, for example, *Crossborder Monitor*, April 21, 1993.

20. See Turner and Karle, 1992.

21. See Rosenberg, 1993.

22. From Barks, 1994.

SELECTED REFERENCES

Albrecht, Karl. *The Only Thing That Matters.* New York: Harper Business, 1992.

American Chamber of Commerce in Mexico. "Setting Up a Distribution Operation: How Amway Adapted Its Direct Sales System to Mexico." *Business Mexico*, 2 (January–February 1992), pp. 22–23.

Barks, Joseph V. "Penetrating Latin America." *International Business*, February 1994, pp. 78–80.

Boddy, Clive. "The Challenge of Understanding the Dynamics of Consumers in Korea." In *Meeting the Challenges of Korea: The 1994 AMCHAM Marketing Seminar.* Seoul: American Chamber of Commerce in Korea, 1994, pp. 7–12.

Brooke, James. "More Open Latin Borders Mirror an Opening of Markets." *New York Times*, July 4, 1995, p. 47.

Chadwick, Michael, and Sue Won. "Toys-R-Us in Japan." Project report, Waseda-Georgetown program, Summer 1994.

Czinkota, Michael R., and Jon Woronoff. *Unlocking Japan's Markets.* Chicago: Probus, 1991.

Dreifus, Shirley B., ed. *Business International's Global Management Desk Reference.* New York: McGraw-Hill, 1992.

Fields, George. *The Japanese Market Culture.* Tokyo: The Japan Times, 1989.

Fornell, Claes. "A National Customer Satisfaction Barometer: The Swedish Experience." *Journal of Marketing* 56, no. 1 (January 1992), pp. 6–21.

Johansson, Johny K. "The Sense of 'Nonsense': Japanese TV Advertising." *Journal of Advertising* 23, no.1 (March 1994), pp. 17–26.

Johansson, Johny K., and Ikujiro Nonaka. "Customer Satisfaction in Japan." Working paper, School of Business, Georgetown University, 1993.

Johansson, Johny K., and Masaaki Hirano. "Japanese Marketing in the Post-Bubble Era." *International Executive* 38, no.1 (January–February 1995), pp. 33–51.

Kerin, Roger A.; P. Rajan Varadarajan; and Robert A. Peterson. "First-Mover Advantage: A Synthesis, Conceptual Framework, and Research Propositions." *Journal of Marketing* 56, no.4 (October 1992), pp. 33–52.

Kotler, P.; L. Fahey, and S. Jatusripitak. *The New Competition.* Englewood Cliffs, N.J.: Prentice Hall, 1985.

Papadopoulos, Nicolas, and Louise A. Heslop, eds. *Product-Country Images: Impact and Role in International Marketing.* New York: International Business Press, 1993.

Rosenberg, Sharon Harvey. "Burger King Maps Move into Latin America." *Miami Daily Business Review,* December 13, 1993, p. A1.

Sanchez, Jacqueline. "Some Approaches Better than Others when Targeting Hispanics." *Marketing News,* May 25, 1992, pp. 8, 11.

Smith, Geri. "Why Wait For NAFTA?" *Business Week,* Dec. 5, 1994, pp. 52–54.

Taylor, John. "The Critical Elements of Sales and Distribution." In *Meeting the Challenges of Korea: The 1994 AMCHAM Marketing Seminar.* Seoul: American Chamber of Commerce in Korea, 1994, pp. 23–28.

TeleVeronique and TV 10. "Launch of Dutch Commercial TV Good News for U.S. Distributors." *Television/ Radio Age* 36 (July 24, 1989), p. 19.

Tse, David, and W. Lee. "Evaluating Products of Multiple Countries-of-Origin Effect: Effects of Component Origin, Assembly Origin, and Brand." Working paper, Faculty of Commerce, University of British Columbia, Vancouver, Canada, 1989.

Turner, Rik, and Delinda Karle. "Shops See Unity of Latin America." *Advertising Age,* April 27, 1992, pp. I-4, I-38.

Updike, Edith Hill, and Mary Kuntz. "Japan Is Dialing 1 800 BuyAmerica." *Business Week,* June 12, 1995, pp. 61, 64.

Womack, James P.; Daniel T. Jones; and Daniel Roos. *The Machine That Changed the World.* New York: Rawson Associates, 1990.

WuDunn, Sheryl. "Japanese Do Buy American: By Mail and a Lot Cheaper." *New York Times,* July 3, 1995, pp. 1, 43.

Chapter 10

Local Marketing in Emerging Markets

"Sleeping giants wake up"

After studying this chapter, you should understand the following global marketing issues:

1. To take advantage of the opportunities in emerging markets, the marketer needs to get back to basics of what marketing is supposed to bring to people.

2. In emerging markets there are a variety of marketing environments that a local marketer might encounter, and every national market is different. However, emerging countries are usually characterized by political uncertainty, and a lot of business in them involves countertrade.

3. A functioning marketing infrastructure, especially an effective distribution system, is crucial. When one is lacking, the local marketing effort has to help build one up.

4. The political heritage of the NDCs means that middlemen and consumers often have a very ambivalent feeling about free markets, simultaneously both expecting too much and not wanting to accept the uncertainties they bring. The local marketer from abroad becomes an educator about free markets.

IN THIS, THE SECOND of two chapters on different marketing environments, the challenges posed by emerging markets are discussed. *Emerging markets* include the newly democratized post-communist nations, including China (still communist but with a more open economy), India, and other developing countries. Although some of the discussion will cover developing countries in general, the focus will be on "newly democratized countries" (NDCs). In these markets the heritage of a centralized planning economy means that marketing activities are suspect, marketers need to be legitimized, and there is a traditional supremacy of producers over consumers. Marketing becomes an act of rebellion against the old order and places people's mindsets under stress. The standard injunction of good marketing practice—satisfy the customers with good products and services—still applies. However, there is a lot of basic education about the workings of the free market system needed—among competing producers, middlemen, and customers—before marketing action can be effectively implemented. Marketing is a tool of the capitalist system, and the marketing manager becomes its foot-soldier and standard-bearer.

Partners and Persistence Are Leaven for Chinese Bakery

For Ray Tsaih, an American businessman born in Taiwan, operating a $2.2 million bakery on the outskirts of Shanghai, China, is full of surprises. In fact, *surprise* (his own word) is a positive way to think of the challenges Tsaih has faced since he first began negotiating arrangements for the business.

Knowing that personal relationships are key to marketing success in China, Tsaih started by signing on a joint venture partner—a company owned by the city government. For its share of equity in the enterprise, the partner contributed a plot of land and no cash. However, not even a local partner could guarantee good service from the electric company. A month before the factory was scheduled to open, the utility said it was still building the power grid and would be late plugging in the factory. Once the plant was operating, a freezer and some electric dough mixers were destroyed in two power surges.

With new parts from Japan, the bakery got running again, but the Shanghai government informed Tsaih that his company, Shanghai Cheerful Food Company, needed a permit before it could use its delivery trucks. Unfortunately, the number of permits is limited. Tsaih had to pay another company to "borrow" its unneeded permits.

By then, seven months had passed, and many small bakeries had sprung up in Shanghai. Tsaih had to scrap his initial small-scale marketing plan to sell frozen dough to local retailers. He needed a less-crowded niche, and that meant operating on a larger scale. He negotiated an arrangement to sell buns to Kentucky Fried Chicken outlets in Shanghai. To win the contract, Tsaih had to agree to several changes, including replacement of his (new) ovens and quadrupling his delivery fleet.

Finally, Shanghai Cheerful Food Company was in business, selling 80,000 hamburger buns, cakes, and other products a day. Still, the "surprises" continue. Turnover is high, and government officials are apt to look for special favors.

Tsaih's challenges are hardly unique or limited to small businesses. General Motors, too, depended on local partners to establish a foothold in China, and GM had to give the Chinese extensive access to its advanced technology. With challenges like these, why are businesspeople flocking to China? The economy's growth and its sheer size offer a potential that is just too mouth-watering.

Sources: "In Shanghai, Executive Finds, Success Requires a Thick Crust," *Journal of Commerce*, May 17, 1995, p. 6A; Edwin McDowell, "Business Travel," *New York Times*, September 20, 1995, p. D6; Edward A. Gargan, "Asia Guide Calls Local Partners Key to Success," *New York Times*, November 14, 1995, p. D4; Keith Naughton and Pete Engardio, "How GM Got the Inside Track in China," *Business Week*, November 6, 1995, pp. 56–57.

INTRODUCTION

Emerging markets as defined here comprise the newly democratized postcommunist nations, China (whose communist government has eased central control over the economy), India, and other developing countries. Among typical **developing** countries are many of the poor nations in Africa (Nigeria, Zambia, Tanzania), Asia (Pakistan, India, Philippines), and Central America (Nicaragua, Guatemala). They are defined primarily by *low per capita income levels* and are discussed here together with the newly democratized countries (NDCs) mainly because they share a severe *lack of marketing infrastructure*.

This chapter will first deal briefly with some general problems of marketing in developing countries and then concentrate on marketing in the newly democratized countries (NDCs), especially Russia and Eastern Europe. We then discuss the special cases of marketing in China and India.

LOCAL MARKETING IN DEVELOPING COUNTRIES

Marketing in the typical developing country faces a number of special problems engendered by the poor economic conditions, the low educational levels and high illiteracy rate, and the general apathy of the populace. Western marketing activities tend to assume a substantial and economically strong middle class, something usually lacking in developing countries. Local marketing in such countries becomes a special challenge.

The macroenvironment in the typical developing market is characterized by *uncertainty*, and thus "environmental scanning" becomes part of the job for the local marketer. Radical political change can develop quickly, and financial risk tends to be great. Convertibility problems, black markets, and exchange rate fluctuations tend to lessen the value of revenues. The possibility of abrupt changes in tariff rates and other trade-impeding measures creates a need for constant vigilance. It becomes necessary for the local marketer to work with international lending agencies such as the World Bank and the International Monetary Fund (IMF) and to use insurance agencies such as the Overseas Private Investment Corporation (OPIC).[1] And a lot of the business involves some form of countertrade.

Countertrade

Countertrade is the term for transactions in which all or part of the payment is made in kind rather than cash. The practice has been known as barter trade throughout recorded history, but in the last few years new and ingenious wrinkles on the practice have emerged. The primary moving force has been the shortage of hard currencies available to developing countries, in particular those lacking a strong export sector to generate foreign earnings.

It is useful to distinguish between five kinds of countertrade: barter, compensation deals, counterpurchase, product buy-back, and offset.

Barter is the oldest form of countertrade. Barter is the direct exchange of goods between two trading partners. A famous barter trade was the huge deal between Occidental Petroleum of the United States and the Soviet government back in the 1970s to exchange superphosphoric acid (from Occidental) for urea and potash (from the Soviet Union), an agreement valued at about $20 billion. No money changed hands and no third party was involved—a classic Armand Hammer transaction.

For barter to make economic sense, the seller must be able to dispose of the goods received in payment. In the case of Occidental this was no problem since the company could use the urea and potash in its own manufacturing plants. To assist companies who engage in barter trading and cannot count on such arrangements, several barter houses have been established primarily in Europe where many of the barter exchanges are negotiated.

Compensation deals involve payment both in goods and in cash. In one case GM sold locomotives to former Yugoslavia for $12 million and was paid in cash plus Yugoslavian machine tools valued at approximately $4 million. The introduction of the cash portion is to make the deal more attractive to the seller, and most companies faced with the possibility of a countertrade agreement will in fact insist that at least some portion of the bill be settled in cash. As in the case of barter, the goods portion of the payment has to be sold in a third market, and the added transaction costs should logically be added to the original amount invoiced.

Counterpurchases represent the most typical version of the countertrade. Here two contracts are usually negotiated, one to sell the product (the initial agreement) at an agreed upon cash price, and a second to buy goods from the purchaser at an amount equal to the bill in the initial agreement. This type of contract simply represents one way for the buyer to reuse valuable foreign currency and force exports and is usually introduced relatively late in the exchange negotiations. In practice the seller gets his money and then has a limited period of time (usually 6 to 12 months) before his purchases from the country must be completed. In some of these cases the second contract is sold (at a steep discount) to a third party (a barter house, for example), but this is not always feasible. McDonnell Douglas, for example, had to buy and then resell ham from China in order to sell a few of its aircraft there.

Product buy-backs come in two types. Under one type of product buy-back agreement the seller agrees to accept a certain amount of the output as full or partial payment for the goods sold. Alternatively, he can agree to buy back some of the output at a later date. Levi Strauss is accepting Hungarian-made jeans (bearing its brand name) in partial payment for setting up a jeans factory outside Budapest. Another Western company has established a tractor plant in Poland and agreed to buy back a certain number of Polish-built tractors as part of the deal.

In **offset** deals, the seller contracts to invest in local production or procurement to partially offset the sale price. In aircraft, for example, it is not uncommon for a national airline buying aircraft to demand that the aircraft manufacturer procure certain components, parts, or supplies in the buyer's country, or invest in some assembly operation there. This helps justify the purchase price paid to the manufacturer from cash-strapped nations.[2]

BUSINESS EVALUATION   There are many multinational corporations and exporters who have found themselves in a situation where a countertrade represents the only feasible alternative for the buyer. In general, settlement in cash is preferable to the seller. Where there is no competition, the seller can insist on a cash settlement. But companies such as Coca-Cola and Ford have been forced to accept the "realities" of the international marketplace and will do countertrading if necessary. GM has even gone so far as to create its own in-house barter subsidiary, General Motors Trading Company. For Japanese companies, the close ties with the large trading houses have proved to be of vital importance for countertrade, giving the Japanese an edge in the marketplace.

Similarly, European companies rely on barter houses to provide the necessary expertise and contacts to sell the goods received. In the global marketplace of the 1990s, with the huge China market opening up and the former Soviet republics suffering because of slow economic progress and currency problems, the acceptance of countertrade proposals might be necessary in order to be able to compete at all.

A countertrade option means not only that the value of the offered goods must be assessed but also that the extra costs associated with the negotiations and future sale be considered. It is usual, therefore, for the agreed upon price to rise considerably higher than the cash price. But for the buyer the gains are important—and in many situations the value to the buyer of the seller's products is much higher than the sacrifice in terms of domestic products, so the higher "price" is only a nominal figure.

For the seller evaluating a countertrade proposal, the following points are important to consider:

1. Is this the only way the order can be secured?
2. Can the received goods be sold?
3. How can we maximize the cash portion?
4. Does the invoiced price incorporate extra transaction costs?
5. Are there any import barriers to the received goods (so that we will have trouble disposing of the goods at home, say)?
6. Could there be currency exchange problems if we try to repatriate the earnings from sales in a third country?

If these issues receive a positive evaluation, countertrade might be a useful alternative. When the opposite happens, the firm might be better off curbing its appetite for foreign sales.

Market Analysis

Because developing markets have typically not had access to many consumer products in the past, consumer needs tend to be basic and easy to identify. However, the same lack of products has also made for a poorly advanced **marketing infrastructure.** Distribution channels are few and show low productivity, and communication media are limited in reach and coverage. Marketing research, therefore, rather than focusing on the buyer, is more usefully focused on the feasibility of various marketing activities. The well-known problems Nestlé faced with its baby formula products in African countries underscore this point. Although mothers were pleased with the product, the lack of clean water with which to mix the formula made the product dangerous for the infants.[3]

In these markets *income level* represents the basic segmentation criterion, and the market for upper-end status products from the West is often potentially lucrative because of an uneven income distribution. But the effective income measure is not necessarily defined in terms of salary or wages per household but rather in terms of *access to foreign or convertible currency.* For example, government bureaucrats may not be paid much in Uganda, but they may have better access to convertible currency than a local small entrepreneur. On the other hand, the secondary (or the black) market for foreign currency may offer the small entrepreneur access to hard currencies but at a price premium.

Once income level has been identified, the standard demographics may be used to segment the market. But the relatively low level of customer sophistication makes segmentation unnecessary on any other basis than geography. "Where" the customers are is the second question after income has been taken care of. And usually the most promising market is the urban population of big cities.

Marketing Decision Making

PRODUCT   The developing market environment makes product policy a key issue. Because customer needs tend to be basic and domestic alternatives weak, the initial offering usually consists of standardized simpler selections from the existing product lines. Limited features also make it possible to sell through low-service outlets; the reliability that comes with standardization alleviates the need for extensive after-sales service. General Motors uses this strategy. The company has developed a special automobile for use in rural areas in Southeast Asian countries such as the Philippines, where dirt roads are common. The chassis can be constructed from steel bars that come in a kit and require only simple tools for assembly. The engine and transmission are then mounted on the frame together with two seats and a canopy. The vehicle is cheap, runs high off the ground, and is easy to repair. It's perfect for the market (although with rising incomes and better roads, countries such as Malaysia have increasingly turned to more sophisticated Japanese cars assembled in neighboring Indonesia or Thailand).[4]

It is important not to be too casual about the emergence of more sophisticated tastes and preferences on the part of the customers. In most markets even relatively poor buyers have some aspirations concerning emotional satisfaction, a desire to get more than just functional performance from a product. Contrary to popular belief, high prices may not be such an impediment to market success in these countries as one would expect. For example, by focusing their spending on a few items, Russian consumers are able to spend for luxuries, and, at the upper end of the market, some of the successful new Russian entrepreneurs and Western expatriates can be targeted. In such instances, a low price can be a drawback, since a luxury image is automatically associated with a high price. American Standard's experience in Russia is instructive (see box, "American Standard in Russia").

It is useful to recognize that upscale positioning, targeting an upper, more status-oriented niche of the market, can play an important role in newly democratized markets. But in *developing* markets such desires tend to be exactly that, only developing. Gradually, as the markets shift into growth, the consumers will develop their individual preferences.

PRICE   Price policies in developing markets are dominated by the balance between affordability and upper-end positioning. Thus, pricing often fluctuates between maintaining a *skimming price*, which will yield a high-end positioning

AMERICAN STANDARD, the New Jersey–based multinational, is the world's largest manufacturer of bathroom furniture, with strong market presence in many countries. Its entry into Russia has not been so successful, however.

An initial market survey of demand in Russia in early 1991 suggested that the main market, new construction, would be slow and closed to outside vendors for the time being. The company decided to target reconstruction, the renovation and upgrading of old apartments in Moscow and St. Petersburg to offices for Western firms.

The firm decided that the Russian private entrepreneurs who took on the renovations would mainly be interested in the low-end equipment, which would lower building costs. Accordingly, the company brought in their low-end product line, priced competitively. The products did not move. The entrepreneurs wanted the top of the line. They went to European competitors for their top products. Price was no object. The reason? The builders figured that the Western companies would be willing to pay top dollar for their offices. They were right. In 1994 central Moscow was perhaps the world's most expensive business district, where prices of $15 to 20 thousand dollars per month for a small office were not unheard of.

Sources: Lloyd, 1994; Personal interview with Eric Crabtree, VP and Director, CMT Moscow, Construction Marketing and Trading, Inc., Washington, D.C., October 20, 1994.

and possibly quick payback, and a lower *penetration price*, which ensures affordability but also lowers margins and endangers the most desirable position. Striking a middle ground, many companies opt for a relatively high price that eliminates some buyers but offers the firm first-mover advantages in terms of image and brand loyalty.

The lack of purchasing power means that the marketer often must find innovative ways of offering a simpler product paid for through innovative financing. A washing machine can be sold to a communal village, for example, with several families helping to foot the bill. Smaller and less-expensive packages of shampoos sold by Unilever are popular in many of these markets. Soft drinks and packaged foods often come in smaller sizes as well, as do cigarettes (it is not unusual for someone to buy or sell one cigarette, for example) and beer cans. Store credit to customers is common, forcing manufacturers and distributors to offer liberal credit terms in turn.[5]

PROMOTION Promotion in developing markets is initially limited because of the lack of broadcast media available. However, as such media become available, the effectiveness of promotional messages can be considerable because of the lack of other advertising—there is less clutter. Of course, this is not true for outdoor advertising, which is an often effective means of establishing brand awareness and image. It is important to keep in mind the level of literacy—in developing countries the notion that "a picture is worth a thousand words" should be taken literally.

Gillette promotes its blades in New Delhi, India. Using buses with prominent displays and offering giveaways of shavers with free samples of blades, Gillette has adapted well to the weak infrastructure in many emerging markets.

Pablo Bartholomew/Gamma-Liaison.

DISTRIBUTION AND SERVICE   Distribution is usually the most critical area facing the local marketer in the developing country. In fact, unless effective ways of distributing the product can be found or created, market entries might be thwarted and the economic growth of the developing markets will not take off. On the other hand, cheap labor and personal service are usually readily available in developing markets. Where established logistical systems are weak one can often pursue alternative routes using cheap domestic labor.

For example, where telephone systems are unreliable, messengers on bicycle or Vespas are often able to carry on. Lack of fast road systems can be compensated for by slower river traffic and hand-carry services. Overcrowded mass transportation systems are avoided by taking taxis to faraway destinations. In developing markets personal service is a "convenience good" for many people and a necessity for the upper crust of society, including the expatriate manager in a multinational firm.[6]

Marketing organization and control is a difficult management problem in overseas business, regardless of the environment. In developing markets things get particularly difficult, since the local professional skills tend to be lower than elsewhere.

LOCAL MARKETING IN NEWLY DEMOCRATIZED COUNTRIES

From a marketing perspective, there are three major features that set **newly democratized countries'** (NDC) markets apart from those of the typical developing country.

1. *Basic needs satisfied.* Although these countries may be poor in per capita income by Western standards, the most basic needs of the population have in the past been satisfied through the government planning system. The consumers in these countries have not been starving (except during some drought years), and they have been able to buy clothing, shoes, housing, soap and detergent, and sometimes even televisions and automobiles. Since most of these products have been produced domestically, they may not be up to world standards, but the people had their needs met. This is especially important considering that some of the NDC countries have very large populations (Russia and China, for example).

2. *Education and social control.* These countries have usually offered their citizens a solid basic education, strong social control, and a secure life. At the same time, they have inculcated, intentionally or not, an aversion to the capitalist system and free markets. The people in these countries are not illiterate, they understand logic and numbers, and they have considerable pride in past accomplishments by their country. They have some hope for a better future and can be energized by the new prospects for individual growth.

3. *No free market.* What these people don't have, on the other hand, is a clear understanding of what a free market system entails, and they have trouble appreciating the magnitude of the changes of mindset required. Placing the consumer ahead of the producer is inconceivable to someone reared on the Marxist theory of labor value. Teaching Russian retail clerks that customers are important takes a lot of patience. For consumers, making a choice between three alternative coffee brands is a new and sometimes disconcerting experience.

These factors make the marketing manager's task different in NDC markets. But these markets also share characteristics with other developing markets, adding further complexity. The marketing infrastructure is typically weak. Channels of distribution are few and provide few service functions. Communications media are often still controlled by the state, and advertising is frowned upon. Customers do not have much purchasing power, and foreign currency is difficult to come by except for a few privileged groups.

International Support

NDC economies share many of the typical problems of developing countries—underdeveloped legal and financial institutions, uncertain political leadership, generally low purchasing power for foreign products, and so on. As in the case of developing countries generally, assistance from **international agencies** plays an important role in economic progress.

International institutions such as the United Nations, the World Bank, and IMF play important roles in many NDC markets. The functions of these international agencies—lending capital, technical assistance, and economic planning help—have been mobilized to support the transformation of many of the Eastern European countries into free market economies. The European Bank for Reconstruction and Development (EBRD), created by the European

Union, was developed expressly to support the Eastern European countries. These international agencies are important facilitators and guarantors of foreign investments in improving the basic infrastructure (road construction, electric power, and telephone service) and factories. From a marketing perspective they can be seen to help create a more favorable demand situation. The markets for products and services in the construction and telecommunications industries, for example, depend directly on loans from international agencies such as the World Bank.[7]

Regional trade and economic cooperation groupings can also be important factors for the foreign marketer in an NDC economy. Thus, even though Comecon, the former Soviet and East European economic community, is disbanded, trade relations between the countries are maintained and mutual trade is still often easier than trade with the West. These national markets tend to be at the same stage of the product life cycle. Because of this, for some consumer products it can be possible to treat Eastern Europe as one regional market.

Political and Legal Factors

In NDC markets it is necessary to treat political and legal factors as part of the economic landscape. Since communism banned private property, a complete legal system required to create and sustain orderly free markets is often not in existence. The result is that some fundamental marketing activities have a loose legal basis.

For example, marketing usually involves the exchange of products and services for money (or other goods and services). When the transaction is completed, the ownership of a product passes from the seller to the buyer. Each has important rights—based on explicit and implicit contracts—concerning product use, fulfillment of payment obligations, delivery times, return rights, and so on. This legal machinery is often not yet in place in NDC economies, making binding transactions difficult to enforce.

Export controls are another political-legal problem area for the marketer. During the Cold War it was important to control trade with adversarial nations, especially in technology-intensive products. In the West, export controls became common for goods traded to any communist country, and even some nonaligned nations such as India.

The administration of the control regime was the task of COCOM, the multilateral coordinating committee for export controls. After the fall of the Berlin Wall, the importance of export controls diminished, and in the spring of 1994 COCOM was dissolved. This did not mean the end of export controls, however, since there continues to be a need to control the proliferation of various weapon systems to belligerent countries. A new international control regime is being developed by the United States and other countries, and the marketer of technology-intensive products should not expect an export license to be automatically granted for NDC markets.[8]

The **political risk** in these countries primarily involves the chance that the regime will revert to communist rule or some similar centralized economic system. Although most commentators seem to agree that such a reversal is unlikely, the local marketer needs to keep close watch on these developments.[9] It is important that contacts with knowledgeable insiders be established so that developments can be monitored. This is not only the job of the general manager of a local subsidiary or branch. Since marketing is the function in the firm that consistently relates to the external world, it is incumbent on the marketer to demand that salespeople and distribution channel members track and report new developments.

Politics also influences NDC peoples' **attitudes toward the free market system.** The situation in NDC markets varies to some extent between countries. Central European countries have a different political heritage from the former Soviet republics in Asia. Some of these differences have marketing implications. For example, in China communism came into power only in 1947, while the Russian October revolution was in 1917. As a consequence, in China the precommunist days of more free market entrepreneurship, including the Kuomintang of Chiang Kai Shek, can be remembered by a part of the population. In addition, there are many Chinese living and working abroad, with sustained ties to relatives in the homeland. The overseas Chinese are successful in many free market economies, and they can help the transformation to a free market system in China. This is less true for the countries of the former Soviet republics, including Belarus and Ukraine.[10]

Because of the length of the period of communism in Eastern Europe, there are fewer remnants of the capitalist past in these countries. Education in economics by its reliance on Marx has been effective in discrediting the free market system. In addition, the obvious successes of Soviet Russia—Sputnik, military weaponry, the achievements in high culture, the strong sports teams—have inspired justified pride in the communist system. The dismantling of the Berlin Wall was a result of economic failure—but for many of the people in these countries, economics is not everything. Marketing is not well understood by these people, and when they see it in action, they don't always like it. "Hard sell" promotions, for example, are likely to backfire, not only among older consumers.[11]

Market Analysis

The local marketer in NDC economies may find it useful to define the market served in terms of **ethnic market segmentation** of subgroups among the population in each of the countries. For example, the ethnic Hungarian minority in Slovakia may have preferences similar to those in Hungary and Moravia. Despite the breakaway of many countries from the former Soviet Union, Russia is still home to many ethnic minorities who are represented also in other eastern European countries.[12] In China, the province of Sichuan with its 350 million inhabitants and different food and cultural traditions from the rest of China may provide a sufficient market by itself.

....
EXHIBIT 10.1   A Psychographic Segmentation of the Russian Market

	Kuptsi (merchants)	Cossacks	Students	Business executives	"Russian souls"
Percent of all men	30%	10%	10%	25%	25%
Percent of all women	45%	10%	5%	10%	30%
Dominant traits	Reliant, nationalistic, practical, seeks value	Ambitious, independent, nationalistic, seeks status	Passive, scraping by, idealistic, practical	Ambitious, Western oriented, busy, concerned with status	Passive, follows others, fears choices, hopeful
Likely preferences	*Car:* Volkswagen	BMW	2CV	Mercedes	Lada
	Cigarettes: Chesterfield	Dunhill	Marlboro	Winston	Marlboro
	Liquor: Stolichnaya	Rémy Martin	Local vodka in Smirnoff bottles	Johnnie Walker	Smirnoff

Sources: *The Russian Consumer*, 1992; Elliot, 1982.

As the transition toward a market economy progresses, the NDC consumers will undoubtedly move closer to their Western counterparts. A 1992 market segmentation study of Russian consumers found that more than half of all men and women could be categorized as independent, ambitious, or self-reliant, all traits uncommon in communist days (see Exhibit 10.1). As the exhibit shows, the 150 million consumers in the Russian market can be segmented into five different segments.[13] Apparently Western products are often preferred in some segments of the Russian market. If economic progress proceeds smoothly, one would expect actual sales to follow in the not too distant future.

For many NDC economies, the relevant *market definition* needs to be done with care. The local marketer needs to remember that national borders may be very new impositions on previously integrated markets and, at the same time, that a large total population may hide several different market segments. This naturally affects marketing decision making directly. While the marketer in advanced markets tends to think of market segmentation in terms of different lifestyles and preferences freely developed, in many NDC markets segmentation needs to start much more on an ethnic or cultural basis or to reflect ingrained habits of mind in groups.

Product and Price

One question for the new local marketer in an NDC market is whether to lead with the upper or lower end of the product line. Most indicators—income, usage conditions, needs—would suggest that these markets would be best

𝒢etting the Picture

Exporting Vodka to Russia?

A SURPRISING success story of a Western company entering an NDC market is the case of Rasputin, a vodka brand exported from Germany to Russia. Exporting to the large Russian market, the company's importer limits the negative effects of a 25% tariff by declaring only the value of the drink, not the bottle and packaging. It offers dealer margins of 25% as compared to the domestic companies' fixed 15%, inducing the dealers to stock up on the brand. The company does not demand payment in advance as the domestic companies do, and the empty bottles need not be returned. Consumers are charged 3,700 rubles (about $2) for a .7 liter bottle, comparable to the same price for a domestic Stolichnaya .5 liter bottle. The domestic vodka distilleries are slowly learning to grapple with competitive marketing strategies of their own, but are hindered by old habits and "favorable" regulations placing burdens on the dealers.

Source: Babakian, 1995; "Rasputin Is Alive and Bottled," *The Economist*, April 9, 1994, p. 68.

served with a more basic product at the low end of the price scale. But this forgets that becoming the first company to offer a more advanced product can yield first-mover advantages. Furthermore, the lower end typically pits the entrant squarely against existing domestic brands, however uncompetitive they may be.

In NDC markets customers tend to feel ambivalent about their domestic products. On the one hand, they know that new offerings from outside are often superior. Still, they do not necessarily want to give up the old brands. The reasons are not only sentimental remembrances of things past, or country-of-origin affections. They also realize that if the products are not bought, the domestic factories can't stay open, and they will lose their jobs. And it is not easy to evaluate the many competing brands when previously only one or two choices have been available.[14]

Many domestic producers that have been privatized are still in a favored position with government and labor leaders and perhaps also with loyal consumers. However, such a "favored" position may, in the longer run, be a drawback since it prevents the domestic companies from making the necessary changes in product and market strategies. The success of Rasputin, an imported vodka that outsells the domestic variants because of the dealer support given, is one striking Russian example (see box, "Exporting Vodka to Russia?").

There is some advantage in adopting a "follow the leader" strategy and introducing products only after other foreign competitors have done so. Several foreign entrants will legitimize an entry, and consumers generally find it easier to accept a new product as more brands are introduced. There is an advantage in numbers, even if the competitive rivalry becomes more intense.

It is also important to keep in mind that in many cases these foreign competitors are engaged in an infrastructure build-up effort that creates synergies for other companies as well.

Marketing Infrastructure

A big problem that the new local marketer faces in typical NDC markets is a wasteful and dysfunctional distribution system. Because the economies were closed off to outside competition, ineffective systems for delivery of products and services have been left in operation. Marxist ideals hold that only production has value, and unfortunately distribution was seen as unworthy of serious attention. Furthermore, the priority was on industrial products over consumer products, which means that the entire marketing infrastructure (the logistics of distribution, the media of communications, and the means of transferring payments) in consumer goods is particularly weak.

It is mostly the deficiencies of the marketing infrastructure that make it difficult for the local marketer to penetrate NDC markets. The functions provided by middlemen are weak or nonexistent, and the local marketer can't expect to rely very much on independent middlemen. This creates a need for localization by augmenting the product sold. For example, since electricity is often in short supply and rationed with frequent blackouts, electric appliances might need to be redesigned with a buffer battery that kicks in when cutoffs occur. Similarly, digital alarm clocks, radios with push-button station memory, coffeemakers with preset timers, and rice cookers with warming features are all products that might need to be redesigned. In some cases complete battery function is preferable—battery radios without a recharger are still best sellers in many NDC markets.[15]

It is important to find out what functions the existing channel members can and can't perform, and to what degree it is necessary to create entirely new channels for products, services, and communications. Procter & Gamble's experience in Russia is instructive (see box, "P&G Goes to Russia").

To accomplish the job, the local marketer sometimes has to think about reconfiguring the firm's *value chain*. For example, in addition to localizing the product, services that at home are provided by independent operators may need to be added to the value chain. To service vacuum cleaners and other household appliances, Western firms at home often depend on small entrepreneurs who run their own independent operations and service several makes. In NDC markets, the required know-how may not yet be diffused enough to rely on independents. Instead, the Western entrant has to help create such a service network and train the service staff.[16]

The Marketer as Teacher

In NDC markets the marketing manager needs to be prepared to do a lot of on-the-job training and **educating of middlemen** and others in basic marketing principles and practices, in how to distribute, sell, and service the product effectively. There is also a secondary audience consisting of actual and potential customers, as well as domestic competitors. Finally, many government bureaucrats need to be informed about free markets, although this part of the

Getting the Picture

P&G Goes to Russia

WHEN RUSSIA opened up its borders to Western products, the giant multinationals in consumer packaged goods quickly started to reconnoiter the potentially huge market. But the initial delegations of top marketing executives soon came to realize the difficulty of selling through the existing distribution channels. Weak transportation systems, inferior storage facilities, and out-of-date warehousing operations created costly inefficiencies in the delivery of the products to the stores. And in the stores the limited shelf space, the dull grey atmospheres, and the sullen clerks made for a dreary shopping experience, even though the stores had been recently privatized.

Accordingly, the first tasks for a company such as P&G in Russia involved creating a much more efficient and modern distribution network. Investing in existing facilities and new warehouses, helping to improve transportation fleets and parking space, and training store employees were some of the measures taken. As efficiency grew, so did the sales of P&G products. But with growth came new problems, since the product throughflow put a big burden on all aspects of the distribution. For example, with increasing shipments from the West into Russia, the lines of trucks waiting to get their papers processed at the border grew increasingly long. The solution for P&G was to invest in improving port facilities in St Petersburg and sending its products by ship. Needless to say, P&G executives are carefully monitoring the political developments in Russia, attempting to balance the need to invest against the threat of a return to a closed market.

Sources: *New York Times*, July 23, 1994, pp. 1, 43; Lloyd, 1994.

educational process is usually handled during the initial negotiations about starting to do business in the country.

Broadly speaking, the aim of the education is to demonstrate the role of marketing in the free market system. It is necessary to elaborate on principles taken for granted and self-evident to the Western marketer. Thus, before the marketer can serve as a teacher, he or she may have to study some of the basics of the system at home.

The marketer first of all has to explain the basic functioning of a product or service to the middlemen involved in the distribution chain. Many products have no counterpart in the NDC markets, or their advanced character requires explanation and instruction in use and service. Further, how to listen to customer questions, how to offer product information, and how to give after-sales support are all "naturals" for the Western marketer that he or she must now give some thought to. The Japanese incursion into American and Western markets has served to educate even Western middlemen about these basic prerequisites of effective marketing.

The marketer in NDC economies needs to be able to explain how the roles in the distribution chain have changed with the emergence of free markets. Now the idea is to perform efficiently—to help move the products through the chain with speed, respond quickly to demand shifts, and be alert to competitors'

McDonald's employees in Moscow learn the ropes of a new system. In communist Russia the consumer was an endangered species and service was virtually extinct, so when Western companies arrived native workers had to be trained in effective service delivery and customer satisfaction.
Somov Novosti/Gamma-Liaison.

moves. Gone are the days when the suppliers and the customers were captive—now only the best can survive. The marketer needs to explain—"teach"—that in the free market system costs need to be controlled and revenues have to cover expenses. It is "Welcome, brave new world," for the middlemen.

The new teaching will be heresy to many and will seem to go against many things in their past experience. The middlemen will have ingrained ideas about what is appropriate and may find it difficult to accept the new message. It becomes important that the "teacher" explain why these changes are necessary. Of course, the market and competitors are the new "teachers," but the manager can't wait for mistakes to show up before taking action. Luckily, people are generally willing to try the changes, having seen how badly the previous system performed. For example, the successful Western cosmetics firms' marketers in Eastern Europe indoctrinate the in-store sales personnel, teaching them how to care for a customer—and, in the process, teach them how to take care of themselves.[17]

Practically speaking, the local marketer needs to:

1. Develop training programs for store personnel, focusing on how to treat customers.

2. Prepare manuals and pamphlets describing products and services and helping middlemen devise appropriate facilities and procedures for the transportation, storage, and shelving of the product.

3. Help the middlemen develop a tracking and cost accounting system to make it possible to trace shipments and locate where in the chain there may be a problem such as overstocking.

$\mathcal{G}$etting the
Picture

Advertising to
the Russian
Consumer

DURING THE INITIAL years of perestroika, the markets for Western products in Russia consisted mainly of Western expatriates, whose companies were evaluating the prospects of entry. The expatriates were the only ones with sufficient hard currency to buy many of the imported products. As economic progress has quickened, the markets are now enlarged to include many Russians who constitute an NDC middle class.

The emergence of this new class of consumers has meant that advertising strategy has to be changed. Using inexpensive radio ads, previous market communications were directed toward the expatriates in English and on English-language programs. Gradually there has been a shift toward Russian-language commercials and Russian-

language programs. This has meant a bonanza for Russian radio programs, and a decline in the demand for English-language spots. Some of the English-language radio announcers have returned home as work opportunities have dwindled, while Russian announcers are moving in. At the same time, the stores that tended primarily to the expatriates are now seeing a shift to Russian customers. For some exclusive supermarkets, the customers today are 80% Russian. And business is good.

Sources: "Radio Advertisers Tune In to Russia's Middle Class," *New York Times*, August 12, 1994; "Advertising: Russian Ad Market Offers Options," *Business Eastern Europe*, Nov. 1, 1993.

4. Make sure that product localization in terms of design and packaging also takes into account the needs of the middlemen. This often involves educating the home office about special requirements, such as different sizes and packaging of existing products.
5. Distribute instructional videotapes and other educational material to various members of the distribution channel, explaining why customers are so important in the free market system and why marketing is as important as manufacturing.

Communication Strategy

Marketing communications often have to be revised in NDC markets. The common advertising media—television, magazines, newspapers—may not be available or may have only limited reach. Because of the immaturity of the market, many products are new to the market and any communication needs to stress simple functional explanations. People who have not seen a 10-speed bike need some instructions and explanation of its advantages over the domestic clunker that has served so well for 30 years—and justification for the high price. The solid education of the people, however, will make the requisite advertising copy quite easy to develop. The average Russian is quite capable of processing information (see box, "Advertising to the Russian Consumer").

Credibility of advertising claims is a problem. In previously totalitarian countries people maintain a healthy disrespect for public announcements and mass communication. This naturally reduces the power of advertising, at least in the short run until its benefits in terms of new products and services materialize. By contrast, word-of-mouth is often considered more reliable and effective than mass media. This can have its own negative consequences. In Poland, for example, a rumor that P&G's "Head and Shoulders" shampoo made your hair fall out turned out to be particularly difficult to put down. In some of these markets, domestic companies sometimes resort to such "dirty" campaign tricks as they see their protected advantage dissipate.[18]

When the political, economic, and social fabric is undergoing the kind of revolution seen in newly democratized countries, old values are crumbling along with the political system. There is a need for the country and its people to learn what a free market system is about. To change the old order, communications have to be open and the old implicit understandings reexamined. The American insistence on transparency of transactions helps tear down the labyrinthine networks and closed systems that in many NDCs have made corruption and exploitation of the common man and woman prevalent. The American way with marketing is an agent for democracy.

Still, the hardhitting approaches used in some American advertising could lead to a backlash when applied in an NDC market. On the one hand, cynicism and suspicion can be a problem. On the other hand, people are not used to the "puffery" associated with much of American promotion and may take assertions of "best" and "most" at face value. This potential downside risk of the free market experience will taper off in intensity as the people become gradually more insensitive to preposterous assertions and reap the benefits of new ideas and new products. In the meantime, the local marketer will do well to temper some of the more obvious excesses of American advertising.[19]

TWO SPECIAL CASES: MARKETING IN CHINA AND INDIA

The discussion so far has dealt with marketing in developing countries and with marketing in the newly democratized countries, emphasizing Russia and Eastern Europe. The objective has been to present some of the main determinants of local marketing in these environments, to show the differences and similarities between them, and to highlight the role of the local marketer in creating functioning free markets.

Two large and important emerging markets deserving further treatment are China and India. Both countries can be viewed as "developing," and both have features similar to NDCs. But China is not (yet) a democracy, and India is not a *new* democracy. They present some very special problems for the local marketer. These problems have mostly to do with the political legacy of the countries, and much of the discussion about the NDCs above is relevant for China and India. In what follows, only the additional peculiarities of the marketing environment in the two countries will be highlighted.

MARKETING IN CHINA[20]

China's Market Potential

China has 1.2 billion people to feed. The large population plus the growing economy make China a large importer of machinery, production equipment, technology, telecommunication equipment, aircraft, and raw materials for industrial production. The Chinese government has recently expanded its importation of agriculture-applied technology, fertilizers, industrial raw materials, and technologies and equipment for energy, transportation, telecommunication, and industrial renovation programs. Importation of consumer products is expected to grow because of recent tariff reductions. The 1995 granting of continued MFN status by the United States promises to help the Chinese economy to achieve further export-driven growth. In 1994, China's import value totaled US$95.27 billion; the imports from the United States accounted for $9 billion.[21]

Despite the size and nominal potential of the Chinese market, its fast-growing purchasing power is still low. The per capita income in 1992 was equivalent to US$224, in 1993 $380, and in 1994 $490.[22] The relatively low per capita income makes China and the Chinese price-sensitive customers. For example, in 1991, the United States was a large polypropylene supplier to China, but the next year the market was dominated by Korean producers because of their lower price. In 1994 the American imports from China totaled close to $39 billion, making for a bilateral trade imbalance of roughly $29.5 billion.[23] As economic progress continues, the huge market potential for Western products will presumably come closer to realization.

Entry Barriers

The Chinese government is by most measures the greatest entry barrier into China. The Chinese government controls importation mainly through the following measures: import license controls, protective tariffs, foreign exchange control, and government-controlled foreign trading companies.

Import license controls. The Ministry of Foreign Trade and Economic Cooperation (MOFTEC) is the main regulatory organization governing the current import-licensing system. China uses a centralized system to restrict imports of consumer and luxury goods in order to conserve foreign exchange for other items. Among the 10,000 import product categories, 53 are on the import license control list, covering various consumer products, raw materials, and production equipment. In 1992, 16 categories were removed from the list in an effort to meet World Trade Organization (WTO) requirements, and the Chinese government promised to eliminate two-thirds of the listed categories in the next two years.[24]

Protective tariffs. From 1986 to 1990, China adjusted tariff rates 18 times and continues to do so. The tariff reduction in January 1993 brought the average tariff level to 22.5 percent. However, this rate is still much higher than both the average 5 percent for the developed countries and the average 13 percent for the developing countries. In 1992, the government promised to continue tariff reduction until it meets the average level of the developing countries. At the Asia-Pacific Economic Cooperation Forum in November 1995, Chinese President Jiang Zemin pledged to cut import tariffs by 30 percent.[25]

Foreign exchange control. In January 1994, China implemented a new exchange rate system. Its official exchange rate was brought into line with the more market-driven rate that applied on the foreign exchange swap market. After the unification the rate stayed stable at around 8.4 to 8.5 yuan to the U.S. dollar, compared with a trading rate at 8.7 to the dollar just before the change.[26]

Foreign exchange is controlled by the State Administration of Foreign Exchange Control, which supervises the allocation of the foreign exchange quota and the operation of the Foreign Exchange Swap Center. The swap center makes it possible for enterprises to have access to foreign exchange. With a foreign exchange quota, one can obtain foreign exchange at the official exchange rate. The quota is allocated based on criteria such as the importance of the project and the enterprise's record of foreign exchange generation.

The Foreign Exchange Swap Center is an institution through which entities with excess quota or foreign exchange trade off their foreign exchange with those who need it. Contrary to the stable official exchange rate, the swap rate varies from day to day. For example, during the month of July 1993 the swap rate changed from 8.0 to 10.5 to 8.5 per U.S. dollar.

Foreign trading companies. With the ongoing reform of China's foreign trade system, the government-controlled trading companies have lost their monopoly to the mushrooming local trading companies and the industrial firms. The foreign-invested companies are automatically granted foreign trade rights.

In general, China's foreign trade system is undergoing a big reform and most of the effort is geared toward the goal of resuming WTO status. To reenter the WTO, China needs to:

- Unify its foreign trade policies, laws, and regulations.
- Clarify its foreign trade policies, laws, and regulations.
- Reduce tariff and nontariff barriers.
- Promise a price reform timetable.
- Accept selective protection provisions prior to price system reforms.

All the reforms or readjustments have to be made if China wants to become a WTO member.

Hong Kong's Role

Many European and American companies enter China from Hong Kong, where many sophisticated **Hong Kong trading companies** are familiar with both Western business practices and Chinese language and culture. Trade fairs, exhibitions, and technical seminars are commonly used to promote awareness among trading middlemen and mainland customers.

To identify potential customers, the in-charge industrial ministries in China need to be approached, which is difficult to arrange without a strong and well-connected Hong Kong intermediary. Although the ministries can no longer decide which products to buy, they are still influential over the factories and purchasing decisions. In addition, much information, such as plant size and capacity, purchasing potential, financial records, can be found in the ministries.

A few critical products, such as natural rubber, tobacco and pesticides, are still centrally controlled. The suppliers of these products usually deal with a small number of big state-owned import/export companies. The import/export companies will distribute the products to their end-users.

Most foreign companies find themselves in a difficult position. They have to deal not only with their Hong Kong agent and the foreign trading companies in China, but also with their Chinese end-users' requests for service. In general, the end-users select the foreign supplier and the foreign trading companies sign the contract as agents for the factories. Even with the use of the Hong Kong traders, the local marketer from abroad needs to consider employing a Chinese national to balance the decision-making power. With a Chinese employee, it is possible to communicate directly with the end-users and get feedback from the market without relying entirely on the intermediate traders. The Hong Kong trading company can then concentrate on handling the administrative and organizational arrangements with the Chinese trading company, while the marketing manager gathers market information and stays close to the customer.

Joint Ventures

Another mode of entry for foreign companies is a **joint venture with Chinese partners,** with the Chinese partner usually contributing some assembly to reduce the effect of tariffs and other barriers. In autos, for example, an import tariff of 180 to 200 percent for vehicles coupled with restrictive government policies force the joint venture route and shared assembly. The Chinese partner is usually in charge alone of the marketing effort.

The quality gap between foreign and local products is still large, but the technology transfer in the joint ventures helps reduce the difference. Prices are still high for products with imported content. For example, a Chinese-assembled Volkswagen Santana car costing around US$14,000 on world markets sold in China for 180,000 yuan ($20,000) in April 1994.[27] For pure imports, the difference is even greater. Nevertheless, one of every two cars running on Chinese roads is imported.

The foreign competitors mostly compete on the promotion scheme, after-sale service, product delivery, and price. Compared with Japanese and Korean companies, delivery is a disadvantage for the European and American suppliers due to the long supply line. Quality is less important because the quality difference between foreign companies means little to Chinese customers so far.

Getting the Picture

Pirated Rock Music

WALKING AROUND the streets of Beijing or Shanghai—as well as New York and Paris—it is easy to spot the vendors who sell cheap copies of many branded products from watches to compact disks. Most of these pirated copies come from Southeast Asia, where small entrepreneurs have long found it lucrative and relatively risk free to produce knockoffs of well-known products. China's recent economic growth has made the "home market" especially enticing, and the market opportunity has led to even more availability of pirated copies. Compact disk copies of famous rock stars are a common target since the artists are very popular in China and since digital equipment is now relatively easy to acquire and allows copying without a loss of sound quality.

As the Chinese market opens up and the potential is recognized, Western record producers have started to engage private investigators to track down factories and vendors guilty of these copyright violations. But nothing much happened until the U.S. Trade Representative decided to press the issue just before China's MFN status was up for review. In what was called a landmark agreement, the Americans managed to get strong Chinese commitment to eliminate product counterfeits and piracy. In one case, Walt Disney Company won a victory in Beijing Intermediate Court with a $77,000 judgment against Chinese companies that were producing children's books based on Disney's animated films.

Even so, Chinese government officials have been reluctant to engage in active prosecution. The reason? The legal system is not yet ready to handle these cases, and going to court is complicated. Furthermore, many of these entrepreneurs have good contacts with the ruling party—and even though the China market is opening up, the communists are still in power.

Sources: Ecenbarger, 1994; *New York Times*, August 18, 1994; May 17, 1995.

Five **Special Economic Zones** (SEZs) have been established by the Chinese government. They are Shenzhen, Zhuhai, Shantou (all in the Guangdong province in the South), Xiamen (in Fujian province), and Hainan (in Hainan province). Besides these five, the Pudong New Area in Shanghai is entitled to similar preferential policies as an SEZ. To attract investment, the corporate tax rate within SEZs is only 15 percent compared with a national rate of 33 percent. Also, enterprises within the zones enjoy some tariff exemptions.[28]

The SEZs serve to bring in foreign manufacturing jobs, with Chinese workers staffing the assembly lines. Furthermore, the products are intended for reexport, helping the government to generate hard foreign currency. But it has also meant increased penetration by foreign products in China. Although the products imported into those areas are not allowed legally to be used outside the areas' borders, many are smuggled across the zones' borders into China, copied, and sold. The difficulty of controlling this black or grey trade and widespread **copyright infringement** means that the authorized distributors find themselves competing with local **counterfeits and pirated copies.** Pirated compact disks are a case in point (see box, "Pirated Rock Music").

Avon salesladies with their bicycles in Guangchou, China. Avon's method of selling women's cosmetics door-to-door in the West has been transplanted successfully to the East.

Courtesy Avon Products.

The Chinese Customer

Out of habit, most mainland Chinese customers are price oriented. They are not willing to pay more for superior quality because of the uniformly low quality level they associate with products across the whole product range. The fast-growing economy also means that many products are in short supply and some domestic companies are still in the "quantity, not quality" frame of mind nurtured during the central planning era.

Personal contacts play an important role in sealing a transaction. The Chinese customers value "old friends." The good friendship can even offset a negative price impact. This sentiment has been successfully exploited by new foreign entrants into China's insurance market (see box, "Selling Life Insurance in China").

Once a Chinese company chooses a foreign product, it is unlikely to change unless there is a big price difference. Firms who contact the Chinese customers before their competitors gain first-mover advantages.

As is typical in NDCs and other developing markets, Chinese customers cite two reasons for buying a foreign product: (1) no availability of similar products on the domestic market; and (2) the superior quality of the foreign product. Because of high tariffs, a foreign product can seldom compete with a

---

Getting the Picture

Selling Life Insurance in China

IT MAY COME AS a surprise in a country where communists are in power and food and housing are in principle guaranteed, but China has long had a viable life insurance industry. A traditional family focus has encouraged savings and risk sharing, and when the one-child-per-family policy was enacted by Chairman Mao, the demand for life insurance to protect the one offspring rose further.

Naturally, in the past, the industry has been a government monopoly. Not surprisingly, service was deficient. Each month, a person would have to stand in line to pay the premium, and if late, a penalty would be charged. Only a straight insurance policy was available, with no interest and no options to borrow against the policy.

Enter the American International Group, whose chairman had wooed the Chinese government officials since his first visit to China in 1975. American International, or "Friendly Nation" in its Chinese incarnation, is the only foreign insurance company allowed to market its product in China. In Shanghai it sells life insurance policies which pay interest after 5 years, can be borrowed against after 3 years, and is fully refundable after 20 years. The sales agents are Chinese young ladies who have adopted a door-to-door approach to the Chinese situation. Door-to-door selling is relatively new in China, although Avon Products pioneered cosmetics sales that way in the southern city of Guangchou in 1990; Mary Kay Cosmetics entered in 1994.

The "Friendly Nation" ladies are easily identifiable on the streets by their careful grooming and thick briefcases and bicycles. They visit offices, at which underemployed workers do not mind being interrupted. They sell to the boss first, so the authority-conscious employees know it is acceptable to buy. They appeal to parents to buy insurance for their children. And they sell to women.

"I go for the women," says Lily Hua, an agent, flashing a mischievous smile. "You sell a policy to a man and the next day he may come back and ask for a refund because his wife objected. That never happens when I sell to a woman."

Sources: *New York Times*, April 4, 1995, pp. D1, D5; Yuen, 1995.

Chinese product on a price basis. However, the situation may change after China reenters the WTO.

There seems to be no particular country preference among the Chinese customers. While the United States, Japan, and Europe are respected for their product quality, Korea and Taiwan are credited for their prices. What country-of-origin effect there may be will sometimes come from the central government. When France was caught selling Phantom fighter planes to Taiwan, many government-controlled trading companies were warned not to purchase French products.

A large number of importers are foreign-invested joint ventures, who have import/export rights and access to foreign currency. One main challenge of these ventures is to keep the product quality consistent with that of their foreign partner's, so that reexporting is possible. There are also export-oriented Chinese enterprises, which will pay for superior quality of imported parts because their products have to compete on the world market. Such companies, for example, manufacturers of bicycles, electronic measuring instruments, and sports equipment, are given tariff reductions on imported parts because of their exports.

For most Chinese acquiring foreign-made products is a novel experience. With very few choices for four decades, the Chinese are eager to see what is in the stores. Their limited experience leads them, predictably, to rely on famous brand names. In a wide range of goods surveyed, well-known brands accounted for as much as one-half of intentions to choose.[29] The Chinese consumers are also very brand loyal. Fancy displays and shelf placement are less important, since the consumers have time to browse and search for brands in the stores. They will look for a brand they have heard of—even though the information came through advertising on commercial TV stations. Their lack of experience with variety leads them to trust a brand they know, have tried, and found satisfactory, generating a strong first-mover advantage for foreign entrants.

Continuous Change

As news media report, China continues to change. This change is reflected not only in a two-digit economic growth rate but also in the frequent revisions of government policies, the privatization of state-owned monopolies, and reform in the foreign trade system.

These are some highlights of recent events:

- In 1992, China promulgated a law to protect intellectual properties and pipe-line products.
- Since the end of 1992, many state-owned enterprises have carried out a wide variety of reforms, and a large number moved towards market-oriented management. In 1980, 90 percent of the national economy was planned by directives from the central government. That portion was reduced to 12 percent by 1992.
- Since January 1993, foreign trade is no longer monopolized by the government-controlled foreign trading companies. Over 900 industrial firms were permitted to contact foreign companies directly.
- In January 1993, the Chinese government reduced import tariffs for 3,371 categories of products, bringing the tariff rate down by 7.3 percent.
- In July 1993, the Chinese government lifted the ceiling rate control on the foreign exchange swap market.
- After March 1992, the devaluation of the RMB (Chinese currency) was alarming. The following 18 months witnessed a more than 40 percent loss in the value of the RMB against the U.S. dollar.
- The car industry is opening up very slowly, with the Chinese government wanting to protect inefficient domestic producers while

importing more modern technology. The government is forcing the small automakers to merge and aims to create approximately 10 major groups, each of which will get government assistance to develop joint ventures with foreign automakers. Needless to say, most foreign automakers are eagerly trying to assess the promise and pitfalls of tying up with a Chinese partner, but they may have no choice if they want to enter the market.

Change brings fresh opportunities. The economic growth in China has opened up a vast potential market. Change also brings problems, as the Tianamen Square events of 1989 demonstrated. Most foreign marketers find it challenging to operate on such a moving stage, but the stakes may well be worth it.

MARKETING IN INDIA[30]

Market Potential

India has close to 900 million citizens. Since 1947, when British colonial rule ended, it has been the world's largest democracy. Despite religious and ethnic violence in India, the country's leaders have continued to be elected through a democratic process, without the military coups that have plagued less fortunate Third World countries.

A heritage from British colonial rule is India's educational system with advanced English-language education that is the envy of many other countries. Unfortunately for the country, a large portion of its elite can't find an outlet for their productive capability in the developing home country and have found it necessary to emigrate to Western countries, where their education is put to good use. In these Western countries the Indian immigrants constitute a large ethnic minority at the upper end of the income scale. For example, in 1990 Indians were the ethnic segment of the U.S. population with the highest median income. As socialist policies and government controls give way to privatization and free markets, domestic opportunities for India's citizens will multiply and one can expect the country to show much stronger economic growth than in the past.

The Socialist Era

Indian industry did not develop much under British colonialism, which exploited the country's raw materials, precious gems, textiles, tea, and exotic foodstuffs. When the British granted independence to India in 1947, the country split into predominantly Muslim Pakistan (East and West) and India. The two main industries, cotton and jute, suffered tremendously as the manufacturing and raw material supplies were split between the two countries.

After 1950, when Nehru became prime minister, India developed a socialist leaning attempting to develop industry on three fronts: a massive public sector based on the Soviet experiments with state-run industry; a small joint sector with private participation; and a private sector consisting of business houses that had made it rich during British rule. Because of their traditional regional monopolies, the private sector companies were the only successful part of the economy. Lack of competition led to little development.

During the next three decades, India had very high tariff and nontariff barriers against foreign imports. Both the public and private sectors developed considerable corruption and bureaucratic inefficiencies, remnants of which still plague the political and economic functioning of the country.[31]

Domestic products were of poor quality and marketing activities aimed mainly to inform the customer of the existence of products. The Indian consumer had very little choice. What mattered to the consumer was mainly that the products be durable. There was some foreign participation, and several multinationals, including Coca-Cola, Colgate, Ciba-Geigy, and GE, had limited presence through equity collaborations with Indian firms. However, during those three decades most information coming to India about foreign goods was via the Indian emigrants abroad, who sent back gifts of higher-quality foreign goods. Consequently, in popular imagination, anything having a foreign-made label was seen as having high quality.

During this period not only were there restrictions on the flow of products but, more importantly, also on inbound **technology transfer into India.** The private companies advertised the fact that they had been in business for 30 years and they often had regional monopolies. The advertising media were limited to radio and print. There were little or no market segmentation efforts except along geographic lines. There was almost no research and development into new technology with the exception of government-sponsored R&D into weaponry and nuclear power. *Products on the Indian market hardly changed from 1950–1980.*[32]

Free Markets

In 1977 the left-wing party led by Morarji Desai came to power and soon implemented even more extreme socialist policies. Foreign equity shares had to be decreased and multinationals' technology shared. These policies caused a mass exodus of foreign companies from the Indian market, led by Coca-Cola. Desai's party was defeated in the next election.

From 1980 onwards, in an effort to modernize the economy, then Prime Minister Indira Gandhi started to allow foreign investment, alliances, and technology transfers. Foreign firms were allowed to have a stake of up to—but no more than—26 percent in the equity of a joint venture. Among the first collaborators to enter India were Japanese motorcycle companies, Yamaha, Kawasaki, and Honda, creating competition with domestic automakers. Later, Japanese electronic firms began to enter. To maintain market share, almost all domestic companies started collaborating with multinationals. Market success

A Kellogg's box of basmati flakes in India. In countries where cold cereal and milk are not standard breakfast items, the box needs to explain where to pour the milk and how to eat the cereal.

Kellogg's ® is a registered trademark of Kellogg Company. Photo used with permission.

during this period depended directly on which company had the best international collaboration. Goods were expensive, since the foreign firms wanted to make sure that their returns were sufficient, given the uncertain prospects in the Indian market. The technology offered, although advanced according to Indian standards, was internationally substandard.

The further **liberalization in India** in the early 1990s led by Prime Minister Rao has eliminated the ceiling on the share of foreign ownership. The return of Coca-Cola, General Electric, and other Western companies has been a tremendous boost to the Indian economy. Although the **political risk in India** remains high because of ethnic and religious violence, the country is showing strong economic progress and revitalized domestic firms. The United States Department of Commerce has proclaimed India one of the new export priorities and has led trips of businessmen to the country.

The New Market

During the 1980s the Indian market started to divide into two large segments—a still impoverished rural population and an increasingly well-off urban middle class. As the new opportunities pulled people away from the countryside, cities became huge metropolitan markets, and towns grew into cities. This trend was strengthened after the further market-opening measures of the early 1990s. The disposable income of the Indian middle class has increased considerably. Not only has there been strong economic growth but

Getting the Picture

Basmati Flakes in the Morning

KELLOGG COMPANY, the American cereal maker that made corn flakes a staple of many Western kids' breakfasts, is scoring again. This time they are having success in India with corn, wheat, and basmati rice flakes, which are selling faster than hotcakes in Bombay. The company estimates that by 1997 its sales in India will have grown from $2 million a year to $26 million annually. The key is an intensive advertising and promotional campaign designed to make Indian consumers change their breakfast eating habits.

A $450,000 multimedia campaign included three 30-second TV spots featuring a family around the breakfast table addressing the problem of overeating as well as the effects of a bread and butter diet and skipping breakfast. The campaign "does leave behind a suggestion that current fried breakfasts are not the best you could provide your family to begin the day," says Anil Bhatia, senior VP-general manager at Hindustan-Thompson Associates.

Kellogg also plans to sponsor a TV special featuring a panel of nutritionists, dieticians, and physicians on the government-run Doordarshan Network. The company is already sponsoring "Kellogg's Breakfast Show," a morning talk show that runs daily on radio. The first guest celebrity was Sushmita Sen, Miss Universe 1994.

Kellogg is also sponsoring two message boards on the main Bombay commuter thoroughfare featuring healthful advice from medical experts. Informative and copy-heavy ads are being placed in English and local-language newspapers and women's and health magazines.

"The Indian market is similar to the Mexican market because the Mexicans also used to consume a hot, savory breakfast," says Damindra Dias, Kellogg India's managing director. "We are saying, 'Take the right food. Don't fill yourself with fat the first thing in the morning.'"

Sources: Dubey, 1994; *Advertising Age*, November 14, 1994, p. 60.

---

trends in family planning have changed, with households having fewer children than traditionally. This has also meant that in many families the wives, many well educated, have started contributing to the family income. Traditional habits are changing, and the Indians are even starting to have cold cereal for breakfast (see box, "Basmati Flakes in the Morning").

Exposure to new products and services has increased the appetite for further purchases. The Indian consumer who was earlier focusing on the durability of products has now started buying products as symbols of status and success. Consumers are becoming more demanding. Products that were earlier a luxury now have become necessities. Cable TV has entered Indian homes and households have more than one car. Foreign automakers compete for the privilege of tying up with domestic automakers (see box, "Foreign Cars in India").

These developments have come so fast that aggregate demand still outstrips supply. Even large companies like Procter and Gamble cannot yet completely fulfill the demand in India, although new investments in plants suggest this will change in the near future.[33]

*G*etting the
Picture

Foreign Cars
in India

SINCE THE FREE-MARKET liberalization measures of 1991—which lowered tariffs and allowed foreign companies to open plants—India's 250 million–strong middle-class has scooped up brand name consumer goods now produced inside the borders. Foreign automakers are trying to follow the success of their counterparts in electronics, but the size of the investments needed make it a riskier business.

The car industry was one of the last to be liberalized. The need for imported oil forced the previous Indian government to place a ban on the number of cars produced domestically and to ban imports of cars. Economic progress has made Indians better prepared to pay for the necessary fuel, and demand for cars is at an all-time high. Foreign carmakers are trying to get on the bandwagon, working with various domestic partners who better understand the marketplace.

Foreign Car Companies Now Coming to India

Company	Model	Estimated Cost
General Motors (Through Hindustan Motors)	Opel Astra	$18,000
Mercedes-Benz (Through TELCO)	E-220	$50,000
Chrysler (Through Mahindra & Mahindra)	Jeep Cherokee	$34,000
Daewoo (Through DCM-Toyota)	Racer	$16,000
Peugeot (Through Premier)	309	$13,000
Rover (Through Sipora)	Montego	$31,000

Source: Government of India, company executives, Indian newspaper and magazine articles. All prices are preliminary and subject to change.

But the foreign automakers face several problems. The Indian customer is reluctant to incur installment debt for a purchase, a result of many years' experience with uncertain incomes. Another is the state of the roads in India, hardly such that the advanced suspension of modern cars is functional. There is also a dearth of qualified repair shops with the necessary training and equipment.

Not surprisingly, for some Indian buyers the inexpensive old Ambassadors are preferable to the new Nissans. As one customer says: "What do you do when the power steering and power windows break down? With an Ambassador I know that any fool with a piece of string and chewing gum can make it move."

Sources: Michaels, 1995; *Washington Post*, September 17, 1994.

Domestic Resurgence

As competition has increased, domestic companies have become more aggressive in their marketing policies to meet the challenge. Advertising in India does not include direct attacks on the competition (it is prohibited by law) but more of it is implied. Competition is now on the basis of product features and quality, image, price, and so on. The price is still not prominent because there is high demand and there aren't enough companies to fulfill it. Showing how marketing can help reposition previously protected companies, giant industrial conglomerates like Tatas and Birles—companies that make and sell everything from candy to industrial machinery—advertise defensively what they do for local communities.

As the liberation of the economy continues, Indian companies are being forced to become more efficient. Drawing on the large pool of talented and well-educated people, the domestic industry is now surging ahead. Foreign companies are also eager to utilize the local expertise. Motorola, the American cellular phone company, has been awarded a plum contract to provide cellular phone service to the Indian public and can easily find local engineers and MBAs who are familiar with both the technology and the market.

Companies are finally starting to deliver products to suit consumers' needs rather than expecting the consumer to adapt to their products. Distribution channels and stores are developing more efficient networks, and capacity is expanded. Advertising and marketing agencies are now booming. Consumer choices are multiplying. A leading industrialist, Rahul Bajaj of Bajaj Autos, proclaimed in the preliberatization period: "We are a Third World country, our consumers do not expect very high quality."[34] Unless political forces intervene, such sentiments are a thing of the past in India's marketplace. The Indian consumers have developed expectations similar to those in more advanced economies.

....

SUMMARY

Developing countries are characterized by low disposable incomes, low educational levels, and a general apathy among the people. Market potential in these countries is often low, and trading with these countries often involves intermediaries such as specialized trading companies and international financial institutions such as the World Bank and the IMF. Also, the local marketer has to be prepared to evaluate and accept countertrade offers.

Internally, these countries have an overriding need to develop a more effective marketing infrastructure, in particular a function-ing distribution network. But to accomplish this more is needed than a mere infusion of capital and know-how. The local marketer has to become a teacher of sorts, educating middlemen as well as consumers about how to do effective marketing.

The NDC markets differ from other developing markets in that the political systems have long attempted to provide the basic conditions of a decent life and good elementary education but have also emphasized production instead of consumption and have pursued a consistent strategy of hostility to capitalism. These background factors make these markets different and in some ways more difficult to penetrate. The idea of consumer sovereignty, so basic to the Western market systems, is foreign to people who have been taught that labor is the supreme value. The notion that consumers must be satisfied by producers is hard to accept, and a service orientation is difficult to inculcate in retail clerks. The local marketer in these nations becomes a foot-soldier and a teacher in the struggle to bring the marketing concept to these budding free markets.

But consumer psychology in NDC economies is changing rapidly as economic progress continues. As new products appear, people change their attitudes and preferences, and traditional habits give way to new lifestyles. Over time, unless the political situation reverses itself, customers in the NDC markets can be expected to become more similar to their compatriots in more mature markets.

KEY TERMS

Attitudes toward free markets in NDCs p. 353
Barter p. 345
Compensation deals p. 345
Copyright infringement in China p. 364
Counterfeits and pirated products in China p. 364
Counterpurchase p. 346
Countertrade p. 345
Credibility of advertising p. 360
Developing markets p. 344

Educating middlemen p. 356
Ethnic market segmentation p. 353
Export controls p. 352
Hong Kong traders in China p. 362
International agencies in NDCs p. 351
Joint ventures with Chinese partners p. 363
Liberalization in India p. 370
Marketing infrastructure p. 347

Newly democratized countries (NDCs) p. 350
Offset p. 346
Personal contacts in China p. 365
Political risk in India p. 370
Political risk in NDCs p. 353
Product buy-back p. 346
Special Economic Zones in China p. 364
Technology transfer to India p. 369

DISCUSSION QUESTIONS

1. How strong would you say the evidence is that the emerging markets will sooner or later have the same kind of consumers as mature markets? What will the role of national differences and culture become? How do entry barriers stall the process toward similarity?

2. What are the basic functions of an effective distribution system in mature markets? How well and by whom are these functions likely to be performed in an NDC market such as Russia?

3. From trade press reports and newspaper articles, trace the distribution path of an im-

ported product of your choice into one of the developing markets.

4. What factors would you think are particularly important for a marketer of cosmetics to teach retailers about in the stores of NDC markets? Of automobiles?

5. What factors in your own country's typical consumer advertising do you think will not be the same in an NDC economy? How do consumers in your country and the NDC learn about new product features?

NOTES

1. This is of course much too brief a discussion to do justice to the range of agencies and services available and what the firm can do to mobilize support for its overseas endeavor. The extent of support differs by region, country, and industry. More will be said below in the context of the newly democratized countries (NDCs), but this chapter can only scratch the surface. There are specialized books and directories available, and the interested reader can start by consulting, for example, the sources listed in Chapter 4.

2. These are only highlights of the countertrade options. The book by Alexandrides and Bowers, 1987, can be suggested for further reading.

3. See "Nestlé Alimentana S. A.—Infant Formula," Harvard Business School case no. 9-580-118.

4. This example is from "General Motors' Asian Alliances," Harvard Business School case no. 9-388-094.

5. See *The Russian Consumer*, 1992, and "A New Brand of Warfare," 1994.

6. For more on this perspective, see "Gillette Keys Sales," 1987.

7. These brief paragraphs on international support for NDCs can be pursued further by the interested reader—see note 1 above.

8. See Czinkota, 1994.

9. Events in Russia have created some anxiety, but as of mid-1995 progress is still being recorded. See, for example, "In Polish Shipyard," 1995.

10. See "GE's Next Century," 1993.

11. See *The Russian Consumer*, 1992.

12. See, for example, "Cosmetics Companies," 1994.

13. From Elliott, 1992, and *The Russian Consumer*, 1992.

14. See "A New Brand of Warfare," 1994.

15. See Yan, 1994, and also "What Clinton Won't Find," 1994.

16. See "A New Brand of Warfare," 1994.

17. See ibid. and "Cosmetics Companies," 1994.

18. From "A New Brand of Warfare," 1994.

19. For an informative view on advertising strategy in the new Russia, see *The Russian Consumer*, 1992.

20. Thanks are due to May Guo for drafting this section and to Mingxia Li for reviewing and updating it.

21. Sources: "China: Special Report," 1995, and "China Summit Opportunity," 1995.

22. Sources: "China's Low-Cost Loans in Doubt," 1995, and *Walden Country Report*, 1994.

23. Sources: See note 21 above. Also, "Chinese Bikes," 1995.

24. Source: "China: Trade Regulation," 1995.

25. Sources: "China Tariff Cut Seen," 1995, and "Peugeot Chief," 1995.

26. See "China Pledges," 1995.

27. Source: "China Expert," 1994.

28. Sources: *Walden Country Report*, 1995, and "No Holiday," 1995.

29. From Yan, 1994.

30. Thanks are due to Ashwani Gujral for drafting this section and to Sachin Anand for reviewing and updating it. Unless otherwise noted, the country statistics are from United Nations and the U.S. Department of Commerce publications.

31. The recent problem with the massive power project in the state of Maharashtra is a reminder of the political risks involved. American company Enron was awarded the contract by the Indian government, but a new state government challenged the agreement and forced a renegotiation. See "Enron, India to Begin Talks," 1995.

32. This is the popular imagination in India. There were changes—for example, already by 1980, India did have electronic word processors and some personal computers, brought in by expatriates from abroad. But the relative stagnation in, for example, automobiles, where the models remained unchanged over a 30-year period, is a striking testament to the power of trade barriers to retard economic growth.

33. See "GE's Next Century," 1993.

34. From "Foreign Car Makers," 1994.

....

SELECTED REFERENCES

Alexandrides, C. G., and B. L. Bowers. *Countertrade: Practices, Strategies, and Tactics.* New York: Wiley, 1987.

"A New Brand of Warfare." *Business Central Europe,* April 1994.

Babakian, Genine. "Smirnoff Pop Chart Causes Russian Flap." *Adweek* 36 (August 7, 1995), p. 14.

"China Expert Sees 'A Car in Every Garage' by 2010." *Reuter European Business Report,* April 6, 1994.

"China Pledges Three-Stage Currency Convertibility." *Reuter Asia-Pacific Business Report,* February 11, 1995.

"China's Low-Cost Loans in Doubt." *The Age (Melbourne),* March 30, 1995.

"China: Special Report—The Long March to Market Economy Continues Unabated." *Lloyds List,* November 24, 1995.

"China Summit Opportunity." *Washington Times,* October 22, 1995.

"China Tariff Cut Seen to Slash Surplus by $10 Billion." *Reuters, Limited,* December 10, 1995.

"China: Trade Regulation." *EIU ViewsWire,* October 30, 1995.

"Chinese Accused of Pirating Disks." *New York Times,* August 18, 1994.

"Chinese Bikes Being Dumped in U.S." *Los Angeles Times,* May 20, 1995.

"Cosmetics Companies Stake Out Eastern Europe." *New York Times,* October 11, 1994.

Czinkota, Michael R. "Export Controls: Providing Security in a Volatile Environment." Working paper, MKTG-1777-13-994, School of Business Administration, Georgetown University, 1994.

Dubey, Suman. "Kellogg Invites India's Middle Class to Breakfast of Ready-to-Eat Cereal." *The Wall Street Journal,* August 29, 1994, p. 83B.

Ecenbarger, William. "There's No Escaping Us: The Sun Never Sets on America's Pop-Culture Empire." *Chicago Tribune Sunday Magazine,* February 13, 1994, p. 16.

Elliott, Stuart. "Sampling Tastes of a Changing Russia." *New York Times,* April 1, 1992, p. D1.

"Enron, India to Begin Talks." *The Oil Daily,* November 3, 1995, p. 5.

"Foreign Car Makers Make Drive for India's Middle Class." *Washington Post,* September 17, 1994.

"Gauging the Consequences of Spurning China." *New York Times,* March 21, 1994.

"GE's Next Century: China, India, and Latin America." *Business Week,* April 12, 1993.

"Gillette Keys Sales to Third World Tastes." *The Wall Street Journal,* April 2, 1987.

"In Polish Shipyard Signals of Eastern Europe's Revival." *New York Times,* July 4, 1995, pp. 1, 46.

Lloyd, John. "Survey of Russia." *Financial Times,* June 27, 1994, p. VIII.

Michaels, James W. "The Elephant Stirs." *Forbes,* April 24, 1995, pp. 158–59.

"Missing Out on a Glittering Market." *New York Times,* September 12, 1993.

"No Holiday for HK Pro-Labor Group." *United Press International,* December 16, 1995.

"Peugeot Chief Urges China to Protect Car Market." *Reuters, Limited,* December 8, 1995.

"Radio Advertisers Tune In to Russia's Middle Class." *New York Times,* August 12, 1994.

Siegle, Candace. "Crap Shoot." *World Trade* 6, no. 10 (November 1993) pp. 64–66.

The Russian Consumer: A New Perspective and a Marketing Approach. New York: D'Arcy Masius Benton and Bowles, 1992.

Walden Country Report, January 30, 1994.

Walden Country Report, January 30, 1995.

"What Clinton Won't Find in Russia." *New York Times,* January 10, 1994.

Yan, Rick. "To Reach China's Consumers, Adapt to *Guo Qing.*" *Harvard Business Review,* September–October 1994.

Yuen, Darrel K. S. "China: The Next Life Insurance Frontier?" *National Underwriter* 99, May 22, 1995, pp. 2, 17.

Case 1

WARNER COSMETICS: RALPH LAUREN IN SAUDI ARABIA?

hat's the problem," sighed Mike Wilson[1] as he sank down in his chair. "How can we expect the same advertising to be as effective in the Middle East as in the United States?" He glanced at his watch. "Let's go for lunch—maybe we'll get some good ideas over a quiche Lorraine." Sue Perkins, his assistant who was sitting across the room, stood up and, as they departed, extended the thought: "Perhaps lunch at 'Cedars of Lebanon' down on 30th Street would help us figure out whether Arab users of men's cologne are really that much different from our American customers."

Company Background

Warner Cosmetics, headquartered in New York City, was a successful manufacturer and marketer of two major lines of cosmetics, one aimed at women, one at men. Among the men's brands marketed were Ralph Lauren's "Polo" and "Chaps" brands of colognes, after-shave lotion, soaps, and related toiletries. The arrangement called for the Ralph Lauren organization to receive a royalty on sales of the

[1]Personal names are disguised.

products—about 7% of gross revenues. The "Polo" brand was used for top-of-the line products, the "Chaps" name used for a less expensive line of toiletries. For both lines the Ralph Lauren designer identification was displayed prominently, to considerable success.

Mike Wilson was sales promotion manager in the international group at Warner. The international group was tied closely to the domestic operations but played largely a step-sister's role in the total operations. Product policies and promotional approaches were generally developed with a clear focus on the domestic American market, and the international group was then charged with selling the product abroad with minimal adaptation of promotional messages. This ethnocentric approach had worked well enough in the more than 20 countries entered so far, and "Chaps" had become a leading shareholder in men's cologne in several markets, including the large Middle Eastern market.

Repositioning

The problem faced by Mike and Sue had to do with a repositioning strategy recently implemented in the U.S. market. The "Chaps" cologne packaging had been redesigned, keeping the shape of the original glass bottle but without the expensive leather covering and with no leather straps dangling from the package box. The new packaging is shown in Exhibit 1.

Extensive test marketing in the United States had shown the new package to be equal to, or even better than, the original leather-covered bottle in terms of customer acceptance. The repackaging was but a first step in the gradual shift of the product into a mass-market segment, away from a strong "macho" image into a more broad-based, "active lifestyle" segment. The repositioning was not accompanied by a shift downward in price, but because of the lower production costs the net contribution was substantially higher. The introduction of the new package had gotten under way only a month earlier, and results were so far on target.

. . . .
EXHIBIT 1

Ahmed Ben Gassan, the Saudi Arabian representative of "Chaps," had just visited New York and was quite upset about the package change. "The packaging is the most important feature of this product," he had claimed, "and the new package just does not have the same strong style as the original one. My customers will be very disappointed. They want the American dream, not the American lifestyle."

Another complication was the issue of TV advertising. The opening of a new commercial TV channel in Saudi Arabia had made the use of TV advertising feasible and competitively necessary—and the New York head office had already decided that any advertising abroad would have to use the same basic material as developed domestically. The two alternative commercials used in the domestic market had just been reviewed for the umpteenth time by Mike and Sue. The original commercial used the old macho packaging and positioning, featuring cowboys from a make-believe "Marlboro"-style country, while the new version incorporated the positioning shift and the new packaging, featuring active young men and women in outdoor gear, with the voiceover explaining, "Chaps cologne is not just for men who ride horses." Given the restricted choices, the question was how the introduction of the new package in Saudi Arabia should be handled—and how should Ahmed be mollified?

Product Market

The market for men's cologne had a relatively recent origin in the United States as well as other markets. The idea of a man's perfume had not penetrated and become acceptable to the majority of males in the mass market, but largely remained a specialty item for a particular type of status-conscious, "macho" type of fellow with money to spare and old enough to want to make sure that his impression upon others reflected his own self-perception correctly. And, to him, it was always important to surround himself with glamorous and beautiful women, at least for others to see. This man was not necessarily married, possibly divorced, and had more time for himself than for his children, if any.

The shift in the positioning attempted by the Warner company in the U.S. market represented a conscious shift over into a much larger segment consisting of young adults, married or unmarried, leading active lives and cherishing their independence. This target group seemed quite similar to the one depicted in commercials for premium beers such as Heineken and Michelob, and the Warner commercials clearly represented an attempt to generate a broad acceptance of the men's cologne concept. It also, not coincidentally, went very well with the general thrust of Ralph Lauren's designer style, emphasizing outdoor settings and rough but well-made products used by individuals who like sports.

The Saudi Arabian target buyer was less well delineated. From his conversations with Ahmed, Mike Wilson had a picture of a person with plenty of money to spare, a heavy user of colognes (and, at times, even women's colognes), who belonged to the upper stratum of the society by birth, or else occupied an important government position or worked as a bureaucrat, in either case possessing a Western education. These were people who traveled freely and often spent big money on Western luxury products. Given the hot climate in their home country, they used cologne freely, splashing generous amounts over face and hands, as well as their chests, and even on top of their clothes.

In terms of fragrance, the "Chaps" brand had been positioned somewhere between the "animal" scent of musk, typified by the "British Leather" after-shave lotion, and the more refined and feminine floral fragrance typical of many women's colognes. It was strong and distinctly "spicy," yet softer than the "Polo" brand which emphasized the musk. The "Chaps" fragrance had found favor with many men, even those who were new to the cologne market, and seemed in no need of modification in foreign markets.

Competition

Although there were a number of competitors in Saudi Arabia, also from women's products, the one standout seemed to be Paco Rabanne from France's Yves Saint Laurent. At the lower end there was Old Spice, the British cologne, but Mike felt their threat was less dangerous. In the domestic market, brands such as "Grey Flannel" by Geoffrey Beene and "Eau Savage" by Dior had garnered some sales but the "Polo" line by Lauren had taken the brunt of that attack. Mike was not sure whether these brands had been introduced into the Saudi market as yet.

....

DISCUSSION QUESTIONS

1. What are the arguments in favor of staying with the original package in the Saudi market? What are the arguments against such a strategy?

2. Do you trust Ahmed's contention that the new package will not be accepted in the Saudi market? Why, or why not? What additional research about the Saudi Arabian customer would be useful before reaching a decision about the package?

3. Given the apparent buying motivations among Saudi customers, which of the two commercials seems to have the better chance of succeeding in the Saudi market? Explain fully.

4. What additional research would you suggest Mike undertake before deciding about the commercials?

Case 2

DALOON A/S (C): MARKETING ORGANIZATION IN GERMANY

*H*emming Van, managing director of Daloon A/S, was the first to admit that the company's success in Germany during 1989–91 had been facilitated by the reorganization and strengthening of the sales and marketing organization.[1] Before 1988 the local sales organization was very thin, and managers in Germany were assigned very wide responsibilites which made their activities very diffuse. This he had changed.

Strengthening the Local Organization

Daloon's German sales subsidiary was in charge of all sales in Germany to both the retail and the catering markets. In 1988 the subsidiary had a Danish manager and three regional salesmen (German nationals). Since 1989 the staff of the German sales subsidiary had been increased substantially. This increase had been made possible by the increased earnings from the German market.

When Aldi became a steady customer in 1989–90, it was decided to invest earnings in an intensification of the sales and marketing activities in the German market, particularly the catering market. By 1992 there was a Danish manager, three sales managers, four junior salesmen (customer advisers), as well as two

secretaries (the latter nine were German). The new employees in the sales subsidiary had resulted in much more intensive Daloon customer contact.

The three sales managers supervised direct sales to the catering market and were responsible for negotiations with catering wholesalers as well as retail chains. In addition to this, they participated in general sales drives, and helped to prepare the magazine *Daloon Report— Informationen, Ideen und Tips*, posted to all customers in Germany. The three junior salesmen were all fully trained cooks and were in direct contact with Daloon's most important target groups in the German catering market. It was their job to visit chefs and other decision makers at the customers to demonstrate new products, advise the customers in the applications of Daloon products, put up advertising signs and the like in canteens, cafeterias, and so on, and furthermore to be in constant touch with minor catering wholesalers.

Increased Sales Effort

Daloon influenced the canteen decision makers more and more actively. The firm had started to visit wholesalers to get the names and addresses of the wholesalers' most important customers. Daloon then offered to join the wholesaler's salesmen when calling on customers and was allowed to visit the chefs to

[1]For more company background, please see Daloon (A).

Source: Daloon A/S parts (A), (B), and (C) were prepared in 1993 by Professor Tage Koed Madsen, Department of Marketing, Odense University, as a basis for discussion rather than to illustrate either effective or ineffective management. The case is based on information made available by Daloon A/S. The case is not to be used or reproduced without prior permission.

influence them with information on the application of the products (recipes, etc.). This initiative had been welcomed by the wholesalers. The four junior salesmen each typically visited about 200 canteens every month. In addition to their advisory activities they also took orders during these visits. The orders were then forwarded to the wholesaler. It was Daloon's experience that this direct customer influence had been definitely advantageous. The direct influence was supported by advertisements in professional papers and by direct mail campaigns forwarding new recipes to selected target groups among the customers. Finally, the *Daloon Report* magazine supported the influence on canteen decision makers.

The junior salesmen also participated in the so-called house fairs and together with the sales managers they influenced the wholesale salesmen at meetings where Daloon tried to familiarize these salesmen with Daloon products and their applications by means of video shows and tastings. The same things took place at meetings in various chef clubs.

Customer Feedback

Being cooks, the junior salesmen were able to look at thing from the customer's point of view and thus contribute greatly to the customers' understanding of opportunities offered by Daloon products, as well as to feed important information from the market back to the Daloon organization.

The model for this form of organization was transferred from the Danish market. In Daloon's opinion it offered a number of advantages. First, it had a much more effective influence on customers, as it was very easy to get out into the field and test new ideas and support the Daloon program. Second, the close contact to catering customers ensured that the feedback from the market was exploited very quickly and much more efficiently in Daloon's internal organization. The market information went directly back to Daloon and did not "disappear" in a report from one of the wholesaler's salesmen. The information obtained from Daloon's own salesmen was considered more reliable and thus carried greater weight internally than information received from an external agent. It was not that Daloon did not trust its representatives in other markets, but naturally could be much more responsive when the information about the market came from somebody "in the fold."

Close to the Customer

The close contact to the catering market customers had been of great importance. The personal contact with chefs at university canteens had, for example, resulted in a material change of the soufflé products. Previously, the soufflés had been sold in aluminum dishes and were to be baked on location in the canteen kitchen. This meant that the canteens had the problem of discarding several thousand aluminum containers. The students had found this great waste of aluminum environmentally wrong. Daloon changed the product so that it was now prebaked in Nyborg, and the aluminum packaging was no longer required.

It was Daloon's opinion that the personal contact to the market was an important advantage for development. The feedback from the market was by and large received through the personal contacts of the sales force in the market. When feedback on product drawbacks had been channeled to Daloon through independent wholesalers' salesmen reports, it had not had the same effect on Daloon's internal product development group. Actual formal market analyses were very rare.

DISCUSSION QUESTIONS

1. How well did Daloon adapt its marketing organization to the requirements in the German market?

2. What market research was done by Daloon? What else could the company do?

3. How did Daloon try to create a strong relationship with and loyalty among its customers?

Case 3

IKEA'S UNLIKELY EXPANSION (B): IN THE U.S. MARKET

*I*KEA, the Swedish furniture store chain virtually unknown outside Scandinavia two decades ago, had drawn large opening crowds to its stores as it pushed rapidly into Europe, North America, and Asia.[1] It was now faced with the challenging task of making its United States entry a success.

Initial Problems

The most pressing problem for IKEA entering the U.S. market was the creation of a stable supply chain. By taking an incremental approach, starting with a few stores on the East Coast of the United States with its relative proximity to European suppliers, the company ensured a successful transition from its Canadian beachhead. The company soon opened a store in southern California also, much farther away, but a large market with the kind of customer demographics—young and active—which favored IKEA'S modern designs and assemble-it-yourself strategy. The California entry was precipitated by the emergence of a local imitator, "Stør," which had opened ahead of IKEA, capitalizing on the word-of-mouth generated by IKEA'S new concept.

IKEA'S early effort showed up problems because of less adaptation to the American mar-

[1]For company background, please see the IKEA (A) case.

ket than customers desired. For example, IKEA decided not to reconfigure its bedroom furniture to the different dimensions used in the American market. As a result, the European-style beds sold by IKEA were slightly narrower and longer than standard American beds, and customers' existing mattresses and sheets did not fit the beds. Even though IKEA European-sized stocked sheets in the stores, bed sales remained very slow.

The American suppliers, whom IKEA gradually recruited to reduce the dependence on imports, also proved in need of upgrading and instruction in IKEA'S way of producing furniture. IKEA sent its people to the suppliers' plants, providing technical tips about more efficient methods and helping the suppliers shop around for better-quality or lower-price materials.

Promotion

While some managers helped establish the supply side of the stores, IKEA'S marketing staff were busy with the promotional side of the business. Store locations had generally disadvantaged IKEA relative to competitors. Because of the huge size of the stores (typically around 200,000 square feet), the need to keep a large inventory so that customers could get the purchased furniture immediately, and the

Source: Richard W. Stevenson, "IKEA'S New Realities: Recession and Aging Consumers," *New York Times*, April 25, 1993, p. F4; Kate Fitzgerald, "IKEA Dares to Reveal Gays Buy Tables, Too," *Advertising Age*, March 12, 1994, pp. 3,41.

EXHIBIT 1

EXHIBIT 2

It's a big country.
Someone's got to furnish it.

amount of land needed for parking around each store, most stores were located in out-of-the-way places—next to the airport in New Jersey in one case, and in a shopping mall 20 miles south of Washington DC in another. Thus, advertising was needed to make potential customers aware of the store location. It was thought that lower prices and selection would do the rest—positive word-of-mouth had proven the best advertising in most other markets.

But in the United States' competitive retail climate IKEA found that more focused media advertising was needed. As one manager stated: "In Europe you advertise to gain business; in the United States you advertise to stay in business." The diversity of the consumers made word-of-mouth less powerful than in ethnically more homogeneous countries. Management decided that a strong slogan and unique advertising message were going to be necessary to really bring awareness close to the levels in other countries.

The Moose symbol of IKEA, (see Exhibit 1) although successful in Germany and Canada, was considered strange and too provincial for the U.S. market, and would project the wrong image especially in California. Instead IKEA, in collaboration with its New York-based advertising agency Deutsch, developed a striking slogan that combined the down-home touch of the company philosophy with the humorous touch of the Moose: "It's a big country. Someone's got to furnish it" (see Exhibit 2).

Following the success of this advertising strategy, the company ventured further to establish itself as a pioneering store and to attract new kinds of customers. IKEA and Deutsch developed a series of eight TV advertising spots which featured people at different transitional stages in their lives, when they were most likely to be in the market for furniture. One spot featured a young family who had just bought a new house, another a couple whose children had just left home, and so on. IKEA even developed one spot that featured a homosexual couple, two men talking about furnishing their home. It was a daring step, applauded by most advertising experts and impartial observers. The campaign had a positive impact on IKEA'S image—and on IKEA'S sales. The company has continued the trend. One 30-second TV spot showed a divorced woman buying furniture for the first time on her own.

The privately held company won't reveal sales figures, but it is successful in each of the market areas where it has located its U.S. stores. It is credited with being partly responsible for a shift in furniture buying behavior in the United States. Choosing furniture has become a matter of personality, lifestyle, and emotions in addition to functionality. IKEA'S managers like that—they want IKEA to be associated with the "warmest, most emotional furniture in the world."

DISCUSSION QUESTIONS

1. What are the reasons behind IKEA'S success in the United States market?
2. Why is advertising so important in the U.S. market?
3. What are the risks associated with the kind of TV advertising campaign initiated by IKEA?
4. Describe how IKEA'S arrival has reenergized a mature market and changed the competitive situation.

Case 4

OCEAN SPRAY (A): THE SCANDINAVIAN MARKET

*I*n late 1990, the marketing department of Ripella A/S, Denmark's largest juice producer, was gathered to make a decision regarding the introduction of Ocean Spray Cranberry Drink on the Scandinavian market with Denmark on the lead market. The meeting had been called to consider an attractive proposal from Ocean Spray that Ripella become the Scandinavian agent, and, if the answer was yes, to decide what the next action should be.

Ocean Spray Cranberries

Cranberries are small, ruby red fruits slightly bigger than peas. They have a very long ripening period of approximately 20 months from pollination to harvest. Their contents of vitamins, minerals, fiber, and organic acids are substantial, extremely wholesome, and in some cases may prevent infections. Cranberries contain very little water and sugar. The pure juice from the fruit is loved by very few people; its taste is as tart and bitter-sour as pure lemon juice. About 85 percent of the world production of cranberries is in North America owing to the optimum climatic conditions there.

The cranberry is one of the few present-day fruits that was also grown by Native Americans. The Native Americans used the fruit as food, as medicine, and as a dye. In modern times cranberries have traditionally been used

Source: The Ocean Spray case was prepared by Professor Tage Koed Madsen, Department of Marketing, Odense University.

as a side dish, for example for Thanksgiving Day and Christmas. These holidays coincide with the fresh cranberry season from October to December. Until 1960 about 95 percent of all cranberry sales were related to these holidays. History and tradition bear great impact on the American use of cranberries.

Ocean Spray Cranberries dates back to 1912 when Marcus L. Urann, a young cranberry grower, observed that few people outside New England had ever tasted the unique little fruit. He started to sell his cranberry sauce in tins under the name of Ocean Spray Cape Cod Cranberry Sauce. At that time, the individual grower acted in his own name. Financial problems did, however, have the effect that the most important growers in Massachusetts in 1930–31 formed a cooperative under the name of Ocean Spray Cranberries, Inc. Urann was one of the promoters of this project. Today about 800 members constitute the cooperative of Ocean Spray.

Through Ocean Spray the growers invested in intensive market-oriented product development. The result showed up in the early 60s in the development of a clear, ruby, diluted juice—Cranberry Juice Cocktail—which is still Ocean Spray's core product. Many growers were skeptical about this "diluted" cranberry juice, but their skepticism was proved wrong by developments. Cranapple ® Cranberry Apple Juice Drink, a blended product, which is sweeter than Cranberry Juice Cocktail and thus appeals to a much larger clientele, was launched in 1964.

Today a number of drinks are marketed under the brand name of Ocean Spray. The most important part of the product range is based on cranberries in the form of juices, sauces, and so on. In addition, a number of blended products have been developed with cranberries blended with raspberries, apples, oranges, and grapes. Some drinks contain more sugar than others. Ocean Spray also markets pure citrus juices (starting in 1976) and apple juices (starting in 1982). The

launching of the "foreign" juices was a result of the wish to better exploit the brand name of Ocean Spray. Finally, cranberries as well as citrus fruits are sold as fresh fruit. As a result of the comprehensive product development, now only about 25 percent of annual cranberry sales take place at Thanksgiving Day and Christmas.

Ripella A/S

Looking to expand abroad, in 1990 Ocean Spray contacted Ripella A/S and offered the company the Cranberry Drink agency for the Scandinavian market, combining Denmark's 5.2 million people with Norway's 4.2 million and Sweden's 8.2 million for a market size of 17.6 million people. The generous offer looked promising to Ripella management. Cranberry Drink had been a great success on the American market; it was a product with a high price and a good profit margin. Product development costs would be minimal if no adaptation to the Scandinavian market was necessary.

Ripella A/S was established on March 8, 1989, through a merger between Rimi (Ringe on the island of Fyn) and Apella (Odder on Jylland, Denmark's largest island), both leading juice brands in their respective local markets. Up through the 1980s both Rimi and Apella had shown strong growth. Competition was fierce, however, in the Danish market, where the consumer prices of juice were low. The idea of a merger therefore had not been unwelcome to either party. Following the merger, Rimi was applied as the premium brand name for high-quality products, and low-price products were sold under the name of Apella or as private labels. In addition, Ripella had active-sounding brand names like "Læske" for refreshing drinks to be diluted and "Pinard" for French red and white wines. Under the Rimi brand, Ripella had recently launched three new products, "Skolejuice" (School Juice), "Morgenjuice" (Morning Juice, a blended juice with oranges, apples, and pine-

EXHIBIT 1   Danish Lifestyle Eating Habits (June 1987)

	The renewers	The unworried	The traditional	The careless	The old-fashioned	The passive	Total
Fresh fruit	*100%*	*100%*	*100%*	*100%*	*100%*	*100%*	*100%*
Daily/almost daily	78.1%	51.7%	63.0%	35.5%	51.6%	8.5%	54.6%
At least once a week	96.3	87.0	91.9	67.4	77.6	18.7	81.5
At least once a month	98.2	96.5	98.3	87.1	88.5	23.9	90.3
At least twice every half year	98.8	97.9	98.9	93.7	91.4	30.4	92.7
Never	98.9	98.3	99.0	95.4	91.8	33.7	93.3
Fruit/Orange juice							
Daily/almost daily	23.6%	20.1%	16.8%	10.5%	8.4%	1.4%	15.8%
At least once a week	52.4	48.4	42.2	24.9	18.9	4.5	37.4
At least once a month	79.7	74.3	75.1	45.1	34.4	8.2	61.0
At least twice every half year	90.1	89.0	89.1	57.4	46.3	12.4	73.2
Never	92.8	92.6	93.3	65.7	56.4	14.0	78.4

apple), and "Dansk Æblejuice" (Danish Applejuice).

Ripella had a dominant position in the Danish juice market with a market share of about 50 percent. Exports accounted for about 20 percent of total sales of about DKK 400 million.[1] The export markets were primarily found in Scandinavia. Ripella had a staff of about 200 people, with production activities being increasingly concentrated in Ringe on the island of Fyn. Sales and marketing functions employed slightly over 20 people.

The Danish Juice Market

In Europe, the consumption of juice had been steadily increasing up through the 80s. Germany was the dominant market with about 40 percent of overall European sales. This was partly due to the large population, partly to a per capita sale of as much as 40–50 liters annually. Only Switzerland and the Netherlands came close with per capita sales of 20–35

liters. Great Britain and the Scandinavian countries consumed about 20 liters per capita, whereas countries like France, Italy, Spain, and Portugal were as low as about 5 liters per capita.

Data on Danish consumption habits as of 1987 are given in Exhibit 1 for six lifestyle segments. Danes annually drink about 3,600 million liters of liquid corresponding to about 700 liters per capita. The dominant drinks are coffee (about 33 percent), beer (about 20 percent), and milk (about 16 percent), followed by tea, lemonade/mineral water, tap water, and blended juice ("saft")/refreshing drinks ("læskedrik") in drinkable dilution (each about 6 percent); wine represents about 3 percent and juice almost 3 percent. The consumption of juice is about 50 percent orange juice, just under 40 percent apple juice, and the remaining 10 percent juice blended of various fruits and vegetables.

The latter juices are the most expensive at a consumer price of DKK 12–13 a liter, whereas orange juice usually costs DKK 7–8 and apple juice DKK 6–7. The price of apple juice is today at the same level as the price of orange juice. The cheap products (typically

[1] In 1990, the exchange rate was approximately DKK 5/U.S. $1.

private labels) are generally 25–30 percent below this price level. The retail profit is 10–30 percent, depending on the brand, whereas the wholesale profit is typically 5–15 percent.

The consumption of blended "saft" and "læskedrik" to be diluted with water is about twice as large as the consumption of juice when you estimate the quantity in drinkable condition. The consumption is about equally distributed between blended "saft" and "læskedrik." As these products are to be diluted with about four times water, the sale of pure "saft" and "læskedrik" is somewhat lower than the sale of juice. To the consumer the prices of these products are, however, much lower. Typically one liter of blended "saft" costs DKK 8–12 in the store, depending on the quality. After dilution, the consumer price is therefore only about DKK 2 per liter of diluted drink. It is Ripella's opinion that a major part of the "saft" and "læskedrik" is consumed to quench thirst. Children often drink juice to quench their thirst. The juice consumption of adults is, however, considered the result of a desire to drink something wholesome and nourishing, particularly in the morning.

Most Danes drink juice only every once in a while. About 28 percent of all households drink juice at least once a day (heavy users); nearly 22 percent drink juice at least once a week. Quite a few (about 30 percent) drink juice about once every three months whereas about 20 percent never drink juice. As Exhibit 1 indicates, juice drinking habits vary considerably.

Generally, milk and coffee are the most common drinks, consumed daily or almost daily by about 80 percent of all households. Beer consumption is more concentrated on heavy users. Tea and lemonade are likewise consumed relatively frequently (about 30 percent of all households daily or almost daily).

DISCUSSION QUESTIONS

1. What are the main differences in juice consumption between the U.S. market and the Danish market?

2. How attractive is the Danish market as a lead market for Scandinavia?

3. How should Ripella position Ocean Spray Cranberry Drink in the Danish market?

4. What is the next step for Ripella?

Case 5

OCEAN SPRAY (B): THE FOCUS GROUP RESEARCH[1]

*I*n early spring of 1991, the marketing department of Ripella A/S, Denmark's largest juice producer, was again gathered to make a decision regarding the introduction of Ocean Spray Cranberry

[1]For background information on Ocean Spray and Ripella, please see Case 4, Ocean Spray (A).

Drink on the Danish market. The meeting had been called to consider the results from six focus group interviews with Danish consumers. The research was undertaken to establish what the positioning and the unique selling proposition of the Cranberry Drink should be on the Danish market.

Positioning Concepts

It was natural for Ocean Spray as exporters to want the positioning of the product transferred unchanged from the American market to the new market. First, costs would be saved by not having to adapt the concept; second, Ocean Spray could use its core competence in the best possible way as the company's accumulated experience from the sale and marketing of Cranberry Drink could be fully exploited. For Ripella it seemed more natural to work with the positioning decisions from a Danish point of view, particularly since Cranberry Drink had to fit into Ripella's existing line of products, adding an extension of strategic value.

Ocean Spray's proposal for the product positioning in Denmark was to launch Cranberry Drink as a unique, especially wholesome juice. The actual product was to be Ocean Spray's flagship, the Cranberry Juice Cocktail. The reason for picking this product was that it constituted the core of the unique "cranberry concept": the wholesome, the pure, the special taste. Based on Ocean Spray's experience in the United States, the extension of the product line with "blended products" could be effected simultaneously (few variants) or when the main product was well introduced on the market. Ocean Spray suggested the same glass packing as in the United States. In the retail outlets the product should be shelved together with other juice products. The strategy should aim for the widest possible distribution. The price level of the product should equal that of the most expensive juices, that is, a liter price of about DKK 13.[2]

Ripella's product positioning concept was based on the following reasoning: The consumers were likely to perceive Cranberry Drink as a wholesome and refreshing special

[2]In 1991, the exchange rate was approximately DKK 5/U.S $1.

product of high quality. Cranberry Drink would probably be consumed in two very different situations: First, as a refreshing and wholesome product following physical exercises such as sports and gardening; second, in a cozy and relaxed environment where cranberry had the character of a nonalcoholic drink, sipped rather than gulped down. The target group of the product was envisaged by Ripella to be households/people over 18 years of age living in cities, having at least a bachelor's degree and an income above average (i.e., about 20 percent of the Danish population). The company planned to market Cranberry Drink in a Pure-Pack 0.75 liter carton, priced between orange juice and special juices. An advertisement and promotion budget of just under DKK 2 million was considered necessary in the case of a product like Cranberry Drink.

At first, Ocean Spray suggested that the target group should be heavy users of juice, that is, persons drinking juice at least three times a week and preferably persons who had tasted juice based on different fruits. As their actual target group Ocean Spray wanted to focus on married women from 25 to 40 years of age, with 1 or 2 children. Furthermore, the women should have passed at least their university entrance exams and have medium-high incomes.

Focus Group Interviews

To test their alternative concepts, Ripella and Ocean Spray agreed to run six focus group interviews with a total of 48 consumers, taking about two months to complete. Ocean Spray's ad agency prepared rough sketches of advertisements showing eight alternative positioning themes and unique selling propositions.

The first focus group interviews were very general with the objective of achieving an introductory understanding of how Cranberry Drink might become part of Danish juice-drinking habits. Another objective was to illustrate the consumers' terminology related to drinks.

The subsequent focus groups were more specifically aimed at consumer reactions to Cranberry Drink and various communication concepts. The precise objective was to generate ideas about how Cranberry Drink could be fitted into the Danish market (product acceptance, target group, positioning, and so on).

The focus group interviews indicated that Danes have a different way of categorizing drinks than Americans. In the United States the concept of juice includes all drinks consisting of juice squeezed out of or extracted from fresh fruit. It is characteristic of Denmark that the consumers' terminology is more varied in this area.

The English concept of "juice" is to Danes almost exclusively attached to apples and oranges, and to Danes "juice" means 100 percent pure juice from these fruits. Actually "juice" might cover the same meaning as "saft" (syrup). However, the concept of "saft" in Denmark gives cause for some confusion. Historically, it is closely attached to home-made products and consequently the term "saftevand" has for generations been applied to drinks involving home-made "saft" diluted with water. Later "saftevand" became closely attached to industrially manufactured "blandet saft/læskedrik" (blended syrup/refreshing drink). The latter terms seem to communicate that it involves a blended product based on various fruits and containing quite a lot of sugar and possibly artificial additives. Danes attach higher quality to the concept of "blandet saft" than to the concept of "læskedrik," the latter being considered more "artificial."

Finally, the Danish vocabulary contains another concept: "most" (a sort of unfermented cider), which to Danes indicates very high-quality and pure raw materials. According to Danish law the term "most" must be applied only to cider from fruit or berries grown in Denmark. This applies for example to apples ("æblemost") and black currants ("solbærmost").

The first six advertisement concepts emphasizing the unique taste, freshness, and power of the small cranberry, were quickly discarded by the first focus groups. Practically all participants were negative about their contents, calling them "too smart", "sickening," "over-American," "irrelevant," "unrealistic," and the like. One comment was, "This little berry cannot contain all that." The two concepts that were most positively received were "Goodness born of sun, sand, and ocean" and "The Cranberry country." It was considered positive to tell about the origin of the fruit. Many people were in doubt, however, as to where to find "The Cranberry country" (Canada, the United States, Japan, and northern Sweden were suggested). The small, hardy berry arouse interest. Because the text was factual, "bitter-sweet" did not seem incredible. Many got associations to a drink that was good at quenching their thirst. Illustrations of applications of the product were well accepted by all participants.

When the participants saw the actual product (in a glass bottle) and tasted it, their reactions became clearer. The look was generally judged as negative; many participants thought that the product looked thin and artificial. Some expressed the opinion that a good and wholesome juice was characterized by its content of pulp. The ruby red color seemed to signal something synthetic with lots of additives. One comment was, "It looks like a cheap summer drink." Simultaneously, to many the color red indicated something sweet and consequently not refreshing and thirst-quenching. Because of the glass bottle and the color, some people got associations to beetroots.

The taste was assessed by most participants as sourish and fresh (not sweet). The word "sourish" was perceived by most participants as a positive word whereas "sour" was negative. The word "bitter" was perceived very differently and might therefore be dangerous to apply. After having seen the advertisement concepts and Cranberry's strong color, quite a few of the participants were disappointed by its taste. Everybody agreed to characterize the taste as weak. Cranberry Drink was considered by practically everybody an adult drink as children would not like the peculiar taste and aftertaste that even many of the participants (adults) found unacceptable.

Cranberry Drink was perceived by most participants as a good thirst quencher that could be enjoyed alone or as a cocktail with a touch of some kind of liquor. To quench your thirst you need something cold; some mentioned ice water and others plain water. Obviously, there are two perceptions of the term "thirst." One is the thirst in which a biological need for liquid is to be satisfied, another is the lesser thirst for which you can drink something delicious. In the former case of true thirst, many thought that water was required, as otherwise it would be too expensive. There was general agreement that Cranberry Drink did not go with food with which many participants drank water. Basically, there was also agreement that Cranberry Drink was not a health drink and that it was actually not a juice, but more like a "saft." Color, taste, and consistency affected this judgment.

DISCUSSION QUESTIONS

1. How would you evaluate the reliability and validity of the research?

2. Judging from the focus group findings, how transferable is the U.S. positioning to the Danish market?

3. What adaptation of product and unique selling proposition, if any, would you propose for the Danish market?

4. After this research, how would you evaluate the potential for Ocean Spray Cranberry Drink in the Danish market?

Case 6

WHITE DOVE SHAMPOO (A): MARKETING IN THE PHILIPPINES

According to industry sources, shampoo was first introduced in the Philippine market by a multinational company after World War Two. Since then the product has grown in popularity and usage largely due to massive advertising and extensive distribution. While specific figures on shampoo production and consumption were unavailable from national or local government agencies, a survey of Filipino family expenditures in 1988 was available from the National Census and Statistics Office (NSCO). It

Source: The next two cases were written by Renato S. Esguerra, Assistant Professor of Marketing at De La Salle University in Manila. He is a former president of two national associations, the Philippine Marketing Association and the Entrepreneurs Society of the Philippines.

showed that a family spent 3.3 percent of its annual income for personal care products, which included shampoo. Based on this percentage of expenditures, the value of the personal care products industry would be close to 11 billion pesos. Knowledgeable persons involved in the shampoo business put its value at about 10 percent of that, or 1.1 billion pesos.

Shampoo is distributed nationwide by several companies, with more than a dozen brands of shampoo in the market. Shampoo is sold in sari-sari (sari-sari is a Filipino word meaning variety store) stores, drugstores, department stores, supermarkets, superettes or minimarts, beauty specialty shops, salons or beauty parlors, and, megamalls. Its users, both male and female, young, and old, come from all income levels.

In the subcategory of hair care products (from the class of personal care products), a companion item to shampoo was developed called hair conditioner or simply conditioner. Celia Torres, production manager of White Dove Philippines Company (WDPC), explained the distinction between the two: "Shampoo is a chemical preparation for cleaning scalp and hair, while a conditioner is a chemical preparation applied to hair to help restore the strength of, and give body to, hair."

The Company

The beginning of White Dove Philippines Company can be traced back to 1973. Koji Izumi, president of White Dove Company of Japan, was a visitor to the Philippines looking for a company that could be a distributor of his company's products. While he was having his hair cut in the barbershop of a five-star hotel in Manila, the brand of the barber's chair caught his eye. It was a very familiar brand: Nikko-Montand. He thought then that if a Japanese-made barber's chair could be sold here, then his White Dove shampoo also would find a good market. In Japan, White Dove products had been extensively marketed through beauty salons. He sought the barber's

help to locate the distributor of the Nikko-Montand barber's chair. The distributor was Leonardo Paras' Commercial Company, a firm engaged in the importation and distribution of barbershop and beauty shop equipment like steamers, hair dryers, shampoo bowls, chairs, and other accessories from Japan. Paras was an architect-businessman.

When they met, Izumi explained the purpose of his visit and quickly offered the distributorship of White Dove products in the Philippines to Paras. Izumi believed that, as a distributor of barbershop and beauty salon equipment and accessories, Paras' company would be the right organization to distribute White Dove products in the Philippines. Paras' immediate reaction to Izumi's offer was, "But I don't know anything about shampoo."

Izumi assured Paras of all technical assistance, necessary as well as assistance in marketing and research. He invited Paras to Japan.

As an importer of Japanese products, Paras went to Japan every quarter. During one of those trips, he called on Izumi and was given a tour of the White Dove plant. Before leaving for Manila, Paras was given samples of White Dove products. Back home, he distributed the samples to beauty salons. Happily for him, the feedback from the beauty salons' owners and their customers was positive.

Research and Development

It took three years before White Dove Philippines Company (WDPC), established by Paras, became a licensee of White Dove Japan. WDPC was as interested and concerned as its Japanese licensor was in the production of hair care products of high quality and standards. Before the formulations were developed for the products to be marketed in the Philippines, samples of various types of water from many areas in the country were sent to Japan for testing and analysis. Specimens of Filipinos' hair strands were also collected for study. Since White Dove products' formulations were made for Asians, it was not necessary to test for sensitivity of the Filipinos' skin. However, in the matter of essence or scent, it was found that the Filipinos had a preference for stronger scent while the Japanese preferred a milder scent.

Thus, it was 1976 before White Dove Philippines Company officially started. Its first factory was a 60-square-meter backyard space at the Manila residence of Paras. It was there that its initial products—shampoo, rinse, and hair treatment—were packed. Packaging was done in plastic bottles made in the Philippines from molds lent by White Dove Japan.

After four years in Manila, the factory had to move to a suburban town to streamline its operations with modern machinery from Japan. That modernization increased WDPC's production tenfold. The installation of the machinery and the training of manufacturing personnel were supervised by a Japanese technician. To assure that product quality standards set by the licenser were adhered to, White Dove Japan sent a chemist to WDPC every quarter to check on the formulations and the finished products.

Advertising and Promotion

The promotion of White Dove products started with free sampling in beauty salons. This was done in keeping with the system used by White Dove Japan. In Japan, White Dove products were classified as institutional products and sold to and at beauty salons, not directly to the consumer.

Sampling was followed by other promotional activities. A hairstyling show and seminar featuring a foreign hairdresser were held in a five-star hotel in Manila. They were attended by more than 1,000 amateur and professional hairdressers. The success of the promotion made White Dove Philippines Company a byword among hairdressers and beauty salon patrons.

Eventually, White Dove became a regular sponsor or cosponsor of hairstyling shows and competitions, and national and international beauty contests, and a regular exhibitor at cosmetics and beauty products' fairs. The Hair and Cosmetologists Association of the Philippines (HACAP) had become a regular beneficiary of White Dove's sponsorship of tie-in advertising and promotional shows.

Advertising of WDPC products had been limited to cinema advertising, radio, and print media. A larger bulk of its annual advertising budget, roughly 4 percent of its national annual sales, went to print media, specifically daily newspapers and weekly and monthly magazines, especially those read by women and young girls. (See Exhibit 1.)

White Dove had used more testimonial advertising than any other type. In its ads, professional hairdressers' photos, the names of shops, and their testimonials on White Dove's products were featured. The hairdressers were very happy about these testimonial ads, which they often posted in their shops for their customers to see. The success of White Dove's testimonial advertising eventually induced other shampoo manufacturers to do similar types of advertising.

To tap the retail market, WDPC set up display counters in selected department stores and supermarkets, especially in Metro Manila.

Distribution

The initial promotional sampling of WDPC products in beauty salons, hotels, and motels set the pace of the company's distribution. For several years, more than half of WDPC sales were made through these institutions.

According to the WDPC marketing department, there were about 10,000 beauty shops in the Philippines in 1991. Twenty-five percent of them and their customers had been using WDPC products. One of the WDPC products contributed about 60 percent of the beauty salons' annual income, according to WDPC research department.

EXHIBIT 1   White Dove Philippines Company Print Media Advertising
Expenditures* (in percent)

Publication	1989	1990	1991	1992[†]
Newspapers:				
Manila Bulletin	40%	35%	40%	40%
Philippine Daily Inquirer	15	20	15	15
The Philippine Star	5	5	5	5
Magazines:				
Mod	10	10	15	15
Woman Today	15	15	10	10
Miscellaneous	10	10	10	10
Woman's Quarterly	5	5	5	5
Total	100%	100%	100%	100%

*In selected media only.

[†]Projected.

EXHIBIT 2   White Dove Philippines Company's Other Hair Care
Products (1992)

1. Avocado Cream Rinse
2. Lemon Cream Rinse
3. Hair Treatment Liquid
4. Hot Oil Treatment
5. Hair and Scalp Rejuvenator Tonic
6. Hair and Scalp Rejuvenator Tonic (with pump spray)
7. Fashionable Gel
8. Hair Styling Gel
9. Hair Spray
10. Styling Mousse

Beauty salons were classified into A, B, and Upper C as markets for WDPC products. Class A and B salons were usually bigger, had more personnel, were air-conditioned, offered more services than just hair trimming and styling, and carried inventory of WDPC products. Class A beauty salons carried an inventory of White Dove products worth P30,000 and up; Class B, P10,000 to P30,000; and Upper C, P3,000 to P10,000. (See Exhibit 2.)

The average annual sales of White Dove shampoo and conditioner during the period of 1989–1992 was P27,000,000. This figure represented about 40 percent of the company's national annual sales. (See Exhibit 3.) The remaining 60 percent represented sales of other WDPC products. According to the sales department of WDPC, its annual sales of shampoo and conditioner were roughly equal to about 5 and 4 percent, respectively, of the Philippine market.

....
EXHIBIT 3   White Dove Philippines Company Annual National Sales,
1989–1992 (in percent)

Area	1989	1990	1991	1992*
Greater Manila Area	76.58%	76.31%	75.74%	67.58%
North Luzon	8.74	9.47	10.82	12.25
South Luzon	6.20	4.39	5.90	9.31
Visayas	7.63	8.20	5.16	7.03
Mindanao	.85	1.63	2.38	3.83
Total	100.00%	100.00%	100.00%	100.00%

*The 1992 figures were based on projections by the company.

....
EXHIBIT 4   White Dove Philippines Company's Suggested Retail Prices of
Shampoo and Conditioner (1992)

Product	Bottle size		
	100 ml.	200 ml.	600 ml.
Avocado Oil Shampoo	P34.00	P59.50	P165.00
Lemon Shampoo*	31.00	54.00	148.00
Oil Shampoo	31.00	54.00	148.00
Treatment Shampoo	30.00	52.00	†
Treatment Conditioner	30.00	55.00	†
Balance Shampoo	†	52.00	†
All Over Bath Shampoo	(Sold in 175 ml. size only for P29.00)		

*Also available in 1.000 ml. bottle for P195.00.
†Not available in this size bottle.

WDPC distributed its products nation-wide through retail outlets that included supermarkets, department stores, drugstores, grocery stores, minimarts, superettes, beauty salons, and barbershops. These outlets were serviced by 11 sales representatives and 16 distributors covering the retailers; 7 sales representatives, 6 territorial representatives, and 18 subdistributors servicing the salons; and 1 corporate distribution outfit serving as marketing arm in the Metro Manila area.

Pricing

The pricing policy of White Dove had been governed by its Mission Statement. Each WDPC product was priced primarily for the Class A and Class B markets. However, according to Ruben Panlilio, White Dove's marketing director, the prices of WDPC products were set at a competitive level, allowing the company a fairly reasonable return on investment and a margin of profit. (See Exhibit 4.)

DISCUSSION QUESTIONS

1. Why do you think it took three years before the Japanese company appointed White Dove Philippines Company its licensee?

2. Do you think testing water, hair strands, and scent preferences of the Philippine market is a correct research approach? Why?

3. How would you view the company's concern for product quality and the licensor's similar interest in the same?

4. What do you think are the marketing objectives of the company?

5. What do you think of its channels of distribution? Should they be changed at all? Why?

6. How would you compare its promotional activities with those that you are familiar with?

7. Why do you think the company was not using television as much as it was using print media?

8. Why was the company pricing its products to the level of the A and B markets? Was it a sound pricing policy? Why?

9. On the whole, how would you evaluate the company's marketing performance?

Case 7

WHITE DOVE SHAMPOO (B): NEW PRODUCTS

In early 1993, Ruben Panlilio, a retired Philippine marketing executive, accepted the invitation of Leonardo Paras, president and general manager of White Dove Philippines Company to be its full-time marketing director.[1]

Eighteen months earlier, WDPC had retained the personal services of Panlilio as marketing consultant on a part-time basis. During that period, Panlilio had worked with Paras on the company's marketing operations. The latter had to oversee his company's marketing operations for lack of a senior marketing executive.

[1]For information about the White Dove Company, see Case (A).

During Panlilio's part-time involvement, Paras had asked Panlilio to make a thorough study of the company's operations and submit his recommendations. It was after Paras had read Panlilio's report that he invited Panlilio to assume the post of marketing director.

One of Panlilio's recommendations was for WDPC to introduce new products to increase sales volume and improve its market position and profitability in pursuit of its corporate mission. (See Exhibit 1.) Two products were recommended by Panlilio. One was a hair cream that would serve as a quick setter and, at the same time, would work as a hair darkener whose effectiveness would be reached

....
EXHIBIT 1   White Dove Philippines Company Mission Statement

> White Dove Philippines Company will strive for leadership in the personal care products market by providing the best quality products, with particular emphasis on products for the care of hair, to Philippine consumers, ensuring that any addition to the product line or mix offering will contribute desirably to the company's volume and market position and, ultimately, its profit standing.

after repeated usage. The other was a combination shampoo and conditioner.

Paras and Panlilio both agreed that the two products would be launched in late 1994. Sometime in the middle of 1993, however, a multinational company launched a product described as "2-in-1," which was a combination of shampoo and conditioner. The introduction of the new product was heavily supported by mass-media advertising. Toward the end of the year, about six months after the launch of this new product, Paras called Panlilio to remind him about their meeting to finalize the plans for the two WDPC products' launch.

After receiving the call, Panlilio went over his files of the latest sales figures. The figures showed that the introduction of the "2-in-1" shampoo-conditioner of one of WDPC's competitors had not had any adverse effect on WDPC sales to its institutional customers, beauty salons. At the same time, the shampoo-conditioner's sales at the retail outlets had been increasing, and were, in Panlilio's view, threatening WDPC's sales to beauty salons. To him, it seemed that sales through retail outlets would far exceed sales to beauty salons, thus reversing the trend established over the past many years.

As Panlilio mulled over the market situation revealed by WDPC sales figures, the memory of his conversation with a White Dove Japan chemist, on his quarterly quality inspection trip to the Marikina plant, came to mind. The chemist had said, "Shampoo is shampoo, Panlilio-san, and conditioner is conditioner. We do not believe they should be mixed."

Panlilio was a liberal arts graduate of the University of Santo Tomas and had majored in literature. He thought that what the chemist had said was something like the line of the poet, "East is East, and West is West, and never the twain shall meet." He gathered his files, walked out of the room, and went down the passageway toward Paras' office, where they would review the WDPC planned launch of a 2-in-1 shampoo and a 2-in-1 hair cream.

....

DISCUSSION QUESTIONS

1. Were the planned product launches consistent with its marketing objectives?

2. Do you think the company should introduce its own shampoo-conditioner? Should it secure the licensor's approval before doing so?

3. Between the 2-in-1 shampoo with conditioner and the dual-purpose cream, which do you think the company should launch first in the face of its competitor's move?

Atlas

Your Window to the World

Contents

MAP 1 Language

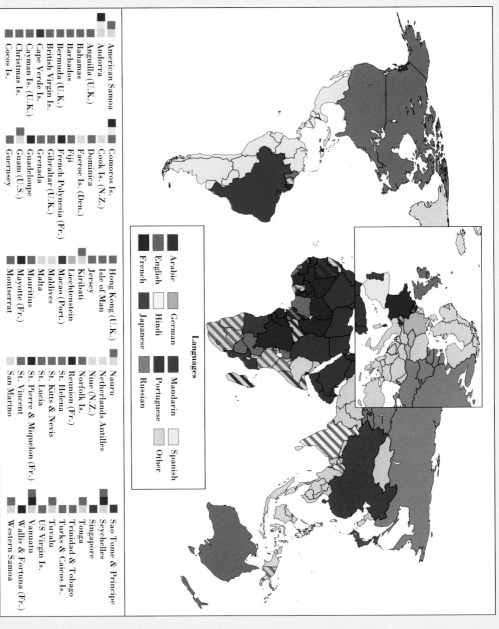

Languages

Arabic	German	Mandarin
English	Hindi	Portuguese
French	Japanese	Russian
	Other	Spanish

American Samoa
Andorra
Anguilla (U.K.)
Bahamas
Barbados
Bermuda (U.K.)
British Virgin Is.
Cape Verde Is.
Cayman Is. (U.K.)
Christmas Is.
Cocos Is.

Comoros Is.
Cook Is. (N.Z.)
Dominica
Faeroe Is. (Den.)
Fiji
French Polynesia (Fr.)
Gibraltar (U.K.)
Grenada
Guadeloupe
Guam (U.S.)
Guernsey

Hong Kong (U.K.)
Isle of Man
Jersey
Kiribati
Liechtenstein
Macao (Port.)
Maldives
Malta
Mauritius
Mayotte (Fr.)
Montserrat

Nauru
Netherlands Antilles
Niue (N.Z.)
Norfolk Is.
Reunion (Fr.)
St. Helena
St. Kitts & Nevis
St. Lucia
St. Pierre & Miquelon (Fr.)
St. Vincent
San Marino

Sao Tome & Principe
Seychelles
Singapore
Tonga
Trinidad & Tobago
Turks & Caicos Is.
Tuvalu
US Virgin Is.
Vanuatu
Wallis & Fortuna (Fr.)
Western Samoa

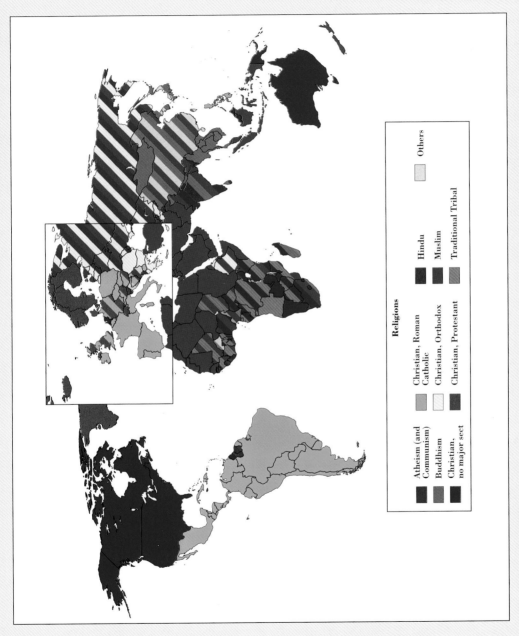

MAP 2   Religions

Religions

Christian, Roman Catholic

Christian, Orthodox

Christian, Protestant

Hindu

Muslim

Traditional Tribal

Atheism (and Communism)

Buddhism

Christian, no major sect

Others

MAP 3 **Population Density and Growth**

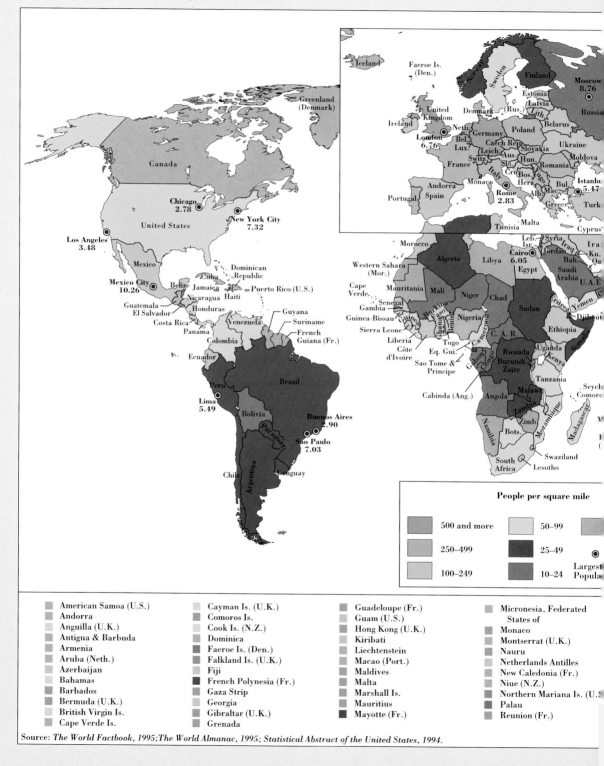

Iceland

Faeroe Is.
(Den.)

Greenland
(Denmark)

Norway Sweden Finland Moscow
8.76

United Denmark (Rus.) Estonia
Kingdom Latvia Russia
Ireland Neth. Germany Poland Lith. Belarus
London Bel. Czech Rep. Ukraine
6.76 Lux. Leich. Slovakia
Switz. Aus. Hun. Moldova
France Slo. Romania
Andorra Italy Cro. Bos. Yugo. Istanbul
Monaco Herz. Bul. 5.47
Portugal Spain Rome Alb. Mac.
2.83 Greece Turk.

Tunisia Malta Cyprus

Morocco Leb. Syria Iraq Ira
Isr. Jordan Ku.
Western Sahara Algeria Libya Cairo Bah.
(Mor.) 6.05 Egypt Saudi Qa
Cape Arabia U.A.E
Verde. Mauritania Mali Niger Chad
Senegal Eritrea Yemen
Gambia Sudan Djibouti
Guinea-Bissau Burkina Nigeria Cameroon
Guinea Faso Benin C.A.R. Ethiopia
Sierra Leone Ghana Togo
Liberia Eq. Gui. Gabon Uganda Somalia
Côte Congo Rwanda Kenya
d'Ivoire Sao Tome & Burundi
Principe Zaire
Cabinda (Ang.) Tanzania Seych
Comoro

Angola Malawi
Namibia Zambia Mozambique
Zimb. Madagascar
Bots.

South Swaziland
Africa Lesotho

Canada

Chicago
2.78

New York City
7.32

United States

Los Angeles
3.48

Mexico Dominican
Cuba Republic
Mexico City Belize Jamaica Puerto Rico (U.S.)
10.26 Haiti
Guatemala Nicaragua
El Salvador Honduras
Costa Rica Guyana
Panama Suriname
Colombia Venezuela French
Guiana (Fr.)
Ecuador

Peru Brazil

Lima
5.49 Bolivia
Buenos Aires
2.90
Paraguay Sao Paulo
7.03

Chile Uruguay
Argentina

People per square mile

500 and more	50–99
250–499	25–49
100–249	10–24

Largest
Popula

Source: *The World Factbook, 1995; The World Almanac, 1995; Statistical Abstract of the United States, 1994.*

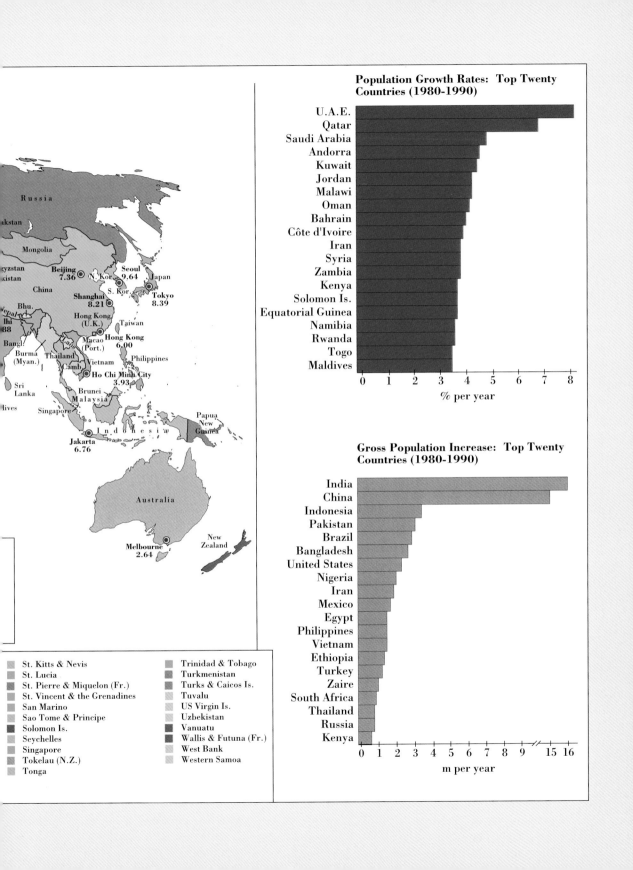

Population Growth Rates: Top Twenty Countries (1980-1990)

U.A.E.
Qatar
Saudi Arabia
Andorra
Kuwait
Jordan
Malawi
Oman
Bahrain
Côte d'Ivoire
Iran
Syria
Zambia
Kenya
Solomon Is.
Equatorial Guinea
Namibia
Rwanda
Togo
Maldives

% per year

Gross Population Increase: Top Twenty Countries (1980-1990)

India
China
Indonesia
Pakistan
Brazil
Bangladesh
United States
Nigeria
Iran
Mexico
Egypt
Philippines
Vietnam
Ethiopia
Turkey
Zaire
South Africa
Thailand
Russia
Kenya

m per year

Russia

Mongolia

China

Beijing 7.36

N. Kor.

Seoul 9.64

S. Kor.

Japan

Tokyo 8.39

Shanghai 8.21

Hong Kong (U.K.)

Taiwan

Macao (Port.)

Hong Kong 6.00

Bhu.

Nepal

lhi 88

Bangl.

Burma (Myan.)

Thailand

Vietnam

Camb.

Philippines

Ho Chi Minh City 3.93

Sri Lanka

Brunei

Malaysia

Singapore

Indonesia

Papua New Guinea

dives

Jakarta 6.76

Australia

Melbourne 2.64

New Zealand

St. Kitts & Nevis
St. Lucia
St. Pierre & Miquelon (Fr.)
St. Vincent & the Grenadines
San Marino
Sao Tome & Principe
Solomon Is.
Seychelles
Singapore
Tokelau (N.Z.)
Tonga

Trinidad & Tobago
Turkmenistan
Turks & Caicos Is.
Tuvalu
US Virgin Is.
Uzbekistan
Vanuatu
Wallis & Futuna (Fr.)
West Bank
Western Samoa

MAP 4   Economic Strength

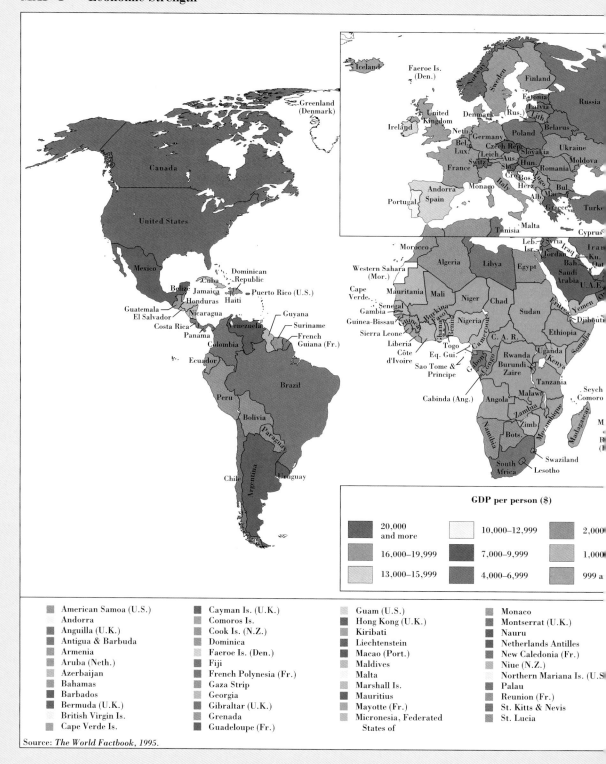

GDP per person ($)

20,000 and more	10,000–12,999	2,000
16,000–19,999	7,000–9,999	1,000
13,000–15,999	4,000–6,999	999 a

American Samoa (U.S.)
Andorra
Anguilla (U.K.)
Antigua & Barbuda
Armenia
Aruba (Neth.)
Azerbaijan
Bahamas
Barbados
Bermuda (U.K.)
British Virgin Is.
Cape Verde Is.

Cayman Is. (U.K.)
Comoros Is.
Cook Is. (N.Z.)
Dominica
Faeroe Is. (Den.)
Fiji
French Polynesia (Fr.)
Gaza Strip
Georgia
Gibraltar (U.K.)
Grenada
Guadeloupe (Fr.)

Guam (U.S.)
Hong Kong (U.K.)
Kiribati
Liechtenstein
Macao (Port.)
Maldives
Malta
Marshall Is.
Mauritius
Mayotte (Fr.)
Micronesia, Federated
   States of

Monaco
Montserrat (U.K.)
Nauru
Netherlands Antilles
New Caledonia (Fr.)
Niue (N.Z.)
Northern Mariana Is. (U.S
Palau
Reunion (Fr.)
St. Kitts & Nevis
St. Lucia

Source: *The World Factbook*, 1995.

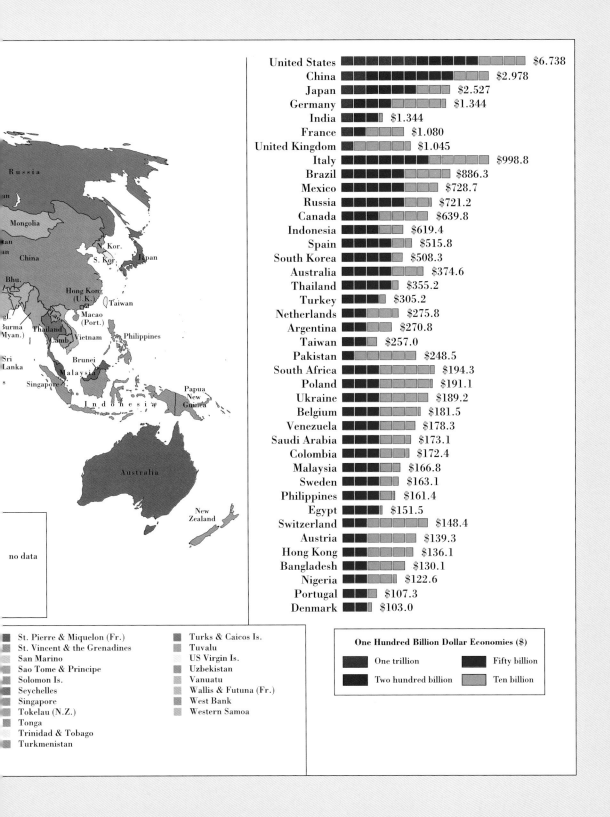

United States	$6.738
China	$2.978
Japan	$2.527
Germany	$1.344
India	$1.344
France	$1.080
United Kingdom	$1.045
Italy	$998.8
Brazil	$886.3
Mexico	$728.7
Russia	$721.2
Canada	$639.8
Indonesia	$619.4
Spain	$515.8
South Korea	$508.3
Australia	$374.6
Thailand	$355.2
Turkey	$305.2
Netherlands	$275.8
Argentina	$270.8
Taiwan	$257.0
Pakistan	$248.5
South Africa	$194.3
Poland	$191.1
Ukraine	$189.2
Belgium	$181.5
Venezuela	$178.3
Saudi Arabia	$173.1
Colombia	$172.4
Malaysia	$166.8
Sweden	$163.1
Philippines	$161.4
Egypt	$151.5
Switzerland	$148.4
Austria	$139.3
Hong Kong	$136.1
Bangladesh	$130.1
Nigeria	$122.6
Portugal	$107.3
Denmark	$103.0

no data

St. Pierre & Miquelon (Fr.)
St. Vincent & the Grenadines
San Marino
Sao Tome & Principe
Solomon Is.
Seychelles
Singapore
Tokelau (N.Z.)
Tonga
Trinidad & Tobago
Turkmenistan

Turks & Caicos Is.
Tuvalu
US Virgin Is.
Uzbekistan
Vanuatu
Wallis & Futuna (Fr.)
West Bank
Western Samoa

One Hundred Billion Dollar Economies ($)

One trillion
Two hundred billion
Fifty billion
Ten billion

MAP 5   **Raw Materials and Manufactures Trade**

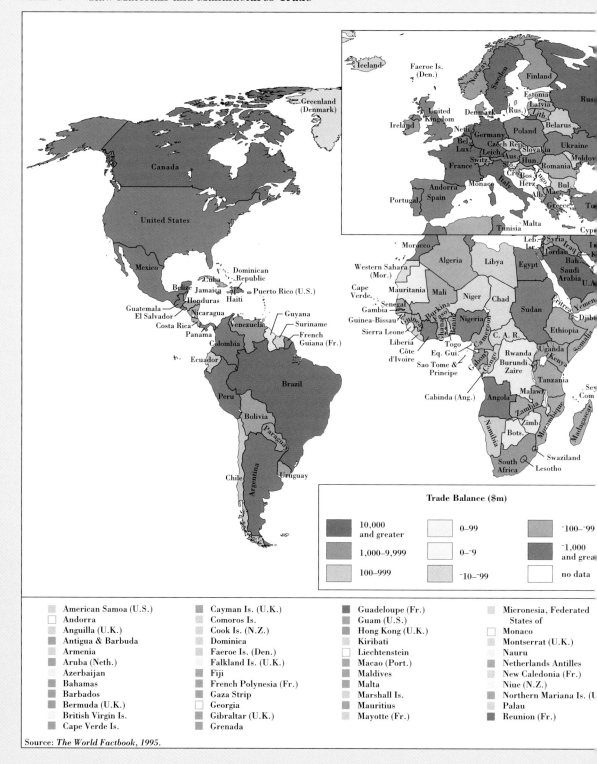

Trade Balance ($m)

10,000 and greater	0–99
1,000–9,999	0–9
100–999	⁻10–99

⁻100–99	
⁻1,000 and grea	
no data	

American Samoa (U.S.)
Andorra
Anguilla (U.K.)
Antigua & Barbuda
Armenia
Aruba (Neth.)
Azerbaijan
Bahamas
Barbados
Bermuda (U.K.)
British Virgin Is.
Cape Verde Is.

Cayman Is. (U.K.)
Comoros Is.
Cook Is. (N.Z.)
Dominica
Faeroe Is. (Den.)
Falkland Is. (U.K.)
Fiji
French Polynesia (Fr.)
Gaza Strip
Georgia
Gibraltar (U.K.)
Grenada

Guadeloupe (Fr.)
Guam (U.S.)
Hong Kong (U.K.)
Kiribati
Liechtenstein
Macao (Port.)
Maldives
Malta
Marshall Is.
Mauritius
Mayotte (Fr.)

Micronesia, Federated
  States of
Monaco
Montserrat (U.K.)
Nauru
Netherlands Antilles
New Caledonia (Fr.)
Niue (N.Z.)
Northern Mariana Is. (U
Palau
Reunion (Fr.)

Source: *The World Factbook*, 1995.

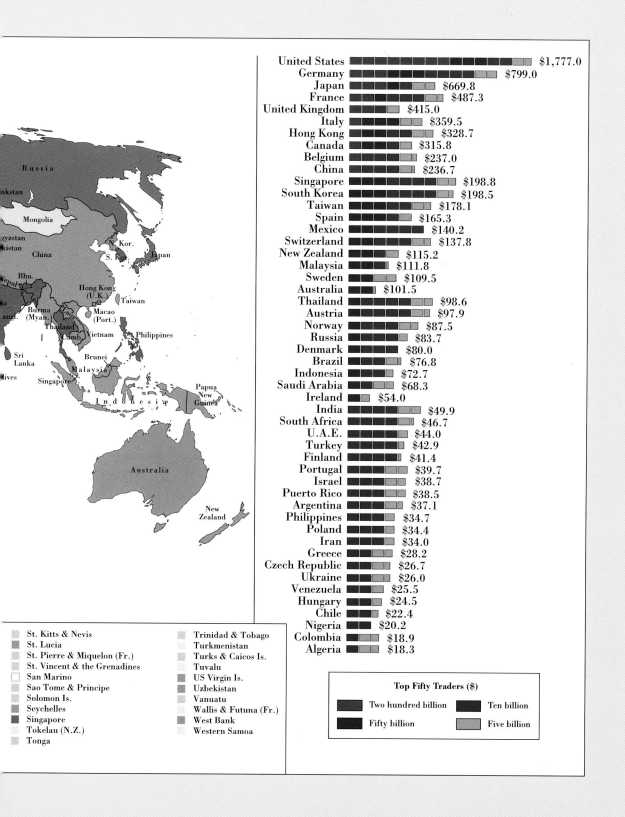

Top Fifty Traders ($)			
United States			$1,777.0
Germany			$799.0
Japan			$669.8
France			$487.3
United Kingdom			$415.0
Italy			$359.5
Hong Kong			$328.7
Canada			$315.8
Belgium			$237.0
China			$236.7
Singapore			$198.8
South Korea			$198.5
Taiwan			$178.1
Spain			$165.3
Mexico			$140.2
Switzerland			$137.8
New Zealand			$115.2
Malaysia			$111.8
Sweden			$109.5
Australia			$101.5
Thailand			$98.6
Austria			$97.9
Norway			$87.5
Russia			$83.7
Denmark			$80.0
Brazil			$76.8
Indonesia			$72.7
Saudi Arabia			$68.3
Ireland			$54.0
India			$49.9
South Africa			$46.7
U.A.E.			$44.0
Turkey			$42.9
Finland			$41.4
Portugal			$39.7
Israel			$38.7
Puerto Rico			$38.5
Argentina			$37.1
Philippines			$34.7
Poland			$34.4
Iran			$34.0
Greece			$28.2
Czech Republic			$26.7
Ukraine			$26.0
Venezuela			$25.5
Hungary			$24.5
Chile			$22.4
Nigeria			$20.2
Colombia			$18.9
Algeria			$18.3

St. Kitts & Nevis
St. Lucia
St. Pierre & Miquelon (Fr.)
St. Vincent & the Grenadines
San Marino
Sao Tome & Principe
Solomon Is.
Seychelles
Singapore
Tokelau (N.Z.)
Tonga

Trinidad & Tobago
Turkmenistan
Turks & Caicos Is.
Tuvalu
US Virgin Is.
Uzbekistan
Vanuatu
Wallis & Futuna (Fr.)
West Bank
Western Samoa

Top Fifty Traders ($)

Two hundred billion   Ten billion

Fifty billion   Five billion

MAP 6   International Groupings

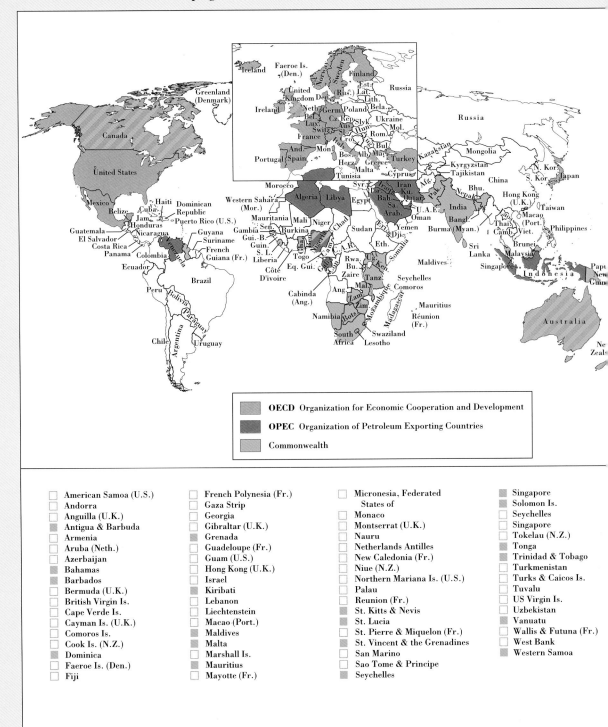

OECD Organization for Economic Cooperation and Development

OPEC Organization of Petroleum Exporting Countries

Commonwealth

American Samoa (U.S.)
Andorra
Anguilla (U.K.)
Antigua & Barbuda
Armenia
Aruba (Neth.)
Azerbaijan
Bahamas
Barbados
Bermuda (U.K.)
British Virgin Is.
Cape Verde Is.
Cayman Is. (U.K.)
Comoros Is.
Cook Is. (N.Z.)
Dominica
Faeroe Is. (Den.)
Fiji

French Polynesia (Fr.)
Gaza Strip
Georgia
Gibraltar (U.K.)
Grenada
Guadeloupe (Fr.)
Guam (U.S.)
Hong Kong (U.K.)
Israel
Kiribati
Lebanon
Liechtenstein
Macao (Port.)
Maldives
Malta
Marshall Is.
Mauritius
Mayotte (Fr.)

Micronesia, Federated
   States of
Monaco
Montserrat (U.K.)
Nauru
Netherlands Antilles
New Caledonia (Fr.)
Niue (N.Z.)
Northern Mariana Is. (U.S.)
Palau
Reunion (Fr.)
St. Kitts & Nevis
St. Lucia
St. Pierre & Miquelon (Fr.)
St. Vincent & the Grenadines
San Marino
Sao Tome & Principe
Seychelles

Singapore
Solomon Is.
Seychelles
Singapore
Tokelau (N.Z.)
Tonga
Trinidad & Tobago
Turkmenistan
Turks & Caicos Is.
Tuvalu
US Virgin Is.
Uzbekistan
Vanuatu
Wallis & Futuna (Fr.)
West Bank
Western Samoa

Source: *The World Factbook, 1995.*

Europe Trade

- **EU** European Union
- **EFTA** European Free Trade Association

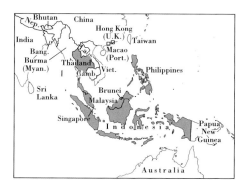

Pacific Basin

- **ASEAN** Association of South East Asian Nations

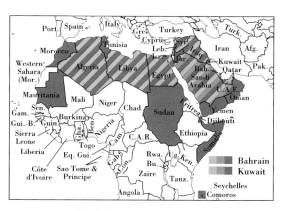

Middle East

- **OAPEC** Organization of Arab Petroleum Exporting Countries
- **Gulf Cooperation Council**
- **Arab League**

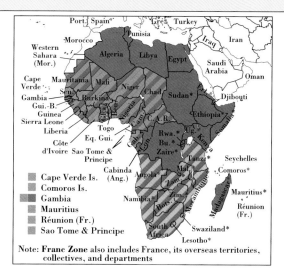

- Cape Verde Is.
- Comoros Is.
- Gambia
- Mauritius
- Réunion (Fr.)
- Sao Tome & Principe

Note: Franc Zone also includes France, its overseas territories, collectives, and departments

Africa

- **OAU** Organization of African Unity (nonmembers)
- **SADC** South African Development Community
- **ECOWAS** Economic Community of West African States
- **Franc Zone** Countries whose currencies are linked to the French Franc
- * **COMESA** Common Market for Eastern and Southern Africa

- Antigua & Barbuda
- Anguilla (U.K.)
- Aruba (Neth.)
- Bahamas
- Barbados
- British Virgin Is.
- Cayman Is. (U.K.)
- Dominica
- Guadeloupe (Fr.)
- Grenada
- Montserrat (U.K.)
- Neth. Antilles
- St. Kitts & Nevis
- St. Lucia
- St. Vincent & the Grenadines
- Trinidad & Tobago
- Turks & Caicos Is.
- US Virgin Is.

Latin America and the Caribbean

- **LAIA** Latin American Integration Association
- **Andean Group**
- **CARICOM** Caribbean Community and Common Market

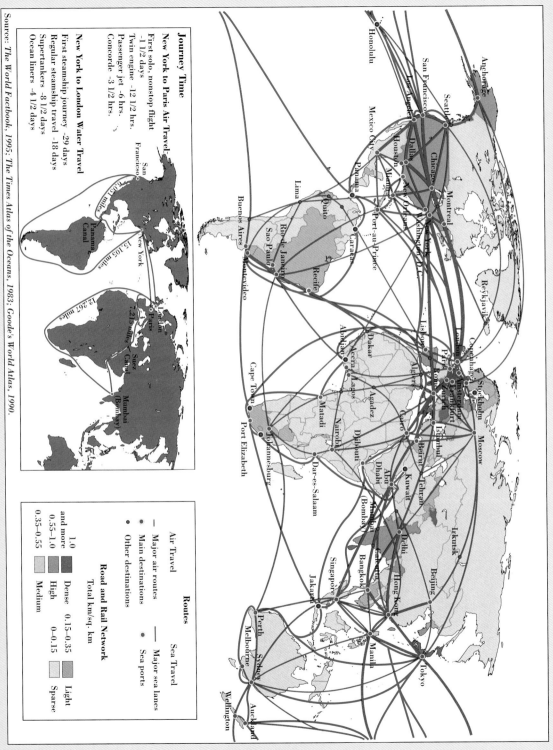

MAP 7 Trade and Travel Networks

Journey Time

New York to Paris Air Travel
First solo, nonstop flight
 -11/2 days
Twin engine -12 1/2 hrs.
Passenger jet -6 hrs.
Concorde -3 1/2 hrs.

New York to London Water Travel
First steamship journey -29 days
Regular steamship travel -18 days
Supertankers -8 1/2 days
Ocean liners -4 1/2 days

San Francisco
New York
13,105 miles
London
Paris
7,215 miles
12,367 miles
Suez Canal
Bombay
Mumbai
Panama Canal

Routes

Air Travel
— Major air routes
● Main destinations
● Other destinations

Sea Travel
— Major sea lanes
● Sea ports

Road and Rail Network
Total km/sq. km

	1.0 and more	Dense 0.15–0.35	Light
	0.55–1.0	High	0–0.15	Sparse
	0.35–0.55	Medium		

Source: *The World Factbook, 1995; The Times Atlas of the Oceans, 1983; Goode's World Atlas, 1990.*

Global Management

After the company has expanded into foreign markets and become a confident marketer in several local markets, there is usually a need to integrate the global network and develop a global strategy. There are many reasons for this. On the cost side, unnecessary duplication (meaningless differences in product designs, separate advertising campaigns, different brand names) is wasteful of resources. On the demand side, global communications make for homogeneous preferences and positive spillovers from global brand names. Global competitors often force other firms to go global as well.

Part Four deals with the globalization of marketing management, that is, how a firm coordinates and integrates its local marketing efforts globally. Chapter 11 focuses on the standardization question and how a globalized marketing mix can still satisfy customers and be effective against local competitors. Chapter 12 discusses global products and services and explains why global brands have been successful in a variety of industries. Chapter 13, which covers global pricing, shows how companies have tried to come to grips with price coordination across borders, including the problem of arbitrage opportunities because of fluctuating exchange rates. Global distribution is covered in Chapter 14, including a discussion of the massive changes in global logistics technology.

The next two chapters deal with global advertising and promotion. Chapter 15 on advertising gives the pros and cons of globally uniform ads and shows how the emergence of global agencies has facilitated global advertising. Chapter 16 covers other promotional tools, including public relations, publicity, and trade fairs, and also discusses personal sellling and the increased importance of direct marketing for global expansion. Chapter 17 treats the organizational problems which arise when global marketing is undertaken and the question of how to motivate local subsidiary managers. Chapter 18 concludes coverage of global management and ends the book by discussing the future potential of global marketing, including the threat from protectionist forces and the potential of the Internet as a global marketplace.

Globalizing Marketing

"Global markets, global competitors"

After studying this chapter, you should understand the following global marketing issues:

1. Standardization, which together with overall coordination forms the core of a globalized strategy, has strong benefits and should be seriously considered at all levels (for groups of similar countries, trade regions, continents, the globe).

2. Even if market analysis reveals that markets are essentially multidomestic, the marketer has to assess the probability of future convergence of preferences, especially in response to the introduction of globally standardized products.

3. Global competitive analysis needs to take into account the strategic intent of global and domestic competitors in each local market and the wide repertoire of fast and flexible marketing actions usually available to resourceful global companies.

4. Global marketing strategies are appropriate only when industry conditions are favorable, and to successfully implement such strategies it is important that the cooperation of local representatives be solicited early on.

F O R M U L A T I N G   A N D   I M P L E M E N T I N G   a global marketing strategy is a complicated task. Even an accomplished marketing manager with experience in local markets abroad can have trouble sorting out the many complex issues involved. Good market data on customers and competitors across the globe make the task easier. But insightful analysis of such data requires some managerial rethinking about customers and competitors.

As we saw in Chapter 1, there are a number of market factors that drive companies toward global strategies—common customer needs, global customers, global channels, transferable marketing, and leading markets. This chapter deals with these factors in more depth and also covers competitive analysis.

Some Books Are Really Black, White, Read All Over

Each fall in Frankfurt, Germany, publishers gather to offer their products to the world. To do this, they sell foreign rights, that is, the right of a foreign publisher to produce and sell a book in one or more countries. Publishers at the Frankfurt Book Fair set up exhibits and spend their days negotiating with representatives from firms in other countries.

Foreign rights sales are important because many books have global appeal. Fiction, in particular, interests readers throughout the world. James Redfield's novel *The Celestine Prophecy*, published by Warner Books, was a best-seller not only in the United States but in Brazil, Denmark, Canada, and other countries. Besides fiction, business titles and New Age books interest a global readership.

Publishers do have to tailor their offerings to local needs. There's the obvious issue of language differences; when customers speak another language, the book must be translated. In addition, tastes and outlooks vary from one region to the next. Italian publishers are reluctant to buy the rights to biographies because Italians tend to read about famous personalities in magazines instead. The poison gas attacks in Tokyo's subway spurred an interest among the Japanese in books on terrorism. And at a recent book fair, a Dutch editor hesitated over Hillary Rodham Clinton's book on raising children, *It Takes a Village*. The editor remarked that she would have to see the book first because "American values are so different."

The market for many books has, of course, long been global. Writers such as Umberto Eco, Milan Kundera, Jorge Luis Barges, Kazuo Tshiguro, and Salman Rushdie are established best sellers even in a country such as the United States, where foreign futures have found the going tough. Similarly, American books are often on foreign best-seller lists, and the number of countries involved in buying foreign rights is growing to include more developing nations. Rights to books by John Grisham have been sold to over 30 countries, including Estonia.

Books, of course, are not the only product with worldwide appeal. Marketers such as Nestlé and General Electric Lighting are successfully offering a variety of products to the world. In the case of Nestlé, those products include chocolate, mineral water, and iced tea; GE markets light bulbs and other lighting products. Products with global appeal enable companies like Nestlé, GE, and Warner Books to come out on top in a world where the globalization of markets has ignited a business revolution.

Sources: Mary B. W. Tabor, "Book Deals: Losing Nothing in Translation," *New York Times*, October 16, 1995, pp. D1, D8; John Tagliabue, "Nestlé's Aim: New-Market Growth," *New York Times*, October 15, 1994, pp. 37, 39; Thomas A. Stewart, "Welcome to the Revolution," *Fortune*, December 13, 1993, pp. 66–68.

INTRODUCTION

The globalization of marketing usually takes place after the company has international experience in multiple markets. At the corporate level, globalization typically involves three separate activities:[1] (1) Integrate sourcing, production, and marketing; (2) Allocate resources to achieve a balanced portfolio and growth; and (3) Coordinate marketing activities across countries and regions. At the business level, this coordination is usually accompanied by a certain degree of standardization of the marketing mix. In fact, a large number of globalization questions in marketing center on the issue of standardization versus locally adapted products.

This chapter first examines the pros and cons of standardization. We then discuss in further detail the most common obstacle to standardization, multidomestic markets, and show how such markets can still be targeted by standardized products. How does a marketer analyze markets to identify opportunities for globalization? We describe customer analysis first and then competitive analysis, focusing on what separates globalization analysis from more traditional market analysis. There are limits to a completely globalized marketing strategy; a "pattern standardization" approach (that leaves execution in the hands of local management) is emerging as the typical solution. A final section on pan-European marketing illustrates the emergence of globalized marketing for one region.

THE PROS AND CONS OF STANDARDIZATION

Globalizing marketing involves global *coordination* of marketing activities. It involves taking a *global management perspective* on the marketing operations in any one country. Most typically it involves a certain degree of marketing *standardization*, maintaining a degree of *uniformity* in product, advertising, distribution, and other marketing mix elements across country markets.

To evaluate the potential benefits of a globalized marketing strategy, it is useful to assess the advantages and drawbacks of standardized offerings. There are several pros and cons of marketing standardization.[2]

The Advantages of Standardization

COST REDUCTION   Cost reductions gained by **scale economies** constitute the primary benefits from standardization. Because of the longer production series there are considerable savings to be gained in manufacturing as well as purchasing. Product development costs can be spread over a larger number of units. Centralizing the purchase of media spots for advertising generates quantity rebates and other savings. When one global brand name is used in several countries, there are savings in media advertising and sales efforts. Furthermore, there are **scope economies** in marketing. The use of a globally standardized advertising campaign makes it possible to exploit good creative ideas to their fullest potential. Benetton's goodwill can be extended from apparel to sports gear. Advanced technology and new features can be used across a whole product line. New carbon material can be used for all tennis rackets, not just the upper end of the market.

ENHANCED CUSTOMER PREFERENCE   The firm can also enhance customer preferences by standardization. Positive experiences with a product in one country naturally encourages a consumer to buy the same brand elsewhere. One attractive feature of a camera can be that the same model is available in other countries, increasing the chance of getting service. Standardized advertising messages and slogans capitalize on spillover effects in marketing communications. Seeing attractive ads for the same camera at home and in a foreign country reinforces a customer's purchase decision. Canon, capitalizing on the recognition value of Andre Agassi, the tennis player, features him endorsing Canon cameras in airport advertisements around the world.

IMPROVED QUALITY   The standardized product or service is likely to offer improved quality in terms of functioning. Since additional resources can be focused on the product development effort and the design, the standardized product or service is likely to be more thoroughly tested. Investment in state-of-the-art production processes is justified. This leads to higher quality in terms of durability and reliability. The customized product may have more status and extra quality features—an expensive luxury car, for example, may have more expensive wood on the dashboard—but in terms of functionality, a standardized product is more likely to function well.

GLOBAL CUSTOMERS   There is also a special advantage to standardization because of global customers who demand uniform quality and services wherever they happen to be and buy. In consumer goods, global communications and the

An advertisement for an international alliance between three airlines. The air travel market is a classic example of a mature global market.

Courtesy Swiss Air Transport Company Ltd.

growth of international travel and tourism have helped spawn global markets for products as diverse as chocolate, watches, and apparel. In business-to-business markets, as firms grow more global and their purchasing function is centralized on a global basis, standardization of requirement specifications becomes necessary.

GLOBAL SEGMENTS   Finally, standardization has the advantage that it fits with the emergence of global customer segments. As we have seen, the customer segments in one market can often be similar to those in other markets. In technology-based product categories—computers, cameras, televisions—there are customer segments in various countries who all want similar products, and as these segments grow, the potential benefits of standardization grow as well.

The Drawbacks of Standardization

OFF-TARGET   The greatest drawback of standardized products, services, and promotional mix is that they are likely to miss the exact target in terms of customer preferences in any one country. Where needs and wants across countries are homogeneous, this is not such a severe problem. The problem is exacerbated in mature markets in which customers in different countries have widely different tastes or needs.

Standardization means that some of the segments are not targeted explicitly, and the resulting positioning of many global products may be in the larger core segments of the market (the typical American and Japanese case) or in specialty niches (the more common approach for Europeans). Thus, IBM, Microsoft, Xerox, Sony, Panasonic, and Toyota tend to offer standardized products for core market segments in many countries, while Mercedes, Armani, Chanel, and Leica offer standardized products to upscale segments everywhere.

LACK OF UNIQUENESS   There is also a drawback in the lack of uniqueness of standardized products. If customization or exclusivity is one of the overriding purchase considerations, a standardized offering is by definition in a weak position. As markets grow more affluent, uniqueness is likely to become increasingly salient. By contrast, in a period of recession, the luxury of being "special" might be foregone by the consumer.

SENSITIVE TO PROTECTIONISM   In order to reap the benefits of standardization open trade regimes are necessary. The scale economies are difficult to realize unless production can take place in one or two countries, with plant capacity at least of the minimum efficient scale and with the standardized product exported globally. Where country markets are protected by trade barriers, local manufacturing may be necessary and the scale benefits from standardization can't be reaped. Then it may be better to target the local market specifically with an adapted product in order to avoid mispositioning.

STRONG LOCAL COMPETITORS   Globalization can also fail simply because local competitors are capable and manage to mount a strong defense. By working closely with local channel members and offering special services, the local competitor can hold off an attack from a global company. If, in addition, the global company is not able to execute effectively at the local level, the global strategy is likely to fail.

Empirical research tends to show equivocal results as to the benefit of standardization. One study found that when standardized strategies were properly matched against homogeneous markets, sales growth improved, but ROI did not.[3] Another study reported similar results, with sales growth affected positively by standardization strategies, but with return on assets worse.[4] This study also found that the attractiveness of product standardization declined when market growth was slow—customization seems more promising in mature markets. In general, standardization seems to be associated with increased sales, while the effect on the bottom line is less clear.

MULTIDOMESTIC VERSUS GLOBAL MARKETS

Marketing people in the past tended to argue that product adaptation was necessary in foreign markets because consumer preferences vary across countries.[5] In many cases preferences do vary, and it is important for the global marketer to understand why these differences exist, why they may or may not persist over time, and why global standardization can still succeed.

Consumer Differences

It is clear to any observer that consumers in different countries think, speak, and behave differently in many ways. The salient product beliefs, attitudes, and social norms vary considerably between markets. The extent to which quality concerns are important, the attitudes toward foreign products, and the degree to which individuals comply with social norms all affect consumers' decision making differently across countries. For example, if a Japanese shopper is often fastidious and examines a product carefully in the store, an American consumer may be more impulsive and respond to in-store promotions of new brands.

There are variations in tastes as well. If a European prefers a car with a stick-shift and tight cornering, a Japanese likes a light touch and easy controls. If a Canadian wants a beer with a certain "body," an American may be happy with a light beer. If a Latin American woman wants strong and dark colors, the Northern Europeans dress in lighter colors. These are preferences based on tradition, culture, or simply fashion. They are malleable within limits—but it is not at all clear whether any one firm can effect any changes alone or how long it will take. These are the differences that have made marketers say products have to be adapted.

Multidomestic Markets

Multidomestic markets are defined as product markets in which local consumers have preferences and functional requirements widely different from one another's and those elsewhere.[6] The typical categories include products and services such as food, drink, clothing, and entertainment, which tend to vary considerably between countries and in which many consumers prefer the local variants.

Multidomestic markets reflect underlying religious, cultural, and social factors and also climate and the availability of (or lack of) various foods and raw materials. Japanese prefer rice and dried fish for breakfast, while Europeans eat ham and cheese or coffee and croissants. Drinking beer with food is strange for the French, while tea is the standard drink at Chinese dinners. The thin-soled shoes favored by stylish Mediterranean men do not fare well in the American setting with its rugged Western traditions. And so on. These differences are based on long traditions, education, and upbringing. Western people might think that sweets are liked by young and old—but even the children in Asian countries often prefer salty snacks to sweet chocolate cake. One's taste is educated, not something one is born with.

The firm selling into multidomestic markets needs to *localize and adapt* its products and services to the different requirements and preferences in the serious markets. Levels of salt and sugar in food products might need to change, and color patterns and sizes of packaging may have to change and even be redesigned for attractiveness and taste. Drinks need to be taste-tested and perhaps given strong communication support, educating the local consumers and trying to change their preferences, as Seven-Up has tried to do in the United States. In clothing, redesigning jeans to fit the different bodies of Asian people, widening the shoes, and shortening the sleeves are necessary steps, but the multidomestic marketer may also have to create new colors, different styles, and alternative materials. Before globalization, firms were generally multinational for a reason: The products had to be adapted to each country's preferences. Marketing could not be uniform.

Global Markets

At the same time, there are many product markets that are *not* multidomestic, such as televisions, telephones, automobiles, and personal computers. Generally speaking, these markets are not multidomestic because of the products' high technology content. People's preferences for these kinds of products are not formed by underlying cultural or religious traditions or by climate but by differences in individual needs and wants. In multidomestic markets, segmentation by countries is natural. Not so in more technology-based products, which are naturally global markets.

Global markets are defined as those markets in which buyer preferences are similar across countries. Within each country, several segments with differing preferences may exist, but the country borders are not important segment limits. The typical characteristics of a *global market* have both customer and competitive aspects. The major *global* features to look for are the following:[7]

In customers:

- Increasingly common consumer requirements and preferences as gaps in life-styles, tastes, and behavior narrow.
- Global networks with a centralized purchasing function among business customers.
- Disappearing national boundaries as customers travel across borders to buy wherever the best products and/or prices are found.
- Increasing agreement among customers across the globe about how to evaluate products and services and recognition of which brands are the best.

In competitors:

- Competition among the same world-class players in every major national market.
- Declining numbers of competitors in the core of the market as domestic companies defend their turf by specialization or merge with larger firms.

- Increasing use of national markets as a strategic tool for the benefit of the firm's global network.

With global communications and spreading affluence, many previously multidomestic markets are becoming more susceptible to globalization. People all around the world now know and like ethnic foods, such as Middle-Eastern hummus, Spanish paella, and Beijing duck. Stylish clothes from Armani, Levi's, and Benetton are bought in many countries. Japanese sake, German beer, and French wine compete directly as a dinner drink in many local places. Larry King broadcasts his TV talk show from Hong Kong to a worldwide audience. As multidomestic markets open up and become more global, the rest of the world is able to pick and choose among the best that the multidomestic markets are offer. Increasing affluence generates a desire for variety and creates opportunities for local specialties from foreign countries in leading countries.

The main differences between multidomestic and global markets are highlighted in Exhibit 11.1.[8] As can be seen, most marketing parameters in the multidomestic case are determined by national borders, as opposed to the global case where borders matter much less.

EXHIBIT 11.1   **Multidomestic versus Global Markets: Key Differences**

	Multidomestic Markets	**Global Markets**
Market boundaries	Markets are defined within country borders. Customers and competitors are of local origin.	Markets transcend country borders. Customers and/or competitors cross frontiers to buy and to sell.
Customers	Significant differences exist among customers from different countries; segments are defined locally.	Significant similarities exist among customers from different countries; segments cut across geographic frontiers.
Competition	Competition takes place among primarily local firms; even international companies compete on a country-by-country basis.	Competitors are few and present in every major market. Rivalry takes on regional or global scope.
Interdependence	Each local market operates in isolation from the rest. Competitive actions in one market have no impact elsewhere.	Local markets operate interdependently. Competitive actions in one market impact other markets.
Strategies	Strategies are locally based. Little advantage exists in coordinating activities among markets.	Strategies are regional or global in scope. Great advantage exists in coordinating activities within regions or worldwide.

Source: Kashani, 1992.

GLOBAL CUSTOMER ANALYSIS

Growing Homogeneity

A strong argument for companies to standardize marketing was made by Ted Levitt, who in 1983 argued that markets were globalizing because of two factors: **global communications** and **technology diffusion**. With satellite TV broadcasts beaming the same programs all over the world and with instantaneous global telecommunications, the world is moving inexorably toward greater **homogeneity of markets.** At the same time, the increasing speed of technological innovation and diffusion makes today's products soon outdated by the onslaught from global competitors able to incorporate the latest product inventions. The joint effect of these two forces makes product standardization not only a possibility but the preferred alternative.

This point of view has met with resistance among some marketing academicians as well as practitioners.[9] Granted that these forces are at work, the world's markets are as yet far from homogeneous. Many domestic producers are still marketing competitive products that could only be dislodged by even more attractive offerings tailored to local conditions and tastes. Further, the advantages of scale have become diminished with the emergence of computerized flexible manufacturing systems that can produce many different product models and versions without incurring extra costs. The experience in the European appliance industry suggests that standardization has some limits (see box, "Globalization Frustrated").

When global standardization does not work, the solution is usually to increase the variety in the product line while still keeping the possible standardization possibilities in mind. For example, Electrolux has attempted to deal with its difficulties in Europe by developing a family of models that appeal to cross-country segments. The electric appliance company has retained the Arthur Martin brand in France for core segment targeting of one local market, uses the Zanussi brand for pan-regional mass products, and targets individual niche segments across Europe with products and brands (Atlas, Zoppas) with Italy as a lead country.[10]

It is also important to remember that over time some differences may disappear, and markets can become more homogeneous. With the increase in per capita incomes in many countries one can discern increasing similarities among, for example, young families across the globe in their use of cameras, VCRs, automobiles, and vacation travel. This is one development that has made globally standardized products successful—a development that in turn has reinforced a trend towards homogeneity of tastes.

Whether or not the world's markets are homogeneous, many have indeed been conquered by globally standardized products. As obstacles to globalization, such as trade barriers and government regulations, have been lowered or dismantled, country-specific industry standards have become regionalized or globalized, and, in turn, there has been an increase in the number of competitors contesting any one market. Many of the new competitors feature

Getting the Picture

Globalization Frustrated

GLOBALIZATION failed in a case presented by Baden-Fuller and Stopford in 1991, who analyzed the performance of regional and national competitors in the domestic appliance industry in Europe. Here was an industry seeming to offer great promise for standardization as the EU integration proceeded with removal of tariff barriers and tedious customs procedures and the creation of common technical standards. It was an industry in which analysts predicted a convergence in consumer tastes, and in which large companies (such as Swedish Electrolux and Italian Zanussi) had joined forces to gain scale advantages and rationalize production, marketing, and distribution.

The researchers found that during the 1980s the firms focused on one national market (such as Hotpoint in Britain and Thomson in France) and exporters such as Merloni in Italy outperformed the large global players (Electrolux and Philips) in terms of return on sales and on capital employed. The reasons were several. First, the predicted convergence of tastes failed to materialize. Tastes did change in the various countries but not toward the same standard. For example, in the 1960s the British preferred top-loading washing machines, while the French demanded front-loaders. By the 1980s the preferences had changed in both countries but, curiously enough, in opposite directions. The researchers are at a loss explaining this development, except to blame it on the traditional rivalry between the two countries!

Another important reason for the weaker performance of the global players was that the local companies maintained high standards in distribution and after-sales service, making it costly and time consuming for the global firms to enter the national markets. Along the same lines, the retail sector in Europe was not regionally integrated, which limited the possibility of transferring systems and know-how to support retail sales. The scale returns and cost savings to standardization could therefore not be realized.

Source: Baden-Fuller and Stopford, 1991.

products standardized on a global or regional basis and have been quite successful, as the Gillette experience indicates (see box, "Gillette's World View").

Business Markets

Some industrial products have long been sold in global markets. This is especially true of raw materials such as petroleum, rubber, and minerals but also true of fabricated products such as steel, semiconductors, and plastics. Of course, tariff barriers protecting domestic producers have tended to create artificial local markets with high prices, but these business markets tend to be inherently global.

Since most industrial products are bought as intermediate goods and used to produce final goods, the degree of globalization of their markets depends

Getting the Picture

Gillette's World View: One Blade Fits All

GILLETTE, the American razor blade manufacturer, is one company that believes in global standardization. As Mr. Alfred M. Zeien, the chairman and CEO, states: "The most important decision that I made was to globalize. We decided not to tailor products to any marketplace, but to treat all marketplaces the same. And it worked in most countries."

Mr. Zeien's globalization principles were honed when he ran Gillette's German subsidiary Braun, maker of electric razors and appliances such as coffeemakers and hi-fi equipment. When he arrived in Frankfurt in 1968, the German home market accounted for 90% of Braun's revenues. When he left for Gillette's headquarters in Boston in 1978, Braun revenues had more than tripled, with 65% coming from non-German sales. Mr. Zeien discovered that he could sell Braun merchandise outside Germany on the strength of the brand name without redesigning the product (except for localization aspects such as electrical rewiring). Traveling out of Frankfurt and exploring markets on every continent, Mr. Zeien learned about different kinds of people. "But," he says, "I did not find foreign countries foreign. They have distinctive characteristics, but they are not foreign. When people shop they do not think very differently from each other."

This simple insight is perhaps not equally apt for all products, but Mr. Zeien gambles that shoppers in Malaysia and Singapore, the site of Gillette's regional headquarters for Asia, will buy the same upscale Parker fountain pens (a Gillette product) as French shoppers at Printemps—and for the same price or more. "We are not going to come out with a special product for Malaysia," he says.

Sources: Uchitelle, 1994; Lim, 1993.

---

intimately on the degree to which manufacturing technology is widespread. Purchasers of automobile or electronic components have similar requirements in most parts of the world and the sellers of these components are forced to shift from a multidomestic to a global perspective.

Globalization is indeed pervasive in some of these industrial markets, and the marketer needs to recognize that competition can come from anyplace. High-quality suppliers to Japanese automakers have now begun selling components to American and European carmakers. Volvo buys transmissions from an Isuzu supplier, and Ford's small engines come from a Mazda subsidiary. Strong European and American suppliers counter by marketing their products to Japanese companies. Air conditioning units in Hondas are manufactured by Americans, and German Bosch sells its ABS braking system to Japanese auto manufacturers. The Bosch systems come from its manufacturing subsidiary in Japan, whose quality control is up to Japanese standards. This has created a problem for Bosch at home, since its German customers (Mercedes and BMW) have requested braking systems to be supplied from the Japanese subsidiary, not from the local plant, which initially had lower quality standards.[11] Customers in global markets are likely to look for the best deal anywhere.

Preference Convergence

Because of the soft and impressionistic data that usually underlie a proposal for global marketing, the global marketer needs to develop and present a more qualitative argument in favor of a global approach. The focus should be the degree to which a **convergence of preferences** is under way.

There are at least three important driving points in an analysis of the global convergence of preferences:

1. Recognize that customer preferences are dynamic and changing.
2. A major driver of changing preferences is new products on the market.
3. The new standard-setting products are first introduced and tested in leading markets.

CHANGING PREFERENCES   Much of standard marketing thought is based on the assumption that customer preferences are stable or at least predictable. Most market research is designed to find out what consumers want, not what they might want. Consumers themselves find it hard to articulate what they want. Few people could have conceived of a hand-held calculator before Hewlett-Packard introduced it. New Zealand's Kiwi fruit was not desired until it appeared. Negative surprises such as lack of acceptance of a new product are often ascribed to faulty market research when the real problem lies in changing customer preferences.

This means there is little point arguing whether customers in a particular local market have different preferences from those elsewhere. They do, probably. The appropriate question is, In what way and how fast will these preferences change? To think that the Japanese will never drink wine is the same as assuming Americans will always drive big cars. Sure, there are differences between countries today, but what about tomorrow? When and how did the Americans become the largest market for opera and Brie cheese?[12]

NEW PRODUCTS   There are many drivers of changing preferences. Word-of-mouth, mass communication, usage experiences, and store visits are some of the typical sources of information that change preferences. They have something in common—they all involve exposure to new products. Customer preferences are changed as new products are introduced.

New products make preferences change, especially innovative new products. Where new products are based on assessed customer preferences, they tend to represent only incremental modifications, such as the New Coke or this year's new Buick. Only rarely can customer desires be more than a general guide to new product development. The incrementally modified product can be dominated by a new innovative product that changes customer preferences in unexpected ways. When the sporty new Buick Reatta was introduced in 1988 after painstaking and sophisticated consumer research on desired features, it was quickly derailed by the introduction of the Mazda Miata, a much smaller

Frieda Caplan (center), founder of Frieda's Inc., a wholesaler of exotic fruits and vegetables, is the main person responsible for the introduction and success of New Zealand's kiwi fruit in Western markets. As California growers became major suppliers of kiwi, Frieda's has moved into Asian pears, kiwano melons, and yellow tomatoes, keeping ahead on the growth curve.

© Steve Goldstein.

and less expensive sports coupe that changed the nature of the market. The Miata was designed "on a hunch" by a British racing fan who convinced Mazda's management to take a chance on a new concept.[13]

LEADING MARKETS The new products and marketing programs underlying global marketing do not have to be "shots in the dark," however. When it comes to product specifications, companies use leading markets to identify what features to include—and which to exclude—for their globally uniform product lines. Leading markets can be found in the countries with the most demanding customers and the most advanced technology. For most companies, identifying the leading markets in the industry is easy: It is usually one or two of the largest markets, with the most mature market and most intense competition. In autos, Germany is one leading market; in consumer electronics, Japan; and in computers, the United States.[14]

Leading markets are important in determining which new products will be successful and which company's design will set the next standard. These markets help the global marketer, who can suggest the new designs to the local follower markets. Even though global marketing often involves standardization of a product, this does not mean that the company compromises on features. Rather, the best designs from a leading market, the ones with outstanding ratings on the major salient attributes, are the successful standardized products. This goes for cars, ice cream, movies, computers, hotels, consumer electronics, and many other categories. Scale and scope economies make it possible to offer state-of-the-art features at affordable prices.

Leading markets are not useful to the same degree for the other ingredients of the marketing mix. The analysis to assess which advertising theme can be globalized, for example, is very much a trial-and-error process. Creative ideas that have worked in one country can sometimes be used elsewhere with some adaptation for language and culture. Promotions effective in one place can be candidates for use elsewhere. Most companies content themselves with proto-types of campaigns and promotions, which are then adapted by the local country heads. Whether a particular idea turns out to work or not is often anyone's guess. But rather than emphasize the negative where uniformity has failed, the more surprising thing is that some global campaigns have succeeded "against all odds."

GLOBAL COMPETITIVE ANALYSIS

In addition to the analysis of common customer needs there is, as always, also a need to analyze competition.

The analysis of **global competitors** adds a level of complexity to the analysis of domestic-only competitors. The essence of competitive analysis is the assessment of competitive strength and prediction of competitive moves. The global competitor usually has available a wider repertoire of competitive actions, which makes for a stronger competitor and also makes prediction more difficult.

The standard competitive analysis distinguishes between five different sources of competition: new product substitutes, supplier power, buyer concen-tration, new entrants, and the rivalry between existing competitors.[15] For purposes of the present chapter, the analysis will center on the last two factors. Global competitors are always a threat to enter any local market where they presently might not have a presence. For any company contemplating a global strategy, the main rivalry will usually be with other global companies.

Competitive Strength

Global competitors tend to possess greater financial and other **competitive resources** than other companies, partly because it takes money to go global, but also because their presence in many countries makes it easier to raise funds in the most favorable location. Because of the challenge involved for manage-ment in a global company and the possibility of drawing on a larger pool of talent, the global competitor also tends to have access to better managerial capability. If one also remembers that the global network can be a hidden competitive asset, it is not surprising if local firms need protective legislation to be competitive.

The analysis of competitive strength should also deal with the **strategic intent** of the global competitor in any one particular local market.[16] U.S. firms used to considering North America their primary market should remember that so do many multinational companies from other countries, Sony and Honda from Japan, Volvo and Saab from Sweden, and Unilever and Shell from Europe. When a global competitor enters a certain market its intent is not necessarily profit making, and as we saw in Chapter 4, "Country Attractiveness," the strategic objective can include a number of other goals. Since what matters to a global competitor is usually the total leveraging of the assets invested in the global network, the global firm can accept losses in one or more markets as long as the spillover to other markets is positive. And since the financial strength of the global competitor makes a long-term view feasible, such a company can wait a long time for the turnaround.

Competitive Repertoire

The broadened **competitive repertoire** of the global competitor includes first of all the capability of attacking a competitor in several markets, and, in the same vein, the capability of defending a market by countering elsewhere. The global competitor can also engage in **integrated competitive moves.**[17] For example, selected price wars can be started in a few markets to occupy competitors, while new products are tested and introduced in other markets. This was the tactic used by the Japanese television manufacturers as they moved into Western markets, using their home market as a testing ground for technical innovation. The global competitor can also sequence new product introductions and the roll-out of a new campaign around the globe, maximizing the effect from word-of-mouth and spillover gains from global mass communication.

It is important to recognize that the skilled global competitor does not have to yield much to domestic companies in **local presence**. The global competitor employs natives who gain considerably when the global competitor does well. Honda and Toyota dealerships have been tickets to riches for their American dealers, for example. In most countries the locals who have the territorial distribution rights for global companies such as Dunlop, Coca-Cola, and Caterpillar have done very well.

Finally, it is difficult for a domestic manufacturing company to retain the loyalty of the natives when raw materials, parts, and components are imported from foreign locations. Honda is likely soon to employ more Americans than Chrysler, as Honda strives to become an insider in the United States and Chrysler enlarges its supplier network in Asia.

Marketing Actions

The increased strength and widened repertoire of the global competitor mean that the scope of marketing competition is enlarged. The Kodak–Fuji story is illustrative (see box, "The (Continuous) Kodak–Fuji Battle").

The Kodak–Fuji illustration shows how the global competitor can use its **global network** and its presence in many markets to make surprise competitive

Getting the Picture

The (Continuous) Kodak–Fuji Battle

BY THE EARLY 1980s Fuji film, the Japanese "poor second" competitor to American Kodak, had long tried to make a dent in Kodak's home market. Despite competitive products and successes in Europe and other foreign markets, Fuji had never been able to muster the brand awareness necessary to make it big in America. But in 1984 all that changed. As the Los Angeles Olympic Committee approached Kodak about becoming the "official" film for the 1984 Summer Olympics, Kodak managers vacillated. The potential incremental gains to Kodak awareness and goodwill hardly justified the steep $20 million price tag suggested by Peter Ueberroth, the business-oriented leader of the Olympic Committee. A small notice reporting the conflict in a British newspaper caught the attention of a Fuji manager in London, who promptly telephoned the Fuji U.S. headquarters in New Jersey. Within hours the Fuji home office in Tokyo agreed to offer Ueberroth what he asked, and Fuji became the official sponsor of the Olympics.

The story does not stop there. The Kodak managers realized that their reluctance had inadvertently opened the door for their main global competitor. Their evaluation of the benefits and costs of the sponsorship had failed to take competitive considerations into account. A counterattack seemed necessary, partly to rejuvenate the flagging spirits within the company. Kodak management decided to launch a marketing offensive in Japan, Fuji's home market stronghold. Developing a revamped but still recognizably "Kodak yellow" package with Japanese print, and capitalizing on a superior new "200" film, Kodak saturated Tokyo with street giveaways and storefront displays. The full-court press worked. Fuji had to refocus its energies from the U.S. market and protect its home turf by matching the new film and its promotions (and as we saw in Chapter 9, this was done successfully by working closely with channel members, even though the methods used are being challenged by Kodak).

Sources: Johansson & Segerfeldt, 1987; *Washington Post*, June 26, 1995, p. A12.

moves. *Global advertising* is also a competitive weapon that can pay off nicely for the global company. The Coca-Cola experience in Russia is an example. Pepsi-Cola, its arch rival, scored a coup in the 1970s when President Nixon helped Pepsi get the lone license to bottle cola in the Soviet Union. When the Russian market opened up after the fall of the Berlin Wall, Coca-Cola had to come from far behind to catch up with ensconced Pepsi. Using globally broadcast commercials on satellite TV emphasizing "The Real Thing" and saturating advertising on CNN's global news channel, Coca-Cola established itself as the cola of the new times and relegated Pepsi to inferior status as an almost domestic Russian brand, reminiscent of the communist past. Within months, Coca-Cola had captured chunks of market share from Pepsi.[18]

Global competitors can elect in which markets to battle a competitor. They can elect how to attack a dominant shareholder in a given market. Global competitors need always to be taken into account even when they are not yet present in a given market or segment. Defending against global competitors can involve some deft maneuvering and some loss-leading efforts where company actions are by themselves unprofitable. The aim is often to neutralize the global threat.

For example, Esco, a small American manufacturer of components and replacement parts for earth-moving machinery, has long had a licensing agreement with Mitsubishi Heavy Industries, a large company member of the Mitsubishi keiretsu in Japan. Rather than attempting to enter Japan and sell to Komatsu, Kubota, and Caterpillar Japan, Esco has ceded the market to Mitsubishi. Despite the drawbacks, the contract allows Esco to keep a check on Mitsubishi and its possible expansion into Asian markets where Esco is strong. For example, as the contract was renegotiated in the late 1980s, Esco lowered its royalties claim and the control it exercises over actual sales in order to maintain the prohibitions against Mitsubishi sales in Korea and other Asian countries. The alternative was to cancel the licensing agreement, which would have opened the door for Mitsubsihi to go abroad—using technology learned from Esco to start with. Anticipating similar problems in the future, Esco has since engaged in a policy of creating much stronger ties with its Asian distributors, a process that means the company is becoming more and more global.

THE LIMITS TO GLOBALIZED MARKETING

Even though there might be a trend toward more global markets and toward globalized strategies, it is important to keep in mind that global is not always the right answer.

When Not to Use Global Marketing

There are three important points to realize about globalized marketing:[19]

1. Not all industries have the right characteristics for a global strategy.
2. Not all companies have the required resources (managerial, financial) to implement global marketing effectively.
3. Not all marketing mix activities lend themselves to a global treatment.

INDUSTRY FACTORS   The conditions under which the industry operates may not be supportive of a global approach. That is, the four "globalization drivers" discussed in Chapter 1 (market, competition, cost, and government) may not be conducive to a global approach. In particular, lack of homogeneous markets and persistent differences in customer preferences across countries may prohibit globalization of marketing.

INTERNAL RESOURCES   Even if the aim is cost savings because of less duplication and larger scale in production, instituting a global marketing strategy requires some financial resources up front for the necessary investment in advertising prototypes, benchmark designs, and global communication capabilities. Even more importantly, it requires managers with international experience, patience, and administrative skills to deal with the unavoidable managerial conflicts and threats against morale at local units. It is partly because of the increased complexity of the global marketing manager's job that a stint abroad is necessary for today's manager. The organizational requirements of a global marketing strategy will be dealt with in Chapter 17.

DIFFERENT MIXES   Usually, not all marketing mix activities can—or should be—globalized to the same extent. While product design can often be uniform across several countries, language and cultural barriers make it difficult to standardize salesmanship. Regulations about allowable in-store promotions and the extent to which independent dealers will cooperate still vary across countries, making uniform promotions difficult even as media advertising beamed via satellites is standardized. For example, the usual tie-ins for contests ("Look for details at your local dealer") have to be scrapped in countries where the dealers refuse to cooperate.

Differentiated Globalization

Consequently, a global marketing strategy that totally globalizes all marketing activities is not always achievable or desirable. A more common approach is for a company to globalize its product strategy by marketing the same product lines, product designs, and brand names everywhere but to localize distribution and marketing communications. This is the standard approach in consumer durables such as automobiles, cameras, and electronics. By contrast, consumer packaged goods companies have often gone further in their globalization effort, with worldwide ad campaigns and frequent in-store promotions in addition to a standardized product line.

Studies of the extent to which successful companies' marketing mix activities are globalized have revealed a fairly consistent pattern. A company's packaging and brand names are most likely to be globalized, followed by its media message and distribution; activities become, more localized for in-store promotions, and the pattern ends with very localized personal selling and customer service functions.[20] This pattern holds for American as well as Japanese and European firms. A firm's global marketing strategy has to be flexibly implemented and take account of the different degrees to which the activities need local adaptation and personnel. Canadian and Japanese customers may prefer the same automobile, for example, but they may have different needs when it comes to after-sales support because of the different conditions of use in the two countries.

In general, the closer a marketing mix activity is to the point of purchase or after-sales service, the more need for customization. The coining of the term **global localization,** which has become a new code word in marketing strategy, is a recognition of the fact that the marketing job is not finished until products and services are used and consumed.

Two examples from a global ad campaign for the Visa card, one for Latin America and one for North America, drawing on the company's Olympic sponsorship. By judiciously selecting the featured sports, the ad can work well in a number of countries.
Courtesy of Visa International.

Stated another way, while strategy *formulation* and *implementation* may be globalized, strategy *execution* has to be local. "What" to do and "how" to do it can follow uniform plans and guidelines, but "doing it" requires that one "speak the local language." This is why the expatriates who serve as general managers in the local foreign subsidiaries of various global companies rarely get into the action but serve more as figureheads and headquarters liaisons. For example, the management style called MBWA, management by walking around, which directly affects strategy execution, can be counterproductive when language and cultural differences prohibit effective personal communication between top managers and local employees. Even a global marketing strategy needs to keep execution local.

Some Pitfalls of Global Marketing

Because of one factor or another bearing on whether a global marketing strategy will be successful, some global campaigns have failed. By systematically comparing winning and losing campaigns, one researcher found that five factors explain why global campaigns fail:[21]

1. Insufficient market research.
2. Overstandardization.
3. Poor follow-up.
4. Narrow vision.
5. Rigid implementation.

INSUFFICIENT MARKET RESEARCH   Good marketing research helps a global strategy in two ways: by identifying commonalities but also differences across markets and by winning support from the local organizations involved in the research. By contrast, insufficient research means not only that similarities among customers are assumed rather than proven but also that the local subsidiaries feel stepped on. For example, when Polaroid introduced its path-breaking SX-70 camera in Europe, the company employed the same advertising strategy—including TV commercials and print ads—it had used in its triumphant launch in the United States. When the local Polaroid executives protested that TV testimonials from unknown people would not be very useful for consumer perceptions in Europe and asked for a chance to do more research on possible replacements, headquarters refused. The subsequent lack of awareness and acceptance of the camera in Europe did not come as a surprise to the disenchanted local heads.

OVERSTANDARDIZATION   Even though many technologically intensive products lend themselves to standardization, the same is not necessarily true of their positioning. The Canon AE-1 camera, the first automatic single-lens reflex camera introduced in the mid-1970s, was first positioned as an expert's choice in all markets. After a less than successful entry, the company decided to gamble and reposition it as a fun camera in the United States, taking on the then prevailing 110 standard Kodak camera. TV commercials were used, the first time ever for a single-lens reflex camera, using as a spokesman tennis player John Newcombe. The success of the new strategy led the company to reposition the camera in other markets as well, creating a much larger market for single-lens reflex cameras worldwide.

POOR FOLLOW-UP   Impressive kickoff meetings, splashy presentations to country heads, and the personal appearance of the CEO are important attention-getters at the start of a global campaign. But these efforts need to be followed up diligently by communications, visits, and local effort if the campaign is to succeed. When, for example, after the German company Henkel to great fanfare launched a global campaign for its stick glue brand "Pritt" as an umbrella brand for related products, it failed to capitalize on the initial momentum. Instead of supplying extra resources and incentives to local units the company left the implementation to be covered under the normal budget, forcing country heads to cut existing programs. Needless to say, as initial results proved weak, the resources were quickly reallocated back to existing brands.[22]

NARROW VISION There are two main approaches to organizing global campaigns. One is to direct the campaign from headquarters, the other to designate a lead country, usually an important market for the product. Both approaches have their strengths, the main advantage of each being the clear focus of responsibility. However, the vision at the headquarters or in the lead country should not be narrow and inflexible. When Unilever introduced a new household cleaner, "Domestos," in the pan-European market, the UK unit took on the lead role for global implementation. The problem was that the product was most successful in West Germany, where the local subsidiary had shifted the positioning from a "germ killer" to a "dirt remover." But this change in positioning was ignored by the UK organization, and its potential was lost, since other countries' organizations were not informed of it.

RIGID IMPLEMENTATION When uniformity of marketing programs is dictated from the center, there needs to be some flexibility in implementation retained by local units. Although not all local requests for deviations need to be accepted, shrewd managerial judgment is required to judge how far to go. Even though differences in customer preferences may be malleable, competitive differences may require local adaptability. When the U.S. subsidiary of Lego reported that an American competitor, Tyco, offered toys in a plastic bucket that could be easily used for storing the toys and requested to be allowed to replace its existing paperboard cartons with similar buckets, the Danish headquarters refused. After a two-year slide in market share, the headquarters finally relented. The Lego toys are now sold in buckets worldwide.

GLOBAL LOCALIZATION

As we have seen, globalizing marketing typically involves some kind of standardization, maintaining a degree of *uniformity* in product, or advertising, or distribution or other marketing mix elements across country markets. But globalization is broader than simply standardization of marketing programs. It involves *global coordination* of marketing activities, regardless of degree of uniformity. It involves taking a *global management perspective* on the operations in any one country, including the home country, making decisions to the benefit of the global system and not just one country's operation.

Today, there are some firms that still adhere to complete global standardization—Gillette, the razor blade manufacturer, is one, as we showed. However, most new globalized marketing solutions tend to be more limited, tempering the desire for uniformity and cost savings with a recognition that ours is not yet one world. Some firms, such as Goodyear, Procter and Gamble, and Volvo, have been successful with *pan-regional* standardization of marketing programs, using trading blocs as natural market areas with sufficient size to ensure the scale advantages can be achieved. Even when marketing is globalized or "regionalized," some room is left for local adaptation. Cars are assembled from common components or "platforms" with variations unique to each market. Globalized advertising campaigns revolve around commercials as prototypes that can be adapted, or, pattern standardization with guidelines for how new advertisements may be created. Pattern standardization lays down the basic idea—the platform, the prototype, and the theme—around which local adaptation can be pursued.

Two factors have been instrumental in the shift of focus from global uniformity to global localization. One is the fact that increasing affluence in the world's markets has been accompanied by an increase in diversity of preferences. Markets have surely become more similar, as Levitt suggested, and one is likely to find a lot of commonality between, say, the young-family segments in different countries. But at the same time, at least at the upper end, the local markets have become fragmented, affluent young families not all wanting the same things. This should not be so surprising, since increasing affluence tends to generate a desire for variety and uniqueness.[23] It means that standardized products need to be aimed at smaller, localized segments of the market.

A second factor reinforcing the new trend toward more local input to the marketing program is that overseas affiliates today often comprehend the world-wide nature of their business. With advances in global communications, increasing cross-cultural awareness, and more obvious interdependencies between the countries of the world, managements at local subsidiaries are more aware of how developments elsewhere affect the local markets and can be both willing and able to adopt a global perspective.[24] With today's rapid diffusion of information, local managers are even likely to regard the parent's business as their business and to know a great deal about other units in the global network. It is no longer necessary to assume that the local manager is only parochially interested in his or her unit's survival. Consequently, the global manager can allow more room for local autonomy and help the spreading of useful new ideas that come from locals throughout the network. The best ideas for standardization of the various marketing mix elements may in fact come from foreign subsidiaries, especially those in leading markets.[25]

As long as free trade and free market fundamentals stay in place throughout the world, globalized marketing will be an important option. Standardization through uniform marketing mix elements is always going to be one main component of a globalization strategy. But standardized products or promotions need to be localized to appeal to some subsegments of the total market; scale economies will be gained by targeting similar segments across countries in the trading bloc or (in special cases) across the globe. And the standardized offering is as likely to come from a subsidiary as from the center.

SPECIAL CASE: PAN-EUROPEAN MARKETING[26]

The 1992 European integration stimulated many companies to analyze the potential of **pan-European marketing** strategies. Although pan-European marketing is not truly "global," the experiences of companies in the EU demonstrate many of the problems and opportunities associated with globalizing marketing.

Background

The decision in 1986 to establish a single European market within the EU by 1992 led to a completely changed strategic environment for most businesses, European and others. Tariff barriers and customs duties were scrapped and goods and labor were to move freely between countries. Product standards would be harmonized between countries. Cumbersome border controls were abolished and a common European passport was created. Commercial vehicles needed a single loading document for shipments across Europe where before each country had its own set of documents and standards. The resulting savings were estimated at $5.8 billion. National price controls were to be eliminated, helping to create a large and unified market with competitive prices. Cars were estimated to be reduced in price by 13 percent in France, 4 percent in Germany. Prices on electric equipment were projected to come down an average of 15 percent in most countries. The increased trade and competition would foster higher productivity and an increased standard of living. A common figure quoted was that the average GDP in EU countries would be given a 5 percent boost.

Although not all the national differences in regulations were eliminated by the 1992 deadline, EU has moved steadily closer to a fully integrated marketplace. The 1989 fall of the Berlin Wall slowed down the momentum toward EU unity as the question of Eastern European countries' membership took precedence. Rather than moving ever closer to full political union and a single currency, EU has instead began expanding its membership by positively encouraging Eastern European affiliations and new members from former

Heineken's alcohol-free beer Buckler is an example of a new product designed as pan-European from the start. With Holland's strong reputation in beers, plus the cachet of imported beers overall, the positioning is clearly premium.

© Michael J. Hruby.

European Free Trade Association (EFTA) countries. Even though full economic and political integration still seems elusive, Europe is steadily becoming
a very large single market approaching 400 million consumers.

Needless to say, for many of the large multinational companies with a
long-established presence in a fragmented Europe, the changes have presented
an exciting challenge. In addition to the need to coordinate marketing strategy
(segmentation and positioning) and tactics (the marketing mix) across EU,
there have been questions about the appropriate organizational structure to
implement the changes. Paradoxically, the challenge has been greatest for the
European companies themselves.

Organizational Response

The proposed integration forced large European corporations to start coordinating previously independent national operations. Partly for historical reasons,
with great wars having been fought between neighboring countries, the
European multinationals had often allowed their separate national operations a
great deal of autonomy. The EU integration, in fact, aimed to minimize the risk
of such wars in the future. But for the companies, the new rules meant that
national subsidiaries had to be given stronger central direction to gain the
projected savings from eliminating unnecessarily costly national differences in
product designs, brand names, and promotions. It also meant that smaller
plants in local countries would be closed and more efficient larger scale units
created. With decades, even centuries of hostility between countries, all this was
no easy task.

By contrast, many large non-European companies were unburdened by old
and outdated affiliations and practices. With an existing manufacturing foothold in the EU market and global brand name recognition, many were well
placed to take advantage of the integrative opportunities, be they low-cost labor
in Italy, financial problems for middle-sized business as in Austria needing
solutions, or no-longer-protected electronics businesses in France. It looked as
if the creation of the single market would benefit non-European companies
most.

For smaller European companies—and even the many large firms—the
threat from these foreign entrants had to be met by the creation of larger and
stronger companies. The result was a spate of mergers and acquisitions. Stella
Artois and Jupiler, the two dominant Belgian beer brewers, merged. Heineken
in Holland bought Amstel. German Siemens, the large maker of electronic
machinery, bought Nixdorff, a computer maker. Asea, in the large-scale power
transmission business, bought Brown-Boveri, a Swiss competitor. Virgin
Records in London bought FNAC, a French retail firm. Where acquisitions
failed or were disallowed, alliances were formed. German Lufthansa agreed
with United Airlines to share routes and frequent fliers. Similarly, Swiss Air,
Caledonia, and SAS agreed to cooperate. In fact, at the corporate level, there
seemed to be only one strategic response possible for European firms: Get

bigger and go pan-European. The response of large European retailers is one case in point. Exhibit 11.2 shows some of the retailer alliances entered into.[27] As the exhibit shows, the alliances tend to be initiated by organizations based in the larger markets, such as Germany and France. These retailers are more likely to have the financial and managerial resources required to go pan-European.

By the end of the 1980s most of the foreign as well as the European multinational firms had established representation in Brussels from which to monitor and lobby the EU Commission and its deliberations. Companies wanted a say in formulating the new regulations, and non-European firms used their existing European plants to argue that they were also "European insiders." American firms added staff in their European subsidiaries and positioned "Europe-watchers" at headquarters. Japanese companies tried to decide whether a full-fledged European subsidiary was necessary and where to locate it. While Toyota made do with an enlarged presence in Brussels, Nissan established European headquarters in Amsterdam to be close to port and warehousing facilities and thus be able to coordinate a pan-European approach better. But most Japanese companies established European headquarters in the English countryside, where language and simple village customs made the transition from Japan easier.

Within Europe the Americans shifted and centralized responsibilities. Ford pulled some of the decision-making power from country heads to its European headquarters in Dagenham outside London. Product design responsibilities were centralized, and pan-European design teams were assembled in Dagenham. Financial controls and reporting back to headquarters in Dearborn, Michigan, were tightened up by a new European head, sent in from the United States. The head of Ford Werke AG in Cologne quit rather than lose power.

Rather than centralizing decision-making power within Europe, the Honeywell corporation, manufacturer of electronic measurement devices and computer controls, decided to adopt a **distributed headquarters** model with each country organization taking the European lead in certain functions. The French unit would focus on R&D, the British would handle the marketing, and the Germans would handle the existing customer support and service functions. This reorganization met with some resistance. The Xerox corporation was able to attract some of the top German development engineers from Honeywell to its German subsidiary in Duesseldorf. The Germans did not want to relocate to France and play second fiddle to the French.

The European distribution networks of most companies came under close scrutiny. With border controls eased, transportation was speedier and local warehousing capability of parts and final products became less critical. Large-scale dealer units, which could offer representation in several countries supplied from a central warehouse, promised to save manufacturers a lot of money on sales contacts, order-filling, and invoicing. Again, the contemplated rationalizations were met with resistance. Pioneer, the Japanese audio products company with European headquarters in Antwerp, Belgium, decided to buy out the independent dealers in three countries so the savings could be realized.

....
EXHIBIT 11.2   Pan-European Retailers

Retailer expansion		Cross-border alliances	
Name (origin country; turnover $billion)	**Countries active in**	**Group (turnover $billion)**	**Member (countries)**
Tengelmann (Germany) ($25)	Austria; France; Italy; GB; Germany; Netherlands	European Retail Alliance ($24)	Ahold (NL); Argyll (Safeway) (GB); Casino (F)
Metro (Germany/Switzerland) ($25)	Switzerland; Germany; Netherlands; (also GB; France; Italy; Denmark; Belgium; Greece; Spain; Portugal; Turkey)	Associated Marketing Services ($52)	Ahold (NL); Argyll (GB); Casino (F); Dansk (DK); Hagen (N); ICA (S); Kesko (SF); Rina-Scente (L); Mercadona (E); Migros (Gr)
Carrefour (France) ($13)	France; Switzerland; Spain	EMD ($60)	Markant (D, NL); Selex (I, E); Uniarme (I); Socadip (F); Euromarche (F); AS-ECOL (F); Baud (F); Codec-UNA (F); Nouvelles Gal (F)
Auchan (France) ($11)	Germany; Belgium; Netherlands; Denmark; France; GB; Austria; Spain; Italy	Spar/Bigs ($26)	Spar cooperatives (D, GB, DK, A, I); Unigro (NL); Dagels (S); Tuko (SF); Unil (N)
Promodes (France) ($10)	France; Germany; Spain; Italy; Portugal	Deuro Buying ($42)	Metro (D, CH); Makro (NL); Asda (GB); Carrefour (F)
		Eurogroup ($48)	GIB (B); Vandex (NL); Rewe (D); Coop (CH); Paridoc (F)

A = Austria
CH = Switzerland
D = Germany
DK = Denmark
E = Spain
F = France
GB = Great Britain

Gr = Greece
I = Italy
L = Luxembourg
N = Norway
NL = Netherlands
S = Sweden
SF = Finland

Source: Halliburton and Huenerberg, 1993, p. 89. Reprinted by permission of Michigan State University Press.

Rather than antagonize the heads of the independent country dealer units, Volvo's Penta unit, a manufacturer of boat engines, involved them in the rationalizations and attempted to create informal as well as formal linkages between the individual heads. The appeal was obvious: When a prospective buyer of a boat engine can travel from Barcelona to Marseilles in less than three hours, buy a Penta engine, and bring it back across the border with no customs duty, the Spanish and the French organizations are forced to coordinate whether they like it or not.

The integration became a boon for the large multinational advertising agencies, which could represent clients in all of the new Europe. The big American agencies—J. W. Thompson, Young & Rubicam, BBD&O, and especially McCann-Erickson with the largest international network of all—were already well positioned with European representation in all large centers, including London, Paris, and Frankfurt. In many cases they transferred staff from existing operations to centralized locations, in particular to Brussels, which became a center of advertising activity. A new BBD&O office in Brussels with 15 professionals, for example, was started by staff from its London operation, English rather than French being the lingua franca of the advertising world even in Europe.

But European agencies did not sit still. Instead, they attacked with the same weapon used by their European manufacturing counterparts—mergers and acquisitions. Saatchi & Saatchi, a small London agency, became the largest agency in the world by taking over Ted Bates, an American agency. Later it was overtaken as number one by Interpublic's acquisition of J. W. Thompson. As other European and American agencies merged or were acquired in their efforts to go global and big, the agency business became increasingly concentrated. Typically the acquired units were left intact, with only limited change of personnel and some imposition of financial controls. Even though some of these large units have since been dissolved, most European and American ad agencies are today able to execute pan-European advertising and promotion.

Strategic Response

As most companies developed organizational capability for a pan-European strategy, the businesses' segmentation and positioning plans followed predictably. Europeanwide target segments were identified and targeted. Pan-European product designs and marketing communications were created to achieve the same synergistic positioning in all countries.

On the *segmentation* side, the experience of Volvo Trucks, one of the largest truck manufacturers in the world, is instructive.[28] Before the integration, segmentation of the European market had been localized and specific to each country. It had been up to the marketing manager of each country subsidiary to develop a segmentation scheme for the customers in that country. Because each country had special traffic regulations and transportation laws, there had been no effort to use the same segmentation scheme elsewhere. The only criterion common across countries was the carrying capacity—large trucks above 16 tons, medium-sized trucks between 10 and 16 tons, and small trucks under 10 tons. This division was dictated by Volvo's manufacturing plants, but served no particular marketing purpose.

As the single market demanded greater market orientation, Volvo commissioned market research that would lead to a more in-depth market segmentation scheme that could be used across countries. The research helped to identify different customer segments based not only on tonnage transported but also usage situation, type of shipment, and differences in performance criteria. The usage situation discriminated between urban and long-haul transportation, allowing the company to develop special features (such as small turning radius) useful in Europe's narrow streets. Identifying common types of shipment (heavy machinery versus electronic components, for example) allowed the company to add certain loading features. Differences in performance criteria, such as speed versus fuel efficiency, helped salespeople advise the customer which engine options to choose. These segmentation criteria were "portable" between countries, allowing the company to run a series of training and support sessions where the local managers and sales staff were shown how the segmentation scheme could be adapted to help their operation.

This same shift to a pan-European market segmentation focused around the customer has taken place in many other European markets as companies find it worthwhile to analyze and target the enlarged customer base in the single market. Positioning has followed suit, partly by sheer force of the drive to a single market. There are very few products today that can maintain different images in different countries of Europe. Whereas before French wine might have been expensive, associated with a high-status image in some high-tax European countries, today most Europeans judge French wine as the French themselves do—by drinking it. Germany has had to relax its ban on artificial ingredients in beer, leaving its market open for Carlsberg, Budweiser, Molson, and other foreign beers and allowing its outstanding German beers to stand out—and the other German beers to falter.

Before integration a product such as Swatch might have had different images in different European countries; now gradually the differences are between cross-border segments, not nations. In pan-European marketing, product positioning is the same across countries, but different product lines or models target different customer segments. There are Swatches for upscale consumers and for teenagers, for business and for play. Similarly, there are different clothes, foods, drinks, for these segments. These segments are not limited by nationality.

One researcher has identified six basic segments, with another four groupings added as the EU expands.[29] As can be seen from Exhibit 11.3, these clusters of countries form large markets by themselves, making it possible to gain many scale advantages without necessarily operating across the whole EU region.

EXHIBIT 11.3 Six Basic Plus Four Potential European Segments

> *Cluster 1.* United Kingdom and Irish Republic (total population 60.350 million)
>
> *Cluster 2.* France, French-speaking Belgium, and Switzerland (total population 54.518 million)
>
> *Cluster 3.* Iberian Peninsula (total population 56.363 million)
>
> *Cluster 4.* Italy and Italian-speaking Switzerland (total population 71.498 million)
>
> *Cluster 5.* South Mediterranean, including Greece, southern Italy, and Island of Sardinia (total population 31.252 million)
>
> *Cluster 6.* Northern Europe and the Scandinavian Peninsula including the northern part of Germany, Flemish-speaking Belgium, The Netherlands, Denmark, Sweden, Norway, and Finland (total population 57.618 million; if former East Germany is added to this cluster, the total population will be 74.242 million)
>
> *Cluster 7.* East European countries: present Czechoslovakia, Hungary, and Poland (total population 63.771 million)
>
> *Cluster 8.* Balkan states: Turkey, Albania, Bulgaria, old Yugoslav Republics, Romania, Moldova, Cyprus, and Malta (total population 113.142 million)
>
> *Cluster 9.* Black Sea region: Russian Federation, Ukraine and Caucasian states (Armenia, Azerbaijan, Georgia) (total population 205.729 million)
>
> *Cluster 10.* Baltic region: Lithuania, Estonia, Bylerus, and Latvia (total population 17.767 million)

Source: Dalgic, 1992, p. 37.

But a pan-European strategic response is not necessarily the correct approach for all companies in all industries. Given the right industry and company conditions, there is also opportunity in niche strategies. Research has shown three viable strategic alternatives, given in Exhibit 11.4.[30] Some companies have actually benefited by simply retreating from the market, cashing in on the existing brand and company equity and allocating funds elsewhere. More common, the alternative to a pan-European approach is to seek out a niche, or create one. Since the unification of Europe in economic terms has not been accompanied by a similar unification in terms of politics and national borders, there will undoubtedly be good opportunities for smaller firms who wish to cater to ethnic tastes and traditional preferences.

Tactical Response

The marketing mixes of the European marketers have moved toward uniformity as the pan-European strategies are implemented.

Many companies have attempted to develop pan-European products and brands. One of the earliest examples was Procter and Gamble's "Vizir" brand name for a new liquid detergent, whose development process and success record have been used as a model for other similar efforts.[31] The lead country

....
EXHIBIT 11.4 Three Strategic Options

Options	Strategies	Remarks
1. Market retreat	• Sell out to pan-European player (example Nabisco) • Seek a different, less-competitive market (example Nokia Data)	• May be preferable to a stuck-in-the-middle position
2. Pan-European competition	• Identify true pan-European market segments (example Perrier) • Organic penetration from existing national markets (example Pilkington) • Aggressive policy of acquisitions to complete European portfolio (example BSN) • Cooperation with other national players to form pan-European organizations (example Carnaud-Metal box) or alliances (example European Retailers Association)	• May be few true segments • Excessive time required • Few winners • Complex and risky but increasingly important in "post-1992" Europe
3. Niche position	• Consolidate national position through realignment, merger, or acquisition (example Mannesmann-VDO) • Identify new Euro-regions • Identify segments across limited number of countries (example Campbells Biscuits) • Seek economies at component level while retaining niche brands (example Electrolux) • Become an OEM supplier to pan-European companies	• Vulnerable to standardized Euro-products if national differences are marginal • Information access • Need to accumulate scale benefits • Organizational complexity • Vulnerable to pan-European EOM suppliers)

Source: Halliburton and Huenerberg, 1993, p. 85. Reprinted by permission of Michigan State University Press.

for Vizir was Germany, with the biggest market and the most promising test results. A global product team was organized with representatives from several European countries. Despite difficulties with cross-country coordination of introductions, delays by headquarters back in Cincinnati, and uneven support from the various country heads, the launch was a success in most countries (even though the delays allowed Henkel, the main German competitor, to catch up quickly with a me-too product).

Today such Euro-brands are common and are becoming global. And even though brand names may vary because of language differences (the Snuggle fabric softener comes with at least 15 different brand names), the product itself may be identical across countries. Most packaged goods in Europe feature packaging in at least four languages: English, French, German, and Spanish. Euro-designs of durable products are also common. France's Thomson, Italy's Olivetti, and Swedish Electrolux have long designed household appliances and office products aimed primarily at the European market. But now other companies follow suit. In its Bordeaux plant Pioneer makes loudspeakers with a European design (thinner, sharper lines); Sony make some design alterations for the European market with slimmer and elongated shapes and less flashy colors; the Mercedes product line in Europe has more models than in the United States, making finer discriminations in the intermediate range; Japanese camera makers make their European product lines unique by adding a few features demanded by customers and deleting other features (partly to enable the companies to control the gray European trade in cameras from Hong Kong and the United States).

Another striking development is the increasing use of pan-European TV advertising, taking advantage of the satellites beamed across previously closed borders. As public ownership of TV broadcasting lessens and commercial air time is made available, even previously "protected" countries such as Norway and Sweden are exposed to the same mass media messages as the British, the French, and the Italians, who have long had commercial TV. Language differences are overcome by limiting copy to voiceovers, making it possible to quickly adapt a given commercial to broadcasting in a different language. This allows the local branches of the agency handling the Honda account to use the same commercial everywhere. Coca-Cola does not need many words to put across its message, and in some cases even the American English stays intact. The satellite channels feature commercials with a limited number of words, usually English. To appeal to the many different nationalities with a common theme, American Clairol uses rapid scans over pictures of women from easily recognized places in Europe, all using the same Clairol shampoo.

In addition to the rationalization of the manufacturers' sales network, retail and wholesale distribution is gradually being transformed, from locally based smaller units, to large integrated organizations resembling those common in North America. The French hypermarket chain, Carrefour, has expanded throughout the EU, as have Standa's Italian-based Euromercatos. Marks & Spencer, Britain's clothing chain, is developing a pan-European presence.

Belgium's Delhaize supermarket chain is attempting to expand using mergers and acquisitions in addition to new store investments. Germany's Kaufhof department store chain is also developing a pan-European strategy.

These new large units help facilitate the introduction of pan-European strategies among manufacturers. The savings created through large centralized negotiations between the manufacturer and a large distribution chain are well known in the American marketplace but are relatively new in Europe. From a marketing viewpoint, this development is likely to generate the same kind of interest in, and need for, more relationship marketing as it has in the United States.

Other tactical marketing mix decisions are also being adapted to the new reality. Pan-European pricing is a particularly complicated issue because of its antitrust implications, the floating exchange rates, and the direct effect on domestic competitors. Companies need to—and want to—lower the price differentials on their products in different countries to avoid the gray trade complications, with exported products reimported to take advantage of changes in exchange rates and differences in price levels between countries. But long-standing practices are not easily changed, especially since in many protected local markets the high prices have made some products cash cows for the distributor. Astra, the Swedish pharmaceutical company, is faced with controlled prices in many markets, with governments reimbursing patients' medical expenses. But if, because of these controls, its drugs can be bought less expensively in some countries, there is nothing to prohibit massive purchase by a foreign pharmacy for resale at higher prices. Telecommunication equipment manufacturers face similar complications, as in the case of Finnish Nokia and Swedish Eriksson. More will be said about the pricing problems in Chapter 13, Global Pricing.

The Future

After the fall of the Berlin Wall, some of the pan-European marketing efforts have been slowed down while firms try to assess the opportunity in the East. Because of the slow economic growth and the subsequent political problems there, the outlook for Eastern Europe is still unclear and it is not easy to foresee what will happen. But the drive toward the single market is well under way, and will only be reinforced by the success of the companies with pan-European strategies.

SUMMARY

Global strategies are increasingly necessary as free-trade regions proliferate, markets grow more similar, and international competition grows more intense. Global marketing

management involves coordination of tactical marketing mix decisions, strategic decisions about segmentation and positioning, and the development of organizational capabilities to effectively implement global marketing.

The analysis justifying a global marketing program involves managerial intuition and imagination. It is important to recognize that global markets often emerge when prodded by new product entries. Even though markets are multidomestic today, with different local preferences, such things do not stay constant.

Global competitors have several advantages over domestic-only firms. They tend to be stronger in terms of financial resources. They have experience operating in several countries, building the capability of their managers. They can select where and how to initiate an attack or to counter an attack. Analyzing such competitors involves identifying their strategic intent and their competitive repertoire, recognizing that actions in one local market are conditioned on the role of the market in the competitor's global strategy.

Depending on customer requirements, tastes, and industry conditions, different marketing activities will sustain different levels of standardization. Not all firms need to globalize their marketing activities, and even for the increasing number of firms that do, not all marketing activities should be standardized to the same extent. There are numerous examples of firms' global marketing failing because the industry and market fundamentals were wrong or because the global program did not generate enough organizational commitment or involve the country subsidiaries in strategy formulation.

KEY TERMS

Competitive repertoire p. 413
Competitive resources p. 412
Differentiated globalization p. 416
Distributed headquarters p. 423
Global communications p. 407
Global competitors p. 412
Global localization p. 416

Global markets p. 405
Global network p. 413
Homogeneity of markets p. 407
Integrated competitive moves p. 413
Local presence p. 413
Pan-European marketing p. 420

Pitfalls of global marketing p. 417
Preference convergence p. 410
Scale economies p. 401
Scope economies p. 401
Strategic intent p. 412
Technology diffusion p. 407

DISCUSSION QUESTIONS

1. What are the major reasons for the increasing need to globalize marketing strategies?

2. How can you extend the traditional market analysis to deal with (*a*) changing customer preferences and (*b*) new global competitors?

3. Identify three product categories for which you think the markets are global. What mar-

ket data would you need to support your assertion?

4. Identify three brands that seem to be backed by successful global marketing strategies. Can you find three brands which would *not* be promising candidates for globalization?

5. What are the typical causes of global marketing failure?

NOTES

1. See Douglas and Craig, 1989.

2. This section draws on Buzzell, 1968, and Yip, 1992.

3. See Carpano and Chrisman, 1995.

4. See Samiee and Roth, 1992.

5. The discussions following Levitt's 1983 article followed this line of attack. For an alternative counterpoint, however, see Boddewyn et al., 1986.

6. The term "multidomestic" was first proposed by Hout et al., 1982.

7. This list draws on Yip's original work, 1992.

8. Adapted from Kashani, 1992.

9. See note 5 above.

10. This example comes from Halliburton and Jones, 1994.

11. From a personal interview with Mr. H. Ahnefeld, Corporate Planning, Bosch A.G., Stuttgart, January 17, 1989.

12. These and similar changes are reported every day in television news programs and print media. A good data source for up-to-date market information on spending patterns is the *Global Scan* publication from Bates Worldwide, and other sources listed in Chapters 4 and 8.

13. The Reatta case discussion is from Urban & Star, 1991 and the Mazda Miata information from a class project report by H. Schumpert, Georgetown University, Spring 1992.

14. From Johansson and Roehl, 1994.

15. See Porter, 1980.

16. The emphasis on strategic intent was first suggested by Hamel and Prahalad, 1989.

17. From Yip, 1992.

18. From *The New York Times*, May 11, 1995, pp. D1, D9.

19. This section draws on Quelch and Hoff, 1986, and Yip, 1992.

20. See Johansson and Yip, 1994.

21. From Kashani, 1989.

22. From Robert J. Dolan, "Henkel Group: Umbrella Branding and Globalization Decisions," Harvard Business School case no. 585-185, 1985.

23. For example, in mature Western markets one-to-one database marketing has become a way of targeting single households and individuals, important when tastes differ between individuals. (Halliburton and Jones, 1994).

24. This enhanced global awareness on the part of the local managers has resulted in a shift in the power balance between headquarters at the center and the local subsidiaries (Hanni et al., 1995). This impacts the organizational structure of the globalizing firm, as we will see in Chapter 17.

25. This is the perspective adopted by Bartlett and Ghoshal, 1989, in their book on the "transnational" organization. A good example of how the subsidiaries can generate superior ideas for standardization is the "ultrathin" disposable diaper from Pampers, which was developed by Procter & Gamble's Japanese subsidiary.

26. This section is based on Cecchini, 1988; on Quelch et al., 1991; on Johansson, 1989; and on updated material from various newspaper sources.

27. From Halliburton and Huenerberg, 1993.

28. From "Volvo Trucks Europe," case no. 17 in Kashani, 1992.

29. See Dalgic, 1992.

30. From Halliburton and Huenerberg, 1993.

31. See Bartlett, 1983.

SELECTED REFERENCES

Albrecht, Karl. *The Only Thing That Matters*. New York: Harper Business, 1992.

Axelsson, Bjorn; Jan Johanson; and Johan Sundberg. "Managing by International Traveling." Chapter 7 in Forsgren, Mats, and Jan Johanson, eds. *Managing Net-*works in International Business. Philadelphia: Gordon and Breach, 1992.

Baden-Fuller, Charles W. F., & John M. Stopford. "Globalization Frustrated: The Case of White Goods." *Strategic Management Journal* 12 (1991), pp. 493–507.

Bartlett, Christopher A. "Procter & Gamble Europe: Vizir Launch." Harvard Business School case no. 384-139, 1983.

Bartlett, Christopher A., and Sumantra Ghoshal. *Managing Across Borders: The Transnational Solution.* Cambridge, MA: Harvard Business School Press, 1989.

Boddewyn, Jean J.; Robin Soehl; and Jacques Picard. "Standardization in International Marketing: Is Ted Levitt in Fact Right?" *Business Horizons*, November–December, 1986, pp. 69–75.

Buzzell, Robert D. "Can You Standardize Multinational Marketing?" *Harvard Business Review*, November–December: 1968 pp. 102–13.

Carpano, Claudio, and James J. Chrisman. "Performance Implications of International Product Strategies and the Integration of Marketing Activities," *Journal of International Marketing*, 3, no. 1 (1995), pp. 9–28.

Cecchini, Paolo. *The European Challenge 1992.* Aldershot, UK: Woldwood House, 1988.

Chadwick, Michael, and Sue Won. "Toys-R-Us in Japan." Project report, Georgetown-Waseda Graduate Management Program, Tokyo, 1994.

Dalgic, Tevfik. "Euromarketing: Charting the Map for Globalization." *International Marketing Review* 9, no. 5 (1992) pp. 31–42.

D'Avieni, Richard. *Hypercompetition.* New York: Free Press, 1994.

Douglas, Susan P., and C. Samuel Craig. "Evolution of Global Marketing Strategy: Scale, Scope and Synergy." *Columbia Journal of World Business*, Fall 1989, pp. 47–59.

Halliburton, Chris, and Reinhard Huenerberg. "Pan-European Marketing—Myth or Reality?" *Journal of International Marketing* 1, no. 3 (1993), pp. 77–92.

Halliburton, Chris, and Ian Jones. "Global Individualism—Reconciling Global Marketing and Global Manufacturing." *Journal of International Marketing* 2, no. 4 (1994), pp. 79–88.

Hamel, Gary, and C. K. Prahalad. "Strategic Intent." *Harvard Business Review*, May–June 1989.

Hanni, David A.; John K. Ryans; and Ivan R. Vernon. "Coordinating International Advertising—The Goodyear Case Revisited for Latin America." *Journal of International Marketing* 3, no. 2 (1995), pp. 83–98.

Hout, Thomas; Michael E. Porter; and Eileen Rudden. "How Global Companies Win Out." *Harvard Business Review*, September–October, 1982.

Johansson, Johny K. "Japanese Marketing Strategies for Europe 1992." Paper presented at the Conference on "The New Japan–U.S. Relationship," New York University, New York, April 4–5, 1989.

Johansson, Johny K., and Izrael D. Nebenzahl. "Multinational Expansion: Effect on Brand Evaluations." *Journal of International Business Studies* 17, no. 3 (Fall 1986) pp. 101–26.

Johansson, Johny K, and Jan U. Segerfeldt. "Keeping in Touch: Information Gathering by Japanese and Swedish Subsidiaries in the U.S." Paper presented at the Academy of International Business Meeting in Chicago, October 1987.

Johansson, Johny K., and Thomas W. Roehl. "How Companies Develop Assets and Capabilities: Japan as a Leading Market." In Bird, Allan, ed. *The Future of Japan's Business.* Greenwich, CT: JAI Press, 1994.

Johansson, J. K., and George Yip. "Exploiting Globalization Potential: U.S. and Japanese Business Strategies." *Strategic Management Journal*, Winter 1994.

Kashani, Kamran. "Beware the Pitfalls of Global Marketing." *Harvard Business Review*, September–October 1989.

———. *Managing Global Marketing.* Boston: PWS-Kent, 1992.

Levitt, Ted. "The Globalization of Markets." *Harvard Business Review*, May–June 1983.

Lim Say Boon. "The Shave of Things to Come." *The Straits Times*, April 11, 1993, Sunday Review, p. 4.

Mintzberg, Henry. "Patterns in Strategy Formation." *Management Science* 24 (1978) pp. 934–48.

Ohmae, Kenichi. "Getting Back to Strategy." *Harvard Business Review*, November–December 1988.

Porter, Michael E. *Competitive Strategy.* New York: Free Press, 1980.

Quelch, John A., and Edward J. Hoff. "Customizing Global Marketing." *Harvard Business Review*, May–June 1986, pp. 59–68.

Quelch, John A.; Robert D. Buzzell; and Eric R. Salama. *The Marketing Challenge of Europe 1992.* Reading, MA: Addison-Wesley, 1991.

Samiee, Saeed and Kendall Roth. "The Influence of Global Marketing Standardization on Performance," *Journal of Marketing*, 56, no. 2 (April) 1992), pp. 1–17.

Sorenson, R. Z., and U. E. Wiechmann. "How Multinationals View Marketing Standardization." In D. N. Dickson, ed. *Managing Effectively in the World Marketplace.* New York: Wiley, 1983 pp. 301–16.

Uchitelle, Louis. "Gillette's World View: One Blade Fits All." *New York Times*, January 3, 1994, p. C3.

Urban, Glen L., and Steven H. Star. *Advanced Marketing Strategy.* Englewood Cliffs, NJ: Prentice Hall, 1991.

Yip, George. *Total Global Strategy.* Englewood Cliffs, NJ: Prentice Hall, 1992.

Chapter 12

Global Products and Services

"Best in the world"

After studying this chapter, you should understand the following global marketing issues:

1. There is a difference between *localization* of a product or service to fit local regulations and usage requirements and *adaptation*, which is a matter of fitting the product to buyer preferences.

2. A *standardized* global product or service is not adapted to customer preferences but must still be localized.

3. The advantages of global products and services lie in the cost savings from long series and large scale but also from their ability to change customer preferences.

4. The market success of global products and services is based on their "best value" characteristics, offering state-of-the-art features at competitive prices and the added value from their strong brand names.

5. Local products and services still have opportunities in the marketplace, above all in specialty niches and as alternatives for variety-seeking consumers.

O NE OF THE FIRST questions arising in global marketing management is "Can this product (or service) be standardized and sold globally?" While a customized offering is closest to the marketing ideal, there are cost savings in large scale that make global standardization preferable. There are also demand spillover effects from a uniform approach—in brand-name recognition, trade support, prestige, and word-of-mouth. This chapter discusses why global products and services have been successful.

Montblanc Bets on World-Class Reputation

When is a pen not a pen? When it is an "art form." This is how Switzerland's Compagnie Financière Richemont positions its Montblanc pens. The fancy writing instruments boast individually numbered gold nibs and are topped with a white mark representing a bird's-eye view of snow-capped Mont Blanc, a mountain in the Alps. A single fountain pen will set you back $235 to $13,500 (for one made of platinum).

Apparently, the pen's style and quality have succeeded in making it more than just a status symbol. The upscale readers of *Robb Report*, a monthly magazine that rates products associated with an affluent lifestyle, voted Montblanc the best writing instrument in the world.

For Richemont subsidiary Montblanc North America, this reputation presents an opportunity to extend the product line. The company recently announced plans to open stand-alone boutiques offering jewelry and leather accessories such as wallets, briefcases, organizers, and garment bags.

To support the brand extension, the company plans marketing communications reinforcing Montblanc's image of fine quality. This promotional effort includes magazine advertisements that link the Montblanc pen with the "art of writing." Newspaper ads announce the opening of the boutiques and the introduction of new products. Cultural events at the boutiques include displays of rare manuscripts, letters, and autographs. Together, such efforts are intended to convey, in the words of the ad agency's creative director, "an image that Montblanc isn't only a writing-instrument company, but a European luxury brand . . . We hope that the Montblanc brand will stand not just for a pen, but for a certain lifestyle."

Decisions about product design and image are also at the core of other marketers' efforts to expand international product lines. At Reebok International, Angel R. Martinez is leading an effort to rejuvenate the company's Rockport subsidiary, a maker of comfortable casual shoes. Martinez, formerly Reebok's vice president for global marketing, is betting that more exciting styles, coupled with advertising that conveys the shoes' high quality, will fuel a big upturn in sales and make Rockport a global brand. And at General Motors, management hopes that sharing design ideas across brands and national boundaries can help the company design "world cars" from Germany that will appeal to buyers on more than one continent. The stakes are high, but so are the expected rewards.

Sources: Glenn Collins, "Montblanc Expands on Gertrude Stein to Suggest that Sometimes a Pen Is More than a Pen," *New York Times*, July 27, 1995, p. D9; Glenn Rifkin, "Does This Shoe Fit?" *New York Times*, October 14, 1995, pp. 33, 36; David Woodruff, "Can Opel Deliver the 'World Cars' GM Needs?" *Business Week*, December 4, 1995, pp. 52–53.

INTRODUCTION

A common question in global marketing is whether the product or service should be standardized. A perhaps more useful question is *which features* of a product or service should be standardized and to what degree. For most companies some standardization is unavoidable. Cost savings from longer product series often outweigh the disadvantages of not being perfectly adapted to customers' precise requirements. At the same time, the customer satisfaction advantages of a high level of adaptation are well understood by most companies. Where the two countervailing forces cross (see Exhibit 12.1) is the optimal level of standardization. Finding this point in practice is often a delicate balancing act.

This chapter first compares "global" and "regional" standardization, and then describes briefly how products and services differ. It clarifies the distinction between localization and adaptation, after which the market reaction to a standardized offering is analyzed and reasons why globally standardized products succeed are identified. We spell out how the effect in the marketplace varies according to the stage of the product life cycle and discuss the threat of counterfeit products. This is followed by a discussion of services and the specific marketing problems encountered in globalizing services. The final section suggests how local companies can still survive and prosper in competition with global brands and services.

PRELIMINARY DISTINCTIONS

Marketers generally make little distinction between "global" and "regional." **Global products** are standardized with uniform features in all countries. Examples include Gillette razor blades, Sony television sets, and Benetton sweaters. By contrast, **regional products** are unique to a particular trading region, such as Honda's "European" car model Concerto, the Mexican beer

EXHIBIT 12.1   The Trade-off between Standardization and Adaptation

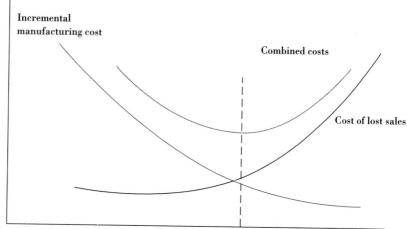

brewer Corona's "pan-American" market, and Korea's ginseng tea makers covering the Asian market. These regional products are latently global, as global expansion occurs and customers learn more about the products. Also, the marketing issues raised by regional products are similar in *kind* to those raised by global products—only the *degree* of complexity and the magnitude of the task are different. Where the regional market is large enough to offer the cost savings associated with standardization—reaching a "minimum efficient scale"—the marketing issue is to what extent the local markets can accept one standardized product. "Pan-European standardization" poses the same problem as "global standardization."

Whether management should approach the standardization of services and of products the same way is more questionable, however. One can view products as "embodied" services—a car "offers" transportation, a coffeemaker "serves" coffee—and thus there may be no generic distinction in core benefits of products and services. On the other hand, the "delivery" of embodied services is usually mechanical and impersonal (even though on a cold winter's morning it might seem that your car is against you), while "true" service delivery typically involves a human element (with the associated risk of human error). Even a bank's cash machine or a voice mail system, however mechanical, offers a semblance of human interaction.

Given the cultural diversity in the world, the human element becomes an obstacle to **service standardization.** Thus, the consensus among many service marketers has come to be that one can globally standardize the "back room" aspects of the service—quality control in fast-food restaurants, computerized bookings within a hotel chain, inventory control of retailers—but not necessarily the customer interactions "up front."[1] The front-line personnel in even the most global service companies are usually natives, whose command of language and customs enables them to deliver the service appropriately.[2]

LOCALIZATION VERSUS ADAPTATION

Successful companies often find that even the most standardized product or service usually requires some local changes. Every country has a few regulations not found elsewhere. For example, a country may demand certain product information on a package not needed in other countries. A case in point is the U.S. warning on cigarette packages about the health hazard associated with smoking, not required in many Asian countries. Cars in Sweden need to drive with the parking lights on, and the lights are turned on automatically when the ignition key is turned. The United States is particularly confusing to foreign entrants since the individual states often feature separate requirements—such as the stricter pollution controls on cars registered in California compared to most other states.

Basic Requirements

But these differences do not mean "no standardization." Adhering to them involves **localization** more than true "adaptation," an important difference in global marketing. *Localization refers to the changes required for a product or service to function in a new country.* For example, when a fax machine is fitted with a new type of telephone jacks for a foreign country, it is "localized." *When products are "adapted," changes are made to match customer tastes or preferences.* When the fax machine comes with a lighter handset for the Italian market, it is "adapted." Generally speaking, localization avoids having potential customers reject the product out of hand, while **adaptation** gives customers a positive reason for choosing it. Localization is a positive for all potential customers in the country, while adaptation aims to target some special segment or segments. Localization is necessary for consumers to even consider the product; adaptation tries to make them prefer it over other choices.[3]

In practice there is sometimes not a sharp and definite distinction between localization and adaptation as the Kentucky Fried Chicken experience in Japan shows (see box, "KFC Goes to Japan"). Nevertheless, the distinction is very useful in analyzing the pros and cons of standardization. *Even a "globally standardized" product needs to be localized.* It would basically offer an unchanged core design and simply be refitted to a country's requirements.[4]

Compatibility Requirements

"Localization" is in many ways equivalent to compatibility. It represents the adjustments in the product specifications necessary for the product to function

<table>
<tr>
<td>

*G*etting the Picture

KFC Goes to Japan

</td>
<td>

IN THE EARLY 1970s when Kentucky Fried Chicken entered Japan, it faced the task of creating a market for its version of fast food. The Japanese fast-food market consisted mainly of small noodle and sushi restaurants with lunch served at counters and with free home or office delivery (on moped or bicycle). The original recipe for KFC chicken was left unchanged (it is still the same worldwide, in the more than 9,500 KFC restaurants in 18 countries KFC has entered since 1995). But developing a market for KFC in Japan involved some changes in side dishes to

</td>
<td>

appeal to the Japanese palate, such as, lowering the sugar content of the coleslaw. KFC also added fish to the menu, redesigned the outlets, and stressed the American origin in the advertising. Appealing especially to children, a lifesize plastic model of Colonel Sanders was placed outside the restaurants, creating an immediately recognizable mascot. In many respects—the logo, the visual layout, the buckets and bags, the appearance of the servers, the food, and the drinks—the stores remained true to the original concept.

</td>
</tr>
</table>

in the foreign environment. With TV broadcast systems differing between European countries and the United States, VCRs need to be adapted. The sleeves of Western clothing need to be shortened for the Japanese market. Shampoos for the softer Northern European hair are chemically different from those for Southern people's thicker hair. Effective skin care products need to be biogenetically different depending on the food of a nation's people. And so on.

A lack of compatibility sometimes adds a cachet among a select group of customers. In autos, the dysfunctional left-hand steering and large size of American imports to Singapore bolster the owner's pride. Elegantly dressed Swedes trot in the snow in Italian-made tasseled loafers. For sustained successful operations, such small niches are usually not sufficient. The product needs to be adapted to the functional needs of a larger portion of the market. Localization is necessary. But this does not mean that a different product is necessary. Using the same basic design, localization can often be accomplished with a minimum degree of changes. Furthermore, compatibility can be achieved by incorporating multiple options.

Multisystem Compatibility

In many products today, localization is accomplished by building in compatibility with multiple systems at the outset. Thus VCRs and TV sets are designed to operate in many system environments. Wordprocessing software offers multiple formatting options making it possible to transfer files between programs. Hardware developers offer built-in adapters and transformers that help make fax machines portable worldwide.

Multisystem compatibility ensures that localization requirements are satisfied. Products designed for easier manufacturing are usually modularized, making the manufacturing more of an assembly task than before. Thus,

A Kentucky Fried Chicken outlet in Japan. A classic example of global standardization, the KFC name and logo are easily recognizable anywhere in the world, even though the menu (apart from the chicken) varies slightly across countries.

Courtesy Kentucky Fried Chicken.

building a camera or a motorcycle becomes something resembling the kit assembly of a model airplane. It is easy, then, to separate out those components requiring localization and incorporate multiple options for those components alone. Laptop and notebook computers now come with adapters for various electric voltages as standard equipment. PCs offer expansion slots for floppy discs, soundcards, CD-ROM, and various other accessories, letting the buyer do the customization. IKEA, the furniture store chain, offers modular systems the customers can use to design different living environments in their homes. Multisystem compatibility makes it possible to generate the savings associated with long and standardized product series—even without the use of advanced robotics and flexible manufacturing systems.

GLOBAL PRODUCT POSITIONING[5]

To understand how global products and services affect customers, the typical product positioning framework is useful. Although the discussion will focus mainly on "products," the same principles are valid for "services." The special problems in globalizing services will be dealt with below in a separate section.

It is useful to distinguish between three psychologically different effects on buyers when a globally standardized product or service is introduced on a local market. In one, customers' existing perceptual maps of the product category remain intact; in another the product space is altered; and in a third, buyer preferences are changed. In practice all three processes are often at work simultaneously.

No Change in Perceptions

As mentioned earlier, a drawback of a standardized product is that it is not adapted to the particular preferences in the foreign market. In standard marketing language this means that it is mispositioned relative to the **ideal points** of the consumers in their perceptual space.[6] This situation often leads local managers to claim that adaptation is necessary because "in our market customers are different."

Exhibit 12.2 shows a product space map of the American automobile market in the beginning of the 1980s.[7] The Japanese makes Toyota and Datsun (now Nissan) are positioned inside the third-largest segment in the market. This segment desires good gas mileage and a car that is both sporty and fun to drive—preferences that the Japanese-made cars had already targeted in their home market. But even though these two makes were well positioned relative to American makes, there is also a "gap" open in the back of the Japanese makes—segment 3—a gap that Honda was to fill.

Why would customers buy a mispositioned offering if they have alternatives closer to their ideal? The usual answer is a lower price. But as many marketers have learned, inducing the customer to purchase a less-desirable product by offering a discounted price often leads to lower customer satisfaction, as the favorable discount is soon forgotten but the less desirable product remains.[8]

....
EXHIBIT 12.2   **Market Positioning Map of Selected Automobile Brands (1984)**

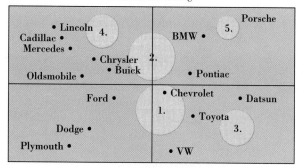

*G*etting the Picture

Bunge & Born: Creating Brand Awareness

BUNGE & BORN S.A. is South America's largest consumer goods company, a multinational especially strong in food products. As the Latin American market improves, the company is facing increased competition from domestic producers and imports in the various country markets. Says Ricardo Esteves, a director of the company: "During high inflation the fear was simply to be able to get the products, and you did not worry about quality or price. Now the shopper is comparing local goods with imported goods and other brands. So we have to produce better products at more competitive prices."

The solution? Standardization of products from the various country subsidiaries. And establishing strong regional brand awareness. "Before people would buy whatever pasta was on the shelves, even though they did not know what little company made it," says Mr. Esteves. "But people want to feed themselves better; they are looking for better taste, more purity, as well as a company that will stand behind the product. We want them to look for our brand."

Sources: Nash, 1994; Robinson, 1989.

GLOBAL BRANDS   Another and more common reason why mispositioned standardized products are attractive to potential consumers is *brand image* and status. While local products and services may be better adapted to the market, the globally standardized competitor with a strong brand name offers "value-added," which the locals can't easily match. For conspicuous consumption, to impress someone special, or simply to lower perceived risk and cognitive dissonance, a well-known global brand name will often do much better than a local brand (see box, "Bunge & Born").

In consumer psychology terms, such a brand effect means that for certain products or usage situations the social norms might favor the globally standardized brand. If the buyer's motivation to comply with social norms is high—a matter of cultural factors as we saw in Chapter 7—the global brand will be preferred. In Exhibit 12.2, Mercedes, whose positioning relative to segment 4 is weaker than Lincoln's, is a good example. The **mispositioning** is not compensated for by price—the Mercedes being more expensive than the Lincoln—but by brand image and the status conferred upon the owner.[9]

Exhibit 12.3 shows the world's best-known brands as tabulated from one large-scale survey in the United States, Europe, and Japan.[10] Other surveys tally roughly the same set of brands—although the ranking varies by region. As can be seen, all of the brands belong to companies that market globally standardized products.[11]

The growing impact of global brands makes global brand management of crucial importance.[12] While brand managers in individual markets still manage the local execution of the marketing strategy, global brand management is necessarily a strategic function at headquarters. In many successful companies, the responsibility of **global brand management** rests in fact with top senior managers rather than the traditionally young brand managers. The reason

EXHIBIT 12.3 The World's Best-Known Brands

1. Coca-Cola	3. Pepsi-Cola	6. Toyota	8. Disney
2. McDonald's	4. Sony	7. Nestlé	9. Honda
	5. Kodak		10. Ford

Source: Reproduced from *Managing Global Marketing*, by Kamran Kashani with the permission of SouthWestern College Publishing. Copyright ©1992 PWS-Kent Publishing Company. All rights reserved.

is that the companies' principal brands are a major force, worth billions to their companies. In a 1995 study, the median value assigned by 153 senior managers to their principal brand was $5.3 billion.[13] Fully 91 percent of the executives had a "definite plan or strategy" for enhancing their brand in the next two years. The basic thrust of these plans was similar across the companies. With quality and functional performance comparable across brands and therefore expected by the customers, differentiation would come from customer service and increased promotional support for the brand image.

In the same study the senior managers ranked the 10 most effective global brand managers (see Exhibit 12.4). The results confirm Coca-Cola's preeminence as a global marketer. In fact, the most striking fact about Exhibit 12.4 is perhaps the sharp drop-off after the leader. Managing a global brand is not necessarily easy.

The creation of brand awareness can have its drawbacks. Intel, the PC chip maker, used a "piggybacking" approach to promotion of its name by asking hardware manufacturers to indicate "Intel inside" on promotional materials, but the consumer awareness helped exacerbate the negative public relations

EXHIBIT 12.4 The 10 Most Effective Global Brand Managers*

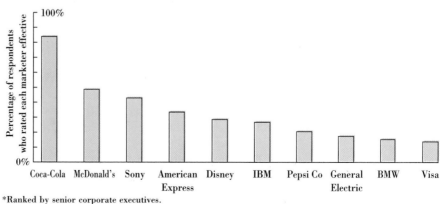

*Ranked by senior corporate executives.
Source: Elliott, 1995, with data from the *Brands at the Crossroads* study by Bozell Worldwide and Fortune Marketing, New York, 1993.

An advertisement for Wedgwood fine bone china. When art and design matter, tradition often has a cachet.

Courtesy Waterford Wedgewood USA, Inc.

damage when the company had problems with its Pentium chip. Procter and Gamble has long avoided the use of company-identified brand names—there is no "P&G" detergent, for example, only several global or regional brands: Tide, Cheer, Vizir. This helps when difficulties occur—such as when its sanitary napkin brand "Rely" was found to induce toxic shock. On the other hand, the goodwill from a linkage to a reputable company is lost. Although in American markets this factor can count for less because mergers and acquisitions blur the connection between ownership and market presence, in other markets the connection is more valuable. For example, in Japan it is customary for the company to identify itself in its brand advertisements to assure the Japanese consumers that the company stands behind the brand. This has forced P&G Japan to place its company name and logo on promotional materials and to add a tag line with its logo at the end of its commercials on Japanese TV.

COUNTRY OF ORIGIN   Similar to a brand effect, the "made in" label of products—which identifies the country where the product was manufactured—will often have a so-called *country-of-origin effect*. A number of research studies have been conducted on the impact of "made in" labels.[14] In general, the studies show a pronounced effect on the quality perceptions of products, with country stereo-types coloring consumers' evaluative judgments of brands. There is also evidence that these effects do not go away over time. Because of increased global communication consumers learn more about foreign countries, and they learn what technologies and products firms in the countries are good at. But even if country-of-origin effects do not go away, country perceptions do change over time. For example, while American products enjoyed a reputation for high quality after World War II, they slipped badly in the 1970s and 1980s as superior foreign products raised customer expectations. British quality percep-tions largely followed the same path only earlier and quicker, while Japanese products showed the opposite trend and the German quality image remained strong. However, given the intense global competition in many markets, there is, not surprisingly, evidence of a convergence of quality ratings in the 1990s.[15]

Country-of-origin effects differ by product category. They are less pro-nounced in products for which technology is widely diffused across the globe and products from different countries consequently are of similar quality. In apparel, for example, made-in labels ("made in" Malaysia, China, Portugal, Hungary, and so on) tend to have less effect because consumers are becoming accustomed to seeing similar quality clothes from various places. By contrast, in advanced medical equipment, electronics, cosmetics, and wine, country of origin still counts for a great deal.

Another thing that matters is whether a country produces at widely different quality levels. If companies in a country tend to adhere to strict quality standards, that country stands to gain from country-of-origin effect, just as a global brand name means the company "guarantees" a certain performance level. Consumers come to trust imported products from countries such as Germany, Japan, and Sweden, because they show relatively low quality varia-tion. On the other hand, products from Britain, the United States, and Italy may or may not be of high quality because these countries feature producers at widely different quality levels. This renders the made-in label useless for quality judgments (just as variable quality would ruin a brand name).

The country-of-origin effects on quality perceptions are generally justified on the basis of objective data. In autos, for example, performance tests and expert ratings confirm that German cars are well engineered with superior handling and performance, similar to the standard stereotype of German products. Japanese cars are reliable and fuel efficient, the way most consumers see them. But there are also **country-of-origin biases** that have effects. As research has shown, there is a tendency on the part of consumers to overstate positive and negative product attributes. Japanese cars may not be quite as fuel efficient as people think, German cars not quite as outstanding technologically as many expect, and American cars not quite as bad as some would say.[16] Over time, as global competition intensifies and objectively the products become more comparable, many of these misperceptions are likely to be corrected. Still they may linger on for some time, rewarding or penalizing a country's companies accordingly.

There is also an emotional aspect of country-of-origin effects, when people feel pressured to buy (or not buy) products from a certain country. This can happen, for example, because of a media campaign ("Buy American") or because of social norms operating on the buyer. Research shows that in most countries, people like to buy products from their own country, everything else being equal.[17] The "everything else equal" condition is naturally the key—imported products will in general offer something special, and as experience has shown, it is imprudent for the domestic company to rely on the emotional attachment of people to homegrown, but inferior, products.

When Perceptions Change

In practice it is unlikely that customers' perceptual maps stay unchanged when a globally standardized product enters the market. More often than not the introduction of new "stimuli" (again using the standard consumer psychology terms) will change the perceived product space. The space gets elongated or compressed, and new dimensions might be added.

EXTENDED PRODUCT SPACE   The elongation of the dimensions defining the product space occurs when globally standardized products offer more of the salient features. This happens frequently, since the globally standardized products incorporate the newest technology.

An illustration of extending the product space was the introduction of the Honda Accord in the U.S. auto market. Exhibit 12.5 shows a positioning map

Exhibit 12.5   **How the Honda Accord Extended the Product Space**

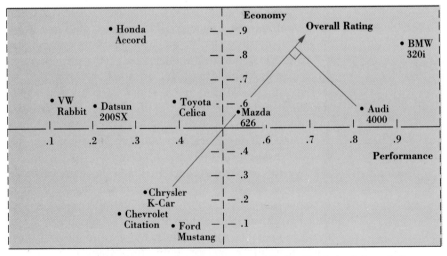

Source: Johny K. Johansson and Hans B. Thorelli, "International Product Positioning," *Journal of International Business Studies*, vol. 16, no. 3, (Fall 1985), pp. 57–75. Reprinted by permission of the *Journal of International Business Studies*.

from 1982 with the Accord and several competing models included.[18] As can be seen, the Accord offered a unique mix of characteristics, being much more economical than even the Japanese competitors. As the overall rating vector shows, the BMW was the preferred choice—but the price was much higher for that car. The American makes were not competitive in this segment without large rebates.

With extended spaces the benefits desired by consumers are available in greater amounts than before. The convenience, functioning, storage, shopping, and other aspects of the purchase and use of the product have improved because of advances in technology incorporated in the new products.

ADDITIONAL FEATURES   Because of the advances in technology, there is also a strong possibility that the globally standardized product offers new features as well. This means that the product space is changing, with new salient dimensions added. Products that do not offer the new features (digital audio, anti-lock brakes, no cholesterol) will be left out of the consumers' evoked sets. Older brands, often local, are now not just mispositioned—they do not register in the appropriate evoked set. The players are global.

The advances in technology restructure the space in another way. Features that in the past could be had only by giving up other features can now be accommodated without sacrifice. In the product space previously mutually exclusive features have become independent dimensions, enlarging the benefit space. In automobiles, comfort can now be had without compromising fuel economy. Safety does not require heavy car bodies. Noiseless air-conditioning is available. These innovations are not necessarily limited to globally standardized products—but the advantage of the globally standardized product is that it can incorporate these advanced features at a reasonable cost to the consumer.

Again the American automobile market offers an instructive illustration. Exhibit 12.6 shows the market in 1968, before the two oil crises in the 1970s. As can be seen, there is little evidence of miles-per-gallon or economy as a buying criterion. This can be contrasted with the earlier map in Exhibit 12.2. In Exhibit 12.2 "economy" was emerging strongly, opening up a window for the Japanese entrants. At the same time, there was no need to give up on sporty performance, as would have been the case in 1968.

Changing Preferences

A third phenomenon associated with the success of globally standardized products involves **changing customer preferences** over time. The shift in preferences can be bought about by various factors, including global communications, changing fashions, and social and national movements, such as the emergence of a "Green" political platform. Japanese carmakers received a "windfall gain" when the oil crises of 1974 and 1978 made consumers look for more fuel-efficient cars. L.L. Bean, the U.S.–based catalog retailer of outdoor gear has been boosted internationally by the increased emphasis on healthy living and extended amounts of leisure time.

....
EXHIBIT 12.6   **Illustration of Joint Space of Ideal Points and Stimuli (1968)**

Sporty	

Ford Mustang •   AMC Javelin
                              •
    Plymouth   Mercury
    Barracuda •   • Cougar

• Jaguar Sedan

* Ideal point for subject I

• Ford Thunderbird V8

Luxurious

• Chevrolet Corvair

* Ideal point for subject J

• Ford Falcon

• Lincoln Continental

• Chrysler Imperial

• Buick Le Sabre

Source: Paul E. green, and donald S. Tull, *Research for Marketing Decisions*, 3d ed. (Englewood Cliffs, NJ: Prentice Hall, 1975), p. 601. © 1975. Adapted by permission of Prentice-Hall, Inc., Upper Saddle River, NJ.

As often as not, the driving factor behind the changes in preferences is the emergence of products offering more value for the money and new advanced features embodying the latest technology. The change might not be immediate, and, in fact, the first reading may be negative. Early market reactions to the "Swatch" fashion watch were negative. Honda's Acura Legend was considered a "failure" one year after its U.S. introduction. Toshiba's laptop computers were rated low at first because of weak picture resolution, but their portability and ease of use soon converted users. These products set new standards and became the preferred choices for some segments, often creating new markets in the process. It is not efficient to manufacture such products in small quantities—they have to be standardized and, if possible, marketed on a global scale.

Embryonic Markets

Product space maps used to disentangle the multiple effects of globally standardized brands assume that consumers have a well-articulated view of the marketplace for a given product or service. So far our discussion has reflected this assumption, which is likely to hold strictly only in the *mature* stage of the product life cycle. Since many foreign markets will be in the early stages of the life cycle, a natural question is how global products perform in these markets.

A foreign market in the embryonic stage offers the standardized product the opportunity to be a first mover and create demand. Since domestic competition is weak or nonexistent, the marketing tasks are to demonstrate how the product fills a need and to educate potential customers in its use. This generic marketing task can be challenging and expensive, with reluctant

*G*etting the
Picture

Citibank Looks
to Emerging
Markets

BANKING, both retail and commercial, has been one of the slowest areas of the economy to change in Eastern Europe. But in 1994, Citibank, the large American multinational, opened its first branch in Budapest, and its flashy decor, lavish services, and plastic cards are having an effect on traditional banking there.

Entering Hungary, Citibank decided that the best strategy was to offer upscale services not matched by any competitors. This made the bank less dependent on building volume, and the bank's research suggested that there would be enough customers for higher-margin service packages. The bank offers cash machines, still rare in Eastern Europe, but to qualify the customers need to maintain a minimum balance of $250, a little less than the average salary in the country. So far 4,000 accounts have been opened, 70%

Hungarians, the rest foreign residents of Budapest.

At the high end, the bank offers special privileges to customers who maintain balances of $100,000. Beyond the rich wood veneer, peach carpet, and potted palms in the main lobby, these customers are given access to a third-floor wet bar with free drinks adjacent to the safe-deposit boxes. The bank has found 12 customers who qualify—hardly sufficient for a very profitable operation—but well suiting a prestige-raising business that generates favorable word-of-mouth advertising and intimidates potential competitors.

Sources: Bobinski, 1995; Saul Hansell, "Citicorp Announces High-Level Personnel Shifts," *New York Times*, July 1, 1995, p. D5; Jane Perlez, "Citibank in Budapest: A.T.M.'s and Potted Palms," *New York Times*, June 22, 1995, p. D7.

learners and a need for special promotional material and personal selling. But the brand has a chance to develop brand loyalty before competitors enter.

Entry into an embryonic market does not need *adaptation* to preferences in the traditional sense, since these are still being formed. But it requires imaginative *localization* to demonstrate fully the utility of the new product. Citibank's early entry into Eastern Europe is suggestive (see box, "Citibank Looks to Emerging Markets").

Growth Markets

Growth attracts competitors. A major strategic goal of competitors is to establish their offering as the standard against which all other brands are compared. Toshiba in laptop computers, Microsoft in operating software, Volkswagen's Beetle in economy cars are examples of companies whose products set new standards.

Even if not a first-mover, when a global product is introduced it will sometimes become the accepted standard.[19] The IBM PC late entry is a well-known example. After Apple had created a new market for the personal computer, IBM's entry made DOS the new PC standard. A similar example is the VHS videocassette. Too sure that it was in command of the market standard, Sony invested heavily in the Betamax video format, only to see the market shift to the VHS format when Matsushita threw its weight behind that format.

First-Mover or Follower?

In both the embryonic and growth stages, being a first-mover can create advantages but can also be hazardous. The **first-mover's advantages** relative to followers include:[20]

- Higher brand recognition.
- More positive brand image.
- More customer loyalty.
- More distribution.
- Longer market experience.

The drawback for a first-mover is that the market is not yet developed, which means that:

- Channel members may need training.
- Customers might have to be educated.
- Advertising has to be more generic.
- Tastes and standards are unknown and perhaps unformed.

Because of the uncertainties involved, some firms decide to become followers, waiting to see how the first entrant does before entering a new market. When they then enter, it is usually with a kind of me-too approach, trying to capture some of the first-mover's customers and also help grow the new market. When Saab entered the U.S. market, it positioned itself as "the other Swedish car," trading on Volvo's image. The leading French beer, Kronenbourg, attacked the same market through a campaign slogan that claimed it to be "Europe's largest-selling beer," trying to capitalize on Dutch Heineken's and German Beck's rising popularity. Mastercard has been playing catch-up with some success in the global market for credit cards (see box, "The Global Card Game").

The Success of Global Products

The key to success of the globally standardized products is not that they are especially cheap or that every consumer wants the same as everyone else. They are often the best-value products because they offer higher quality and more advanced features at better prices. They also tend to be stronger on the intangible extras such as status and brand image. But mostly they embody the best in technology with designs from leading markets and are manufactured to the highest standards. As much as they satisfy customers, they as often create new desires. In terms of the product life cycle, global products will often generate new growth in mature markets, as customers return sooner for upgrades and more modern features.

Such products need to be global because they achieve success by being tested against the world's most demanding customers wherever they may be.

Getting the Picture

The Global Card Game

FIRST CREDIT CARDS, then cash cards and smart cards, and now cards for the Internet—the world is turning (virtually) plastic.

The globalization of the American Express card was followed by Visa, which beat Mastercard to the global punch. Visa still has a larger global presence than Mastercard, with extensive advertising campaigns presenting Visa as a welcome alternative to the American Express card (which is not usually as attractive because of higher fees for the merchants).

Playing catch-up, Mastercard developed its own innovative strategy. Embracing the new concept of co-branded cards, Mastercard has been in the forefront of offering credit cards jointly with General Motors, AT&T, and General Electric. Purchases charged to the cards automatically add up to discounts for products from these firms, just as frequent flier miles are accumulated when flying. Coupled with another Mastercard strategic push to make people use their card for everyday shopping including supermarket purchases, Mastercard is gaining considerable business in its prime market, the U.S. As the necessary infrastructure develops in other countries' stores, the plan is to introduce similar features there.

Now there are also the so-called "smart cards." Already available in Europe, these cards derive from the prepaid telephone cards widely used in Europe and Asia (but still not available in the fragmented American telecommunications market). The smart cards are embedded with microchips that store cash and, when used, automatically subtract from the face amount on the card. Easier to use than typical credit cards, since the balance is visible, these cards are preferred by many merchants as well as customers when paying for purchases. Several American companies, including Microsoft, the software developer, are working on developing smart cards to be used on the Internet for making payments.

Sources: Saul Hansell, "The Man Who Charged Up Mastercard," *New York Times*, March 7, 1993, sec. 3, pp. 1, 8; "Microsoft Developing Electronic Cash Card," *New York Times*, June 12, 1995, p. D4; "Revolutions: The Card that Could Rule our Lives." *Asiaweek*, Nov. 3, 1995, p. 52.

They also need to be standardized so that they can be offered at competitive prices and become core players in these leading markets. But the explanation behind their success is not their global or standardized aspects as such—but that they are the best buys in the core segments of the various country markets. That is also why they have become targets for counterfeiters.

COUNTERFEIT PRODUCTS

Counterfeits or knockoffs are fake products designed and branded so as to mislead the unwary customer into assuming that they are genuine.[21] Counterfeit products should be distinguished from "gray trade" or parallel trade. **Gray trade** is parallel distribution of genuine goods by intermediaries other than

U.S. customs agent in Miami drives a steamroller over confiscated counterfeit watches. Manufacturers and authorized dealers have to be vigilant in checking serial numbers and documentation of every shipment.

Bettmann

authorized channel members. Gray trade as a pricing problem will be discussed in Chapter 13, Global Pricing, and gray trade as a distribution problem will be discussed in Chapter 14, Global Distribution.

Extent of Problem

Counterfeit products pose an ominous problem in the global marketplace. According to expert estimates, worldwide company losses due to counterfeit products are over $20 billion annually. The traditional cases of counterfeit products involve luxury products with global brand names. Gucci wallets, Louis Vuitton bags, Cartier watches, and Porsche sunglasses are typical examples. But counterfeit products are no longer confined to designer jeans and watches. Products now routinely counterfeited include chemicals, computers, drugs, fertilizers, pesticides, medical devices, military hardware, and food—as well as parts for airplanes and automobiles.

Counterfeiters operate at all levels of the economy. As foreign direct investment transfers technology and manufacturing to new countries, these countries acquire the skills to turn out bogus goods. But not all counterfeits come from developing countries. For example, experts estimate that perhaps 20 percent of all fakes are made in the United States by producers who can't make a profit otherwise or who see the opportunity of a quick kill.

*G*etting the
Picture

Counterfeit
Goes
High-Tech

As computerized CAD-CAM techniques become ever more sophisticated in design and manufacturing, the possibility of producing exact copies of apparel designs increases proportionately. This poses a headache for global brand names in particular, because of the price premium they fetch.

The counterfeit products from Hong Kong's and Taiwan's many small factories have long been a problem for global brands. But even in New York's Soho district, the heart of the city's large business in the fashion trade, high-tech machinery is used by some business operators to produce illegal copies of branded apparel. Given a specimen of a new Polo shirt, for example, the new machinery has the capability to photographically analyze the material, the design, and the stitching, and then "reverse engineer" the process to produce an almost exact copy, including the logo stitching of a polo player and the label inside the collar.

Only a specialist will be able to spot the copy's minor differences from the original. Buyers from the stores can't usually tell the difference, much less a regular customer. Of course, since there is no discernible difference, the consumer might well be satisfied. For the owner of the brand name, however, the sale of the counterfeit items means a considerable loss of revenues, and the companies pay to have guards go through merchandise and interrogate store owners to find the illegal makers, prosecute them, and destroy fake merchandise.

Sources: *New York Times*, December 13, 1994; *Business Week*, December 16, 1985, pp. 48–53.

Some knockoffs can be as good as the original, especially since they use the same label (see box, "Counterfeit Goes High-Tech"). For the global marketer trying to build and sustain a global brand name's equity, such practices are naturally alarming. In Korea knockoffs of designer clothes are sold in some stores with various designer labels offered separately so the customer can stitch the label on at home.

A particularly intriguing case is that of software piracy, the duplication and sale of software programs for personal computers. The practice of copying diskettes is widespread, and it is very difficult to enforce the copyright limitations indicated on the packages. One research study, however, found that the quicker diffusion of the software programs made possible through pirating can actually help penetration. In England, where six of every seven adopters of popular spreadsheet and word-processing programs utilize pirated copies, the pirates were responsible for generating more than 80 percent of new software buyers.[22]

Actions against Counterfeits

What can the global marketer do? For some, the counterattack has been a two-pronged "search and destroy" mission. Firms make an effort to find the factories that turn out the counterfeits, and they track down the fakes in the

---

*G*etting the
Picture

China's Video
and Audio
Pirates

IN THE SPRING of 1995, the U.S. Trade Representative's Office scored a major diplomatic victory, convincing China's government to agree to strongly enforce a ban on copyright and trademark violations in that country. China entrepreneurs had long copied popular videotapes and compact disks from the West for resale on the streets and small shops of Beijing and Shanghai, as well as being trucked or shipped by boat into Hong Kong and other Southeast Asian cities. The American government had been pressured by the artists' organizations to help stop the practice, since it resulted in lost revenues and undermined the authorized distributors.

Although in principle this was a victory for the United States, many observers remain skeptical about the real effect of the agreement. For one thing, the amount of lost revenues is hardly great, given China's difficulty in paying hard currency. In addition, with regular prices many of the products would have a hard time making it against local competition: Mandarin and Cantonese artists are more popular than Western artists, and their CDs, many of them also pirated copies, cost a fraction of Western CDs at regular price. A third difficulty is the sheer number of small factories and outlets. New factories are easily established, and the manufacturers and the street salesmen are often entrepreneurial young people eager to come back.

While Western companies concede that the effect is probably minimal, they consider the principle important for the development of a better business climate in China.

Sources: *New York Times*, February 27, 1995, pp. D1, D6, and May 17, 1995, pp. D1, D5; "Business Beams on IPR Breakthrough," *South China Morning Post*, March 17, 1995, p. 7.

---

stores. Private investigation outfits have emerged to offer their services to multinational companies.

To help identify fakes, some companies have resorted to various coding devices. Levi Strauss, the jeans maker, weaves into its fabric a microscopic fiber pattern visible only under a special light. To deter pirates, Microsoft launched a $1.09 million print media campaign in Hong Kong, claiming that Windows 95 is coded so that counterfeits can be tracked.

Many companies also appeal to their government for assistance, although the cases have to be well documented before most governments react. The recent agreement between the United States and China concerning piracy in the entertainment industry has received much publicity, although the ultimate success is uncertain (see box, "China's Video and Audio Pirates").

GLOBAL SERVICES

Services marketing has received increasing attention in the last few years as its importance in the developed economies has grown considerably. The share of GNP attributable to services has increased over the last few years, and in

Getting the Picture

Any Vacancy?

THE BUSINESSMAN IN East Berlin going to Prague on the early morning train can reserve a hotel room in Prague by simply calling the local Marriott phone number in Berlin. There might be no hotel with the Marriott marquee in Prague, but the American hotel chain has a number of affiliates in Eastern Europe. These independent hotels have allied with Marriott to attract customers from abroad. In turn, Marriott can provide foreign visitors with Marriott-warranted accommodations abroad. In the future, when people from East Europe want to travel in the United States, Marriott will be able to draw on the same network to attract them to Marriott hotels in the United States.

An important ingredient in this global expansion has been the creation of efficient telecommunications and computerized reservation lines. If the Berlin connection is attempted after-hours, reservations can still be made. In fact, many of Marriott's international reservation calls, from Eastern Europe, Japan, or Buenos Aires, are routed through its central reservation office in Salt Lake City, Utah, where telephone operators with different language capabilities serve the customers. The operators can check room availability through the computer and confirm the reservation. The local hotel staff receives confirmation via e-mail from Utah.

Source: Bruce Wolff, Vice President of Distribution Sales, Marriott Hotels.

particular the employment share in the service sectors has increased a great deal in the advanced economies. The international trade and foreign direct investment in services have grown considerably over the last few years, as new communications technology makes global service delivery possible (see box, "Any Vacancy?").

The service industries include hotels and other lodging places; establishments providing personal, business, repair, and amusement services; health, legal, engineering, and other professional services; educational institutions; membership organizations; finance, insurance, and real estate (including rent and imputed rent for owner-occupied dwellings); wholesale and retail trade; and general government, transportation, communication, and public utilities. Although some of these services are not very significant globally, only a few have no international involvement.

Our discussion will first center on the issues that make global services marketing different from physical goods marketing abroad; then on how service quality is determined and how a service concept can be globalized; and finally on two illustrative examples, franchising and professional services. (It should be pointed out that this section does not deal with services associated with the sales and support of products. The after-sales service guaranteed with the sale of an automobile, for example, or the in-store explanations offered by a camera salesman, both important activities for customer satisfaction, are not the focus of this section.)

A Marketing Equivalence

From a marketing viewpoint there are actually many similarities between physical goods and services. For example, a "product is a bundle of benefit-generating attributes" in one standard definition. There is nothing inherently physical about this bundle. The same definition can be applied to an intangible service such as an insurance package. In fact, the similarities can be so strong that for some purposes there is no difference. In many ways the *product* is simply the packaging of a problem-solving *service*. For example, a book replaces the telling of a story, a car offers transportation, a cash machine replaces a teller, and so on.

The similarities and differences that affect the marketing management of services can be identified clearly with reference to the traditional product discussion in standard marketing texts. Adapting the product discussion of these texts, we distinguish between the "core service," the "basic service package," and the "augmented service."[23] Exhibit 12.7 demonstrates the relationships between these three concepts of the service.

The **core service** is what the buyer is "really buying." For instance, the person getting a tune-up for her car is really buying trouble-free operation and transportation. The individual checking into the Hilton in Manila is really buying comfort and reliable service. The first job of the global services marketer is to make sure that these service benefits can be delivered in the foreign markets. While this task establishes a necessary condition for expansion, it is not sufficient by itself for success.

The **basic service package** refers to the specified services offered the customer, which include service features, the price, the packaging, and the guarantees offered. The basic service package of a bank involves the various "products" the bank offers and their features, including free checking, high-interest certificates of deposit, and so on. An airline provides a set of more or less tangible in-flight services (food, drink, duty-free sales, special baby care, movies). The second job of the global services marketer is to develop a service package that can be appropriately localized and replicated in the various markets around the world. Offering innovative and hard-to-duplicate service packages, such as the Club Med all-inclusive vacations in its own villages in different parts of the world, can help develop a loyal customer base and a sustained competitive advantage.

The **augmented service** is the totality of benefits that the individual receives or experiences when buying the product. These benefits revolve around the service delivery, the way the provider is dressed, the tone of voice and body language used, the confidence and credence imparted, and so on. They also involve the brand image and status of the service provider, and the physical surroundings of the service encounter. The third job of the global services marketer is to create a customer-oriented augmented service package.

Although they do play a role also for physical products, in relatively standardized services these augmenting features can make a big difference.

EXHIBIT 12.7   The Service "Product"

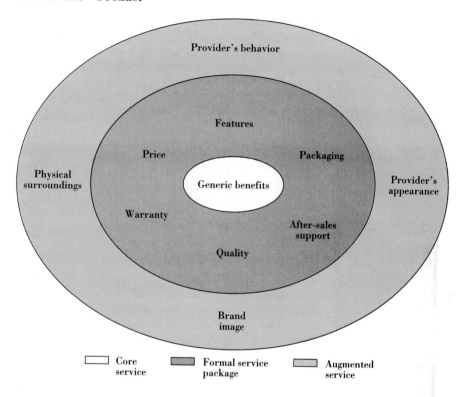

They can become the FSAs. For example, the beautician's appearance, the salon's furniture, the music played, and the other customers seen are all factors contributing to whether the hair styling itself will seem acceptable or not.[24] These augmenting benefits are often so inextricably linked to most services that without them the service can't be replicated properly elsewhere. Without such duplication, exporting to other countries is less likely to succeed. One key factor in global services marketing is not whether the core benefit is desired or whether the basic service package can be replicated but whether the total *service delivery system* can be successfully transplanted abroad. If not, quality and customer satisfaction are jeopardized.

Service Quality

The intangibility of services is typically assumed to make consumer evaluation of quality more difficult than for tangible products.[25] This view is based on the natural hesitation of people to evaluate things they can't touch. The intangibility of services makes them much more *subjective* "products." Quality is a matter of how we feel and of our particular taste.

This dependence on subjective feelings means that what is perceived as high-quality service may differ between individuals. *Customer satisfaction*, a subjective state of mind, is often the best—or even only—guide to whether a service was high quality or not. This can inhibit direct comparisons or word-of-mouth advice, or perhaps should, though it often doesn't. We may feel it is easier for us to rate cars than dentists, easier to evaluate cameras than legal services. We may lack technical knowledge about whether the doctor or the lawyer is really good, and we have to take a lot on faith (the credence factor is high). We know it if we like how a camera or car performs. But nothing is more vivid and impressive than our subjective feelings. Given a certain amount of experience and confidence, our subjective feelings can be quite sufficient for evaluation. Customer satisfaction can be very real—if you don't experience it, you know it. So in fact we often have little or no hesitation about recommending (or not recommending) our dentist, car repair shop, or tax accountant to friends. Even medical services, of which the actual quality is supposed to be especially hard to judge because we don't know how good the doctor really is, can be judged on the basis of how good we feel after the visit. A bungled root canal treatment does not take long to make itself known, and later we recount it.

In one way, services are easier to judge. What we like—our taste—is largely determined by culture and by past experiences with products or services. The standard against which both products and services are judged contains a subjective element. But for products, standards are in addition based on more objective data, to obtain which customers read car or camera magazines or check out ratings in *Consumer Reports*. Although generally of less importance, such data can also can be obtained for many services. Restaurant ratings, hotel comparisons, recommendations about doctors, rankings of accounting firms are all relatively "objective" guides to quality in that opinions have been carefully filtered and corroborated. We are taking experts' subjective opinions. Because of the intangibility of a service, and because of the consumer participation in its "production," subjective feelings can be sufficient for evaluating services. We are willing to accept the subjective opinion of a restaurant or movie critic. For people with experience, service evaluations are sometimes easier than product evaluations—because the latter require knowledge of the objective data—and so in many areas we are all more willing to rate a service than we would be to rate many products.

In global markets the difference between physical goods and services carries special relevance. What constitutes "high-quality service" can differ considerably between countries while what constitutes a "high-quality good" often does not. The case of personal and cultural judgment about services comes into play.

In personal services, quality is apparently determined partly by factors such as language spoken, tone and choice of words, body language (hand gestures, stance, distance), and ability of the provider to listen well, avoid confrontational argumentation, and use other interpersonal communication skills. By comparing

Getting the Picture

Rude Service in China

THAT THE WELCOME of the multinationals in China is sometimes less than hearty is becoming a cliché. While the Chinese authorities invite foreign companies to bring technology, they also insist on joint ventures, sharing of technology, and exports. They even use blunt language, as when Microsoft was threatened by a ban on Windows 95 unless a local partner was selected and a promise was made to help develop a Chinese software industry.

The same pattern can be recognized in the personal service offered in many Chinese stores. Past habits die slowly, and the top-down, in-your-face attitude toward customers is still alive. It has gone far enough that the Chinese government, true to its style, recently banned 50 common phrases that the rude clerks are not to use when dealing with customers. The list is instructive as a reminder of the changes a market orientation imposes on a noncapitalist society. Select items are:

1. If you don't like it, go somewhere else.
2. Ask someone else.
3. Take a taxi if you don't like the bus.
4. I don't care whom you complain to.
5. If you're not buying, what are you looking at?
6. Buy it if you can afford it, otherwise get out of here.
7. Are you buying or not? Have you made up your mind?
8. Don't you see I'm busy? What's the hurry?
9. I just told you. Why are you asking again?
10. Why didn't you choose well when you bought it?
11. Go ask the person who sold it to you.
12. If you don't like it, talk to the manager.
13. The price is posted. Can't you see it yourself?
14. No exchanges, that's the rule.
15. If you're not buying, don't ask.
16. It's not my fault.
17. I'm not in charge. Don't ask so many questions.
18. Didn't I tell you? How come you don't get it?
19. If you want it, speak up; if you don't, get out of the way. Next!
20. Why don't you have the money ready?
21. What can I do? I didn't break it.

Sources: Faison, 1995; Engardio, 1996.

two culturally different places (say, New York City and Tokyo) great differences in approach—and "service"—can be easily seen. The direct, explicit, and "professional" approach of a New York department store clerk is far away from the Japanese clerk's kind and indirect demeanor. It is clear that one person raised in a particular service environment might be surprised by what passes for high-quality service in another environment—even though the attitudes of Chinese store clerks are likely to please no one (see box, "Rude Service in China").

Keeping the cultural factors well in mind and localizing where necessary, the global entrant can educate local customers about what services in banking, restaurants, hospitals, hotels, and so on can potentially be, revealing to the local customers how culture and past experiences have limited their perspective unnecessarily. Just as past choices color what the customer has come to expect, new choices from global firms can open the eyes of local-only customers. New service opportunities can be created. And, as people say, once you have tasted luxury, it is no longer a luxury but a necessity.

SERVICE GLOBALIZATION POTENTIAL

The feasibility of globalizing a service business depends on some factors that are unique to services.

Life Cycle

As with product cycle, development over time of a business service follows a cycle from birth through growth and maturity to decline. In the typical marketing illustration, the product life cycle follows an S-curve, with the growth period corresponding to the where the S has its steepest ascent. This is when a new product is often introduced in foreign markets to capture first-mover advantages. However, for services, it is in the maturity stage that the potential for global expansion of the service concept is the highest.

In the early and growth stage of the cycle, the "production process" employed by the service company is often still under development. The concept is still being created. In maturity, the soft- and hardware ingredients in the service have been fully developed, and the standardization of key components and features takes place. It is this *standardization*—whether it be in advertising, medical care, fast-food restaurants, accounting, or hotels—which is the basis for global expansion of the service. FSAs in services are often in innovative standardization—from McDonald's strict procedures for cleanliness and friendliness, to Hilton Hotels' training of how to greet guests, to Boston Consulting Group's growth-share matrix.

Infrastructure

The global applicability of a service depends on whether the **infrastructure** through which the service is offered exists in foreign markets. In brokerage firms, for example, a very sophisticated service concept that works very well under a certain type of regulatory and economic environment might lose all relevance when the financial regulations and/or the institutional members change character. The buying and selling of call and put options or other derivatives, for example, is not feasible where there is no futures market.

Localization

Another important inhibitor of services exporting is that many service systems exist as ingenious solutions to very special problems faced in the home country.

Getting the Picture

Where Are the Japanese Services Industries?

SINCE JAPANESE CORPORATIONS like Sony, Toyota, and Canon have been so successful in penetrating Western markets, one might have expected Japanese service firms to do equally well. After all, Japanese banks, brokerage houses, ad agencies, construction companies, hotel chains, and department stores are among the largest in the world in terms of assets and revenues. But so far there are only scattered signs of a "service invasion" abroad.

Japanese hotel chains, such as Nikko, have bought up properties on Hawaii and own hotels in various metropolitan centers such as Hong Kong, London, and Paris. Department stores, such as Takashimaya and Mitsukoshi, have opened some overseas branches. How-ever, most of the customers of the hotels and the stores are Japanese tourists and expatriates. Japanese banks, such as Sumitomo in California, and brokerage firms, such as Nomura in New York, do some business with foreign clients, but have trouble competing against the Americans. Dentsu, one of the world's largest advertising agencies, has a successful joint venture with Young & Rubicam, but is not very visible outside Asia.

The basic problem limiting these companies' foreign expansion is the special conditions in their main domestic market. For example, the larger hotel chains are part of the keiretsu groupings, which virtually guarantees high occupancy rates. Established department stores are shielded from competition by laws limiting new stores' entry. Japanese banks can draw on a favorable savings rate, which has made abundant deposits available at low interest rates. Brokerage firms are protected by strict regulations preventing foreign competition. Ad agencies can control media in addition to producing advertising.

Yes, Japan has large service companies, and, yes, they have great service skills. But their ability to operate in a more open and free marketplace has simply not had a chance to develop. As Japan deregulates, this is likely to change—but only gradually, and with much pain for the established players.

Sources: Aaker, 1990; Johansson, 1990.

The typical supermarket in the United States developed partly as a response to the growing availability of automobiles and parking lot space in many suburban areas of the nation. Similar idiosyncratic factors determine the specific shape of the service organizations found in many countries. This helps explain why Japanese service firms have been very slow in globalizing (see box, "Where Are the Japanese Services Industries?").

What is needed for services export is (1) a reasonable similarity to the home country situation, (2) a distillation of exactly what the *key features of the service* concept are, and (3) the *localization of these* to another environment while still maintaining the FSAs of the firm.

Since the "production" of the service is typically inseparable from the distribution of the service, FDI is usually needed to transfer the complete **service delivery system.** In particular, if the FSAs are lodged in augmented personal service, to globalize without loss of FSAs one needs to train the personnel delivering the service as well. For example, it is difficult to provide the restaurant "service" of the fast-food joints in New York's financial district without also training the workers behind the counter to throw hamburgers and soft drink cans in the air to wherever they are requested by the other servers. Exporting this fast-food "service" would involve not only the shipment of the foods sold or the recipes and the packaging but also the unique "style" of delivering the food in the air.

Globalizing this type of service becomes tantamount to establishing a whole separate "production" unit in the market country—a stark contrast to exporting a physical good. Of course, since the style of throwing hamburgers and Coke cans from one server to another represents a solution to the high rents and cramped quarters of downtown New York, one would expect the potential for this service to be very limited outside other crowded downtown areas of the world.

TWO SPECIAL CASES

To show the variety in global services it is useful to examine two in more depth, global fast food for its amazing success and professional services for their unlikely globalization.

Fast-Food Franchising

The *franchising* of fast-food restaurants has witnessed an unprecedented growth in the last two decades. The brand names McDonald's, Kentucky Fried Chicken, Dunkin' Donuts, Wendy's, and others are well known the world over. How and why have these "exports" proven so viable?

The basic and necessary first step in franchising abroad is analogous to that of developing any geographically dispersed franchise organization. The core service features of the service system and the firm's specific advantages have to be identified and then formulations developed that travel well. These features will form the basic building blocks for the system as exported. In the case of McDonald's it consists not only of the cooking method and serving procedure but also of the training of the workers, their attire and attitude, and the management and bookkeeping system (see box, "The McDonald's Way").

Successful fast-food franchising firms provide a lot of preplanning tools to help the prospective local investor. These include analyses of key factors in choice of location (traffic patterns, competition and synergy from similar outlets, offices versus residential), checklists of positive and negative attraction factors in the market area (population mix, income levels, age and family size), and building advice (size, layout, construction materials).

Needless to say, these tools have to be localized to the conditions in the foreign markets. "Traffic pattern" in one country may refer to cars, in others to motorcycles, in still others to bicycles or pedestrians. "Population mix" is a nonfactor in homogeneous countries such as Norway but important and based

Citibank branch in Hong Kong. Global expansion into retail banking is demanding, but Citibank has successfully expanded by offering more convenient access to funds and longer opening hours.

Mary Beth Camp/Matrix.

on religion in countries such as Malaysia. "Building advice" in the desert sands of Kuwait is far different from that in North Dakota—not to speak of the building permits which of course differ not only across countries but even between municipalities.

Professional Services

Despite local regulations that vary between countries, **professional services** have recently expanded in step with the expansion of global firms. A gradual move toward making regulations more homogeneous has also played a role. In the EU region, for example, certification of lawyers and doctors in one member country is recognized in other EU countries as well. As accounting standards converge, large Western firms, such as Arthur Andersen and Price & Waterhouse, are also going global. Their main customers are still multinationals from their own countries, but even this is changing. Large European firms such as Siemens and BMW retain American accountants, and Japanese firms such as Canon and Sony are now clients of the Tokyo offices of American accounting firms.

The global expansion of professional services has been facilitated by the increased sophistication in creating strategic alliances. Traditionally, professional services went global through the establishment of local branch offices managed by expatriates who would come and spend a few years as the country head. The system worked but always made the branch office subservient to headquarters, not a useful arrangement to attract the best local professionals. Today, the firms often expand through the use of looser affiliations such as strategic alliances with local firms, allowing the local firm to keep much of its identity—and the fees. Even though sometimes this makes the service offered to global customers

Getting the Picture

The McDonald's Way

PERHAPS THE MOST successful franchising system of all time is McDonald's. Since the company has been very successful duplicating its early U.S. success elsewhere, its franchising system is of special interest for a global marketer.

Franchisees may invest as much as $600,000 (or the equivalent) in initial start-up costs for a franchise. Many investors form teams to raise the money, and it is common for a successful investor to own more than one outlet. However, each store manager should have an equity stake in the restaurant. McDonald's charges a 3.5% service fee and a rental charge of 8.5% of the franchisee's volume. The franchisees are also required to attend "Hamburger University" in a suburb of Chicago for three weeks to learn how to manage the business and how to train the staff. This has become a good way for incipient entrepreneurs in emerging countries to learn quickly about the capitalist way.

The franchisees must also adhere to certain procedures in buying materials and in preparing and selling the product. This has created problems in places such as Tokyo and Moscow where the company insistence on American style forces importation despite tariff barriers and, especially in Russia, protests from domestic suppliers. The solution in Russia has been to allow the domestic variants but to insist on rigorous quality control, while in Japan Idaho potatoes are now an American success story.

With more than 11,000 outlets in 50 or so countries and more than $17.5 billion in annual sales, McDonald's sells more than double the hamburgers of its nearest rival, Burger King. Worldwide more than 19 million customers pass through the golden arches each day, and the company is rapidly expanding. In 1990, when McDonald's opened its first Moscow outlet, its 700-seat restaurant served 30,000 meals in one day. It is hardly surprising that some non-Americans—as well as some Americans—consider McDonald's a threat to a country's traditions.

Sources: Barbara Marsh, "Franchise Realities: Sandwich-Shop Chain Surges, But to Run One Can Take Heroic Efforts," *The Wall Street Journal*, September 16, 1992, pp. A1, A5; Michael Specter, "Borscht and Blini to Go: From Russian Capitalists, an Answer to McDonald's," *New York Times*, August 9, 1995, pp. D1, D3.

uneven in quality, the client is served in name by the same firm everywhere. The result is a lower-cost global reach for the main office and a motivated local force in the field.

LOCAL PRODUCTS AND SERVICES

The success of global products and services does not mean that locally adapted products or services have no opportunity.

As the experiences of many travelers attest, even in open markets many local products and services survive and prosper next to global brands. Restaurants serving local specialties thrive. In audio products, shoes, apparel, and other consumer goods, local products coexist with well-known world brands. In

Getting the Picture

This Bud is Not for You, Anheuser

ITS MARKET saturated in the U.S., St. Louis–based beer maker Anheuser-Busch, the world's biggest brewer, is trying to market its leading Budweiser brand globally. But the rights to the Budweiser name in Europe belong to a much smaller beer maker, Budejovicky Budvar, the original Czech brewer of Budweiser. The Czech company has the leading market share at home and has a growing export business to other European countries as well.

Since beer marketing is very brand oriented, Anheuser-Busch has long made efforts to acquire the rights to the Budweiser name globally, all in vain as the government-owned company has always refused to negotiate. But after the fall of communism, when the Czechs started to privatize industry and sell off government-owned businesses, Anheuser-Busch figured it had another chance and decided to try again to buy the little beer maker and the trademark.

But the Czech managers and workers were not about to be bought up by the American giant. They did not want any part of a company that they suspected would only pull the plug on their operation, siphon the profits away, and try to take their beer off the market. And they did not like the idea of replacing their own great beer with the lightweight watery-tasting beer of the American namesake.

To soften up the folks, Anheuser-Busch opened up a $1 million cultural center in Ceske Budejovice, the town where the brewer is located, inaugurated baseball and basketball teams, opened a marble-floored cafe, and offered scholarships and English lessons. But to no avail. Listen to Frantisek Nedorost, a 52-year-old electrician: "I absolutely disagree with the Americans buying part of our company. I like Americans, their culture, their films. But I know American beer doesn't reach the quality of Czech beer. It's much poorer, much weaker."

After years of courtship, Anheuser-Busch has just about given up hope of ever being able to sell their Budweiser in Europe.

Sources: Perlez, 1995; Koenig, 1995.

business-to-business markets local vendors do well with custom software and supplies. Local beers are successful throughout North America and Europe, even though in some cases their market is directly targeted by global competitors (see box, "This Bud Is Not for You, Anheuser").

The typical reason for the success of local products and services is the customization involved. In *industrial goods* markets, personal attention, fast delivery, and prompt after-sales service are all factors tending to favor local products. This advantage is diminished to the extent global manufacturers pay attention to the localization of their offerings. With the growing trend toward global integration and coordination in customer organizations, industrial marketing tends to follow suit and favor global standardization. Selling to a globalized customer forces suppliers to globalize as well.

In *consumer goods*, the sameness of globally standardized products creates a potential for local products in special niche segments of the market. These niches comprise consumers who are looking for ethnic color, uniqueness, and local tradition. There are people who still like stickshifts, cigarettes without filters, and hair spray. Local products and services provide variety for consumers in special situations for which the standardized brand is not suitable. Thus, while global brands may capture a large segment of the market, local variants can coexist underneath the standardized umbrella.

SUMMARY

This chapter has discussed the emergence of global products and services. It emphasized the distinction between localization to a country's infrastructure and adaptation to customer preferences. Localization is necessary, adaptation to customer preferences more a matter of tactics. Tastes can change over time, as conditions evolve and new products and service businesses enter a market. The advantages of a global offering in quality, cost, and image are often sufficient to shift customer preferences toward its position.

Successful global products often set new standards. Then the global marketers naturally emerge as dominant market players rather than operators in marginal niches. Domestic-only producers can still build a following in niche segments with loyal traditionalists. Even core segment members often

have a desire for variety and novelty in usage because of situational factors and may turn to local specialties. Thus, successful global core brands often leave room for domestic players and may expand the market for them as well.

A global service is generally a more intricate and fragile export than is a physical good. The difficulty for the marketer is re-creating the quality level of the existing service abroad. Issues that arise when going global are defining what the service concept is "really about," how the same service delivery system can be reproduced abroad, whether the necessary localization to the new markets can be made without jeopardizing the firm-specific advantages, and how the necessary local personnel can be properly trained. Judging from the successes, many companies are up to the challenge.

KEY TERMS

Adaptation p. 438
Augmented service p. 457
Basic service package p. 457
Changing customer preferences p. 447
Core service p. 456
Counterfeits or knockoffs p. 451
Country-of-origin biases p. 445

Extended product space p. 446
First-mover advantages p. 450
Global brand management p. 442
Global products p. 436
Gray trade p. 451
Ideal points p. 441

Infrastructure p. 461
Localization p. 438
Mispositioning p. 442
Professional services p. 463
Regional products p. 436
Service delivery system p. 461
Service quality p. 457
Service standardization p. 437

DISCUSSION QUESTIONS

1. What are the factors behind Disney's global success? What can other entertainment businesses learn from Disney about standardizing products and services?

2. Analyze the reasons why some local products (such as local beers) might have an enhanced potential when standardized global products enter the market.

3. What country-of-origin *biases* do you think affect people's perceptions about these products: autos; rock music; classical music; hotels; shoes; stereos. To what extent do you think the biases are justified by the facts? Are they changing over time?

4. In what ways are services different from products? How do these differences affect global expansion potential?

5. Why is most personal service not easily globalized? Give some examples that show how a service has to be standardized before going global—and how standardized service is almost always *impersonal*.

NOTES

1. See, for example, Normann, 1984.

2. More on how to globalize services will be presented later in the chapter.

3. This difference is similar to the split between "practical" and "emotional" preferences cited by Du Preez et al., 1994. Practical preferences are desires associated with a country's infrastructure, climate, or physical environment (a desire for air-conditioning in a desert country, say). Emotional preferences involve more subjective taste, such as a preference for a certain color or designer name. Incorporating air-conditioning in an automobile is more of a localization strategy, while offering a pink cabriolet version is more of an adaptive strategy to target some niche in the market.

4. In PC software, the word "localization" is commonly used, but the word "adaptation" is rare. Software is generally a globally standardized product. Adding umlauts and hyphens to word-processing programs or changing from English to a native language in a spreadsheet are typical localization practices. Like changing the steering wheel of automobiles to the right side for countries where people drive on the left side of the road, such changes are not really a matter of preferences. There is always, of course, a "lunatic fringe" or "status at any price" part of every market who take pride in weird and dysfunctional features.

5. The standard terminology is here with "product positioning" also covering services.

6. In an interesting study of consumers in France, Korea, and Spain, Du Preez et al., 1994, showed how ideal points and attribute importance in automobiles differed between the countries. A standardized car model offering similar features in all three countries would have been mispositioned in at least two.

7. This illustration is adapted from Koten, 1984.

8. This is the problem of extrinsic versus intrinsic motivations, a topic researched in consumer behavior. See, for example, George J. Szybillo, and Jack Jacoby, 1974.

9. Global brand names also give the manufacturers more clout in international channels, a topic we will return to in Chapter 14.

10. From Kashani, 1992.

11. This does not mean that all standardized products are sold under global brand names. For example, the Unilever fabric softener called "Snuggle" in the United States uses the same logo and packaging in most countries but its brand name is different everywhere (Yip, 1992, p. 98).

12. The value of global brands has not escaped potential global marketers. Although a 1989 study found that only about one-half of the top brands in the United States were used abroad (and some of them only in neighboring Canada), the strategic intent is for more global branding (Rosen et al, 1989; Simmons, 1990).

13. These and the subsequent figures are from the "Brands at the Crossroads" study by Bozell Worldwide and Fortune Marketing, as reported in Elliott, 1995.

14. A good early review is that by Bilkey and Nes, 1982. For more recent studies, see Papadopoulos and Heslop, 1993.

15. See, for example, LaBarre, 1994. In this survey covering respondents from North America, Japan, and Europe, Japan was rated overall highest in quality of manufactured products, followed by Germany and the United States. Broken down by respondents from the various regions, however, Germany scored highest among Europeans, the United States among the North Americans, and Japan among the Japanese.

16. See Johansson and Thorelli, 1985.

17. The Papadopoulos and Heslop 1993 volume offers several examples of this effect.

18. Adapted from Johansson and Thorelli, 1985.

19. Schnaars, 1994, documents 28 cases where followers have taken the market from the first-mover.

20. This section draws on Liberman and Montgomery, 1988, and on Schnaars, 1994.

21. These definitions and much of this section draw on "The Counterfeit Trade," 1985.

22. See Givon, et al., 1995.

23. In Kotler's version, the product definition now takes five levels: core benefits, generic product, expected product, augmented product, and potential product (Kotler, 1994, p. 433). For global services, the more standard three-level split is sufficient.

24. See, for example, Bitner, 1992.

25. See, for example, Zeithaml, 1981.

SELECTED REFERENCES

Aaker, D. "How Will the Japanese Compete in Retail Services?" *California Management Review* 33 (1990), pp. 54–67.

Albrecht, Karl. *The Only Thing That Matters.* New York: Harper Business, 1992.

Andrews, Edmund L. "A.T.&T. Reaches Out (And Grabs Everyone)," *New York Times,* August 8, 1993, sec. 3, pp. 1, 6.

Bilkey, Warren J., and Eric Nes. "Country-of-Origin Effects on Product Evaluations." *Journal of International Business Studies* 8, no. 1, (Spring–Summer 1982), pp. 89–99.

Bitner, Mary-Jo. "Servicescapes: The Impact of Physical Surroundings on Customers and Employees." *Journal of Marketing,* April 1992, pp. 57–71.

Bobinski, Christopher. "Polish License for Deutsche Bank." *Financial Times,* July 4, 1995, p. 24.

Boddewyn, J. J.; Robin Soehl; and Jacques Picard. "Standardization in International Marketing: Is Ted Levitt in Fact Right?" *Business Horizons,* November–December 1986, pp. 69–75.

Carlzon, Jan. *Moments of Truth.* Cambridge, MA: Ballinger, 1987.

"The Counterfeit Trade." *Business Week,* December 16, 1985, pp. 48–53.

Czepiel, J. A., "Managing Customer Satisfaction in Consumer Service." Marketing Science Institute, working paper, September 1980, pp. 80–109.

Du Preez, Johann P.; Adamantios Diamantopoulos; and Bodo B. Schlegelmilch. "Product Standardization and Attribute Saliency: A Three-Country Empirical Comparison," *Journal of International Marketing,* Vol. 2, No. 1, 1994, pp. 7–28.

Elliott, Stuart. "Advertising." *New York Times,* June 21, 1995, p. D9.

Engardio, Pete. "Rethinking China," *Business Week,* March 4, 1996, pp. 57–65.

Faison, Seth. "Service With Some Bile," *New York Times,* October 22, 1995, sec. 4, p. 4.

Feder, Barnaby J. "The Unorthodox Behemoth of Law Firms." *New York Times,* March 14, 1993, sec. 3, pp. 1, 6.

Givon, Moshe; Vijay Mahajan; and Eitan Muller. "Software Piracy: Estimation of Lost Sales and the Impact on Software Diffusion," *Journal of Marketing* 59, no. 1 (January 1995) pp. 29–37.

Green, Paul E.; Arun Maheshwari; and Vithala Rao. "Dimensional Interpretation and Configuration Invariance in Multidimensional Scaling: An Empirical Study." *Multivariate Behavioral Research,* 4 (April 1969), pp. 159–180.

Hanssens, D. M., and J. K. Johansson. "Rivalry as Synergy? The Japanese Automobile Companies' Export Expansion." *Journal of International Business Studies* 22, no. 3, (1991) pp. 503–26.

Johansson, Johny K. "Japanese Service Industries and Their Overseas Potential," *The Service Industries Journal*, Vol. 10, No. 1, Jan. 1990, pp. 85–109.

Johansson, Johny K., and Hans B. Thorelli. "International Product Positioning." *Journal of International Business Studies* XVI, no. 3 (Fall 1985), pp. 57–76.

Kashani, Kamran. *Managing Global Marketing*. Boston: PWS-Kent, 1992.

Koenig, Robert L. "Bud War: 2 Budweisers Square off in Czech Republic," *St. Louis Post Dispatch*, Oct. 22, 1995, p. 1A.

Koten, John. "Car Makers Use 'Image' Map as Tool to Position Products." *The Wall Street Journal*, March 22, 1984, p. 31.

Kotler, Philip. *Marketing Management*. 8th ed. Englewood Cliffs, NJ: Prentice Hall, 1994.

Levitt, Ted. "The Globalization of Markets." *Harvard Business Review*, May–June 1983, pp. 92–102.

LaBarre, Polly, "Quality's Silent Partner," *Industry Week*, Vol. 243, No. 8, April 18, 1994, pp. 47–48.

Lieberman, Marvin, and David Montgomery. "First-Mover Advantages." *Strategic Management Journal*, Summer 1988, pp. 41-58.

Lovelock, C. H. *Services Marketing*. Englewood Cliffs, NJ: Prentice Hall, 1984.

Nash, Nathaniel C. "Bunge & Born: More Mindful of Latin-America." *New York Times*, January 3, 1994, p. C5.

Normann, R. *Service Management*. New York: Wiley, 1984.

Normann, R., and Rafael Ramirez. "From Value Chain to Value Constellation." *Harvard Business Review*, July–August 1993, pp. 65–77.

Papadopoulos, Nicolas, and Louise A. Heslop, eds. *Product-Country Images: Impact and Role in International Marketing*. New York: International Business Press, 1993.

Perlez, Jane. "This Bud's Not for You, Anheuser." *New York Times*, June 30, 1995, pp. D1, D4.

Robinson, Eugene. "In Argentina, Private Firm a Power Player; Bunge & Born, a Multinational Wields Clout in Nation's Economy." *The Washington Post*, Dec. 6, 1989, p. G1.

Rosen, Barry Nathan; Jean J. Boddewyn; and Ernst A. Louis. "US Brands Abroad: An Empirical Study of Global Branding," *International Marketing Review* 6, no. 1, (1989) pp. 7–19.

Schnaars, Steven P. *Managing Imitation Strategies*. New York: Free Press, 1994.

Shelp, R. K. *Beyond Industrialization: Ascendancy of the Global Service Economy*. New York: Praeger, 1981.

Simmons, Tim, "A Global Brand of Dialog," *Supermarket News* 40, no. 28 (July 9, 1990) p. 2.

Szybillo, George J., and Jack Jacoby. "Intrinsic versus Extrinsic Cues as Determinants of Perceived Product Quality." *Journal of Applied Psychology*, February 1974, pp. 74–78.

Thomas, Robert J. *New Product Development*. New York: Wiley, 1993.

Uchitelle, Louis. "Gillette's World View: One Blade Fits All." *New York Times*, January 3, 1994, p. C3.

Vernon, R. "International Investment and International Trade in the Product Cycle." *Quarterly Journal of Economics*, May 1966.

Yip, George. *Total Global Strategy*. Englewood Cliffs, NJ: Prentice Hall, 1992.

Zeithaml, Valarie A. "How Consumer Evaluation Processes Differ between Goods and Services." In James H. Donnelly and William R. George, eds. *Marketing of Services*. Chicago, IL: American Marketing Association, 1981.

13

Global Pricing

"There are limits"

After studying this chapter, you should understand the following global marketing issues:

1. Keeping the same global price in major markets is rarely possible unless the product is a big-ticket item sold to industrial users. Locally varying prices are generally preferable from a marketing perspective.

2. Although centrally coordinated prices are difficult to implement and although they interfere with the local subsidiary's ability to target its market, it is necessary and possible to coordinate pricing at least by regions or trading areas.

3. The desired price position in a market is not always feasible because of institutional constraints (such as tariff barriers or government regulation) on the level of prices.

4. Transfer prices between a global company's plants in different countries can seldom be arbitrarily used to shift profits, but should be used to motivate subsidiaries and measure performance, while remaining supportable to local tax authorities.

PRICING GLOBALLY is much trickier than pricing in the home market. In the domestic market, deciding on price levels, promotional rebates to middlemen, and consumer deals requires careful analysis, but once the decisions are made the implementation is straightforward. The opposite generally holds true for markets abroad. The level of price is often a minor headache compared with the problems of currency fluctuations and devaluations, price escalation through tariffs, difficult-to-assess credit risks, f.o.b. versus c.i.f. quotations, dumping charges, transfer prices, and price controls—all common issues in global pricing. In global marketing the actual height of the product price is sometimes less important than currencies quoted, methods of payment, and credit extended.

Global Forces Create Pricing Challenges for Mercedes-Benz

For customers of Mercedes-Benz, "made in Germany" has long signaled high quality. Lately, though, it also signals a drag on profits.

One reason has to do with exchange rates, the relative value of nations' currencies. In the mid–1990s, the value of the German mark has risen, meaning more and more dollars are needed to exchange for a given number of marks. For Mercedes, higher and higher dollar prices are needed to profitably sell a car valued at a certain price in marks. Or, if the price is fixed in dollars, the money Mercedes earns is worth less when converted to marks. The company therefore has to choose between continually raising prices or earning lower and lower profits.

The strong mark also makes German employees relatively expensive; Mercedes pays them in high-value marks, rather than in a weaker currency. However, this is only one of several factors contributing to high costs for Mercedes. Like other German automakers, its factories are less efficient than Japanese or American plants. Until recently, German producers were able to tout their superior engineering instead of keeping up with productivity improvements their foreign competitors were adopting to lower costs and reduce defects.

These environmental pressures have forced Mercedes to take a harder look at how to earn a profit without raising prices. The exchange rates have hurt sales somewhat, but Mercedes can minimize the damage by holding prices steady. To profit with this policy, Mercedes must cut its costs.

The company is therefore establishing production facilities outside Germany; almost all the new cars it is developing will be made in foreign plants. It is also making product-related decisions such as simplifying designs so that they involve fewer variations among cars.

Eventually, Mercedes may regain its competitive edge. Other market forces may help. For example, the U.S. government recently threatened (and later withdrew), a punishing 100 percent tariff (tax on imports) on Japanese luxury cars. Since the tariff effectively doubled the price of a Japanese car, it would have given Mercedes a relative advantage. Of course, the performance of Mercedes over the long haul depends more on how well the company can rebuild its own competitive advantage through innovation, product/development, and other decisions, and recent market share figures show it bouncing back very well.

Sources: Nathaniel C. Nash, "Loss by Daimler Shows Danger of Strong Mark," *New York Times*, July 29, 1995, pp. D1, D7; "Daimler-Benz Posts $1.06 Billion Loss," *New York Times*, September 12, 1995, p. D4; Nathaniel C. Nash, "Luxuries They Can't Afford," *New York Times*, September 13, 1995, pp. D1, D22; David Greising, "Weak Dollar, Strong Profits," *Business Week*, July 11, 1994, p. 39; Robert Hanley, "Car Buyers Play a Game of Beating the Tariff," *New York Times*, May 18, 1995, pp. D1, D5.

INTRODUCTION

In theory, the student of microeconomics is well equipped to handle pricing problems. Given fixed and stable demand and cost curves, the derivation of optimal price allows the simultaneous identification of optimal quantity to produce. A wonderful situation, since other company functions become anciliary and the "firm's problem" is solved.

The "next-generation" texts in applied areas such as marketing then go on to demonstrate that the basic price theory learned in normative economics is not very practical. Demand and cost curves are not easily estimated, they are not stable over time, the competitors influence the demand function unpredictably, the firm produces for more than one market, and prices and output can't be set simultaneously because of organizational constraints. Even though the economists are patching up some of these holes, their theories (if not their terminology) have been largely abandoned by pragmatic price makers in the firm's marketing function. Instead, new procedures much closer to heuristic rules-of-thumb have been devised for the job.

These practical heuristics are also prominent in global pricing. Here the conditions that limit the value of microeconomics are further magnified when new limitations stemming from cross-border transactions are encountered. As a result, the pragmatic guidelines for price setting that have been developed over the years for the home markets need to be revised and augmented. New approaches have evolved—and keep evolving—under pressure from legal and governmental forces in the various countries in addition to the traditional market forces, and they represent truly eclectic combinations of practical experience and more or less theoretical suggestions.

It is perhaps fair to say that it is in pricing that the existing know-how from domestic marketing is least valuable for global operations. Market segmentation and product positioning principles can be extended abroad. Advertising and sales campaigns can be standardized for foreign markets. But the practical and institutional know-how required for global pricing decisions is of a wholly different order of magnitude.

INSTITUTIONAL LIMITS

Many of the problems in global pricing concern host country institutional limitations (legal and financial) that constrain strategy.

It is useful to distinguish at the outset between pricing considerations facing the company as an exporter and the pricing problems specific to global coordination and integration. Primary among the export pricing concerns are the currency exchange risk exposure and the credit risks, which can combine to make customer-oriented easy credit terms in local currencies financially irresponsible. Problems also arise relating to such matters as how to quote prices (f.o.b. vs c.i.f.), and whether all of the price escalation due to the tariff (and nontariff) barriers should be passed on to the customer, lowering competitiveness. As for positioning strategy, high prices and an "import" status image necessitate niche targeting but also slow down market growth and leave competition strategic windows. On the other hand, choosing a low *penetration price*, the firm runs a risk of being accused of *dumping*, that is, selling its products below cost.

For the global company, there are similar problems of strategic constraints. The first strategic task is that of determining *transfer prices*—the prices charged country subsidiaries for products, components, and supplies—which are fair in terms of performance evaluation between country units and still optimal from the overall network perspective, including a desirable profit repatriation pattern. But foreign tax authorities have grown increasingly impatient with pricing schemes that rob a country of "fair" tax returns, and subject transfer prices to great scrutiny. The second problem is that of coordinating pricing across countries, to satisfy multinational customers, without imposing a straitjacket on local subsidiaries and illegally fixing prices for independent distributors.

These and related issues will be discussed in detail in this chapter. As always, it is in the end the "final" price of the product as viewed by the buyer that matters, regardless of what ingredients have come together to make it up. Differences in trade barriers make some prices escalate abnormally, and a great competitor in some markets might simply be priced out of other markets. Foreign cars have long been more or less shut out of the Italian market by virtue of high tariffs and quotas to protect Fiat, Alfa Romeo, and the other domestic producers, a situation that is gradually changing as the EU integration proceeds. The stage of the PLC will differ between countries for the same product. Inflation and the selective price regulations imposed by governments will vary.

The chapter will also discuss "systems selling" and the questions that arise when pricing a complete system of hard- and software. In global markets there are many "turnkey projects," which pose their own peculiar kind of marketing problems. For instance, one typical headache for management is whether the components should be priced separately or whether one system price should be quoted.

The chapter will start with the basics of pricing in marketing generally, then move to the issues of price escalation. Various financial issues, such as price quotes and *hedging* against exchange rate risks, will be dealt with next, followed by transfer pricing, dumping, and *systems pricing*. The roles of the price-quality relationships and the product life cycle in positioning strategy are discussed next. This is followed by an assessment of the feasibility of a global or regional coordination of prices with particular emphasis on firms' "gray trade" experiences in the integrated European market. The last section of the chapter deals with the relative merits of *polycentric, geocentric,* and *ethnocentric* pricing strategies in the global firm.[1]

PRICING BASICS

The basic principles of global pricing derive from the traditional pricing approaches in home markets. These revolve around production costs, competitive factors, and demand considerations.

The Role of Costs

The standard pricing procedure for exporting consists of a **cost-plus** formula. The firm arrives at export prices by adding up the various costs involved in producing and shipping the product (cost-based pricing), and then adds a markup ("plus") to this figure to achieve a reasonable rate of return. The cost components include manufacturing costs, administrative costs, allocated R&D expenditures, selling costs, and the transport charges, customs duties, and requisite fees to various facilitating agencies (see Chapter 5).

There is a longstanding argument about whether full costs should be used or whether only direct costs should burden the product or, the ideal case from a theoretical viewpoint, whether the firm should not simply attempt to estimate marginal costs and then use those. In practice most firms seem to use all or a combination of these and other related methods. The emphasis varies with the company strategy and the market situation. For an existing product entering a new market, direct costs tend to be a natural choice, since overheads are already covered at home and investments have been recouped. If the product is new but relates directly to the firm-specific advantages (FSAs) of the company, marginal costs will be more important and the potential of grooming a "star" dominates the strategy. In the decentralized company where profit center accountability is featured, the tendency is to let the individual product carry itself and to load it down with its full share of overhead and contribution requirements.

The sole reliance on a cost-based pricing system is acceptable only in rare circumstances. It is frequently resorted to in the firm starting its exporting, since the know-how and the financial resources are not yet sufficient for market-oriented pricing. In most cases, however, it becomes absolutely necessary that competition and demand be factored into the decision process.

Experience Curve Pricing

The use of a cost-based price has become more common after the discovery of the "experience curve" effect. The **experience curve** shows how unit costs go down as successively more units of a product are produced. Through the "learning by doing" that comes from experience, the company's employees develop skills and capabilities that translate into lower costs.[2] Thus, a firm entering new foreign markets will gain in capabilities and scope economies from accumulated production and market experience.

Under this scenario, the entry into a new local market might well be accompanied by a lower price than that maintained in other markets, even at home. With the new market providing a chance for increased output and thus lower unit costs, the anticipated gains might be passed along to the customers in the form of low introductory prices ("penetration" prices in the early stage of the PLC). Whether the introductory price will be raised later or not depends directly on the correctness of the anticipated cost declines. If experience effects are smaller than anticipated, costs might certainly rise later—but a very low "cutthroat" entry price might stay down for a very long time (because of competition) and still generate positive profits because of the experience curve decline.

Experience curve pricing has been adopted primarily by companies entering an existing market in the maturity stage. Many Japanese firms operate with this strategy, since it allows them to maintain a penetration price level in foreign markets.[3]

Competition

The competitive analysis might be as simple as finding out what global and domestic competitors in the particular country market charge for their products. These prices tend to set the "reservation" prices in the local market, that is, those limits beyond which the firm's product will not be considered and people will avoid buying. The analysis can go further and attempt to isolate the differential advantages that the firm's product might have over these existing offerings, so-called "perceived value" pricing.[4] One way to do this, developed by DuPont, the U.S.-based manufacturer of artificial fibers and related products, consists of dividing price into a "commodity" part and a "premium price differential" part. The commodity portion of price relates to underlying demand factors while the premium differential focuses specifically on the competitive factors.

The **premium price differential** refers to the degree to which the firm might be granted a higher price by the market because of the particular strengths of its product. To find this out, the company needs to do market research in the local market, identify how important various product attributes are to customers, and assess how competition is perceived on the salient attributes. A company such as Caterpillar uses this approach to price its products in relation to those of Komatsu, its large Japanese competitor.[5] Although in domestic markets such research is typically done via comprehensive and in-depth marketing research, in foreign markets softer data from existing customers, distributors, and country experts can usually offer a preliminary guide.

Demand

Naturally, demand also needs to be considered when setting prices, and most firms do, however implicitly, pay attention to what the various local markets "will bear."

The **price elasticities** associated with the demand curve in economic theory identify how many customers are willing to buy how much of the product at various price levels. This curve yields the "commodity" price in the DuPont approach, reflecting the underlying willingness to buy and ability to pay among the potential customers across the market. In many cases the assessment of this "generic" demand can be done using statistical analysis; in other cases, especially when the product is new on the market, the analysis has to be judgmental (see Chapter 4 for some of these techniques).

The more seasoned manager will tend to base prices on an analysis of the costs involved and adjust the emerging prices in view of competitive and demand conditions in the market country. This naturally leads to an approach in which prices are set on the basis of costs plus a variable markup. Where demand is strong and the competitive differential large, the markup can be higher. In countries where the premium price differential is weaker because of strong competition, and especially where demand is relatively soft, the markup will come down correspondingly. This type of variable markup is common among companies with global strategies since it lends itself well to global coordination.

PRICE ESCALATION

In general, prices abroad can be expected to be higher than prices at home for the simple reason that there are several cost items faced by the exporter not encountered in domestic sales. The factors relate to transportation costs, tariffs and other duties, special taxes, and exchange rate fluctuations. The resulting increase in price overseas is commonly denoted "price escalation." An example of how **price escalation** works is presented in Exhibit 13.1. As can be seen, there are several added cost items incurred when selling overseas. Shipping

EXHIBIT 13.1   International Price Escalation Effects (in U.S. dollars)

International marketing channel elements and cost factors	Domestic wholesale-retail channel	Export market cases			
		Case 1 (same as domestic with direct wholesale import c.i.f./tarrif)	Case 2 (same as case 1 with foreign importer added to channel)	Case 3 (same as case 2 with V.A.T. added)	Case 4 (same as case 3 with local foreign jobber added to channel)
Manufacturer's net price	$ 6.00	$ 6.00	$ 6.00	$ 6.00	$ 6.00
+ insurance and shipping cost (c.i.f.)	*	2.50	2.50	2.50	2.50
= *Landed cost* (c.i.f. value)	*	8.50	8.50	8.50	8.50
+ tariff (20% on c.i.f. value)	*	1.70	1.70	1.70	1.70
= *Importer's cost* (c.i.f. value + tariff)	*	10.20	10.20	10.20	10.20
+ importer's margin (25% on cost)	*	*	2.55	2.55	2.55
+ V.A.T. (16% on full cost plus margin)	*	*	*	2.04	2.40
= *Wholesaler's cost* (= Importer's price)	6.00	10.20	12.75	14.79	14.79
+ wholesaler's margin (33 1/3% on cost)	2.00	3.40	4.25	4.93	4.93
+ V.A.T. (16% on margin)	*	*	*	.79	.79
= *Local foreign jobber's cost* (= Wholesale price)	*	*	*	*	20.51
+ jobber's margin (33 1/3% on cost)	*	*	*	*	6.84
+ V.A.T. (16% on margin)	*	*	*	*	1.09
= *Retailer's cost* (= Wholesale or jobber price)	8.00	13.60	17.00	20.51	28.44
+ retailer's margin (50% on cost)	4.00	6.80	8.50	10.26	14.22
+ V.A.T. (16% on margin)	*	*	*	1.64	2.28
= *Retail price* (= what consumer pays)	$12.00	$20.40	$25.50	$32.42	$44.94
Percent price escalation over: Domestic		70%	113%	170%	275%
Case 1			25%	59	120
Case 2				27%	76
Case 3					39%

*(asterisk) indicates "not applicable."
Source: Becker, 1990. Reprinted by permission of Butterworth-Heinemann, Ltd., and the authors.

costs are only part of the problem—added are applicable tariffs and customs duty, insurance, and value-added taxes. Also, the fact that several middlemen (importer to take the goods through customs, freight forwarder to handle the shipping documents, dock workers) are involved in the channel adds to the costs and cuts into the profit margin unless prices are raised.

The escalation of price means not only that prices become higher than intended, it also makes it more difficult to anticipate what the final price in the market will be. The methods used to cope with the problems are several. Companies attempt to redesign the product so as to fit it into a lower tariff category, sometimes by shifting the final stages in the assembly process abroad. For example, truck tariffs for completed assemblies are usually much higher than for semifinished autos, and the industry has responded by creating a "knockdown" (KD) assembly stage consisting essentially of putting the flatbed on the chassis, "knocking it down" into place. The same formula has been applied with success to passenger autos, so that FDI in auto production now might simply means a "KD plant" with perhaps 20 employees.[6]

Another solution to the escalation problem has been to lower prices and thus absorb some of the trade barrier cost on the part of the company. It also means that duties that are paid on value ("ad valorem") will be lower. The problem is then that the host country subsidiary will show large profits and repatriating these funds might be a problem (see section "Transfer Pricing" below). When entering the newly opened Russian market, many companies are tempted to quote low prices for goods sent to their Russian operation in order to avoid taxes. The problem is that this tends to inflate profits unrealistically, since costs will be low and consequently profit margins will be high for the Russian sales. This makes for a very profitable operation in rubles, but rubles are not so easily turned into Western currency.

It is also important to consider the possibility of FDI to assemble or manufacture in the market country, thus avoiding the escalation problems entirely. This is exactly what many trade barriers are intended to make firms do. Such FDI could also be made in a third country with more favorable tariffs compared to the market country. The problem with relying too heavily on the tariffs as the only justification for FDI is that such barriers can be removed or changed on a moment's notice and it becomes important to recognize that escalation as a reason for FDI is simply too shortsighted.

In the end, most exporters have learned to live with the escalated prices and to avoid more outrageous customs duties by modifying the escalated products, shipping semifinished goods, and, in general, making such moves as will allow the product to fall into a relatively moderate transport and tariff classification. Having done that, they are generally on par with other importers, if not the domestic producers, and given the existence of at least some unique FSAs they are able to avoid further costly redesigns or shifting production location.

FINANCIAL ISSUES

Price Quotes

Export pricing quotes are considerably more complex than domestic quotes. Most of these complications are covered in special discussions on exports and imports—see Chapter 5. Here it is sufficient to point out that the firm selling abroad would generally be in a stronger competitive position by quoting prices *c.i.f.* (cost-insurance-freight, that is, by accepting the responsibility for product cost, insurance, and freight, and factoring these items into the quote) rather

A buyer from Super-Valu, the large U.S. food and grocery wholesaler, inspecting a sample of grapes from Chile before negotiating a price for the shipment. As Chile's reliability as a supplier of quality fruits has grown, the country's growers are able to claim higher prices for their produce.

Courtesy SuperValu Stores, Inc.

than *f.o.b.* (free-on-board), which means that the buyer has to arrange shipping to his country. Quoting c.i.f. still leaves the buyer with the responsibility for checking and adding tariff charges and other duties, and if, in addition, the buyer has to arrange transportation from the seller's country, the transactions costs will be very high.

For products where value is high relative to weight and size, air transportation is often used. Computer software, for example, is sometimes shipped overseas by air, cash on delivery (c.o.d). In many cases the seller will force these shipments to be prepaid, however, especially after a few mishaps and, in particular, when the buyer is from a less-developed country. In this way price quotes for overseas markets are very much tied into the question of trade credit.

Trade Credit

The importance of the level of price quoted depends very much on what credit arrangements can be made. A high price can often be counterbalanced by advantageous **credit terms,** especially where the seller takes the responsibility for arranging the trade credit. For many foreign buyers, governments as well as companies, the actual price is of less concern than what the periodical payments will be. This is nothing very peculiar to specific countries, but rather hinges on the magnitude of the money involved. Credit is of particular importance in exchanges that involve large items such as turbines, industrial plants, aircraft, and so on, in which no buyer can realistically be expected to pay the total bill in cash.

What makes the credit question particularly interesting from a global marketing perspective is that in many cases the competitive advantages depend critically on this question. For the seller to have strong support from a dominant international bank is of unquestionable advantage in many of these cases. The Japanese trading companies are provided such support through their affiliated keiretsu banks, which can also help organize financial support from related companies. If, in addition, the government in the home country can be persuaded to use its financial leverage to provide further credit the competitiveness of the seller can be increased dramatically. For example, the Airbus sales are generally made at relatively high prices per plane but are accompanied by advantageous loans extended by the governments involved in the consortium (France, U.K.). To compete against the Airbus it might not be sufficient to offer lower prices but more important to offer good terms for credit payments. The Boeing aircraft company undertakes a heavy lobbying and advertising effort supporting the Export-Import Bank in Washington, D.C., partly because the Bank helps the company offer competitive credit terms.[7]

Exchange Rates

Fluctuating exchange rates will routinely create problems with revenues and prices in a foreign market and can affect the performance of local subsidiaries powerfully. A particularly potent threat is the chance of a government **devaluation** as happened in Mexico (see box, "Mexico's Peso Problems").

In less severe cases, **exchange rate fluctuations** do not always affect prices in the manner postulated by economic theory. A rising currency does not necessarily mean higher prices, weakened competitiveness and less exports. A simple example helps illustrate what might happen.

Take the case of trade between Germany and Japan. If the German mark depreciates against the yen, theory says that German automobiles will be cheaper in Japan while Japanese automobiles will be more expensive in Germany. Because of existing inventories of automobiles and lags between ordering and delivery times, the effect may not be immediate, but gradually the trade balance will shift. German automobiles will sell better in Japan, while Japan's market shares in Germany will diminish. The extent of the shift depends on the price elasticities in the two countries for the automobiles traded and thus on available substitutes from domestic producers and other foreign producers.

From a managerial perspective, this scenario depends on prices being set by the headquarters in the home country currency—and that they stay unchanged. In other words, German exporters are assumed to quote prices to their Japanese importers in terms of the same D-mark (Deutsche mark) price as before the currency depreciation. Similarly, the Japanese are assumed to stay with the same yen prices to their German subsidiaries as before. Neither case is necessarily realistic for the company with global operations.

Getting the Picture

Mexico's Peso Problems

THE DEVALUATION of the Mexican peso in January 1995 was a prime example of how difficult pricing in foreign markets can be in an era of exchange rate volatility.

During the early years of the 1990s, Mexico was a fast-growing market and a very attractive market for foreign products. The economy was spurred by the creation of NAFTA, the North American Free Trade Agreement, which ensured free access for Mexican goods in Canada and the U.S. Foreign direct investment flowed in as companies were producing for the internal Mexican market and also for exports. With the peso pegged to the U.S. dollar, the purchasing power of the Mexicans increased apace with growth, and imports grew rapidly.

However, as the peso grew increasingly overvalued, the Mexican exports became high priced and uncompetitive, and foreign investment slowed down. As the import surplus grew, the country's foreign exchange reserves were depleted, forcing a devaluation only days after a new government was installed. By mid-1995, the peso had lost in the neighborhood of 30% of its original value.

For the foreign marketer in Mexico, the booming sales to Mexican consumers suddenly lost their luster. In the short run, revenues were the same in pesos—but back home at headquarters, they often did not cover production costs. Over the next few months, as pending orders from Mexican sales subsidiaries were filled at foreign prices, they became too expensive for the Mexican consumers to buy with their devalued pesos, and the multinationals faced the question of whether to support the Mexican market positions by introducing lower prices. Most opted to maintain prices, forcing the Mexican consumers to forgo imports. Firms with local manufacturing or assembly fared better, since their costs came down— which will help make exports from Mexico become competitive again.

This experience is not atypical for firms doing business abroad. The famous German carmaker, Porsche, did brisk business in the United States in the first half of the 1980s, with its strong dollar-to-mark ratio. The company received about half of its annual revenues from U.S. sales alone. However, in 1985, the so-called Plaza Accord to lower the dollar's value against other currencies ruined Porsche's performance, and the company lost its status as an independent company and was sold to Volkswagen.

Sources: Lustig, 1995; Thurston, 1995; and various newspaper reports.

First, the Japanese may decide that the German market is too important for them and therefore keep their D-mark prices in Germany unchanged in an attempt to maintain market share. This strategy was common for the Japanese after the Plaza Accord in 1985 led to a yen appreciation of nearly 40 percent. Since the revenues from the automobiles sold in Germany will be lower than before, profits for the Japanese will tend to fall even as volume sales stay steady.

Second, the shrinking profitability will induce the Japanese to shift supply routes. Instead of shipping to Germany from Japan, which is now a more expensive producer, the Japanese companies will look for supplies from their manufacturing subsidiaries in a third country whose currency has moved with the German mark. This is one reason why many Japanese companies have started to supply Europe from their North American–based subsidiaries.

Third, when the shift in the exchange rate is judged to be more or less permanent, management will explore the option of investing in production in Germany (or in an EU country, where the currency is closely aligned with the D-mark). Although currency rate fluctuations are notoriously difficult to forecast and thus rarely "permanent," the relatively small appreciation of the Japanese yen of about 10 percent at the beginning of the 1990s had this effect, since it coincided with long-term structural changes in the Japanese economy.

As for German companies faced with a depreciating D-mark, they become more price competitive in Japan and their exports are stimulated, much in the way economic theory suggests. Their incentive to invest abroad is reduced, and no trade-substituting foreign direct investment (FDI) is likely to occur. Nevertheless, to the extent that the German automobiles rely on components produced abroad, perhaps in their own foreign subsidiaries, the cost of such components may rise. The tendency will be for such components to be replaced by German domestic supplies where feasible, and German value added will be increased.

Thus, a depreciating currency often leads to an increased ability to lower prices abroad and increased competitiveness for the exporter. By contrast, an appreciating currency does not necessarily lead to higher prices and lower competitiveness, since the company can often shift supply routes and invest in overseas manufacturing.

This asymmetrical pattern is even more pronounced for the company that has a global network of manufacturing locations and a presence in many markets. Not only can alternate supplier locations help limit the damage from currency fluctuations, but a presence in multiple markets makes it possible to shift emphasis from one market to another. As their competitiveness in German markets decreases, Japanese companies can simply allow their shares to go down and instead focus on other markets where the currency rate against the yen is more favorable. This was happening in the late 1980s as the weak U.S. dollar made American markets less attractive and the then stronger D-mark made Germany a particularly attractive market.[8]

In the big picture, the effect of exchange rate fluctuations on the market prices of the products sold is limited not only by what managers can do but also by what they can't do. Prices can't be changed overnight, even if exchange rates do. Purchasing contracts for industrial products may be negotiated months in advance and remain in force for a prespecified period. Suppliers of high quality components are sometimes asked to work closely with the company's designers and engineers and can't be easily dismissed. There are considerable start-up costs in organizing and managing a distribution channel in a foreign country, and a shift in exchange rates will often be viewed as a "windfall" profit or loss to the channel members without any adjustment in prices and costs quoted. To avoid the risk of wide fluctuations in short-term profits, the global company will often turn to hedging.

Hedging

Hedging involves the purchase of insurance against losses because of currency fluctuations. Such insurance usually takes the form of buying or selling "forward contracts" or engaging in "currency swaps" with the help of financial intermediaries (banks and brokerage houses).

A **forward contract** refers to the sale or purchase of a specified amount of a foreign currency at a fixed exchange rate for delivery or settlement on an agreed date in the future, or, under an options contract, between agreed upon dates in the future. A **swap** may be defined as the exchange of one currency for another for a fixed period of time. At the expiration of the swap each party returns the currency initially received. While the forward contract represents a simple insurance policy against downside risk—the firm buys today so as not to lose by deteriorating exchange rates—the cost of the contract reduces the gain from a favorable change in rates.

Various combinations of these contracts are possible and hedging has become a major financial activity of the international division in many MNCs. From a marketing viewpoint, the most desirable arrangement would be for the seller to assume responsibility for currency fluctuations and quote prices in the local currency. This is not done very often by Western companies, however. Their prices, especially in commodities and industrial markets, tend to be quoted in the "hard" currencies, in particular the U.S. dollar. A company such as Boeing, for example, quotes prices in U.S. dollars only and lets their customers worry about the exchange rate fluctuations and the conversion from the local currency.

Government Intervention

Different countries exhibit different rates of inflation, some like Israel and Argentina in the past showing hyperinflationary patterns. The currencies of such countries will continuously be losing their value against stronger currencies and their governments intervening into the workings of the financial system in order to bring some stability to prices. The standard solution is selective **price controls**. For the global marketer, price controls mean that prices can't be changed as frequently as might be desirable—in particular, inflationary erosion of revenues can't so easily be avoided.

Under price controls, increases in prices usually need to be officially sanctioned. To obtain such sanction it is typically required that price increases be directly related to costs. Accordingly, companies with exemplary accounting records tend to have a much better chance of getting their requests for increases in price sanctioned. But where inflation is very rapid, it is unlikely that cost increases alone are sufficient to justify price increases. In such a case, the company has to resort to the kind of currency management discussed above under the exchange rate heading, getting involved in forward contracts and swap deals. Needless to say, such matters are best handled by financial, not marketing, officers of the firm.

There are other types of government intervention that affect pricing. Chief among these are the antitrust laws, in particular as they relate to price fixing and discrimination. Not much can be said here about these matters—the interested reader is referred to any international law book. The firm's legal counsel is the person most likely to be involved in these matters. In terms of price fixing it is important to point out that in certain countries price cartels are not forbidden per se as they are in the United States and that there are several instances of cartels in, for example, Japan. Under the current trend toward open markets and free international trade, however, cartels will be increasingly under attack. The 1994 flat glass agreement, in which American trade negotiators managed to break open a Japanese cartel to allow foreign firms to bid on new construction, is an example of how protective barriers gradually fall.

In terms of **price discrimination,** there are very few laws of the American Robinson-Patman type that prohibit discrimination unless justified by cost savings. However, many laws do question discounts not tied to specific functions performed—the issue of bribery surfaces easily. The firm needs to get some legal advice on what is acceptable and what is not in the particular country. In Japan, for example, it is customary to give large functional rebates to the many middlemen handling the product in that country's complex network of distribution.[9] It is usually necessary to offer such rebates for any newcomer who wants to enter the market.

TRANSFER PRICING

With a considerable amount of some countries' trade accounted for by shipments between headquarters and subsidiaries, the question of what the value of these shipments is and what the prices mean naturally arises. This is the problem of "transfer" prices.

Definition

The basic reason for **transfer pricing** is simple: There has to be a price paid for the products shipped between units of the same organization when the shipment crosses national borders so that the correct duties and related fees can be paid. However, since the transfer prices charged directly affect the amount of purchases in the cost accounting of a foreign subsidiary, they have a direct influence on the subsidiary's financial performance. Because of this they have also become a mechanism for the multinational company to shift profits from one country to another. If the headquarters of a company sets a high price on the shipment to a subsidiary in an African country, say, this subsidiary will have trouble showing a profit—and if the (quite arbitrary) price is set low, the subsidiary will be very profitable.

The use of transfer prices for the purpose of profit repatriation has come under the close scrutiny of many governments whose tax revenues have

Getting the Picture

How to Transfer Income? Carefully

BECAUSE OF the tax and dumping implications of transfer prices and governments' insistence on transparent accounting rules, public accounting firms have developed strict guidelines for the transfer pricing process in large multinationals. The following 10 steps are typical of the recommended process:

1. Before the beginning of annual business cycle, meet with outside advisors and agree on a game plan.
2. Compare third-party (arm's-length) transactions with "related party" transactions. Adjust prices.
3. Prepare a financial model to test the method agreed on.
4. Make sure senior management understands the transfer pricing audit process, issues, and exposure.
5. Prepare internal documentation.
6. Prepare external documentation.
7. Spot-check the process within the company.
8. Simulate a transfer pricing audit by outside advisors.
9. Evaluate year-end or cycle-end tax position against goals.
10. Prepare tax returns.

Sources: Davis, 1994; Weekly, 1992.

diminished because of it (see box, "How to Transfer Income?"). Reputedly, the use of transfer prices for tax-shifting purposes is not as widespread as it once was because the governments have now caught on to past abuses. Transfer prices have taken on an additional role as control mechanisms, however.

Arm's-Length Price

From a theoretical point of view, the transfer prices set should reflect the prices the subsidiary might encounter in the open market—so-called **arm's-length prices.**[10] In this way the costs of the goods to the subsidiary will give the right "signals" to the buyer about how much to buy, and the consequent operating criteria (such as return on investment and profits) will be valid indicators of the subsidiary's performance. In the practical world there are times when such market prices are difficult to identify, usually because there are no substitutes in the open market. The practice also goes against the use of transfer pricing to shift profits from one country to another.

Judging from their public statements, many global American companies have given up trying to repatriate profits in this fashion and do indeed attempt to set market-related transfer prices. Several companies have even taken the logical step of introducing an option for the subsidiary to buy on the open market, should price and quality there be more favorable. Many of Ford Motor Company's subsidiaries around the world now have this option—to exercise it requires, however, a quite rigorous demonstration that the quality of components and parts is up to par.

Because of the "signaling" function of market-based transfer prices, these prices also serve as "arm's-length" control devices, yielding correct indicators of

The Hertz company's uniform pricing approach appeals to global business customers who travel to many countries and want to simplify control over expenses. However, local customers in countries with weak currencies against the dollar may find Hertz relatively expensive.

Courtesy The Hertz Corporation.

performance. But when headquarters wants the individual subsidiary to "fall in line" behind an overall global strategy, the market-related transfers will usually have to be adjusted. An example will explain why. The global strategy might call for one country's subsidiary to concentrate on the manufacturing of a certain component or subassembly. Management in that subsidiary might well have other plans, however, having spotted a good opportunity for the introduction of a new product in their local market. Given the market-based transfer prices, the subsidiary would make more money pursuing this opportunity. In principle, they should then suggest to headquarters that the components the subsidiary had been assigned should be supplied from the open market—the opportunity lost otherwise being too great. Headquarters might be unwilling to do that for various reasons, but in forcing the subsidiary to adhere to the global strategy, headquarters should raise the transfer prices on the components so as to compensate the subsidiary for the lost opportunity.

Shifting Resources

There are other factors influencing the level of transfer prices, most related to the flow of funds between headquarters and the subsidiaries. Where the country suffers from rapid inflation, there is usually an attempt to keep the operating funds at a minimum. The shipments of intermediate goods going to the subsidiary in the country will be charged at a higher rate than otherwise, for example. This was the effect of the problems firms faced in Brazil in the 1980s. If a country suffers from currency shortages (rationing of dollars, for example) this approach will not work since the payments are not convertible. Options then include currency swaps, forward contracts, countertrade, and so on. In the end, the global firm will attempt to reduce its dependence on the country, possibly pulling out its investments. This was why the Mexican devaluation in early 1995 was so threatening to Mexico and other countries in Latin America.

Transfer prices can also be used to support a subsidiary's competitive position in a local market. Where the market position is strategically important for the global position of the MNC, headquarters might well transfer more funds to the subsidiary by simply charging low prices for some key product components or parts. The approach is equivalent to government subsidies, but in this case it is carried out within a corporation. An example is the entry of many Japanese companies into the U.S. market. In the initial stages at least, the American offices are usually staffed by people paid directly from Japan without any attempt to make the subsidiary a profit center.

The biggest headache in designing the levels of transfer prices is often the organizational repercussions of the prices. For example, one company in the pharmaceutical industry whose highly directive transfer pricing caused a disproportionate share of income to arise overseas could not stop the obvious boasting of some country heads about their "contribution" to overall profits. In fact, these profits were "allocated" to them through the system of transfer prices used. At the annual retreat, the company's head of international was finally compelled by distraught managers at headquarters to distribute "revised" earnings based on transfer prices more in line with actual costs. Unfortunately, this also meant that the "global view" the company had attempted to encourage was replaced by a recognition on the part of the country heads that the company was still basically ethnocentric. It is these organizational repercussions that have caused many companies to retreat to the "arm's-length" transfer prices, for which profitability is a more valid indication of performance.

DUMPING

Even though pricing on the basis of costs alone is not commonly done, cost-based pricing (including experience curve pricing) has one strong justification: It is the pricing procedure easiest to defend against dumping charges.

Dumping is commonly defined as selling goods in some markets below cost. There are sometimes good management reasons for doing that. A typical case is an entry into a large competitive market by selling at very low prices; another case is when a company has overproduced and wants to sell the product in a market where it has no brand franchise to protect. "Reverse dumping" refers to the less-common practice of selling products at home at prices below cost. This would be done in extreme cases where the share at home needs to be protected while monopolistic market positions abroad can be used to generate surplus funds ("cash cows" in foreign markets). Regardless, dumping as defined is often illegal since it is destructive of trade, and competitors can take an offender to court to settle a dumping case. The usual penalty for manufacturers whose products are found to violate the antidumping laws is a **countervailing duty** that brings the prices back up over production costs and also imposes a fine.

The manner in which the relevant costs are used to define dumping varies between countries, reflecting the fact that economists have difficulty agreeing on a common definition. Most countries and regional groupings have established their own particular version of antidumping regulations. Under the new WTO (World Trade Organization) trade laws, the antidumping rules that are to apply to all members are more liberal than usual, making penalties more difficult to assign.[11] The new rules, developed with the intent to support emerging countries' exports, feature: (1) stricter definitions of injury, (2) higher minimum dumping levels needed to trigger imposition of duties, (3) more rigorous petition requirements, and (4) dumping duty exemptions for new shippers.[12]

To enforce rules against dumping, the injured party can file a complaint with the appropriate government agency, in the U.S. the Department of Commerce. Countervailing duties are imposed only if the DOC finds that dumping has occurred and if then the U.S. International Trade Commission (ITC) makes an affirmative determination that the dumped goods are causing injury. There are problems in enforcing antidumping laws caused by the difficulty in ascertaining the exact height of the costs involved, regardless of definition, and dumping cases are notorious for their protracted duration. The 1968 case against Japanese TV producers in the U.S. market, for example, took three years to decide, and by 1977 the assessed extra dumping duties were not yet fully collected. At this later date the U.S. low-price importers had already shifted their sources of supplies from Japan to Taiwan and South Korea.

Because of the inefficiency of the enforcement and the fact that many countries have excess capacity and overproduction (especially in steel, shoes, TVs, and textiles, where diffusion of production technology has made many countries capable manufacturers), dumping is a continuous headache for domestic industry and host governments in the 1990s. Efforts to generate stepped-up government enforcement and more rapid resolution of legal conflicts are currently under way in several countries, but dumping is close to becoming a way of life in the freely competitive local markets.

SYSTEMS PRICING

One pricing issue of frequent relevance in global markets is the question of systems pricing. **Systems selling** or **turnkey sales** refers to the notion that in many instances the firm is selling not only some particular physical product or offering a single service but also is providing the buyer with a complete

Siemens workers delivering a turnkey switching system in Bangkok. The sale of a modern telecommunication network involves not only equipment installation but also training of operators, maintenance, and service support.

Courtesy Siemens AG.

"package." Examples include the turnkey plants being built by firms from developed countries in many LDCs—for instance, the paper and pulp mill built in Japan and floated to the Manaus free trade zone on the Amazon river in Brazil.[13] Fiat's auto plant in Russia is another example. Many computerized office systems are sold as complete turnkey operations because of compatibility requirements. The German computer firm Nixdorf, now part of Siemens, has long specialized in complete information systems for banks in Europe. The driving force in these sales is not the hardware itself but the added value produced by wedding hardware and software into a functioning and complete system. The question is how such a system should be priced.

Exhibit 13.2 demonstrates how one firm has gone about analyzing this pricing problem.[14] The company deals with a varied set of customers in Southeast Asia in the telecommunications industry. The specific hardware sold is a mobile telephone, but the final sales to many customers also involve switching networks, computerized accounting and billing facilities, the construction of physical facilities, and the training of supervisors. The firm does not manufacture the switches or the telephones but serves basically as the prime contractor for the turnkey system, carries out the initial feasibility studies, develops the administrative software, and selects the hardware components and

EXHIBIT 13.2 Pricing a Turnkey Package

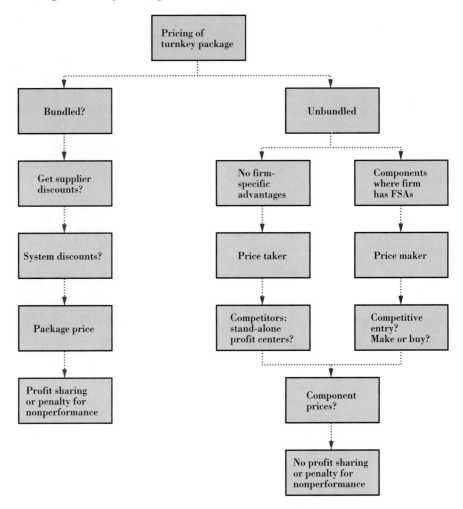

the construction subcontractor for the physical facilities. Its know-how and FSA lies in the experience accumulated in running these types of systems in the United States.

As Exhibit 13.2 demonstrates, an initial decision is made between offering an unbundled system versus a complete turnkey operation. The unbundling option is less preferable from the seller's point of view and is only resorted to when the customer insists he has certain skills that can be used for parts of the project. The seller attempts to direct the participation of the buyer into areas where the seller has no firm-specific advantage (FSAs), partly in order to protect against dissipation and also because alternative suppliers are available. This is done by pricing such components high—while areas where the firm's proprietary know-how (its FSAs) are lodged are priced more aggressively so as to discourage customers from going outside or doing their own. Thus, system design, an area in which the firm claims a great deal of expertise, tends to be sold aggressively, while the telephone hardware is less of a concern and accordingly priced higher.

In the preferred case the customer does not attempt to unbundle but allows the firm to become the supplier for the complete turnkey operation. In such a case the firm will identify the overall price by negotiating for possible supplier discounts, using its previous connections with suppliers to obtain special discounts if possible. Where desirable, these discounts can then be passed on to the customer. The ability to obtain these special discounts is one argument used to convince the customer not to unbundle the package.

When the complete system is handled, the firm is in a position to guarantee its performance—a guarantee customarily not offered when unbundling has taken place (to accept responsibility the firm needs to be in complete control of the project). In its home market the firm has been willing to accept business risk on some projects, receiving full payment only after successful installation and marketing of the mobile telephone system. Such an exposure has not been deemed acceptable in foreign markets.

THE FINAL PRICE

Before deciding on the final price, some basics of pricing and positioning need to be kept in mind. In the final analysis, price is important because it represents the sacrifice for the potential customer contemplating a purchase. As such, price is no different whether we think of a consumer in Tanzania, in Thailand, or in Turkey. Most of the pricing discussions in traditional marketing texts are relevant at this stage. A few issues, however, do not translate so directly from the domestic to the foreign and global markets and need to be considered carefully when going abroad. They include the question of price-quality relationships in positioning of the product and the role of the product life cycle with its skimming versus penetration price.

Price-Quality Relationships

In many markets where the positioning objective of a product is for a high-quality niche in the market, it goes without saying that price has to be relatively high. What is assumed, often correctly, is that customers will attribute high quality to a product with high price. It would generally cost more to produce a high-quality product and thus its price will be higher. Research has shown that this **price-quality relationship** varies in strength by products, standardized products being less affected. Also, a strong brand name or a strongly positive country-of-origin image can nullify the negative quality effect from a low price.[15]

The price-quality relationship is also weakened in markets protected by trade barriers. In such markets imported products will usually show an artificially high price (the price escalation phenomenon), and thus a high price signals an imported product, not only or even necessarily a high-quality product. In many cases such imports will be of higher quality (if they were not, why would they be imported?), so the high price is in a sense justified. In other cases, however, the escalated prices are simply too high to render a product competitive and the imports will make no inroads against established domestic brands. An example is the situation in the Japanese market where high nontariff barriers have made many markets "dualistic," with a domestic and an import segment.[16] The majority of the market falls to the domestic producers, between whom competition is intense, while the imports garner a small fringe segment of the market whose primary buying appeal is "status." A typical case is cameras, where a Swiss Leica is priced at approximately 2.5 times the price of Nikon, a high-priced Japanese rival, or autos, where a BMW is priced at double its American price. Perhaps not surprisingly, for both companies Japan is their most profitable market.[17]

In this type of distorted marketplace, the assumption that high prices necessarily imply higher functional quality no longer holds and the consumers will by and large learn this fact. Status is what matters. A high-priced Western luxury car, such as a Cadillac, is not equipped for right-hand drive, for example, even though the Japanese drive on the left. In Japan, the customers can usually buy more functional quality products at relatively low prices, by staying with domestic offerings.

The PLC Impact

It is generally agreed that in the introductory stage of the product life cycle (PLC) customers are relatively insensitive to price levels. The innovators and pioneers who venture to try the new product are not very much concerned with price but act out of a desire to experience new things. Thus, the firm entering a market in the early growth stage could possibly maintain a relatively high **skimming price,** charging what the market will bear.

This logic becomes much less clear in global markets. Even though a given local market might be new so that the product is in the introductory stage technically speaking, it might already have reached the maturity stage in other local markets and certainly in leading markets. If so, the existing producers in those countries will be potential entrants in the new market and thus serve to put a limit on prices. Further, a "demonstration" effect serves to speed up the introductory phase of many products—potential customers are prepared for the eventual arrival of the new product by exposure via television and related global media.

Consequently, the best entry pricing strategy in many markets will be a relatively low-priced **penetration** approach. This is also the one followed in recent years by most companies, including companies as diverse as Microsoft

IN 1994 some car models cost 30% to 40% less in Italy than in Germany because of the recent devaluation of the lira. The flood of reimports prompted one German automaker to drastic action. To control reimports from Italy where prices were much lower than at home in Germany, the company bought back a number of reimported cars from the gray traders and offered them as a "special series model" to authorized German dealers at gray import prices. Next, headquarters limited the number of cars to the Italian dealers, who were no longer able to supply both local customers and gray trade demand. With a limited supply the prices in Italy moved up, and with the exception of a few gray reimports by private owners, the so-called "pipeline control" worked out well.

Sources: Assmus and Wiese, 1995; Simon, 1995.

Getting the Picture

Checking Gray Trade the Hard Way

with its office products, Compaq in PC hardware, Mercedes' new model, Olympus cameras, and Xerox copiers. The competitive rivalry is potentially intense, the buyers in the global village already know much about the product, and the producers use the experience curve argument to justify very low prices based on marginal costs. If the competitors consider the new entry to be in the potential "star" category, they will price aggressively for global strategic reasons.[18] All in all, the role of a skimming strategy in the introductory stage in the PLC is severely limited, although in the mature stage of the cycle a well protected position can possibly still be used to generate cash in the short term.

GLOBAL COORDINATION

When a company manufactures in several nations and sells its products in many countries, the same product might appear on the market in different countries at widely different prices.

For many products there is a need to develop a formula for coordinating prices and avoid creating confusion among customers and opportunities for gray trade. A global customer does not usually like to pay different prices for the same product in different parts of the world. If he finds he does, he might simply concentrate purchases where the price is lowest, ship to his subsidiaries elsewhere, and cut costs. Or he might opt to put pressure on the manufacturer. For example, a leading manufacturer of consumer products distributed through large local and pan-European retailers had its biggest retail customer request that all products be supplied at the lowest European price. The company had to comply, but the 20 percent price decline across Europe resulted in a profit disaster.[20]

A coordinated pricing policy is obviously desirable but not so easily implemented. Generally, one can identify a polycentric, a geocentric, and an

....

EXHIBIT 13.3 The Hamburger Standard

| | Big Mac prices | | | | |
	Prices In local currency*	Prices in dollars	Actual exchange rate 13/4/93	Implied purchasing power parity† of the dollar	Local currency under (-)/ over (+) valuation**,%
United States‡	$2.28	$2.28	—	—	—
Argentina	Peso3.60	3.60	1.00	1.58	+58
Australia	A$2.45	1.76	1.39	1.07	−23
Belgium	BFr109	3.36	32.45	47.81	+47
Brazil	Cr77,000	2.80	27,521	33,772	+23
Britain	£1.79	2.79	1.56 ‡‡	1.27 ‡‡	+23
Canada	C$2.76	2.19	1.26	1.21	−4
China	Yuan8.50	1.50	5.68	3.73	−34
Denmark	DKr25.75	4.25	6.06	11.29	+86
France	FFr18.50	3.46	5.34	8.11	+52
Germany	DM4.60	2.91	1.58	2.02	+28
Holland	Fl5.45	3.07	1.77	2.39	+35
Hong Kong	HK$9.00	1.16	7.73	3.95	−49
Hungary	Forint157	1.78	88.18	68.86	−22
Ireland	I£1.48	2.29	1.54 ‡‡	1.54 ‡‡	0
Italy	Lire4,500	2.95	1,523	1,974	+30
Japan	Y391	3.45	113	171	+51
Malaysia	Ringgit3.35	1.30	2.58	1.47	−43
Mexico	Peso7.09	2.29	3.10	3.11	0
Russia	Rouble780	1.14	686§	342	−50
S. Korea	Won2,300	2.89	796	1,009	+27
Spain	Ptas325	2.85	114	143	+25
Sweden	SKr25.50	3.43	7.43	11.18	+50
Switzerland	SwFr5.70	3.94	1.45	2.50	+72
Thailand	Baht48	1.91	25.16	21.05	−16

*Prices may very locally

†Purchasing-power parity: local price divided by price in United States

**Against dollar

‡Average of New York, Chicago, San Francisco, and Atlanta

‡‡Dollars per pound

§Market rate

Source: *The Economist*, April 17, 1993, p. 79, with data from McDonald's. © 1993 The Economist Newspaper Group, Inc. Reprinted with permission.

ethnocentric approach. But first companies have to decide what to do about gray trade.

Usually, the problem relates to exchange rate fluctuations. A good example is the pricing of a McDonald's hamburger. Although the company attempts to position the products as affordable and targets broad-based segments in most local markets the resulting prices vary a great deal, as Exhibit 13.3 shows. The 1993 Big Mac prices ranged from $1.03 in China to $3.69 in Switzerland, and even between two relatively comparable countries such as Singapore and Korea the range is from $1.90 to $2.84.

Pricing Actions Against Gray Trade

The problem of gray trade is particularly acute in trade areas where barriers have recently been dismantled and exchange rates fluctuate—the EU being one example. According to one report, for identical consumer products, prices typically deviate 30 percent to 150 percent, creating big **arbitrage** opportunities.[19] By the mid-1990s, if you lived in France but bought your car elsewhere in Europe, you could have saved 24.3 percent on a Citroen, 18.2 percent on a Peugeot, or 33 percent on a Volkswagen Jetta (see box, "Checking Gray Trade the Hard Way"). Against this background it is not surprising if the drive towards a common European currency (the "Euro") is sustained despite many countries' misgivings.

As will be seen in Chapter 14, on "Global Distribution," controlling gray trade involves more than trying to set prices that eliminate price differentials between countries, an impossible task in a world of floating exchange rates. Nevertheless, some pricing actions can be taken to help reduce the gray trade problem.

Four approaches to coordinating prices under the threat of gray trade can be identified.[21] They are not mutually exclusive; a company can pursue a combination:

- *Economic controls.* The company can influence price setting in local markets by changing the prices at which the product is shipped to importers or by outright rationing of the product as in the German auto case (described in the box.) This usually is most feasible in the case of transfer prices to wholly owned subsidiaries.
- *Centralization.* The company can attempt to set limits for local prices. This can involve so-called "price corridors," ranges of prices within which all local prices in a trading area must fall. The corridor should consider market data for the individual countries, price elasticities in the countries, currency exchange rates, costs in countries and arbitrage costs between them, plus data on competition and distribution.[22] The United Distilleries example (see box below) shows how the process can be implemented.

EXHIBIT 13.4   Coordinated Pricing Strategies

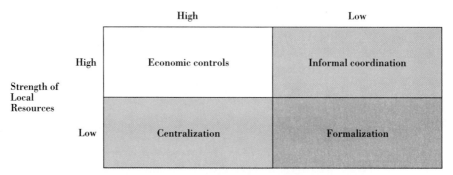

Source: Gert Assmus and Carsten Wiese, "How to Address the Gray Market Threat Using Price Coordination," *Sloan Management Review*, 36, no. 3 (1995), pp. 31–42. Reprinted by permission of publisher. Copyright 1995 by the Sloan Management Association. All rights reserved.

- *Formalization.* The company can standardize the process of planning and implementing pricing decisions at the local level.
- *Informal coordination.* The company can institute various informal coordination mechanisms, including explicit articulation of corporate values and culture, human resource exchanges, and frequent visits to share experiences in other markets.

The choice between these approaches is affected by many factors, but two have been identified as particularly important: level of marketing standardization and strength of local resources. The diagram in Exhibit 13.4 helps identify how these factors affect choice of method.[23]

When marketing standardization is high, target segments and the elements of the marketing mix are known well enough for headquarters to help set local prices. If local resources are on a high level, economic controls tend to be preferable, since raising and lowering transfer prices or rationing will send clear signals to local representatives without imposing final prices. But if local resources are weak, centralization of the pricing decisions may be necessary, creating limits beyond which prices may not deviate.

In the low standardization case, when marketing is multidomestic in orientation, with locally adapted mix elements, headquarters' role will be less directive. Local managers are likely to be better informed about local conditions than headquarters. When local representatives are less resourceful, formalization of procedures can be helpful in ensuring that the appropriate factors are taken into account when local prices are set. With strong local resources, informal coordination is likely to be preferable, preserving local

Getting the Picture

Informal Coordination: Using the Carrot and the Stick

ONE COMPANY in high-tech medical equipment was faced with a sticky problem. In some countries, doctors needed extensive service support to operate the equipment, while in other countries hospitals had more trained staff. The transfer prices to these latter countries were set higher since sales costs for the subsidiaries were lower. But hospital purchasing managers in these countries were able to lower procurement costs by ordering equipment directly from subsidiaries in countries with lower transfer costs.

To solve the problem, headquarters first organized discussion groups with subsidiary managers to find an acceptable solution. After several meetings, the following strategy was adopted. First, the three most important markets were defined as lead countries. The main pricing authority was given to the local managers in the lead countries, who were to set prices so that gray trade would not be lucrative. Second, the country managers were trained and rotated between countries to better understand local competition and profit responsibility. Third, the reward system was changed by basing part of the local manager's annual bonuses on the success of the whole group. Managers who were uncooperative and hindered progress toward more coordination were laid off.

After one year, the problems were solved. Prices were coordinated, and profitability increased by more than 10%.

Source: Assmus and Wiese, 1995.

autonomy—but still using a stick if the carrot is not enough (see box, "Informal Coordination").

One implication of the diagram in Exhibit 13.4 is that firms in the same industry may choose to use different coordination methods. In one example, two competing European producers of housebuilding equipment had highly centralized production, with country subsidiaries mainly serving as distribution centers so the level of local resources was low. The smaller of the two competitors carried a very broad product range to meet widely different construction standards in the various markets—marketing standardization was low. According to the diagram in Exhibit 13.4, the solution would be to formalize pricing rules, and the firm developed simple pricing rules that tied its prices to local competitors'. The company showed its country managers a way to calculate the value of its brand image relative to competitors and then set prices above or below the competition. In addition, since the company's main market was in Germany, the country managers were instructed to consider the German price levels and adjust their prices so there would be less incentive for German customers to buy from outside.

The larger competitor faced a different situation. It had anticipated European integration and used a leadership position to simplify its product line in all its European markets. It then collected market data, including demand elasticities, in the various countries for its main products. This meant that the company possessed better information about the local market than its subsidiary did. These two steps made marketing standardization possible, and the company proceeded to set prices by a strongly centralized approach.

Polycentric Pricing

In a polycentric organization, prices are set at their appropriate levels in each local market separately, without constraints from headquarters. Naturally, prices might vary considerably between countries in **polycentric pricing.** On the other hand, there is the undeniable advantage of really being able to adjust prices to the particular conditions facing the product in any one country.

Geocentric Pricing

The most common **geocentric pricing** scheme revolves around the use of a global or regional standard plus a markup that is variable across countries. The comparison price is derived for the home country or some other lead country for the world or a regional trading bloc. This base price is computed from a cost-plus formula. The markup is then adjusted for the particular situation the product faces in each country. When demand is strong and competition is weak (a "cash cow" situation) the added-on markup will be high; if competition is strong the markup will come down. A Swedish pharmaceutical company with a successful ulcer drug uses this approach in its European markets.[24] The coordination is not easy, because the company has to take into account not only competition and demand but also regulatory factors and reimbursement formulas that differ between countries. Of course, the possibility of gray trade across country borders also needs to be taken into account, especially after the EU integration. The overall consistency across EU countries is ensured by periodically reviewing the prices at headquarters and comparing to the base price.

The biggest headache in geocentric pricing is the question of **product line pricing.** The markup deemed reasonable for one product in the line might not be very appropriate for another item in the line with a different competitive situation. Consequently, the assigned markup will differ across products in a local market. The strategy followed by United Distillers is instructive (see box, "Portfolio Pricing of Spirits").

Philip Morris, the American tobacco company, tried for years to maintain a premium price image for its world-leading Marlboro brand. Because of widely varying tariffs and pricing regulations—and tobacco tax differences—the actual prices on Marlboro varied considerably across countries but the premium image was consistent across the Philip Morris product line. This policy was finally abandoned in 1993, when competitive pressure and increased taxes in some states in the United States forced the company to discount Marlboro.[25] The

UNITED DISTILLERS of Britain, one of the most profitable spirits companies in the world, reanalyzed its pricing policies in order to optimize global performance. Because the organization was formed through successive mergers between several smaller distillers, it had been natural to maintain a brand management system, where each brand was run by a brand manager with sales and profit responsibility. But taking a global approach, the company realized the need for a more coordinated pricing system.

A careful analysis of the demand structure of several local markets based on historical sales and marketing data for the various brands showed that:

1. The specific price elasticities of brands were much different from the generic price elasticities of a market as a whole. Brand loyal customers followed a brand as its price went up, even if as a whole consumers were sensitive to the price level in the product category. For example, rising beer prices might shift some buyers to other drinks—but raising the price of a favored beer brand would not make many customers shift to another brand.

2. There were price ranges within which each brand could move without much effect on sale (price elasticity was low), but with wider swings price elasticity could suddenly jump, as the brand moved into another set of competitive brands.

3. Sales of one brand without a loyal following could be affected greatly by shifts of prices of competing brands with higher awareness. Similar cross-elasticities (i.e., sales response of one brand when another brand changed price) held for a majority of the markets investigated. It was possible to find an optimum set of prices where each brand attracted a different set of consumers.

United Distillers used the results from the statistical analysis to first develop subsets ("portfolios") of brands whose cross-elasticities were high and who therefore justified coordination on a global scale. Then brand managers for the various brands involved got together in global groups to agree on price ranges or **price corridors** that maximized the portfolio's overall sales and profit performance rather than the performance of the individual brands.

Sources: Sims, Phillips, and Richards, 1992; Simon, 1995.

premium positioning is still attempted in foreign markets, but the global coordination of prices is no longer in effect.

Product line pricing is very much influenced by varying competitive conditions. When IBM competes with Digital Equipment Corporation (DEC) in some particular country, only minicomputers might be involved. Accordingly, IBM could lower its prices on these units alone in the countries in question. The problem is that in terms of the overall product line, lower prices for the large-scale units will make its smaller scale units seem overpriced. Further, if the unit prices are lowered in some countries but not others (where

---

Getting the Picture

Hewlett-Packard's New Global Pricing System

IN 1992, faced with a globalizing marketplace, Hewlett-Packard, the computer maker based in Cupertino, California, realized that its international pricing system no longer worked. H-P's old system relied on two parts. The first was a *base* price, quoted in U.S. dollars and derived on the basis of production costs at home and estimated price elasticities in the U.S. market. On top of the base price each country's sales organization would charge an "uplift," taking into account price escalation due to transportation, tariffs, and their own sales costs. There was little attempt to analyze the differences in demand between countries and across the various products (minis, PCs, notebooks, printers, and so on).

In changing the global pricing system, the first move was to make each product division into a business unit responsible for pricing and profits worldwide. The U.S.-based formula was discarded in favor of a globalized price structure. The base price was changed to reflect transfer costs to the various countries, and the local subsidiaries set final prices on the basis of their own sales costs, demand conditions, and competitive situations. But headquarters has final say in pricing, over possible protests by locals, in order to be able to optimize worldwide performance. Held responsible for worldwide performance, business unit managers at headquarters are expected to set transfer prices and sales incentives to local managers so as to maximize overall profits.

Global coordination of prices does not mean one global price. Instead it has led to widely varying prices of identical products overseas, since local sales costs vary widely. To limit the gray trade potential, the local operations are encouraged to bring costs in line with market-based prices. Also, the global head of a business unit will adjust transfer prices to the various country sales organizations to reflect fluctuating exchange rates.

Sources: "The Price Is Right at Hewlett-Packard," *Financial Executive* 10, no. 1 (January–February 1994), pp. 22–25; Gates, 1995.

DEC does not have a sales office, for example), some large MNC might easily concentrate its computer purchases in the lowest-price country, and do its own distribution to different countries—parallel trade again. The solution adopted by IBM is to avoid changing prices but rather increase the marketing (including service) support in the countries under competitive attack.

In contrast to IBM, Hewlett-Packard, another computer maker, has shifted from a "standard plus markup" approach to a more global system (see box, "Hewlett-Packard's new Global Pricing System").

Ethnocentric Pricing

In **ethnocentric** pricing the same price is charged to all customers regardless of nationality. It provides a standard, worldwide price, usually derived on the basis of a full-cost formula to ensure that general overhead, selling expenses, and

R&D expenditures will be covered. This type of pricing approach is most useful when the company is producing a relatively standardized product with uniform usage patterns across many countries.

This is the typical pricing scheme for large-ticket items in industrial goods. Examples include aircraft and mainframe computers. IBM maintains this type of pricing policy, partly for the reasons stated above. Boeing, the aircraft company, is pricing all its commercial aircraft in this fashion, only making adjustments because of special customization requirements and quantity discounts—and Airbus competition.[26] Ethnocentric pricing is also a natural pricing procedure when the company is small and the international sales are few and far between. This is also the kind of pricing scheme most acceptable to global customers since homogeneity of prices worldwide makes planning easier and concentrated purchases from central headquarters possible.

Choosing the Approach

The ethnocentric approach to pricing in global companies has the great advantage of simplicity and allows headquarters to coordinate prices at the subsidiaries. But its drawbacks, primarily in terms of nonadaptation to the individual local markets, usually make it not useful to the multinational facing multidomestic markets and different competitive situations in each country. The polycentric approach is the one favored by most local managers of subsidiaries since it increases their control and allows complete attention to competing in the local market. Nevertheless, the lack of control and coordination from headquarters makes the polycentric strategy suboptimal in the global context, missing out on potential synergies and advantageous trade-offs. It also leaves the company open to the arbitrage possibilities of gray trade with entrepreneurial middlemen buying up products in a low-price country, transporting the shipment back to a high-price country, and undercutting regular resellers at a profit. Many different product categories such as cameras, watches, jeans, and compact disks suffer from parallel imports. Even though these middlemen in a sense help markets become more efficient and equalize prices, they create a headache for multinationals trying to manage their regular distribution channels and motivate authorized resellers to support and service their products.

Geocentric pricing, especially as regionalized by trading blocs, emerges as a well-balanced compromise between global coordination and local adaptation. The variable markup, or the use of price corridors, allows the subsidiaries to adapt to the specific conditions within their particular local markets, including the threat of parallel imports from a neighboring country. The markup adopted for a particular product and country can be based on both the demand conditions in the country and on the role the subsidiary is supposed to play in the MNC's overall global strategy. In this way it allows synergies to emerge and a global perspective is naturally adopted by both headquarters management and managers at local subsidiaries.

SUMMARY

This chapter has dealt with the many complex pricing issues facing the global marketer, showing how institutional limitations constrain purely strategic considerations in global pricing. The discussion dealt with export pricing issues and also the problems related to global coordination of prices. We first briefly discussed the role of the standard factors in price determination, that is, production cost (including experience curve effects), competition, and demand factors.

The institutional limitations involved in global pricing include problems of dumping, price escalation due to tariffs, exchange rate problems, and international credit arrangements. These factors combine to determine what the actual price of the product will be when it finally appears on the market abroad. This final price might be quite different from the intended positioning—in global marketing it is not always easy to control what the final price in the market will be because of regulatory limitations, the number of independent middlemen and facilitating agents, and the need to sustain the autonomy of a local subsidiary. The need to provide cost-based justifications against dumping accusations also constrains the possibility of implementing penetration price strategies in foreign markets. Transfer prices to local subsidiaries have various functions, in particular a role in performance evaluations of the subsidiaries.

The chapter dealt briefly with the positioning questions of how customers evaluate high and low prices in different countries and why the pricing know-how from the home country might not be applicable abroad. We discussed the pricing aspect of the gray trade problem with special reference to the EU market, along with various schemes that companies use to counter gray trade. In the last section of the chapter we described the relative merits of polycentric, geocentric, and ethnocentric pricing strategies in the global firm.

KEY TERMS

Arbitrage p. 495
Arm's-length prices p. 485
Cost-plus pricing p. 474
Countervailing duty p. 488
Credit terms p. 479
Devaluation p. 480
Dumping p. 487
Ethnocentric pricing p. 500
Exchange rate
fluctuations p. 480
Experience curve
pricing p. 475

Forward contract p. 483
Geocentric pricing p. 498
Hedging p. 483
Penetration price p. 492
Polycentric pricing p. 498
Premium price
differential p. 476
Price controls p. 483
Price escalation p. 476
Price elasticities p. 476

Price discrimination p. 484
Price-quality relationship
  p. 491
Price corridor p. 499
Product line pricing p. 498
Skimming price p. 492
Swap p. 483
Systems selling p. 488
Transfer pricing p. 484
Turnkey sales p. 488

DISCUSSION QUESTIONS

1. What are the reasons why prices on imported products do not necessarily fluctuate in step with changes in exchange rates? Why would there be a delay in reactions?

2. Why are so many foreign-made products cheaper in the United States, while very few American-made products are cheaper abroad?

3. As a marketing manager for a non-European business, what obstacles would you face in attempting to coordinate prices between European countries? Why would you attempt it?

4. From a marketing viewpoint, what are the advantages and disadvantages of allowing local units to set their own prices?

5. What are the problems in implementing a coordinated pricing system to control gray trade?

NOTES

1. Two other topics that could be viewed as part of a global pricing chapter are countertrade and gray trade (discussed here briefly). *Countertrade* was discussed in Chapter 10 dealing with marketing in emerging markets, where countertrade is particularly important. *Gray trade* is very much a matter of alternative distribution channels as well as price, and is discussed further in Chapter 14 on global distribution.

2. See Abell and Hammond, 1979, ch. 3.

3. Because the experience effect can't be documented in advance, companies that price on the basis of anticipated costs can be convicted of dumping based on historical costs.

4. See Anderson et al., 1993.

5. See Kotler, 1994, pp. 501–2.

6. The host country governments have gradually grown in sophistication and try to stem this "loophole" in the trade barriers by requiring a certain percentage of "local content" in the value of the imported product. In autos, figures around 60–80 percent are typical.

7. See, for example, "U.S. Says Talks," 1987.

8. See Johansson, 1989, for the Japanese reluctance to raise prices after the yen appreciated. The trade conflict between the U.S. and Japan in mid-1995 concerning luxury cars again illustrated that exchange rate shifts alone will not necessarily change prices—see Pollack, 1995, and Tagliabue, 1995.

9. This practice lies behind the charges from foreign entrants that Japan's market is closed—as in, for example, the ongoing battle between Kodak and Fuji. See "Fuji Denies," 1995.

10. This discussion of transfer prices draws on the excellent discussion by Rutenberg, 1982, ch. 5.

11. Effective enforcement of the new rules is of course still in question, especially since individual countries may not agree to the binding arbitration stipulated through the new DSM (dispute resolution mechanism). See Horlick and Shea, 1995.

12. These are only the main changes. For further information, see, for example, Horlick and Shea, 1995 and Suchman and Mathews, 1995.

13. Because of the difficulty of transportation into an area such as Manaus and the standardized manufacturing processes involved, most of the plants built for this booming free trade zone are basically turnkey operations. See Brooke, 1995.

14. Adapted from Mattsson, 1975.

15. See Chao, 1993.

16. See Johansson and Erickson, 1986.

17. See Terry, 1994.

18. The pressure of aggressive competitive pricing at entry is perhaps most commonly observed in new electronics products. See, for example, "The Fight for Digital TV's Future," *New York Times*, January 22, 1995, section 3, pp. 1,6 and "Digital Innovator Pays a Price for Being First," *New York Times*, Febarury 1, 1995, p. D4.

19. The figures for the European Union come from Simon, 1995.

20. From Simon, 1995.

21. The following discussion draws on the excellent study by Assmus and Wiese, 1995.

22. See Simon, 1995.

23. Adapted from Assmus and Wiese, 1995.

24. See "Pharma Swede: Gastirup," case no. 14 in Kashani, 1992.

25. The move to discount Marlboro was seen gloomily as the "end of the brand names" in the advertising world. More recently, however, brand names, including Marlboro, have staged a comeback—see Elliott, 1994.

26. See "Boeing Launches Stealth Attack on Airbus," *Business Week*, January 18, 1993, p. 32.

SELECTED REFERENCES

Abell, D. F. and J. S. Hammond. *Strategic Market Planning.* Englewood Cliffs, NJ: Prentice Hall, 1979.

Anderson, James C.; Dipak C. Jain; and Pradeep K. Chintagunta. "Customer Value Assessment in Business Markets: A State-of-Practice Study." *Journal of Business-to-Business Marketing* 1, no. 1, (1993) pp. 3–29.

Assmus, Gert, and Carsten Wiese. "How to Address the Gray Market Threat Using Price Coordination." *Sloan Management Review* 36, no. 3, (1995) pp. 31–42.

Becker, H. "Price Escalation in International Marketing," Reading no. 43 in Thorelli, Hans B., and S. Tamer Cavusgil. *International Marketing Strategy.* 3rd ed. New York: Pergamon Press, 1990, pp. 523–26.

Brooke, James. "Brazil Looks North from Trade Zone in Amazon." *New York Times, August 9, 1995, p. D3.*

Chao, Paul. "Partitioning Country of Origin Effects: Consumer Evaluations of a Hybrid Product." *Journal of International Business Studies* 24, no. 2, (Second Quarter 1993), pp. 291–306.

Davis, H. Thomas Jr. "Transfer Prices in the Real World—10 Steps Companies Should Take Before It Is Too Late." *The CPA Journal* 64, no. 10 (October 1994). pp. 82–83.

Elliott, Stuart. "From the Optimists' Ball, a Consensus that Happy Days Are Indeed Ahead." *New York Times,* December 6, 1994, p. D22.

"Fuji Denies Kodak's Contention of Unfair Trade." *New York Times,* August 1, 1995, p. D2.

Gates, Stephen. "The Changing Global Role of the Marketing Function: A Research Report." The Conference Board, report no. 1105-95-RR, 1995.

Hofmeister, Sallie. "Used American Jeans Power a Thriving Industry Abroad." *New York Times.* August 22, 1994, p. A1.

Horlick, Gary N., and Eleanor C. Shea. "The World Trade Organization Antidumping Agreement." *Journal of World Trade* 29, no. 1, (February 1995), pp. 5–31.

Iritani, Evelyn. "For Japanese, Hawaii's Hottest Spot May Be a Discount Mall." *Los Angeles Times,* September 25, 1995, p. D1.

Johansson, Johny K. "Stronger Yen and the United States–Japan Trade Balance: Marketing Policies of the Japanese Firms in the United States Market." In Agmon, Tamir, and Christine R. Hekman, eds. *Trade Policy and Corporate Business Decisions.* New York: Oxford University Press, 1989.

Johansson, Johny K. and Gary Erickson. "Price-Quality Relationships and Trade Barriers." *International Marketing Review* 3, no. 2, (Summer 1986).

Kashani, Kamran. *Managing Global Marketing.* Boston: PWS-Kent, 1992.

Kotler, P. *Marketing Management.* 8th ed. Englewood Cliffs, NJ: Prentice Hall, 1994.

Lustig, Nora. "The Outbreak of Pesophobia." *Brookings Review* 13, no. 2, (Spring, 1995), p. 46.

Mattsson, L. G. *Systemforsaljning.* Stockholm: Marknadstekniskt Centrum, April, 1975).

Pollack, Andrew. "U.S. and Japan Again Pull Back from the Brink." *New York Times,* June 22, 1995, pp. 31, 34.

Royal, Weld, and Allison Lucas. "Global Pricing and Other Hazards." *Sales & Marketing Management* 147, no. 8 (August 1995), pp. 80–83.

Rutenberg, D. P. *Multinational Management.* Boston: Little, Brown, 1982.

Shulman, J. S. "Transfer Pricing in the Multinational Firm." Reading no. 40 in Thorelli and Becker, *International Marketing Strategy,* pp. 316–324.

Simon, Hermann. "Pricing Problems in a Global Setting." *Marketing News,* October 9, 1995, p. 4.

Sims, Clive; Adam Phillips; and Trevor Richards. "Developing a Global Pricing Strategy." *Marketing & Research Today* 20, no. 1, (March 1992), pp. 3–14.

Suchman, Peter O., and Susan Mathews. "Mixed News for Importers." *China Business Review* 22, no. 2, (March/April 1995), pp. 31–34.

Tagliabue, John. "For Japan Auto Makers, It's Tougher in Europe." *New York Times*, June 28, 1995, p. D4.

Terry, Edith. "Japan: Where the Prices are Insane!" *Fortune*, October 31, 1994, p. 21.

Thurston, Charles W. "Surprise! It's Devaluation Time Again." *Global Finance* 9, no. 2 (February 1995) pp. 48–50.

"U.S. Says Talks with Common Market over Airbus Subsidies Are Deadlocked." *The Wall Street Journal*, December 18, 1987.

Weekly, James K. "Pricing in Foreign Markets: Pitfalls and Opportunities." *Industrial Marketing Management* 21, (1992), pp. 173–179.

14

Global Distribution

"Here, there, everywhere"

After studying this chapter, you should understand the following global marketing issues:

1. Global logistics are important—and dynamic.

2. Parallel distribution and gray trade are problems for the global distributor.

3. The wholesale and retail structure of a local market reflects the country's culture and economic progress and the way business is done in that country—but new channel modes may be successful if timing and conditions are right.

4. Channel management is very much a matter of local execution, and therefore local managers need to play important roles in implementing any global strategy.

T HE GLOBAL MARKETER faces a complex problem in designing globally coordinated channels through which to market the product. The distributors and agents used for initial entry may not be suitable any longer when global expansion proceeds further, and new channels may have to be found. Which alternative intermediaries are available and what functions they perform vary across different local markets. The channel strategies successful at home might not be effective abroad—and might not even be feasible. The global logistics of transporting products between various countries increase in speed and flexibility but also become more difficult to manage, with diverted gray trade creating problems for manufacturers as well as local distributors. The global marketer attempting to create synergies and cost savings by rationalizing global distribution faces a formidable task.

Retail Chains Seek to Clothe the World

For marketers who want to serve consumers around the world, channels are often already in place. Retailers, like producers, have been going global as never before.

Woolworth credits responsiveness to global changes for much of its recent growth. To serve its international customers, Woolworth identifies product categories that will be profitable, then sets up stores targeting those categories. A Woolworth format popular in many countries is Foot Locker and Lady Foot Locker—specialty stores offering athletic footwear and clothing.

Stocking U.S. brands can give these stores an edge. Explains Woolworth's president and chief operating officer, Frederick E. Henning, "Consumers worldwide recognize and want American labels like Nike." The demand, Henning says, is fueled by the popularity of American movies and television. Woolworth therefore designs stores that reflect the images promoted by these media.

For The Gap, successful global retailing involves offering American fashion not only in clothing but also in store design. The chain has determined that the way products are presented to customers is even more important in Europe than in the United States, and Gap stores apply that knowledge. In London, The Gap's interiors are white with light wood floors and chrome fixtures. This striking design, which is not typical of British retailers, has generated attention—and sales.

In contrast, Wal-Mart's global expansion has capitalized on the chain's exceptional management of logistics and distribution. The discounter is the first retailer in the United States to have its own foreign trade zone. Located in Buckeye, Arizona, where Wal-Mart has a massive distribution center, the zone allows the company to receive imports without paying duties until the products are shipped to stores, to avoid paying duties on exports and on any imports it rejects, and to pay lower duties on products assembled from imported components. Wal-Mart requested government approval of the free trade zone not only as a way to save half a million dollars a year, but also to fulfill what it called its "ultimate goal of truly global distribution and sales."

Of course, U.S. retailers are not the only ones with global ambitions. Thailand's two largest retailers merged as a way to strengthen their ability to compete in China and other Asian countries. By joining forces, the two chains (Central Department Store and Robinson Department Store) became Southeast Asia's largest department store chain. Management completed the merger to help the stores fend off increasingly heated competition. In distribution, bigger definitely seems to be better.

Sources: Jai Ok Kim, Mary Barry, and Carol Warfield, "Gaining Ground in a Globalized Market: U.S. Clothing Industry," *Bobbin*, Bobbin Blenheim Media Corp, May 1994, p. 60; Arthur Markowitz, "Wal-Mart Zones In on Foreign Trade," *Discount Store News*, April 19, 1993, p. 1; Ron Corben, "Thailand Megamerger Is Expected to Shake Up Retail Trade in Asia," *Journal of Commerce*, May 22, 1995, p. 5A.

INTRODUCTION

In Chapter 5, "Export Expansion," the importance of finding good distributors for an exported product was emphasized. The capability of the distributor chosen is critical for two reasons. One, the distributor is the gateway to the new country market, the "face" of the exporter's firm, and the avenue through which the marketing effort in the market is channeled. Two, because of contractual obligations it is difficult to change distributors later when a global strategy favors an alternative.

In this chapter this issue will be faced by the global marketer who wants to impose some coordination on local distribution channels. We'll show how the attempt might involve reconfiguring channels by introducing new alternatives or by establishing parallel channels. Multiple distribution channels are often a fact of life anyway for the global marketer because of the growth of gray trade. As for the distribution of products between countries, technological development and competition have made independent global logistics companies crucial players in the firm's global strategy.

The chapter starts with a discussion of *channels in different countries* and the possibility of rationalizing local distribution channels. It also covers *globalization of retailing*. Then we shift our attention to *global logistics* and recent advances in global transportation. We then turn to the issue of gray trade and the threats and opportunities from multiple channels in *parallel distribution*. The chapter finishes with a discussion of the potential for coordinated *global channels*.

RATIONALIZING LOCAL CHANNELS

Channel networks designed once do not stay the same forever. It is in the very nature of the open market system that competitive and countervailing forces assert themselves and force change. The global marketer will want to try to rationalize distribution by introducing some uniformity across countries.

Changing Distributors

The distribution channel configuration created for entry into a foreign market is rarely optimal once the product is established on the market. In some cases the success of the distributor in selling the product contains the seeds of his or her undoing. Then the exporter may move aggressively to usurp some of the power of the distributor and grab some of the profits. But the traditional reason for termination of a distributor is the sense on the part of the principal that the distributor is not doing a good enough job in the market.[1] Nike's experience is a case in point (see box, "Nike's 'Do It Yourself' Switch").

As in the Nike case, typically the channel changes initiated by the manufacturer involve the termination of independent distributors' or authorized dealers' contracts and creating a wholly owned sales subsidiary. But termination often involves conflict.[2] As we saw in Chapter 5, it is useful to formulate the distribution contracts in such a fashion that conflicts are resolved in an orderly manner. And we saw in Chapter 6, some joint-venture distribution agreements even go so far as to include "divorce clauses" specifying how the dissolution of the "marriage" should take place if necessary.

When conflicts do arise, some painful and scarring experiences often result. One reason is the different view that people from different countries have of proper conflict resolution methods. In the United States, legal proceedings are resorted to rather quickly. By contrast, in many foreign countries such proceedings are invoked only as a last resort. Whereas certain cultures view the business relationship between manufacturer and middleman in terms of antagonism that readily engenders conflict, others view it in terms of cooperation and are willing to forgo immediate individual gratification for the benefit of a harmonious relationship in the longer run. When these two viewpoints clash as they often do in global channel agreements, the whole channel design is in jeopardy.

The channel changes that occur do not necessarily involve termination of contracts. In some cases multiple channels emerge or are created.[3] For example, Lucky Goldstar's entry from Korea into the U.S. television market was made via OEM agreements with retailers such as Sears, but later a **dual distribution** system was initiated with sales under its own brand name Goldstar. Often the manufacturer tries to differentiate the offerings in different channels. Italian apparel maker Giorgio Armani has set up a number of stores in the West under a separate name, AX Exchange, carrying more casual clothes and lower-priced

*G*etting the
Picture

Nike's "Do It
Yourself" Switch

NIKE, the Oregon-based athletic-shoe maker, first entered foreign markets in the late 1970s using independent distributors. But as the company grew successful at home, it began putting pressure on overseas distributors to invest more in the sales of its brand. But whereas Nike spent about 8–9% of sales on advertising, overseas distributors were reluctant to spend more than 4%. Since the distributors in many cases handled more than one brand, the long-term building of Nike brand equity was, unavoidably, less important to them than short-term sales.

So, starting with Europe in the early 1980s, Nike began to establish overseas sales subsidiaries and take control of its overseas distribution. It now controls all of its distribution in Europe and has marketing subsidiaries in Australia, New Zealand, Hong Kong, Malaysia, and other Asian countries. In some countries the subsidiaries were created from acquired distributors, while in other cases they were started from scratch.

Going direct naturally cost Nike more. Apart from the direct costs for the subsidiary operations, there is need for recruiting, hiring, and training new sales people in each local market. To maintain high-quality service and support for the trade, these sales people need to be kept up-to-date with the latest advances in show design and features. Since athletic shoes represent a very fast-moving and competitive global market, Nike feels it is necessary to bring the sales people to headquarters for briefings and product training four times a year.

Sources: *Business Asia,* July 27, 1992, p. 263; M. S. Salter and M. J. Roberts, "Nike: International Context," Harvard Business School case no. 9-385-328.

items than the regular Armani's at his own specialty stores and department stores.

Changing to direct sales might solve the overseas distribution problem for the industrial goods multinational. The global marketer of consumer goods, however, also has to deal with the wholesalers and retailers that provide the link to the ultimate consumer.

Wholesaling

Wholesalers sell to retailers or industrial users. Their main functions involve making contact, negotiating, buying, selling, warehousing, but they might also be involved in shipping, financing, and packaging as well as other middleman functions. Wholesaling is a major component of a country's infrastructure and its structure reveals important clues as to the country's stage of development. The data presented in Exhibit 14.1 demonstrate how the number and size of wholesalers vary in different countries.

Perhaps the most striking fact about the numbers in Exhibit 14.1 is the large number of people employed in wholesaling in Japan. While most European countries are on par, relative to the population, and the United States has relatively few establishments, each of larger scale, the Japanese have a lot of

EXHIBIT 14.1   Size and Number of Wholesalers in Selected Countries

	Number of enterprises (thousands)	Persons employed (thousands)	Turnover (billions ECU)
Belgium	48.0	201.8	85.0
Denmark	35.8	166.2	60.0
Greece	28.0	115.4	—
France	132.4	1,049.0	312.0
Ireland	3.5	40.4	12.0
Italy	192.6	1,084.0	—
Luxembourg	1.9	10.8	5.0
Netherlands	71.9	360.0	135.0
Portugal	31.3	200.0	—
United Kingdom	142.7	921.0	310.0
United States	469.5	4,578.0	1,260.0
Japan	436.4	4,332.0	2,651.0

Source: *Retailing in the European Single Market, 1993*. These figures are adapted from Table EUR1a: "Importance of Commerce in the EC—absolute values (1987–91)."

units and a large number of people in wholesaling. The notoriously complex Japanese distribution system involves at least three levels of wholesalers.[4] This system is gradually being streamlined under pressure from direct imports and new technology, and the savings can be considerable even for a relatively mundane product such as Italian spaghetti, as Exhibit 14.2 shows. Initiatives for direct imports (buying directly from overseas suppliers, bypassing the established importer) come not only from foreign entrants into the Japanese markets but also from individual Japanese entrepreneurs as well as established channel members who recognize and capitalize on the new trends.

Vertical Integration

POWER AND COMPETITION   The size distribution of wholesalers in many countries seems to approximate the well-known "80-20" rule: 80 percent of the transactions are handled by 20 percent of the firms. In Malaysia, for example, fewer than a dozen European merchant houses handle over half the import trade while hundreds of small local trading companies handle the remaining volume. The giant Israeli wholesaler Hamashbir Hamerkazi handles all kinds of products and has full or partial ownership of 12 major industrial firms, representing approximately one-fifth of all Israeli wholesaling trade.[5]

The financial power of large wholesalers coupled with a good infrastructure and lack of government regulation has meant that in some countries they operate on a nationwide basis—Japan, Israel, and Australia are only a few examples among many. In other countries, however, the preponderance of small wholesalers means that in order to cover the whole country more than one

Exhibit 14.2   Japanese Import Distribution Alternatives—Distribution Route of
Italian Spaghetti

Conventional Route

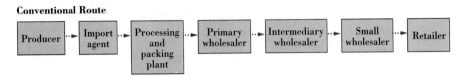

Retail price: 170 yen/300g package

Restructured Route

Savings: 25%   Retail price: 128 yen/300g package

Source: Allied Import Company, as reproduced in Michael R. Czinkota, and Jon Woronoff, *Unlocking
Japan's Markets*. Chicago, IL: Probus, 1991, p. 104. Used with permission.

wholesaler is used—the smaller ones cover at most a regional portion of
countries such as Italy, Turkey, and Egypt.

The U.S. trend toward vertical integration in channels—with large food
wholesalers such as SuperValu and Associated Grocers controlling the production and distribution of farm produce, for example—has now spread to other
countries. There are cases in which wholesalers have organized retail chains (in
Britain for soft goods, for example) and also cases in which wholesalers have
integrated backward into manufacturing (as in Japan for certain food products).[6] This integration sometimes makes it difficult for an importer to gain
access to a wholesaler. In India, the large wholesalers in several markets are
entrenched "monopsonists," monopolistic buyers. If you don't deal through
them, you don't deal.

EFFIENCY   The trend toward integration is based on the technological developments that have made large-scale economies and technical coordination
feasible. It is an example of technological diffusion across the globe. The
emergence of freezing equipment, automatic (and computerized) materials
handling, models of optimal inventory control and large-quantity reordering,
and reliable and fast communications (telecommunications and transportation)
has made the growth of the large individual wholesaler possible and economically desirable. As the infrastructure in various countries has improved with
economic development, the introduction of these technical innovations has
become feasible. As entrepreneurial wholesalers adopt the new technology they
leave others behind—and if the wholesalers don't do it, there are always eager

retailers and manufacturers who are keeping a watchful eye on possible cost-savings or improved service in the middleman levels. In many countries the wholesalers have, in fact, been too slow to innovate and been pushed aside by aggressive retailers integrating backward and manufacturers eager to simplify their distribution channels.[7] The functions carried out by the wholesalers still remain necessary for the movement of the product from producer to consumer—it is just that wholesalers are not always the most efficient at it, especially with the new direct importers providing stiff competition.

Types of Wholesalers

In most developed countries it is customary to identify a wide variety of wholesalers, and one can usually count on finding some wholesaler that will fill the bill when it comes to distributing the product. But this variety reflects more the aggressive nature of the entrepreneurial instinct and the particular nature of the market system in each of the countries rather than a homogeneous trend toward which all economies move. In general, the so-called **full-service wholesalers** can usually be counted on in most countries. But because of their size and tie-ins with existing brands and chains they might not be willing, or the best ones, to distribute the firm's product. The "full service" concept should be carefully assessed for each country entered. "Full-service" might mean "take title" (and thus ownership) to American sellers, but it might not prohibit a Middle Eastern wholesaler from returning a product that does not sell well in expectation of a full refund. "Full service" might not include service backup in European countries, but in India retailers expect to be able to hand over defective products to the wholesaler rather than the manufacturer.

Even practices in developed countries can vary considerably—see Exhibit 14.3. As can be seen, in a country such as Japan it is common that unsold goods can be returned to the manufacturer. This is in stark contrast to Western countries' practice. While European countries offer some open and fixed rebates on purchases, and the United States allows functional discounts, Japan has a much more complex system of rebates, some of which are not open but only extended to favored customers. Suggested retail prices do not exist in principle in Europe (although price competition is usually less intense than in the United States), are allowed in the United States, and are not only common in Japan but quite vigorously enforced by some manufacturers (although the practice of cutting off supplies to uncooperative retailers has been successfully challenged in court). Manufacturers in Japan have also engaged in forward integration to a greater extent than elsewhere and tend to offer more sales support to the distribution channel members. Needless to say, complete standardization of channel design across these countries by a global marketer is not feasible without creating a new channel.

Between-country differences are perhaps even more common for the various limited-line wholesalers who specialize in one or two of the wholesaling functions. For example, a very unique institution in the United

....
EXHIBIT 14.3   International Comparison of Wholesale Trade Practices

Practice	Japan	United States	Britain	France	Former West Germany
Returned goods	• Returning unsold goods is common	• Doesn't exist except for imperfect or damaged goods	• Doesn't exist except for imperfect or damaged goods	• Doesn't exist except for imperfect or damaged goods	• Doesn't exist except for imperfect or damaged goods
Rebate system	• Various and complicated structure (volume, fixed date, evaluation, promotion) • Long term in pay unit (yearly, half-year, etc) • Rebates are not necessarily open	• No rebates but discounts and allowances exist • Open rule • Pay unit depends	• Quantitative and date fixed rebates exist • Open rule • Pay unit depends	• Quantitative and date fixed rebates exist • Open rule • Pay unit depends	• Quantitative and date fixed rebates exist • Open rule • Pay unit depends
Quotations	• Manufacturer's suggested retail prices exist • Written materials and certain drugs and cosmetics are allowed to maintain resale prices	• Manufacturer's suggested retail prices exist	• Doesn't exist in principle • Books and drugs are allowed to maintain resale prices	• Doesn't exist in principle • Books and certain cosmetics, ski equipment, and some consumer electronics are allowed to maintain resale prices	• Doesn't exist in principle • Books, newspapers, and magazines are allowed to maintain resale prices
Forward integration	• Exists (consumer electronics, auto, cosmetics)	• Uncommon	• Exists (auto)	• Exists (auto)	• Exists (auto)
Others	• Loaned sales staff • Frequent and small-amount delivery • Perpetuates business relation • Unclear contracts	• Uncommon	• Uncommon	• Uncommon	• Uncommon

Source: Distribution Economics Institute, *Survey on International Comparison on the Distribution Industry*, May 1990.

States economy is the rack jobber, the wholesaler who delivers the product to the retailer's shelf directly. Many supermarkets overseas do not have this system, and the chain drugstores (another semiunique U.S. invention) where products such as compact disks and women's hosiery might be sold through displays rented to, and stocked by, the rack jobber are not yet common in many other countries. The reason a product such as L'eggs pantyhose has been accepted only slowly in overseas markets is not resistance to the product among buyers. A greater obstacle has been that the innovation (the firm-specific advantage) lies in the convenient packaging and the "front-door" delivery system via rack jobbers through which the product is distributed.[8] Without the same channel linkage operating well in other countries, market penetration is difficult.

Retailing

Retailers are those middlemen who sell directly to the ultimate consumer. They fulfill similar functions as other middlemen, including ordering, creating assortments, presenting the merchandise, storing and packaging, and perhaps also shipping and financing. The variety in retailing across countries is, if anything, greater than in wholesaling. In some countries such as Italy and Algiers, retailing is composed largely of small specialty houses carrying a narrow line of products. By contrast, in the Northern European countries there are many stores with a broad assortment of products. The large Japanese chain of department stores, Mitsukoshi, maintains stores around most major capitals in the world and attracts an average of 100,000 customers per day. The bazaars of the Middle East, on the other hand, contain as many shops as customers on some days.[9]

Exhibit 14.4 presents a statistical picture of the number of retail outlets in a selected number of countries. The United States has an unusually large number of people employed in retailing (relative to the population), with each store relatively large (the United Kingdom is the closest country in this regard). Most European countries have fewer people in retailing relative to the population and have smaller stores. Japan is quite similar to the British pattern, with more stores than the United States but relatively few persons employed in each store.

Retailing and Life-styles

Because retailers cater to the individual consumer it is hardly surprising that there are so many of them, and such wide differences between countries. The retailing structure has to adapt to the varying living conditions (the life-styles) of individual households. Shopping represents both a tiresome job and a leisure activity for individuals everywhere and is both a reflection of and a formative influence on the life-style of the people in a country. Where living standards differ between countries, one would therefore expect retailing structures to

EXHIBIT 14.4　Size and Number of Retail Outlets in Selected Countries

	Number of enterprises (thousands)	Persons employed (thousands)	Turnover (billions ECU)
Belgium	127.8	274.7	35.0
Denmark	48.1	199.7	24.0
Greece	175.0	338.2	20.0
France	461.8	2,090.0	260.0
Ireland	29.3	131.4	11.0
Italy	929.7	2,401.0	230.0
Luxembourg	3.5	18.1	3.0
Netherlands	95.0	637.5	45.0
Portugal	173.3	366.3	20.0
United Kingdom	348.2	3,030.0	280.0
United States	1,503.6	19,085.0	1,350.0
Japan	1,619.8	6,851.0	682.0

Source: *Retailing in the European Single Market, 1993.* These figures are adapted from Table EUR1a: "Importance of Commerce in the EC—absolute values (1987–91)."

differ—and where life-styles are similar, these similarities will be reflected in more homogeneity in the respective retailing structures. Retail stores are, in a sense, the most obvious indication of a country's economic achievement and thus are a most informative indicator of the life-styles of a country's citizens.[10]

Over time, economic progress is likely to lead to a convergence of the retail structures, as the large chains globalize their operations (see below). In the meanwhile, however, the global marketer has to face the differences and learn to work through them. For example, the standardized Gillette blades sold through drugstores in the United States are sold in tobacco shops in Italy, department stores in Germany, on the street in Moscow, at movie counters in Thailand, and from traveling vans in India.

One implication of these differences for management is that the same channel strategy can't be followed in all countries. While convenience goods are largely "presold" through advertising of brands in the United States and other countries that rely heavily on supermarkets and convenience retail outlets, an Italian housewife shopping for food might very well be swayed by in-store factors including the persuasion of the store clerk. In some countries the convenience products become, in fact, very similar to shopping goods in other countries.

Similarly, the firm that draws on its advertising expertise to sell its canned food products in this new environment might not do very well unless the strategy is aided by considerable support for the store owners. Thus not only is it necessary to use different types of stores in different countries; the stores most suitable for the product will require widely different marketing support in

A 7-Eleven outlet in Denmark decorated for the Christmas season. Even as the store chain introduces new forms of retailing, its exterior design, display windows, and entrance attempt to meld into the existing surroundings, facilitating local customer acceptance.

Courtesy of The Southland Corporation.

various countries. It becomes necessary to learn in detail the particular nature of the retailing structure and the way consumers make decisions in the particular country based on life-styles.

Creating New Channels

But retailing is dynamic. As economic growth takes place and global trade expands, new alternatives emerge. Even the least-developed countries experience dramatic changes in distribution channels as innovations such as self-service, discounting, vending machines, mail-order houses, and fast-food outlets are diffused globally.[11] Today, convenience stores such as 7-Eleven and its emulators, fast-food restaurants such as McDonald's and its similar offshoots, discount stores such as Tower Records and Virgin stores, and catalog merchandisers such as L. L. Bean and Eddie Bauer can be found in a number of countries around the globe.

Some of these developments entail a change in life-style—something customers can be educated about and persuaded to undertake—more than an increase in economic development. It does not require a high level of per capita income to make vending machines pay off, nor does it take much money to eat at fast-food restaurants. Innovations may require the infusion of new capital— the coolers for soft drinks, the large cooking ovens for Kentucky Fried chicken—but because of the promise of a large market, foreign investment of this kind is attracted to poor countries. There are many companies that have been successful creating new channels along the lines used at home. Avon and Mary Kay, two American firms that sell cosmetics door-to-door, have entered Asia using the same techniques. Despite the newness of door-to-door selling in Asia, the companies have been able to adopt the same selling system as elsewhere, recruiting and training housewives and young women as sales people. Amway is another company that has had success abroad using its own network-style distribution arrangements, where new customers are recruited to become distributors marketing the company's wide selection of merchandise to neighbors, friends, and relatives.

Global Retailing[12]

Retailing is, in fact, being globalized at a fast rate. Helping to spark this trend, in addition to increasing affluence in global markets, is the logistical and operational know-how of leading retailers around the world. As was mentioned in the section on wholesaling, throughout the 1980s the rapid deployment of point-of-purchase information technology, including barcoding, scanner data, and inventory controls, shifted the power in the channel toward large retailers. Leading stores, such as Wal-Mart and Kmart in the United States, Marks & Spencer in Britain, Carrefour in France, Delhaize in Belgium, and Daiei and Ito-Yokado, owner of 7-Eleven, in Japan, integrated upstream, established their own sourcing abroad, introduced p-o-p technology, and created data banks on product and brand turnover that gave them power over both wholesalers and manufacturers. The sheer volume of product channeled through these large store chains, coupled with immediate access to sales data, gave the retailers a strong hand in negotiating for functional discounts and preferential services. Global expansion has become large retailers' avenue to growth in the 1990s.

Wal-Mart, the world's biggest retailer, now operates 67 discount stores and Sam's Clubs in Mexico along with a Mexican partner, Cifra. Although further expansion is on hold until the Mexican peso problems clear, Wal-Mart will open three stores in Brazil and two in Argentina in 1995. The company has three joint-venture stores in Hong Kong and is planning to enter China. By 1998 Wal-Mart's overseas sales should top $10 billion (still only 10 percent of total sales).

In China, Wal-Mart will run into Yaohan, the Japanese retailer that has built the largest shopping center in Asia, the 21-story Nextage Shanghai Tower, just east of Shanghai's harbor. Opened in December 1995, the shopping center has more than a million square feet under one roof. Yaohan's main owner and chairman, Kazuo Wada, in fact believes so strongly in the Chinese market that he moved his company's headquarters from Tokyo to Hong Kong as other business people were moving out in anticipation of the 1997 communist takeover. He was the first foreign retailer to receive a license in China, and Yaohan intends to open more than 1,000 stores in China, in addition to expanding in the United States and into Europe.

Perhaps the largest retail group in Southeast Asia is Dutch-owned Makro, a wholesale club operator specializing in warehouse stores. Its sales in the region topped $2 billion in 1994, and the chain has revenues of more than $10 billion worldwide. Other Europeans are also active globally. Carrefour, the French hypermarket chain, is a leading retailer in Brazil and Argentina. Marks & Spencer, the English chain that sells good quality clothing under its own

Getting the Picture

Benetton's Turnaround

IN THE EARLY 1980s, Benetton, the Italian apparel maker that had been very successful in Europe, was poised to enter the U.S. market. The company quickly expanded using its tried-and-true formula of franchising individual owners, providing them with supplies from Benetton's own factories in Europe. But the distance between Europe and the U.S. created delays in shipments, and even with the company's rapid market feedback system it proved difficult to replicate the European success. Benetton franchised too many dealers too fast (and too close to each other), information about the fast-selling (and slow-selling) items was not always timely or accurate enough from the novice franchises, and shipments were slow in coming.

Regrouping, Benetton reengineered the whole business system. Focusing on apparel design, its original strength, the company exited manufacturing and shifted to contract manufacturing with centralized warehousing in Italy. It stopped franchising dealers and instead became a wholesaler to independently owned stores around the world. It operates one huge distribution center in Castrette, Italy, from which its robots can supply the latest fashions to 120 countries within 12 days—very fast for the apparel industry. Benetton is no longer in retailing, but in "apparel service" as the company brochure has it. And its controversial advertisements seem to put its name in the headlines even more often than before.

Sources: Rapoport, 1995; "Benetton (A)," Harvard Business School case no. 9-685-014, 1984.

brand names at good prices, has six stores in Hong Kong even more profitable than the high 12 to 13 percent profit on sales the chain racks up in Britain. The trend now involves not only retailers in the "triad" countries, but also in other countries, such as Thailand.[13]

Of course, global expansion is not always successful. France's Carrefour has introduced the hypermarket concept to the East Coast of the United States with little success so far. Japan's Takashimaya department store has established a store on Fifth Avenue in New York but has still to turn a profit. Its compatriot Isetan has developed an only slightly more successful collaboration (joint venture) with Barney's of New York for men's and women's upscale apparel and has brought a Barney's store to Tokyo. Belgium's Delhaize, a successful top-of-the-line supermarket at home, has had trouble in the United States, where its Food Lion's supermarkets have tried against odds to penetrate the market in the South. Marks & Spencer, which seemed a sure bet in Canada, encountered a lot of difficulties and has pulled out. Timing is important—and so is focusing on what you do best (see box, "Benetton's Turnaround").

Even though the emergence of global retailers would seem to offer the global marketer a chance for central coordination of worldwide channel activities, it is important to remember that these retailers tend to become powerful "channel captains." It is more than likely that the manufacturers (and wholesalers) will have to adapt to their needs—they want to be treated as customers. Selling through them will involve "relationship marketing"—

offering special services, discounts, emergency supplies as necessary, and so on. To tilt the balance to a more even playing field, the manufacturer with a strong global brand has an advantage. Then the giant retailers need them as much as they need the retailers.[14]

The global marketer who wants to avoid the power of the large integrated retailers by "going local" needs to realize that coordination advantages are not easy to achieve. Trying to impose a uniform channel configuration in each country can easily run afoul of the existing local management and their way of doing business. Against the backdrop of each local market's unique pattern of wholesalers and retailers, not to speak of ways of doing business in general, it is hardly surprising if the local managers, whether natives or expatriates, will argue for headquarters' keeping their hands off the existing local channel setup. This is another reason why the development of alternative distribution channels, parallel to the existing ones, is sometimes better than trying to change or get rid of existing channel members.

GLOBAL LOGISTICS

Global logistics can be defined as the transportation and storage activities necessary to transfer the physical product from manufacturing plants and warehouses in different countries to the various local market countries. Global logistics is a subset of **global distribution,** which also involves the management of the channels *within* a country. It is a useful distinction for the global marketer, since the management of channels within a country requires a lot of interactions with local subsidiaries, distributors, and agents. By contrast, the distribution *between* countries is usually a matter for headquarters and the trading partners alone.

The global marketer has to make some decisions about channels and their coordination even in the foreign entry stage. As we saw in Part Two, "Foreign Entry," the firm can opt to "externalize" its foreign marketing by hiring an export management company (EMC) or an international trading company to carry out the functions necessary to sell the product abroad. Alternatively, it can engage in direct exporting and try to find independent distributors and agents to represent it in the local market. In either case, the logistics function, transportation and storage between countries, is almost always contracted out to specialists, such as freight forwarders, ship lines, and customs agents. These alternatives were discussed in Chapter 5.

Coordinating and rationalizing the global logistics function of the firm involved in many markets is not a simple task. The manufacturing side alone is often complex. The company might have located manufacturing facilities in various countries, each specializing in only part of the complete product line, so that a particular local market needs to be supplied from a number of countries. The Nissan trucks sold in France might come from the company's United States plant in Tennessee, the Micras from its Sunderland plant in England, while the Maximas are imported from Japan by its European subsidiary located in Amsterdam. Complicating the logistics function further is that the parts, components, and subassemblies for each product in the complete line are sourced from different countries as well. Although many components initially might have come from Nissan's Japanese factories, local content requirements lead to more and more sourcing from local suppliers. This in turn forces the company to locate more manufacturing, and not just assembly, abroad. But a manufacturing plant needs to have enough capacity to gain economies of scale, which often means that its output has to be exported to other plants in the company's global network. Nissan's engine plant in the U.K. might be supplying engines to its American and its Spanish plants, for example. From a marketing perspective this might seem quite irrelevant, but it means that parts for after-sales service and repairs have to be ordered from factories in several different countries, and where to locate warehouses becomes a crucial marketing decision. Global logistics in the heavily globalized automobile industry might be particularly complicated, but similar problems afflict most companies that attempt to implement a global strategy.

Competition and Technology

Considering the difficulties involved, many firms are reluctant to try to reengineer their global logistics. A decentralized solution, building on whatever localized solutions have gradually emerged during the global expansion, seems preferable, especially since the local managers know their customer requirements better anyway. But this goes counter to two external forces pushing the company: competition and technology.

As we have seen throughout this book, global competition requires more efficient operations, greater flexibility, and quicker response time. Global *transportation* is an area where considerable savings are often possible. Consolidating shipments, eliminating duplication in cross-border procedures, including shipping documents and customs declarations, and investing in specialized equipment at transfer points are only a few of the areas in which reengineering can help. Furthermore, inventory management can often be improved through rationalized global logistics, creating savings through just-in-time practices and adding customer value by reducing delivery times.

Also, because of new technology—global communication possibilities and computerized operations, in particular—more efficient logistics operations have become possible. Benetton, the Italian apparel company, has long been known for its fast market response. A competitor such as Levi's is now using point-of-sale terminals in some European locations, linked directly to regional headquarters in Brussels. Transactions and sales of its apparel can be traced quickly and new and revised orders transmitted to factories as demand fluctuates and according to work loads. Order lead time is lowered, faster response is made possible, and inventories are reduced.[15]

The technology has spawned a number of new global distribution options available for the global marketer. Freight forwarders, ship lines, air express outfits, and airlines now offer more reliable and faster services than before and also offer services not available before, such as tracking of shipments and overnight delivery.

Air Express

Technical innovations in computerized inventory systems and numerically controlled machines for goods handling, including robotics, coupled with the speed and reliability of the jet aircraft, made possible the growth of **air express** systems exemplified by American-based Federal Express, DHL, UPS, and Airborne. Typically, the logistics involve shipment systems offering local pickups, the transportation of packages in the evening to a single transshipment point, sorting according to addresses during the night, and then shipping out to their destination by the early morning for local delivery.

These new air freight services are growing rapidly. With the increased penetration of modern telecommunications and fax machines in developing and newly emerging markets, these shipping services have been very active in foreign markets. Overnight delivery is usually not available, since there is a need for a transshipment point in the country of destination. Typically, one or two more days are needed. For example, Atlanta to Frankfurt requires two days, while Detroit to Hiroshima takes three days. As technology is applied further, these limits are likely to change (see box, "UPS on the Next Flight Out").

Today, shipping computer software, cameras, many consumer electronic products, and even apparel overseas often starts with a call to the local express mail office for a pickup. Instead of taking one to two weeks or much more in the case of ocean shipping, the shipment can arrive in a couple of days. The goods are cleared through customs faster by using the express carrier's dedicated access ports at the point of transshipment, usually away from crowded entry ports for general merchandise. The computerized system makes it possible to track the packages, monitor the progress, and resolve obstacles or trouble.[16]

Ocean Carriers

The development of fast and efficient air transportation has opened up new international distribution channels, in particular for items high in value per unit weight. For shipments of bulky and low-value-per-unit products, such as automobiles, produce, dry goods, beer, and softdrinks, **ocean-going vessels** are still the most economical carrier alternative overseas. A few of these products— autos, oil, grain—are shipped in specially designed ships owned by the producers, but the shipping is done largely by independent ship lines through containers, ship-to-truck or rail. But even here global requirements have made for changes.

Getting the Picture

UPS on the Next Flight Out

TO GAIN a (possibly short-lived) competitive edge on its international rivals, UPS (United Parcel Service, an American express delivery carrier based in Atlanta) has started a round-the-clock, next-flight-out service from the United States to Europe, Asia-Pacific, and Latin America.

UPS's new service is intended as another weapon in the fierce international express war being waged between UPS, Federal Express, DHL Worldwide Express, and TNT Express Worldwide. As business finds new markets abroad, these companies are indicating a need to add rush premium service they're now offering domestically.

"No one knows how big the demand for this new service will be," says Greg Smith, vice president of the Colography Group, a transportation consultancy in Marietta, Georgia. While convenient, the new service is not cheap. It will cost $365 for the first 10 pounds according to a company spokesman. It is targeted toward people who are trying to get merchandise moved on an emergency basis and who have to get the package there as soon as possible. Most companies attempt to avoid such shipments in order to keep costs down, and the market may be small. But there is a strategic angle to it. As Mr. Smith says, "You don't want to be in a position of a shipper telling you: 'Here, this is my most critical package,' and you having to tell them: 'Well, I don't do that. Call someone else.' "

Moral: Global competition requires speed and flexibility.

Sources: Johnson, 1995b; "DHL Worldwide Express," Harvard Business School case no. 9-593-011.

Because of the savings involved in sharing resources and the advantage in providing integrated one-stop services to the shipper, there have been a number of **global carrier alliances** in the shipping industry. American President Lines (APL), Orient Overseas Container Line from Hong Kong, and Mitsui O.S.K. Lines from Japan have joined in a global alliance consortium. APL and Matson Navigation Co., another American ship line, plan to share vessels in a U.S.–Hawaii–Asia service beginning in 1996. In another alliance, Sea-Land Service in Seattle and Maersk Line of Denmark have announced a world partnership to begin soon.[17]

The advantages of these alliances are similar to those in the airline industry. Sharing routes, vessels, and port facilities, better utilization of fixed assets is made possible, cargo destinations are expanded, and economies in documentation and customs clearing can be realized. The larger scale makes investment in specialized assets economically justified, reducing transfer costs further and offering lower prices to users.[18] These specialized assets, involving large-capacity lifting cranes, up-to-date storage facilities, and ever larger and faster ships, put pressure on competitors and ports as well. While competitors respond with alliances of their own, the future of ports is thought to depend on the building of "megaports," which can accommodate huge ships, speed up container loading and unloading, and reduce the "dwell time" while the unloaded containers wait on the dock for further transportation via truck or rail.[19]

A DHL advertisement explaining how its EasyShip program works. The offer to install hardware and software at no cost in the customer's office for easy shipment via DHL shows the extent to which logistics specialists can help the individual company go global.

EASYSHIP®

List management, tailored shipping history, charge back capability

Pre-printed airbills or labels

Management reports, commercial invoices

Inbound and outbound shipment details via bar code scanning

DHL will install a free EasyShip® shipment processing system in your office.

These days, we're all looking for ways to work smarter, faster. EasyShip, DHL's user-friendly and easily customized shipment management system, can help. Designed to simplify the processing of both domestic and international shipments, EasyShip allows you to pre-print airbills, create management reports and maintain your own database of customer addresses.

DHL will install an EasyShip computer in your office at no cost to you. If you prefer, we can also provide the software to run on your existing DOS-based PC. And if you're using a third party system, we'll work with you to determine the most effective method of accessing DHL's service.

With automation, you have control over your shipments because you manage the processing on your own premises. And you save money because less staff time is required to handle your shipping needs.

Within the U.S. and Canada, Zip-Ship capabilities cut the processing time of your shipments to U.S. destinations even further. With Zip-Ship, a zip code is all that's required to route your shipment to its destination.

Ask your DHL sales representative how you can qualify for this free shipment processing system.

**EasyShip Customer Service
1-800-527-7298**

DHL WORLDWIDE EXPRESS®

Courtesy of DHL Worldwide Express.

Overland Transportation

The increasing volume of international trade has put the system under pressure not only in ports but also inland. There is of course a direct link. For example, containers with tobacco products from Richmond, Virginia, are unloaded in Bremerhaven, put on trucks, and speeded overland to Poland on the German

A bulk container is lifted onto a flat railroad car in a Rotterdam railroad yard. The economics of logistics hinge on the extent to which transitions between transport modes are required and the speed with which they can be accomplished.

Don Spiro/Tony Stone Images.

Autobahn—creating traffic problems, safety hazards, and long lines at the border. With so many new products entering the Eastern European markets, the traffic problems are getting worse, and German authorities are contemplating placing a steep toll on trucks.[20]

One North American solution to this problem has been the **roll-on-roll-off (RORO) system,** in which a loaded container is simply rolled onto a railcar, and shipped by rail for part of the way, avoiding congested freeways. Even quicker is the new **RoadRailer** system, in which a rail wheel carriage can be attached to the bottom of the trailer carrying the container on the road. Then the container can go directly on the rail and be hooked up to a train without the need for a railcar.

These North American solutions have not yet been introduced in many places elsewhere, mainly because of the costs involved in transferring from the existing systems. In Europe, the typical overland transportation involves trucking, and the changeover to rail requires a special truck/rail terminal with a capability of lifting the container off the trailer and then placing it on a railcar. The special equipment required and the time lost in the transfer mean that European roads are likely to be clogged by trucks for some time to come.[21]

Warehousing

The competitive need on the part of global companies to be "close to the customer" and provide fast and efficient service has not only placed increased demand on transportation but also on warehousing and **inventory management.** While increased speed on the part of independent carriers has made it possible to fill orders faster and cut **response time** for parts requests, increased competition has escalated customers' demands for service. SKF, the Swedish roller-bearing company, has centralized its European distribution system, reducing its distribution points in Europe from 24 to 5 and creating a new distribution center in Belgium, thereby cutting costs, increasing speed, and improving service.[22]

Thus, locating several warehouses close to customers is not necessary any longer for the customer-oriented firm. And if the company does not want to invest in its own distribution center, some of the middlemen in global logistics provide inventory services. For example, Federal Express, DHL, and also smaller outfits offer warehouse space for rent at their transshipment points.[23] Companies rent the space to store products in high demand. A company such as Eddie Bauer can stock some of the more popular items in its catalog in Memphis at the FedEx central location and ship directly from there, lowering the shipment time significantly.

Such options are useful for the company attempting to cut down the time required to respond to customer requests. In addition, companies attempt to speed up the manufacturing-to-market process further, not only by reengineering inventory management but by streamlining their own handling of shipments to multiple markets. The Kodak approach is instructive (see box, "Kodak's Own Air Freight Hub").

It is not surprising that senior managers from major manufacturing companies now consider logistics one of the key areas for company profitability.[24] The cost savings and the value-added made possible by rationalized global logistics can be considerable.

PARALLEL DISTRIBUTION

Developments in logistics coupled with floating exchange rates and widely different prices in different countries have led to the emergence of gray trade through **parallel distribution** channels.

Gray Trade[25]

As mentioned in our discussion of counterfeits in Chapter 12, *gray trade* is parallel distribution of genuine goods by intermediaries other than authorized channel members. Gray marketers are typically brokers who buy goods overseas either from the manufacturer or from authorized dealers at relatively low prices and import them into a country where prevailing prices are higher. The gray marketers sell the merchandise at discounted prices in direct competition with authorized local distributors, often advertising the lower prices openly in print media and direct mail. The practice is not illegal per se except under certain circumstances, but the activities tend to disturb existing trading relationships and are usually fought by manufacturers as well as authorized distributors.

Getting the Picture

Kodak's Own Air Freight Hub

EASTMAN KODAK, the world's largest maker of photography products, has formed its own air freight hub at home in Rochester, NY. To minimize product handling and shipping errors, Kodak, which ships its products worldwide, is consolidating all outbound air freight at an on-site gateway in Rochester with the help of MSAS Cargo International, Inc., a California-based shipping and logistics specialist, which began handling the lion's share of Kodak's worldwide air freight in January 1994. After consolidation, the shipments are loaded on trucks at Rochester bound for different airports, and all customs documentation and shipping paperwork are completed at Rochester. Flight approval is obtained electronically before the shipment arrives at the airport.

The shipments run the gamut of Kodak products, from its consumer and professional films and processing chemicals and papers to its photocopiers, microfiche and microfilm machines to X-ray film and health and sciences supplies. In the past Kodak's air shipments were cobbled together at New York's John F. Kennedy International Airport. But this proved unwieldy because shipments were repeatedly handled, sometimes came up short, or airlines rejected certain Kodak products—such as certain processing chemicals—as unsafe. In addition, some shipments were being pilfered on the way to or at the airport.

An added benefit of the Rochester gateway is that the company can choose which airport to go through. Since Chicago to the west offers better service to the Asia-Pacific (home of Fuji, the arch rival) and is not that much farther from Rochester than New York, Kodak is now shipping a large amount of product to the Orient through Chicago's O'Hare airport.

Source: Johnson, 1995a; *Washington Post*, June 26, 1995, p. A12.

As we saw in Chapter 13, "Global Pricing," gray trade tends to serve as an arbitrage mechanism, equalizing prices between markets in different countries. Three main factors motivate entrepreneurs to engage in gray trade:

- There are substantial price differences between national markets (see Chapter 13).

- There is limited availability of certain models or versions in one market. Demand outstrips supply and is likely to push local prices even higher relative to other markets. Certain Mercedes-Benz and Porsche models are unavailable in the United States, for example, as were originally some Lexus models in Japan, which stimulated gray trade. Localization requirements, such as local certification of emissions controls on cars, have a dampening effect, but with sufficient margins gray traders will invest in conversion equipment (although sometimes the buyer gets stuck with the job).

- Transportation and importation can be accomplished with relative ease. The increased availability of global modes of transportation and the added services offered by carriers and freight forwarders have meant that the logistics problems are usually few. Gray traders can use the independent middlemen as well as any manufacturer.

Exhibit 14.5 shows some of the ways in which gray traders infiltrate the global distribution of Japanese cameras. The Japanese companies export cameras to the importer, often a sales subsidiary, in the various countries. From there the cameras are shipped to the distributors and on to retailers. These are the authorized channels where the company offers merchandising support and sales training and in turn demands service support.

EXHIBIT 14.5   Seiko's Authorized and Unauthorized Channels of Distribution

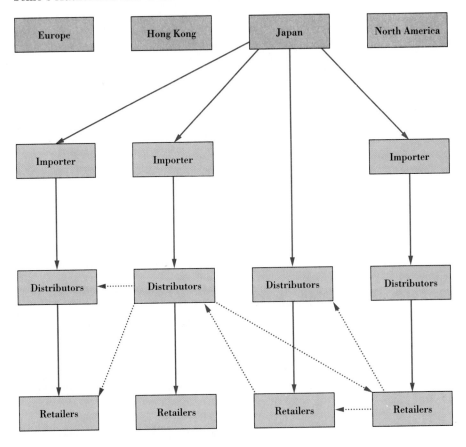

⋯⋯▶ Broken arrows denote the flow of Seiko watches through authorized channels of distribution.
⟶ Solid arrows denote the flow of Seiko watches through unauthorized channels of distribution.

Source: Jack Kaikati, "Parallel Importation: A Growing Conflict in International Channels of Distribution." Symposium on Export-Import Interrelationships, Georgetown University, November 14–15, 1985.

As can be seen in the exhibit, the gray trade arises from several sources. Some of the distributors in price-competitive markets, such as Hong Kong, will divert part of their shipment to more lucrative markets. They may sell directly to unauthorized (or even authorized European or American distributors or retailers, getting higher prices which more than offset any transportation charges. Alternatively, Japanese distributors and retailers backed by a strong yen can go abroad to get cameras from overseas distributors or retailers for sale at home. And for new models in great demand, a Hong Kong distributor may send people to Tokyo to buy at retail, sometimes in duty-free shops, and bring back cameras that fetch premium prices.

The company's control over distribution is lost when gray trade proliferates. Sales statistics for individual country markets are misleading or meaningless. The Japanese camera makers try to do something about it. Apart from monitoring their independent importers and authorized distributors more closely, they also change model names, mix features differently, and generally make the styles for different regions (Europe, North America, Asia) slightly different. Such as solution represents "cosmetic" localization, since it does not involve adaptation to consumer preferences or needs.

Gray trade is extensive for global brands in certain product categories. Although exact figures are hard to come by, since identification of gray goods is uncertain and the volume varies annually by exchange rate changes, the following are some estimates from U.S. industry sources:[26]

- 10% of IBM PC sales.
- 20% of Sharp electronics.
- 22% of Mercedes cars.

Total volume has been estimated at $10 billion. In cameras, a notorious gray trade product category since value per unit is high and brands are well recognized, the average manufacturer might have recently lost sales of about $7.4 million annually. The volume is increasing as the opening of the communist blocs has further stimulated gray trade (as well as piracy). However, firms are reluctant to discuss gray trade since the legal recourse is uncertain, and the fear is that as the general public learns more, the practice may become more widespread.

Effects of Gray Trade

The damage from gray imports falls into four categories. Gray trade threatens to:

- Erode brand equity.
- Strain relationships with authorized channel members.
- Lead to legal liabilities.
- Complicate global marketing strategies.

The eroding of brand equity can happen if the gray goods do not perform to the level expected. For example, products with date marks, such as film and

Getting the Picture

Do Gray Goods Get Serviced?

JAPAN'S NOTORIOUSLY tight distribution system has been jolted throughout the 1990s by the appearance of gray goods in several product categories. Taking advantage of the strong yen, which has cheapened imports, the reduction in tariff rates, and the reluctance of existing distributors to pass savings on to consumers, Japanese entrepreneurs have set up purchasing offices overseas and established direct import channels that sell products at savings as high as 50%.

One example is Steinway grand pianos from New York and Hamburg, whose regular price is much higher than the domestic leader Yamaha, but which can be had as direct imports at prices competitive with Yamaha's. The ensuing surge in sales of Steinways has created problems for Steinway's sole authorized distributor in Japan. Rather than reducing prices to compete with the direct imports, the distributor has opted for a more subtle strategy.

The gray pianos, easily identified because of their serial numbers, are placed last in line for service. This means long waiting times for a repairman or a piano tuner and repeated failures to show up. These can seem minor problems at the point of purchase, since grand Steinways are a good example of a globally standardized product and a grand piano requires comparatively little service except for tuning. But there are some localization matters to take care of. The high humidity of Japan's summers requires expensive reconditioning of grands prepared for European conditions. In severe cases the entire soundboard, the key to the grand's sound, may have to be refinished. Also, tuning the pianos during the initial 1–2 break-in years requires specialists trained by Steinway, and they are now suddenly in "short supply." Disgruntled Steinway owners in Japan have taken the distributor to court. But since service is not denied, only delayed, the legal outcome is uncertain. Japan's "impenetrable" distribution system may yet win another one.

Sources: *New York Times*, June 23, 1995, p. D1; Assmus & Wiese, 1995.

batteries, may be resold in gray markets with dates changed or obliterated, and the unwary buyer will find photos ruined and batteries dead. The strain with channel members arises from the fact that they will face intrabrand competition, the identical brand sold at lower prices elsewhere, and they will be asked to do service and repairs for gray imports. They may not have a legal basis for refusal and will have to be inventive (see box, "Do Gray Goods Get Serviced?").

The legal liabilities problem usually involves warranties that can't be honored and performance criteria which can't be fulfilled. These problems are especially acute for pharmaceutical products because of the potential injuries involved. Taking medication that has expired or whose dosages are meant for adults can severly harm children.

Gray trade affects global marketing management in a number of ways. Forecasted sales in a market may not be realized when there is a sudden influx of gray goods. Roll-out campaign plans for new product introductions might have to be changed if gray traders introduce the product prematurely, as happens frequently in film videos and popular music. And as was seen in

Chapter 13, "Global Pricing," while gray trade means that the need for uniform pricing across countries grows, exchange rates need to be monitored and fluctuations may force a realignment.

Channel Actions against Gray Trade

What can global marketers do in the distribution channels about gray trade? There are a number of actions available to help reduce the volume of gray trade and limit the damage done.

- *Supply interference.* Most companies engage in some interchange and relationship building with their distributors in various countries, asking them to help stop gray trade at the source by screening orders carefully and being careful how they dispose of surplus inventory. Lotus, the American software maker, in an effort to stop dealers from ordering large quantities of its popular 1-2-3 program at volume discounts and then selling the excess to gray traders, has announced its determination to terminate any distributor who supplies the product to unauthorized dealers. These practices have to be done with care, since putting pressure on suppliers can easily turn into an illegal restriction of trade.
- *Dealer interference.* A more drastic measure is to search for gray imports at the gray traders' outlets in the importing country, then asking the dealers—or helping them—to get rid of their inventory. Companies sometimes attempt to simply destroy gray merchandise in the stores. This kind of "search and destroy" action requires a substantiated legal justification, such as an illegal change in the valid dates or improper packaging, and is more common for counterfeit goods (see Chapter 12).
- *Demand interference.* Some firms use advertising and other promotional means to educate potential customers about the drawbacks of gray goods and the limitations on warranties, returns, and service. Companies such as Rolex, Seiko, Mercedes, Microsoft, and IBM have engaged in these practices. There are two problems. One is the legal problem of threatening to limit service to products sold through authorized dealers only, not an acceptable practice in most countries. Second, firms are reluctant to call attention to the gray trade phenomenon and create hesitation on the part of potential buyers of the brand.
- *Strategic attack.* A more constructive solution is to go on the attack and create stronger reasons for customers to patronize authorized dealers. As we saw in Chapter 13, this might involve aggressive price cutting, but other measures should be considered as well. Supporting authorized dealers in offering innovative credit plans, improved service, and other customer-oriented initiatives are possible tactics. Caterpillar, the heavy machinery company, helped authorized dealers develop customized warranties the individual buyer could tailor to his or her own special needs.

Manufacturers also support their dealers by regionalizing their offerings, differentiating model features and numbers between trade areas to make it possible to spot gray imports and restrict servicing liability. Most Japanese camera makers use different model numbers and introduce slight differences in features between their Asian, North American, and European markets. By stressing features and model numbers in the advertising, their global advertising copy can remain uniform with the same brand name (Minolta, Canon, Nikon) while at the same time alerting buyers when a gray import does not correspond to an "authentic" model.

Multiple Distribution Channels

Given the increased speed and service in global logistics, the breakdown of single-channel distribution regimes, and the prevalence of gray trade, it is not surprising to find that multiple distribution channels are now common. The initiators are sometimes middlemen who decide that attack is the best defense. While authorized intermediaries appeal to the manufacturer to help block parallel importing, they also attempt to bypass some middlemen on their own. Local distributors, wholesalers, or retailers can now order directly from overseas distributors, bypassing one or more of the levels in the local link between the manufacturer and the ultimate consumer. In fact, these options are not only available to middlemen but often to ultimate consumers as well. There is an increase in **direct buying,** with consumers in different countries ordering directly from overseas stores and catalog houses, which ship the products through independent carriers.[27]

This means that there are many ways for a buyer to purchase a particular product or brand. For example, a Madrid father of two, busy filming his small children playing, could have bought his Sony videocam in any one of the following outlets:

- A Madrid specialty store (expensive but secure).
- A Madrid discount house (cheaper but outside of town).
- In Portugal across the border, duty free and no sales tax.
- In Frankfurt, at the airport, duty-free and with all-Europe service.
- In Barcelona from a street vendor who smuggled it off the Hong Kong ship in the port (cheap but risky—could be a knockoff).
- By fax order from 47th Street Photo in New York (cheap and no fake—and freight at $45 might be acceptable for a $700 videocamera).

In the not-so-distant future, the Madrid father's videocamera might in fact have been bought on Internet.

Some of these alternative channels, which may seem minor and of limited potential in the large picture, can become important under special circumstances. An example is **duty-free shopping** as done in the Philippines (see box, "Duty-Free Shopping in Manila").

Although some manufacturers do try to control their channels completely by a strong in-store sales effort—Swatch and Rolex are two who do—for many manufacturers the job is too big, and they concentrate on trying to keep the

---

Getting the Picture

Duty-Free Shopping in Manila

IN THE EARLY 1990s Philippine authorities changed the standard duty-free shopping regulations, which make duty-free alcohol, tobacco, and perfume available only to departing airline passengers. Recognizing that a large portion of the more than four million Filipinos working overseas returned home on vacations and holidays with food and household appliances for relatives, the government decided to get some of that business for itself. Now, at the airport in Manila, *incoming* passengers can spend up to $1,000 ($2,000 for returning Filipinos) as the duty-free stores and bring the goods duty-free into the country. The only requirements are that the shopping be done within 48 hours of arrival and that payment be made in U.S. dollars. Residents can come and see the merchandise before purchase, saving the incoming traveler the problem of not knowing what exactly to buy.

Most travelers would have trouble recognizing the duty-free scene that has grown up around the Manila airport. The shops have spread beyond the main international airport. Much of the mer-chandise would never fit into an aircraft cabin's overhead storage bins: motor-cycles, big-screen TV sets, brass beds, freezers, washing machines, air-conditioners, even farm equipment. The grocery section includes large packages of Kellogg's Rice Krispies, Kool-Aid, Cheez-Whiz, Budweiser beer, and other mainstream American brands.

While it make a lot of consumers happy, the new system has infuriated Philippine manufacturers and retailers who are crying unfair competition.

"We're getting battered by duty-free," says Roberto S. Claudio, vice president of the Philippine Retailers Association. "It makes a mockery of re-tailing." People break the rules with false or borrowed papers, he says. One regular store in Manila was found stocked with illegally diverted imports, still bearing duty-free tags.

Whether viewed as a boon for con-sumers or a bust for local retailers, duty-free sales are soaring. Duty-free has passed the Shoe Mart chain as the Philippines' number 1 retailer.

Source: Lambert, 1995; Foster, 1995.

---

abuses and damages at acceptable levels. By managing global logistics they try to steer these forces—via slight model changes, pricing and advertising support, and interpersonal appeals—in a direction that minimizes interchannel conflict and enables synergy to develop between the parallel channels through which the product moves.

GLOBAL CHANNEL DESIGN

Despite the idiosyncracies of each individual country's channel structure it can still be possible to identify what middlemen should be used in a country to ensure that the strategic objectives of the marketing mix—the target segmentation and the desired product positioning—are reached. To do this requires an analysis of what the important functions in the channel network are—identification of what the key success factors are as they relate to channel choice—and then ensuring that the chosen intermediaries in each country

*G*etting the Picture

Swatch's Globally Limited Distribution Strategy

SWATCH, the Swiss watch company whose fashionable but well-functioning watches appeal to a mainly young mind-set across national boundaries, practices what it calls "global but limited distribution." The company's national sales organization works closely with local distributors and dealers to control distribution, build and sustain the brand image, and avoid retailer discounting. The global strategy is to maintain a sense of scarcity: "When you see a Swatch, you better buy it, because it will be in limited supply."

In Europe, Swatch watches are sold by the few existing up-market department stores, but mainly through traditional jewelers and some specialized sports, gift, and fashion boutiques, mail order houses, and duty-free shops. A successful launch at a prestigious jeweler on Rue de la Paix in Paris followed by the acceptance of Swatch at similar stores expanded the French market penetration while raising the Swatch image. In the United States, Swatches are sold mainly through "shops-in-shops" at up-market department stores, some specialized watch retailers, sports shops, and boutiques.

Discounting by distributors is not allowed and the trade is warned repeatedly about counterfeits. In-store merchandising is considered fundamental to the strategy, and retailers are assisted with sales promotions that include color-coordinated display racks, in-store videos, upbeat music tapes, and ample supply of product brochures. As new collections are launched and old lines retired, parties are organized for the trade with the aim of inducing a feeling of belonging to a "Swatch Club" and creating an acceptance of the lower margins offered by Swatch. The economic reasons for the trade acceptance are also important: a very low rate for warranty returns (0.3% compared with an industry average of 5%), higher customer satisfaction, and less after-sales service problems.

Sources: Christian Pinson, "Swatch," Insead-Cedep case no. 589-005-IN, 1987; Susan W. Nye and Barbara Priovolos, "The Swatch Project," Imede, 1985.

measure up on those criteria. The Swatch watch strategy demonstrates how this means that the same intermediaries might not be used everywhere (see box, "Swatch's Globally Limited Distribution Strategy").

The FSAs Revisited

To identify the channel requirements, the natural first step is to decide whether any of the firm-specific advantages are uniquely lodged in the distribution channels to be used. In the case of fast-food franchising, the answer is clearly yes: Without control over the outlets afforded by the franchising contracts, there would be little point in expanding globally. The product sold is a homogeneous (and therefore reliable) meal located at a convenient place. A less-obvious example would be automobile sales. Without a strong dealer network providing after-sales service, some auto exporters find it difficult to export. Part of the problem that British cars like MG, Triumph, and Rover faced in the United States was the weak service network available. Companies recognizing that such drawbacks will make sales difficult and might give the product a bad reputation sometimes refuse delivery into the countries where no service network exists. Toyota avoided Algiers as a market for its trucks until a sufficiently strong service network was built (in the meantime the Mitsubishi trading company sold its trucks in the country in a kind of gray import market).

Key success factors and FSAs may vary across countries. For example, many of the convenience products in Western markets (packaged foods, cigarettes, soft drinks, and so on) require intensive distribution coverage, precisely because customers want them to be conveniently available. One might infer, therefore, that the absence of such intensive convenience channels in some countries would lower the sales of these products there. But as has been mentioned, what constitutes a convenience good in one country might be a shopping good (or even a specialty good) somewhere else. Consequently, there might really be people who would be willing to "walk a mile" just to buy a Camel cigarette.

Availability of Channels

Once the critical features of the channel network have been identified, the question is whether the country market analyzed possesses channels that will provide the necessary service. If local franchisees are necessary, are there financially strong franchisees available? Can dealers provide after-sales service? Are there boutiques where designer apparel is sold to an upscale market niche? Are there middlemen who can store frozen juice in sufficient quantities?

Where the answer is no, the firm needs to consider whether such outlets can be created, that is, whether the firm might invest in a dedicated network in order to supply the market. This is usually a big investment question, and as we have seen there is no certainty of success. When the market is sufficiently large, as the U.S. market almost always is, it might pay for the company to develop its own distribution network, as Honda has done for its motorcycles. But where the market is smaller and the gains consequently less, the investment might not be worth the risks involved.

Channel Tie-Up

Where channel members are available to provide the functions necessary, they still might be unwilling to sign on with the new product unless special trade allowances bigger than those offered by the competition are made. There are reasons for making sure at this stage that the best units available are tied into and it is customary for new entrants to pay a premium to established dealers to get them to accept the new product. One reason for the resistance on the part of auto dealers in the United States to small cars was the lower margins offered on them. Cognizant of this fact, the Japanese small car makers entered with higher dealer margins than customary for that size of car. The thrust behind signing up good distributors and dealers is not only that sales will be high but that they are the ones most likely to sustain the FSAs identified as necessary for the competitive success of the company.

Coordination and Control

With a good distribution network established, **coordination and control** from a centralized headquarters location might now be feasible. The task is large even in small firms, making sure that shipments arrive on time, that the distributors are notified, that a standardized advertising campaign to middlemen across a number of countries is on schedule, that the sales reports for the last quarter have all been received, that the required reporting format is followed so that comparisons between budgeted and actual sales can be made, and so on. It is quite clear that before the advent of global telecommunications and LAN computer networks the control and coordination of distribution across different countries was a very difficult task.

In terms of channel management, global coordination means that physical distribution and logistics have to be controlled to the greatest extent possible. Parts for servicing products, components used in global production plants, and so on, have to be shipped, and then consistent reporting from middlemen in different countries has to be instituted. These reports focus on sales results, broken down by various channel types—sales via supermarkets, drugstores, variety stores—specific enough to provide guidance as to what channels are doing well. The most important part of the control mechanism, however, hinges on getting information about the movement of the product through the various channels. It is not sufficient to know that the warehouse in Abadan has received the shipment, or that the wholesalers have been stocked up, or that the product is on the retail shelf. What is needed, but difficult to achieve, is the final sales results. "How much of the product has been bought?" and "What is the reaction among buyers?"

It is the emphasis on control and frequent reporting that distinguishes the global from traditional multinational companies. The global marketer has to insist that reports are frequent and exact and must make sure that headquarters knows what is happening. But reports are not enough—the global marketer has to travel to the various local markets and deal with local managers directly. This is done to solicit their full cooperation in implementing a global distribution strategy and also to help alleviate problems with actual or potential parallel channels.

SUMMARY

In this chapter various aspects of a global distribution strategy have been discussed: first some of the differences in wholesaling and retailing in various countries, the feasibility of rationalization and creation of new channels, and the emergence of global retailing; then the independent organizations that facilitate global logistics between countries, emphasizing how competition and technology have pressured them to increase speed, reli-

ability, and service; next problems with parallel distribution, especially gray trade, showing how multiple channels into a country have become a fact of life; and finally issues of coordinated global channel strategies. In the end, the degree to which channel policy in different countries should be made consistent through a global strategy hinges on the degree to which FSAs are explicitly lodged in distribution channels and the degree to which the channel members' activities can be coordinated and controlled. If channels are very important because of FSAs, the company has to evaluate the alternatives very carefully and decide whether the available channels provide sufficient support. If they do not, the firm might have to establish its own distribution network, or else forgo entry. The channel strategy is only part of the overall business strategy of the global firm, and where the costs of control and coordination are too high, the global approach might have to yield to a polycentric approach in which the company takes a different angle on distribution in each local market.

KEY TERMS

Air express p. 522
Coordination and control p. 536
Direct buying p. 532
Dual distribution p. 509
Duty-free shopping p. 532
Full-service wholesalers p. 513

Global carrier alliances p. 523
Global distribution p. 520
Global logistics p. 520
Inventory management p. 525
Ocean-going vessels p. 522
Parallel distribution p. 526

Response time p. 526
Retailers p. 515
RoadRailer system p. 525
Roll-on-roll-off (RORO) system p. 525
Wholesalers p. 510

DISCUSSION QUESTIONS

1. Compare and contrast the food retailing system in two countries you are familiar with. Why have the differences occurred? Is a convergence under way?

2. Why is coordination of global logistics so complex? What technological innovations have made coordination more easy?

3. Discuss how the phenomenon of gray trade affects the ability of the global marketer to control distribution. How can the difficulties be overcome?

4. What are the gains from coordinating distribution globally? When are these gains not sufficient to justify changing an existing, well-functioning, multidomestic approach?

5. Using library resources, investigate one of the successful cases of an introduction of a new approach to channels in foreign countries (Avon, 7-Eleven, Toys-R-Us, or L. L. Bean, for example). What customer factors were important determinants of the success? What did competition do? What are some lessons for other companies?

NOTES

1. See Rosson, 1987.

2. Rosson, 1987, demonstrates some of the conflicts that can arise between manufacturers and independent distributors and how they lead to termination of contracts.

3. As the empirical study by Bello et al., 1991, demonstrates, where the multiple channels are not in direct competition, independent distributors can still provide strong benefits to the manufacturers in terms of market knowledge and specialized services.

4. This does not mean, however, that the Japanese system necessarily exhibits low productivity. Although this is a common assumption, and is the case for most productivity measures, it can be argued that because of high value-added relative to low wage rates, Japan's complex and multilayered distribution system is not particularly inefficient by international standards—see Maruyama, 1993.

5. Although this consolidation has perhaps gone furthest in the United States, even Japan with its notorious large numbers and levels of wholesalers is moving toward larger units—see Czinkota and Kotabe, 1993.

6. See Munns, 1994.

7. Typical examples include, from the retailing end, Kmart and Sears in the United States, Virgin stores in Britain, and the FNAC chain in France. Manufacturers moving forward include Compaq and Dell in personal computers, both selling their products mainly through telemarketing, Benetton with its franchised stores, and many luxury goods makers such as Cartier, Louis Vuitton, and Dunhill with their boutiques (see also the global retailing section below).

8. See "L'eggs Products, Inc," Harvard Business School case no. 9-575-090, 1979.

9. Alexander, 1990, discusses the variety among national retailers in more detail.

10. A good example of the kind of difficulty created in retailing by different consumer in-store behavior and different expectations about store service is the early resistance to computer stores in Europe, overcome only gradually. See "What's Holding Back Computer Chains," 1984.

11. For a striking example, see "Dell," 1992.

12. This section draws on the excellent survey by Rapoport, 1995.

13. See Corben, 1995.

14. This power advantage has become one reason why manufacturers aim to develop more global brands—see, for example, Simmons, 1990.

15. See "How Levi's Works," 1993.

16. The emphasis on speed has made even small savings important. For example, in mid-1995 Federal Express induced the U.S. Trade Representative to pressure Japanese authorities for landing rights at Kobe's New International Airport even though other Japanese airports were available and landing in Japan was no longer a necessity on Far Eastern routes from FedEx's hub in Memphis. Rather, Federal Express, which got access, plans to use Kobe from its new hub in Subic Bay in the Philippines. See Pollack, 1995.

17. See Tirschwell, 1995.

18. Price competition among ocean carriers is guided by "conferences," loose agreements between industry participants, sometimes aided by governments, which attempt to regulate competition. These conferences have at times lost power as individual carrier lines refused to go along, but deregulation is not as far-reaching as in the airline industry, and there are still successful attempts to control prices. See, for example, Fabey, 1995.

19. These megaports may have to be built away from existing port sites because of a lack of land area, and they may also be built by the global alliance partners rather than the port authorities since the latter are limited in their actions by local governments. See DiBenedetto, 1995.

20. See Koenig, 1995. As was discussed in Chapter 10, when P&G found its truck shipments delayed at the border, the company helped invest in improved port facilities in St. Petersburg and shipped products to Russia from Germany by boat across the Baltic.

21. Change is possibly under way, however. As of 1995, the RoadRailer system is being tested in Bayern in the south of Germany, with the first train going from Munich across the Alps through the Brenner pass with BMW cars destined for Milano and Verona in Italy, a trip of eight hours (see Barnard, 1995a).

22. See "SKF," 1993.

23. The smaller companies can be competitive by focusing on certain key routes and terminals and offering specialized services, a niche strategy—see Barnard, 1995b.

24. From a study reported in *The Journal of Commerce*—see Johnson, 1995c.

25. This section draws on Cavusgil & Sikora, 1988.

26. Figures from ibid.

27. Direct marketing will be discussed in more detail in Chapter 16, "Global Promotion, Direct Marketing, and Personal Selling."

SELECTED REFERENCES

Alexander, Nicholas. "Retailers and International Markets." *International Marketing Review* 7, no. 4 (1990), pp. 75–85.

Assmus, Gert, and Carsten Wiese. "How to Address the Gray Market Threat Using Price Coordination." *Sloan Management Review* 36, no. 3 (1995), pp. 31–42.

Barnard, Bruce "RoadRailer Trailer to Make European Intermodal Debut." *Journal of Commerce*, May 18, (1995a,) pp. 1A, 2A.

———. "Jan Jansen Leading Ogden's 'Ground Troops' Into Europe." *Journal of Commerce*, June 19, 1995, p. 14A.

Bello, Daniel C.; David J. Urban; and Bronislaw J. Verhage. "Evaluating Export Middlemen in Alternative Channel Structures." *International Marketing Review* 8, no. 5 (1991), pp. 49–64.

Cavusgil, S. Tamer, and Ed Sikora. "How Multinational Can Counter Gray Market Imports." *Columbia Journal of World Business*, Winter 1988, pp. 75–85.

Corben, Ron. "Thailand Megamerger Is Expected to Shake Up Retail Trade in Asia." *Journal of Commerce*, May 22, 1995, p. 5A.

Czinkota, Michael R., and Masaaki Kotabe. *The Japanese Distribution System*. Chicago: 1993.

"Dell: Mail Order Was Supposed to Fail." *Business Week*, January 20, 1992, p. 89.

DiBenedetto, William. "Giant Ship Terminals are Coming; The Question Is: Who'll Build Them?" *Journal of Commerce*, June 21, 1995, pp. 1A, 2A.

Fabey, Michael "TACA Finds Cargo Surge Making Up for Rollback." *Journal of Commerce*, June 19, 1995, pp. 1A, 8A.

"How Levi's Works with Retailers." *Business Europe*, July 19, 1993.

Foster, Peter. "The Capital of Duty-free," *The Times*, Sept. 28, 1995, Features, p. 1.

Johnson, Gregory S. "Eastman Kodak Forms Own Air Freight Hub." *Journal of Commerce*, May 17, 1995a, pp. 1A, 7A.

———. "UPS Leaps Ahead with Next-Flight-Out International Service." *Journal of Commerce*, May 25, 1995b, p. 3A.

———. "Survey: Companies Consider Logistics a Key to Profits." *Journal of Commerce*, May 31, 1995c, p. 2B.

Kale, Sudhir H., and Roger P. McIntyre. "Distribution Channel Relationships in Diverse Cultures." *International Marketing Review* 8 (1991), pp. 31–45.

Kim, Jai Ok; Mary Barry; and Carol Warfield. "Gaining Ground in a Globalized Market: U.S. Clothing Industry." *Bobbin* 35, no. 9 (1994), p. 60.

Koenig, Robert. "Tenfold Increase in Truck Traffic Fuels German Plans for Toll Hike." *Journal of Commerce*, June 7, 1995, p. 1A.

Lambert, Bruce. "In Philippines, Duty-Free with a Difference (or Two)," *New York Times*, June 24, 1995, p. 34.

Lyons, N. *The Sony Vision*. New York: Crown, 1976.

Markowitz, Arthur. "Wal-Mart Zones In on Foreign Trade." *Discount Store News* 32, no. 8, (April 19, 1993), p. 1.

Maruyama, Masayoshi. "The Structure and Performance of the Japanese Distribution System." In Czinkota and Kotabe, *The Japanese Distribution System*, pp. 23–42.

Morita, Akio. *Made in Japan*. New York: NAL Penguin, 1986.

Munns, Peter J. S. *Marketing and Distribution in Japan Today*. Master's thesis, Graduate School of Management, International University of Japan, 1994.

Pollack, Andrew. "U.S. and Japan Again Pull Back from the Brink." *New York Times*, June 22, 1995, pp. 31, 34.

Rapoport, Carla, with Justin Martin. "Retailers Go Global." *Fortune*, February 20, 1995, pp. 102–8.

Rosson, Philip. "The Overseas Distributor Method." In Rosson, P., and S. Reid, eds., *Market Entry and Expansion Mode*. New York: Praeger, 1987.

"SKF to Centralize Distribution." *Business Europe*, April 12, 1993, p. 7.

Simmons, Tim. "A Global Brand of Dialog; Food Products Manufacturers Moving to Market Products Globally," *Supermarket News* 40, no. 28, (July 9, 1990), p. 2.

Tirschwell, Peter M. "APL Seeks Shift to Terminal Adjacent to Partners." *Journal of Commerce*, June 23, 1995, p. 1A.

"What's Holding Back Computer Chains in Europe?" *Business Week*, November 12, 1984, p. 120.

Chapter 15

Global Advertising

"One voice, many languages"

After studying this chapter, you should understand the following global marketing issues:

1. As the affluence of countries grows, new products and services appear, and customers need more information. Advertising becomes more important, and advertising expenditures as a percent of the GDP increase.

2. As markets integrate, global communications expand, and customers become more similar, pan-regional advertising campaigns will become increasingly cost efficient and more effective than multidomestic advertising.

3. Rather than trying for complete uniformity, global advertising tends to follow a pattern standardization approach with unified slogan, visualization, and image but with local execution in terms of language, spokespersons, and copy. This helps to avoid the pitfalls of standardized and translated messages.

4. The global advertising agency is often at an advantage over local rivals when global or regional advertising is contemplated. But independent local advertising agencies have combined with others to form multinational networks and can sometimes offer stronger local talent.

5. The development of a global campaign takes time, effort, and planning. The process should involve headquarters and ad agency managers but also local representatives whose knowledge will help formulate the global communication strategy.

GLOBAL PROMOTION involves a variety of activities, ranging from in-store point-of-purchase displays and Sunday newspaper coupons to satellite TV advertising to sponsorship of symphony orchestras and athletic events such as the Olympics, soccer's World Cup, and major tennis tournaments. The most visible promotional activity is perhaps *global advertising*, the topic of this chapter. *Global sales promotion, public relations, and publicity* have also become powerful promotional tools because of developments in global communications and the opening up of new markets. Then there is participation in *international trade fairs, direct marketing, and personal selling*, the last typically much more localized, but still important. These other promotional tools will be discussed in Chapter 16.

This chapter will start by discussing the extent of advertising and media spending that exists in various countries, and then we will focus on global advertising issues. We'll discuss the pros and cons of global versus multidomestic advertising, what is involved in doing global advertising, the role of the advertising agency, and the problems of global advertising management. We conclude with an illustration of how one company has gone about developing a pan-regional advertising campaign.

Provocative Ads Give Benetton Global Impact

"Do you play safe?" asks an advertisement for Benetton Sportsystem, picturing Ektelon eyeguards on one page and a condom on the other. Other ads juxtapose an Asolo climbing boot with a picture of Jesus's crucifixion ("Do you play alone?") and Kastle skis with photos of German and American Olympic athletes giving Nazi and black-power salutes in 1936 and 1968 ("Do you play race?").

These ads are undeniably provocative; many people find them offensive. They build on Benetton's experience that controversial images give the retailer worldwide recognition despite modest advertising budgets. These benefits convinced Benetton to stick with the provocative ad campaigns for the company's clothing stores as well as its sporting goods.

The earlier Benetton campaigns were classic examples of global marketing. They paired multicultural groups of models with the logo "United Colors of Benetton," promoting global harmony as much as Benetton's clothing. Because of the ads' ethnic diversity and freedom from words, they worked around the world, and Benetton gained a reputation for caring about high-minded values like global unity.

Extending the focus on values, Benetton's ads became more hard-edged. One showed a man dying of AIDS, another a priest and nun kissing. Some consumers bristled, and many critics doubted the messages could stimulate sales. In the United States, where sales slipped, Benetton began using more conventional advertising that concentrated on ensuring that consumers know what its stores offer. A television ad describes a minidress as "your best dress . . . the one you sometimes think you love more than your boyfriend." Provocative as that message is, it's a lot more like other fashion ads than the earlier Benetton billboards were.

Even as Benetton diversifies its advertising, debate continues over whether global advertising can succeed. To promote the Flore line of fragrances, New York agency Ally & Gargano and Spanish agency FMRG collaborated on a global campaign with the theme "a world within." The ads use soft-focus photos of a woman—images the agencies believe universally convey intimacy. Eastman Kodak, too, uses global advertising, although it allows local ad agencies to adapt campaigns to local needs. In contrast, Colgate-Palmolive Company shifted from a global strategy to advertising tailored to each country for some of its brands. Kellogg Company also targets its advertising—a logical step in its Latin American markets, where eating breakfast cereal (or breakfast, for that matter) is not part of the culture.

Either way, marketers need advertising agencies with international expertise. The ideal agency? One that knows whether to use a single global message or to target messages geographically. That kind of knowledge is literally worth its weight in gold.

Sources: Stuart Elliott, "Benetton's Unrepentant Adman Vows to Keep Pushing the Envelope," *New York Times*, July 21, 1995, p. D4; Marshall Blonsky and Contardo Calligaris, "At Benetton, a Retreat from Revolution," *Washington Post*, April 30, 1995, pp. H1, H7; Stuart Elliott, "Creative Agencies That Feel at Home in the Global Village Are Writing Their Own Tickets," *New York Times*, September 30, 1994, p. D17; Laurie Freeman, "Colgate Axes Global Ads; Thinks Local," *Advertising Age*, November 26, 1990, pp. 1, 59.

THE GLOBAL ADVERTISING JOB

The global advertiser faces a complex task. The communication has to be appropriate for each local market while at the same time there is a need to coordinate campaigns and control expenditures across the globe. Because of the varying media availability in different countries and differing effectiveness of global media, the feasible channels for advertising will differ. Further, the variations across country markets in customer behavior make for variable receptivity to advertising and message construction. But customizing the advertising to each individual country leads to increased costs and unwieldy control procedures. This chapter deals with these managerial issues in-depth and attempts to show how the optimal balance between the two extremes of ethnocentrically global and polycentrically multidomestic advertising can be achieved.

Global advertising can be defined as advertising more or less uniform across many countries, often, but not necessarily, in media vehicles with global reach. In many cases complete uniformity is unobtainable because of linguistic and regulatory differences between nations or differences in media availability, but, as with products, **localized advertising** can still be basically global. In contrast, **multidomestic advertising** is international advertising deliberately adapted to particular markets and audiences in message and/or creative execution.[1]

There are several traditional problems facing the decision maker in global advertising. One is how to allocate a given *advertising budget* among several market countries. Another is the *message* to use in these various markets. A third is what *media* to select.

But even before tackling these management decisions, the advertiser needs to define the *objectives* of the advertising in the different countries. And before doing that it is imperative that the decision maker identify what can conceivably be expected from the global advertising effort. Thus, the logical starting point in global advertising management is the assessment of the *role of advertising* in the country markets and the availability of alternative advertising media.

THE INTERNATIONAL WORLD OF ADVERTISING

Advertising Volume

Judging from most published figures, there is a role for advertising to play in all economies, socialist as well as capitalist. At the same time, there is little doubt that the role of advertising in the United States is considerably greater than in many other places. The advertising-to-GDP percentages in Exhibit 15.1 illustrate this and other interesting facts.

- Advertising intensity varies a great deal between countries. Advertising is simply not a very common form of communication in some countries and may not be an effective promotional tool there.

- Generally the higher the GDP, the more is spent on advertising in percentage terms. The more developed the country, the more money is allocated to advertising. The association is not necessarily uniform across the globe, and Brazil, for example, shows a higher figure than most European countries, possibly reflecting its large geographical spread.

- Religion matters. Muslim countries such as Indonesia tend to show low figures for religious reasons. Since advertising attempts to stimulate desire for products it runs counter to Muslim religious convictions.

- Advertising is an unusually important medium in the United States, probably a result of the cultural diversity that makes social norms and interpersonal communication (word-of-mouth) relatively less influential. This has now been recognized by many foreign companies, which find that they have to spend much more on advertising in the United States

EXHIBIT 15.1 Advertising Intensity in Selected Nations 1993

Country	Advertising as percent of gross domestic product
North America	
Canada	1.17%
United States	2.49
Latin America	
Argentina	1.08
Mexico	0.16
Asia	
India	0.28
Indonesia	0.39
Japan	0.82
Malaysia	0.85
South Korea	1.21
Australia	1.20
Europe	
Belgium	0.54
France	0.65
Germany	0.82 (1990)
Italy	0.57
Sweden	0.63
United Kingdom	1.35

Sources: Calculated from *International Marketing Data and Statistics* 1996, and *European Marketing Data and Statistics*, Euromonitor Plc, 1996.

than elsewhere. To illustrate, for German BASF and Siemens, both in industrial products, corporate advertising in the United States far outstrips that done by the two companies elsewhere.[2]

The global advertising manager needs to remember that different cultures and target segments have different receptivity to advertising. This affects the desirability of having a job in advertising as well. In parts of Asia and the Middle East, advertising agencies have difficulty hiring the best people.[3] Things are changing over time; free-market advertising crowds out traditional norms and inefficient ways of communicating. Even Italians are taking to voice-mail. But differences persist.

The point is one can't assume that global market receptivity to advertising is already the same everywhere, because it isn't. Global advertising allocated equally across countries will lead to misallocated resources. Allocating so that the last dollar spent yields equal returns everywhere, a good rule of thumb, means that there will be widely different levels of coverage across countries,

EXHIBIT 15.2 Media Usage in Various Countries*

Nation	TV	Print	Radio	Cinema	Transit
Argentina	148	155	43	16	47
Brazil	126	77	10	—	4
France	2,712	4,717	611	57	1,108
Germany	2,826	13,423	641	157	550
Japan	13,434	12,900	1,913	—	5,231
South Korea	1,083	1,755	188	—	708
Spain	2,386	4,569	873	62	384
Sweden	143	1,560	—	13	82
United Kingdom	4,621	9,071	287	84	530
United States	45,410	67,536	14,022	—	1,672

*In U.S. dollars

Sources: *International Marketing Data and Statistics 1995* and *European Marketing Data and Statistics 1995*, Euromonitor Plc, 1995.

with countries like Korea and the U.K. getting more than their GDP share, and Italy and India less (using the figures in Exhibit 15.1). At the same time, the global marketer has to judge whether historical data for a country such as India are a good guide for the future; there might be a good opportunity for an expanded advertising effort there.

Media Spending

It is useful to sketch out what media are important in different countries. In Exhibit 15.2 expenditures in five basic media types (TV, print, radio, cinema, and outdoor/transit) are shown for selected countries. Some differences stand out:

- *Outdoor* advertising is much more important in Japan and South Korea than in the West, probably a reflection of the fact that such media can reach the large number of people in the big cities.
- Special media such as *cinema* can be of great value in some countries such as Argentina and India (not shown) where films are popular pastimes and advertisers have access to theaters.
- *Print* media in France, Germany, and Sweden are strong, probably attributable to a high literacy rate and relatively limited commercial broadcasting.
- The Europeans avoid the use of *radio* for advertising. This is perhaps primarily a reflection of lack of opportunity. Many of the European radio stations are still government-controlled near-monopolies with no commercial base.

- *Television* advertising is strong in the United States, Asia, and South America. A unusually large share of Japanese advertising expenditures are for TV advertising, reflecting the complete penetration of that medium in Japanese homes. The Latin American figures reflect a general tendency among Spanish-speaking countries to rely heavily on audio-visual rather than printed communication.

Global Media

The figures in Exhibit 15.2 do not show the degree of global advertising spending nor do they depict the emergence of truly global media. Global media are emerging:

- In *television;* for example, Cable News Network (CNN) reaches into many of the globe's remote corners. The British Skychannel can be seen in most of the EU countries.
- In *magazines* such as U.S.-based *Time, Newsweek, Cosmopolitan,* and *Playboy,* which have overseas editions in the English language with editorial content adapted to the local country. For major markets they also have more completely localized editions and offer, for example, Japanese-language editions.
- In *newspapers* such as *The Financial Times* and *The Wall Street Journal* that have global reach—*The Wall Street Journal* has an Asian and a European edition.
- In the *Internet* and the *World Wide Web*, whose arrival heralds further developments in global media. Although the future is uncertain, publishing houses and broadcast networks are already teaming up with on-line services to create a global multimedia environment.

By and large, however, global advertising does not depend on the emergence of global media. Even the most global advertising campaigns have to be scheduled in local media vehicles with the help of media planners in the local ad agencies. A global 30-second television commercial for British Airways, which may run unchanged in a dozen or so countries (with some voice-over translation), still needs to be scheduled in the local media in these countries. Although cross-country media ownership is growing, at the present advertising space in foreign media is still largely bought and paid for locally.

Strategic Implications

The global statistics are indicators of important differences between country markets. They have some important strategic implications:

1. Advertising expenditures create barriers to entry into an industry. A new firm bent on entering a market usually needs to match the advertising

expenditures of existing firms in order to enter successfully. A global firm with established presence can use high advertising spending to make competitive entry difficult.

2. There are some countries where a scarcity of available media has made advertising a competitive weapon of limited usefulness. Since advertising represents mass communication and thus requires mass media, successful advertising campaigns are very dependent on a well-developed and functioning infrastructure.

3. The communication objectives realistically achieved through various media differ among countries. The so-called **hierarchy of effects,** which traces the effects of advertising through brand awareness to knowledge, attitude, liking, trial, and adoption, illustrates this fact nicely. Whereas television is a true mass medium in the United States and Western Europe and thus a reasonable avenue for creating *awareness* for a new product, television in many other countries (including some European countries with limited time availability) provides a status association for the brand and is thus better as an *attitude change* agent. Similarly, radio is a true mass medium in many countries and thus useful for awareness campaigns but is very focused on specific segments in the United States and aimed at the direct action or *trial stage* rather than more general objectives. Newspapers are the only available medium in some countries and will thus have to fulfill their standard role (in Western markets) of a direct action influence as well as establishing more general *knowledge* and *liking* of the brand. Where literacy levels are low (such as in Bangladesh), broadcast and outdoor advertising plus relatively odd media such as cinema advertising will outweigh print media in importance regardless of objectives of the campaign.

WHAT DOES GLOBAL ADVERTISING INVOLVE?

It is helpful to distinguish between four components of global advertising:

1. *Message and creative:* Global advertising is basically uniform in copy and visualization across markets. The ads can be identical, with language voice-over changes and simple copy translations. Pan-European advertising featuring Exxon gasoline's tiger in the tank and Marlboro cigarettes' cowboy are examples of such global advertising. Then there are **global prototypes** in which the voice-over and the visual may be changed to avoid language and cultural problems and the ad reshot with local spokespeople but using the same visualization. Drakkar Noir, a man's fragrance, in an Arab print ad shows a woman's hand caressing a man's hand holding the product; in the United States the same hand grasps the man's wrist. Colgate-Palmolive and Coca-Cola often use prototypes of actual commercial and advertisement samples that demonstrate what headquarters wants in the ads with written specific guidelines for acceptable deviations from the prototypes in terms of story and message

Continental Airlines uses pattern standardization to unify its message across different regions—in this case Latin America, left, and French-speaking countries, right.

Courtesy Continental Airlines.

(usually limited flexibility) and creative (layout, color, symbols—usually more flexibility) and with suggestions for appropriate media.

A similar but less structured global approach involves **pattern standardization,** in which the positioning theme is unified and some alternative creative concepts supporting the positioning are spelled out but the actual execution of the ads differs between markets. This has become perhaps the most common approach, since it allows creative flexibility at the local level. In particular, it allows the local execution to reflect differences in the use of copy versus visuals. The European ads of Xerox, the copier maker, often carry more copy than their corresponding ads in the United States, for example.

2. *Media:* Global advertising draws on media with global reach such as satellite TV and international editions of magazines and newspapers to create spillovers in two ways: (1) crossing borders to reach customers in different countries and (2) following traveling customers around the globe.

3. *Strategy:* Global advertising often involves products and services which are positioned similarly across markets, that is, whose advertised benefits can be the same. It is not necessary that market segments or usage conditions be identical, but the product's appeal should be the same. The positive spillover won't happen unless certain elements of the product are standardized. Brand name should be identical or recognizably similar.

4. *Organization:* Global advertising is managed globally by managers at headquarters and with the help of advertising agencies with access to a global network.

Globalization Examples

There are many examples of successful campaigns based on global advertising. For many of its cola brands, Coca-Cola develops prototypes of advertising messages and layouts in the United States and ships them to its representatives abroad. The local offices are allowed to make changes so as to accommodate language differences and possible differences in regulations but are generally expected to follow the main script for the campaign. The result is a congruent presentation of the product throughout the world in a manner that is judged to yield the best payoffs. The synergy is naturally high, and unless the slogans are totally inappropriate for the target market, the possible loss due to lack of local adaptation is more than counterbalanced by the instant recognition of the brand name and the slogans (sometimes in English even in non–English language countries). Added to that are the savings from the use of similar materials across the globe and the scale returns to globalization. It is easy to see that globalization might well pay off.

Other companies (and products) that are practitioners of global standardization of advertising are the Revlon company (cosmetics), Philip Morris (tobacco) with its Marlboro brand, the Ralph Lauren Polo and Chaps brands (men's clothing and accessories), Kodak film products, most high-fashion companies such as Yves Saint-Laurent and Dior, and home electronics companies such as Sony. There are others from which one might expect globalized campaigns but which do not use them. The Canon AE-l, a "world camera," employs different campaign material in Japan, Europe, and the United States, and so do the Japanese automobile companies. The European car manufacturers develop special campaigns for their North American markets even though many of the selling propositions remain the same.

Investigating a cross section of 30 print campaigns and 16 television campaigns from ad agencies in the United States, Germany and Japan, one researcher found that standardization is more common for advertisements transferred between Western markets than for messages transferred between Western and Eastern markets.[4] Interestingly, the product type played a much smaller role than did the market distance. Message standardization was much more common for television commercials than for print ads, regardless of country, probably due to the relatively higher cost of producing TV commercials.

Naturally, global advertising is not always the correct strategy. By far the most advertising spending in the world is for ads adapted to the local marketplace. In a recent study of 38 European and U.S. multinationals, it was found that only three practice complete standardization of advertising.[5] Another three reject any attempts at standardization completely. The majority of the companies practice some degree of standardization, from "standardizing strategy but not execution" (23.5 percent) to "limited standardization" (31.5 percent) to "standardize in most cases" (29.5 percent). The most common approach was that of "pattern standardization," employing a unified positioning theme but allowing local variation.

PROS AND CONS OF GLOBAL ADVERTISING

There are several reasons why global advertising might be beneficial—and why it might not be. The most immediate benefit usually centers around the cost advantages of unified campaigns.

Cost Advantages

From a cost viewpoint a globally uniform campaign is usually advantageous.[6] The creative ideas once developed can be used globally; the illustrations and messages can be developed once and for all or employed with only minor modifications. Media availability forces some changes, since a broadcast approach might not be directly translatable into print, but generally costs can be held down below those generated by original work for the local market.

Globalized campaigns can also be the basis for savings in media buying. Several media provide global services, especially print, through its international editions. Because media ownership is becoming multinational (so that newspaper owners, for example, in one country control newspapers in others—Murdoch's string of newspapers in Australia, the United Kingdom, and the United States), there are sources of scale returns available to a globalized campaign not easily tapped by local buyers.

The Role of Global Markets

In general, global advertising will be most useful when the market itself is global. Air travel is a case in point. International airlines offer a typically standardized "product"—or service—and compete for passengers in a global marketplace. The various international airlines attempt to differentiate themselves by superior preflight, in-flight, and postflight service. Global advertising has become an important competitive weapon and a prime source of differentiation. British Airways' famous "Manhattan landing" TV commercial from 1982 has become a landmark in global strategy.

Desperate to make inroads in a competitive market, airlines have pushed the limits of what can be accomplished within a relatively limited range of possibilities. Singapore Airlines offers unparalleled in-flight service based on an extensive customer satisfaction program and uses global ads in business magazines to emphasize the attractiveness of its stewardesses. The drive to be noticed and stand out was taken to new heights by South African Airways as it tried to break into the European and American markets (see box, "The Airline that Cares").

The Role of Global Products

It might be assumed that global products need global advertising. This is often true. The campaigns for Swatch watches, Club Med, Benetton, and Reebok are very similar across continents. But there is often a need to do some local

*G*etting the Picture

The Airline That Cares

AFTER SOUTH AFRICA rejected apartheid and Mr. Mandela became president, the country started a drive to convince companies that had left to return and to attract tourists and new business. One side benefit was increased air travel between South Africa and the advanced economies. South African Airways wanted to be the airline of choice—and needed to establish a much better-known image in an industry where anonymity is associated with lack of safety.

A global advertising campaign seemed the best vehicle to create awareness and a caring image for the airline. To carry the message, a TV commercial was created that drew on a 1982 event on a South Africa Airways 747 en route from Johannesburg to London. A passenger, assisted by flight attendants, gave birth to a healthy baby boy. The spot, produced by Sonnenberg Murphy Leo Burnett, the South African affiliate of the Leo Burnett Company of Chicago, shows a woman, seven months' pregnant, going into labor as her husband watches nervously. After a successful delivery, and as the aircraft continues aloft, the pilot says: "Ladies and gentlemen, this is your captain. We'd like to welcome a new passenger on board."

The commercial was broadcast in the major European and American markets and received considerable attention. The spot's drastic departure from the standard "feel good" airline advertising and its graphic coverage of the birth led to highly negative reviews among creative agency directors, who felt it had gone beyond the bounds of good taste. In *Adweek*, one critic stated: "I don't see flight assistant–assisted birth as an appropriate selling tool, unless you are trying to promote Lamaze Airlines," referring to the well-known birthing technique.

Consumers in various countries were divided, but not along country lines. For every consumer who praised it as heart-warmingly on target, there was another who damned it as tasteless and irrelevant. But in all countries, the awareness goal was reached and surpassed. The negative press coverage in fact helped— so that even though the image conveyed was not entirely positive among all target consumers, on balance the follow-up research showed consistently high ratings for the commercial's being noted and liked. And traffic on the routes between the points where the commercial has aired has never been higher.

Sources: Elliott, 1995a; Wentz, 1994.

adaptation of global campaigns. For example, a global product and brand such as Levi's jeans targets specific segments with different appeals in each local market, since the positioning of the product and brand varies as the target markets differ (see box, "The Localization of Levi's").

Sometimes a global brand's global campaign has misfired and the company has retreated back to a more multidomestic adaptation. Parker Pen, a globally recognized American brand name, shifted to global advertising in the mid-1980s only to return to multidomestic advertising (and renewed success) after sales slumped badly. The cause of failure was the lack of cooperation on the part of the company's country subsidiaries, whose previously successful campaigns were discontinued.[7]

*G*etting the
Picture

The Localization
of Levi's

LEVI'S JEANS are among the most global of products and brands. But Levi's advertising is not global.

In North America Levi's are part of a particularly active, outdoors life style and advertised as such, showing healthy, slightly square individuals pursuing their version of the American dream in a variety of outdoors settings. By contrast, in Japan Levi's are fashionable and emphasize this by using James Dean as a symbol. Levi's in Japan are for the young and restless "shinjinrui", the new generation of men and women. In turn, Levi's advertising in Britain stresses (as so common in British ads) the humorous and cheeky aspects of the product, with a male in his underwear washing his Levi's in a laundromat. Levi's in Britain are targeted toward young college students and their ilk having fun. Same product, different images.

Sources: David B. Montgomery, "Levi Strauss Japan K. K.," Stanford Business School case, 1994; Clio International Awards, 1992: TV commercials from Japan and Britain.

In summary, global advertising is most powerful under the following conditions:

- The *image* communicated can be identical across countries.
- The *symbols* used carry the same meaning across countries.
- The product *features* desired are the same.
- The *usage* conditions are similar across markets.

If all of these conditions hold, as they do in the case of the airlines, global advertising is a natural. When one or more are not fulfilled—as in the case of Levi's—even standardized products may need adapted multidomestic advertising. If the conditions are not right, global advertising will fail—which helps explain why there is still so much controversy about global versus multidomestic advertising.[8]

THE GLOBAL ADVERTISER'S DECISIONS

To describe what is involved in global advertising decision making, we start with the basic mass communication process as it has to be adapted for the international context. This will help explain why the advertiser has to rely to a large extent on local people (agency people and local representatives of the firm) when doing global advertising. Advertising, being so close to the cultural traditions of a country, was long one of the more decentralized decisions in the multinational company. Headquarters would perhaps be setting the budget, but the basic positioning strategy would be determined by the local subsidiary and approved by headquarters. When it came to execution, including message creation and especially media selection, the advertising agency and its local branch were the prime movers.

The global advertiser, aiming to gain some benefits from a unified approach, has to take charge of this process more effectively. Positioning strategy has to be unified across countries and the unique selling propositions of the brand made clear—and the same—everywhere. That is the strategy part. As for execution, the global advertising manager needs to work closely with local personnel in the subsidiaries and in the agency network to get consensus on a message that transcends borders, reflects the brand accurately, and has punch everywhere. As for media, although the agency still must be the main actor, the global advertiser will want to make sure that cost factors such as media discounts are properly taken into account. While doing all this, the global advertiser also needs to keep an open eye and open mind to suggestions from the local people, to quickly diffuse information through the various local affiliates, and to be flexible enough to change when new information and market research suggest so. A challenging task!

The International Mass Communication Process

Communicating well through mass media is hard enough when populations speak the same language and come from the same culture. When such homogeneity is missing, everything becomes even more complicated. The global advertiser starts with the same basic communications model—then adapts it by introducing cultural context and language differences as added noise (see Exhibit 15.3, which uses the common "sender–encoding–channel–decoding–receiver" paradigm, but also shows what the specific tasks are at

EXHIBIT 15.3   **A Model of the International Mass Communication Process**

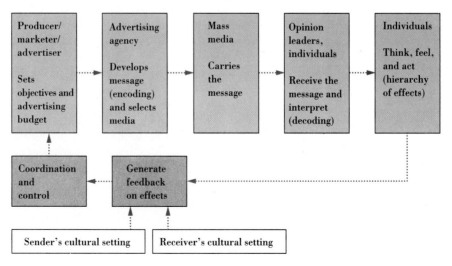

different stages). The *encoding* involves the formulation of translated messages that properly reflect the underlying positioning themes selected by the advertiser. Needless to say, there are problems putting into exact words what the communication is trying to achieve, especially since themes for foreign markets can need a subtly different slant. Then there are language problems. For example, an English word such as "assertive" has no counterpart in many foreign languages, which also means that the sentiment is hard for people in those cultures to recognize and feel. By contrast, the many-hued variations in the meanings of the multipurpose English word "love" need to be precisely translated into languages in which "love" has a certain and unmistakable connotation and various synonyms and alternatives can be found as needed. It's crucial to be clear not only about what the advertising is supposed to convey but about whether this has been adequately translated into another cultural and linguistic context.

The *decoding* on the part of the receiver is similarly complicated by differences in context. While the encoding translation may be correct and apt, the receiver's situation may be very different from what has been envisioned by the sender. For example, television messages are usually intended to be one-on-one with the viewer but in societies where television watching is more of a social activity as in many emerging markets, intimate-sounding messages about feelings tend to be less effective and in danger of being interpreted with snide remarks when the audience is a group. Even if the language is correct and the message is perfectly well understood at one level, hidden or double meanings may surface. Having a good-looking blond female show her perfect smile and white teeth in a magazine ad for a man's cologne might not increase the attractiveness of the product for males in certain cultures. While pink for a baby boy's shirt might not seem wrong to many Asians, increased exposure to Western cultures has made them more sensitive. Some of such problems can be caught by diligent pretesting of ads, but it is difficult to predict audience reactions when cultural distractions from a message are not well understood.

The decoding is likely to involve word-of-mouth from *opinion leaders*, and to follow the so-called *two-step-flow of communication*.[9] This means that the message is first decoded (the first step) by individuals with special interest or expertise whose opinions are valued by other members of the same social groups. These peers evaluate and then pass on (the second step) their version of the message to followers in the groups, creating positive or negative *word-of-mouth* information. The advertiser needs to find out who the opinion leaders are, at what level they should be spoken to in the message, and what selling propositions they would judge important. This requires clear understanding of the cultural context. Even though the majority of ultimate buyers in a country may be without particular product expertise, their opinion leaders are likely to be very knowledgeable. Marketing PCs to upper-level European households, for example, might be very much a matter of creating image and status but the advertising needs to provide information useful to the opinion leaders of the target segments.

Given these complications, it is not surprising that complete standardization of message and visualization is usually unrealistic. Some adaptation is usually necessary, and pattern standardization allowing local variation has become the norm.

In the end, these communications problems mean that the quality of the local talent in the ad agency is very important. The agency's local branches and the firm's local representatives have to be depended on to bridge the gap between different cultural contexts.

Strategic Objectives

Most managers approach global advertising with the intention of using the global reach of media and the similarity of message to enhance the awareness and unique positioning of the brand or product. The boost to the **brand image** is usually the most immediate benefit. When the target market involves global customers, the ability to reach these customers in many places on the globe helps sustain a positive image of the brand. The traveler who recognizes a brand advertised in a foreign resort location may pay more attention to it than at home. Global advertising helps create goodwill.

But the effect of global advertising can also be more direct and come closer to **buyer action.** Global customers, such as businesses with a multinational spread, will usually be able to act on buying intentions even when away from the purchasing center. The manager visiting a plant in Malaysia can still place purchase orders through the head office in Honolulu, New York, or London. Global communication—telephone, fax—makes this possible and even likely, considering the global manager's typical traveling schedule. In fact, the effect of advertising might be enhanced when the manager encounters it overseas, simply because of the pleasant surprise of recognition. For global customers, global advertising can be a trigger to action, not just goodwill.

What about consumers exposed in their home country? Does global advertising make any difference? Does locally adapted advertising get closer to the buying stage while global advertising is good for image only? Again, the answer is perhaps surprising. Yes, local advertising in newspapers and on local broadcast stations can run a tagline with local outlets' phone numbers and addresses, which is harder and more expensive to do—although it can be done—with globally directed advertising. Also, where technical information on attributes needs to be passed along, the copy may have to be redone in the local language, changing voice-overs may not be sufficient. The visual memory, seeing the words, will enhance the consumer's aural memory from the voice-overs. But global ads are often superior in execution. Since more money and creative resources can be spent on global ads, they can support more special effects. In addition, global ads tend to use only the best creative ideas. In all likelihood, the consumer exposed to a global ad will see something more impressive than in a local effort (see box, "Global Ads Taking Flight").

Getting the Picture

Global Ads Taking Flight

ONE OF THE FIRST examples of global advertising, the "Manhattan Landing" TV commercial by Saatchi & Saatchi for British Airways, has achieved legendary status in the advertising world. The commercial, developed in 1982, was inspired by the success of the Spielberg film, *Close Encounters of the Third Kind*. The long 90-second commercial showed Manhattan, with its well-known skyscraper skyline, landing slowly in an English village, landing lights blinding astonished onlookers, engines decelerating, and no voice-over during the first 40 seconds. As the island spaceship lands, the announcer intones, "Every year, we fly more people across the Atlantic than the entire population of Manhattan." The commercial ended with the slogan "The world's favorite airline." A major objective of the campaign was to increase the awareness of British Airways as a worldwide leader in air travel.

Although British Airways attempted to induce all its country managers to run the commercial, not all cooperated. In India, there were questions about the relevance of Manhattan to Indian customers. In other former British colonies the slogan "favorite airline" was mocked. The Japanese manager rejected the commercial as inappropriate because the challenge for advertising was first to make Britain attractive as a destination, then turn to British Airways as the best choice. The Saatchi & Saatchi local branches also objected in some cases. In South Africa, 90 seconds were not available for commercial time. Others objected on the grounds that three 30-second commercials would surely be preferable.

In the end, the commercial was launched in 20 countries. The results were very good, with positive improvement in most local markets.   the United States, especially, awar   ss of the company rose significantly   d unaided recall of the advertising was high. British Airways' image also improved, although according to market research consumers still had some negative perceptions of customer service. Most important for the advertising industry, the campaign showed that the extra money spent on superior execution of global TV commercials could produce strong effects in local markets even without adaptation.

Sources: Quelch, 1984; Stuart Elliott, "British Air Joins a Flight to New Saatchi," *New York Times*, May 3, 1995, pp. D1, D9.

More recent than the "Manhattan Landing" commercial, the Coca-Cola commercial with a huge number of young people on a hilltop in Italy or the similar British Airways commercial with thousands of extras creating a mosaic flag pattern somewhere in India are ads people talk about and are not easily forgotten.[10] Global advertising carries more emotional impact.

Further, as we saw in Chapter 14, people in many parts of the world are starting to buy more items over the phone or from catalogs, using credit cards and avoiding stores. This means the advantage of localized advertising will diminish. Chinese customers in Hong Kong call—or fax—L. L. Bean in the state of Maine to place orders for outdoor boots using their Visa cards. They learn about L. L. Bean (and Eddie Bauer and REI) from travel in the United States, from Hong Kong media reports, and from advertising in international editions of English-language magazines. Global sources of information are available everywhere, in airplanes, dentists' offices, stores, and in homes.

This is why global advertising in many cases can reach the consumer at the point of purchase as effectively as local advertising is able to. There is no reason to relegate global advertising just to the role of sustaining goodwill. A toll-free phone number, a fax number, or a small order form—all globally centralized with local communication switches to make access easier if need be—can be tagged to any global ad or commercial. The extra cost for the advertiser is minimal, since communications have in most cases become globally organized anyway. Local credit checks of cards actually use global check points; local hotel reservations can be made for any global location; and express mail through DHL and Federal Express is already globally available.

In many instances, the local advertising may be seen as the supporting arm of the global advertising effort, quite the opposite of what one might expect. Global brand names, such as Coca-Cola, Sony, Mercedes, and Chanel, are developed and sustained primarily by global advertising. As global media proliferate and markets become globalized, this tendency will continue with increased intensity. New global brands such as Armani, Beck's, Panasonic, and Microsoft are only the tip of the iceberg. These companies and their brands use local advertising primarily to establish local presence—to make customers feel they are not insensitive to local needs and to ensure that customers can get after-sales service and new supplies as needed.

Budgeting for Global Advertising

In *domestic* markets, a common method for advertising budgeting is **percentage-of-sales,** setting a certain percentage of last year's sales as next year's budget. The figure arrived at can be adjusted by considering a changing competitive situation, increasing growth objectives, or a squeeze on company profits, but percentage-of-sales has the advantage of establishing a stable and predictable expenditure level tied to revenues. The percentage chosen can be calibrated against the industry average ratio of advertising-to-sales, making for easy comparisons with competitors.

Although percentage-of-sales is popular among firms from most countries, it is not a very useful method for setting *global* advertising budgets. Even if total worldwide revenues can be used as a base, it is not clear what the appropriate percentage would be. Which country's industry average should be used as a starting point, for example? Different countries show widely different levels of advertising-to-sales ratios for the same industry, depending on media availability, competitive situation, and so on. Since the percentage-of-sales approach sets advertising on the basis of past sales, it is of little use when a shift from multidomestic to global advertising is contemplated. **Competitive parity** approaches,

German and American advertisement for Omega, the Swiss watchmaker. As with most global products, the advertisements involve a standardization of pattern, although the spokespersons featured are different. But the brand and a unique benefit—"vertraut," or "trust"—are the same.
Courtesy Omega Corporation.

where advertising budgets are set on the basis of what competitors spend, are also of less relevance in global advertising. The main difficulty is to identify the appropriate parity to actual and potential competitors from different countries, many of which have very different FSAs and market presence. Competitive parity is most appropriate when the major global competitors are from the same countries, as with Coca-Cola and Pepsi-Cola, or with Sony, Matsushita, Sharp, and other Japanese players in consumer electronics.

Budgeting for global advertising typically involves some version of the so-called **objective-task** method favored domestically by more sophisticated marketers. In this method the objectives of the advertising are first made explicit and quantified, after which the requisite media spending to reach the required exposure levels is specified. Although precise calibration of spending is difficult because of the uncertainty in gauging worldwide audiences of media vehicles, the basic logic is sound. After the initial specification of the job to be done by advertising (target percentages for awareness, for example, or certain reach and frequency figures), the creative solutions and the media schedules likely to attain the levels desired are developed.

This is work requiring the expertise of a global ad agency. The budgeting done for global advertising involves an unusually large amount of agency input, since assessing the feasibility and cost of global campaigns requires input from the local branches in the agencies' global network. Partly for this reason, the drive toward global advertising is often spearheaded by an agency with global reach.[11]

Since global advertising involves much higher production costs and total media expenditures than local advertising, many companies that start advertising globally draw advertising funds away from local subsidiaries. The local country head quite naturally will oppose the budget reduction. There are many arguments why the local effort should be sustained at previous levels: There are undoubtedly local differences in customer receptivity to advertising, local media buys will have to be forgone, and the global ads will negatively enhance the company's image as being foreign. The global advertiser should consider these objections seriously—but also remember that it is always difficult to prove the need for globalization from existing data. The promise of global advertising is always simply a promise, whose success is not easily demonstrable before the fact. But it is based on trends and competitive successes hard to ignore, which need to be taken seriously.

Cooperation from the country heads is absolutely necessary for the successful implementation of a global campaign. In advertising budgeting, this means that companies almost always maintain a balance between global and local ad budgets. Not all the ad money will be allocated to the global campaign, not even when the main ad agency has a strong global network that promises local adaptation.

The local country heads need to have an ad budget over which they have spending authority. Too much centralization leads to lukewarm support, demotivated country employees, and even destructive countermeasures derailing the global effort. In the case of Henkel's Pritt glue product, the corporation found its standardized campaign efforts derailed by local efforts promoting other product lines. Even if the global campaign is limited to one of many product lines, local support makes a big difference and not all the campaign money can be spent on global media.

THE GLOBAL ADVERTISING AGENCY

As mentioned earlier, the drive toward global advertising has to a large extent been spearheaded by **global advertising agencies** that have developed worldwide networks of subsidiaries or affiliates.

Agency Globalization

Most large agencies in the United States and Europe today have more or less global reach (by contrast, the Japanese agencies, including large Dentsu, are very minor players outside of Asia), but the ability to execute a global campaign can vary because of uneven local capability. A more established and tightly knit network of branches and joint ventures around the globe has paid off very well for large integrated agencies in the new global environment. This meant that a firm such as McCann-Erickson, the largest global player before the mergers, gained business in the early 1990s from independent local agencies in Europe and Asia. In 1994, IBM centralized all its advertising to the global network of Ogilvy & Mather Worldwide, one of the large New York–based agencies.[12] However, as always, some buck the trend (see Exhibit 15.4, "Coca-Cola's Agency Network").

As ad agencies expanded their global reach, many advertisers started to centralize their advertising spending and appointed a single firm as the global agency. This meant that many smaller agencies lost accounts as large firms consolidated their ad spending in one agency. As a result, smaller agencies merged and became part of larger global networks. Even large agencies were gobbled up—the WPP Group, in 1992 the world's largest, consisted of J. Walter Thompson and Ogilvy & Mather in the United States; Brouillard Communications in France; as well as Scali, McCabe, Sloves; Fallon McElligot; and the Martin agency—all of Britain. Among the largest global agencies now are Cordiant (which includes Saatchi & Saatchi) and the WPP Group PLC in Britain; Publicis and BDDP Group in Paris; Dentsu and Hakuhodo in Tokyo; and Interpublic Group and Omnicom (now owner of Chiat-Day) in New York (see Exhibit 15.5).

With the members of the groups being large agencies in their own right and often with a proud history, most mergers have retained the independence of the individual units as far as possible. This strategy has been all the more important as many mergers placed accounts from competitors under the same roof. But it also means that the combined units, although large and well represented in many countries, tend to have some difficulty in making the parts work together. The Saatchi & Saatchi breakup is an example (see box, "Saatchi & Saatchi's Global Management Problems").

The Agency's Job

The global advertiser will generally develop the message and media schedule working intimately with an advertising agency with local representation in the various markets. The creative development and the production of a prototype ad or standardized commercial are usually centralized to an agency with headquarters in the company's home country and branch offices in the relevant market countries.

The large multinational with entries in many country markets will generally find it advantageous from a control and coordination perspective to rely on a worldwide agency. Unilever, the large packaged-goods company headquartered in London, employed J. Walter Thompson, now part of the WPP Group, to handle most of its products and markets. Volkswagen was so impressed by Doyle Dane and Bernbach, an American agency, in its handling of its U.S. account that Volkswagen gave the agency responsibility for its other country markets, including the home market in Germany.

EXHIBIT 15.4 Coca-Cola's Agency Network

A growing cast

Since 1991, the Coca-Cola Company has changed its relationships with Madison Avenue. Instead of using a handful of advertising agencies to create campaigns for its brands, the company has hired almost a score, including Creative Artists Agency, the powerful Beverly Hills, California, talent agency.

Before 1991 . . .

Principal assignment(s)	Agency
Ads aimed at black consumers	Burrell Communications Group
Diet Coke/Coca-Cola Light	Lintas Worldwide
Sprite, Mello Yello, Fresca, Minute Maid, Hi-C	Lowe & Partners
Coca-Cola Classic/Coca-Cola, Fanta, Cherry Coke, Mr. Pibb	McCann-Erickson Worldwide
Ads aimed at Spanish-speaking consumers	Sosa, Bromley, Aguilar & Associates

Since 1991 . . .

Principal assignment(s)	Agency
Special projects	Bartle Bogle Hegarty
New products, other brands	Batey (Hong Kong)
Local service, Italy	Leo Burnett S.R.L. (Milan)
Local service, Scandinavia	Leo Burnett (Oslo)
Ads aimed at black consumers	Burrell Communications Group
Aquarius	Casadevall Pedreño & PRG
Fruitopia	Chiat/Day (New York)
Cherry Coke	Chiat/Day (Venice, Calif.)
Coca-Cola Classic/Coca-Cola	Creative Artists Agency
Fanta, Latin America	D'Arcy Masius Benton & Bowles/Americas (Mexico)
Fanta, Asia-Pacific, and local service	D'Arcy Masius Benton & Bowles (Hong Kong)
Local service, Japan	Dentsu
Coca-Cola Classic/Coca-Cola, campaigns promoting contoured bottles	Fallon McElligott
Local service, Japan	Hakuhodo
Coca-Cola Light	Lintas Paris
Fanta, Europe	Lowe Howard-Spink
Diet Coke, Sprite, Fresca, Minute Maid, Hi-C	Lowe & Partners/SMS
Fresca (sugared)	Lowe/SMS de Mexico
Mello Yello, Mr. Pibb	The Martin Agency
Georgia Coffee	McCann-Erickson (Japan)
Powerade	McCann-Erickson (Seattle)
Five Alive	McKinney & Silver
Caffeine-Free Diet Coke/Caffeine-Free Coca-Cola Light	Publicis Conseil (Paris)
Ads aimed at Spanish-speaking consumers	Sosa, Bromley, Aguilar & Associates
OK Soda	Wieden & Kennedy

Source: *Advertising Age.*

EXHIBIT 15.5   The World's Largest Ad Agencies (in $ millions)

Rank			Worldwide gross income			Worldwide capitalized volume		
1994	1993	Advertising organization, headquarters	1994	1993	% Change	1994	1993	% Change
1	1	WPP Group, London	$2,768.2	$2,627.5	5.4%	$20,025.4	$18,644.3	7.4%
2	2	Interpublic Group of Companies, New York	2,211.0	2,125.2	4.0	14,866.0	14,353.7	3.5
3	3	Omnicom Group, New York	2,052.6	1,909.1	7.5	16,058.9	14,268.5	12.5
4	4	Dentsu, Tokyo	1,641.7	1,403.2	17.0	12,325.9	10,846.3	13.6
5	5	Cordiant, London	1,431.5	1,340.0	6.8	11,355.2	10,624.4	6.8
6	6	Young & Rubicam, New York	1,059.7	1,008.9	5.0	7,989.8	7,559.0	5.6
7	7	Euro RSCG, Levallois-Perret	813.3	864.8	−6.0	6,115.9	6,508.9	−6.0
8	8	Grey Advertising, New York	808.7	765.7	5.6	5,428.1	5,161.7	5.1
9	9	Hakuhodo, Tokyo	774.2	727.9	6.4	5,766.5	5,336.0	8.0
10	10	Leo Burnett, Chicago	677.5	622.4	8.8	4,592.0	4,223.5	8.7
11	11	True North Communications, Chicago	619.0	615.5	0.6	5,140.9	5,198.3	−1.1
12	13	D'Arcy Masius Benton & Bowles, New York	608.4	553.6	9.9	5,338.5	4,770.1	11.9
13	12	Publicis Communication, Paris	529.3	555.8	−4.8	3,601.8	3,745.5	−3.8
14	15	Bozell, Jacobs, Kenyon & Eckhardt, New York	329.6	269.9	22.1	2,530.0	2,135.0	18.5
15	14	BDDP Groups, Paris	243.8	279.6	−12.8	1,622.0	1,855.4	−12.5

Source: *Standard Directory of Advertising Agencies* (no. 233), July, 1995. New Providence, NJ: National Register Publishing, p.xxi.

It is also common for companies to allot their advertising money to agencies in the local market when conditions in a country are particularly difficult or unique. Thus, Japanese multinational companies rely on the giant Dentsu or Hakuhodo agencies of Tokyo to handle many of their markets in Asia, but not the American market. Most of the personnel in a particular branch office (even a wholly owned subsidiary) of a multinational agency will be natives of the branch country. Even so, the avoidance of the home country agency by the Japanese is simply a step to ensure that the campaign will have no ethnocentric overtones. At the same time, the tendency for the U.S. multinationals is to prefer dealing with American agencies abroad. This practice might be questioned, since in the annual Clio awards given by an international jury to well-crafted and imaginative advertising, American advertising tends to fare less well. But then, American-based advertising agencies rely largely on local talent in their offices abroad.

Research shows that the extent to which local branches focus on global advertising is relatively limited. In a survey of 347 foreign branches of U.S. agencies it was found that about two-thirds (232) had at some time participated in multicountry advertising initiated by the home office.[13] Of these multicoun-

IN EARLY 1995, Saatchi & Saatchi, one of the world's largest advertising agencies and the one that spearheaded the drive toward global advertising, was in trouble. Three years of recessionary economies around the world had led to lowered billings. The expansion of the agency business into marketing consulting had to be cut short. The acquisitions of several large agencies, including Compton's and Ted Bates, had placed a heavy debt burden on the London-based home office. And the bond- and stock-holders of the publicly listed company included professional money managers of pension funds who demanded high returns on their portfolios. In a coup engineered by American shareholders, Maurice Saatchi, an advertising wizard who had founded the agency in 1970 together with his brother Charles, was ousted as chairman.

Global advertising campaigns, the force behind the creation of powerful global brands, are difficult to implement without the help of agencies like Saatchi with global reach. But these wide-reaching organizations that try to combine creative talent and business skills are difficult to manage. As analysts tried to diagnose Saatchi & Saatchi's problems, one thing stood out: A large company might need strong financial managers, but could it allow enough freedom for the creative people in a successful ad agency?

Sources: *Washington Post*, January 4, 1995; *New York Times*, January 12, 1995.

---

try campaigns, most were regional in scope, followed by major-markets-only campaigns, with less than 10 percent truly global (see Exhibit 15.6). According to the researchers, the emphasis on **pan-regional** campaigns (evidenced by the figures in Exhibit 15.6) is mainly due to the emergence of regional groupings and trading blocs.

Local agencies are often preferable (and sometimes the only ones willing to accept the assignment) when the account is small. The reason is that global agencies, owing to their sheer size, tend to neglect smaller accounts. Even though payment agreements differing from the standard commission fee of 15 percent can be negotiated, the multinational agencies still tend to concentrate on the more important large accounts. This drawback of small local campaigns can be eliminated with the help of globalized campaigns directed from headquarters and managed through the local branch office of a multinational agency. Even though a particular country shows a small account size, the globally pooled advertising budget can be substantial.

One particular headache of agency-advertiser relations is the across-country variability in financial arrangements and payments. Advertisers in some countries insist on paying for the agency services with the product advertised or some other type of "countertrade." The agency then has to arrange the media payments. It is not surprising that some of the highly leveraged global agencies exhibit rather low levels of profitability, creating pressure from irate bond- and shareholders as the Saatchi & Saatchi experience demonstrates.

....
EXHIBIT 15.6   Scope of Advertising Agencies' Participation in Multicountry Campaigns

Market scope	Number of agencies	Percent of total
Agencies doing one type of multicountry campaign		
Global	15	6.5%
Major	35	15.1
Regional	103	44.4
	153	66.0
Agencies executing more than one type of multicountry campaign		
Global-major	5	2.2%
Global-regional	16	6.9
Major-regional	29	12.5
Global-major-regional	29	12.5
	79	34.1
Total	232	100.0%

Source: Adapted from Hill and Shao, 1994, p. 39.

Message Creation

For good reasons, message creation and language translation are the aspects most consistently and thoroughly discussed in the literature on global advertising. Even experienced advertising people commit mistakes with ease. And once committed the faux pas are painfully obvious. The examples are legion (see box, "Translated Messages Have Their Pitfalls").

But there are also examples of successful advertising messages used in many different countries with only a modicum of modification. A classic example is Exxon's "Put a tiger in your tank." Unilever's Lux soap was long advertised around the world as "the soap used by 9 stars out of 10"; "Coke is refreshing" in many countries of the world; Sony positions itself as "the innovator" in most country markets; and Marlboro is from the same "cowboy country" whether you are in Asia, Europe, or Latin America.

Message translation is complicated because of the cultural diversity among the various countries of the world. Language difference is only the most obvious manifestation of this diversity. Other factors, more subtle and therefore treacherous, include the use of idiomatic expressions to signify other matters than the ones literally expressed. An example is the slogan "Avoid embarrassment—use Quink" for an ink product, which translated into Spanish became "Avoid pregnancy—use Quink." Cultural symbolism makes darkened teeth very attractive among some Asian people, creates difficulties in employing an animal as a trademark across cultures (even the tiger had to be given up by Exxon in some countries such as India), and forces close scrutiny of numbers

SMALL NUANCES in words sometimes matter a lot. An American manufacturer in the auto industry advertised its batteries as "highly rated." In Venezuela the translation made it "highly overrated." A shirt manufacturer advertising in Mexico also had trouble with the Spanish language. Instead of declaring, "When I used this shirt I felt good," the character in the advertisement asserted, "Until I used this shirt I felt good."

Sexual connotations under the surface of day-to-day language create pitfalls. Chrysler tried to use its American slogan "Dart is Power" in Latin American markets only to find that the message implied that drivers of the car lacked sexual vigor. An airline advertising its "rendezvous lounges" on its flights did not realize that to many Europeans a rendezvous carries the distinct connotation of meeting a lover for an illicit affair. Otis Elevators pro-

moted parts of their line in Russia as "completion equipment," which in Russian became "tools for orgasms."

Brand names are well known stumbling blocks. Chevrolet's Nova car meant "won't go" in Spanish markets. In Mexico "Fresca" is slang for "lesbian." "Pinto," the Ford car, had to be renamed "Corcel" in Brazil after it was discovered that pinto was slang for the male appendage. The Japanese, on the other hand, have maintained several of their domestic names (in order to maintain the Japanese connection) even though experts warned them that names such as "Facom" and "Datsun" ("That soon?") elicit snide remarks among English-speakers. Such examples demonstrate why it is desirable to employ local agencies rather than rely on a home country agency that works at a distance from the market.

Sources: Ricks, 1993, and personal interviews.

and colors (4 is the number of death in Japan; so is 3 in the Philippines; 13 is not acceptable in the United States and Western Europe; black *and* white are funerary colors in Asia; white is happiness in Europe; red is a masculine color in Italy and feminine in Northern Europe; and so on).[14]

Media Selection

If message creation needs the collaboration of the agency and the advertiser (to ensure a unified positioning theme), media selection is one area where the agency rules. The reason is primarily expertise. Local knowledge of the availability of media alternatives is absolutely necessary so that the optimal media, given the constraints, are chosen. It might be possible to direct an advertising campaign from overseas insofar as budgeting, message creation, and general direction go, but the media choices must be negotiated and made locally.

Varying media usage across regions was shown in Exhibit 15.2. As noted earlier, rates of media usage are determined by a number of factors such as availability of commercial TV and radio, level of economic development, literacy rates, religion, and so forth—and reflect directly, of course, the actual

A video van visits a village in Maharashtra to advertise soap from Hindustan Lever. While television commercials can reach most urban households in India, the inhabitants of rural villages still wait for these vans to provide visual entertainment and product information.

Raghu Rai/Magnum Photos.

media selection decisions made by the advertisers and agencies for the country in question.

What type of media to select hinges (within the availability constraints) very much on the objectives and target segment(s) of the campaign.

For *awareness*, television serves well in many countries where it is generally available. In countries with lower rates of TV penetration, radio can often be used to supplement television advertising. Television in most cases has the advantage of a high-attention value, especially in countries where it is relatively rare.

Effective communication of *knowledge* about a product usually requires the use of words, whether spoken or written. If illiteracy is a problem, knowledge will have to be transmitted through the spoken word—radio would be a logical candidate. Where literacy is high but the number of appropriate magazines low, newspapers might have to serve. In most Western nations the best medium for knowledge creation is the magazine, where specific selling points about the product can be well communicated. It is no coincidence, as noted earlier, that it is in these same countries that "rational," multiattributed product evaluations seem to be most applicable.

For *attitude* change and *image* building, newspapers and radio advertising are generally inferior to television and magazines. Cinema and outdoor advertising are important in certain countries. In Argentina, cinema is an important medium precisely because of the affective spillover from the movie's context and, of course, because of the captive audience (Argentines unlike Americans don't seem to mind). In most countries television is the most important medium for emotional communication, since it combines visual and verbal stimuli.

To affect *behavior* directly, the media chosen have to be timely and reach the audience near the time of purchase. Newspapers fulfill this function well in most cultures. Magazines (and TV) tend to be less useful here, unless the product can be sold through the special direct marketing channels opened up in some countries. An example of the latter is the United States where credit cards are used to pay by telephone for goods advertised on TV.

Once the media types have been decided upon, the particular vehicles to be used within each type are usually selected on the basis of some efficiency criterion, such as "cost-per-thousand" (CPM). The use of an efficiency criterion requires information about how much advertising in a vehicle costs and how many people (in the target market) will be reached. Here a major problem is encountered in many markets. The available audience measurements are either incomplete (lacking audience demographics, for example) or unreliable or even nonexistent. Even in developed countries it is sometimes hard to find accurate figures properly validated by independent agencies. As a result, it is often very difficult to be very precise about the computation of an index such as the CPM. Again, local people with in-depth knowledge of the various media vehicles should be consulted before choices are made.

On the cost side, the rate schedules for advertising may provide great discounts for large quantity and special rebates, often to domestic agencies over foreign agencies. Again the local connection becomes important in negotiations about proper pricing and payment procedures.

GLOBALIZING ADVERTISING: GOODYEAR IN LATIN AMERICA

The way in which the headquarters managers, the local subsidiaries, and the ad agency work together to generate a global advertising campaign can be illustrated through Goodyear's development of a pan-regional campaign for Latin America.

Goodyear, the large American tire company headquartered in Akron, Ohio, has long taken a standardized approach to its advertising. Under the assumption that customer needs and wants in tires are largely dependent on basic factors such as climate and road conditions, the company has coordinated its international advertising centrally since the early 1970s. Goodyear's present regional approach has evolved into a prototype standardization program that involves the local subsidiaries in decision making more than previously. Its Latin American market advertising gains global scale advantages while remaining responsive to local conditions.[15]

Planning for a unified regional advertising strategy that properly involves local subsidiaries needs to start early. For Goodyear, prompted by a reorganization in 1992, the process began about 12 months before the new campaign rolled out. The planning process involved six stages (see Exhibit 15.7).

....

EXHIBIT 15.7 Goodyear's Latin American Campaign Development Stages

1. Preliminary orientation, September 1992

Subsidiary strategic information input on business and communications strategy on country-by-country basis. Home office review

2. Regional communications strategy definition meeting, October 1992

Outputs: Regional positioning objective, communication objectives, and creative assignment for advertising agency.

3. Advertising creative review meeting, November 12, 1992

Outputs: Six creative concepts (storyboards). Research questions regarding real consumer concerns to guide research.

4. Qualitative research stage, November–December 1992

Consistent research results across five counties on purchase intentions and consumer perceptions of safety.

5. Research review meeting, January 15, 1993

Sharply defined "consumer proposition" identified and agreed upon with new creative assignment for agency.

6. Final creative review meeting, March 12, 1993

Campaign adoption.

Source: Adapted from Hanni, Ryans, and Vernon, 1995, p. 88. Reprinted by permission of Michigan State University Press.

1. *Preliminary orientation* (September). The beginning stage was an educational one, allowing both headquarters and local subsidiary staff to understand each other's perspectives. Headquarters informed the subsidiaries of the benefits expected from a pan-regional approach, and the subsidiaries were asked to provide information about their current and planned communication strategies. To emphasize the pan-regional benefits, the regional director of Latin American sales and marketing described the cost reductions from lower trade barriers for advertising materials and the advantage of having available a bank of high-quality standardized commercials. Each national sales director was asked to provide answers to several strategic business questions, including brand image perceptions in their respective markets.

2. *Regional meeting to define communications strategy* (October). An informal two-day working conference was organized in Miami where the communications strategy could be developed. From headquarters came the regional vice president for Latin America, the director of sales and marketing communications, and the manager of marketing research. From the subsidiaries came the sales director and the advertising manager for each country. Also participating were regional account executives and creative directors from Leo Burnett Worldwide, the recently appointed global ad agency based in Chicago, and its offices in Latin America.

The purpose was to develop an "umbrella" campaign theme that would fit all countries but with subsidiary autonomy to prepare retail, promotional, and

<table>
<tr><td rowspan="2">*G*etting the Picture

Smile and Say "Tires"</td><td colspan="2">G O O D Y E A R has identified four different ways to say "tires" in Latin America, and a fifth way to say it in Puerto Rico. In some of these countries one of the expressions occurs less frequently, while in other countries expressions other than the main one either will not be understood or may convey an entirely different meaning. It's important to pick the right word for each local market.</td></tr>
</table>

Spanish word for tires	Countries using each word
Cauchos	Venezuela
Cubiertas	Argentina
Gomas	Puerto Rico
Llantas	Mexico, Peru, Guatemala, Colombia, and elsewhere in Central America
Neumaticos	Chile

Source: Hanni, Ryans, and Vernon, 1995, p. 96.

product advertising to meet local requirements. The umbrella theme would make sure that local creative concepts reinforced common positioning and would make possible centralized (and thus cost-effective) production of a pan-regional pool of television commercials and print advertisements.

Everyone involved at the October meeting was requested to look at tire advertising afresh, disregarding previous regional campaigns to the extent possible. The various participants were happy to discover that no one country's problems were in fact unique, a common base soon emerged, and participants were able to agree on a unified positioning strategy to build brand equity throughout the region. At the same time, needs for local adaptation of local execution were uncovered. For example, even though Spanish is a common language among all the countries except Brazil, national differences in word choice and pronunciations made localized voice-over necessary (see box, "Smile and Say "Tires""). Using local talent would enable the country units to employ spokespeople with regional appeal. On the basis of the subsidiaries' input, a pattern standardization solution of the regional advertising campaign seemed logical.

Involving the ad agency at this early stage facilitated development of the creative brief for the pan-regional ads. To follow up on the development of creative alternatives, a task force was organized, consisting of advertising managers and sales directors from each country, the regional sales and communications directors from headquarters, and agency people (including creative teams from five countries).

3. *Advertising creative meeting* (November). The task force met to consider six alternative concept or storyboards developed by the creative teams. Each of the

five creative teams explained and defended its particular concept or storyboard and lengthy discussions ensued. The outcome was a decision to collect more data on the concepts from customers in the respective countries. Specifically, more marketing research was judged necessary to identify the extent to which the campaigns were targeted correctly at real consumer concerns.

4. *Qualitative research stage* (November–December). The research on the proposed concept storyboards focused on two main issues. One was customers' degree of concern about safety and security of the tires. The second issue involved consumer reactions to four different creative themes:

a. Authority based on an emotional appeal.

b. Leadership positioning.

c. Technology transfer.

d. Advanced technology with rational appeal.

Using focus groups in five countries (Brazil, Chile, Colombia, Mexico, and Venezuela) to test the alternatives, the company found that the results were consistent throughout the region, with safety and security a strong theme everywhere, and with support for an emotional authority-based approach. It was also found that the typical "we are not the same" local sentiments were overstated: The respondents in each country rated their roads "the worst in Latin America."

5. *Research review meeting* (January). The task force met to consider the research results. The aim was to reach a consensus on one unique selling proposition, a convincing argument why consumers should change their beliefs about tires and choose Goodyear. This theme would be the recurring motto serving to unify the various local executions.

The outcome of the meeting was a succinctly worded "consumer proposition," a theme that was assigned to the ad agency for the development of a full pan-regional campaign. In a subsequent meeting, the task force reviewed the creative proposals from the agency and its local creative teams, and further directions for the work were issued.

6. *Final creative review* (March). At this final decision-making meeting of the task force, each team's concept was presented without indicating the team identity or the country in which the campaign originated. A regionwide creative team presented all the proposals, with the supporting material reflecting an entire campaign from print to outdoor media. This was done to avoid the "not invented here" syndrome and reduce the inclination to defend one's own particular proposal at all cost.

The process worked smoothly, as one of the campaigns was judged clearly superior in capturing the positional theme and creative concept. This campaign was adopted, and the agency and its local offices were instructed to proceed with full-fledged development of the campaign material and local executions. The production of the commercials, advertisements, and other support material took place through the summer months and media buys were completed by the start of the campaign at the end of August.

LESSONS   There are several points to emphasize about this illustration of a recent approach to pattern standardization in pan-regional advertising.

First, by focusing on regions it may be possible to reap the scale benefits and cost efficiencies of global advertising without sacrificing too much on the side of local adaptation. The recent emergence of new trading blocs suggests that this perspective can be useful generally.

Second, the early involvement of country subsidiaries and agency professionals not only facilitates later acceptance of unified themes but helps broaden the sources of powerful campaign concepts. This is especially useful since in most cases the local subsidiaries can be expected to have greater market knowledge than headquarters.

Third, and very important, the process by which pattern standardization is arrived at needs to allow open and free exchange. In the Goodyear case, it is striking how local differences seemed to be based on misperceptions that vanished once participants interacted without pressure to defend the home turf. By the same token, headquarters can't assume to know more about the markets involved than its local units know but should focus on explaining carefully why standardization might be beneficial to the local units. The way the local operation fits into the whole needs to be clarified, and headquarters should not expect local units to sacrifice for the common good without a compelling rationale. Then headquarters should be flexible when the local units suggest alternative options.

Fourth, even when the company has operated for years in a market, marketing research is still necessary, especially when conditions are changing. Yesterday's solutions were perhaps good for yesterday's problems—but new times need new information and new solutions. A planning process that is systematic, thorough, and flexible—such as the one implemented by Goodyear—is far more likely to generate successful advertising campaigns than one based on a static and unchanging perception of the environment.

....

SUMMARY

Despite the pitfalls of standardized and translated messages, global advertising has become an important alternative to adapted multidomestic advertising. The technological advances in global communications, the growth of global media, and the strength of global advertising agencies have combined to make global advertising possible. And the positive spillovers from unified messages and the increasing homogeneity of many markets have made global advertising desirable.

As the affluence of countries grows, new products and services appear, and customers need more information. Advertising becomes more important, and advertising expenditures as a percentage of the GDP increase. For the global marketer, faced with increasing spending needs in all markets, a coordinated effort with synchronized campaigns, pattern standardization, and unified image across trade regions is usually more effective and cost efficient than multidomestic campaigns. We took note of the advantages, problems, and pitfalls of global advertising and discussed how the advertiser and ad agency can jointly develop a regional or global campaign, using as illustra- tion a case study of how one company, Goodyear, went about developing and imple- menting a pan-regional campaign.

KEY TERMS

Brand image p. 555
Buyer action p. 555
Competitive parity p. 557
Global advertising agencies p. 559
Global prototypes p. 547
Global advertising p. 543

Hierarchy of effects p. 547
Localized advertising p. 543
Media selection p. 565
Message translation p. 564
Multidomestic advertising p. 543

Objective-task p. 558
Pan-regional advertising p. 563
Pattern standardization p. 548
Percentage-of-sales p. 557

DISCUSSION QUESTIONS

1. Using library sources of daily foreign media, find three examples of global advertising. What characteristics make these campaigns global?

2. Using the same sources, can you find ex- amples of global advertising for which the markets are not global but "multidomestic"?

3. Discuss what an advertiser may do to avoid conflicts with country managers when a glo- bal advertising campaign is contemplated.

4. Discuss the reasons why *pan-regional* advertis- ing campaigns are more effective than multi- domestic advertising. Why would they be more effective than globally standardized ad- vertising?

5. Rather than enforcing complete uniformity, global advertising tends to follow a "pattern standardization approach." What does this mean? How does this help avoid the pitfalls of standardized and translated messages?

NOTES

1. These definitions are necessarily crude. Some "global" advertising, such as the pan-European advertising done by Pioneer car audio products, is perhaps better seen as "regional." Even the most multidomestic advertising, such as that done for Budweiser beer in many countries, retains a cer- tain similarity across markets, with the featured packaging and brand name remaining constant. As in the case of product standardization, global ad- vertising is a matter of degree.

2. From Greyser, 1992.

3. See DeMooij and Keegan, 1991.

4. See Mueller, 1991.

5. From Harris, 1994.

6. Although not always as advantageous as one would initially assume. In one case an American company wanted to use the same TV commercials abroad as the ones used at home, without any dubbing or change of language. But the actors employed for the U.S. commercials demanded so high a compensation for the world rights that reshooting the commercial with local talent became the cheaper option.

7. From Lippman, 1988.

8. See, for example, the contrasts between Banerjee, 1994, and Elliott, 1995c.

9. The two-step-flow communication model, first developed in sociology, is usually attributed to Austrian sociologist Paul Lazarsfeld and his colleagues at Columbia University in the 1940s—see Kotler, 1994, p. 610.

10. These were TV commercials aired during 1994–95.

11. See, for example, the role of Saatchi & Saatchi in the British Airways' decision to use global advertising.

12. See Johnson, 1994.

13. From Hill and Shao, 1994.

14. Many of these culturally based idiosyncracies are documented by Ricks, 1993.

15. The following account draws on the excellent article by Hanni et al., 1995.

SELECTED REFERENCES

"Advertisers Seek Global Messages." *New York Times,* November 18, 1991.

Banerjee, Ashish. "Global Campaigns Don't Work: Multinationals Do." *Advertising Age* 65, no. 17 (April 18, 1994), p. 23.

DeMooij, M. K., and Warren Keegan. *Advertising Worldwide.* London: Prentice Hall International, 1991.

Elliott, Stuart. "What's in a Name? Perhaps Billions," *New York Times,* August 12, 1992, p. D6.

_____. "South African Air Gets Results from a Much-Debated Commercial." *New York Times,* January 11, 1995a, p. D9.

_____. "At Coke, A Shift to Many Voices," *New York Times,* January 20, 1995b, pp. D1, D6.

_____. "Creative Agencies That Feel at Home in the Global Village Are Writing Their Own Tickets." *New York Times,* September 30, 1995c, p. D10.

"Firms Opt for Pan-Regional Marketing Strategies in EC." *Business International,* October 29, 1990.

Freeman, Laurie. "Colgate Axes Global Ads; Thinks Local." *Advertising Age,* November 26, 1990 sec. 1, pp. 1, 59.

Greyser, Stephen A. *Siemens: Corporate Advertising.* Harvard Business School case 593-022, 1992.

Greyser, Stephen A., and W. S. Schille. *British Airways: The World's Biggest Offer.* Harvard Business School case 592-051, 1993.

Hanni, David A.; John K. Ryans; and Ivan R. Vernon. "Coordinating International Advertising—The Goodyear Case Revisited for Latin America." *Journal of International Marketing* 3, no. 2, (1995), pp. 83–98.

Harris, Greg. "International Advertising Standardization: What Do the Multinationals Actually Standardize?" *Journal of International Marketing* 2, no. 4 (1994), pp. 13–30.

Hill, John S., and Alan T. Shao. "Agency Participants in Multicountry Advertising: A Preliminary Examination of Affiliate Characteristics and Environments." *Journal of International Marketing* 2, no. 2 (1994), pp. 29–48.

Johnson, Bradley. "Tumult Ahead for IBM, Ogilvy." *Advertising Age* 65, no. 23 (May 30, 1994), pp. 36–37.

Kotler, Philip. *Marketing Management,* 8th ed. Englewood Cliffs, NJ: Prentice Hall, 1994.

Lippman, Joanne. "Marketers Turn Sour on Global Sales Pitch Harvard Guru Makes." *The Wall Street Journal,* May 12, 1988, p. 1.

Mårtensson, Rita. *Innovations in Retailing.* Lund, Sweden: Liber, 1983.

Mueller, Barbara. "Multinational Advertising: Factors Influencing the Standardised versus Specialised Approach." *International Marketing Review* 8, no. 1 (1991), pp. 7–18.

Quelch, John. *British Airways.* Harvard Business School case 585-014, 1984.

Ricks, D. A. *Blunders in International Business,* Cambridge, MA: Blackwell, 1993.

Solomon, Michael R. *Consumer Behavior.* 2d ed. Needham Heights, MA: Allyn & Bacon, 1992.

Sorenson, R. Z., & U. E. Wiechmann. "How Multinationals View Marketing Standardization." In D. N. Dickson, ed., *Managing Effectively in the World Marketplace.* New York: Wiley, 1983, pp. 301–16.

Wentz, Laurel. "Global Village." *Advertising Age,* Nov. 21, 1994, p. I3

"World's Top 50 Advertising Organizations." *Advertising Age,* April 15, 1992, pp. 5–10.

Global Promotion, Direct Marketing, and Personal Selling

"In your face"

After studying this chapter, you should understand the following global marketing issues:

1. In addition to global advertising (covered in the previous chapter), there are now a number of alternative promotional tools for creating global presence and visibility. But marketing communications need to be integrated so a unified image and message is communicated.

2. The global promoter should be aware that local regulations can kill the implementation in any one country. Use local representatives to find out exactly what the limits are.

3. With advances in telecommunications, express mail, the development of address lists, and the availability of credit cards, direct mail is transformed from a simple promotional tool to a low-risk direct marketing option, a new mode of entering a market, and a new way for small business to promote and sell its products abroad.

4. Personal selling may be the last frontier of globalization, with local people necessary for the implementation and execution of sales strategies. But with the globalization of industries, the locally well-adapted sales person will have to offer more expertise, information, and service. "How to do business" customs might converge under pressure from globalization, and cultural bonds and personal likes and dislikes are no longer a sufficient basis for a buyer-seller relationship.

THE MAIN COMPONENTS of the promotional mix besides advertising are sales promotion, public relations, and publicity, as well as personal selling. This chapter will cover these plus some special international promotions, including international trade fairs and the use of direct marketing in a global setting.

Because of widely different local trade regulations and the obstacles of local customs and culture, at first sight many of these promotional activities don't seem good candidates for globalization. Global coordination of promotion is complicated by implementation and execution being in the hands of local employees. Local sales people are necessary for running promotional schemes such as in-store displays, free samples, and contests. But globalized promotional activities have become very important in global marketing. The main reasons involve the globalization of markets, the growth of global media reach, and the resulting emergence of megastars and megabrands. Globally recognized endorsers and brand names are opening doors for global promotions.

The Windows 95 Launch: Promotion as Global Event

When you introduce a product that retailers forecast will boost overall sales by 20 percent, expect them to make a fuss over it. When you spend $200 million on promotion, expect the media to make a fuss, too. That's just what happened when Microsoft Corporation launched its Windows 95 operating system.

What the *New York Times* called "the splashiest, most frenzied, most expensive introduction of a computer product in the industry's history" started in New Zealand. Microsoft had announced it would release Windows 95 on August 24, and it kept that promise to the minute. Windows 95 went on sale at midnight in the first English-speaking country to greet the new day. As midnight arrived in one time zone after another, stores joined the hoopla with late-night hours, balloons, and special sales.

In the United States, CompUSA kept stores open past midnight for the first time in its history. The stores offered free pizza and discounts on American Airlines tickets. Computer City Super-center ran late-night specials on Windows-related merchandise, such as discounts on a Microsoft mouse from eleven o'clock till midnight.

Microsoft didn't rely on its retailers to generate all the excitement. In New York, the company arranged for the Empire State Building to be lit with spotlights in colors from the Windows logo. In Toronto, the landmark CN Tower bore a Windows 95 banner. And in a move that dismayed some, Microsoft underwrote the cost of distributing the *Times of London*. A box at the top of the first page read, "Windows 95 Launch—Today The Times Is Free Courtesy of Microsoft." At the bottom of the first page was this ad: "Windows 95. So Good Even The Times Is Complimentary." The paper also carried an editorial supplement sponsored by Microsoft.

Meanwhile, in the Redmond, Washington, home of Microsoft, Bill Gates was throwing a party. Jay Leno hosted the introductory ceremonies, the product's theme song ("Start Me Up" by the Rolling Stones) was played, and commemorative T-shirts sold briskly. Those who didn't get an invitation could attend electronically. Microsoft made the party's sights and sounds available over the Internet (thereby promoting the product's easy-to-use Internet connection, known as the Microsoft Network). Forty-five Microsoft employees wielded digital cameras, sound digitizers, and other electronic equipment to record the festivities for anyone able to navigate the World Wide Web. And though the real-world party was a day long, the on-line version lasted over two weeks.

Perhaps the clearest indicator of Microsoft's promotional success was that other companies bought advertising on the infomercial introducing Windows 95. Who would run ads on an ad? Coca-Cola Company, Compaq Computer Corporation, CompUSA, and Eastman Kodak Company. Explained a Coca-Cola spokesperson, "The whole launch is a happening . . . a place we ought to be."

Sources: Carey Goldberg, "Midnight Sales Frenzy Ushers in Windows 95," *New York Times*, August 24, 1995, pp. A1, D6; Richard W. Stevenson, "Software Makes Strange Bedfellows in Britain as Microsoft and Murdoch Team to Push Windows 95," *New York Times*, August 24, 1995, p. D6; Peter H. Lewis, "Microsoft Has Windows 95 Party; the Internet Shows Up," *New York Times*, August 25, 1995, p. D4; Stuart Elliott, "So Much Stock, but So Little Liquidity," *New York Times*, August 25, 1995, p. D4. Amy Cortese, "The Software Resolution" *Business Week*, December 4, 1995, pp. 78–90.

INTRODUCTION

While global advertising has been around for a few years, other global promotions have only recently come into their own. While companies have long sponsored sports and arts events, including World Cup soccer, tennis tournaments, auto racing, and painting exhibitions, recently companies have taken to creating events and news with the promotions being the main purpose. Disney's gala film openings or video releases, Swatch's parties when launching new lines, Benetton's ultrahip advertisements, and Microsoft's launch of Windows 95 are global events created for the purpose of maximum visibility for products. In the beginning they may have reflected the 1980s unabashed hedonism, but their continuation into the 1990s suggests that they reflect a structural change in the way promotions will be done in the future. With the emergence of the Internet as a genuine global and accessible communications medium, one can only assume that these promotional stunts will increase in frequency over the next few years.

But global promotions also involve more mundane and traditional tools, such as point-of-purchase merchandising, public relations, and personal selling. There is also the new development of global direct marketing, emerging from the old direct mail campaigns, and, of course, the "tried and true" international trade fairs where prospective buyers and sellers get together to check out new products and establish ties. It is the purpose of this chapter to discuss these various promotional tools and give the global marketer a sense of where they can be most useful.

The chapter will start by discussing global *sales promotion*, covering in-store promotions, events and sponsorship, and cross-marketing. Then the discussion will shift to *publicity*, recently emerging strongly in global marketing communications, and global *public relations*. The role of international *trade fairs* will be dealt with briefly before discussing *direct marketing*, a tool enabling even the smallest firm to go global. The last part of the chapter will focus on *personal selling* and the problems and opportunities in a global sales effort. Since its emergence is so recent, the Internet and its promise will be dealt with in Chapter 18, "The Future of Global Marketing."

GLOBAL SALES PROMOTION

Sales promotion involves a variety of activities, ranging from point-of-purchase displays and trade promotions to Sunday newspaper coupons to the sponsorship of symphony orchestras and athletic events such as the Olympics, soccer's World Cup, and major tennis tournaments.

In-Store and Trade Promotions

In-store or point-of-purchase (p-o-p) **promotions** refer to promotional activities inside the store; trade promotions are targeted at channel intermediaries ("the trade"). Both are important in the U.S. market and are becoming more important in many other markets as well.

Typically, in-store sales promotion is a much more localized activity than media advertising, which can be broadcast using global media such as cable television and international magazines. Sales promotion needs to be localized because its use is often more rigidly regulated than advertising. Cents-off coupons, free samples, and two-for-one offers can be prohibited in some countries where regulation is aimed at ensuring orderly markets and steady margins for local retailers. Premiums, gifts, and competitions are sometimes allowed but with major restrictions. As Exhibit 16.1 shows, outright prohibition is unusual, but most countries impose limits on what can be done. These

....
EXHIBIT 16.1   Regulations Regarding Premiums, Gifts, and Competitions in Selected Countries

Country	Category	No restrictions or minor ones	Authorized with major restrictions	General ban with important exceptions	Almost total prohibition
Australia	Premiums	x			
	Gifts	x			
	Competitions		x		
Austria	Premiums				x
	Gifts		x		
	Competitions		x		
Canada	Premiums	x			
	Gifts	x			
	Competitions		x		
Denmark	Premiums			x	
	Gifts		x		
	Competitions			x	
France	Premiums	x			
	Gifts	x			
	Competitions	x			
Germany	Premiums				x
	Gifts		x		
	Competitions		x		
Hong Kong	Premiums	x			
	Gifts	x			
	Competitions	x			
Japan	Premiums		x		
	Gifts		x		
	Competitions		x		
Korea	Premiums		x		
	Gifts		x		
	Competitions		x		
United Kingdom	Premiums	x			
	Gifts	x			
	Competitions		x		
United States	Premiums	x			
	Gifts	x			
	Competitions	x			
Venezuela	Premiums		x		
	Gifts		x		
	Competitions		x		

Source: Jean J. Boddewyn, *Premiums, Gifts, and Competitions*, New York: (International Advertising Association, 1988). © 1988 International Advertising Association.

<table>
<tr><td>

*G*etting the
Picture

Going Against
the Rules—
In Germany

</td><td>

AFTER SUCCESSFUL ENTRY
into Switzerland against entrenched do-
mestic retailers, IKEA, the Swedish
furniture retailer, decided in the late
1970s to go for the big prize and enter
(then) West Germany, Europe's largest
market. The low-price store chain, with
a business concept of fiberboard furni-
ture sold in kits for home assembly, was
not welcomed by the German retailers.
But they were not worried—they
"knew" that the German consumers
would not take easily to lower prices for
unfinished furniture. The German con-
sumers knew quality and would not be
taken in by any promotional stunts.

  It turned out quite differently. The
Swedish company defied tradition and
entered with a high promotional pro-
file. It positioned itself as "the impossi-
ble store" from Sweden, sporting a
Moose as a spokesman. At the first store
opening it offered all comers an early
morning breakfast, contests, and free
samples. It emphasized its Swedish ori-
gin by flying the Swedish flag and
stressed the easy-to-assemble furniture
by simplifying instructions and relying
entirely on pictures drawn partly from
European traffic symbols. Its opening
in Munich drew more people than the
local football champions, the Bayern

</td><td>

Muenchen with national hero Franz
Beckenbauer.

  The German retailers were not slow
to retaliate. They sued the Swedish
company for upsetting an orderly mar-
ket and for false advertising. One claim
was that most of IKEA's products were
not make of solid wood and could there-
fore not be sold as wood furniture.
Another argument was that the Swedish
origin was misleading since most of the
products came from East European
suppliers. It was also argued that since
the free breakfast did not include eggs,
it was misleading to serve it as a break-
fast.

  The arguments were of course for-
mally correct and were all accepted by
the court. But IKEA won the market bat-
tle, its success led to a revision of indus-
try regulations, and the final blow came
when one of the largest German chains
established its own chain of low-priced
unassembled furniture, reasoning that
"if you can't fight them, join them." The
German market is one of IKEA's strong-
holds, but a much more competitive mar-
ket today than previously.

Sources: Mårtenson, 1983; Christopher A.
Bartlett and Ashish Nanda, "Ingvar
Kamprad and IKEA," Harvard Business
School case 390-132.

</td></tr>
</table>

restrictions vary between countries. In France, for example, a gift can't be worth
more than 4 percent of the retail value of the product. In Germany, requiring
proof of purchase for participation in a competition is illegal.[1]

  It is important to identify such regulatory differences and adapt to them—
but also to realize that they are not set in stone. IKEA'S experience in Germany
is illustrative (see box "Going against the Rules").

  Apart from severe regulations in some countries, several factors influence
the effectiveness of in-store promotions:

- In-store promotions to the consumer need to be supported by trade
  promotions, that is, promotions to channel intermediaries. The aim of
  in-store promotion is to "move product," and retailers and upstream

wholesalers need to be induced to cooperate and increase the product flow. This is usually done through trade discounts, cooperative advertising, and sales support. If the trade is not compensated, middlemen may not cooperate. For example, A. C. Nielsen tried to introduce cents-off coupons in Chile, but the nation's supermarket union opposed the project and asked its members not to accept them.

- The retailers need to handle promotions such as coupons professionally and not embarrass the consumers, often an impossibility in countries with a history of producers dominating the consumers.

- Since distribution infrastructure is often different between countries, some promotions may simply not be feasible. Procter and Gamble tried to introduce its Cheer detergent in Japan using the type of trade promotion employed in the United States, including coupons, cents-off, and trade discounts. The stores in Japan, however, were too small to handle the necessary volume and quickly ran out of stock. Consumers were disappointed, retailers were frustrated, and the introductory campaign was a failure.

- In-store promotions work best when the consumer expects to make choices in the store. In some cases the choice is already made before entering the store—preselling a product through advertising or newspaper coupons, for example, often means that no in-store choice is necessary. Brand loyalty has the same effect. But when channels are dominated by manufacturers (as used to be the case in Japan), stores may feature only one brand and the store choice dictates which brand will be bought.

Trade promotions have their own problems. When General Electric broke into the air-conditioning market in Japan, the company offered overseas trips to outstanding dealers and a free color TV set to purchasers of high-end models. The successful campaign drew complaints from the trade association, and new rules to limit promotions were approved by the Japanese Fair Trade Commission. A limit was set on the size of the premium that could be offered, and no overseas trips were allowed as dealer incentives for any home appliances.[2]

Calculating the cost of a promotion relative to its revenue-raising potential is not always easy. Involved is not only the actual cost of the promotional material and the accompanying marketing communications and a forecast of anticipated sales, but also an estimate of the amount of sales that would have been made without the promotion. Simple mistakes can ruin the projections. One British firm created a very successful promotion by offering free airline tickets to buyers of its home appliances. However, the firm neglected to eliminate some longer routes from the offer and found that most customers opted for an expensive trip from London to New York. Once the losses started to mount, the promotion had to be broken off, leading to legal entanglement and the promotional manager out of a job.

Events and Sponsorship

With the advent of global media the possibilities for global **sponsorships** are opening up. Sponsoring a World Cup match by plastering the brand name on the bleachers and piggybacking on the television broadcasts has helped companies such as Hitachi, Kodak, Siemens, and Volvo establish a strong identity in the global marketplace.[3] More direct spending involves sponsoring tennis tournaments (Volvo, Virginia Slims), Formula One race cars (Coca-Cola, Marlboro), single-man treks to the South Pole (Nordic track), and athletic team wear (Nike, Reebok). The Olympic sponsorship, which reached new heights in Los Angeles in 1984, has spilled over into promotional sponsorship of Russian hockey players (Visa) and Italian basketball teams (Sony). It is somewhat unsettling to see newspaper pictures of Jüergen Köehler, the all-German national player from Koeln AS, and to find Toshiba, the name of the Japanese electronics company, on his jersey. Global promotion knows no boundaries.

The global reach of **events,** which has created possibilities for products to become associated with globally recognized sports figures, has made the sports figures rich in addition to famous. Michael Jordan, the basketball player, receives more money from his endorsements than from his playing. Andre Agassi, the tennis player, might be an effective spokesperson for Reebok tennis gear and for Canon cameras but can put his name on his own line of products.

Swatch is a somewhat unlikely sponsor of the Atlanta Olympics, as Swatch watches are associated with fashion rather than timekeeping. But the sponsorship may reflect the notion that the Olympics are becoming more of a global entertainment event and not just a sporting meet.

Courtesy Swatch/SMH (U.S.A), Inc.

The product line needs to be marketed well and can't stretch too far—Bjorn Borg's adventure in personal hygiene products and leisure wear was not successful, for example.

The use of well-known personalities has its downside. The Pepsi-Cola company used Michael Jackson as a global spokesman until his legal troubles started. Luciano Pavarotti was used by the American Express card until his fee became too high. O. J. Simpson, Magic Johnson, and Bo Jackson are three athletes whose subsequent problems limited their usefulness, to the despair of sponsors like Hertz and Nike.

The 1995 track and field world championships in Gothenburg, Sweden, represented another step in the increasing promotional role of athletic events. For the two-week event the Swedish organizers created a number of exhibition booths, restaurants, and well-equipped business offices in a city block across the street from the main entrance to the stadium. For a fee, businesses could rent a space, invite existing customers, potential prospects, or employees for business entertainment as well as serious negotiations, interspersed with attendance at the events and meals in the restaurants. The available spaces were quickly snapped up, mostly by European firms. The Mercedes-Benz company entertained a number of its salesmen and their spouses during a two-day visit.[4]

Companies also help arrange events at which their brands can be promoted. An extreme example of creating an "event" associated with a brand was the launch of Microsoft's Windows 95, its new operating system for personal computers as described at the beginning of this chapter. Similar strategies, although perhaps less extravagant, are used by other companies. The Swiss watchmaker Swatch relies extensively on sponsorship of special events. The company has a policy of spending a major share of its promotional budget on special events promotion. Exhibit 16.2 shows the range of events sponsored by the company. As can be seen, some events, such as the large Swatch on a Frankfurt building, are simply "happenings" created to draw attention to Swatch and generate free publicity for the brand. The company organizes "launch parties" in various countries, such as the one in Barcelona in November 1985, when a new collection of Swatches is introduced. The company has positioned its watches as fashion products, and its product policy is to keep the Swatch designs fresh by introducing new styles twice a year, in the spring and in the fall.[5]

Cross-Marketing

As markets have globalized and regulations have been harmonized, promotion has become a very active area of competition. The varied promotional tactics in the globally successful American entertainment industry are illustrative. The **cross-marketing** of related products from successful events and stars represents one of many tactics. There is a big global business in selling products associated with Elvis Presley, the rock king, James Dean, the actor, and various successful films (*Beauty and the Beast, Forrest Gump*) and TV shows ("Star Trek,"

EXHIBIT 16.2   **Major Special Events Organized or Sponsored by Swatch**

Date	Country	Event
March 1984	Germany	13-ton giant Swatch on Commerzbank building, Frankfurt
April 1984	France	"Urban Sax" saxophonist group at the "Eldorado" theater in Paris to celebrate launch, first *Swatch* Magazine
August 1984	USA	Ivan Lendl U.S. Tennis Open
September 1984	USA	World Breakdancing Championship: "The Roxy" New York
September 1984	France	First street art painting show with the French artists "Les Fréres Ripoulin," "Espace Cardin" theater, Paris
November 1984	USA	The Fat Boys music sponsorship, "Private Eyes," New York, to introduce "Granita di Frutta" to the trade
Oct 84 - Jan 85	USA	New York City Fresh Festival: breakdancing, rapping, graffiti artists
January 1985	USA	World Freestyle Invitational/Celebrity Classic, Breckenridge, Colorado
March 1985	France	IRCAM "copy art" show, Paris; limited edition (119) Kiki Picasso design watches; second *Swatch* Magazine
Spring 1985	USA	Hi-fly freestyle windsurfing team sponsorship
May 1985	England	Second street art painting show, Covent Garden, London, with "Les Fréres Ripoulin" and English street artists
June 1985	Switzerland	Art fair in Basel; third street art painting show with 50 European artists
Summer 1985	Sweden	Oestersjö Rallyt (Segel-Rallye)
September 1985	France	Cinema festival, Pompidou Center, Paris with Kurosawa's film, *Ran*; Mini City Magazine
September 1985	France	"Le Défilé": Jean-Paul Gaultier & Régine Chopinot fashion/dance show, "Pavillon Baltard," Paris
September 1985	England	Andrew Logan's Alternative Miss World, London
October 1985	Belgium	"Mode et Anti-Mode" fashion show, Brussels
Fall 1985	USA	Thompson Twins concert tour sponsorship
November 1985	Spain	Swatch launch party, the "Cirque," Barcelona

Source: Pinson and Kimball, 1987. Copyright © 1987 INSEAD-CEDEP, Fontainebleau, France. Reproduced with the permission of INSEAD-CEDEP.

"Sesame Street"). It is possible to buy T-shirts, lunchboxes, pencils, hats, bags, puzzles, music tapes, and a CD-ROM game featuring Disney's film *The Lion King*.[6] The cross-marketing leveraging of a strong brand name by product-line extension has been done for a long time by luxury brands such as Dunhill, Gucci, and Burberry. Other brands are getting into the act, combining global advertising to sustain the brand name with product-line extensions that make it economically feasible to open separate boutiques.

The practice of using popular success for promotion has spilled over into media advertising and has been adopted by non-U.S. companies. Honda, the Japanese auto company, introduced its new minivan Odyssey using characters based on the art of Keith Haring, the New York artist—and sold more units than forecasted despite a premium price.[7] Japan Air Lines, a most staid organization, has painted two of its 747s used on the Hawaii route in bright and irregular patches of color. The sky is the limit—if regulation opens up.

PUBLICITY

An increasingly important part of global companies' promotion function lies in the careful nurturing of general media contacts and the release of positive news about the company then featured in the press and broadcast media. **Publicity** is a very important global promotional tool for many companies, since much of the global expansion effort is inherently more newsworthy than expansion at home. Many of the products and services involved represent high technology, of importance for security reasons or for national competitiveness, which enhances potential reader interest. Managing the promotional angle of publicity is important when foreign direct investments or trade barriers become news, as they often do.

Publicity has the advantage that there is no need to pay for air time or press coverage. It is less expensive than sponsorship and media advertising. On the other hand, publicity requires some management and can be labor intensive. Press coverage of the opening of a plant or warehouse in a new market involves travel, food, and sometimes lodging for journalists. The preparation of press releases requires skill, especially when the information is about a technical breakthrough. Making top managers available for personal interviews takes their time and diverts their attention. Still, the payoff in goodwill and free advertising can be considerable and the investment well worth it (see box, "Total Communication Inc.").

A good example of the way free publicity can be used (and manipulated) for the benefit of the company was Microsoft's periodically releasing tantalizing bits of information about the features of new software Windows 95, including a controversial direct access to Internet and making company spokesman Bill Gates available for interviews on TV shows such as "Larry King Live." The company generated massive publicity for its simultaneous new product launch across the globe in August 1995. As one example of the free publicity generated, the *New York Times* ran three articles on the launch in its business pages on August 24 and three more on August 25, the launch date, including a feature on the front page. As many observers have been quick to point out, the ultimate success of such "hype" depends critically on the subsequent performance of the product, a failure made potentially more damaging to the company image than otherwise.[8]

Even "negative" publicity can have its rewards since it serves to keep the brand name in the public eye. Through its famous (or infamous depending on one's views) realistic TV commercials and large full-page magazine ads of a man dying from AIDS, a priest kissing a nun, an automobile ablaze after a car bomb, and a boatload of refugees without copy but with the brand logo displayed after the commercial or below the picture, Benetton, the Italian

Getting the Picture

Total Communication Inc.

IN THE WORLD of high technology, global publicity counts as a major promotional medium. The announcement of new technological discoveries, the introduction of a new product, the exploration of frontiers such as Internet are some of the more obvious examples. The introduction of the Macintosh personal computer was accompanied by a "full-court" media blitz with Apple press conferences, customer contests, educational "give-aways," appearances of software producers (Microsoft, Lotus) giving assurances of program designs, and of course personal interviews with *Time's* "Man of the Year," Steve Jobs, Apple's chairman. The international press duly reported on the American developments, in fact preparing an entry mat for Apple into many European and Asian countries.

High-tech companies often create news as a matter of course in their daily business and the press is a ready channel to tell the world about it. The industry has not been slow in capitalizing on this potential. Annual and semiannual fairs and conventions in multimedia technology, computers, new telecommunications, and automotive technology take place in Cologne, Las Vegas, Hong Kong, and Sydney. The release of a new product occasions a press conference, where pictures, models, technical summaries, and prototypes are available for publicity purposes. The hoopla and excitement are orchestrated to create an event and atmosphere worthy of Hollywood—and of news coverage. Charismatic leaders of companies, such as Bill Gates and Mick Kapoor, are company assets—and the worldwide media help give well-recognized public persona a global impact.

Consulting firms are created to help companies manage this important function. The large PR firms, such as Hill & Knowlton in the U.S., have global reach, following their customers around the world. Smaller companies that specialize in certain countries and industries offer specialized services.

San Francisco–based Autodesk, which sells LAN software for networked PCs, uses smaller publicity consultants extensively in its global markets in addition to the large global media relations firms. Autodesk offers new and highly technical products and services requiring product demonstration and customer education for acceptance. By releasing newsworthy items about its products, the company aims to create curiosity among potential customers in order to get a foot in the door. Using local consultants, the company is able to draw on people with intimate ties to local journalists who can adapt the global press releases to the needs of the local media. Using frequent traveling and personal appearances at conferences and industry seminars, the president of Autodesk makes herself available for local interviews.

Sources: Smith, 1994; *New York Times*, June 14, 1994; Jan Segerfeldt, personal communication.

apparel maker, has garnered plenty of publicity, mainly negative. The ads seem to be in bad taste, and Benetton has been accused of exploiting human suffering to sell its products. In Germany, irate store owners refused to stock Benetton products unless the ads were withdrawn, claiming that the ads kept customers away. But the company argues that it is doing a positive thing, and to help prove it, it has opened a new store in war-torn Sarajevo.[9]

Surrounded by well-known industry people, Microsoft chairman Bill Gates (center) conducts class in the use of his company's new Windows 95. The simultaneous global introduction of Windows 95 set a new standard for product launch publicity.

Bettmann

GLOBAL PUBLIC RELATIONS

Global public relations, which focuses on creating goodwill toward the corporation as a whole, is a form of indirect promotion of products and services. The corporate communications staff at headquarters and its counterpart in the various host countries serve as promoters of the corporation to various stakeholders interested in the company's foreign expansion. These stakeholders can include a wide variety of groups:

Stockholders	Financial community
Employees	Media
Customers	Activist groups
Distributors	General public
Suppliers	Government

These groups can lay some legitimate claim on a company to conduct itself ethically and to operate with a certain level of transparency in accordance with the free market system. However, because of the many countries in which a global company is likely to do business, ethical standards and customary business secrecy can vary considerably. This easily creates conflicts between host country stakeholders' claims and headquarters' policy guidelines. One job of the public relations staff is to make sure that such potential conflicts do not erupt, and when they do, to carry out "damage control."

Conflicts typically arise when a firm enters a new country by acquiring a local company or by investing in manufacturing. When American companies such as Ford and GM, IBM, Xerox, Honeywell, and General Electric became big investors in Europe in the 1950s and 60s, Europeans became alarmed by the "American challenge."[10] As Japanese companies Nissan in trucks, Mitsubishi in real estate, Matsushita in electronics, and Honda in automobiles established presence in the United States by large investments, many Americans voiced misgivings.[11] Even though the economic justifications of these and other FDI entries are usually sound, and the host countries also benefit, the companies' PR departments have to work hard to establish the "good local citizen" image among stakeholders such as the general public. This involves compiling statistics about the number of natives employed, the local content of the products, and the tax contribution made to the local municipality—and publicizing this information.

From the global marketing perspective, the critical issue is whether alarm or misgivings about corporate strategy spill over into a negative brand evaluation and lower sales. According to company research, the negative evaluation against Japanese investments in the United States did lead to some temporary loss of American market share for Honda in the early 1990s.

Effective damage control requires both public relations and timing. When a Volvo TV commercial in the United States was found deceptive because the car used in a demonstration of Volvo's body integrity was reinforced, the company first publicly admitted the mistake, retracted the advertising, and then moved to dismiss the advertising agency.[12] The German automaker Audi, by contrast, stood firm in defending its Audi 4000 model design against repeated accusations of malfunctioning. Several accidents had happened because drivers mistakenly (as the courts found) stepped on the gas pedal instead of the brakes. The Audi engineers won their court case, but consumer PR damage was not contained, and Audi market share slipped badly.

A recent example of how a company can mishandle public relations was the problem Intel had with its Pentium chip at the end of 1994. At first belittling the importance of the flaw, which led to miscalculated long divisions, the company rallied after a week and offered apologies to the public, explanations to media, and free replacements to users.[13] This quick about-face in a relatively straight-forward case can be contrasted with the much more complicated PR problem of Nestlé's infant formula in the Third World (see box, "Nestlé and Babies").

INTERNATIONAL TRADE FAIRS

As we saw in Chapter 5, participation in **international trade fairs** is a way of identifying potential distributors in a new local market. But the 1,500 or so international trade fairs that take place in over 70 countries each year also serve other purposes. Whether at the traditional Fotokina photo show in Cologne, Germany; or the famous Hannover fair, also in Germany, "largest in the world"

*G*etting the Picture

Nestlé and Babies: Who Was Right?

THE LARGE SWISS multinational Nestlé is a major global company in the food industry. Its Nestlé instant tea, Nescafe coffee, Libby's juices, and Carnation milk products are household names all over the world.

The company got its baptism in global PR by fire. In the latter half of the 1970s, having developed a superior infant formula that could effectively supplant a breast-feeding mother, the company saw great potential among malnourished Third World mothers. Distributing the formula through clinics and wet-nurses, the company was able to tap into the market effectively. There was only one problem. Some mothers, partly to offset the relatively high cost of the formula, took to diluting it with water. As a consequence, many babies on formula did not get the requisite nourishment, and in a few cases, the water used for the dilution was infected and there were some deaths.

Through various sources, activist groups in Europe and North America soon learned about the situation. As initial appeals to the company in Vevy, Switzerland, were rebuffed, the groups started a massive international campaign against Nestlé and its products. The target was not limited to the baby formula in Third World markets only but expanded to consumer boycotts of all Nestlé products, direct appeals to doctors and nurses in the West to avoid recommending Nestlé products, and the amassing of scientific evidence presented at international conferences.

This public relations nightmare went on for months before Nestlé gathered its forces and mounted an effective counterattack. The company, more accustomed to its high standing in the European corporate elite than to defending itself against consumer activists, decided to fight it out. Through press conferences and media releases as well as in direct meetings with activist leaders, the company argued that withdrawing a beneficial product would do more harm than good. The company undertook scientific research projects designed to establish the superiority of the product against weak mothers' milk and projected the expected death rates should the product be withdrawn. The findings were disseminated in various ways to a global audience. For example, a Harvard business case was developed about the events, and the company disseminated findings and their side of the story to professors likely to teach the case.

In the end, the activists were fought off and the company prevailed, succeeding in maintaining its product in the Third World markets and reducing the damage to its brands. But the process, which extended for several years, was a lesson for the company and should be a lesson for other global firms as well. Ethical conduct and corporate standing that might seem spotless and self-evident at home need to be explained, justified, and defended actively in other places. And in all cases, flexibility and respect for local norms are a must.

Sources: Shirk, 1991; C. B. Malone and N. Harrison, "Nestlé Alimentana S.A.—Infant Formula," Harvard Business School case no. 9-580-118.

with its 5,000 or so major exhibitors, or the annual New England Auto Show in Boston; or the Comdex computer fair in Las Vegas; or any of the other large events, the fairs' attraction is the chance to introduce a company's latest products and models, to discover industry trends, and to spot new competitive developments. This holds true whether the fair is open to the general public, quite common in the United States, or attendance is limited to industry members, the more common European approach.

For the global marketer, fairs are an excellent promotional avenue. Participation enhances and sustains visibility and local presence. The Comdex computer fair, for example, is the major avenue through which new hardware and software companies get known and where established players such as Microsoft, Novell, and Lotus show their coming products. The prestige of Comdex has grown to the point where 90 percent of the exhibition space is let one year in advance, and the fair returns a sizable profit to the organizers. In 1995, the fair was sold to a Japanese investor, Masayoshi Son, for $800 million. Mr. Son plans to expand the fair by holding Comdex shows in Asia and Europe in addition to the traditional Las Vegas location.[14]

Because of the press coverage and media publicity generated by major fairs, many companies view participation as an effective alternative to media advertising. But this also means that the price for exhibitors can be high. Apart from the rent for a booth, the company needs to be prepared to invest in displays, demonstration mockups, translations of pamphlets as appropriate, and proper training of the people manning the exhibit.

Fairs offer a natural opportunity for a company to nurture relationships with existing customers and suppliers. Visiting with major customers to develop interpersonal ties and gather feedback is a useful activity that can be pursued more efficiently when everyone has gathered in one spot. These occasions are also used by companies to build morale among local representatives, with headquarters and subsidiary people freely exchanging ideas and sharing information.

Because of the importance of trade fairs in global business, government agencies such as the U.S. Department of Commerce often assist businesses with participation. This usually takes the form of organized industry delegations to the larger fairs. For the annual Paris Air Show, for example, the DOC will organize business representatives from the aerospace industry to travel to the show and exhibit their products. Assistance is also given by government representatives in the various countries, and for some ambassadors the main job is to help forge economic rather than political links with the host country.

DIRECT MARKETING

Direct marketing refers to sales from the producer directly to the ultimate consumer, bypassing the channel middlemen. Direct marketing is not so much a promotional tool as a new distribution channel, but it grew out of direct mail, which is a traditional advertising medium. The traditional direct mail promotions of various products often offered "direct response" options, including requests for more information, redeemable cents-off coupons, and participation in contests and lottery drawings. It was only a small step to a completed sale and especially since credit cards became common, direct mail has become an important sales and promotion channel.

The standard direct marketing medium is **mail order**, with catalogs and sales offers sent directly to individual households who then order via mail. The names and addresses are drawn from various lists—in the beginning often subscription lists of newspapers and magazines but today more often commercial databanks that can screen for keywords and develop lists of qualified prospects. In recent years **telemarketing**, selling via the telephone, has grown fast in the United States, and so has **direct response television (DRTV),** where TV commercials will list telephone numbers to let viewers call for purchases.

Direct marketing is growing fast because it is fast, safe, convenient, and low cost—and eliminates the job of going to the store. Express mail delivery means most goods can arrive within one or two days. Return privileges are generous. Payment can be made by simply giving a credit card number. The liability for improper use of a card number is limited. Toll-free 800 numbers make it possible to use the telephone free of charge.

Can direct marketing be globalized? The answer, despite the need for fast delivery and efficient communications, is an emphatic yes. First of all, the postal systems of many countries, despite otherwise weak infrastructures, seem to function quite well. Second, countries' telephone systems are growing increasingly reliable and have in many cases penetrated into remote rural areas. This has not escaped the attention of international long-distance carriers. AT&T

Clerks in Montego Bay, Jamaica, handle hotel reservations called in from toll-free numbers in the United States. With the advent of digitalized electronic transmissions, the physical location of communications facilities is becoming less and less important.

Brian Smith/Outline Press.

*G*etting the Picture

In Global Direct Marketing, Small is Beautiful

TO GET A GRIP on how global direct marketing works, have a look at Acton Ltd. for an object lesson. A typical company in global direct marketing, Acton is a small (48 employees) direct marketer in the publishing and financial services industries. The company is located in Lincoln, Nebraska, in the heart of Buffalo Bill and Wild Bill Hickock country.

Acton's direct marketing operation started by marketing U.S. client banks' checking accounts and related services across the country and gradually developed or acquired address lists of prospects and leads at home and in overseas markets. One of the lists it has exclusive rights to includes 14 million households in Japan, developed from client contacts over a few years. The address files are digitalized and can be transferred back and forth on the Internet. For any particular direct marketing campaign, the company will work with a local agent who is part of Acton's emerging global network.

About 70% of the company's clients are large banks on the East and West Coasts of the United States who are primarily interested in expanding their credit card customer bases overseas. Says Cheri Pettet, vice president of international sales: "Our marketing programs for credit cards . . . work so well we can almost guarantee the client will gain customers."

Sources: Kelly, 1994; Egol, 1994a.

International Service 800 S.A. now offers toll-free dialing to more than 50 countries on five continents. Third, as we saw in Chapter 12, credit cards have gone global, and people pay by American Express, MasterCard, or Visa all over the world. Finally, as we saw in Chapter 14, the express carriers have globalized their operations and now reach most places on the globe.

Because of advances in communications technology, the number of conversations handled by the transatlantic cable between Europe and North America has increased from 138 per hour in 1966 to over 100 million per hour in 1994. It is estimated that the volume will triple by the year 2000.[15] The increase in coverage of global communications has meant not only that customers almost everywhere can be reached but that the marketer can be located in any small place on the map, not needing a major metropolitan location for its headquarters nor a large staff (see box, "In Global Direct Marketing, Small Is Beautiful").

Regional Developments

Direct marketing opportunities in mail order have been boosted by the recent privatization of many postal services around the world. Direct mail is one of their top cash-generating "products." In Germany, for example, newly privatized Die Deutsche Post A.G. or "Bundespost" is moving quickly to become a major international player, with the rich U.S. market as a key target. The new executive team at the top of Bundespost—mostly from private business—has charged a wholly owned subsidiary with the task of easing entry into the German market for prospective U.S. companies interested in gaining a foothold in the German market.[16] The subsidiary updates address lists, develops new lists working with Bertelsmann (the world's second-largest media company), and sells computer software to help with presorting mail and bulk-mail preparations. The Bundespost offers a 25 percent discount on bulk mailing, provided the presorting corresponds to official regulations. The postal subsidiary even offers assistance with shipments to 14 other European countries. A shipment to France, for example, can be sent via air to Frankfurt and loaded there—without time-consuming inspection—on trucks for Strasbourg on the French border where they are inserted into the the French mail stream. Packages can reach Paris or Marseilles within a day or two, depending on the shipper's choice—one day being more expensive.

Latin America is another area where the direct marketing possibilities are opening up as a result of improved infrastructure.[17] The telecommunications system in Chile is said to be world-class. The Brazilian postal service is, perhaps surprisingly, famous for its service and efficiency. Cable TV has excellent penetration in Argentina with more than 50 channels available to most subscribers. Databanks with address lists are being developed at a rapid pace, often with technology transferred from U.S. database companies in alliances with local software firms.

Japan with its high per capita income, well-developed post and telecommunications, and complex distribution system has become a natural target for direct marketers. Foreign catalog sales are booming. The U.S. Department of Commerce has even organized a unit that offers lists of catalogs to Japanese consumers in three locations, Tokyo, Osaka, and Sapporo. Consumers can browse through the list and then pay about $5 for any one catalog they are interested in. Catalog houses pay the Commerce Department $600 to participate in the program. Japanese language information about ordering, payment, and return policies is available. Credit-card orders can be faxed to the companies the same day they are filled out by Japanese customers, and customers usually receive their packages within a few days, depending on the delivery option chosen.

About 200 American companies participate in this program, ranging from jewelry to candy to sporting goods catalog houses. For many of them, this is a first-time entry into the Japanese market, and many plan to invest more, perhaps in a Japanese-language catalog, if sales take off.[18]

Japan is not the only Asian country with promise. Even though China so far seems to be less promising because of a lack of infrastructure and few lists, other countries show more potential (see box, "Asia").

Global Strategy

Although direct marketing is relatively new, early experiences suggest that there are basically three alternative ways of implementing a global strategy.[19]

- *"Do it yourself."* The most obvious method is the company developing the market and the necessary contacts on its own. This involves time, travel, and expense plus, at some point when volume justifies it,

---

Getting the Picture

Asia: Direct Marketing Requires Smarts

MANY COUNTRIES in the booming Asian economy offer good potential for direct marketers, even though China is still "problematic." But to get the most out of the effort the marketer has to be smart, according to James Thornton, managing director of Mailing Lists Asia. He recommends a two-step entry strategy, first testing multinational lists that include several countries to find out which countries are responsive to your offers. Only after that determination has been made does he recommend step two, which involves going after a specific local market. For example, he suggests skipping Hong Kong, Singapore, and Malaysia if the offer involves merchandise rather than publications. In Singapore and Hong Kong, especially, financial offers and self-improvement books and courses seem to work well, while catalogs with merchandise will usually fail. By contrast, consumers and business people in Indonesia and Thailand seem to be responsive to all products regardless of type or country of origin. And a bonus for global direct marketers, many people in the region are English-speaking or at least readers of English.

Sources: Egol, 1994b; "Thais and Indonesians," 1995.

---

developing a relationship with a local company to handle "fulfillment," that is, handling customs when necessary, some delivery, lost goods, and other incidental services. This is a labor-intensive and costly method for a small company, with a typical overseas business trip lasting two to three weeks and costing easily $5,000.

- *Marketing intermediary.* A second way to go is to turn the product over to a direct marketing company specializing in international marketing and to let it act as a general contractor (akin to an export management company). The intermediary will be responsible for establishing infrastructure and setting up local representatives to handle inventory as needed, order taking, and fulfillment. These intermediaries often work through a global network of local entrepreneurs. Going this route, the company will need to establish a consistent global pricing structure, to prohibit reexporting, yet offer the intermediary sufficient margin to realize a profit.

- *Strategic alliance.* A third option is to develop a strategic alliance with a direct marketing company in the local market. Such a company will have better knowledge of the local market and may also be able to help with neighboring country markets. It will also have the required infrastructure capabilities in place.

To date, the second option seems to be the one chosen most often by smaller companies. It enables the direct marketer to get into foreign markets quickly and without major expense. It is the natural alternative when the company is starting out and learning how global direct marketing works. Established catalog houses, such as L. L. Bean and Eddie Bauer seem to prefer the first option since it offers more control over the local marketing effort.

Technology-based companies also seem to favor this option. Sun Microsystems (office computer systems) has created its own direct marketing division in Europe, Sun Express, which currently mails 60,000 quarterly catalogs in three languages along with direct mail, places direct response ad space and fax ads, and participates in local trade shows. Telephone response filters directly to The Netherlands, but callers dial a local number. Orders are fulfilled from the United States usually within three days.[20]

The three options are likely to vary in attractiveness across local markets, and most companies find it useful to examine all three alternatives for any one local market. In Europe, a relatively difficult direct marketing region because of fragmentation of languages and cultures, alliances tend to be common. One American publisher tackled the U.K. market by partnering with Direct Marketing Services, a British firm, which adapted the American promotional material and address list characteristics to those in Britain with good success.

Direct marketing is emerging as a new global option for many companies. It is an option capitalizing directly on the technological advances in global communications and transportation during the last two decades, opening up global opportunities for even the smallest companies.

GLOBAL PERSONAL SELLING

As we saw in Chapter 3, culture affects the people-skills of the global marketer. Because of the importance of personal factors in selling, it is not surprising to find that salesmanship varies across countries. Personal selling is usually the least global of all the marketing activities. As Barnevik of ABB puts it: "When you are selling in Germany, your salesmen have to be German."[21]

Managing a Sales Force

When the company is simply an exporter using independent distributors, management of the sales force is not an issue for the global company. However, when more control over local marketing is desired, the local company agent needs to work with the distributor's sales people, help train them, and offer incentives to push the company's products. When the company takes over distribution in the country, it will usually end up establishing its own **sales force.**

Establishing the company's own sales force in a foreign country requires faith in the market and considerable resources. But some companies, especially those for which the selling function is a key success factor, have decided to take the plunge and have done it successfully. As we've mentioned, companies such as Avon and Mary Kay (cosmetics), Amway (miscellaneous products), and Electrolux (vacuum cleaners) have managed to create viable direct sales forces in various countries by following the selling practices back home. This has typically meant that the sales force has been started from scratch, with the company hiring people whom it can train from the beginning.

In Caracas, Venezuela, this salesperson from U.S.–based Parker Hannifin demonstrates a fluid connector to a customer. Parker Hannifin trains its local sales force in technical support as well as sales techniques and deploys experienced salespeople to other countries as instructors.

Courtesy Parker Hannifin Corporation.

In the more general case, where personal selling is used primarily to sell to middlemen and large customers, the practice is often to hire some of the people who used to work for the distributor in order to avoid high start-up costs and to avoid interruptions in service. When Microsoft decided to open its own sales subsidiary in Japan, the people who previously had worked at ASCII, its distributor, were given the chance to interview for positions in the new outfit. Since switching jobs in Japan is a sensitive matter, following Japanese tradition these interviews were kept secret so as not to jeopardize the person's status in his or her current position.

The major question facing the manager trying to coordinate the global sales effort is the transferability of the selling strategies and techniques used in the home market. Interviews with multinational managers and reviews of published literature have shown that there are basically four factors that affect transferability:[22]

1.   *Geographic and physical dimensions.* The geographical spread of a country, its climate and terrain, as well as roadways and transportation conditions are obvious factors in determining the size of the territories that can be economically covered by one salesperson and the expense of individual calls. In cases such as rural India, for example, a single salesperson will rarely be able to cover more than a village area. Advanced techniques for optimizing territorial limits need considerable adaptation to provide guidance in such countries.

2.   *Degree of market development.* In countries where customers are sophisticated and demanding, with high potential, in-depth training and specialization of the sales force is both necessary and possible. By contrast, where the life cycle is at an early stage, customers are less knowledgeable and require more

information and education. Products tend to be less advanced, and the sales person has to be more broadly trained and sell a wider product line. In the EDP industry, for example, Burroughs compresses its sales territories in smaller markets and each sales person carries a broader line and assumes servicing tasks in addition to sales tasks.

3.   *Differing regulatory environments.* In some countries where fringe benefits, such as medical coverage, severance pay, and pension funding, may be high, the cost for a sales person will escalate. Since such benefits are usually accompanied by a high tax rate on individuals, offering high commission rates to a sales person may be ineffective in comparison with special gifts, a free car, or housing, all of which offer opportunities for tax avoidance.

4.   *Differing human relations.* In many societies the job of a sales person is looked down on as relatively unworthy. Hierarchical cultures such as Hindu India, Muslim Iran, and the Shinto culture in Japan tend historically to be aristocratic, favoring military castes, the priesthood, and feudal landowners over business people or "merchants." Even in more democratic societies there may be some remnant of this pattern, and there is often a subtle ranking that puts a sales person below engineers and the professions. The effect is to make it difficult to attract the best people to a sales job, and for those who accept the challenge it is often difficult to remove a certain aura of defensiveness in them that can mar the sales presentation. Commissions, contests, and bonuses are less effective since they make obvious the extrinsic monetary motivation behind sales people's behavior. Research shows, for example, that in Thailand straight salary is considered more "respectable" than commission-based remuneration.[23]

These fundamental factors affect sales force recruiting, hiring, training, compensation schemes, and territorial allocation. The global marketer also needs to understand more specifically what can be realistically expected from the sales persons in different countries. What constitutes a good salesman?

Personal Salesmanship

Salesmanship is the art of making a sale to another person. There are a few key personal characteristics of good salesmanship. One is enthusiasm, another self-confidence, still another appearance. These and other related factors all refer to the **salesman as a person.**[24]

There is no doubt that *appearance* is a very important factor in international business dealings, perhaps more so than domestically. Since the business relationship crosses cultures, to use a person's appearance as a clue to his personality is much more common globally than at home where it is easier to "look through" the surface appearance. But the important features of a person's appearance are not the same everywhere—even those features that are relevant everywhere are often given a different interpretation. Asian nationals tend to be much less preoccupied with "good looks" and more concerned about appropriate clothing for the occasion than Westerners whose individualism is usually given much more play. Whereas wide, large shoes with thick soles (the much maligned "wingtips") might be viewed by Americans as conservatively masculine, the no less tall or large people of Northern Europe regard such shoes as clumsy and in bad taste. There are naturally a great many such small differences of style (which might make a large difference to the business relationship) and the astute sales person will learn in-depth about the host country's particular customs.

As for enthusiasm and self-confidence, these factors are always important abroad but tend to go over best in "hard sell" situations of the kind typically encountered in New York, Bombay, or Tel Aviv. To the extent that enthusiasm reflects an interest in showing one's company and product in a positive light, enthusiasm is certainly an asset in most countries. But excited delivery, loud voice, and fast talking do not sit well in many cultures. The energy of enthusiasm needs to be carefully tempered in many cases so that it is not released at inopportune moments.

The same is valid for self-confidence, that great asset of Western individualists. In cultures in which group decisions are the norm, the role of *self*-confidence is appropriately reduced. A knowledgeable individual possessing confidence can make his voice heard, but self-confidence is no necessary requirement for an influential presentation: The product and the company are what the individual has to sell, and his "self" should not get in the way of his function.

Especially in high context cultures, there are other characteristics of the salesperson as an individual person quite distinct from his role as a spokesman for the product and the firm that are important in overseas markets. In many cultures the objectives of the business transaction go beyond the immediate business proposition. In such cultures in which the relationship is so important the "personal worth" of the sales person becomes a much bigger issue than it is customarily in the American tradition.

This important point seems paradoxical at first. The salesman and his self-confidence are unimportant since he only represents a company, but his personality and "worth" are important at the same time? This needs to be explained.

Representing the Country

In American salesmanship books one is usually told that "the salesman *is* the company." This means that the customer is presumably identifying the company with the individual—and that the two are indistinguishable. It is the latter part of the presumption that falters in many foreign markets. Yes, the person traveling abroad *is*, in a sense, the company. But to the customer in foreign markets he is so much more. Precisely because this salesman is from another country, he implicitly becomes associated with many of the ideas, facts, stories, and images that the customer has of that country. To see why this is so—for

Americans too—visualize a German salesman visiting a prospect in New York City as a representative of a company like Siemens, the electronics giant. Yes, he is at the moment the company to the American customer. But the latter sees in him much more: "How is the German mark?" "What will happen in the next election?" "I spent last June in Berlin visiting some of the places I saw in the War." Naturally the conversation turns to Germany. The salesman is not just representing Siemens, but to some extent all of Germany, in fact, possibly all of Europe. In this nonbusiness conversation the two persons end up showing much more of themselves as human beings than the standard "good salesmanship" text would suggest.

Imagine the conversation when the same American prospect receives a salesman from an American competitor, say General Electric in Bridgeport, Connecticut. There may be less reason now to spend much time on incidental, nonbusiness matters, since they both possess approximately the same access to information about social, cultural, and political events and don't want to waste time.

The standard approach to preparing for a sales call by focusing on (1) the product, (2) the customer's needs, and (3) the competition needs to be augmented abroad by a wider definition of the "customer's needs." The "good salesman" will have to become a "good individual" in a general sense. At the minimum, one needs to study up on those aspects of one's own country that might be of personal interest to the customer. More broadly, the person sent abroad should get in touch with some genuine interest in nonbusiness matters he or she has that could be of interest to the customer so that the person can show some of himself or herself to the customer. In many countries such "human worth" needs to be established first before more serious, focused business discussions can take place.[25]

Once these discussions start, the sales person then can calmly play down individual worth, repressing his self, as it were, in favor of presenting his or her company and product in the best light. The sales person functions as the conduit through which the company wants to attract the new customer. As a conduit, the sales person's only role is to transmit the necessary information and present the product as well as possible. He needs to leverage the company and the product, not sell himself! The biggest mistake for the individually oriented sales person from the United States in some of these markets is to let enthusiasm and self-confidence place ego in the way of the company and the product.

The Western type of salesmanship, enthusiastic and confident individuals asserting themselves as the "face" of their companies, is successful in Western cultures, in particular, the United States. The opposite type of salesman—a simple conduit when it comes to business, an interesting human being outside of business — is more successful in Eastern cultures, in which individualism is subdued and the ultimate objectives of the business transaction are more than just economic.

The Presentation

The presentation made during a sales visit in domestic markets is typically viewed as consisting of five distinct stages:

Attention: Get the customer to listen to you.

Interest: Get the customer interested in what you have to say.

Desire: Get the customer to desire what you are selling.

Conviction: Get the buyer convinced that the offer is a good deal for him.

Action: Get the customer's signature on the contract.

In global marketing these stages are in a superficial sense still valid but their relative importance and the way an individual salesman goes about moving the customer through them deviate considerably from the home market.

First of all, the attention and interest stages are often less critical when making sales calls abroad. The obvious investment in time and travel plus the "exotic" flavor of the visitor naturally arouse the curiosity of the prospect. The exception to this rule is the salesman representing a country not too well known for the particular product sold, such as a Brazilian visitor to France selling loudspeakers, a new export product from Brazil. In general, however, the first two stages are easier to surmount in global markets.

By contrast, the next three stages are for the same reasons less easily traversed in global transactions. The distances involved, geographically and psychologically, and the consequent difficulties in establishing reliable supply and payment systems, not to speak of future service support, all combine into obstacles for a successful agreement. These global factors create an environment in which the traditional salesmanship virtues of "preparedness," "handling objections," and "closing tactics" take on new and deeper meanings.

Be Prepared!

There is no shortcut to effective sales presentations abroad, and the most fundamental building block in this process is **preparation**. The visitor must be knowledgeable with respect to her or his product and the competition, as well as with the customer's situation and needs, but must also be able to handle questions with respect to tariff and nontariff barriers and other trade complications affecting shipments. In many cases the requirements for an effective sales call are such that a single individual simply can't be expected to handle all the questions alone. Teams of visitors are therefore dispatched (at consequently higher expense), or a representative of the consulate in the country may be asked to join. The important fact here is usually not that specific information can be instantaneously accessed and questions answered right away but that the salesman demonstrates that he has paid close attention to the customer's specific situation and the special requirements for doing business in the country.

Such a demonstration, again, comes down to not only specific knowledge about the "strictly business" aspects of the transactions but also to the "nonbusiness" aspects of the relationship. Learning about Subhas Chandra Bose ("Netaji") and his role in Bengal during the first half of this century is not only "good for business" in India in a narrow sense. For the visitor it generates an understanding of the complex social and political forces at work in the country that in turn leads to a deeper appreciation of similar anticolonial movements and postcolonial societies elsewhere. It tends to make the individual a more compassionate and less prejudiced human being, and that is always useful.

Handling Objections

Handling objections is a difficult task in any sales presentation, and it is not any easier in global settings where communications are more easily garbled. In fact, there is perhaps no other area of the sales presentation in which the cultural differences are more pronounced. The best procedures for handling objections vary considerably from country to country.

Generally speaking, some pointers can be suggested. It is important that the objections not be escalated into an argument. Even in very contentious societies—as in Israel, for example—it is better to allow for the fact that most objections do have merit. Rather than attempting outright refutation and persuasion based on facts and figures it is more effective to suggest the direction in which the answer lies and lead the customer toward it rather than pushing him.

The best way to handle objections is to avoid having them raised in the first place. Whether this can be done hinges very much on the amount of "ego" that the sales person presents. The self-confident sales person so highly praised in American textbooks is told to "keep standing so that the prospect can be dominated" or at least be equal to the customer: "I know you are busy. I am busy myself."[26] It goes without saying that such tactics might be inappropriate in countries where the "customer is the king" and where the use of confrontation and intimidation are highly counterproductive. Even though in many such countries the presentation will meet no overt objections, it is likely to fail miserably. In such cases the unfortunate sales person is often back in the hotel room before long wondering, "What hit me?"

Closing Tactics

The **closing tactics** also vary considerably between countries. Most infuriating for foreigners, it is not always easy to discern when exactly the "decision to buy" is made or when a felicitous moment for closing is at hand. There are times when the senior manager on the customer's side leaves a meeting without any particular agreement with the sales person, who is expected to continue the presentation without his presence. Some quietly whispered words in the native tongue not understood by the sales person, can easily be misinterpreted as a polite way of saying "no" when in fact they mean "yes." A direct question from the sales person to gauge interest and reaction of the customer may be given an evasive answer, again yielding mixed and exasperating signals.

When closing is seemingly within reach, some person with intimate knowledge of the country's customs should be present to assist the sales person. It is in these later stages that the particular cultural norms have been set down most precisely. Generally, cultural norms can be suspended more easily in matters of low importance. Since the signing of the contract is the most serious action to be taken during the whole of the negotiations, most customers (and salespeople) tend to lean on standard, formal procedures when committing themselves and their company. The presence of a knowledgeable person (often with legal expertise) to assist in the final stages therefore becomes very important.

But this same person might be useful throughout in indicating to the sales person what is going on among the customer's people present. This does not only mean that she or he can listen in on their discussions using knowledge of the country's language; she or he may be able to interpret what their nonspeaking, their silences mean. *Silence* has a particularly strong effect in international presentations as a closing technique. Sometimes the "final offer" is modified when the customer remains intimidatingly silent, although the offer would have been quite acceptable. This is common in Japan when American sales people get impatient and give unnecessary concessions—but occurs often enough in Europe and even in the United States. A salesman for industrial products related how he had closed a sale to the U.S. manufacturing operation of a European ski producer: "I had made all my points, laid out the whole situation, answered the questions. I saw he was thinking, thinking hard, so I shut up and just sat there. Seconds stretched into minutes. I sensed that the first man to speak would lose, so I let it ride. We sat there for perhaps 15 minutes, not saying a thing. Suddenly he said, 'Let's do it' and I had a sale."

Global personal selling has to be localized *and* adapted—but with sensitivity, persistence, preparation, and a good product, most cultural obstacles can be overcome.

SUMMARY

Although much of the execution of promotional strategies needs to be localized because of varying regulations in different countries, the growth of global communications, global media, and global events in sports and other areas has made global promotion feasible. Sponsorship and creation of global events, participation in international trade fairs, and a global public relations perspective, including global publicity, are promotional tools for the company's global marketing effort. The increasing feasibility of direct marketing helps even smaller companies capitalize on global opportunities.

As for the promotional regulations that often force localization, the growth of integrated trading blocs are gradually forcing harmonization of regulations. Challenges from global companies to arcane legislation designed to protect local businesses have been successful. The trend has been toward increasing importance of global recognition and reputation, as evidenced by the growth of global brand names. The various promotional tools discussed in this chapter play an important role in developing and sustaining the equity in such global brand names. This is accomplished by integrated global communications, tying advertising images and appropriate copy to promotional messages, sponsorships of events, and appropriate publicity.

Many people around the world do not like the way promotional hoopla seems to have become more important than what is promoted—the game or the product itself. However, with open global markets, democracy, and capitalism, promotion is unavoidably part of the game.

KEY TERMS

Closing tactics p. 600
Cross-marketing p. 582
Direct marketing p. 589
Direct response television
(DRTV) p. 590
Events p. 581
Global public relations p. 586

Handling objections p. 600
In-store promotion p. 577
International trade fairs
  p. 587
Mail order p. 590
Preparation p. 599
Publicity p. 584

Sales force p. 594
Salesman as a person p. 596
Salesmanship p. 596
Sponsorship p. 581
Telemarketing p. 590
Trade promotions p. 580

DISCUSSION QUESTIONS

1. What is it that makes a created media event such as a Disney opening a powerful promotional tool? Trace the effect of such an event on the individual consumer decision process discussed in Chapter 7, "Local Buyer Behavior" (for example, identify to what extent the effect is cognitive, affective, and socially normative). What does this tell you about when such events should (not) be attempted by the global marketer?

2. Think about some of the packaged goods you bought in recent months. How many languages were used to describe their contents? For consumer durables, check how many languages are used in the instruction booklets. What does this tell you about global promotion and which products are more global?

3. Promotion that leads to publicity and high visibility has some drawbacks. What are they?

Why is it that some observers argue that computer software companies are "product oriented"? What are the marketing disadvantages of such an orientation? Any advantages?

4. What are the forces that have led to the success of direct marketing? What are the threats against its continued success? What has helped the globalization of direct marketing? Any obstacles, now or in the future?

5. Drawing on the cultural discussion in Chapter 3 and your own cultural background, compare the salesmanship skills needed to sell an automobile in Germany, in the United States, and in Japan (or some other countries of your own choice). What skills would be most advantageous? Which ones could land you in trouble?

NOTES

1. See Boddewyn, 1988.

2. From Terpstra and Sarathy, 1994, p. 508.

3. Such "serendipitous" advertising, broadcasting of brand names through TV coverage of the events, is coming under scrutiny, at least in the United States. The rental rates for stadium advertising space have risen to reflect the TV coverage, at the same time as broadcasters are starting to complain about the "free ride" they are giving to nonpaying advertisers. But although cigarette advertising such as Marlboro's has been curtailed (see McKinley, Jr., 1995) it will probably be some time before Monica Seles' Yonex stickers disappear from view.

4. From the *Washington Post*, August 12, 1995.

5. The Swatch material is drawn from two case studies, Pinson and Kimball, 1987, and Jeannet et al. 1985.

6. See, for example, the Gump mania discussed in Farhi, 1995.

7. See Bennet, 1995.

8. See Segal, 1995; Goldberg, 1995.

9. See Levin, 1994.

10. Jean-Jacques Servan-Schreiber's *The American Challenge* became a great best-seller in the late 1960s.

11. Many of the negative attitudes have been documented and shown to be based on a one-sided view of Japanese management as all powerful—see Sullivan, 1992.

12. See Stephen A. Greyser and N. Langford, "Volvo and the Monster Mash," Harvard Business School case no. 9-593-024.

13. See Markoff, 1994.

14. From Pollack, 1995a and 1995b.

15. See Parke, 1994.

16. See Weyr, 1995.

17. See McNutt, 1995.

18. See Boyd, 1995.

19. This section draws on Sacks, 1995.

20. See Egol, 1994a.

21. From an interview in *Harvard Business Review* (Taylor, 1992).

22. This section draws on Hill et al., 1991.

23. See Still, 1981.

24. Much of the noninternational material in this section comes from Buskirk and Buskirk, 1992, a leading text on salesmanship.

25. Hall, 1960, has an extended example of a telecommunications deal in a Latin American country that is fun reading as well as instructive.

26. From Buskirk and Buskirk, 1992, pp. 266 and 331.

SELECTED REFERENCES

Bennet, James. "An Auto Maker Uses a Cult Artist's Colorful Images to Make Its Minivans Stand Out from the Pack." *New York Times*, January 19, 1995, p. D23.

Boddewyn, Jean J. *Premiums, Gifts, and Competitions.* New York: International Advertising Association, 1988.

Boyd, Terry. "Sweet Surrender? Candy Company Hopes Federal Program Will Help It 'Invade' Japan," *Business First—Louisville*, 12, no. 1, (August 7, 1995), sec.1, p. 14.

Buskirk, R. H., and B. Buskirk. *Selling: Principles & Practice.* 13th ed. New York: McGraw-Hill, 1992.

Egol, Len. "Europe: Uncommon Market." *Direct* 6, no. 10 (October 1994a), p. 83.

———. "Is China Ready for U.S. Mail, U.S. Direct Marketers?" *Direct* 6, no. 12 (December 1994b), p. 55.

Farhi, Paul. "Selling Is as Selling Does." *Washington Post*, April 30, 1995, pp. H1, H6.

Goldberg, Carey. "Midnight Sales Frenzy Ushers in Windows 95." *New York Times*, August 24, 1995, pp. A1, D6.

Hall, Edward T. "The Silent Language in Overseas Business." *Harvard Business Review*, May–June 1960, pp. 87–96.

Hill, John S.; Richard R. Still; and Unal O. Boya. "Managing the Multinational Sales Force." *International Marketing Review* 8, no.1 (1991) pp. 19–31.

Jeannet, Jean-Pierre; Susan W. Nye; and Barbara Priovolos. "The Swatch Project." Imede, 1985.

Kelly, Gene. "Direct Marketing Going Overseas." *Lincoln Evening Journal*, June 1, 1994, business sec.

Levin, Gary. "Benetton Ad Lays Bare the Bloody Toll of War." *Advertising Age*, February 21, 1994, p. 38.

Markoff, John. "In About-Face, Intel Will Swap Its Flawed Chips." *New York Times*, December 21, 1994, pp. A1, D6.

Mårtenson, Rita. *Innovations in Retailing*. Lund, Sweden: Liber, 1983.

McKinley, Jr., James C. "The Garden Agrees to Curb Cigarette Ads." *New York Times*, April 5, 1995, p. C2.

McNutt, Bill III. "DM in South America Can Be as Easy as ABC. " *DM News*, November 13, 1995, Supplement, "Global Views," p.22.

Parke, Jo Anne. "The Case for Going Global: Globalization in Direct Marketing." *Target Marketing* 17, no. 11 (November 1994), p. 8.

Pinson, Christian, and Helen Chase Kimball. "Swatch." Insead; Cedep, 1987, case no. 589–005–IN.

Pollock, Andrew. "Computer Exhibition Purchased." *New York Times*, February 14, 1995a, pp. D1, D8.

———. "A Japanese Gambler Hits the Jackpot with Softbank." *New York Times*, February 19, 1995b, sec. F, p. 10.

Sacks, Douglas. "Entering the Asian Living Room: Direct Response Television." *Target Marketing* 18, no. 2 (1995), p. 12.

Segal, David. "With Windows 95's Debut, Microsoft Scales Heights of Hype." *Washington Post*, August 24, 1995, p. A14.

Servan-Schreiber, Jean-Jacques. *The American Challenge*. New York: Atheneum, 1968.

Shirk, Martha. "Simple Formula No Answer for Hungry Children." *St. Louis Post-Dispatch*, September 23, 1991, p. 18.

Smith, Dawn. "Putting Soul into the Machine." *Marketing Computers* 14, no.7 (July 1994), p. 38.

Still, Richard R. "Cross-cultural Aspects of Sales Force Management." *Journal of Personal Selling and Sales Force Management* 1, no. 2, (1981), pp. 6–9.

Sullivan, Jeremiah J. *Invasion of the Salarymen*. Westport, CT: Praeger, 1992.

Taylor, William. "The Logic of Global Business: An Interview with ABB's Percy Barnevik," in Christopher A. Bartlett and Sumantra Ghoshal, *Transnational Management*, Homewood, IL: Irwin, 1992, pp. 892–908.

Terpstra, Vern, and Ravi Sarathy. *International Marketing*. 6th ed. Fort Worth, TX: Dryden, 1994.

"Thais and Indonesians Are Good Direct Mail Targets." *Market Asia Pacific*, February 1, 1995.

Weyr, Thomas. "Germany Flexes Postal Muscle, Expects to Become a Major Player." *DM News*, June 19, 1995, Supplement, "Dateline Europe," p. 7.

Organizing for Global Marketing

"Making it all work"

After studying this chapter, you should understand the following global marketing issues:

1. The global network of the multinational firm is a marketing asset that can be leveraged with a global strategy, but only if the appropriate organizational structure is created.

2. The most important aspect of any organizational solution is to make sure that local motivation is not diminished, negatively affecting the implementation of a global strategy. Because of this, local managers need to be consulted early in the strategy formulation process.

3. The local managers not only have better knowledge of the local market but can assume a more global view given the chance. In the "transnational" company, local subsidiaries become centers of excellence, with global responsibilities for a particular product line—local globalization.

4. The coordination mechanisms that companies institute range from creating a common global culture, sharing information, and establishing personal relations to the creation of new organizational units such as global account managers and global teams. All these mechanisms serve to bring the global company closer to the local customer—global localization.

To IMPLEMENT A GLOBAL marketing strategy, the organization's structure—the solid and dotted lines connecting management positions, departmental staff, divisional units, and subsidiaries on the organizational chart—often needs to be changed. The typical multinational organization with an international division and semiindependent country subsidiaries can work well in the multidomestic case when coordination across local markets is of less importance. As markets globalize, the central coordination requirements grow stronger, and country subsidiaries' autonomy must be reined in. In matrixed organizations, where coordination across product divisions and countries is explicit, global marketing can be implemented more easily. However, since a global marketing strategy tends to focus on the "market served" and limit the role of local adaptation, in global companies the product dimension of a matrix tends to dominate the country dimension. It is the global counterpart of "product management." Needless, to say, this creates conflicts at the local country level and firms have to find a way to tilt the balance, for example, by placing strong managers at regional centers.

This chapter deals with the organizational aspects of global marketing. It explains how to structure centralized coordination and integration and how to manage the potential conflicts at the local level. As in all organizations, the *organizational structure*, the *management systems* installed, and the *people* in the organization are the critical ingredients in the successful implementation of global marketing strategies.

ABB Structures Its Way to Success

For almost a century, Swedish Asea was an international leader in the heavy electrical equipment industry. But despite rapid growth, its future was cloudy. Asea had a score of competitors in the European electrical industry, half of them losing money—a sign of substantial overcapacity. Percy Barnevik, Asea's managing director, thwarted decline by pioneering a dramatic restructuring.

The transformation began when Asea merged with Switzerland's Brown Boveri, forming a giant international provider of electrical systems and equipment. The new company, ABB Asea Brown Boveri, acquired or took minority positions in 60 companies, primarily in Europe and the Americas. As ABB grew, it structured itself to simultaneously capitalize on each subsidiary's unique strengths and unite the work of its 240,000 employees.

ABB is what Barnevik calls "multidomestic." Each of its operations maintains deep roots in its home country, yet ABB has managers who specialize in setting global objectives to which the various groups must contribute. Its local plants have global mandates, and the organization shares knowledge and other resources across national boundaries.

Consider the business of transportation, in which ABB is the market leader, selling locomotives, subway cars, trolleys, signaling systems, and more. To serve this market, ABB draws on technology expertise from its international network of labs and facilities. Because it has several specialized facilities among which to allocate production orders, ABB can capitalize on economies of scale and compete by offering exceptional value. Because its operations are in a variety of countries, ABB also offers in-depth knowledge of its markets—for instance, the Swiss concern for the environment, or the effects of a region's temperature changes on its locomotives.

Tying the enterprise together at the top are a few ABB executives in Zürich with a global outlook. For these positions, the company develops and selects people with patience and open-mindedness. To ensure that everyone has equal access to information, they are expected to communicate in English, ABB's official language.

The need for radical change is hardly unique to ABB. Rapid globalization eliminates companies that settle for business as usual; somewhere in the world a competitor will find a way to deliver better value. At AlliedSignal, change has involved reorganizing the company around the core processes that deliver value to customers rather than around functions like marketing or engineering. Illinois-based Thermos has moved away from a functional structure to product development by cross-functional teams that take their cues directly from customers. General Electric, too, uses teams, plus a flatter structure, strategic alliances, and closer links to suppliers, all to break down the boundaries that stifle innovation. Ironically, change is the only certainty in global business. So flexibility is crucial to survive as well as thrive.

Sources: William Taylor, "The Logic of Global Business: An Interview with ABB's Percy Barnevik," *Harvard Business Review*, March-April 1991, pp. 90–101; Stratford Sherman, "Are You as Good as the Best in the World?" *Fortune*, December 13, 1993, pp. 95–96; Brian Dumaine, "Payoff from the New Management," *Fortune*, December 13, 1993, pp. 103–104; Noel M. Tichy, "Revolutionize Your Company," *Fortune*, December 13, 1993, pp. 114–15.

INTRODUCTION

The *formulation* of a global marketing strategy for a product line is primarily an intellectual challenge for managers. The *implementation* of the strategy, by contrast, involves much more interpersonal discussion and persuasion. The global marketing manager needs to become an internal salesman and champion. And the global organization needs to be structured carefully to be able to respond to the challenge. The local units have to be motivated to *execute* the global strategy effectively.

The focus of this chapter is the organizational problems of global marketing. We start by establishing the *context* in which the organizational decisions are made, then spell out the *job* that needs to be done, along with the tools that exist to do it. We discuss some common organizational *structures* found in multinational firms and look at the global *network* as a firm-specific advantage. A section on *globalizing management* leads into a discussion of management *systems* and the role of *people and culture* in global marketing management. We deal with the special case of organizing to serve *global customers*, and finally, we present techniques for *resolving conflicts* between headquarters and local units.

The Context

To see why implementing global marketing is generally difficult, it is important to first understand the managerial context. The typical situation is one where:

1. The company is already present in many markets.
2. The company is successful in at least some of the major markets (global marketing is usually *not* a crisis solution).
3. There is a history of quite successful operations with local autonomy.
4. The country heads have experience and status at home and in the organization. For administrative and control reasons the subsidiaries may be run by expatriates, but the local marketing effort is run by a local marketing manager (and/or by the country head, when a native).
5. The *legitimacy* of the global marketing "imperative" is not all that obvious in the organization—unless successful competitors have forced the issue.
6. The global advantage derives from (*a*) cost savings, (*b*) demand spillover effects, and (*c*) serving global customers. Only in the last category will the benefits be unequivocal.
7. One obvious effect of a global strategy will be less autonomy for the local subsidiary.
8. The initiative for the global strategy comes from the top.

Given this context, it is not surprising if local country managers have to be dragged into globalization against their will.

The Job

There are essentially three main tasks imposed on the organization when a global marketing strategy is attempted. They can be delineated as follows:

- An effective *multiple-way communication system* needs to be set up to carry directives from the center to the local markets and to feed back information to headquarters and other subsidiaries.
- The local country heads need to be given *incentives* to implement the global strategy even though it often involves a reduction in local autonomy and resources.

- The organization structure and/or systems need to be *flexible* so that changing conditions and new developments can be responded to and capitalized on as they arise.

The typical organization has several *organizational tools* to accomplish these tasks:

- *Creating new organizational units.* The most common new units are perhaps *global teams*, drawing members from headquarters and country subsidiaries, with the team leader from a major lead country.
- *Creating new positions* (or reformulating existing position descriptions) that emphasize global responsibilities. A typical example is the creation of a *global marketing director.*
- *Changing the reporting lines.* The organization can change the existing *structure*, that is, the formal lines of reporting and authority. This is in some ways the most clear-cut change toward centralization and the most far-reaching and dramatic change in the local organization. For example, one company wanting to create a pan-European marketing strategy directed its local marketing managers to report to European headquarters instead of the country heads, who saw themselves as losers.
- *Creating new systems.* The organization can create new *systems* and procedures within the given structure. Generally, this means that local managers retain formal authority and reporting lines but are forced to work harder and/or differently. For example, among globalizing firms it is very common to initiate periodic global meetings among country heads to explain and reinforce the global strategy.
- *People adapting.* The organization can rely on *people* to change their behavior and accommodate the changes. In one technology-intensive firm, the global "change agent" was the marketing manager at headquarters who spent most of his time on the road explaining the global strategy and sharing information from other subsidiaries.

ORGANIZATIONAL STRUCTURE

There is no single best way to organize for global marketing. There is simply too much variety in product lines, customers, and country environments. Even companies with similar product lines and global reach will organize differently. The diversity and flexibility of people and existing systems differ between organizations and the global organization is a product of the historical evolution of the company. Naturally, it is easier to implement global marketing when people and systems in the company have previous experience with marketing in foreign countries.

The key issue for **organizational design** tends to be how to strike an appropriate balance between headquarters' need for central coordination and the local subsidiary's motivation for implementing the global strategy.

The firm can organize its international coverage in different ways. Most firms have gone through a sequence of these stages as they change their structure to expand overseas.

- *Export department.* The creation of an **export department structure** is usually the first step in the functional organization toward entry into foreign markets. Export departments are typically cost centers without independent authority in product and marketing mix decisions. The typical export department structure is given in Exhibit 17.1.

- *International division.* As the export revenue share increases (a common threshold value is around 10 percent of total revenues) and there are several countries in the strategic portfolio, the firm changes to a full-fledged **international division structure**, where the general manager has profit-and-loss responsibilities. The international division is often a **strategic business unit** (SBU), an operating unit functioning basically as a free-standing business. It competes with the domestic units for resource allocations, buying services from the central headquarters' staff and demanding a say on product design, product positioning, and other decisions affecting its effectiveness abroad. Exhibit 17.2 shows the typical structure with an international division.

- *Geographical/regional structure.* As overseas sales expand and the management of the countries takes more time and resources, the firm usually subdivides the international division into country groups or trade regions. Typical areas are Western Europe, Latin America, Africa and the Middle East, East Asia and the Pacific, and Eastern Europe and Russia. The international division is still usually intact, and a new organizational level is introduced to

EXHIBIT 17.1 The Export Department Structure

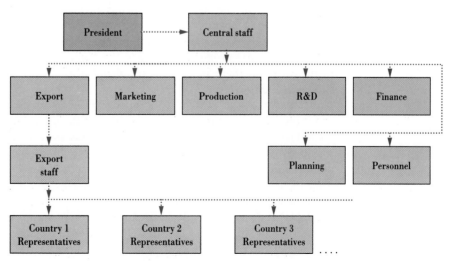

EXHIBIT 17.2 The International Division Structure

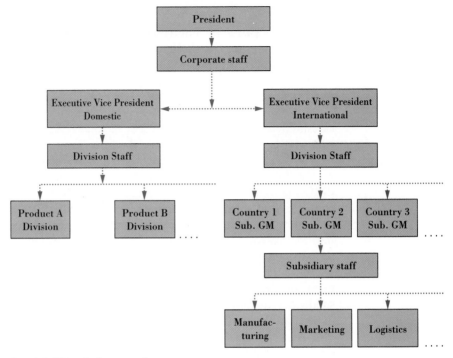

Note: Sub.GM = subsidiary general manager.

coordinate within the newly established regions. This **regional organization** is common among Japanese companies, whose home market is large and structured separately. When the home market is minor compared to the overseas sales, as in many European companies, the home market is simply subordinated in the area and there is no domestic division as such. A regional structure is shown in Exhibit 17.3.

• *Global product divisions.* The attempt to develop a truly global strategy for a firm's product line tends to force a rejection of the international-versus-domestic split. The solution is often a **global product division**, where regional and local managers' authority is subordinated to that of the global division chief, who approves and directs. Although the structure has a strong logic behind it and the implementation of global marketing is facilitated, this structure demands a lot from the division manager.[1] The reason is simple. The division head staff is often too far away from the local market to have a very secure understanding of the local issues and differences. Furthermore, the need for speed and responsiveness

....
EXHIBIT 17.3 **The Regional Structure**

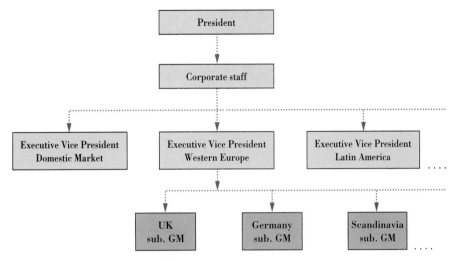

Note: sub.GM = subsidiary general manager.

to local competitive moves and customer requests makes central direction of operations difficult. One common solution has been for the division chief to only set broad policy goals and formulate the global strategy and then allow the local managers a great deal of autonomy in implementing the strategies. Even though global uniformity might be less than otherwise, the positive effect on the motivation of the local country heads often makes up for the lack of uniformity. The global product structure is displayed in Exhibit 17.4.

- *Matrix organizations.* Matrix structures are those in which both country and product receive equal emphasis. Marketing of one product in a given country has to report both to the global product head, who oversees all the countries for that product, and the country head, who is responsible for all the products in the country. The local marketer has to respond to two bosses, an undesirable feature, but often workable if the people are experienced and the management systems are handled flexibly. This is the essence of coordination and integration, and the **matrix organization**, whether formally established or not, is a natural structure for the global marketer. The global matrix structure at Honda Motor Company is shown in Exhibit 17.5.

- *Transnational organizations.* As globalization requirements increase in reach and scope, global strategies involve not only manufacturing and marketing but also R&D, design, and engineering. This has led especially technology-intensive companies to develop organizational structures in which different

EXHIBIT 17.4 The Global Product Structure

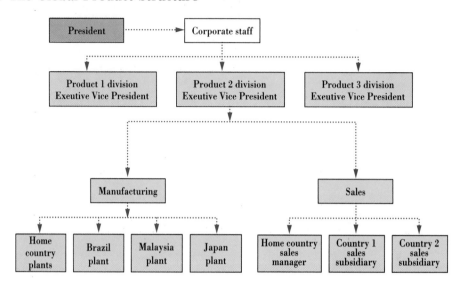

EXHIBIT 17.5 The Global Matrix Structure: Honda's Global Organization

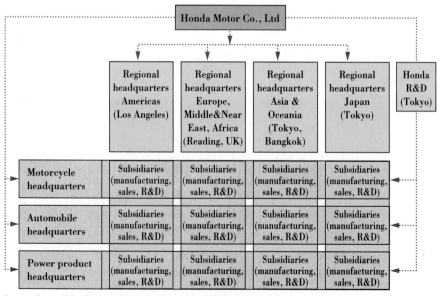

Source: Osamu Iida, Executive Vice President, Honda North-America.

parts of the firm's value chain are located in different parts of the world. These are called **transnational organizations** to emphasize their cross-country network character.[2]

For example, companies such as Ericsson from Sweden in telecommunications can place its R&D for certain products in one country, manufacturing of the product somewhere else, and then do global sales and marketing from a third location. Other firms have gone even further, splitting up country subsidiaries into specialized units. Honeywell, the U.S.-based multinational in electronic measurement, has distributed its functions for design, engineering, sales, and marketing throughout Europe, allowing each country subsidiary to specialize. The reorganization of former full-fledged country subsidiaries into "special resource centers" is not particularly easy on the people displaced because their specialty is now in a new country location. Nevertheless, given some flexibility in the implementation of the new structure, many firms have succeeded in developing global networks with the country units drawing on the particular strengths of the local economy. How the transnational structure involves all units of the global network is shown in Exhibit 17.6.

• *Horizontal networks.* The natural result of the recent emergence of transnational expertise, effective global communications, and the drive toward "lean" organizations, **horizontal networks** have become the new "ideal" type of organizational structure. In these networks, the traditional hierarchical arrangement with a decision maker at the top of the international division or global

EXHIBIT 17.6 Integrated Network: The Transnational Structure

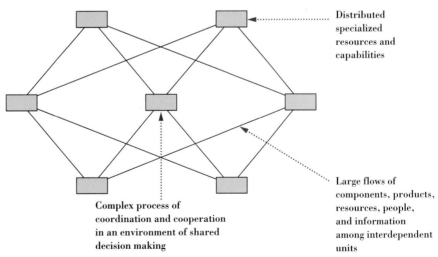

Distributed specialized resources and capabilities

Complex process of coordination and cooperation in an environment of shared decision making

Large flows of components, products, resources, people, and information among interdependent units

Source: Reprinted by permission of Harvard Business School Press. From *Managing Across Borders: The Transnational Solution* by Christopher A. Bartlett and Sumatra Ghoshal. Boston, MA, p. 89. Copyright 1989 by the President and Fellows of Harvard College, all rights reserved.

product division, directives flowing out to the various country subsidiaries, and performance results fed back up has been replaced by a much less pyramidal structure. In horizontal networks, not only do local managers implement global strategies but the local subsidiaries are also involved in the formulation of the strategy, often in fact initiating the global approach. In the horizontal network structure local and central managers are virtually indistinguishable, as flows are generally horizontal from the periphery into the home country center and directly between country subsidiaries. In practice, the picture is not quite so simple, of course (see box on "The Pan-European Effect" on page 621).

Although very few corporations have yet attained the perfect equality implied between all parts of the network, the structure itself is enabling the emergence of such horizontal or "democratic" relationships. In actual organizational life, even if the *structural* reporting lines are horizontal and management *systems* encourage free participation, *people* do not always respond to the implied equality. Leadership and charisma still matter. An organization has a tradition and a culture, which enable certain behaviors and discourage other behaviors. It is not surprising to find the horizontal organization working in new start-up companies, as in computers and software, but not very far advanced even in such high-tech industries as telecommunications, where old and established companies still dominate.

THE GLOBAL NETWORK AS AN ASSET

Many companies think of their global network of country subsidiaries as an "invisible resource" or "hidden asset." The network is their FSA. After the years it has taken to develop presence in the many separate country markets, the companies start contemplating how to further leverage the investment. This is a natural development for entrepreneurial managers. For example, as we saw in Chapter 15, advertising agencies that develop global reach to follow their clients abroad start attracting new business because of their network. Procter and Gamble used its global network to be the first to introduce condensed detergents in major countries, beating the innovator, Japan's Kao, to the market.

The strategic view of the **global network as an asset**, as an FSA, is doubly useful since it tends to make local units more important, helping to counter the problem of country managers' feeling their local authority compromised by a shift to global strategy. Treating the network itself as an asset means that the global strategy becomes more of a "win-win" proposition for both headquarters and subsidiaries.

Painful History

To understand how companies may leverage network resources, we can learn from the past history of multinational expansion. It teaches some painful lessons.

Belgacom is a consulting firm which specializes in helping companies leverage the assets in their global network. Often the first problem is the creation of an effective communication system between the various local nodes in the network.

The increased need for an integrated global strategy has come about partly because of the successful attacks on world markets by newly emerging multinationals, especially the Japanese. A key ingredient in their success has been their lack of existing foreign subsidiaries, allowing their global expansion to take place through well-coordinated exporting from Japan and other home countries. As Western companies have tried to emulate the Japanese successes, their efforts at globalized strategies have been hampered rather than helped by their traditionally independent country subsidiaries. The European multinationals, in particular, had long allowed local subsidiaries to run their own operations, a historical accident partly due to Europeans' bent for respecting different local customs.

American companies have traditionally operated with stronger central authority than the Europeans, which means that many American brand names are well recognized globally while European brand names differ between countries. But even American companies have had trouble coordinating global marketing, involving as it does more limited independence for local subsidiaries. As late as the early 1990s, Western companies still lagged behind Japanese companies in their level of global marketing integration.[3] Subsidiary managers balk and refuse to cooperate, citing differences in customer preferences and the lowered motivation among local personnel as impenetrable barriers to coordination with headquarters. Norelco, the American subsidiary of Dutch Philips, is still largely run as an independent company; the head of Ford's operation in Germany resigned; and even Procter and Gamble's decade-long struggle for pan-European product teams has encountered some fierce resistance.

The Win-Win View

Perhaps not surprisingly given this history, the "win-win" solution to the problems involved in implementing a global strategy against local resistance has come primarily from companies and researchers in Europe. Scandinavian academicians in particular have been active in promoting what has become known as "the network theory" of global enterprise.[4]

The central tenet of the **network theory** is that the linkages between actors in the global network—not only between headquarters and subsidiaries but also between company and suppliers, marketers and channel members, and company and loyal customers—constitute the true source of competitive advantage for the firm. Rather than thinking of the firm as "we" and the other actors as "they," the approach is inclusive. The best way to gain advantages is for the network to be strong, not only the individual participants. "What is good for them is good for us."

In this view, *competition occurs mainly between networks of businesses.* Analyzing Japanese competitors, for example, the network approach suggests that Nissan and Toyota compete not only directly but also through their related keiretsu (or network) suppliers. This view is shared among many business people inside and outside Japan. Another factor of importance in the network view is the enlarged role of a country subsidiary in communicating and supporting other subsidiaries—and not only reporting to headquarters. The role of headquarters, in the network view, becomes one of sharing knowledge, disseminating innovations, and facilitating communication among network members rather than giving orders and directing from the center (see box, "Researching the Power of Networks").

From a global marketing viewpoint, the most striking benefit derived from the network approach is the fresh recognition of *what* the firm's resources and FSAs are and *where* new ideas and innovation might emerge. The existence of the network opens up new possibilities, rather than constraining solutions. The so-called core competencies of the corporation involve not simply what the company can do—but what the network can do. The network can do more things than the individual company can do—and, conversely, an absence of a global network reduces management strategy options.

The ideas for expansion and growth can come from anywhere in a network—which is why communication in the network is so important. As managers inside the network learn about the capabilities of other members, new visions open up and imaginative innovations emerge. It is very much like the acquisition of a home computer and its associated products (CD ROM, modem, laser printer, e-mail). As the user develops experience with the equipment, not

Getting the Picture

Researching the Power of Networks

SINCE THE NETWORK approach places the key competitive advantages in the linkages between players rather than in individual companies, it is natural to replace the topic of organizational behavior with that of network behavior, an approach suggested primarily by Swedish researchers. Network researchers study how networks are created, grow, and change over time. For example, researchers have dealt with how companies get new trade contacts (often quite haphazardly, as through random encounters while traveling), how often and for what purposes face-to-face meetings are necessary (common when a subsidiary adopts an innovation), and how "sleeping" relationships can be activated by new opportunities (such as when the Berlin Wall's dismantling allowed Swedish companies to reactivate past contacts in Eastern Europe).

In the same stream of research, there is relatively little discussion of leadership. The reason is that traditional leadership is typically a top-down activity with followers being motivated by leaders. The network view is much more egalitarian and fits nicely into the newer organizational frameworks of empowerment and decentralized power. The businesses that have shown themselves particularly adept at global networking involve high-technology products or services with skills distributed throughout the network. The so-called "virtual corporation" is one extreme form of the network approach with company employees attached to the center by virtue only of a computerized communications link. It remains to be seen whether such communication links can be strong enough to completely replace face-to-face encounters. But the fact remains that the computer-linked global network competitor is here to stay.

Sources: Forsgren and Johanson, 1992; Hakansson, 1989.

only will operations be easier but new possibilities open up and opportunities for additional extensions appear. In the same way, the global network allows the members to develop experience and skills in operating the network and dealing with its members, and new growth opportunities appear.

As global competition heats up and companies are faced with "hypercompetition," the global network is a key source of competitive advantage and new possibilities.[5] Rather than viewing the network members as out-of-date and obstacles to progress, their local know-how and motivation need to be allowed to impact the member companies and the network as a whole. This takes much less "leadership" from the center than it takes facilitation and sharing of knowledge. The marketing manager whose organization operates with a "network as an asset" view not only uses the most up-to-date telecommunications and videoconferencing equipment but also spends a lot of time on the road, cajoling and persuading and sharing. Global integration is not a matter of centralized command over an army of exporters, as in the Japanese system, but rather of inspiring individual network members to share in the win-win philosophy.

GLOBALIZING MANAGEMENT[6]

Because of the large home market, many American companies come to global marketing with an international division structure separating domestic and international markets. This structure tends to prohibit global integration of marketing effort, since the home country occupies a special position. For integrated marketing, the home country needs to be viewed as part of the global market. To accomplish this, companies are shifting to global marketing directors.

Global Marketing Directors

In companies organized along the lines of global product divisions or separate business units, the **global marketing director** naturally becomes the head of marketing for both the home country and international. Each product division will then have a global marketing manager reporting to the director. Even without a global product structure, global marketing directors may be appointed to operate in a matrix fashion across a geographic structure. In either case, the global marketing director is generally given the following responsibilities:

- Profit accountability for individual lines of business and major product lines.
- Coordination of all functions affecting these lines.
- Strategic planning, budgeting, and implementation with functions and regions.
- Design, creation, and maintenance of global marketing systems.
- Participation in performance evaluation of functional and regional managers.

These are major tasks that may demand that national marketing managers in the main markets report directly to the global marketing director. New product specifications, positioning, advertising, and distribution choices may become centralized decisions, while lower-level execution questions such as local sales and logistics remain a national responsibility. All major accounts are handled centrally.

Even without such a change in the reporting lines of the organization, global marketing directors can still exert considerable influence as staff members by sheer force of personality and access to information. They can bring vast experience to bear on a particular situation. For example, one manager exerted strong influence over the country managers simply by explaining why their advertising ideas had failed in other countries, and sharing where they had succeeded. Arguments about the particular tastes of a local market and the need for special advertising often dissolve when the success of a campaign in a neighboring country is demonstrated.

*G*etting the
Picture

The
Pan-European
Effect

THE EFFECT of global marketing on organization structure is well illustrated by the attempts of companies to get ready for the European integration.

Many companies have developed pan-European structures and processes. Lever Europe, the regional headquarters of Unilever in Europe, added a general manager for strategic development to whom Europewide product group managers report. The strategic European group complements the existing geographic structure with country managers responsible for operating profits. The company is developing Eurobrands for which Europewide product managers have responsibility to develop marketing strategy, package design, and advertising. The Europewide product managers have their own budgets, operate as cost centers, and have to "sell" the country managers on the introduction of the Eurobrands through the existing channels in each country.

Additional reporting lines represent a simple coordinating device. Dell Computer is asking its product marketing managers in the various European countries to report to the pan-European head office in addition to the country managers. Going halfway is sometimes not enough. 3M, the Minnesota-based maker of videodisks and tapes and related products, tried to develop Europroducts by creating small European product teams that had to draw on functional expertise in local units. This structure became too weak, and the company shifted to full-fledged Europewide business units.

When a company dominates its markets and products are standardized, centralized direction is facilitated. Gillette's international headquarters in the USA is responsible for all marketing in Europe, including product positioning, advertising, and public relations. The head man at Gillette spent a long time with Gillette in Germany, so the European market conditions are not unknown at headquarters. Gillette's effort in Japan, which is managed with much more local autonomy, is unfortunately less successful, Schick being the market leader in Japan.

Sources: Gates, 1995; Uchitelle, 1994.

Global Teams

One of the commonest organizational changes for global marketing is to create **global teams**. The responsibilities can vary from specific programs or activities, such as the advertising campaign for a new product, to more wide-ranging responsibilities, including the whole marketing mix. One of the factors behind this development has been the European integration export (see box, "The Pan-European Effect").

For example, a French manufacturer of security devices uses a team of country managers, with the different countries playing the lead role for different products. While this approach is time consuming, the company has found that this reliance on line managers makes it easier for various countries to accept input from other countries.

In response to the European integration, the 3M company initially used "European Management Action Teams," one for each its 50 product lines. Each

A transnational product development team in 3M's European Business Center for medical products in Brussels in 1993. From left: Valori Seltz, a U.S. citizen; Philippe Husson, French; Kurt Wiethoff, German; Inge Thulin, Swedish; and Stig Eriksson, Finnish.

© Steve Niedorf photography.

team had eight to fourteen members representing several functions and different countries and was chaired by a Brussels-based product manager. As the integration proceeded and customers demanded more extensive pan-European sales and services, the teams eventually were succeeded by "European Business Centers" (EBCs). A 3M EBC has responsibility and accountability for managing a business throughout Europe, from panning and manufacturing to selling and delivering the product to the customer. One such business center is the "Consumer and Office Markets EBC." The center's six product lines (Home Care, Consumer Stationery, Do-It-Yourself/Paint and Drywall products, Commercial Care, Visual Systems, and Commercial Office Supply) are managed by separate European Business Units (EBUs) with pan-European responsibility. These six product lines are coordinated in each of 3M's eight European regions, with a local organization that mirrors that of the pan-European structure. For example, the German Consumer and Office Markets EBC manager coordinates sales and marketing for six EBUs in that region.[7]

Although perhaps not as far ahead as 3M, many teams today are moving away from pure marketing functions and becoming more cross-functional. The shift is in response to the increased demands from customers for higher quality, greater customization, and reduced delivery lead times. For example, major industrial customers such as Allied Signal, Ford, GM, Motorola, and Texas Instrument have dropped 20 to 90 percent of their suppliers over the last decade in order to reduce reject rates, improve cycle times, and decrease inventories. To create customer satisfaction and stay competitive, the marketing function must be supported and work closely with new product development, design, and manufacturing for speed, flexibility, and high quality. Cross-functional global teams offer one solution to these demands. The marketing function is tied closer than ever to other functions in the corporation.

MANAGEMENT SYSTEMS

Companies can also implement global marketing within their existing organizational structure by instituting new **management systems** as integrating mechanisms. Global budgeting, global performance reviews, and global accounting are some of the general systems that create a basis for globalized strategies. Companies can also achieve greater global emphasis with integration mechanisms such as meetings and informal networks, committees and task forces, and coordinating staff groups and information sharing on a global basis. The advent of electronic communication media such as videoconferencing and electronic mail has also helped develop a global culture in companies.

The choice of integration mechanism depends on the intensity of the global marketing activity.

Informal Coordination

Information sharing about similar experiences in different markets is a first step in achieving integrated strategies. Most companies today are involved in these types of informal exchanges, and they are one reason why the global marketer has to travel so often and so far. Experiences are rarely the stuff of formal reporting, and it usually takes some time spent in mutual discussion before the relevance of a particular experience is recognized.

This type of informal management interaction is difficult to systematize. It is akin to MBWA (management by walking around) on a global scale. The outsider has to come to the country subsidiary as a consultant and friend rather than as a boss on an inspection tour. Such informal cooperation can't be achieved through telecommunications or through written memos. In one study of managers in Swedish multinational firms traveling to subsidiaries abroad, it was found that as many as 44 percent of the managers traveled without specific problem or action objectives, but in order to "cultivate the network."[8]

Coordinating Committees

A number of companies attempt to achieve more effective implementation systems by creating joint committees of regional or country heads that meet on a regular basis. These high-level meetings serve to reinforce ties at the top levels, creating umbrellas for operational coordination and integration between units. Many large multinationals have used such committees for a long time. IBM, GE, and ITT are some of the well-known examples of this, but so are Philips, Siemens, and Volvo in Europe, and Sony, Honda, and Matsushita of Japan. Swapping new-product information and competitive information, sharing market research, selecting which brands to promote as regional or global, setting international standards for sales performance, and synchronizing product launches—it is from these joint committees that more permanent organizational fixtures such as Eurobrand groups or global advertising units develop.

In many cases the higher-level committee efforts are followed up by regular meetings between functional managers or task forces with professionals at various levels. Temporary personnel transfers are also used, although not so commonly. In one study of 35 European multinationals, only 5 sent their head office marketing managers for a stint in a foreign subsidiary, and only 9 transferred their local marketing managers to the head office.

Coordinating Staff

As the so-called "global imperative" is recognized and endorsed at the higher levels, its implementation usually leads to temporary arrangements of meetings between the various country subsidiary managers. The coordination will initially consist of simple consultation, exchange of information, and informal cooperation, but soon the need for a more systematic approach will be clear.

The emergence of permanent coordinating mechanisms from initial temporary management processes is typical of the incremental character of much of the global integration efforts in companies. For example, product design may require a unified task force of designers and engineers from various countries, drawn together in some central location. In automobiles, many companies from various countries have a design office in Southern California, where many of the new design ideas originate. Similarly, they have engineering offices in Germany, where technology is strong.

The need for global marketing thus often leads to the creation of a new staff group with global integration responsibilities but without line authority. The group may facilitate shared new-product development in lead countries, an approach now common in companies such as Procter and Gamble, Nissan, and Nestlé. The group may also facilitate the wedding of global brands to the existing lineup of brands in local campaigns, such as adding Euro-Vizir to P&G's detergents in Britain. The staff may also help develop a more coordinated campaign across the globe, such as when the Sony Walkman was rechristened replacing the "Soundabout" name already launched in Europe. The global staff group can be responsible for organizing the many global meetings that oil the mechanism of the global management effort. There is a need for travel arrangements, hotel accommodations, alignment of schedules, and simple caretaking that can tax the energies of many organizations. The visits from headquarters are expensive distractions unless real business can be transacted—with global marketing and business decisions made at the meetings.[9]

PEOPLE AND CULTURE

In the end, the implementation of global marketing stands or falls with the capability of the people involved. Because of the complexity of the task and the inherent conflict with local management, **people-skills** matter a lot.

If the organizational *structure* is the body and the chassis that hold the car together and the management *systems* are the engine and the gearbox, *people* provide the necessary lubrication that makes the pistons pump and the car run smoothly. And "people" means everybody in the organization, from top management down.

Under its strong CEO, Harold Geneen, ITT was long famed for its efficient operation of a widely diverse group of businesses spread around the globe. When he stepped down, running the conglomerate became impossible, but Rand Areskog, Geneen's successor, successfully sold off unrelated businesses and focused on a few narrower areas. ITT has shifted from basically a telecommunications company to a company in the global recreation and entertainment industry. Both global strategies are successful—under very different top managers.

Durk Jager, whom we met in Chapter 1, turned the P&G operation in Japan around largely by sheer force of personality. Instead of accommodating the cultural norms of Japan, he imposed the more universal values of Procter and Gamble's corporate culture. The result was a more committed work force, a stronger emphasis on P&G's firm-specific advantages, and a successful attack against a domestic competitor's core market. He showed the corporate home office in Cincinnati that its ideas for the marketplace in Japan needed modification as well. Without a strong leader, the local motivation would have sagged, and the home office would not have listened.

Local Acceptance

Global marketing strategies almost always require a leap of faith on the part of local managers, because local conditions are almost always different from other places.[10] A skilled manager must persuade the local managers about the prospect and motivate them to work for the success of the global strategy. Simply forcing the strategy on the local office leads to surreptitious efforts to undermine the global brand, as Henkel found with its Pritt brand (as we saw in Chapter 11, "Globalizing Marketing"). While paying lip service to the global branding concept, the local subsidiary manager went about supporting the existing brands in direct competition with the new global brand.

Research on the acceptance of global strategies demonstrates the importance of allowing country managers to participate in the global strategy formulation process. The acceptability of a global directive from headquarters is directly related to the perceived fairness of the process.[11] Where local managers have been involved in formulating global marketing strategies, they have been much more likely to accept and to implement them. Regardless of the management incentives and penalties adopted to promote local implementation, the major factor in acceptance was what managers call "due process." If a global strategy did not have sufficient local input, managers felt ignored—and acted accordingly. The "people" factor is important.

Another factor is the degree of recognition of the "global imperative" at the local level. In many globalized firms, the local managers are well aware of their

*G*etting the Picture

P&G's Vizir Experience

T H E 1983 successful launch of Vizir, Procter & Gamble's liquid detergent, in Germany, Holland, and France was spearheaded by a novel organizational innovation, a Euroteam. In order to develop and test the new product, the company had appointed one manager from Germany as the head of a Europewide team of experts and managers. With Germany the largest market in Europe and since the new product development had originated there, Germany became a natural lead country in the product development effort.

Even though the product launch was a success, there were some setbacks in the organization of the team. The local country heads were reluctant to participate, since the periodic meetings were time consuming. As a result, the team members were not always given adequate support in their home countries, participation in the Euroteam changed frequently, and attendance at meetings fluctuated. The solution was to distribute Euroteam responsibilities among the various countries to motivate their participation and to make local managers more sensitive to the difficulties involved in the integrated effort.

Procter & Gamble is pursuing the global team further, and the company is instilling a global perspective in all product managers by regular meetings to share ideas of potential value elsewhere. For example, the product modifications to the Pampers diapers originating in Japan have been introduced globally. The new condensed detergents, also from Japan, have been quickly expanded globally. The global perspective has been further strengthened by the appointment of a CEO with extensive experience abroad.

Sources: Bartlett, 1983; Bartlett and Ghoshal, 1989, pp. 93–94; Yoshino, 1990.

dependency on the global network of the organization and are quite willing and able to assume a global perspective.[12] Giving more global responsibility to local managers, however, requires some organizational changes. The headquarters' role is not so much that of pushing a global strategy as facilitating interaction between various local managers who will be directly dependent on each other. The Eurobrand managers at Procter and Gamble (see box "P&G's Vizir Experience") provide one example of this process.

People-skills and country cultures do not always work in predictable ways. As BBD&O, the advertising agency, expanded its Brussels office in anticipation of Europe 1992, the intent was to draw in talent from several continental countries. Instead, the agency found that British and American employees were much more effective, partly because of the language facility, but also because the continental Europeans tended to remain close to their home culture. Southern Europeans, in particular, with their high context cultures tend to be less flexible when asked to jettison preconceived and culture-bound ideas.[13] The French and Italians' attention to dress, for example, tended to blur their appreciation of easy-going, casual spokespersons.

The people-factor directly affects the execution of global advertising strategies. Telling the local marketing manager to work with the branch office of a global agency and that she can no longer work with a long-time friend in a local agency is not a pleasant job. If handled badly, the local manager will leave the company, as happened when Pioneer, the consumer electronics company, centralized its European marketing in Antwerp with advertising given to BBD&O's expanded Brussels office.

Many of these personnel losses are motivated by personal as well as professional reasons. Ford Werke AG in Cologne lost its top marketing manager in Germany when Ford instituted pan-European product development strategies and pulled in design responsibilities from Germany to its European headquarters in Dagenham, England, even though a promotion to England was offered. The head of market research at Brown Boveri, the Swiss electrical machinery manufacturer, left when Swedish Asea took over to create ABB, not wanting to work for a company dominated by Swedes.

Corporate Culture

The fact is that since global strategies often involve centralization, they are also prone to make a company's culture ethnocentric. While the old-style multinationals, companies like Philips of Holland, Nestlé of Switzerland, Beiersdorf (Nivea) of Germany, and Singer (sewing-machines) of the United States, offered products that many consumers around the world vaguely thought were local brands, the new global emphasis has placed nationality in the forefront. The global marketer who carries the orders from the home office needs a lot of interpersonal skill to get the necessary cooperation. While 20 years ago the local manager for an American multinational in Germany had credibility as a local figure, today the position is undermined by the home office's insistence on direct control. It is hardly surprising if the experienced local managers quit as global strategies get implemented.

A lot of coordination and integration activities involve communication. Firms use people and **organizational culture** to enhance communication in different ways. Good communication can:

- *Build a strong corporate culture internationally.* IKEA, the furniture retailer, does this by fostering its Swedish values of egalitarianism, frugality, hard work, and simplicity among its employees worldwide (and IKEA has had more problems doing this in the United States than in Western Europe and Canada).
- *Build a common technical or professional culture.* Elf-Aquitaine, the French oil company, sets high standards for professionalism and technical knowledge to create group affiliation.
- *Build strong financial and planning systems.* Emerson Electric promotes careful planning, financial reporting, and cost reduction as company values.

HONDA is a company with a strong global vision. The impetus derives partly from its founder, Soichiro Honda, who was blocked out of the Japanese home market by powerful and well-established competitors. This pushed the company overseas, and the United States became its primary market. Recognizing its dependence on foreign markets, the company has attempted to create a corporate culture of "three world headquarters": Japan, U.S., and Europe. The company attempts to be an "insider" in all three areas by assembling cars in several different locations (Swindon, UK and Marysville, Ohio are the major sites) and hiring local workers as well as managers. There is little or no "selling" of the global strategy necessary because the company avoids being "Japanese." Products are standardized but often designed outside of Japan; some are developed for specific non-Japanese markets (such as the Concerto for Europe), and cars built abroad are exported back to Japan (such as the Accord from Ohio). The company also takes workers and supervisors (the "associates" as the company calls its employees) from its plants abroad for stints in factories in Japan—and sends many Japanese workers and managers abroad.

Sources: Sakiya, 1987; Pearson and Ehrlich, 1989.

The key notion is that managers in different countries should be induced to communicate and interact more in line with company values than to rely on their different national cultures. Honda's way is a good example (see box, "Honda's Global Management by Culture").

The Expatriate Manager

The discussion so far has treated the local manager as a native of the country. This is the usual case if the manager in question has the marketing responsibility. But for control and communication purposes, many country subsidiaries are run by **expatriates** from the home country. What is their role in the implementation of the global strategy and the local marketing effort?

Apart from their role as headquarters' envoy, the expatriate country heads in a global company have three typical marketing leadership roles to fill.[14] They must:

- Be a high-level contact with existing customers, prospects, and suppliers *in the local market*. The local marketing effort can then be carried out by locals who can follow up at operating levels on contacts provided by the expatriate. This part of the job relates directly to the "relationship marketing" function so prominent in today's customer-oriented firm.
- Be a champion for the local office at *headquarters*. Local requests such as product modifications, advertising approvals, and additional resources need to be explained and justified back home by the expatriate manager.

- Provide *linkages* with the firm's other offices in the *worldwide network* of the firm. Coordinating product launches in different countries, production scheduling, and exchange of market information are examples of the kinds of issues that require close communication links between the various country heads.

The last two tasks are critical when implementing global marketing strategy. While the local marketing task is often similar to the task of marketers anywhere, it is the linkage with headquarters and other country offices that provides the added sources of advantage for the global marketer. The strength of these linkages depends on the expatriate as much as on the native people.

When strategies are globalized, the expatriate manager is often put in a delicate position, since the strategy often reduces the autonomy of the local subsidiary. Being the connecting link with headquarters, it is natural that the expatriate must be the one to explain and implement the strategy locally. This usually involves limiting the local marketing manager's authority, and may force a change of ad agency, sales effort, and termination of distribution contracts. Since in many cases certain parts of the business are consolidated and placed with other country units or at headquarters, the strategy may involve layoffs and voluntary retirements. Often these measures are a threat to an expatriate's authority in the firm and to the existing network of contacts outside the firm. In one fairly typical case in which the expatriate manager was asked to fire 20 percent of the local work force, the manager decided to quit since his standing in the local business community, as well as the firm, was jeopardized.

When strategies are globalized, expatriate managers may need (or want) to be replaced, rotated to another country, or promoted. It is often more difficult to transfer the native head of the local marketing effort or the country manager if a native. In these cases, the companies have options available, discussed below, which can help avoid the natural demotivation that globalization often incurs.

GLOBAL CUSTOMERS

As we have seen repeatedly throughout Part Four, a very clear-cut rationale for the introduction of a globalized marketing strategy is the emergence of global customers. It is easiest to recognize the advantages of a coordinated offering to multinational buyers who can choose in what country to buy. A consistent image, well-recognized brand, assurance of parts, supplies and service, and coordinated pricing are all obvious benefits to a company selling to global customers. With the emergence of global purchasing on the part of smaller customers as well, the benefits of coordination are increased further. When an individual buyer of a personal computer in Toronto, say, can choose between the local stores, buying through a direct import house, via catalog from New York, or on his duty-free visit to Tokyo's Akihabara district or Frankfurt's airport, the need for the computer company to coordinate product specifications, pricing, warranties, and parts distribution is quite clear.

Global Account Management

In practice, however, the coordination is not that easy. The typical solution for the multinational buyer case is for companies to organize **global account managers** or account groups whose sole responsibility is to serve that customer globally. The account managers serve primarily a coordinative function, usually without direct line responsibility over functions. Their tasks involve the coordination of orders from the customer's various locations, the negotiations for uniform prices, the coordination of communications from various sources inside the firm (R&D, manufacturing, parts) to the various customer locations, and, above all, the provision of consistent after-sales service and follow-up from the seller in all countries. The account managers are the global counterparts to the account groups serving similar functions with domestic customers, such as P&G's large account group (over 60 people strong) focused on Wal-Mart.

Global customers naturally force a coordinated marketing approach, with the marketer's local subsidiaries asked to execute similar strategies as elsewhere. These coordinated strategies involve so-called **relationship marketing**, with the account managers and their groups providing special services to the large customer. Instead of treating the customer as one among many similar nameless consumers, relationship marketing increases customer satisfaction by treating the customer as a special client.

This means that extra services can be offered on demand and that the S-O-Ps (standard operating procedures) may be changed for this customer. Banks change opening hours for their corporate customers, packaged good manufacturers help manage inventories for their top wholesalers, and auto companies offer vacation trips for their largest dealers. For some large and favored customers, the global account manager at the head office is the guy they can squeeze to get the lowest global price.[15]

Needless to say, some of these "relationship marketing" tools can be demoralizing for the local subsidiaries, as the buyer actively tries to play headquarters against local sellers. To carry these activities out on a global scale is a challenge, requiring a lot of information sharing and coordination across the seller's subsidiaries. The global account manager needs to have people-skills not only in dealing with the customer but also in dealing with the managers in the local subsidiaries (see box on "H-P's Global Account Management").

Coordination of marketing activities for smaller customers and individual buyers who buy globally is usually more narrowly focused on avoiding the pricing arbitrage possibilities we discussed in Chapter 13. As for distribution control, rather than relying on innovations in organizational structure, firms tend to attempt coordination via more ad hoc measures and specific interventions in the channels as discussed in Chapter 14.

Global account clients can be selected on the basis of several criteria. They are often industry leaders, both in terms of technology and sales. This creates a competitive advantage where it counts and spreads the awareness of the program throughout the industry. The global accounts should have active

IN 1991 HEWLETT-PACKARD launched a global account management program to meet six customers' need for more standardization and support on a global basis. The global account manager (GAM) reports to the field sales manager and the subsidiary manager in the country of the client's home office and works to achieve coordination and to satisfy the performance goals of the account.

Since GAM often takes over the country manager's best and most profitable client, conflicts arise. After a couple of years, H-P decided to offer the country managers an option to have their performance tied partly to the success of the GAM account. In addition, the directive from the center is strongly worded to the country manager: Cooperate or else.

The GAM contact point at the H-P head office is a headquarters account manager (HAM) who works jointly with GAM on technical, pricing, and strategy issues. They also support business development efforts and share best practices from throughout the H-P organization with the country subsidiaries and with the global clients.

The program has grown from 6 to 26 global accounts in three years. Its success is measured in terms of increased orders and satisfaction among the global clients. Internally, the program's success is attributed to top management support, the dual reporting system from GAM to the field operations and the country manager, and the selling of the system inside as a competitive advantage over competitors.

Sources: Gates, 1995; Royal and Lucas, 1995. See also Cases 7 and 8 in Part Four.

---

operations in several countries, including manufacturing and design. This is the source of the advantage of cross-country coordination. There should be an expressed desire for worldwide procurement, price, service, and support agreements. The global buyer, in effect, needs to be organized for centralized buying.

Global account managers and members of their teams need to be located close to their client's head office (or wherever the buying function is located). They have to be prepared to deliver new products, technological support, cost savings ideas, fast delivery times, and quality assurance. New-product development often requires customer involvement, and the account managers are responsible for organizing the client's early involvement in development efforts.

The global account managers can be profit centers, but the required cooperation of the headquarters sales and marketing staff and the local country subsidiary makes it difficult to sort out appropriate revenue sources and cost allocations. The client's home office does not always do the required purchasing but farms it out to one of its country subsidiaries. This means purchases might depend directly on the seller's local manager in that country and not on the global account manager. Because of these ambiguities on both sides of the buyer-seller dyad, the global accounts are better treated as cost centers with revenue-generating potential.

Retail Trade Groups

A special type of global customer consists of the retailers who are resellers of the manufacturer's product lines. These retailers are also becoming globalized.[16]

In most developed countries, the leading five or six retailing chains control well over 50 percent of the total food and drink volume. They are also expanding abroad. Tengelman, the German retailer, owns A&P in the United States, French Carrefour is a leading retailer in Spain and Brazil, and American Safeway is a leading supermarket in Britain. The heavy investments in computer equipment needed for scanners to streamline inventory control and stock the shelves has required these retailers to hire highly qualified staff people who do not hesitate to make strong demands for service from suppliers. For example, the Wal-Mart success in the United States is partly the result of its managers' insistence that manufacturers supply just-in-time inventory. The success of high-quality private labels and store brands is helping fuel the retail chains' expansion. In some European countries store brands account for more than 30 percent of the total market.

In response, consumer goods manufacturers are creating a special form of **retail trade marketing groups**. These groups attempt to meet the powerful retailers' need for customized product design, advertising, direct marketing, and sales promotions. Trade marketing groups learn which of their company's services and products are most needed by a customer, spot opportunities, and detect problems. Members of these groups include personnel from sales, service, manufacturing, logistics, MIS, and other business activities. Nestlé's cooperation with French retailer Casino and the 7-Eleven experience in Japan illustrate these points (see box, "Manufacturers Pay Attention to Retailers").

CONFLICT RESOLUTION

Coordinating the marketing function on a global basis usually means consolidation of local staff, reduced budgets at subsidiaries, and less local autonomy. This naturally threatens to demoralize country managers, who typically lose control first over manufacturing and then gradually over strategic marketing decisions. What remains is usually more tactical decisions about sales promotions, local advertising, and sales.

The local units are crucial for effective execution of global programs. This is where the middlemen are contacted, advertising media are bought, customers are encountered, and sales are made. Even in the case of global customers, whose negotiations may be with a headquarters global account group, the deliveries of the goods or services are usually local. To counter the threat of lowered morale and to resolve actual or potential conflicts, companies have introduced some or all of the following **conflict resolution** practices:

1. *Let country managers retain local brands and marketing budgets.* In many companies country managers maintain a local product and brand portfolio. While they may have little control over global or regional brands, they have full

*G*etting the Picture

Manufacturers Pay Attention to Retailers

A CONSUMER GOODS company such as Nestlé has unique contributions to bring to its partnerships with retailers. Its leading global brands offer strong appeal. The products offer high quality at competitive prices. The company's market research provides detailed knowledge of consumer habits and requirements, and product R&D generates a stream of improvements and new products.

When Nestlé encountered some conflict about shipments and service with Casino, a large French retailer, the company decided to leverage these resources by establishing a retail trade group focused on Casino. The trade group initiated a series of cooperative meetings to develop joint marketing, logistics, and sales efforts. For example, the partners agreed to test a joint breakfast promotion, with 10 Nestlé brands matched against 10 store brands to help determine which products sell well. The companies will jointly analyze bar code information and scanner data to create a database of how to build customer loyalty for brands and stores while reducing costs. Casino will get help to find out which products need to be stocked more (and which less), while Nestlé will get help to reduce supply channel delays (in France goods-to-market time for breakfast cereals is 11 weeks compared to 3 weeks in the U.S.).

A similar type of alignment that helps manufacturers offer low prices without jeopardizing their clout in regular channels is represented by the various tie-ups arranged by 7-Eleven in Japan. Companies such as Philip Morris, Hershey, and Häagen-Dazs will make specially designed products available for sale in 7-Eleven stores only. For example, under one arrangement, the Kraft division of Philip Morris will sell smaller-sized cheesecakes through the convenience store chain. Although reflective of the power of 7-Eleven in Japan, the alliances are also illustrative of how Western manufacturers seem more able to cope with the new distribution outlets in Japan than their domestic counterparts.

Sources: Gates, 1995; Johansson and Hirano, 1995; Simmons, 1990.

responsibility for the marketing programs of their local brands. They control promotional budget allocations between the brands and the amount allocated to specific tactics such as sales contests and in-store couponing. Also, they have a role to play in global brands. Even though the ad agency choice may be made higher up, they can choose the agency for sales promotions and for direct marketing efforts.

2. *Solicit country managers' input for new-product development.* Country managers, especially in leading markets, are well positioned to develop and test new products. Especially where new products are market rather than technology driven, the local managers' inputs become crucial. Companies in which the local product manager reports to the country head rather than to a global product manager tend to have a higher success rate for new products.[17]

Bausch & Lomb, the optics and glass maker, improved its new-product development success by switching from a global to a regional substructure. Each region has its own product development team, and each local manager participates in the regional level's decisions about priorities for new-product development. New product ideas from local markets are encouraged, and after the idea is presented and evaluated at the regional level, it passes to a global product coordinating committee for worldwide sharing.

3. *Give country managers lead roles in global teams.* To create mutual dependence and improve implementation, it is important that over time different country managers take responsibility for a global brand or at least one component of the global marketing. As in the Vizir case, the country managers are often at the receiving end of the stick, so to speak, when they have to persuade other country managers to participate in a global program, and this helps make them sympathetic in turn to the requests of other global team leaders. It is important that the country managers assume responsibilities in the global teams, so that the local subsidiary's role is endorsed by the boss. Lower-level managers, such as the local product manager and advertising manager, will then have the requisite support and legitimacy to implement the local part of the global campaigns.

4. *Provide international transfers for country managers.*

A clear perspective on foreign local markets helps when making global marketing decisions. Consequently, global marketing groups at the head office would benefit from foreign national marketing team members. Unfortunately, frequent international transfers of marketing managers are still rare. There is even less exchange between subsidiaries in different countries. In a recent study, only 4 of 35 companies reported any regular transfers of marketing people between country subsidiaries.[19]

Foreign marketing managers are caught in a double-bind.[20] A lack of experience at corporate limits the foreign managers from reaching the upper echelons where their different perspective could be very valuable. However,

Matsushita expatriate manager of a semiconductor plant in Washington State. Although the Japanese management style differs from the traditional Western approach, the success of the Japanese has given legitimacy to many of their transplanted practices.

© Alan Levenson.

since most global companies do not offer the marketing managers the opportunity to work at the home office, there is no way to accumulate the required corporate experience.

If neither marketing nor country managers rotate, their experiences remain parochial. This can be a disadvantage since the implementation of global strategies requires local sacrifices for the benefit of the entire company. Creating alternative career opportunities for country managers outside their home market can broaden their perspectives and lessen conflict with global or regional managers.

5. *Involve the country managers in the formulation of the global marketing strategy.*

In the end, the best medicine against local subversion of global marketing is to co-opt the country managers by inviting them to help design the global marketing strategy. The impetus for a globalized strategy is almost always from the top, since headquarters marketers are the ones who most easily notice the potential savings and gains. But once the start has been made, country managers from, at the least, the leading countries and the markets most directly affected should be directly involved in the strategy formulation. The implementation success of global strategies tends to be directly proportional to the level of local involvement in strategy formulation.[20]

There are, of course, obvious problems associated with having managers from several countries involved in the strategy formulation:

- Local managers propose strategies without a full understanding of the global situation.
- Country managers feel forced to put their local interests first.
- Communication between managers of different nationalities is not always easy.

These obstacles have made many companies reluctant to involve too many country managers in their global strategy development. Instead of relying on foreign managers, many companies rely on home office nationals with experience abroad. This is the common style in Japanese corporations, with the global strategies developed in Japan and disseminated to local subsidiaries. The local perspectives are mainly represented through Japanese managers with experience in the various countries, a solution made possible because Japanese multinationals consistently try to develop top career paths that include rotations to overseas sites. Unfortunately, the local perspectives brought to the home office for the formulation of the global strategies are sometimes quite biased and unreliable, especially when based on only one or two individual experiences.

Japanese companies are doing well in the Americas where most of the Japanese corporations can draw on a number of senior internal advisers with direct country experience for the strategy formulations. By contrast, in the European market most companies are dependent on a few individuals with direct experience in any one country, making that country national's expertise more important. But the language and cultural barriers—and the Japanese consensus-style decision making—make such relative outsiders' advice difficult to assimilate. Not surprisingly, the Japanese are baffled by the fragmented European markets, and the EU integration has been warmly welcomed by them.

The **ethnocentricity** of the Japanese corporations is paralleled in some global European companies: Mercedes and Siemens have strong German identities, Philips is Dutch at the core, and IKEA is Swedish while Marks & Spencer is English and Benetton is Italian. This situation arises not only from the desire to avoid conflict in strategy formulation, but also to draw strength from the cultural heritage from the country.

American companies sometimes, though not always, show less ethnocentricity in the handling of their country managers. This is commonly attributed to the openness and multiculturalism of the American society. Regardless, a lack of ethnocentricity becomes desirable and beneficial because the American multinationals do have such a large share of their resources located overseas. As data show, both in absolute value and in terms of proportions, the American global companies have more assets abroad than any other country. About one-fifth of the output of American firms is produced offshore, and about a quarter of all U.S. imports and exports represent intrafirm transfers. There is an accompanying cadre of foreign nationals in management positions in the local subsidiaries, providing a rich source of local market information and know-how. Some observers argue that future American competitive strength will come increasingly from the judicious use of these national managers inside the global organization, and that the absence of promising global careers in European and Japanese companies will make it impossible for them to attract the best local managerial talent.[21]

Involving the country managers in the formulation of global marketing strategies is not only good for the quality of the strategy designed and the collaboration that makes local implementation easier, but also because it makes the country manager's job more interesting, attracting the best local talents.

SUMMARY

The inherent conflict between local country managers and the top-down imposition of global marketing, needs to be recognized and handled very candidly throughout the organization. The limits of the resources allocated to the local marketing budgets need to be justified to the local managers and appropriate compensating measures in terms of new global team responsibilities should be considered. In addition it is important that local managers be consulted early in the global strategy formulation process to get their input and stimulate acceptance of the globalization and to encourage cooperation with the local implementation of the strategy. Not many companies can go as far as GE and ABB, whose strong and single-minded CEOs virtually force local implementation of the global strategy, but any globalizing effort involves a certain overcoming of local resistance.

Of the various organization structures that the large multinational firm can operate with, a split between a domestic and an international division is consistently a negative factor in implementing globalized marketing. Global product divisions without a division between the domestic and the foreign markets is more conducive to a global strategy, but there is almost always a need to consider a strengthening of the foreign market perspective. This has led many globalizing companies into a matrix structure with a geographic dimension cutting across the product divisions, which has meant that local country managers are charged with coordination of the firm's involvement in the country while global product managers are responsible for the global marketing program for each particular product line.

While a firm may globalize marketing strategy, marketing tactics usually need to be adapted to local conditions. Thus, the implementation of a global strategy involves a considerable amount of local activity, and it is important that the local subsidiary manager is motivated to support the global brand. This is often accomplished by the creation of global teams focusing on specific brands, on specific tactical measures, or even special global campaigns. These teams can take the temporary form of task forces rather than becoming permanent fixtures in the organizational structure. However, over time the success of such teams has tended to make them the prime vehicle for global marketing implementation, and companies have come to institutionalize them. The added advantage is that serving on a global team is a good way for a country manager to become familiar with corporate headquarters and other country managers, creating a basis for future promotions up the corporate ladder.

The role of people and organizational culture in the implementation of global marketing is also crucial. Regardless of how globalized the organizational structure and the management systems are, there is always need for people-skills to lubricate the relationships and make the organization function. Global communications require the telephone, faxes, and perhaps multimedia, but in the end the global marketer needs to travel a lot and meet face to face with people. This also has the advantage that the marketer can stay closer to the customer, a particularly important factor when organizing for global customers.

KEY TERMS

Conflict resolution p. 632
Ethnocentricity p. 636
Expatriates p. 628
Export department structure p. 611
Global account managers p. 630
Global marketing director p. 620
Global network as an asset p. 616
Global teams p. 621

Global product divisions p. 612
Horizontal networks p. 615
International division structure p. 611
Management systems p. 623
Matrix organization p. 613
Network theory p. 618
Organizational culture p. 627
Organizational design p. 610
People-skills p. 624
Regional organization p. 612

Relationship marketing p. 630
Retail trade marketing groups p. 632
Strategic business unit p. 611
Transnational organization p. 615

DISCUSSION QUESTIONS

1. Discuss how a global team would work to create the kind of pricing "corridor" to control gray trade discussed in Chapter 13. How would it work with the local subsidiaries to create and implement the kind of global advertising campaign created by Goodyear in Chapter 15?

2. "Global managers are made, not born. This is not a natural process. We are herd animals. We like people who are like us. But there are many things you can do. Obviously, you rotate people around the world. There is no substitute for line experience in three or four countries to create a global perspective. You also encourage people to work in mixed-nationality teams. You *force* them to create personal alliances across borders. This is why we put so much emphasis on teams."

   So says Percy Barnevik, CEO of Asea Brown Boveri (ABB), the large Swedish-Swiss multinational in electrical machinery.[22] Discuss what is gained by such rotation and forced personal alliances. Any risks involved? What alternatives to the team concept are there?

3. The standard approach for multinational expansion for American companies in the past was to establish foreign subsidiaries run by American expatriates, reporting back to headquarters, and treating countries and regions as separate profit centers. Contrast this with the newer ABB and GE approach of treating each local company as a profit center with the market defined globally and with country managers in charge of governmental relations and labor relations. Why is global marketing easier to formulate and implement in the latter structures?

4. Why are people-skills so important in the implementation of global marketing?

5. For a consumer product of your choice (autos, soft drinks, or apparel, for example), take the role of a native country manager and argue why a global marketing strategy could be a mistake. Then take the role of a global team member and argue the opposite.

NOTES

1. The burdensome tasks are well documented by Davidson and Haspeslagh, 1982.

2. This is the terminology proposed by Bartlett and Ghoshal, 1989.

3. There is some evidence that the Japanese managers' people-skills and company commitment help motivate subsidiaries to adopt a global strategy—see Yip and Johansson, 1993.

4. See Forsgren and Johanson, 1992.

5. The "hypercompetition" concept was first advanced by D'Aveni, 1994.

6. Much of this and the following section draws on Gates' excellent review (Gates, 1995).

7. These examples are taken from the review by Gates, 1995, and from 3M corporate publications.

8. From Axelsson et al., 1992.

9. Huddleston, 1990, shows vividly why visits from headquarters can be a real distraction for local management.

10. It is useful to remember that a uniform global strategy more or less explicitly assumes that headquarters has better information than locals. In specific instances, such as the degree of price sensitivity on the part of local customers, the notion that headquarters "knows better" than the locals is debatable—see Assmus and Wiese, 1995.

11. The importance of local "ownership" of the strategy formulation process for fairness evaluations was empirically demonstrated by Kim and Mauborgne, 1993.

12. See Hanni et al., 1995.

13. The example of Goodyear's development process of pan-regional advertising in Latin America discussed in Chapter 15 shows how a global mindset can be instilled—and how local knowledge can be integrated into the strategy formulation—by repeated interactions between local subsidiary managers and headquarters personnel (Hanni et al., 1995).

14. Thanks to Norio Nishi of Canada's Commonwealth Bank in Tokyo for suggesting the three roles.

15. See Royal and Lucas, 1995, for a rather cynical view of global account management.

16. This section relies heavily on Gates' up-to-date research on current practices among multinationals. See Gates, 1995.

17. This was one of the empirical findings of Theuerkauf et al., 1993.

18. This surprising finding is reported by Gates, 1995. Despite the many reasons why experiences in different countries are good for management development, especially in marketing, relatively few companies seem to be able to create effective programs to induce people to take a stint abroad.

19. This dilemma is well illustrated in the *Business International* 1990 report.

20. From Kim and Mauborgne's, 1993 findings.

21. This point is forcefully made by Ferdows, 1993.

22. See Taylor, 1992.

SELECTED REFERENCES

Assmus, Gert, and Carsten Wiese. "How to Address the Gray Market Threat Using Price Coordination." *Sloan Management Review* 36, no. 3 (1995) pp. 31–42.

Axelsson, Bjorn; Jan Johanson; and Johan Sundberg. "Managing by International Traveling." Chapter 7 in Forsgren and Johanson, 1992.

Bartlett, Christopher. "Procter & Gamble Europe: Vizir Launch." Harvard Business School case 384-139, 1983.

Bartlett, Christopher A., and Sumantra Ghoshal. *Managing across Borders: The Transnational Solution.* Boston: Harvard Business School Press, 1989.

Business International. "Marketing Strategies for Global Growth and Competitiveness." October, 1990.

D'Aveni, Richard. *Hypercompetition.* New York: Free Press, 1994.

Davidson, William H., and Philippe Haspeslagh. "Shaping a Global Product Organization." *Harvard Business Review*, July–August 1982, pp. 125–32.

Ferdows, Kasra. "Leveraging America's Foreign Production Assets." Working paper, Georgetown University, School of Business Administration, OPMT-1977-01-293, 1993.

Forsgren, Mats, and Jan Johanson, eds. *Managing Networks in International Business.* Philadelphia: Gordon and Breach, 1992.

Gates, Stephen. "The Changing Global Role of the Marketing Function: A Research Report." *The Conference Board*, report no. 1105-95-RR, 1995.

Hakansson, Hakan. *Corporate Technological Behavior: Cooperation and Networks.* London: Routledge, 1989.

Halliburton, Chris, and Reinhard Huenerberg. "Pan-European Marketing—Myth or Reality?" *Journal of International Marketing* 1, no. 3 (1993), pp. 77–92.

Halliburton, Chris, and Ian Jones. "Global Individualism—Reconciling Global Marketing and Global Manufacturing." *Journal of International Marketing* 2, no.4 (1994), pp. 79–88.

Hanni, David A.; John K. Ryans; and Ivan R. Vernon. "Coordinating International Advertising—The Goodyear Case Revisited for Latin America." *Journal of International Marketing* 3, no. 2 (1995), pp. 83–98.

Huddleston, Jackson N., Jr. *Gaijin Kaisha: Running a Foreign Business in Japan.* Tokyo: Charles E. Tuttle, 1990.

Johansson, Johny K., and Masaaki Hirano. "The Recession and Japanese Marketing." *International Executive*, 1995.

Kim, W. Chan, and Renee A. Mauborgne. "Making Global Strategies Work." *Sloan Management Review*, Spring 1993, pp. 11–27.

Mazur, Laura, and Judie Lannon. "Crossborder Marketing: Lessons from 25 European Success Stories." *Economist Intelligence unit*, February 1994.

Pearson, A. E., and S. P. Ehrlich. "Honda Motor Co. and Honda of America (A)." Harvard Business School case no. 9-390-111, 1989.

Royal, Weld, and Allison Lucas. "Global Pricing and Other Hazards." *Sales & Marketing Management* 147, no. 8 (August 1995), pp. 80–83.

Sakiya, Tetsuo. *Honda Motor: The Men, the Management, and the Machines.* Tokyo: Kodansha, 1987.

Simmons, Tim. "A Global Brand of Dialog." *Supermarket News* 40, no. 28 (July 9, 1990), p. 2.

Taylor, William. "The Logic of Global Business: An Interview with ABB's Percy Barnevik." Reprinted in Bartlett, Christopher A., and Sumantra Ghoshal. *Transnational Management*. Homewood, IL: Irwin, 1992, pp. 892–908.

Theuerkauf, Ingo; David Ernst; and A. Mahini. "Think Local, Organize . . ." *McKinsey Quarterly*, no. 1 (1993), pp. 107–114.

Uchitelle, Louis. "Gillette's World View: One Blade Fits All." *New York Times*, January 3, 1994, p. C3.

Yip, George, and Johny K. Johansson. "Global Market Strategies of U.S. and Japanese Business." Working paper, Marketing Science Institute, Cambridge, MA, 1993, pp. 93–102.

Yoshino, Michael. *Procter & Gamble Japan (A)(B)(C)*. Harvard Business School case nos. 9-391-003, 004, 005, 1990.

18

The Future of Global Marketing

"The future is now"

After studying this chapter, you should understand the following global marketing issues:

1. The main threat against global marketing is a possible rise of protectionism associated with national and international crises—political and military crises more than economic ones.

2. The threat against local marketing, especially in emerging markets, is the naturally unequal distribution of benefits from open markets and free trade among the average citizens. The frustrations can lead to a backlash against free market practices, and thus further restraints.

3. The logic and force of the technological innovations, including the Internet, that drive the global imperative are such that any enterprise operating in a competitive market needs to face them. Marketing management needs to be *global management*, even if foreign entry is difficult and marketing actions need to be localized.

4. In most markets of the future, strong global marketing needs to be localized, and strong local marketing needs to be globalized. This is the task of global localization and local globalization, respectively.

GLOBAL MARKETING is in many ways only at the beginning. Global brands have been around for a long time and globally standardized products are certainly not new. But what has emerged in the last decade is a much more emphatic stress on the centralization and coordination of marketing strategies and tactics around the world to take advantage of scale savings and demand spillovers. Will this development continue and intensify, or are there threats against global marketing that will limit its progress? And how can the firm achieve "global localization," the popular expression reflecting the need to be global and local at the same time?

For most companies, not all large, the answers to these questions are obvious. The global imperative means that marketing in the future has to be global to succeed. Marketers have to adopt a global perspective or else be left behind. Companies from Microsoft in PC software, to Ford in automobiles, to Unilever in toiletries, to Beck's in beer, to Marriott in hotels, to Armstrong in wall paneling, to Bridgestone in water tanks and tires, and innumerable others, all share this perspective. This chapter will examine the global imperative and how developments in computers and information technology may affect global marketing in the future. As the reader will find out, despite threats against foreign entry and problems in local marketing, the future of global management is bright.

Going On-Line Gets Marketers Right to the Customer

Efficient, one-on-one communication with customers anywhere—a marketer's dream. No wonder organizations are exploring the potential of on-line marketing. Electronic messages are bringing marketers right to the customer's desktop. Geographic boundaries fade. Paradoxically, geographic and individual differences become *more* important—on-line customers expect and receive individually tailored products and messages.

For some marketers, on-line services *are* the product. Such services, under brand names like CompuServe and America Online, are common in the United States. Elsewhere, electronic marketers must educate potential buyers. In Europe, slowness to adopt computer technology has challenged Europe Online, which hopes to tap into a growing market by persuading Europeans to view their computers as worthy communication tools. The company is betting that European consumers will prefer a service offering distinctively European information. U.S. providers of on-line services in Europe may face stiff competition from France's Infogrames Entertainment, a standout in multimedia programming.

Someday, perhaps, on-line transactions will become so easy that the location of buyer and seller will be irrelevant. For now, however, the most common application of on-line marketing is offering information about organizations and their products. On the World Wide Web (the part of the Internet where users can send graphic images as well as text), more and more organizations are setting up home pages. These Web sites, combining pictures, graphics, text, and sound, reach a self-selected audience at a relatively low cost. Time Warner used its Web site to promote the release of *Batman Forever* with excerpts from the movie. The home page for Zima alcoholic beverages builds brand loyalty by letting consumers join a virtual club, Tribe Z. Club members can visit members-only Web pages, receive free software, and send e-mail to other members.

Effective on-line promotion is more challenging than it may seem. The medium is new enough that few marketers have tapped its potential. Also, the culture of cyberspace generally despises promotion. Therefore, in promotion as well as products, on-line marketers must deliver value as defined by each customer. Determining who will provide value on-line—and even what value means to these cyber-consumers—will be the tricky part.

Sources: Nathaniel C. Nash, "Europe Online Dealt a Blow as Third Partner Abandons Ship," *New York Times*, November 6, 1995, p. D1; Gail Edmondson, "Will Europe Roar Down the Infobahn?" *Business Week*, March 6, 1995, pp. 48–49; John Markoff, "A Credit Card for On-Line Sprees," *New York Times*, October 15, 1994, p. 37; Elizabeth Corcoran, "The Marketers Are On-Lining Up for You," *Washington Post*, September 27, 1995, pp. F1, F4.

INTRODUCTION

The information society has arrived, and it means global business for computer and software companies. The new products created by high-technology firms need marketing to succeed. Marketing forces the companies to explain exactly what benefits will come from the new technology. And as the new products broaden the market base by entering foreign markets, marketing must be globalized (see box, "The Strategic Value of Information Networks").

High-technology products and the marketing efforts in their behalf tend to follow the Vernon international product cycle that characterized the initial American overseas entries.[1] The inventing company from any country marches abroad, markets its new product in many countries, and over time globalizes its marketing. And in less technology-intensive cases, a similar process occurs, as globalized marketing becomes possible because of homogenized mature markets and global communication capabilities. The promise of global marketing can be fulfilled only with free trade and free investment flows, functioning

*G*etting the
Picture

The Strategic
Value of
Information
Networks

HARDWARE COMPUTER MAK-ERS such as Compaq and PC software companies such as Novell have the same marketing target: the virtual corporation, a networked organization with operations distributed globally. To win the coming battle against software competitors, Novell is turning to marketing and global branding.

Denver-based Novell Inc. is the company behind Netware, a leading PC network operating system. Its product line also includes Wordperfect and the rights to the Unix operating system. The company itself is not well known even among its customer base and does not have the world recognition of Micro-soft, a competitor in crucial product markets.

In order to create better recognition and a stronger global presence, Novell hired a new senior vice president for corporate marketing with global re-sponsibilities in early 1995. Christine G. Hughes came from the Xerox Corporation where she was head of integrated marketing. She understands the role for corporate marketing worldwide: "If you look not just at the industry but at where societies and businesses are going, the ability to get information and to really digest it and make it applicable to what you are doing is the most overriding theme we have had in the computer industry in many years . . . There is a difference between looking at Netware as a component and looking at it as infrastructure. Once you start looking at it as infrastructure it becomes strategic. . . . We have to be higher up in the buyer's organization, and address the chief information officers and the chief executive officers."

Sources: Fisher, 1995; La Polla, 1995.

global communications, and shared economic prosperity. The future of global marketing depends directly on the existence of favorable environmental conditions.

In what follows, the threats and opportunities in the global environment relative to foreign entry will first be discussed. Two critical areas will be covered: the threat from politics and protectionism and the impact of free trade areas. Threats against local marketing in the politically sensitive emerging economies will then be assessed along with ethical concerns in local marketing. Then the role of the emerging information superhighway in enabling global marketing and creating a truly global market will be analyzed. The chapter concludes with a discussion of global localization, the role of strategy execution, and how companies manage to be local and global simultaneously.

POLITICS AND FOREIGN ENTRY

Protectionism

There should be little doubt on the part of a marketer about the threat to the global trade regime from **protectionist forces**, wherever and whenever they arise. Tariff barriers and quotas keep more efficient exporters away from domestic competitors in home markets. There are various ways of getting over

An advertisement placing Novell in the global network picture. With the branding successes of technology-based companies such as Microsoft and Intel, other high-tech companies are using advertising to create recognized and valuable brand names.

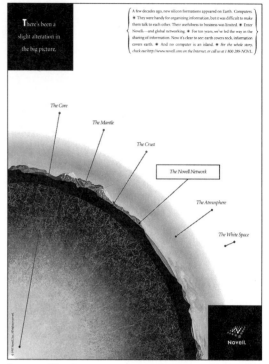

There's been a slight alteration in the big picture.

A few decades ago, new silicon formations appeared on Earth. Computers. ✳ They were handy for organizing information, but it was difficult to make them talk to each other. Their usefulness to business was limited. ✳ Enter Novell—and global networking. ✳ For ten years, we've led the way in the sharing of information. Now it's clear to see: earth covers rock, information covers earth. ✳ And no computer is an island. ✳ *For the whole story,* check out http://www.novell.com on the Internet, or call us at 1 800 289-NOVL.

The Core

The Mantle

The Crust

The Novell Network

The Atmosphere

The White Space

Novell.

Courtesy Novell.

the hurdles, but they invariably lead to higher costs. Investing in overseas manufacturing may not be economically justified unless protective barriers force the issue. Strategic alliance and licensing transfer technologies, but carry risks that need to be compensated. Demands for government equity shares in joint ventures jeopardize entry and complicate management of the local operation.

From a marketing perspective, these issues take on a different color. In principle, it is possible to do global marketing under any mode of entry. Whether exporting (Mazda), licensing (McDonald's), joint venturing (Xerox), or running wholly owned subsidiaries (IBM), a company can globalize its marketing. The problem is that the company's products and services may not be competitive in the protected markets because of the price escalation caused by tariff barriers. As we have seen, global marketing almost always involves a certain amount of uniformity across countries. Trade barriers distort the markets and the positions of the products, making uniform marketing difficult if not impossible. In protected markets, imported low-end products easily become positioned as high-priced luxuries (Chrysler cars in Japan, Budweiser beer in Asia, Levi's jeans in Europe).

With protected markets, most local marketing is necessarily unique to the country environment. It is designed to deal with the markets' distorted price structures and it attempts to nullify domestic producers' artificial advantages. It is hardly a coincidence that in the many protected markets after World War II marketing became a matter of adaptation to local customs. In protected markets, imposing global uniformity on marketing will be suicidal. Open and free markets are a precondition for global marketing.

A protectionist tendency is why the current political difficulties in Eastern Europe, Russia, China, Mexico, and elsewhere, which apparently stem from a nationalistic impulse and a desire to return to a socialist past, are threats to global marketing. By the same token, the liberation of South Africa, the free market conversion of India, the strengthening of democracy in Latin America, and the thrust toward free markets in former communist countries are all positive signs. On balance, the picture looks positive, with WTO, the new GATT, poised to rebuff any threats. The high cost of protectionism has been recognized all over the world.[2] Nonfree markets are a luxury.

Free Trade Areas

The regional free trade areas (EU, NAFTA, APEC) have made "regional" a substitute for "country" and "global." In principle, dividing up the globe into several trade regions is inefficient when compared to pure free trade among all nations. In practice, however, regional trade areas justify globalization strategies, offering sufficient *size* for scale returns in manufacturing and marketing, and sufficient market *similarity* for standardization of products and services and allowing uniformity of the communications mix.

Whether or not regional integration becomes a stepping stone toward further integration remains to be seen. The experience in Europe is positive in this regard. As the EU integration gained momentum, several EFTA countries (members of the European Free Trade Area) initiated negotiations toward EU membership. By the beginning of 1995 most of the seven original EFTA members had become members of the greater European Economic Area (EEA). Countries are apparently not willing to let existing membership loyalties stop them when a better deal is available. From this perspective, one would expect free trade areas to gradually expand to include new members and in the process become more global. The negotiations about NAFTA's inclusion of Chile and other South American countries is a typical example. Free trade areas are perhaps a step on the way toward global free trade, not an effort to place barriers between regional members and nonmember countries.

THE DARK SIDE OF MARKETING

With the failure of the planned economies around the world, marketing is rapidly becoming a household word in the remotest parts of the globe. In advanced countries it is spreading from the field of private business into hospitals, symphony orchestras, and other nonprofit organizations, and into government agencies. Marketing is riding high in markets where it is traditionally viewed with aversion. Some people will still focus on what they see as the dark side of marketing.

Getting the Picture

McDonald's Two Faces

IN ITS MOSCOW fast-food outlets, McDonald's initially introduced a system of two separate entrance doors, one for customers with rubles, one for customers with hard currency only. The customers with hard currency got preferential treatment and were given quicker service and more waiters. Many locals were not served when there were hard currency customers still in line.

As long as the Russians saw only foreigners in the hard currency line, things went relatively smoothly. This was, after all, the ways thing used to be. But as some of the Russians with luck and hard work managed to get access to hard currency, the mood changed. The frustrations and envy on the part of the local currency line began to take their toll,

and the outlets started to encounter some violent reactions. Words were exchanged, and fights between the people in the two lines became a common occurrence.

Rather than change the system, McDonald's outlets introduced security guards to keep problem makers away. The inflation in the local ruble was simply too high not to try to sell as much food as possible for hard currency, especially since many of the ingredients (including some of the potatoes used in the french fries) were imported. As the ruble stabilized, and as Russian competition appeared, the need for the two lines disappeared.

Sources: Saito, 1991; Specter, 1995.

The Legitimacy of Free Markets

Marketing requires free markets, and free markets are proving to be a big headache for many of the emerging nations. **Free markets** require supplies of products, information about demand, and a currency of exchange. Emerging countries have a short supply of these ingredients, because of the planned economy in the past. This means the countries have trouble creating working marketplaces, where exchanges can be transacted. This holds for stock exchanges as well as for retail stores and business-to-business markets. An example of how the marketplace can be distorted by these factors is McDonald's approach in Moscow (see box, "McDonald's Two Faces").

Needless to say, these problems of free markets create frustrations and anger among many people who happen not to be among the lucky ones. In Russia, crime has become a major problem for Western businesses. Shipments to stores regularly get hijacked, store owners have to pay bribery "fees" to distributors to get access to merchandise, and there is a black market for most Western goods. Not surprisingly, various Mafia-style organizations have sprung up, making life and commerce very difficult.[3] The solution clearly lies in economic progress with shared benefits, but that promise is as yet largely unfulfilled. To engage in heavy marketing activities under such conditions is not only bad business, but bad politics. The result is likely to be more regulation, less free enterprise, and a return to the past.

The Ethics of Marketing

There is a question about the extent to which the whole of **ethics of marketing** thinking and practice is acceptable. In many newly opened markets, customers are not used to the ways of Western marketing, and many can be expected to voice opposition to the unabashed trumpeting of a firm's product. It is not just the hard-hitting advertisements that may cause problems; people may find the "everything has a price" mentality abhorrent. Certain promotional activities are likely to become regulated as the free-for-all euphoria in the new countries recedes. It will be important for marketers to correctly read the mood of the populace and to not engage in practices that will stir up negative sentiments. Ethical marketing is likely to be enforced much more in some of these countries than it is in the United States.

The playbook for the company's strategies might well be taken from the company responses to the various problems encountered in the consumer movement in the United States. When Lotus Corporation proposed a database development drawing on individual credit records and social security numbers, the ensuing uproar from privacy advocates forced the company to abandon the plan.[4] The calls for boycotts of brands because of offensive advertising (Camel cigarettes, Powermaster malt liquor), the loss of consumer goodwill on the part of Intel because of the Pentium chip problem, and the imposition of fines for misleading advertising by Volvo are only a few examples.

These issues will seem tame by comparison to the more basic problems in emerging markets. The marketer in China is likely to find it difficult to protect a successful brand from imitators, at the same time as people will challenge the foreign influence of a global brand. When Levi's jeans first attempted to uphold its control of its branded jeans against knockoffs in China, the government questioned the idea that a brand name could be copyrighted and then challenged Levi's to leave the country.[5] Similar anticapitalist sentiments are likely to surface elsewhere, as ethical marketing questions are raised. Global marketers doing local marketing in emerging markets ignore ethical concerns at their peril.

GLOBAL STRATEGY AND INTERNET

The increase in global communications capabilities has facilitated global strategies tremendously. In fact, it is hard to imagine that global marketing would have gotten very far without global telecommunications, satellite TVs, and the ubiquitous fax machines. The new information superhighway of the Internet promises to be another major step in the path toward globalization at the same time that it becomes a new, truly global, marketplace.

Global Communications

The **information superhighway** is the popular name for the new communications technology connecting computers in different countries around the world.

The Internet has become the global information superhighway, and most observers predict exponential growth in the future. Its potential as a marketplace for ideas, products, and services is great, and the uses so far have only scratched the surface.

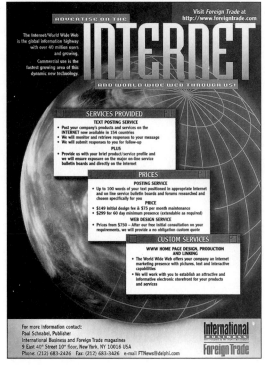

Courtesy International Business and Foreign Trade Magazines.

The basic building block is an electronic connection via telephone lines (or hardwired) between two computers located in different countries and perhaps on different continents. With the advent of fiberoptic cable and digital technology, this connection's capability for carrying voice and video images in addition to text and data increased dramatically. The other part of the equation is the ready availability of personal computers in offices and homes. As the memory and processing capability of these computers have increased with dramatically reduced prices, it has become possible for individual users to tap into the networks linking the computers in different countries.[6]

The result has been a revolution in global communications. The cost of communicating with any overseas location has been cut dramatically—once a basic connection fee is paid, many of these communications cost little more than a local phone call. The communications can be real time, like a telephone call conversation via a keyboard, or the message can be sent as electronic mail ("e-mail"), the message delivered within seconds to the receiver's computer. The feasibility of sending directives, making inquiries, coordinating shipments, and requesting information—all standard administrative items in a global marketing push—has become much greater. Further, not only are global marketing strategies easier to execute through these new implementation tools;

they are more effective as the organization linked electronically necessarily ends up with a common language of communication, usually English. The first task for some country managers today is to learn how to access a computer and how to express themselves in written English.

A Global Marketplace

The ease and efficiency of **internal communications** in the global firm are only one part of the benefits from the information superhighway. The more far-reaching benefit is the emergence of the communication and transaction links between buyers and sellers. The global information highway has created a new marketplace. This development is still in its embryonic stage but is likely to grow immensely in importance in the future.

The **Internet marketplace** started with companies doing market research, typically questionnaire surveys and focus groups, offering general product information, and placing want ads for systems analysts. As the accessibility and versatility of the medium has grown, its capabilities as a true global market are becoming realized.

Firms are now "setting up shop" in networks such as the **World Wide Web (WWW)** part of Internet. Establishing a presence in this "market" means creating software packages with addresses that can be freely accessed by browsers in the same way a shopping mall visitor passes by store windows. The packages describe the firm's products and services and are equivalent to advertisements and catalogs, featuring pictures and text, but can also have audio and video capability in typical multimedia style. Shopping can take place via order forms on the screen and be paid for via a credit card charge.[7]

All the features of a typical buying transaction are in place on WWW, although there are still technological issues to be resolved. One issue is the possibility of fraudulent use of credit card charges. At present, the technology for cross-checking valid credit card numbers and unauthorized charges is relatively primitive, but advances promise to alleviate some of these problems. One solution is provided by First Virtual Holdings, a software company specializing in financial transactions. Exhibit 18.1 shows the purchase process on Internet and the accompanying credit checks as devised by First Virtual[8]— what happens when the consumer sees an ad on Internet, decides to buy, and charges to an account at First Virtual. First Virtual responds by asking for confirmation and if received posts the transaction to the consumer's account. If confirmation is not forthcoming, First Virtual goes through several options to identify the problem, cancels the purchase, and perhaps withdraws the account. As always in the "virtual" world of multimedia, all "actions" are electronically guided and although the process seems cumbersome, the speed of confirmation is no slower than a regular credit card check in a store. In fact, early security concerns about credit card fraud on the Internet are gradually eroding as familiarity increases, and the similarities to any credit card purchase are recognized.

Exhibit 18.1 A Plan for Secure Digital Shopping

A service proposed by First Virtual Holdings promises to permit buying and selling of electronic documents, goods, and services on the Internet without vulnerability to fraud. First Virtual's backers include Electronic Data Services and First USA, a fast-growing issuer of Visa credit cards. Here is how the service would work.

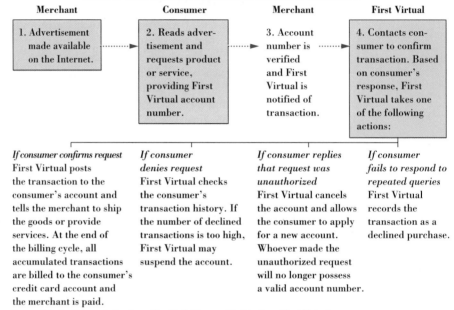

Merchant	Consumer	Merchant	First Virtual
1. Advertisement made available on the Internet.	2. Reads advertisement and requests product or service, providing First Virtual account number.	3. Account number is verified and First Virtual is notified of transaction.	4. Contacts consumer to confirm transaction. Based on consumer's response, First Virtual takes one of the following actions:

If consumer confirms request First Virtual posts the transaction to the consumer's account and tells the merchant to ship the goods or provide services. At the end of the billing cycle, all accumulated transactions are billed to the consumer's credit card account and the merchant is paid.

If consumer denies request First Virtual checks the consumer's transaction history. If the number of declined transactions is too high, First Virtual may suspend the account.

If consumer replies that request was unauthorized First Virtual cancels the account and allows the consumer to apply for a new account. Whoever made the unauthorized request will no longer possess a valid account number.

If consumer fails to respond to repeated queries First Virtual records the transaction as a declined purchase.

Source: Used with permission from *New York Times*, with data from First Virtual.

Virtual Marketing

One of the obstacles for global marketing is the lack of a truly global marketplace. The **virtual reality** of the information superhighway seems likely to change that one day.

Marketing on the Internet is necessarily a global effort. As communication links with all countries, offices, and homes around the world get access to the information superhighway, anyone can log in on a computer and "go shopping" in any "country." It is amazing to imagine a consumer in Japan ordering a briefcase directly from Lands' End in New England, or a Finnish customer buying a video camcorder from Hong Kong. Of course, such transactions are still far from reality but not because the technology is not there. Rather, the availability of terminals and required investments in infrastructure—such as fiberoptic cable—will limit many countries' and individuals' access. As important, trade and tariff barriers will still make some transactions prohibitively expensive.[9] The point here is, however, that a global marketing strategy will prove very beneficial for the company, since it can get a lot of demand spillover effects on the information superhighway.

One interesting aspect of the potential for global commerce on the Internet is that some products can be "digitalized" and sent via electronic mail, bypassing traditional trade barriers that focus on the physical product shipped. Negroponte's book *Being Digital* lucidly explains this process.[10] Good candidates for digitalizing information include newsprint, financial transactions, legal documents, and technical blueprints, all of which are already crossing national borders electronically. More promising (or threatening, depending on one's viewpoint) is the digital transmission of complete books, compact discs, videotapes, and computer software.[11] The digital technology is one reason why piracy of certain products is so common, as the copies can be as good as the originals.

Further into the future, one can visualize the elimination of "exports" and "imports" of manufactured goods such as computer hardware components, including semiconductors, as market-based local plants are guided by remote control. According to Negroponte, that future will come sooner than we think, and companies are now pushing the frontier. For example, the design of some automobile models is already done by global teams working together through terminals located in different countries. The same is happening (or is likely to happen) with apparel design, advertising campaigns, and financial services.

Virtual reality suggests Gertrude Stein's famous remark, "There is no 'there' there." The virtual market in Internet may not be "real" yet—but it will be global.

GLOBAL LOCALIZATION AND LOCAL GLOBALIZATION

The need for companies to have "local presence" even when they are global reflects the fact that most, if not all, markets today are still local. We do our shopping in our hometown or in some airport in a given location, and the company needs to be "there."

In this final section, the question of how to be global and local at the same time will be addressed. **Global localization** refers to the notion that a global marketer needs to be close to the customers locally to be able to compete effectively with local firms. Because of the centralization of many decisions, the firm with a global marketing strategy is in danger of losing touch with the consumer and needs to find ways to avoid this. A key role is played by the execution phase of the strategy.

The Importance of Execution

It is important to recognize that many failures in global marketing are failures of *execution*. Global strategies are not "right" per se. As Swatch, IKEA, Benetton, Honda, and countless other success stories show, decisions are "made right" by luck, persistence, and constant improvement. The foreign entry process might seem scientific and well structured in retrospect, and local marketing analysis is similar to sound analysis elsewhere; in the end, however, failure and success are often determined less by strategy formulation than by implementation—and, in global strategy especially, execution.

Execution means having the nerve and talent (the hidden and not so hidden assets) to do the things the strategy as formulated and implemented intends (remember that implementation has to do with how to do it, while execution is the doing of it). Some examples stand out. The slow and tortured beginning of GM's Saturn project—now a success—was not due to bad strategy or weak implementation—it just asked American management and workers to do things that they had not yet mastered. When IBM ventured into the PC market, its initial execution was not flawed (although it took a special task force project organization separate from the company to do it), but the logical (and strategically sound) follow-up was not executed properly. The many Japanese companies that have successfully entered Western markets have been very careful to tailor their strategies to their execution skills, not the other way around. Their so-called incremental entry strategies are examples of scaled-down aspiration levels and longer-term visions while markets are learned and execution skills are developed.

If the company can't execute, even a good strategy will fail. It also works in reverse. Good execution of bad strategy really demonstrates the flaws of the strategy.[12] The Mitsubishi automobile entry into the United States via Chrysler's dealerships was bad strategy, as has been the strategy of Korean firms to do OEM manufacturing for Sears, GE, and others, and Ricoh's decision to enter OEM with Savin copiers in the United States. The problem is that the effective execution of these strategies has put the companies in a bind. When Chrysler bought Lamborghini, it was bad strategy. Luckily, the deal was not executed properly, and Chrysler got out without major damage.

Localized Global Marketing

Execution is what makes or breaks effective localization. Strategies and systems may be multidomestic or global—in the actual marketplace, what matters is execution.

Companies from Sony to ABB to Microsoft strive hard to become good local citizens wherever they design, manufacture, or market their products. In marketing, this means, as we have seen, that products are localized even if standardized. It means that distribution places the products where consumers can get them easily, even if this is done by Federal Express from a faraway warehouse. It means that pricing is competitive and payment conditions fair, even though the prices are synchronized across the globe and credit checks are done electronically overseas. It means that media advertising speaks in terms that appeal to the target segments, even though the message might be uniform throughout the hemisphere.

The challenge in *global localization* is to make sure that global marketing restraints do not become a disadvantage in the local marketplace. Even though certain options are forced out—no more locally produced slogans, no further modification to the product—standardized features originating from other countries prove more effective also in the local market. To accomplish this is a tall order, but proper execution helps make it come true. And since local country heads will be responsible for the execution of the strategy, their motivation is all-important.

Sony, as one example, attempts to ensure local presence in several ways.[13] Its German subsidiary outside Cologne is a case in point. The German head of the subsidiary came up through marketing. The subsidiary is given a lot of say in product development through, among other things, travel to Japan, visits from Japan, and frequent videoconferences. Product design has partly shifted to Europe, with special European features, styles, and colors added. The advertising draws heavily on Sony's global brand name, using pan-European images, which in contrast to Sony's lighter Japanese advertising emphasizes innovative product features and styling with darker colors suggesting quality. As in other countries, the global slogan "It's a Sony" appears everywhere, in commercials, advertisements, and even as a sticker on many of the products.

Using free publicity about its innovations (Walkman, compact disks, camcorders, videodisks), and creating an aura of higher-end status by consistently pricing slightly above competitors (Matsushita's Panasonic, Toshiba, Hitachi, Philips and others), Sony is positioning its products in Germany and across the globe as a premium brand. In surveys, its brand name is consistently one of the best known in the world, and for many people it is not a Japanese brand. The company does not deny its Japanese roots, but neither plays on them. Sony is a global brand which is local everywhere.

Globalized Local Marketing

ABB (Asea Brown Boveri), the Zurich-based merger of a Swedish and a Swiss company in the electrical and electric machinery business introduced in the opening vignette of Chapter 17, faces an altogether different set of markets.[14] Its customers range from national governments for its hydroelectric power-plants, to local governments for its levitating trains, to large multinationals for its robotics, to local repair shops for its electric draining pumps. Although its size makes the ABB name well known among many of these customers, its global marketing strategy is more limited in scope than Sony's. Strong local presence is absolutely necessary to secure many of the governmental contracts, and in most of the markets, delivery times, service, and repairs need to be quick, with distribution pipelines for components and spare parts well developed.

The solution at ABB has been to place the plants in various countries around the world on a stand-alone profit basis. Each of its 35 plants in Germany is organized as an independent subsidiary with a general manager responsible for profitability. The local marketing is done through the sales force, and market communications, product customization, and pricing are basically each manager's responsibility.

Where does global marketing come in? In two ways. First, the subsidiaries can draw on the ABB distribution networks and sales contacts in other countries, getting access to markets they could not get to before. Second, through global rationalization of production, the subsidiaries have become more specialized, making a globally standardized product for which they have special plant- or country-specific advantages (for example, Strombergs, one subsidiary in Finland, focuses entirely on one important product group, electric drives, for which it is the center of excellence in ABB). That product is then marketed throughout the world using the existing ABB network. This is **local globalization**.

ABB's extreme localization is backed up, in effect, by a global organization. If Sony has localized its global marketing, ABB has globalized its local marketing.

Global Markets

In the Sony and ABB cases the localization depends directly on executing the strategies at the local level. The name of the game is having good local people, good local systems, and good local marketing, classic cases of competing in mature markets.

Microsoft, the PC software producer, is in a different strategic situation.[15] Its global potential depends very much on its dominance in the world's leading market, the United States. Its ventures abroad involve diffusion of new technology into new and growing markets, a classic example of the international product cycle. The software market is also a good example of a fundamentally **global market,** even if local differences in standards sometimes complicate the development of uniform products. The global marketing effort aims at leveraging first-mover advantages and brand reputation overseas.

In these cases the local presence is not so much a matter of skillful execution. Strategic choice in terms of entry mode becomes more critical, especially since it often involves finding independent licensees or joint-venture partners who can provide management know-how and market knowledge lacking at the head office. Microsoft's initial 1983 entry into Japan took the form of a joint venture with ASCII, a small independent software company in Tokyo. Created after a chance meeting on an airplane between Bill Gates of Microsoft and Mr. Nishi, ASCII's founder, the joint venture allowed Microsoft to enter Japan with its Multiplan spreadsheet program before Lotus 1-2-3, making Multiplan the market leader in Japan.

As these markets evolve and customers become more demanding, however, effective local presence takes on a more important role. What worked as an initial setup may no longer be sufficient. The relationship gets strained as local customer preferences for product modifications and new features are passed on to the home office. The selected partner may or may not be able or willing to provide them. Local capability must be increased.

In the Microsoft case, the strain occurred after ASCII demanded that its big customer NEC of Japan be offered special customization of some Microsoft software. Microsoft's home office refused to allow such a close tie to one customer. The company broke off its relationship with ASCII and started up a wholly owned subsidiary in Tokyo in 1987. A wholly owned subsidiary for Europe was also established in London. These two subsidiaries form the centers for the local marketing efforts in Asia and Europe, respectively. A major task of the subsidiaries is also to aggressively pursue copyright infringements, software products being easily copied and distributed.

Microsoft's marketing effort involves standardized products localized by translations done at the company headquarters in Redmond, Washington. Very little adaptation is done locally—the products are basically exported as finished goods from the United States, although display boxes and retail packaging are done locally. Customer information, advertising, in-store displays, and flyers are localized. But there is little input from the local offices to Redmond in terms of product modification, design, or new-product ideas. The American market being the leading market by far, Microsoft's global marketing consists of making its brand names well known through its new-product announcements and the publicity value of its chairman and then introducing the new products abroad as soon as possible. In a global market, being the leader in the largest market simplifies the global marketing strategy.

SUMMARY

It is difficult not to be optimistic about the future of global marketing. The basic philosophy of free markets has proved stronger than the planned economy alternatives. Active marketing efforts to capitalize on the new opportunities by bringing products and services to all corners of the globe are now being locally encouraged. The potential bumps in the road relate to unpredictable political developments, the possibility of slow economic progress in emerging nations, and consequent nostalgia for the past and frustration among local citizens because of unfulfilled promises of free markets. On the upside, the rise of the information super-highway, global mass communications, and innovative product and process technology all combine to make the "megatrends" very favorable.

It seems likely that the drive toward global strategies in marketing will require stronger local presence in the future. No firm can avoid the need to be locally strong. As the information superhighway evolves, it will create a truly global market alternative for some exchanges. In the foreseeable future, however, local conditions will always require localization, if not adaptation, to the customer's situation. Even global marketers have to be close to the customer.

KEY TERMS

Ethics of marketing p. 649
Free markets p. 648
Global markets p. 656
Global localization p. 653

**Information
superhighway** p. 649
Internal communications p. 651
Internet marketplace p. 651

Local globalization p. 656
Protectionist forces p. 645
Virtual reality p. 652
World Wide Web p. 651

DISCUSSION QUESTIONS

1. From newspaper reports, assess how likely it is that trade barriers around the various trade regions (EU, NAFTA, ASEAN) will be raised or lowered. What do you think the impact on global marketing practices will be?

2. Access the World Wide Web and track down some companies' "corner shops." How difficult/easy is it to get to the store? What do they offer—information, games, survey questionnaires, products, services? How big a market do you think they potentially reach? Map out some of the various possibilities for further marketing by the company on the Internet.

3. In marketing journals and newspapers (*Advertising Age, The Wall Street Journal*) find examples of consumer backlash against marketing practices in some emerging market(s). Assess whether these are isolated incidents or whether they represent a trend.

4. In the local consumer market for a product such as beer, global, regional, imported, and local brands (microbreweries) often compete. Discuss how their marketing strategies differ in terms of segmentation (by usage situation, demographics, and so on) and in terms of positioning (high-end, core, and so on). Can you find examples of successful global localization? A not so successful example?

5. Discuss the role of regional integration in creating homogeneous markets. Discuss how successful global marketing campaigns (Swatch, Coca-Cola) have helped make markets more homogeneous. Do you think Levitt is more right now than in 1983, when he argued that markets are becoming less multidomestic and more globalized?

NOTES

1. Vernon's international product cycle was discussed in Chapter 2.

2. In the mid-1990s, several of these threats came from the bilateral disputes between the United States and Japan, spawned by a new "get tough" attitude on the part of the Americans. In the end, free trade sentiment seemed to reign. See, for example, Nash, 1995.

3. See, for example, Shapiro, 1994.

4. See Culnan, 1994.

5. This is only one of the problem areas—see Sanger, 1995b.

6. Every day newspapers are rife with stories about new developments, and for businesses the problem is often just finding their way through the maze. See, for example, Lewis, 1995a. A good guide to the way the communication capabilities influence company organization is "The Virtual Corporation," 1993.

7. See, for example, Hansell, 1994; Lewis, 1994; Markoff, 1994.

8. This illustration is taken from Markoff, 1994.

9. There is also a question whether customers want to buy this way. If history is any guide, however, once there are real advantages to the consumer, whether in the form of convenience, cost, or availability of products, early misgivings are likely to evaporate—see Rushbrook, 1995.

10. See Negroponte, 1995, especially chapter 1 and the Epilogue.

11. As one example of how Internet can bypass official barriers, a book written by the personal physician to the late French President Francois Mitterand but banned by a French judge because of privacy violations, can be downloaded from the Internet.

12. The notion that good execution uncovers strategic flaws is similar to Bonoma's notion that good implementation of a bad strategy unmasks flaws in the strategy—see Bonoma, 1985.

13. The Sony discussion draws on "Sony Corp.: Globalization," 1990, and also on personal interviews in Cologne and Tokyo.

14. The ABB discussion draws on Taylor, 1992.

15. The Microsoft discussion draws on Lewis, 1995b, and "Microsoft Corp.," 1987.

SELECTED REFERENCES

Bonoma, Thomas V. *The Marketing Edge: Making Strategies Work.* New York: Free Press, 1985.

Culnan, Mary. "Privacy Guidelines for the 'New' Direct Marketer." *Privacy and American Business* 1, no. 4 (1994), p. 5.

Fisher, Lawrence M. "A Unifying Force at Novell." *New York Times,* February 5, 1995, p. F9.

Hansell, Saul. "Banks Go Interactive to Beat the Rush of Services." *New York Times,* October 19, 1994, pp. D1, D4.

La Polla, Stephanie. "Compaq Turns Eye on the Enterprise." *PC Week,* October 30, 1995, p. 49.

Lewis, Peter H. "Paperless Cash to Be Tested for Internet Use." *New York Times,* October 19, 1994, p. D4.

———. "Microsoft Has Windows 95 Party; the Internet Shows Up." *New York Times,* August 25, 1995b, p. D4.

———. "Prodigy Is Leading Its Peers onto the World Wide Web." *New York Times,* January 18, 1995a, pp. D1, D7.

Markoff, John. "A Credit Card for On-Line Sprees." *New York Times,* October 15, 1994, p. 39.

"Microsoft Corp.: The Introduction of Microsoft Works." Harvard Business School case no. 9-588-028, 1987.

Nash, Nathaniel C. "The Lonely Americans Isolated in a Trade War." *New York Times,* May 26, 1995, p. D2.

Negroponte, Nicholas. *Being Digital.* New York: Alfred A. Knopf, 1995.

Perlez, Jane. "Fast and Slow Lanes on the Capitalist Road." *New York Times,* October 7, 1994, pp. A1, A12.

Rushbrook, Lewis. "Buying in the Cybermarket." *Marketing,* March 2, 1995, pp. 20–21.

Saito, Akiko. *My Husband Is My Rival.* Tokyo: Yuhisha, 1991.

Sanger, David E. "Trade Fight Aside, U.S. to Sell China More Wheat." *New York Times,* February 8, 1995a, p. D1, D18.

———. "This Is a Trade War! Get Your Popgun!" *New York Times,* February 12, 1995b, sec. 4, pp. 1, 5.

Shapiro, Margaret. "New Russia: A Country on the Take." *Washington Post,* November 13, 1994, pp. A1, A36–37.

"Sony Corp.: Globalization." Harvard Business School case no. 9-391-071, 1990.

Specter, Michael. "Borscht and Blini to Go: From Russian Capitalists, an Answer to McDonald's." *New York Times,* August 9, 1995, pp. D1, D3.

Stevenson, Richard W. "Foreign Investors in Russia Brush Risks Aside." *New York Times,* October 11, 1994, pp. A1, D6.

Taylor, William. "The Logic of Global Business: An Interview with ABB's Percy Barnevik." In Bartlett, Christopher A., and Sumantra Ghoshal. *Transnational Management* (Homewood, IL: Irwin, 1992), pp. 892–908.

"The Virtual Corporation." *Business Week,* February 8, 1993, pp. 98–102.

CASES

Case 1

PERT PLUS (A): A PAN-EUROPEAN OPPORTUNITY

*P*rocter & Gamble (P&G), the U.S. manufacturer of consumer packaged goods, is considering the introduction of a new haircare technology (BC-18) into the European market. The technology combines a shampoo and a conditioner in one product with the same effect as a shampoo and conditioner used separately. The product was launched in the U.S. haircare market in 1986 as Pert Plus and its success provided the impetus to consider a "roll-out" launch in Europe.

Company Background

Procter & Gamble was founded in the U.S. in 1837. Today it is the world's biggest manufacturer of packaged consumer goods and a global leader in health and beauty care products, detergents, diapers, and food. P&G products include Pampers, Ariel, Mr. Proper, Camay, and others. More than one-third of P&G's total profit is generated by its international

operations, which are the fastest growing part of its total business. To strengthen its health and beauty care division, P&G in 1985 bought the Richardson-Vicks Company (with brands like Vidal Sassoon and Pantene) and in 1987 bought the German Blendax Group (dental-care products). These acquisitions resulted in a leading position in health and beauty care products in Europe.

Over its more than 150-year history, P&G has accumulated a broad base of industry experience and business knowledge. A great deal of it has been formalized and institutionalized as management principles and policies. One of the most basic principles is that P&G's products should provide "superior total value" and should meet "basic consumer needs." This has resulted in a strong commitment to research to create products that are demonstrably better than others. In contrast to the conventional product life cycle mentality, P&G believes that through continual product

Source: This case was written by Dr. Wolfgang Breuer and Professor Dr. Richard Köhler, University of Cologne (Germany). It was devised together with the German P&G office. It is based on real facts but the figures have been partly changed for teaching purposes. A more detailed version of the case was published by Sage Publications, Ltd., London, in the volume *Marketing in Europe: Case Studies*, ed. Jordi Montaña, 1994. Reprinted with permission.

development, brands can remain healthy and profitable in the long term.

Perhaps the most widely known of P&G's organizational characteristics is its legendary brand management system. The brand management team, usually a group of three or four people, assumes general responsibility for its brand. They plan, develop, and direct their brand in its market. The group develops business objectives, strategies, and marketing plans. It selects advertising copy and media, develops sales promotion activities, manages package design and product improvement projects, and initiates cost savings. To carry out their responsibilities, members of the brand management team draw on the resources available to them. These include the other disciplines within and outside the organization (e.g., manufacturing, product development, market research, sales, advertising agencies). Summing up, it may be said that they know more about their product than anyone else, and they feel a real sense of ownership as they strive to develop business opportunities in their local market.

But in the early 1980s it became more and more obvious that greater coordination was needed between local markets in Europe. Increasingly, competitors had been able to imitate P&G's innovative products and marketing strategies, and had preempted them in national markets where the local subsidiary was constrained by budget or organizational limitations. Therefore, closer coordination was important, particularly for new brands, to ensure they reached the marketplace first. Marketing strategies had to be thought through from a European perspective. This meant also the possibility of simultaneous or closely sequenced European product introductions. Furthermore, the European approach, through maximizing efficiency across countries, pooling know-how, and manufacturing with better economies of scale, could give a big advantage over the competition.

As a main forum for achieving this goal the Euro-brand team meetings were introduced chaired by the brand management of the so called "lead country." This European perspective did not necessarily mean Europe-wide standardization. Market conditions still vary widely within Europe. P&G's concept is that of "Euro-balancing," meaning as much standardization as possible, as little localization as necessary. A P&G senior manager comments: "It is occasionally better to allow some complexity to get a better overall result."

Pert Plus

The most important P&G shampoo brands were losing U.S. market share in the years up to 1986. Therefore, it was decided to introduce a new technology, called BC-18, in the U.S. market at the beginning of 1986 by replacing the brand Pert with Pert Plus.

The long-term marketing goal of Pert Plus was to take over the leading value position in the U.S. shampoo market, with a market share of at least 10 percent by the end of the fiscal year 1989/90. For the first year the specific target was a market share value of 5 percent.

In order to achieve this, Pert Plus was positioned as the shampoo that offered attractive hair in a convenient way. This was backed up by the unique Pert Plus formula, which combined a mild shampoo with a fully effective conditioner in one wash.

The target group was to be all people. The source of business would also come from the group of people who had not used Pert or a conditioner before. Pert Plus was introduced with a price of U.S. $3.20 (for the 15 oz. size).[1] Pert Plus was an instant success, doubling Pert's market share in one year, and growing steadily after that.

[1] 1 US $ = 2.17 DM; 15 oz. (ounces) = 425 ml.

....

EXHIBIT 1   Market Sizes, Shampoo/Conditioner, Europe, 1988

	West Germany	Great Britain	France	Scandinavia	Benelux
Shampoos					
Value (TDM)	650,000	485,000	700,000	250,000	200,000
Volume (MSU)	20,000	18,000	20,000	7,000	7,500
Use per head (SU/1,000 of population)	325	325	350	300	300
Conditioners					
Value (TDM)	230,000	250,000	100,000	85,000	60,000
Volume (MSU)	4,500	7,500	2,000	1,700	1,500
Use per head (SU/1,000 of population)	70	140	35	70	70

1 MUS 5 1,000 SU (statistical units).

1 SU 5 2.5 litres.

TDM 5 Thousand German marks.

....

EXHIBIT 2   Percentage of Market Shares, Shampoo, Key Brands, Europe 1988

	West Germany		Great Britain		France		Scandinavia		Benelux	
	Volume	Value	Volume	Value	Volume	Value	Volume	Value	Volume	Value
P&G brands										
Vidal Sassoon	0.5	1.3	1.1	3.6	N/A		1.0	2.4	N/A	
Pantene	N/A		N/A		1.0	2.1	N/A		N/A	
Petrole Hahn	N/A		N/A		3.0	2.1	N/A		0.6	
Shamtu	11.0	6.3	N/A		N/A		N/A		N/A	
Head & Shoulders	1.1	1.7	6.5	12.0	1.1	1.6	1.0	1.4	2.9	5.4
Competitor brands										
Timotei (Unilever)	5.0	5.7	8.5	11.8	4.9	5.2	7.5	7.8	3.8	5.3
Nivea (Beiersdorf)	9.0	9.2	N/A		N/A		2.5	2.3	4.4	5.5
Schauma (Schwarzkopf)	21.0	10.0	N/A		N/A		N/A		7.0	4.1
Palmolive (Colgate)	N/A		4.6	2.7	12.3	5.4	7.0	3.0	18.2	10.6
Elsève/ El' Vital (L'Oréal)	3.3	4.6	N/A		4.5	5.8	6.5	8.2	5.0	8.4

N/A 5 product not on offer in this country.

....
EXHIBIT 3   Sizes and Shelf Prices, Shampoo, Europe 1988 (in German marks)

	West Germany	Great Britain	France	Scandinavia	Benelux
P&G brands					
Vidal Sassoon	6.99	6.99	N/A	6.99	N/A
(200 ml)					
Pantene	N/A	N/A	4.99	N/A	N/A
(200 ml)					
Petrole Hahn	N/A	N/A	2.99	N/A	2.99
(300 ml)					
Shamtu	2.99	N/A	N/A	N/A	N/A
(400 ml)					
Head & Shoulders	5.99	5.99	5.99	5.99	5.99
(300 ml)					
Competitor brands					
Timotei (Unilever)	2.99	2.99	2.99	2.99	2.99
(200 ml)					
Nivea (Beiersdorf)	3.99	N/A	N/A	3.99	3.99
(300 ml)					
Schauma (Schwarzkopf)	2.49	N/A	N/A	N/A	2.49
(400 ml)					
Palmolive (Colgate)	N/A	2.49	2.49	2.49	2.49
(400 ml)					
Elsève/El' Vital (L'Oréal)	4.49	N/A	4.49	4.49	4.49
(250 ml)					

N/A = product not on offer in this country.

To simplify matters, the retail prices have been rounded off to a European average. However, price relations within a country have been retained.

Market Development and Competitive Environment

In Europe a steady growth of the shampoo market and the conditioner market could be seen. There was evidence of increased hair-washing. However, the conditioner market was still, compared with the U.S.A., relatively undeveloped. The share of shampoo users who also used conditioner was still below the 44 percent which had been reached in the United States. This was particularly true for Southern European countries. Therefore, the initial fo-cus was on West Germany, Great Britain, France, Scandinavia, and Benelux. An under-developed conditioner market was, however, also evident in France (in terms of sales volume only 10 percent of shampoo consumption). Among the European countries considered, Great Britain, with 42 percent, showed the strongest user share (see Exhibit 1).

With respect to the number of suppliers and brands, the European market was even more crowded than the U.S. market, undoubtedly a function of the different nationalities. The most important competitors for P&G

EXHIBIT 4   Media Spending, Shampoo, Europe 1988 (in thousands of German marks)

	West Germany	Great Britain	France	Scandinavia	Benelux
aP&G brands					
Vidal Sassoon	1,000	3,000	N/A	1,000	N/A
Pantene	N/A	N/A	0	N/A	N/A
Petrole Hahn	N/A	N/A	3,000	N/A	0
Shamtu	4,000	N/A	N/A	N/A	N/A
Head & Shoulders	3,000	3,000	2,000	800	2,800
Competitor brands					
Timotei (Unilever)	6,500	6,500	3,000	3,000	1,500
Nivea (Beiersdorf)	8,000	N/A	N/A	2,000	1,000
Schauma (Schwarzkopf)	10,500	N/A	N/A	N/A	N/A
Palmolive (Colgate)	N/A	4,000	4,000	1,000	1,000
Elsève/El ' Vital (L'Oréal)	5,000	N/A	7,000	2,000	2,000
TOTAL	80,000	80,000	60,000	60,000	50,000

N/A = product not on offer in this country.

were Unilever, Colgate, and L'Oréal. Some brands could be found in all countries, others only in their domestic markets (see Exhibit 2).

The gap between the top and bottom price classes was even bigger than in the U.S. market. Between brands there were price differences of over five times for the same quantity, which meant that the value-based market share of a shampoo brand was very important (see Exhibit 3).

In order to carry through the brand message, media support would be a key driving force (see Exhibit 4).

DISCUSSION QUESTIONS

1. How attractive is the European market for Pert Plus in terms of demand potential?

2. How competitive is the European market? What competitive advantages does Pert Plus have? Disadvantages? Any country-of-origin effect?

3. Which countries are the leading markets in Europe? What are the advantages or disadvantages of entering a leading market first?

4. Do you think Pert Plus should be introduced in Europe? If no, why not? If yes, what country should be selected first?

Case 2

PERT PLUS (B): THE EUROPEAN MARKET TESTS

*T*n 1988, following the success of Pert Plus in the U.S. market, Procter & Gamble decided to introduce BC-18 into the European market.[1] It was clear that the easy, time-saving, everyday use of the product was essential when considering positioning. There was also no doubt about placing the new product in the premium-priced segment. As with Pert Plus, a premium price was necessary to be consistent with the high-quality product concept. The main question was still, however, under what brand name to introduce the product in the individual European markets. There was also the question of whether a 200 ml bottle, used in the United States, would be accepted by the European consumer and the question of price sensitivity at premium pricing.

Consumer Research

It was decided, therefore, to undertake some consumer research. Obviously, it was impossible to test all possible product concepts with respect to brand names, positioning alternatives, pack sizes, pack designs, and price alternatives, for all European countries. So, in a

prescreening phase, the possible brand alternatives were reduced to four. In any case, there was to be a brand which, already present in the United States and several European markets, had so far shown a certain European potential (Vidal Sassoon). The U.S. brand Pert Plus, unknown in the European market, was also to be tested. The two other alternatives were national brands firmly established in their domestic markets (Pantene and Shamtu). Price and packaging alternatives were tested on only two brands: one brand from the lower-price segment and another brand that had a high-quality product concept (i.e., product concepts where possible price sensitivity would be easily detected). An abridged version of the positioning statements can be found in Exhibit 1. The consumer tests were carried out in the relevant European countries (for average results, see Exhibit 2; there were no significant differences between countries).

Economics

The basis for cost planning for the BC-18 introduction in individual European countries was the cost structure of the existing P&G shampoo brands. This also gave an idea of the profitability of the brands tested in the consumer test, which might be one of the deciding

[1]For further information about P&G, see Case 1, Pert Plus (A).

Source: This case was written by Dr. Wolfgang Breuer and Professor Richard Köhler, University of Cologne (Germany). The case was devised together with the German P&G office. It is based on real facts but the figures have been partly changed for teaching purposes. A more detailed version of the case was published by Sage Publications, Ltd., London, in the volume *Marketing in Europe: Case Studies*, ed. Jordi Montaña, 1994. Reprinted with permission.

....
EXHIBIT 1   Consumer Test, Europe

Positioning statement	Price/Pack size
Vidal Sassoon Wash & Go—for great-looking hair in a convenient way	4.99 DM/200 ml
Shamtu 2 in 1—shampoo and conditioner in one—silkiness and bounce in one step	4.99 DM/200 ml
Shamtu 2 in 1—shampoo and conditioner in one—silkiness and bounce in one step	4.99 DM/250 ml
Pantene—shampoo with built-in vitamin conditioner—the perfect hair care in one step	4.99 DM/200 ml
Pantene—shampoo with built-in vitamin conditioner—the perfect hair care in one step	5.99 DM/200 ml
Pert Plus Wash & Go—for great-looking hair in a convenient way	4.99 DM/200 ml

....
EXHIBIT 2   Consumer Test, Europe, Results (*percent*)

	Vidal Sassoon Wash & Go	Shamtu 2 in 1 "silkiness and bounce"		Pantene "perfect care"		Pert Plus Wash & Go
Product concepts	4.99DM/ 200ml	4.99DM/ 200ml	4.99DM/ 250ml	4.99DM/ 200ml	5.99DM/ 250ml	4.99DM/ 200ml
"Would definitely buy"	29%	20%	27%	28%	17%	28%
"Is very new"	41	40	41	39	40	40
"Is very convincing and relevant"	70	73	72	73	72	70

factors in the choice of an introductory brand name for BC-18 (see Exhibit 3).

The costs of producing the new product, including average transport costs, were relatively easy to estimate, since the decision had been made to locate production for the whole European market in England. However, it had still not been decided whether to use the available 200 ml bottle or a 250 ml bottle still in development. Two figures were therefore used in the plans: production costs would be roughly 22 DM/SU[2] for the small bottle and 20 DM/SU for the larger bottle. These figures presumed a work capacity of 50 percent, and it was assumed that working at higher capacity would not generate lower costs because of the special production technology. To determine total costs it was necessary to consider also advertising and sales support budgets, which depended on the individual countries and their chosen introduction program (see Exhibit 4).

Decision Constraints

The first restrictions arose in the available production capacity. For the first year a capacity of 2,000 MSU was available. This could have been increased to 4,000 MSU in the second year and to 8,000 in the third year. Nevertheless, in case of difficulties, with six months notice it would have been possible to get an extra 500 MSU capacity, but with 2 DM/SU higher production costs.

[2]DM = German mark; 1 SU (statistical unit) = 2.5 litres; 1,000 SU = 1 MSU.

EXHIBIT 3   Overview, Economics/Profits, Europe, 1988

		W. Germany		Great Britain	France	Scandinavia	Benelux
		VS 200 ml	Shamtu 400 ml	VS 200 ml	Pantene 200 ml	VS 200 ml	H&S 300 ml
Volume	MSU	100	2,000	300	200	100	400
Shelf price	DM/pack	6.99	2.99	6.99	4.99	6.99	5.99
Manufacturer's list price	DM/pack	4.50	2.40	4.50	3.20	4.50	4.80
Manufacturer's list price	DM/SU	56.25	15.00	56.25	40.00	56.25	40.00
Discount	DM/SU	5.60	1.50	5.60	4.00	5.60	4.00
Manufacturer's net price	DM/SU	50.65	13.50	50.65	36.00	50.65	36.00
Production costs (incl. transport)	DM/SU	30.00	8.00	28.00	22.00	30.00	18.00
Overheads (sales, R&D, etc.)	DM/SU	5.60	1.50	5.60	5.00	5.60	4.00
Advertising costs for trade	DM/SU	2.80	0.75	2.80	2.00	2.80	2.00
Budget for advertising and sales promotion	DM/SU	20.00	2.50	14.00	6.00	14.00	10.00
Profit	DM/SU	−7.75	0.75	0.25	1.00	−1.75	2.00

VS = Vidal Sassoon
H&S = Head & Shoulders
DM = German marks
MSU = 1,000 SU
SU = statistical unit

Lead times for alternative pack sizes and designs were also a restriction. The development of a new 200 ml bottle would take a lead time of 12 months. Although development of a new bottle containing 250 ml was underway, it would still take six months before it could be used. By contrast, using the existing U.S. bottle for Pert Plus would not require any lead time.

DISCUSSION QUESTIONS

1. What does the marketing research tell about the price and positioning decision for Europe?

2. What are the possible alternative brand name strategies? Should the BC-18 technology be introduced with a pan-European name, or with local brand names, or even with a mixture of both approaches? Should a new brand be created, or should an existing brand be relaunched in a new quantity?

3. Should entry be sequential or simultaneous across Europe? Which country offers the best financial promise?

....
EXHIBIT 4   Media and Promotion Costs

	W. Germany	Great Britain	France	Scandinavia[2]	Benelux
Media (TDM per month)[1]					
TV normal advertising month	600	600	600	—	200
strong advertising month	800	800	800	—	250
Radio normal advertising month	400	400	400	—	130
strong advertising month	500	500	500	—	160
Print normal 3-month campaign	3,000	3,000	3,000	1,000	1,000
strong 3-month campaign	5,000	5,000	5,000	1,600	1,600
Samle distribution (DM per piece)					
Sample costs	0.40				
Distribution costs					
Door-to-door	0.10	(s a m e a s f o r W e s t G e r m a n y)			
Hypermarkets	0.20				
Via other products	0.15				
Additional promotions (TDM)					
Hypermarket—display activities	500	600	500	200	200
Consumer competition	100	100	100	50	50
Wheel of Fortune competition	300	300	300	100	100
Additional Costs (TDM)					
Production TV	400	400	400	—	400
radio	30	30	30	—	30
print	50	50	50	50	50
Listing funds	1,000	1,000	1,000	400	300
Material for sales representatives	50	50	50	20	20
Number of households (millions))	26	22	21	10	10

[1]*Strong advertising month means that the frequency (number of spots) is about one-third higher than in a normal advertising month.*

[2]*TV and radio advertising not possible for legal reasons.*

DM = German marks.

TDM = 1,000 German marks.

Case 3

GLOBALIZING A LOCAL STRATEGY: THE ILLYCAFFÉ COMPANY

*I*llycaffé was founded in Trieste, a large city in the northeast of Italy, by Francesco Illy in 1933. Francesco Illy was a true gourmet who sought to provide his customers with the highest quality espresso coffee. By 1990 Illycaffé had a total of 150 employees and its sales had grown from 21 billion lire in 1983 to 67 billion lire in 1990.[1] It was a family-owned company whose shares were divided between Ernesto Illy (the founder's son), his wife, and their four children, all of whom occupied various management positions within the company. Riccardo Illy was marketing manager.

What's Espresso?

Italy is well-known for its history, culture, art, and beauty. But Italian wine and cuisine are also part of the mystique that attracts people from around the world. Espresso coffee is an element of the cuisine and therefore of this mystique. Espresso is a symbol of the Italian culture.

What makes espresso so different from other types of coffee? There are several methods to percolate coffee: the "filter" or "napoletana" method of letting the weight of the water itself (gravity) pull it through the coffee powder; the "moka" method of creating steam

pressure to push water through the coffee; the "espresso" method, which uses water at 194 degrees fahrenheit and 9–10 atmospheres of pressure. The higher the pressure, the less time it takes for the coffee to percolate; the filter method requires several minutes, while the moka method requires one minute, and the espresso method only 30 seconds. The different methods also result in different levels of caffeine in the coffee cup; the filter method (common in North America and in Northern Europe) results in 90–125 mg. of caffeine per cup, while the espresso method produces a cup with only 60–120 mg. of caffeine.

Marketing Strategy

Illycaffé's positioning strategy in the crowded coffee market was based on the quality concept. In order to maintain high standards, the management had patented a packaging system that was able to guarantee high levels of flavor and aroma. But the quality system was also based on the careful selection and control of the coffee beans used in production. Illycaffé used only 100 percent Arabic beans in production and had contributed to the invention of sophisticated machinery that was able to eliminate any defective beans from each batch used in production. The company also dedicated 3 percent of annual sales to research and quality control.

[1]Exchange rates fluctuated considerably during the period of the case. For analytical purposes, 1,100 Italian lire can be set equal to 1 U.S. dollar.

Source: This case was prepared by Pamela Adams, SDA Bocconi, Milano. Used with permission.

The advertising and promotion policies also focused on the quality of the product, linking it to the brand name in order to increase brand loyalty. It was difficult for producers to ensure that coffee served in cafes was identified by brand. But because most consumers believed coffee made in bars and restaurants was better than that made at home, a strong presence in this segment was necessary to build the brand's image in the home segment (food retailing). Illy reinforced its brand name in cafes and restaurants by asking the owners to display Illy signs and logos both outside the premises to attract customers and inside to recall the brand name. The marketing policies and brand image established by the management helped Illy to get a premium price for its coffee, often even doubling the price of the next highest competitor in this market.

The Quality Problem

One of the company's major problems in maintaining its quality image was the high rate of personnel turnover in the bar and restaurant business. Many employees took on temporary positions as they were looking for other lines of work. This was true in most advanced economies, but it meant that bar operators constantly had to train new personnel in the art of producing a quality cup of espresso.

The quality depended as much on the human input and machinery as on the quality of the coffee used. According to Illy, in fact, a good cup of espresso depended on several elements including the quality of the beans, the roasting of the beans, the correct mix of roasted beans, the quantity of coffee powder used to prepare each cup of coffee, the degree to which the coffee was pressed into the filter of the espresso machine, the water temperature, the pressure at which the water was expelled during the preparation, the cleanliness of the filter, the size of the filter holes, and the quality of the water used in preparation.

The company decided that this was a strategic area for innovation and began to offer technical assistance and training/consultancy to its clients. As Riccardo Illy noted, "A good product is not enough in this market . . . You also have to teach the operators of the espresso machines how to use them in the best way if you want to guarantee an increase in sales."

The German Entry

The position of Illy in Germany was somewhat different from its position in other European countries where sales were made through agents and sales subsidiaries. Originally (1974), an exclusive agreement had been signed with a German distributor. Despite the limits of this strategy, the company's sales grew from 10 tons in 1974 to 30 tons in 1978.

In 1978, however, one of the major German coffee producers, Hag, approached the management of Illycaffé with a proposal to form a distribution alliance. Hag was a family-owned and family-run business with a long tradition in the coffee industry. The company produced both caffeinated and decaffeinated filter coffee, as well as a line of supplementary products such as sugar and cream. Hag had an extensive distribution network throughout Germany and had noted a growing interest in espresso coffee among its clients. The company had tried to produce its own brand of quality espresso, but had failed and was now looking for an Italian producer who would be interested in an alliance for the German market.

Ernesto Illy realized that any significant increase in sales in Germany would require much greater investments in both sales force and promotion. But 1977 had not been a profitable year in the domestic market, and the company's financial situation would not permit such investments. Nor was the existing German distributor willing to take on further commitments. Ernesto therefore decided to accept Hag's proposal. As he concluded: "This was a great offer from a significant player in the Germany coffee industry who believed in our product. This was all the assurance that I needed."

The Hag-Goldene Tasse Era

The contract that was signed by the two companies in 1978 gave Hag exclusive rights to the sale of Illy coffee in Germany. Illy's German distributor, in fact, was required to turn over its client lists to Hag. The job of Illy's distributor was reduced to acting as an interface between the two headquarters and to supplying smaller customers.

Illy maintained control over the brand name and the product, while Hag was given responsibility for promotion and distribution decisions in Germany. Rough sales targets were indicated in the contract (80 tons by 1980, 150 tons by 1981 and 250 tons by 1982), although Hag was under no obligation to reach these targets. No provisions were made for Illy to receive any information about the clients.

Three years later, Hag was acquired by another company in the German coffee business, Goldene Tasse. No significant changes were made in the Illycaffé agreement as a result of this acquisition. In fact, the meetings between the two companies during these years were rare and the contract was typically renewed at the end of each period without any direct contact between the two partners.

According to the original contract, Hag had agreed to pay Illy 13.70 DM for each kilo of coffee received. The price was broken down into two parts: one half was pegged to the price of green coffee on the international market, while the other half was pegged to Illy's production costs. Price changes were provided for only the half related to the raw coffee: these changes could be effected only every three months according to the fluctuations in the trading price established on the international market. Requests for price increases due to rising production costs, on the other hand,

could be made by Illy only once at the beginning of each contract year, and had to be supported by documentation explaining the actual cost increases.

Following the signing of this agreement in 1978, Illy witnessed a steady increase in sales. But as Riccardo complained as he looked over the records in 1990, "The sales may have been increasing, but we weren't making any money. Our selling price was too low to earn any margins and we had to absorb the high rates of inflation in Italy. Moreover, as the price of green coffee continued to fall on international markets due to the excess in supply throughout the 1980s, we had no way to raise the price of our product to Hag in any substantial way."

Globalizing the Strategy

As Riccardo Illy took over responsibility for the company's international activities in 1990, he quickly decided to change Illy's strategy in the European market. He was convinced that the move toward a more unified European market provided an excellent opportunity for Illy to appeal to a pan-European consumer through a standardized marketing program in line with the strategy followed in the Italian market. In order to carry out this plan, however, he understood that he needed to create a cohesive team and to bring the various subsidiaries under his direct control. The most effective way he saw to begin this process was to acquire distributors in each major market.

Once the buyout process was completed, Mr. Illy gave one of his export managers, Mr. Giacomo Biviano, responsibility for the company's activities in Europe. Mr. Biviano, a young and decisive manager with a strong background in both international marketing and administration and control, was named CEO for France and Germany, and also appointed to the supervisory board of the new company in Holland. As Biviano described it, "We needed managers who would be loyal to our ideas and would implement a standardized set of policies that were to be decided at the central level."

Ownership Complications

Just about this time, however, Riccardo Illy also learned that Hag-Goldene Tasse had been acquired by General Foods, a diversified multinational in the food industry, which was itself later acquired by Philip Morris International. By 1990, both Kraft, another American-based multinational in the food business, and Jacobs Suchard, a Swiss producer of coffee and chocolate with its own line of espresso, had also come under the wing of the Philip Morris group. As a result, a merger was made between Hag's coffee division, Goldene Tasse, and Jacob Suchard's coffee business in Germany. The new company, called Jacobs-Goldene Tasse, took over Hag's position as Illy's partner in the German market. Riccardo Illy immediately called for a meeting with the new partners to discuss the potential effects of the changes on the distribution agreement between the companies.

Although Hag-Goldene Tasse had its own line of espresso coffee, and Jacobs Suchard had a line of both espresso coffee and espresso pods, all of which were sold to the bar segment in Germany, Riccardo Illy underlined the fact that none of these products were of the same quality as Illy's brand of espresso coffee.

At the meeting the parties agreed to continue the existing arrangement until Jacobs had time to do more research, with one significant change. To protect its quality image, Illy was allowed to have a technical assistant accompany Hag's salesmen during client visits, providing consultancy on the use and maintenance of espresso machines. Although the arrangement lasted only a few months, Illy gained some important insights from these visits. As Biviano noted, "One significant lesson we learned from these direct contacts with the clients was that it was unusual for bar and restaurant operators in Germany to demand

trade credit from small suppliers. Such financing was required only from suppliers whose products represented a large share of the business, such as filter coffee and beer."

The Second Meeting

Riccardo Illy and Giacomo Biviano prepared a list of changes that they wanted made in the contract for the subsequent meeting:

1. The selling price of Illy coffee to Hag-Goldene Tasse should be the same as in other European markets, and with the same payment conditions.

2. All marketing activities (especially advertising to the trade, to the consumer, and at the point-of-sales) would be managed and controlled by Illy's new German subsidiary.

3. Hag-Goldene Tasse would be granted exclusive rights to the distribution of Illy coffee in Germany, contingent on the requirement that Hag-Goldene Tasse distribute only Illy's brand of espresso coffee.

4. Clear growth objectives would be stipulated in the contract. These objectives should be in line with Illy's overall objectives for growth, and Hag should be obliged to achieve the stated objectives.

5. A unit to supervise technical consulting/quality control at the point-of-sales would be created and managed by Illy-Germany.

6. A new policy of communication at point-of-sales would be implemented through the use of Illy cups and billboards. Illy should have the authority to control the implementation of this activity through contracts and regular visits to clients.

By the end of the meeting, Jacobs Suchard and Hag-Goldene Tasse had agreed to points

(1) and (4), but had refused to accept point (3). The companies did not adopt a position concerning points (2), (5), and (6). No new meeting was scheduled between the parties.

Uncertain Future

At the end of the current contract period in June of 1991, the manager of Illy-Germany terminated the contract between Illy and Hag-Goldene Tasse, offering an interim option to renegotiate a new contract. The option was left open until the end of August.

In the meantime, Riccardo Illy and Giacomo Biviano began to study the three major alternatives:

1. Give full responsibility for sales and distribution back to Illy-Germany and work together with the German team to establish an effective sales force.

2. Look for a new partner in Germany who could offer a solid sales network and would agree to the terms outlined in the proposal prepared for Hag-Goldene Tasse.

3. Work toward a new contract with Hag-Goldene Tasse/Jacobs Suchard.

In the latter two cases, given that it was unlikely that all of Illy's request would be accepted by any partner, it would be necessary to rank the requests in order of importance and to establish the minimum requirements for any agreement.

As the next step, therefore, the two managers had to decide whether or not to attempt to revive the piggyback agreement with Hag, to look for a new distributor, or to create their own network in accordance with their new Euro strategy.

DISCUSSION QUESTIONS

1. What created the problems with the existing arrangements for the German market?

2. To what extent do you think the pan-European strategy shift well-founded? For example, is the espresso market global?

3. What would be your recommendation to Mr. Illy?

Case 4

GLOBAL LOCALIZATION: COGNOS INC. IN JAPAN

With FY 1993 revenues of $147.7 million from customers in about 70 countries, Cognos Incorporated was Canada's largest and most international software company. The international scope of Cognos's business followed from Chairman and CEO Michael Potter's view that the computer software industry was global and that, although some differences existed from one country to another, the issues that faced customers and the solutions available to them were fundamentally the same worldwide.

Source: This case was prepared by Professor Philip Rosson of Dalhousie University.

Organization

Cognos had headquarters in three countries. Its world headquarters, R&D laboratory, and product marketing was located in Ottawa, Canada. U.S. operations and much of Cognos's worldwide marketing communications and sales were run out of Burlington, Massachusetts. European operations were centered in Bracknell in the U.K. Cognos operated directly in major markets through sales subsidiaries, often supplemented by branch offices. In smaller markets, customers were reached and serviced indirectly through distributors.

Products

Cognos offered an integrated family of software tools that supported the entire application development cycle for mini- and micro-computing environments. A brief description of each tool gives a picture of the product line.

PowerHouse, the core product, was a fourth-generation computer language for use in professional programming environments. It permitted the development of complete, complex business applications using a minimum of instructions. PowerHouse was priced at $6,500 to $257,000 depending on computer platform and size.

Other products enabled Cognos to offer users a fully integrated set of software tools. *PowerDesigner* addressed the steps that go before program production, namely analysis and design. *Architect* automated the maintenance of PowerHouse applications, generating supporting documentation for any change and indicating the impact of the change on data integrity across a large network. Several reporting tools provided users with quick and easy access to corporate data. *PowerPlay* was a management reporting and analysis tool, displaying data in chart format and permitting successively deeper levels of data examination. Cognos provided tight integration between its tools and the file and database management systems offered by hardware manufacturers and third-party database vendors.

Competitive Strategy

Cognos was one of relatively few companies that offered tools to support each stage of the development process. Its tools were also compatible with a broad range of computer hardware, operating systems, database management systems, and network architectures. This meant that buyers could protect the value of their existing investments in hardware and software when adopting Cognos's application development tools.

Cognos's strategy reflected the fact that organizations were increasingly using information as a source of competitive advantage. With clerical and back-office functions (payroll, financial reporting, etc.) largely automated, computer technology was being used more frequently in front-office operations. This involved tasks such as market analysis, forecasting, and manufacturing planning and control, and depended on accurate and timely information. Many organizations had adopted relational database management systems in the 1980s to deal with this need. These proved to be useful for storing and retrieving data but their associated tools were not adequate for developing complex information systems. More powerful software tools had emerged to fill this need, frequently referred to as computer-aided software engineering (or CASE) tools. These reduced development time, produced higher quality control programs at a lower cost, enabled the adoption of a consistent application development process, and increased end-user involvement.

A number of companies competed with Cognos. The competition came from different sources, ranging from producers of application development tools (such as Information Builders, Inc.), to relational database vendors offering tools to go with their database systems (Oracle Corporation), and hardware manufacturers offering alternative solutions to Cognos (Hewlett-Packard). It was difficult to determine the strength of the product and corporate challenge provided by these and other companies. Cognos' customers were of all sizes and types, but since late 1989, the company had sought larger transaction values by targeting bigger organizations and securing multiple product/service orders.

Marketing and Sales

Cognos used a multichannel distribution system to reach customers and supported these channels with a large number of presales technical experts. In major markets Cognos employed its own direct sales force. The direct sales force was seen as increasing visibility, contact, and add-on sales, and generated 61 percent of product license revenue in FY 1992. Third-party channels were also used to reach customers, including value-added resellers (VARs) and, to a lesser extent, distributors, to extend the company's geographic coverage. VARs used Cognos's tools to develop packaged software applications for sales directly to end-users, and paid a royalty for embedding the company's tools within the application developed. In FY 1992, 300 VARs offered more than 600 such applications.

Cognos also marketed through OEMs (such as DEC and Data General) that were licensed to sell PowerHouse with their computer hardware. In FY 1992, third-party channels accounted for 23 percent of product license revenues, with VARs dominant. The final channel employed by Cognos was telemarketing. This essentially focused on the installed base of customers, from whom sales (16 percent of FY 1992 revenues), support, education, and consulting revenues were earned. All channels were supported by a full program of lead generations and promotion

activities (direct mail, advertising, seminars, trade shows, user group meetings).

Cognos in Japan

By 1985, Cognos was selling in the United States, Europe (from the United Kingdom), Mexico, South Africa, New Zealand, Australia, and Southeast Asia (from Singapore). The major preoccupation of Cognos in 1985 was getting the U.S. operation "firing on all cylinders" and building a stronger European presence from its solid base in the U.K. Other markets were at an earlier stage of development. Given the specific differences noted above and the more general perception that Japan was a "tough" market, Cognos had not seriously pursued sales there. However, circumstances changed in 1985 when Cognos was approached by Yokogawa Hewlett-Packard, Ltd.—a joint venture between Hewlett-Packard (U.S.) and Yokogawa (Japan).

The Japan Market

Like other developed country markets, Japan experienced substantial growth in software sales during the 1980s. Between 1987 and 1988, for example, sales grew by 63 percent to ¥ 1,799 billion or six times the level achieved in 1982. Although it was expected that the Japanese market would become more similar to those in other developed nations, a number of differences impacted on software sales through the 1980s.

Compared to their North American and European counterparts, Japanese buyers preferred custom-built rather than packaged software. It was estimated that less than 20 percent of the software sold in Japan was packaged, versus about 60 percent in Europe and 75 percent in the United States. Opinions varied regarding the prospects for greater sales of packaged software in the future. Some argued that this was a cultural bias that would persist, while others saw the lack of good, adapted software products as explaining the slow penetration.

Packaged software sales were also affected by the greater variety of hardware choices confronting the Japanese buyer. Several Japanese computer manufacturers such as Fujitsu, NEC, and Hitachi had strong market positions. This led to smaller markets for packaged software than in the United States and Europe where, for example, IBM and DEC were major players in mainframe and minicomputer markets, respectively. In the Japanese PC market, the potential for packaged software imports was less than elsewhere because of operating system incompatibilities. NEC was the dominant PC with a market share of about 50 percent. Despite the fact that it used a derivative of Microsoft's operating system (MS-DOS) NEC computers were unable to run most packages developed for the U.S. market without substantial modifications.

The special nature of the Japanese language and its kanji characters also exerted an influence on packaged software sales. Because the prevailing 8-bit processor technology prior to 1986 made it impossible to treat and manipulate kanji as text characters, this had presented a problem for PC software developers. With the advent of 16-bit processors, however, this problem had been resolved. Despite these and other differences, the size and growth potential of the market attracted a number of North American and European software developers to Japan.

Early Development

Yokogawa Hewlett-Packard (YHP) approached Cognos because it discovered a Cognos's product (Quiz) embedded in a computer system it planned to sell in Japan. Without a license from Cognos, it was unable to sell this system legally in Japan. Since this discovery was made at the eleventh hour, YHP was anxious to secure the necessary license. The Cognos executive dispatched to deal with the problem was able to convince YHP that a license for PowerHouse (including Quiz) made more sense than Quiz alone, and a contract was signed on August 30, 1985, whereby YHP would develop sales for PowerHouse on the HP3000 computer.

Cognos' newer markets were the responsibility of Barry Grace, who as manager of offshore operations reported to the vice president of sales. Grace was already covering Lain America (except Mexico), South Africa, and Asia, and the YHP agreement meant that Japan was added to the list. Grace's territory was sizeable, covering 18 time zones and 80 degrees of latitude! Since Grace could at best make three-week market visits once a quarter from his base in Ottawa, he was able to spend little time on individual country markets and was therefore very dependent on distributors such as YHP.

YHP was critical to Cognos's early development in Japan. As well as providing a low-cost, immediate selling capability, the company gave Cognos the "respectability" of size, an important criterion in larger customers' purchasing decisions. It was anticipated, however, that Cognos would eventually open a subsidiary in Japan to support the activities of the existing distributors, to develop new sales channels, and to show that it was serious about the Japanese market.

Increased Localization

The establishment of Cognos Japan K.K. in the spring of 1989 provided concrete evidence of Cognos's commitment to the Japanese market. Grace found an engineer in Ottawa who was interested in assisting with the build-up of the Japanese subsidiary and the search for a general manager. The engineer was put into an "instant office" in Tokyo and, together with Grace still making trips to Japan from Ottawa, helped expand Cognos's operations. An administrator was recruited, a regular office set up, another person hired, and Cognos's technical credibility gradually developed. An experienced Japanese general manager was finally hired in April 1991, after more than a year's search. The fledgling subsidiary now needed a strong new product, appropriately localized, to establish itself in the Japanese marketplace.

When Barry Grace first saw a development version of PowerPlay in Ottawa, he realized this would be ideal for Japan, since "It was intuitive, graphical, and PC-based, all appealing features for Japanese buyers." Whereas PowerHouse needed some explanation before buyers could see its merits, the usefulness of PowerPlay was more obvious. Grace felt that PowerPlay would generate its own interest but also create follow-on sales for PowerHouse. Given this situation, Grace requested that Ottawa produce a version of PowerPlay for Japan. This request came at a time when the research teams in Ottawa were fully engaged in the turnaround period following losses sustained in FY 1989. The fact that this would be the first product fully adapted for Japan also slowed matters down. Grace persisted and, helped by the staff at the Tokyo subsidiary, the request was supported in Ottawa.

The Japanese version of PowerPlay—launched in 1991—was developed informally by a keen group of researchers from the desktop products division in Ottawa. Because it was developed for the PC market and was useful to anyone who had to analyze and present information in organizations, the sales potential was substantial. Cognos's PowerHouse distributors also sold PowerPlay although the differing nature of the market and customers meant that sometimes a separate part of the organization was responsible. By the time a second version of PowerPlay was required, a more formal development process had been put in place, and in late 1992, an Asian language product group (ALPG) was established. This reflected the importance not only of Japan, but also

China and Korea, where differing computer platforms and character handling requirements justified special attention. ALPG was responsible for product development and localization and its director reported to the vice president of R&D. ALPG had a permanent staff of five who covered product marketing, analysis, and programming. One of these persons was physically located in the Tokyo subsidiary. The core group of five persons was supplemented on an "as needed" basis from other areas of the company.

The Future

After some eight years in Japan, Cognos was well-positioned to expand its business. The major barrier to faster development of the market had been Cognos's lack of fully localized or Japanized products. Early versions of PowerHouse sold in Japan had received some localization, as had the first release of PowerPlay. Software releases in 1992 and 1993, however, provided the Japanized product that the subsidiary and local distributors had been waiting for and, it was expected, would spur growth further.

Japanization was critical since, although Cognos products were strong contenders in their fields, most competing products, such as Oracle and Sybase (U.S.) and Uniface (Netherlands), were fully localized. The delays were largely a result of other priorities in Ottawa. Japan was a small market for Cognos and, given the pace of change in the industry and a need for product line upgrades, as well as expansion, it was difficult to allocate R&D efforts and dollars to such an embryonic market. The Cognos style of international development—developing revenues before committing to much investment—meant that new markets did not get much R&D attention, at least initially. Finally, like other corporations, Cognos had been cautious about this culturally dissimilar market.

The Japanese market for hardware and software was growing rapidly as a result of aggressive pricing of PCs by Compaq and Dell, and the release of a Japanized version of Windows by Microsoft. Because of recent product releases and growth in the overall market, Joe Nardi—Vice President of Canadian and Pacific Operations—and other managers were upbeat about Japan. With hard work it was anticipated that sales could be doubled between 1993 and 1995. Expanding sales to this level and further would also require patience for, like other foreign companies, Cognos had discovered that the Japanese market moved at its own pace.

DISCUSSION QUESTIONS

1. To what extent does Japan fit into the Cognos overall global strategy? In what respects is the Japanese market different?

2. What has Cognos done to ensure that the required localization is pursued?

3. What benefits can Cognos expect to gain from its presence in the Japanese market? Can the company transfer its Japanese learning elsewhere?

4. What do you recommend as the next step for Cognos in Japan?

Case 5

BUDGET HOTELS GO GLOBAL

*R*ows and rows of hotels dot the shoreline of Kowloon, overlooking the spectacular skyline of Hong Kong Island, a ten-minute ferry ride across the bay. But not all are at the five-star level. Budget and mid-priced hotel chains have moved in on what used to be an enclave of five-star hotels. Only a few blocks away from the Hilton, Sheraton, Westin, Intercontinental, and Four Seasons hotels, the Holiday Inn conducts a brisk business, accommodating middle-class tourists.

Expansion Strategies

In the same manner that first-class hotel chains first swept the globe, second-tier hotels are now expanding globally. Budget and mid-priced hotels now comprise over a third of all hotels in major cosmopolitan centers. Furthermore, these hotels are the fastest growing segment of the industry. Originally targeting main tourist cities in Europe, current trends show lower-priced hotel construction increasing rapidly in Latin America and Asia. Best Western, the American budget chain, operates hotels in New Delhi and Bombay. The Holiday Inn signboard can be seen in Beijing, China, as well as Temuco, Chile.

Best Western, Holiday Inn, Days Inn, Carlson, and Choice International are examples of American budget and mid-priced hotel chains expanding into Europe, Africa, Asia, and Latin America (see Exhibit 1). Choice Hotels expects to have over 3,000 hotels operating in foreign countries within the next 10 years. Most

Source: This case was prepared by Andrea Alexander under the direction of Professor Johny K. Johansson, Georgetown University. It is based on material from: Edwin McDowell, "Midlevel Hotels Look Abroad; Some U.S. Chains Seek to Expand off the Beaten Path," *New York Times*, August 28, 1995, pp. D1, D6 and Jacqueline Simmons, "Budget Hotels Aren't Bargains Abroad," *The Wall Street Journal*, November 17, 1995, pp. B1, B8.

of the hotel chains expand into foreign markets by franchising their name and, in particular, their electronic reservations network. The company owns very few of the hotels, lessening the need for financing and the risk of foreign exchange exposure.

While first-class hotels tend to locate one major hotel in a metropolitan or tourist area, the new budget hotels pepper each metropolitan area with several smaller hotels and expand further into the provincial areas. This is similar to the strategy employed by McDonald's and other fast-food chains, which initially opened in core country centers and gradually spread across the countryside.

Industry Factors

The growth of budget hotels abroad can be attributed to a variety of factors. The growth of small but global businesses is a major factor. Not able or willing to afford the five-star hotels, smaller companies house their travelling representatives in cheaper three- and four-star hotels. Tourists also are opting for these cheaper alternatives. Furthermore, in many emerging and newly industrializing countries, these hotels remain the only mid-priced alternatives. And in some of these countries, the fall of communism has created a new and previously untapped market.

Like the growing middle class in these countries, small businessmen and tourists do not necessarily want to pay top dollar for a five-star hotel. They can still demand—and receive—a reasonable level of comfort during their stay. Although these hotels often serve only local cuisine, competitive budget hotels are providing air conditioning, television, wake-up calls, and continental breakfasts.

....

EXHIBIT 1   Budget Hotels Expand Globally: *New Hotel Development*

Hotel chain	Location	Open	Under construction	Agreements to open
Best Western	Latin America	34	7	0
	Asia	7	6	0
	Europe, Africa	6	0	0
Carlson (Country Inn)	Latin America	0	1	106
	Asia	0	1	60
	Africa	1	0	0
Choice International	Latin America	20	7	275
(Comfort, Quality,	Asia	23	13	74
Clarion and Sleep Inn)				
Days Inn	Latin America	8	1	0
	Asia	0	8	0
	Africa	0	0	3
Holiday Inn Express	Latin America	23	24	5
	Asia	29	15	0
	Europe, Africa	28	4	16

Technology has also helped to propagate the spread of hotel chains abroad. Even the most remote locations can communicate and make electronic booking for clients. For example, rather than routing reservations and messages through its central New Delhi location, and then forwarding the message to Phoenix, the Best Western system allows a single hotel manager in Bombay to send requests and messages directly to the Arizona headquarters via speedy and low-cost E-mail.

Competition

These hotels compete not only with local domestic chains and single hotels but with budget hotels from other countries. The globalizing trend can be found among international chains not based in the United States. Accor, for example, a giant French hotel chain, competes directly with the American chains in both Europe and the Pacific. Another competitor is European Novotel, with very strong presence in the United States and elsewhere. Globalizing of competitors is a strong driver of further globalization among existing chains.

Even though most budget chains continue to proliferate, some are standing on the sidelines. For example, giant Marriott has refrained from expanding their mid-level—and very successful—Courtyard hotels internationally. Instead the company plans to build its current hotels in key cities throughout the world, preferring to postpone international budget hotel expansion.

Ironically, the budget hotels abroad are often not as much of a bargain as they might seem. A night at a Quality Inn in the United States will cost approximately $65.00. The Rome version can cost over $150.00. A stay at the Beijing Holiday Inn is similarly high-priced. Although high start-up costs and more expensive overhead can account for some of the price disparity, price inflation also gives companies a chance to skim the market. In a transitional period, the new arrival can charge a first-mover premium before competitors move in and put pressure on the prices.

Minor Problems?

In the midst of this optimistic expansion, some problems exist. Many of the newly opened hotels are not yet profitable. Local franchisors can misjudge the market demand, and start-up costs can be high. It is important to create awareness and positive word-of-mouth among customers and taxi-drivers, airport personnel, and so on. Even though the budget hotels tend to refrain from media advertising, in an initial period it is typically necessary to create some awareness of location and amenities in the new market using advertising and various promotions.

Other problems relate to the exchange risks involved. The devaluation of the Mexican peso, for example, made many hotels' Mexican operations a drag on profits.

In spite of these problems, most budget hotel executives contend that the prospects of long-term returns outweigh any current difficulties. The trend toward the expansion of mid-level hotels abroad continues.

DISCUSSION QUESTIONS

1. What factors are fueling the rapid demand for mid-level hotels in Latin America and Asia? What market segments are the hotels targeting?

2. What other conditions can account for this relentless push to expand globally?

3. Why are mid-level hotels charging such high rates? Can these hotels remain profitable without lowering room prices?

4. Why might Marriott be hesitant to expand their middle-class hotels globally?

5. Would you recommend that a budget hotel chain expand globally? Explain your decision.

Case 6

CUSTOMER-DRIVEN GLOBAL ORGANIZATION: THE WILO COMPANY

WILO is an internationally leading manufacturer of pumps for heating systems. The corporation's business spreads over the whole of Europe with 14 subsidiaries and several agencies abroad. WILO's activities are divided into four business units, defined mainly by customer groups and partly by product features:

- Domestic (private one- or two-family houses).
- Commercial (commercial or public builders).
- OEM (original equipment manufacturer = industrial customers).
- Customer service and maintenance (including recycling).

Across and within business units are "systems," including pressure intensifying installations, transfer stations for district heating, filters for private swimming pools, and collectors for the use of rainwater. The OEM-production is located in France, while the main business units are located in Germany.

Until 1990 WILO was organized in the "classical" functional structure, as indicated in Exhibit 1. The functional division "marketing/sales" included departments for sales in Germany, sales abroad, and export. The central marketing department (marketing services) was in charge of market research, advertising, and sales promotion as well as the corporation's representation at trade fairs. Additional marketing specialists were working for the business units, "domestic" and "commercial," just as "OEM" and "customer service" were supported by special marketing and sales units. Exhibit 2 shows this pre-1991 structure.

The functional structure shown in Exhibits 1 and 2 was suffering a significant disadvantage: too many organizational levels between work bench and customer caused coordination problems and time delays. For that reason a fundamental reorganization was implemented in 1991.

Reorganization

The new structure was aiming for the following improvements:

- Priority for market and customer orientation.
- Short distances between market and production.
- Comprehensive process orientation instead of functional departments.

Source: This case was prepared by Professor Dr. Richard Köhler, University of Cologne. Used with permission.

EXHIBIT 1   Functional Organization at WILO until 1990

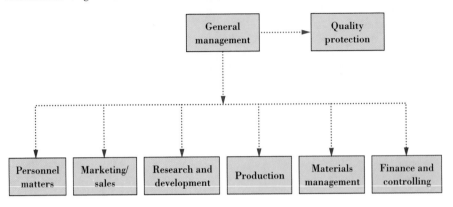

EXHIBIT 2   The Organization of Marketing/Sales at WILO until 1990

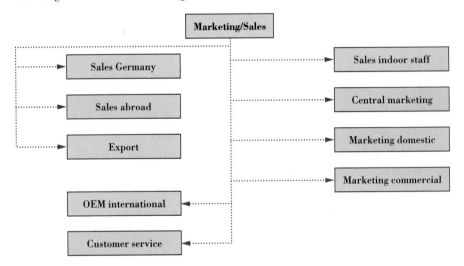

- Delegation of responsibilities to small cooperative groups within the company.
- Higher motivation of the staff.

The CIF-teams. As the main element of the reorganization the so-called *CIF-teams* were created ("CIF" standing for "customer in the focus"; German: "Kunde im Mittelpunkt" = KIM). Each of the above-mentioned business units was assigned its own CIF-team, led

by an expert in marketing/sales or customer service. The rest of the team members were recruited from research and development, materials management, production, and controlling, to ensure that experts from all relevant business functions contributed to the creation of customer benefit throughout the whole value chain of the corporation.

The CIF-teams' work is mainly strategy-oriented: designing market strategies taking into consideration the competitive situation and the market development. However, they are also supposed to supervise the implementation of these strategies (e.g., by introducing new products to the market). In addition, the CIF-teams are responsible for establishing long- and short-term objectives and the supervision of their realization.

The sales force. The immediate contact for closeness to customers is provided by the external organization of WILO, which consists of 16 sales and service teams, three regional managers, and one key account management leader. Since the leaders of the CIF-teams are part of the external organization, strategy development on the basis of the newest information about the market and customer needs is ensured.

The roundtable. The so-called "roundtable" is a further committee, which works as a link between the CIF-teams and the modularly designed production. Members of the roundtable are one delegate from the sales department (indoor staff), one expert from the purchasing department, one manager from the production department, and one controller. They have to ensure that production reacts in a flexible way to market needs and considers the strategic priorities marked by the CIF-teams. The field staff passes customers' orders immediately on to the competent production unit. Exhibit 3 offers an overview of the new CIF-organization.

As can be seen in the new organizational layout in the exhibit, the different roles of the various organizational units are aimed at the

EXHIBIT 3   Customer and Process-Oriented CIF Organization at WILO since 1991

Market	Optimizing closeness to customers	Strategy development and implementation	Improved reactions to the market	High flexibility
	External organization	**CIF-team***	**"Roundtable" as a link between sales and production**	**Factories**
C				
U	Key account management	4 CIF-areas with team members from	1 delegate from the sales indoor staff	Production planning
S				
T	3 regional managers	• Sales	1 member of the purchasing department	Production (motor production, installation, mechanical processing)
O		• Research and development		
M		• Materials management		
		• Production		
E	16 sales and service teams	• Controlling	1 production manager	
R			1 controller	Quality control

*CIF = "customer in the focus" (German: Kunde im Mittelpunkt = KIM).

customer, to signal the need to take a customer's perspective on the unit's work. Even the production units at the factories are asked to improve their flexibility and plan with the customer in mind, not simply respond to requests from engineering or sales.

The "classical" marketing department, to be seen in Exhibits 1 and 2, was given up at WILO. Only "market research" and "advertising" are still centralized. Otherwise, the process organization, which overcomes traditional department limits, provides the framework for market orientation. The reorganization was combined with an intensive "internal marketing" with the goal of creating a customer-oriented mentality among the staff. This new pattern of organization has proved its worth over the last four years.

The Future

The current plan is to group the 14 European subsidiaries into four larger regions: Central Europe, Northern Europe, Southern Europe, and Eastern Europe. The managers of these regions will have a seat and a vote on the CIF-teams, whenever their regions are involved or adjustment to local particularities (e.g., of product innovations) is concerned. The CIF-teams shall guarantee a balance between central control and local adjustments, corresponding to the "transnational marketing" approach (suggested by Bartlett and Ghoshal/Nohria).

DISCUSSION QUESTIONS

1. Compare the advantages and disadvantages of a functional organization over a cross-functional organization similar to the one adopted by the WILO Company.

2. To what extent is the new organizational form better equipped to deal with the European integration and the increase in global competition?

3. What problems would you foresee in going to the planned four regions in Europe? How would you implement such a change to get collaboration from the country organizations?

Case 7

HEWLETT-PACKARD (A): THE GLOBAL SALES PROBLEM

*I*n a November 1989 interview, John Young, president and chief executive officer, Hewlett-Packard, summarized the situation in the computer and electronics industry that was the mainstay of this $11.9 billion multinational corporation:

"Customers no longer want a box, they want solutions."

Source: This case was developed by George S. Yip and Tammy L. Madsen, Anderson Graduate School of Management, University of California at Los Angeles (UCLA). Copyright George S. Yip.

In Young's view, the industry was moving from an era in which the product defined the solution, to one in which the customer defined the solution. A pure technological focus was no longer appropriate as customers were demanding more standardization and support. In addition, industry growth was slowing in the United States, which represented just less than half of the global market for computers and electronics. Challenges were particularly evident in H-P's largest division, the computer systems organization (CSO).

One CSO executive, Greg Mihran, manager, industry marketing, and a fourteen-year H-P veteran, summarized H-P's position as follows:

"H-P has a long history of success with a product-oriented, country-based sales and support organization. While considerable progress had been made during the past two years toward an account focus, ongoing efforts to adjust the balance between account and geographic strategies continued. It seemed evident, however, that the right answer was somewhere in between these two extremes. Both strategies must coexist to ensure success and respond to the complex mix of country and global account priorities."

Company Background

H-P, incorporated in 1947 as successor to a partnership formed in 1939, designed, manufactured, and serviced electronic products and systems for measurements and computation. The company was committed to a set of core values: leadership in technology, quality and customer service, financial stability, and uncompromising integrity in all business dealings. H-P sold nearly all of its products to businesses, research institutes, and educational and healthcare institutions and was one of the United States's largest exporters. H-P's basic business purpose was to provide the capabilities and support needed to help customers

worldwide improve their personal and business effectiveness. In 1990, the company employed over 92,000 people and operated product divisions in 53 cities and 19 countries with over 600 sales and support offices in 110 countries and generated revenues of $13.2 billion. In 1990, net revenue grew by 11 percent following a 21 percent increase in 1989. In 1990, H-P experienced a slower net revenue growth in most of its product areas and declines in operating profit and net earnings when compared to amounts reported in 1989.

H-P maintained manufacturing plants, research and development facilities, warehouses, and administrative offices in the United States, Canada, West Germany, France, Spain, Italy, Switzerland, The Netherlands, Australia, Singapore, China, Japan, Hong Kong, Malaysia, Mexico, and Brazil. H-P had a strong market presence in Europe with net revenue for European operations equal to approximately five billion dollars. H-P's market participation was weaker in Latin America but strong in Asia. The geographic distribution of H-P's orders was as follows: 46 percent—United States, 35 percent—Europe, and 19 percent—Asia Pacific (includes Latin America).

Industry Trends

In 1990 the computer industry was moving away from a geographic focus to more of a customer focus with an emphasis on global strategy. As customers demanded more standardization, hardware producers were being driven into complex and occasionally secret alliances. For example, AT&T, creator and owner of the Unix operating system, teamed up with Sun Microsystems to promote its standard. On the other side of the fence, IBM, Digital Equipment, and a few others were trying to promote another version of Unix, possibly the one used by Steve Jobs, Apple Computer founder, in his new workstation. These two groups then began to discuss working together on a common version of the operating system.

In addition, customers also wanted to work with vendors that provided consistent service and support across geographic regions and industries. Multinational customers demanded that vendors be strategic partners who could demonstrate an understanding of specific international needs and deploy solutions to these needs on a global basis. H-P executives increasingly saw the need for "one platform common across vendors and across many industries." While competitors appeared to be interested in taking a more global approach to the business, one of H-P's senior executives indicated that "the industry looked at 'global' as a buzzword." Many at H-P saw the need to integrate the current geographic approach with a global strategy.

Alternative sales channels such as dealers, two-tier suppliers, systems integrators, or resellers had become prevalent throughout the industry. Thus, companies in the industry needed to identify strategies to maximize these alternative channels and the opportunities presented by them. In H-P's case, the organization needed to couple industry/customer focus with an all-channel strategy as well as develop ways to measure and develop alternative channels.

Account Management Program

In 1990, H-P's account and sales management program was product focused, organized on geographic lines, and supported approximately one thousand accounts worldwide. Under this structure, sales responsibility did not extend beyond geographic boundaries and according to one executive, the amount of business tended to shift up and down from year to year.

The organization structure consisted of four levels. First, there were field operations managers for each of the three worldwide sectors: Europe, Asia Pacific, and the Americas. Second, each sector was divided by coun-

tries and/or regions, and managers were identified for each country or region. The number of country/region managers was a function of country size and business. For example, the United States was divided into four regions: the West, South, Midwest, and East. Each country or region manager reported to the field operations manager.

Third, the regions or countries, depending on size, were further divided into areas. Area sales managers reported to the country or region managers. Fourth, district sales and account managers reported to the area sales managers. Just as area sales manager responsibility did not extend beyond the area geographic lines, district manager responsibility did not extend beyond district lines. District managers were designated as the major account managers for the largest accounts in their districts but were also responsible for the entire geographic area. In addition, there were approximately eight sales representatives per district manager. Distinct geographic boundaries existed within this framework such that sales activity did not cross boundaries. Minimal interaction occurred between regions and districts and there were no mechanisms in the system to encourage interaction across areas, districts, or regions.

In addition to the field operations sales and account structure, headquarters account managers were located at corporate headquarters. Headquarters account managers reported to the product divisions while the rest of the sales staff reported to the geographic operations. Account managers utilized these contacts to gather information and determine if H-P had sufficient resources to support their customers. One of the executives interviewed indicated that since the headquarters account managers reported directly to the different product divisions they did not always act in the interests of the district or region managers. As a result, many of the geographic account managers were not sure if they could trust or would benefit from the use of a headquarters account manager.

Performance Measures

Under the geographic structure, performance measures were based on product quotas. Managers focused on meeting product line targets within their designated region, area, or district. For many years H-P had set sales quotas and tracked performance by product lines solely within geographies. This was an important metric to quantify product performance but lacked clear differentiation of account quotas and expenses. Expenses and account quotas were reported and managed together within all other product quotas and costs in each country and region. As a result, within the product focus structure, it was difficult to differentiate individual account performance at any level and there was a lack of a complete measure of global account performance. In 1990, when H-P began to shift more to a customer focus, one senior executive indicated that it was very difficult to get the sales team to shift to an account focus while they still were required to satisfy product line targets.

The organization structure and the performance measures did not facilitate the development of new accounts outside regional boundaries. Area and district managers had no incentive to provide information to other district or area sales managers regarding new account development, as their primary focus was meeting product quotas in their own designated region or district. In many ways, different regions, areas, and districts competed with each other. Ken Fairbanks, district sales manager, indicated that if managers wanted to help develop business for a customer in another region, the manager was forced to use a "tin cup approach." For example, if an account manager for the Northwest region of the United States needed to coordinate activities for his customer in another region in the United States, he or she had to provide an incentive to the account manager in the other region if they wanted any assistance. Mr. Fairbanks indicated that he had to approach managers in other regions with a "tin cup" or "beg" for support. Managers often spent considerable amounts of time trying to convince managers in other regions of the benefits that would result from their support. Managers in different regions had no incentive to coordinate activities of major customers across regions because their performance was measured only on product quotas for their region and was not differentiated for particular major accounts. Under this system new account development was lacking and product sales fluctuated from year to year.

DISCUSSION QUESTIONS

1. What obstacles to global synergy do you see in the current sales organization?

2. How would you propose to change the sales regions and the performance measures in order to accommodate global accounts?

3. How would you attempt to make the changes acceptable to the current sales managers?

Case 8

HEWLETT-PACKARD (B): THE GLOBAL ACCOUNT SOLUTION

*I*n January 1991, Franz Nawratil, vice president and manager, worldwide marketing and sales, computer systems organization (CSO), Hewlett-Packard, received approval to implement a pilot program based on a proposal for global account management. At this time, Mr. Nawratil asked Alan Nonnenberg, director of sales, Asia-Pacific, to help head the pilot program and appointed Greg Mihran as the new director of sales, global account management, CSO.

Global Account Management

The program proposal envisioned a critical role for the global account manager (GAM). Accordingly, the pilot program focused on providing the GAM with the authority, power, and tools to manage the global account. GAMs were responsible for defining the global account sales and support needs and budget, developing an account plan, and identifying the goals and objectives for the account and the strategies and resources necessary to achieve those goals and objectives.

The first step of the pilot program involved selection of the global accounts based on various criteria. Good executive relationships between the customer and H-P were

required to exist and H-P had to hold a strong defensible position in the account. The global customer needed to be interested in developing a global account program and to also be demanding more global consistency and support than were other customers. From a financial perspective, global accounts were required to have greater than $10 million in current annual sales and support. The first six major global accounts identified were four American companies—AT&T, Ford, General Motors, and General Electric; one Canadian company—Northern Telecom; and one European company—Unilever. Within five of the six accounts, 5–10 percent of each customer's total spending on information technology was allocated to H-P. In the sixth account, H-P was heavily installed with 70 percent of that customer's business.

The dual structure defined in the proposal empowered the GAM to manage his or her sales team to meet the global needs of the customer. The GAM jointly reported to the country manager of the customer's HQ country and to the field operations manager, but was empowered to make decisions independent of geography. In addition, the GAMs were evaluated on worldwide performance of a single account while a country manager was

Source: This case was developed by George S. Yip and Tammy L. Madsen, Anderson Graduate School of Management, University of California at Los Angeles (UCLA). For company background, see Case 7, Hewlett-Packard (A). Copyright George S. Yip.

evaluated on sales performance in a single geography.

To facilitate visibility of the program, a quarterly report, the *Global Account Profile*, documented by the headquarters account managers (HAMs), summarized the status of the global accounts. This report diffused information about the global accounts throughout the entire organization and worked as an internal awareness document. The *Global Accounts Profile* was not a problem-solving tool but informed executives of the opportunities and strategic issues related to each global account. It provided the GAMs with a vehicle to communicate the status of the account to the rest of the organization. In addition, GAMs held quarterly meetings to bring district sales managers together to share best practices.

The HAM Program

The headquarters account management (HAM) program was redefined during the first year of the pilot program and provided a point of contact at H-P headquarters for the customer. The HAMs represented the global account at headquarters, assumed global responsibility and ownership, and were the link between account assigned executives and the global account. In this role, HAMs were seen as an investment by the global sales team to maximize success of the account. HAMs were selected during the development of the pilot program and two were identified by the end of fiscal 1991. Mr. Mihran, Mr. Nawratil, and Mr. Nonnenberg all agreed that sales and field experience was a requirement for all HAMs.

The HAMs worked closely with the GAMs to address technical, pricing, and strategy issues and basically to do whatever was necessary to support the customer. While the HAMs' role was to provide a point of contact at headquarters, they also traveled to customer locations about 30–50 percent of the time depending on the account. Mr. Mihran indicated that initially they did not realize how important it was to keep the HAMs together. But he soon found that locating the HAMs at H-P's headquarters facilitated the sharing of knowledge as well as the development of an important network of resources across industries.

While representing the GAM at H-P headquarters, HAMs also supported business development opportunities presented by the global account and shared H-P best practices with the global account. One headquarters account manager, Teresa Clock, emphasized that the program provided business development opportunities that otherwise might have been missed. For example, Ms. Clock developed an alliance with a third party in Singapore to support the global account with Shell. This would not have been possible without the global account program structure because the country managers previously had no incentive to extend sales operations outside their region. Another HAM, Ann Johnson, on the Northern Telecom account, believed that a main benefit of the program was the sharing of best practices with the customer. In this case, Northern Telecom's operations were organized similarly to H-P's, and the sharing of best practices provided value-added support to the global account.

Internal Acceptance of HAMs

HAMs as well as the entire sales staff for each global account were funded by the global account. During the pilot program, not all accounts funded HAMs and several GAMs were skeptical of the value added by the HAMs' role. Initially many GAMs hesitated to invest in a HAM because of negative experiences with headquarters account managers and sales personnel prior to the GAM program. Within the previous account management organization, headquarters account managers had reported directly to individual product divisions and did not always represent the best interests of the major accounts they supported. As the global account program evolved, most GAMs came to see the value added by the HAMs' role in the new structure, and began utilizing HAMs where funding allowed. HAMs' value-added activities included the development of new business opportunities, sharing of best practices, account visibility at headquarters, and being the eyes and ears of the GAM. Some customers began to recognize the value of having a presence at H-P headquarters.

Other product divisions within H-P also questioned the HAMs' role. Many product division managers initially saw the HAMs as just another layer of management to deal with. Even after the pilot program, many product marketing managers were still not thinking along global lines. But most changed their view once the organization began to better understand the GAM program and the HAMs' role, and product marketing managers began to change their internal approach, emphasizing a more global strategy.

In fiscal 1992, 50 percent of the global accounts funded half a HAM, 20 percent funded a full HAM, and 30 percent did not use a HAM. In contrast, by fiscal 1993, 57 percent of GAMs funded half a HAM while 31 percent funded a full HAM.

Country Reactions to the GAMs

Within the first year, many managers at H-P saw the program as a fad and this presented a large challenge to the GAM team. But by 1993, approximately 80 percent of the people who viewed the program as a fad or did not believe in it were no longer in their positions with H-P. Upper management did not tolerate anyone who did not support the program. Further, individuals in key country management positions that were seen as obstacles to the success of the program were encouraged to pursue other opportunities. H-P did not ex-

pect automatic buy-in from everyone, and gave senior management two or three opportunities to buy into the program.

During the first two years of the program, the difference in performance measurements often created conflict between GAMs and country managers. Country managers continued to focus on their geographic regions and felt threatened by the GAMs. Field operations managers often had to step in to resolve conflicts or assist in negotiations between the GAMs and country managers. Many executives considered this as one of the problems with the performance measurement system. As a result, the global account performance measurements were revised in fiscal 1993. The new system linked the country managers' evaluation to the worldwide performance of global accounts headquartered in his or her country in addition to the geographic region. This change reduced conflicts and provided country managers with an incentive to coordinate and collaborate with the GAMs.

Beyond the performance measurement system, country managers felt threatened by the GAM program as a whole. Outside the United States, the country managers controlled all accounts within their geographic region. With the initiation of the pilot program, some of the country managers' largest and most profitable accounts were now under the control of a global account manager. While GAMs dually reported to country managers, the GAM was empowered to manage the global account to satisfy the account goals. In addition, because the program received a large amount of top-down support and visibility, GAMs were seen as having an advantage over the country managers. Country managers felt their territory was being encroached upon and this adversely impacted coordination between country managers and GAMs. Country managers that did not buy into the GAM program were given several opportunities to accept the program and work with the GAMs. If managers did not eventually buy into the program they were encouraged to pursue opportunities elsewhere in the organization or outside H-P.

Overall, H-P's senior management felt the program was successful, although during the first two years of the pilot program a few global accounts changed. In one case, the customer had funded the account, then pulled the funding out, and the global account manager was no longer needed. In other cases, the global account manager was not the right person for the job. For example, an area sales manager was successful at managing several accounts in one geography but was not effective at managing one account across multiple geographies.

The GAM program had a high profile at H-P and as the program evolved and diffused to more accounts, its success became highly visible. While Mr. Nawratil's proposal was designed to use the current sales force, he did not intend to create an elite group or autonomous division, but this occurred to some extent. During 1992 and in early 1993, the success of the program was heavily promoted and in mid-1993, Mr. Mihran was requested to "tone down" the promotion to avoid conflicts within H-P. As the program received more visibility there was a concern that the success of the program might create tension between the CSO and other product divisions.

Customer Reaction

The initial response from customers was positive. Some customers identified the Global Account Program as a strong differentiator between H-P and its main competitors, IBM, Sun, and Digital. Ms. Clock, headquarters account manager, commented that the global account program positioned H-P as more than just a first-tier or second-tier supplier: "The customers feel value in the linkage with product groups and headquarters executives."

The HAM for Northern Telecom, Ms. Johnson, believed that her customer encouraged the global account concept and wondered why it had taken so long for H-P to develop the program. Ms. Johnson indicated that the program made a significant impact by breaking down barriers between regions and field operations. She emphasized that the strength of the program stemmed from the program promotion and visibility to other levels at H-P, and stated that Mr. Mihran had played a critical role in championing the program with executives. Ms. Johnson commented that this type of headquarters presence was an essential feature of the program.

Overall, H-P believed the program was extremely effective. The pilot program began with 6 accounts, evolved to 20 accounts in fiscal 1992, and 26 accounts in fiscal 1993. Mr. Mihran believed that customers were extremely happy with the program. H-P saw the program as a competitive differentiator and this was reinforced by the company's inclusion in *Fortune*'s 1993 ranking of America's most admired corporations. In the category of computers and office equipment, H-P was identified as the organization with the best managers: "Apple is judged more innovative, IBM a better corporate citizen, but H-P's managers are tops."[1]

DISCUSSION QUESTIONS

1. How does the GAM program solve some of the global synergy problems of H-P?

2. What is the role of the HAM program?

3. How did H-P try to "sell" the program to existing managers?

4. Would you say that the pilot program was a success? Any negatives?

[1]*Fortune*, February 8, 1993.

Case 9

DALOON A/S (D): SUPPLIER TO McDONALD'S

*A*t the end of 1992, managing director Hemming Van looked back at a year that had brought new and great challenges to Daloon A/S. After a couple of years with large expansions and rapid growth, he was proud to note that 1992 was the year when McDonald's, (the American hamburger chain), the flagship within the fast food sector, became a Daloon customer.

Seizing an Opportunity

For a number of years Daloon believed that McDonald's might be a potential customer. Most people within the company considered this idea purely Utopian; however, they were intrigued by the possibility of becoming a supplier to this fast food market flagship. Some years ago, Daloon's sales subsidiary in Germany had a meeting with the McDonald's purchasing department responsible for German outlets, and they presented Daloon's product program. It was not successful at the beginning, but the sales manager in Southern Germany was persistent in his efforts to deal with McDonald's German purchasing department located in Munich.

In February 1991, a request was received from McDonald's to develop a 20-gram pancake roll. Daloon's development department dispatched samples but no agreement was

reached. In November 1991, a renewed request was received which specified the filling of the roll. Daloon replied that they were unable to produce such small rolls within the existing process lines. As a result, Daloon's enthusiasm had cooled off slightly. In Nyborg the general attitude was "Forget it."

Yet Daloon's sales manager in Southern Germany still persisted. After some internal discussions and turmoil, Daloon decided in February 1992 to try again, and the development department was given ten days to test the possibilities. The reply from the department was it would be possible, but only with some investments made in the machinery.

The Campaign Idea

McDonald's Germany wanted to run a trial campaign in September and October of 1992, and so they would need 15 million rolls in August, with an option for an additional 3 million rolls if the campaign became a success. To live up to such requirements, Daloon had to start production in April. Late in February, Daloon hardly knew what product was to emerge from the efforts. Various products were suggested by Daloon, and McDonald's purchasing department selected a vegetarian China roll.

Source: This case was developed by Professor Tage Koed Madsen, Department of Marketing, Odense University (Denmark). For company background, please see Daloon A/S (A).

McDonald's Germany wanted to profile the chain through a "China week," with a special menu consisting of six small Daloon rolls, fresh salad, and Chicken McNuggets "Shanghai." The customers would also be offered a choice of special sauces. The usual assortment of McDonald's products would also be available. Daloon was to deliver the rolls in transparent plastic bags, each containing 48 rolls, packed in cartons with six plastic bags in each. They would be delivered to McDonald's two central distribution centers in Germany that were in charge of the redistribution to the individual restaurants.

After further negotiations, during which a price reduction was made by Daloon and it was agreed that Daloon could have its name and logo on all the material printed for the campaign, an agreement was reached. A Dutch and a Far East competitor to Daloon were not selected, as they could not guarantee the delivery of the quantities requested by McDonald's. The order arrived from McDonald's in mid-April.

The summer was extremely busy at Daloon. Until mid-August, when delivery was to be effected, the production of rolls took place in regular shifts, permanent overtime shifts, and permanent weekend shifts. Production and packaging problems were solved by changes in the machinery as they arose. On the campaign's third day, McDonald's called it a success: the option of the 3 million rolls was ordered, and an extra order for an additional 8 million rolls was also placed. Production plans at Daloon again had to be rearranged drastically, and the good intentions of the staff were challenged, as they had to go back on overtime. Working to the utmost of capacity, Daloon succeeded in delivering the order to the entire satisfaction of McDonald's.

Campaign Execution

The campaign cooperation presented a very intensive and exciting period for Daloon. Mc-

Donald's German purchasing department pursued a very systematic and consistent line when the agreement was concluded. The fundamental attitude of McDonald's was that Daloon had to be prepared to meet all the requirements made: no excuses for delays or any other problems would be accepted. Fortunately for Daloon, no problems arose. Several times during that period the great flexibility in the purchase of raw materials and production turned out to be of great importance; the flexibility and loyalty of the staff likewise. Daloon did not consider it unlikely that McDonald's would like to rerun the campaign in Germany. Considering the good results of the first campaign, Daloon felt confident that its possibilities of becoming the supplier again were good.

At the end of the campaign, McDonald's German purchasing department participated in a strategy meeting in Chicago, together with colleagues from divisions all over the world. The very progressive German department presented its great success with the China week and Daloon's rolls. The result was that Daloon was asked to supply rolls for a corresponding campaign in Britain in February and March of 1993, and the concept (product, prices, printed campaign material, etc.) would be identical to the German concept. Furthermore, McDonald's in the Netherlands and Sweden were very interested in copying the success. For Daloon, this meant that their investments in their special machinery constructions for the small rolls and the general product development could be exploited in full.

Daloon was free to offer the concept of the small rolls to other catering customers, except for direct competitors to McDonald's. Daloon had on its own refrained from selling the small rolls with the McDonald's filling to other customers.

Future Marketing Strategy

The successful McDonald's campaign initiated a number of reflections at Daloon. What if the

German department wanted to repeat the success? What if McDonald's wanted to run corresponding campaigns in all other European countries? What if the success continued, and McDonald's wanted the rolls to become a permanent part of the McDonald's product line—on equal terms with Chicken McNuggets? Should Daloon undertake the substantial investments required to become a supplier? Would it be too risky to become so dependent on one single customer? Could such a situation possibly be exploited to increase sales to other customers? Could Daloon become a substantial producer so that the firm would be better able to match the increasingly larger customers in the retail and the catering markets? How could Daloon protect itself from ending up in somebody's pocket? Would the existing shareholders accept the risk of such a substantial investment? Would they be able to finance it at all? Should Daloon look for injections of external risk capital?

Hemming Van was convinced that the development towards greater dependence on individual customers would continue in the retail and catering markets. It was a relatively new situation for Daloon, which was a company that was more accustomed to acting in a market environment where overall sales were realized according to the principle of "every little bit helps." In the retail market the share of private labels was increasing, so would the future bring about an identical development in the catering market, with the remaining wholesalers becoming more dominant?

DISCUSSION QUESTIONS

1. How did Daloon gain McDonald's Germany as a customer? How is Daloon leveraging this foothold into becoming a supplier for McDonald's in other European countries?

2. What strengths does Daloon acquire as a supplier for a global customer? How can Daloon avoid being taken advantage of by McDonald's?

3. Which of the many questions facing Hemming Van do you think are the most important for the sustained growth of Daloon? How would you advise him?

Case 10

CATHAY PACIFIC AIRWAYS (A): GLOBAL OR REGIONAL?

Introduction

Asia Pacific is the fastest growing region in the world of the airline industry. Cathay Pacific Airways (Cathay) in Hong Kong is strategically located at the "heart of Asia." It is a firmly established international airline repeatedly ranked as one of the most profitable airlines in the world. The economic outlook for the region is extremely promising. However, the competitive environment in which Cathay is operating is challenging. The company is facing the issue of whether to become a truly global carrier, or whether to stay regional by concentrating on the Asian market and awaiting developments after the 1997 Chinese takeover of Hong Kong.

Company Background

Cathay Pacific Airways was founded in 1946 by an American and an Australian who used a DC-3 to offer passenger and cargo services to southeast Asian countries. In 1948, the company was incorporated, and Butterfield and Swire, later the Swire Group, became the largest shareholder. In 1959, Cathay acquired

Hong Kong Airways and became Hong Kong's true "flagship" carrier.

The Swire Group, now one of the two largest British conglomerates in Hong Kong, exercised its control over Cathay through the provision of management support services. Cathay was first listed on the Hong Kong exchange in May 1986. Swire Pacific continued as a holding company, although its shareholding declined from 70% to 54.25%. The Hong Kong and Shanghai Banking Corporation (HSBC) reduced its stake to 23.25%.

Cathay continued to expand rapidly and profitably in the second half of the 1980s. The number of aircraft grew from 21 in 1986 to 41 in 1990, destinations from 36 to 38, revenue passengers carried from 4.2 million to 7.7 million, and consolidated net profit from US$158 million to 384 million.

Apart from benefitting from the emergence of Hong Kong's Kai Tak Airport as an international hub, Cathay's success was also attributed to its good marketing and operating efforts. Cathay won *Air Transport World* magazine's "Airline of the Year Award" in 1987. It maintained an outstanding reputation for in-flight service. Its marketing programs were

Source: This case was prepared by Eddie Yu and Anthony Ko, associate professors, Department of Business & Management, City University of Hong Kong, as a basis for class discussion. It is not intended to illustrate either correct or incorrect handling of administrative problems. The authors gratefully acknowledge case materials provided by Angela Wong and other students in their strategic management class. Copyright 1996 by Eddie Yu and Anthony Ko, City University of Hong Kong, Kowloon Tong, Hong Kong.

EXHIBIT 1   Number of Passengers In and Out of Kai Tak Airport, April 1994 to March 1995 (in 000s)

Markets	Arrivals	Departures
Amsterdam	22.5	28.7
Auckland	40.2	42.4
Bangkok	362	362.3
Kaohsiung (Taiwan)	243.0	236.0
Kuala Lumpur	95.4	87.4
London-Heathrow	160.8	147.8
Los Angeles	113.1	120.0
Manila	335.1	342.2
Melbourne	60.6	63.8
Osaka-Itami	72.4	71.9
Osaka-Kansai	96.9	97.5
Paris-De Gaulle	93.3	90.6
Penang	31.4	34.3
Rome	42.3	44.3
Seoul	178.3	173.8
Singapore	207.8	191.1
Sydney	99.5	94.9
Tokyo-Narita	288.7	274.3
Toronto	34.7	40.4
Vancouver	119.6	130.4
Total (others included)	4,477.6	4,476.2

Source: 1994/95 Annual Report of the Director of Civil Aviation.

designed to secure a major share of the normal full-fare market sector.

By the mid-1990s, Cathay served 46 destinations in 27 countries and territories. The breakdown by destinations of passengers served at Kai Tak from April 1994 to March 1995 is given in Exhibit 1.

The Asian Market

In the past two decades, the Asia Pacific region has undergone significant economic, social, and political changes conducive to the business development of the civil aviation industry.

During this period the region managed to have a relatively stable political climate, which in turn encouraged both local and foreign investments. As a result, the Asia Pacific region was ranked the highest GDP growth region in the world in the period 1970 to 1991, with a compound growth rate of 7.1% against the world average of 3.2%. The region is forecasted to outstrip other regions again in the period 1991 to 2000 at 6.1%, against the world average of 3.4%. Thus, with the region's population representing approximately 55% of the world total, the need for business and leisure travel by air is rapidly increasing.

Other factors have contributed to the substantial growth of airline business in the region. It has vast areas of ocean so that air transport provides a natural means of both commerce and social interaction. As Asia is distant from a number of its major international trading partners, air transport is an obvious choice for businessmen. Asia is also the fastest growing international tourist destination.

Not surprisingly, the region also has the world's highest growth rate in international scheduled passengers' kilometers (9% annually for the next five to ten years), greater than Europe and North America (at 5.6% and 4.0% respectively). The most profitable airlines in the world can also be found in Asia, including Singapore Airlines and Cathay.

Regulatory Entry Barriers

Unlike the United States, liberalization of the airline industry in the region is proceeding very slowly. Access to the Asia Pacific market is closely regulated by governments, and the majority of airlines are state-owned.

Similar to practices in other regions, the rights to fly into and between Asian countries are regulated by bilateral agreements that are a requirement of the Chicago Convention. At the international level, the airline operators are also required to comply with the International Civil Aviation Organization's standards and recommended practices, and at the national level, they are required to comply with the Civil Aviation Acts, Civil Aviation Regulations, and other airport and airline operators' requirements.

Air services agreements are regarded as trade agreements, as they are carefully negotiated between governments, each of which seeks to secure the best possible deal for its designated national airline(s).

Asia Pacific carriers are characterized by their strong national connection, and to some extent their image mirrors national characteristics, such as Singapore Airlines, Korean, Japan Airlines, and Qantas (Australia). They have been able to cope with strong growth, and several are considered dynamic competi-

tors by other airlines in other regions of the world.

Since 1987, there have been some moves towards privatization. Recently, Philippines Airlines was privatized, Thai Air is currently undergoing privatization, and the Government in India also recently announced the privatization plan for Air India.

One feature that reflects developments elsewhere is the move towards deregulation in domestic airline operations. A number of countries in the region are now allowing new carriers to start up to fill market niches and compete with existing flag carriers. Newly emerging carriers, such as Asiana of Korea, EVA of Taiwan, Ansett of Australia, and Japan Air Services, have increasingly exerted competitive pressure to both their countries' flag carriers and other regional airlines.

In addition to the expected 1997 takeover of Hong Kong by China, the early 1990s presented Cathay with some new challenges.

Profitability Squeeze

After a good run in the last years of the 1980s, Cathay started encountering some problems in 1990. A slowdown of the world economy, costs rising due to inflation in Hong Kong, uncertainties caused by the Gulf War, and worldwide excess of capacity led to decline and stagnation of Cathay's profit during the period from 1991 to 1995. The consolidated net profit declined 10% from the peak achieved in 1989. The 1993 profit dropped 23.8% from that of 1992. Cathay was also hit by an industrial action by flight attendants in January 1993, which was estimated to have cost the company around US$31 million.

Strong Route Competition

Cathay also faced increased competition. The market shares for the various destinations are shown in Exhibit 2.

······································

EXHIBIT 2   Inbound (to HK) Market Share Distribution by Place of Origination

	1985	1986	1987	1988
Inbound market share (worldwide) %				
Cathay Pacific Airways	28.7	29.9	30.9	31.5
China Airlines	8.3	8.4	9.2	11.9
Japan Airlines	10.8	10.6	11.6	11.6
Thai International	7.5	7.5	7.2	6.5
Singapore Airlines	7.3	6.7	6.2	4.9
United Airlines	5.6	5.1	5.2	4.2
HK Dragon Airlines	—	—	—	—
China Southern Airlines	—	—	—	—
British Airways	—	—	—	—
Qantas Airways	—	—	—	—
Combined PRC airlines/CAAC (2)	6.2	6.2	6.1	7.4
Inbound market share (S. E. Asia) %				
Cathay Pacific Airways	25.7	24.8	26.8	29.0
Thai International	10.4	9.8	11.1	9.9
Singapore Airlines	13.0	13.7	13.4	12.3
Philippine Airlines	8.3	9.3	10.2	10.5
China Airlines	11.9	12.3	12.0	11.1
Dragonair	—	—	0.3	0.4
Combined PRC airlines/CAAC	5.7	6.2	6.2	6.4
Inbound market share (USA) %				
Cathay Pacific Airways	16.2	18.4	20.2	21.0
United Airlines	18.5	19.2	17.3	17.9
Northwest Orient Airlines	10.7	11.3	11.4	10.5
China Airlines	7.3	6.7	7.6	6.8
Singapore Airlines	11.4	9.6	10.5	9.1
Dragonair	—	—	0.3	1.1
Combined PRC airlines/CAAC	9.7	9.9	9.4	11.0
Inbound market share (Canada) %				
Cathay Pacific Airways	35.9	39.3	44.1	44.1
Canadian Airlines Int'l	9.9	13.6	12.1	15.1
United Airlines	3.2	3.9	3.9	4.2
Dragonair	—	—	0.3	1.0
Combined PRC airlines/CAAC	6.5	6.3	5.0	7.0
Inbound market share (United Kingdom) %				
Cathay Pacific Airways	38.0	36.4	40.9	41.8
British Airways	20.7	22.9	16.4	16.8
Virgin Atlantic	—	—	—	—
Emirates Airlines	—	—	—	—
Thai International	3.7	4.1	4.8	4.4
Qantas Airways	2.6	4.0	4.4	5.8
Dragonair	—	—	0.2	0.5
Combined PRC airlines/CAAC	5.6	5.0	4.8	4.5

Source: Annual Reports by the Director of Civil Aviation, Hong Kong Government.

1989	1990	1991	1992	1993	1994	1995
33.5	33.7	33.4	34.1	32.7	34.0	35.1
11.5	11.7	10.9	11.1	11.6	9.8	9.4
11.3	11.1	11.5	9.5	8.4	8.6	9.3
6.6	5.6	5.5	6.0	5.7	5.9	5.8
4.6	4.4	4.5	4.3	4.3	3.9	4.0
—	—	4.4	3.8	3.8	3.6	3.9
1.5	2.0	2.3	2.5	2.7	3.6	3.8
—	—	2.2	2.4	2.5	2.2	2.1
—	—	2.1	2.4	—	2.0	1.9
—	—	1.9	2.3	3.0	2.7	2.3
5.7	7.6	—	—	—	5.3	4.7
31.3	32.2	27.1	29.2	29.9	29.2	30.9
11.3	10.5	12.3	11.7	10.3	12.0	11.7
10.4	10.8	10.7	10.9	11.1	10.2	11.1
11.9	8.7	8.1	8.8	8.8	7.9	9.8
9.5	11.3	9.9	8.5	8.0	5.6	5.2
0.5	1.0	1.2	1.6	2.2	2.9	2.8
3.4	5.1	5.0	4.6	5.5	4.8	3.7
22.4	20.7	21.5	24.2	24.2	23.0	24.0
17.9	21.0	21.7	20.2	19.1	19.4	21.4
12.1	10.9	8.8	7.6	5.1	5.2	5.5
6.6	7.2	6.5	6.9	7.7	7.3	6.6
10.6	10.1	7.7	7.0	6.3	6.2	6.2
1.3	2.4	3.6	4.3	4.7	5.4	5.6
6.8	8.9	7.0	7.2	8.5	7.1	6.6
45.6	41.8	39.6	42.1	42.0	42.2	41.7
16.6	14.2	18.5	19.8	18.5	15.6	15.7
3.3	9.1	6.7	4.9	5.4	5.8	6.5
1.1	1.7	3.3	2.9	4.4	4.6	5.3
4.2	6.4	5.1	4.9	5.1	4.9	4.5
43.3	45.6	45.8	41.8	36.9	36.5	35.7
25.2	25.0	23.1	21.0	17.9	15.8	15.9
—	—	—	—	—	3.6	8.6
—	—	0.5	2.5	3.3	2.8	3.2
5.0	4.4	4.6	4.2	4.3	3.5	3.0
6.2	4.9	4.3	7.9	13.6	9.4	8.8
0.9	1.5	2.6	2.7	2.9	3.7	4.5
2.8	3.3	2.8	3.4	3.7	3.4	2.9

EXHIBIT 2 *(concluded)*

	1985	1986	1987	1988
Inbound market share (Australia) %				
Cathay Pacific Airways	47.6	48.3	48.9	49.2
Qantas	16.1	23.3	22.5	22.8
Dragonair	—	—	0.2	0.3
Combined PRC airlines/CAAC	3.4	3.1	3.4	3.4
Inbound market share (Taiwan) %				
Cathay Pacific Airways	—	—	26.3	28.4
China Airlines	—	—	42.2	43.1
Thai International	—	—	12.6	6.7
Dragonair	—	—	0.1	0.9
Combined PRC airlines/CAAC	—	—	1.5	11.6
Inbound market share (Japan) %				
Cathay Pacific Airways	33.7	36.8	33.9	33.7
Japan Airlines	42.1	41.3	40.0	42.0
All Nippon Airways	3.0	1.4	2.8	4.7
Dragonair	—	—	0.7	1.8
Combined PRC airlines/CAAC	5.0	5.2	4.7	4.2

As can be seen, the company's strongest competitors on its main routes were some of the major global airlines:

Australian route. Qantas, the Australian national airline was the dominant competitor. Qantas had global ambitions and had established alliances with Swissair and other airlines.

China route. Air China, the Chinese national airline, was the main carrier for customers into China. However, from Hong Kong, the largest market share was held by Dragonair (which is partly owned by Cathay), with China having a controlling interest. In 1990, Cathay had transferred its Shanghai and Beijing routes to Dragonair, de facto withdrawing from the Chinese market.[1] It was not clear, however, what the opportunities would be after the Chinese takeover of Hong Kong on July 1, 1997.

Japan route. An important link in Cathay's global network, the Japan route was dominated by Japan Airlines (JAL). JAL's strongest features were its inflight service and the preferential treatment it received at Narita and Osaka international airports.

London route. This route was another historically important link for Cathay, as its importance was not declining despite the end of British rule, since it linked Hong Kong to Europe. British Airways was the leader on this route, and British-based Virgin Atlantic Airways was a new challenger. British Airways had a strong global network, with high customer recognition, but still lacked a strong ally in East Asia. Virgin Atlantic competed mainly on price, but also provided special services, such as door-to-door transportation and in-flight events.

[1] Case (B) has more information on Dragonair.

1989	1990	1991	1992	1993	1994	1995
52.6	56.0	53.4	50.6	46.3	43.5	45.1
21.1	20.1	23.3	27.1	30.0	28.8	25.3
0.6	1.0	2.0	2.0	2.5	4.1	4.1
2.7	3.0	2.5	2.8	3.7	2.9	3.0
31.1	28.9	33.1	37.7	36.1	42.2	42.4
40.0	41.0	38.4	36.5	39.3	36.0	37.4
5.6	3.6	4.3	5.5	5.3	5.3	5.2
2.7	3.1	3.0	2.4	2.3	2.1	1.6
11.8	17.3	10.7	10.5	10.0	7.1	6.4
34.2	35.8	34.6	35.5	33.2	33.6	35.8
41.9	39.5	40.8	39.5	36.5	36.4	35.4
6.0	5.8	5.1	5.1	7.0	6.7	6.9
1.7	1.8	1.7	1.8	2.1	4.3	5.2
2.8	2.9	2.5	2.9	3.5	3.5	2.9

Singapore route. Although a relatively short distance route, Singapore was an increasingly important link as Asian economies continued to flourish. The main competitor was Singapore Airlines, who had dominant share and preferred landing rights. Singapore had long been viewed as a top service provider, and served as a benchmark when Cathay expanded its own customer satisfaction effort.

United States route. This was a weak link for Cathay's global plans, but was an important route in any global network. This route featured strong competition from national airlines in Asia (including Thai Airlines and Korean Air) and from American airlines, including Delta, Northwest, and, in particular, United Airlines. United's strong domestic presence in the United States, coupled with a strong network across the Pacific (a PanAm heritage), made the company a dominant competitor.

Among the rapidly growing destinations, Japan and China were the most important ones. To be successful, an Asia Pacific air carrier would have to obtain access to the two economic powerhouses of the region, Japan and China. The right to fly from Japan to other Asian nations would thus be an important asset. In addition, the opening of the new Kansai International Airport on Osaka Bay would offer more growth opportunities for domestic and international carriers.

Growth Strategy

Despite its profit problems, Cathay focused on growth during the first half of the 1990s. The fleet was increased from 41 aircraft in 1990 to 57 in 1995, destinations from 38 to 44, and revenue passengers carried from 7.7 million to 10.4 million. It entered into a joint venture to provide ground handling services at Kansai

Airport in Osaka, Japan, in 1990, and acquired 10% of Taikoo (Xiamen) Aircraft Engineering Co. Ltd. to enter the aircraft maintenance services in Xiamen, China. In 1994, it consolidated its position in the cargo business by acquiring 75% of Air Hong Kong, a cargo airline owned by a locally listed company.

The company also started an ambitious fleet renewal and expansion program. Nine Lockheed L1011 passenger aircraft were replaced by newer and more efficient Airbus models in 1995. Between 1996 and 1999, 22 Airbus A340/330s and Boeing 777s will be delivered. Besides making capital investment, Cathay has made other efforts to make management more efficient and to reduce operating costs.

Increased Differentiation

To support its growth strategy, Cathay campaigned vigorously under a "Heart of Asia" slogan, emphasizing its central position in the Asian market. The aim was to increase the differentiation from other global airlines and also to change its British-related image to that of a Asian carrier. The campaign involved TV spots and newspaper ads, press briefings, and executive interviews to broadcast the new message. The airline further differentiated itself by changing in-flight service to include menus with more Asian foods, Chinese-language films, and redesigned seats for the typical Asian body proportions.

To improve customer satisfaction, market research was used to pinpoint areas of concern. As a result, some changes were made, including new counters at Kai Tak Airport to handle customer complaints "on the spot," providing personal TVs in first class, establishment of a frequent flyer program, and club premises at airports. Decision-making power was pushed towards the front-line employees, empowering them to make quick decisions about customer problems. The resulting customer satisfaction

level, measured as the percent of passengers rating themselves satisfied or better with their Cathay flight experience, reached as high as 94%, comparable to the best in the industry.

As Cathay faced the question of whether it should become a truly global airline or stay regional and await the developments after the 1997 China takeover of Hong Kong, a number of issues caused concern.

Alliance Issues

"Mega carrier" was a trendy strategic concept in the international airline industry. To develop an effective market network, international airlines were eager to exchange maintenance services, share ticketing and operations systems, and group together to negotiate better deals from aircraft manufacturers and other suppliers. In early 1992, British Air and KLM Royal Dutch Airlines and Northwest of the United States entered into a strategic alliance. Singapore Airline swapped stakes with U.S.-based Delta Airlines, Swissair had allied with Qantas Airways of Australia, and Japan Airlines allied with Hawaiian Airlines. However, Cathay did not have any alliance arrangement with other international airlines. Should it pursue one?

Marketing Issues

It was difficult to differentiate Cathay from the rest of the Asian airlines. "The Heart of Asia" slogan had been stressed consistently in the past two years. How strong was this in changing the corporate identity from a colonial British image to a modern Chinese one?

How should the cabin crew work force, who came from over eleven nations and cultures, be trained to appreciate and pursue a quality service goal?

How could the company better link up with the various intermediaries, including travel agents, in selling the passenger and cargo space?

Airport Issues

The existing Hong Kong International Airport Kai Tak was saturated and limited the business growth opportunity of Cathay. Cathay represented around 25% of inbound and outbound flights, and this would not be improved until 1998, when the new airport Chek Lap Kok on Lantau island would be finished. What, if anything, should be done in the meantime?

As Kai Tak was located in an urban area, the flight hours were restricted, and only certain low noise aircraft were allowed to fly over the residential areas during early morning and late evening. How could Cathay increase its flights?

Technological Issues

The airline industry was increasingly being driven by technology. Computer reservations systems (CRS) and management information services (MIS) were becoming indispensable competitive tools for the airlines. CRS allowed users, including the airlines, travel agents, and other intermediates, to process bookings for seats on flights anywhere in the network. Travel agents and other sales intermediaries would give preference to airlines who provided efficient CRS access. CRS also enhanced the marketing capability of an airline. When linked to MIS it could also offer a range of product and performance enhancements. Cathay needed to upgrade its system, but MIS and CRS required millions of dollars to develop and maintain the hardware and software systems as well as train the users. Assuming the financing was available, how big would the customer advantage be?

DISCUSSION QUESTIONS

1. Considering "the global option," in which regions should Cathay look for alliance partners, if any? What does Cathay have to offer a potential partner?

2. How does the positioning theme "Heart of Asia" fit in with Cathay's global aspirations? Is the image a plus or minus for going global?

3. What are the advantages and disadvantages of staying regional? How can marketing help leverage the advantages?

4. Considering the increased competition from global players, and the Hong Kong takeover by China in 1997, what are the strengths that can help Cathay survive and thrive? What role does its marketing know-how play in this?

Case 11

CATHAY PACIFIC AIRWAYS (B): CHINA—OPPORTUNITY OR THREAT?

On July 1, 1997, the British Government has to relinquish sovereignty over Hong Kong to the Chinese government. The Joint Declaration and the Basic Law of the Hong Kong Special Administrative Region (SAR) provide for Hong Kong to maintain a high degree of autonomy in aviation matters and "for the maintenance of the status of Hong Kong as a center for international regional aviation." Still, great uncertainties remain for Cathay Pacific Airways, the current flagship carrier of Hong Kong.

Cathay's Nightmare

Putting the best face on a difficult situation, Cathay announced in its 1995 annual report that "We look forward to operating in the new Hong Kong aviation environment and playing our full part as a member of the Chinese aviation community." But inside the organization managers and employees were still wondering about what might happen and what the company should do.

With the British Government's protection vanishing, Cathay's status after 1997 was uncertain to say the least. In the past decade, China, by direct and indirect moves, had sought to have direct influence on the strategic industries in Hong Kong. These industries

included banking, airlines, telecommunications, container terminals, and shipping. In banking, The Bank of China had successfully secured the chairmanship of the Hong Kong Banking Association. The position had been previously monopolized by the two British banks—Hong Kong and Shanghai Banking Corporation and Standard Chartered Bank—since its inauguration. China International Trust & Investment Corporation Hong Kong (Holdings) Limited (CITIC HK), in which China had controlling ownership interests, became a big player in Hong Kong financial markets.

Through CITIC HK and other red chip companies ("red chip companies" was the popular terminology for companies with strong ties to China, if not entirely China funded), the Beijing government was stepping up the holdings in other strategic industries. As all operators of these strategic businesses also had substantial investments in China, the share acquisition processes had been smooth and friendly for most of the cases. But such deals were not necessarily made on a purely commercial basis.

With the Chinese takeover, Chinese airline operators were likely to move into Hong Kong to compete head-on with Cathay. The state-owned airlines could be expected to have

Source: This case was prepared by Eddie Yu and Anthony Ko, associate professors, Department of Business & Management, City University of Hong Kong. For background information on Cathay Pacific Airways, see case (A).

certain privileges hampering fair competition. For example, the China National Aviation Corporation (CNAC), the commercial arm of the regulatory Civil Aviation Administration of China, was widely regarded as the most likely candidate to replace Cathay as the territory's flagship carrier after the transfer of sovereignty. CNAC already owned 51% of start-up carrier Air Macao, the flag carrier of Macao, Hong Kong's neighboring Portugese colony until 1999.

Maintaining a good relationship with the key officials in China and related state enterprises was clearly of strategic importance for the future. Cathay's parent company, the Swire Group, had in the past decade has actively developed an amiable relationship with China. The relationship had grown out of their joint venture, the Dragonair airline.

Dragonair

Hong Kong Dragon Airlines (Dragonair) was founded in 1986 by Hong Kong Macao International Investment Ltd., a company controlled by K. P. Chao and his family, who owned a major textile business. Chao was joined by the prominent Sir Y. K. Pao and other investors in November. However, after Dragonair's initially disappointing performance, the Pao family withdrew from Dragonair in 1989 and sold the shares back to the Chao family.

Realizing the need to get closer to industry insiders and to get better access to the Chinese market, Chao decided to invite the Swire Group and CITIC HK to become partners. In January 1990, Cathay Pacific and Swire Pacific acquired 30% and 5% of Dragonair's issued capital. The cost to Cathay was approximately US$38 million. The Chao family retained 22% of the shares, while CITIC HK with its ties to China became the largest shareholder with 38% (increased to 46% in 1992).

Dragonair's move to invite powerful partners from China was not a novel strategy. Swire Pacific had actually employed the same strategy in February 1987 when CITIC HK acquired a 12.5% stake in Cathay Pacific and thus became Cathay's second largest shareholder. This was the beginning of the close relationship between Swire and Chinese officials.

Cathay also entered into a management service agreement to manage Dragonair. As part of this move, some personnel, including a senior executive, were transferred to Dragonair. Cathay also transferred its China routes, consisting of Shanghai and Beijing services, to Dragonair starting on April 1, 1990.

The China Market

For China, since its inauguration of the Open Door policy in 1979, the rapid growth of economic activities in some 30 cities led to a great demand for air travel. The outbound travel potential of 1.25 billion people, and the several hundred thousands of foreign businessmen going in and out of China each year, presented a great attraction to all regional and international airlines. And as China was speeding up the quest for readmission to the World Trade Organization, China offered the largest potential for airline business development in the next decade.

The Beijing government still controlled key operational areas, such as fares, routes, and aircraft acquisitions of all airlines. However, since the early 1990s, the Civil Aviation Administration of China (CAAC) had gradually decentralized the civil aviation rights to newly established regional airlines in order to meet the increased demand for air travel. In addition to Air China, the flagship carrier, new airlines included China Eastern (Shanghai based), China Southern (in Guangzhou), and China Northwest (based in Xian).

....

EXHIBIT 1 Weekly Schedule of Flights for Hong Kong to China

Route	PRC Airlines	Dragonair
Beijing	28 flights	14 flights
Shanghai	28 flights	16 flights
Xiamen	14 flights	9 flights

Because of the booming Chinese market, the first half of the 1990s was great for Dragonair—in contrast to Cathay and the global airline industry. By 1992, Dragonair was serving 13 cities in China and 4 cities in North and South Asia. It established itself as the preferred carrier for passengers traveling to and from China. With expanding services and high load factors, Dragonair reported record profits in 1993. By 1994, it was providing services to 14 cities in China and 8 cities elsewhere in Asia by a fleet of nine aircraft.

By the mid-1990s, the weekly schedule of flights between Hong Kong and three main Chinese cities showed the relative strength of Dragonair against all the PRC airlines combined (see Exhibit 1).

Troubled Skies

Past history and CNAC's aggressive posture suggested the possibility of international expansion by a new Chinese flagship carrier based in Hong Kong. As the chairman of the Cathay repeatedly emphasized to the press, Cathay would not be afraid of fair competition, as it had already competed successfully with over 61 airlines, many world class. Cathay was simply afraid that the new entrant would have distinct privileges in competing with Cathay, especially since CNAC was also China's regulator of the airline industry. If such worries were realized, no matter how good Cathay's strategic planning, it would have major difficulties in coping with the powerful political forces.

In March 1995, CNAC announced that it had been applying for licenses to operate airline services, initially flying between China and Hong Kong, and Hong Kong and Taiwan (a very profitable route for Cathay) with a new airline company. Sensing that its worst nightmare was coming true, Cathay protested, claiming a conflict of interest in having a regulator run its own airline in Hong Kong. The Chinese rule-maker could easily create obstacles by favoring CNAC and penalizing Cathay, or stripping it of its primary landing slots at the new Hong Kong airport. Unfortunately, Cathay could not rely on Chris Patten, the last British Governor of the colony, to negotiate these issues with China. In addition to his "lame duck" status, the relationship between the Governor and the Beijing government was frayed, due to some last-minute democratic reforms introduced by Patten.

In July 1995, Cathay, in its role as the flagship carrier of Hong Kong, announced that it had reached a preliminary deal with the Taipei Airlines Association to license a second carrier in both Taiwan and Hong Kong. The additional carriers were expected to be Dragonair and Taiwan's EVA Airways. The Chinese were not happy. The general manager of the CNAC, Wang Guixiang, stated that Cathay was not authorized to negotiate the deal, and that the Basic Law had been violated.

In September 1995, CITIC HK sold their holdings of Cathay shares. In mid-March 1996, CNAC was rumored to have off-loaded its 5% stake in Cathay. The market considered these activities as a vote of lack of confidence in the future of Cathay, anticipating that its flagship carrier status would soon be replaced by a powerful China airlines company.

On April 3, 1996, one of the most influential financial newspapers in Hong Kong reported that the Swire Group planned to sell its stake in Cathay. The report claimed that the Swire family had approached five potential buyers, among them United Airlines, Northwest, and Lufthansa. Although the report was categorically denied by the Swire Group's Hong Kong chairman (and chairman of Cathay), Peter Sutch, the rumor persisted.

....

DISCUSSION QUESTIONS

1. How attractive is the China market? How should Cathay deal with the China market—by trying to enter and developing it further, or by focusing on the global market?

2. What objectives should Cathay pursue in the China market—for example, go for market share, or check competitors, or view it as part of the global network?

3. To penetrate the China market, how should Cathay go about it—develop its interest in Dragonair further, or attempt some alliances, for example with Chinese airlines? Any other alternatives?

4. Will Cathay survive? What protection from a direct takeover by CNAC can Cathay count on? To what extent does its firm-specific advantages (including marketing skills) protect it? How?

5. What difficulties do you think a Chinese-run airline might encounter in global competition? How can these be overcome?

Indexes

NAME INDEX

COMPANY NAME INDEX

SUBJECT INDEX